A NEWSPAPER HISTORY OF THE WORLD

A NEWSPAPER HISTORY OF THE WORLD

Michael Wynn Jones

An anthology of famous news stories
from 1850 to the present day,
and a collection of great scoops, leaks,
exposures, crusades, triumphs and disasters
from the pages of the
British and American Press.

David & Charles : Newton Abbot

Above all, I am grateful for the help given to me by the newspaper divisions of the British Museum and the Library of Congress. And to Penny Eyles for her assistance. My thanks, also, to the following newspapers for doing a great deal of the hard work in the first place:

The Chicago Tribune, The Chicago Daily News, Daily Express, Daily Graphic and Sketch, The Daily Herald, Daily Mail, Daily Mirror, The Daily Telegraph, Evening News, Evening Standard, The New Orleans Times-Picayune, The New York Herald, The New York Journal, The New York Times, The New York Tribune, The News Chronicle, The Observer, The San Francisco Chronicle, The San Francisco Examiner, The Sunday Times, The Philadelphia Inquirer, The Times, The World, The Washington Post, The New York Daily News and many others.

Contents

Newspapers from 1650-1850

We expect a great deal in return for those new pence or dimes we hand over for our daily newspaper. For a start, we take it for granted that the news we are purchasing will not be staler than that which we observed on our televisions the night before (if it is a morning paper), or more than two or three hours old if it is an evening paper. We more or less uncritically assume that, granted there are no political barriers, there is nowhere in the world geographically inaccessible to the reporter. All this, almost as of right, we regard as the basic technique of the newspaper trade: any paper that cannot fulfil it satisfactorily is not worth our time of day. But that is only a beginning.

We further expect our paper to be an arbiter of tastes and fashions, a leader and open forum of opinion, detector of trends, critical investigator and seeker-out of corruption and injustice, a guardian of and crusader for the public interest (or at the very least the interest of its readers), and a constant source of entertainment. We have other, rather less tangible, requirements of it too. It should in some indefinable way be an expression of our corporate identity in a society where the voice of the individual can so seldom be heard. Without accumulating power itself, it should be a check on the power of others, whether it is personal, political or presidential. In short, although the chronicler of an imperfect world, it should be the representative of a better one.

Put like that, of course, there would hardly be a newspaperman in the world who would recognise his employer from the description. The ideal seems somehow remote from the practicalities of deadlines, layouts, advertising quotas. Yet when we argue such concepts as the rôle of newspapers and the freedom of the press, these are the things we consider the press 'free' to do — and most papers with a few notable lapses consider it their duty to do. The first two hundred years in the history of newspapers were largely concerned with defining that rôle, and the struggle for the right to fulfil it without repression. Only in the last 120 years or so have newspapers acquired the financial independence, the mass-audience, the technical ability and, most important, the political freedom to attain that goal.

The first English-language newspaper — by common consent The Oxford Gazette — was a publication of modest ambition. Escaping the Plague of 1665 the English Court had gone into voluntary exile at Oxford where, no doubt, it sorely missed these titbits of news that were available in London by word of mouth. To remedy this deficiency Joseph Williamson, an Under-Secretary of State, authorised Henry Muddiman to publish a regular sheet, printed in both London and Oxford: after 23 issues it became The London Gazette. Samuel Pepys found it 'very pretty, full of news' but its diet was heavy with official announcements, leavened only by weekly casualty lists of the plague and such foreign tidings that were brought in on the latest boats and then circulated around the coffee-houses. Apart from its continuity, it differed little from the erratic newsbooks which had preceded it or from the laboriously handwritten newsletters that were sent through the mails to subscribers. Nor could it lay claim to being a pioneer of periodic journalism — weekly papers were already an established feature in the German states, in Holland and France, and the first genuine daily newspaper, The Leipziger Zeitung, had made its debut five years previously. Nevertheless the innovation of The Gazette quickly prompted a rash of imitators. Muddiman himself soon quit to start his own journal, The Current Intelligencer, only to be burnt out of his premises by the fire of London. A great many other efforts succumbed as quickly, whether it was to their own indigestibility or, more frequently, to the heavy hand of government

The Daily Courant.

Bbbb   Numb. 1903.

Wednesday, March 24. 1708.

London, March 24.

MENS Minds being chiefly taken up at pres.. with the Expedition of the Pretender to Scotland, and there being little remarkable in the foraign Prints besides what relates to the Designs France has form'd upon the Success of that Enterprize, We presume it will be acceptable to the Publick to have a true Account of the Condition of the naval Force which the Government has caus'd to put to Sea to oppose the Enemy.

A LIST of the Forty one Ships of her Majesty's, which were with Sir George Byng, when he sail'd last from the Downs for the Coast of Dunkirk, with the Time when last clean'd.

Rates.	Ships.		When Clean'd	
4	Leopard	Grav'd	12	December 1707.
	Jersey	Grav'd	13	
	Crown	Tallow'd	13	
	Swallow	Grav'd	16	
	Antelope	Tallow'd	17	
5	Roebuck	Grav'd	19	} Ditto.
4	Dreadnought	Tallow'd	26	
3	Monmouth	Grav'd	29	
4	Dover	Tallow'd	3.	
6	Cruizer	Grav'd	31	
	Squerril	Grav'd	31	
4	Advice	Tallow'd	1	January 1707 8.
6	Glasgow	Grav'd	11	
4	Worcester	Tallow'd	12	
	Weymouth	Grav'd	12	
3	Berwick	Grav'd	13	
4	Falkland	Tallow'd	15	} Ditto.
5	Tartar	Tallow'd	15	
4	Bonadventure	Tallow'd	16	
5	Gosport	Tallow'd	27	
6	Penzance	Tallow'd	27	
5	Rye	Tallow'd	28	
	Ludlow Castle	Tallow'd	11	Febr. 1707 8
3	Bedford	Grav'd	12	} Ditto.
4	St. Albans	Tallow'd	13	
	Chatham	Grav'd	18	September 1707.
	Exeter	Tallow'd	3	October 1707.
	August	Tallow'd	13	
	Mary	Tallow'd	15	} Ditto.
	Canterbury	Tallow'd	28	
	Dragon	Grav'd	30	
	Monk	Tallow'd	4	November 1707.
	Medway	Grav'd	28	Ditto.
	Salisbury	Tallow'd	1	December 1707.
5	Lyme	Tallow'd	30	June 1707
	Mermaid	Grav'd	16	August 1707.
	Adventure	Grav'd	29	Ditto.
	Lark	Grav'd	1	December 1707.
5	Queenborough		2	Ditto.

	Hunter Fireship	Grav'd	28 October 1707.
3	Shrewsbury	Not Clean'd since she came from the Streights.	

Ships which have been got ready since Sir George Byng Sail'd with the Fleet to the Northward, and are appointed to lye off of Dunkirk under the Command of Commodore Walker.

Rates.	Ships.
3	Swiftsure.
	To bay.
	Oxford.
	Lenox.
	Ipswich.
4	Nottingham.
	Norwich.
	Tilbury.
	Woolwich.
	Anglesea.
5	Sheerness.
	Experiment.
6	Dunwich.
	Maidstone.
	Nightingale.

Deale, March 22. The Queen's Ships mention'd in my last to be remaining, are still here: And Yesterday in the Afternoon came down the Griffin Fire-Ship.

London, March 24.

Yesterday a Proclamation was publish'd, importing, That Information being given that some Persons landed from on board the French Fleet when it appear'd on the Coast of Scotland, and that James Ogilvie the Younger of Boyn Esq; was one of them, and now lies conceal'd, Her Majesty forbids the harbouring him or any of them on pain of being proceeded against for high Treason, and promises 300 pound Sterling to those who shall discover and apprehend the said Ogilvie, and a suitable Reward to those who shall discover and apprehend any of the rest.

For the Benefit of Mr. Booth.
By her Majesty's Company of Comedians.
AT the Theatre Royal in Drury-Lane, to Morrow being Thursday, the 25th of March, will be presented a Play call'd, The Mourning-Bride. The part of the King by Mr. Powell, Gonsalez by Mr. Keene, Osmyn by Mr. Booth, Zara by Mrs. Barry, Almeria by Mrs. Bradshaw, Leonora by Mrs. Porter. And all the other Parts to the best Advantage.
At the Desire of several Persons of Quality.
AT the Queen's Theatre in the Hay-Market, on Saturday next, being the 27th of March, will be presented the last new Opera call'd, Love's Triumph. The part of Barilla to be perform'd by Signiora Maria Gallia Scgione The Dances, Chorus's and other Entertainments, being properly introduc'd as on Foreign Stages Boxes 8s Pit 5s. First Gallery 3s. Upper Gallery 1s 6d Stage Boxes half a Guinea. To begin precisely at 6 ... Person to stand upon the Stage. Being the last time of performing till after Easter
These ... are Sold by J. Knapton at the Crown in St. Paul's Church-yard and B Linton next Nando's Coffee-House, Temple-Bar.

An

---

which insisted upon licensing all printers wishing to put out news-sheets of any kind, and which did not hesitate to revoke its permission and mete out severe punishment whenever it found the 'news' offensive to itself.

One printer who tired of his skirmishes with authority in Britain and emigrated to Boston was Benjamin Harris. He was soon at his press once more and in 1690 issued the first edition of his *Publick Occurrences,* America's earliest attempt at a newspaper. But the Colonies were no more hospitable to his enterprise than London: after the first issue the Governor of Massachusetts suppressed the sheet — for being printed without the necessary licence. The Licensing Act in Britain lapsed in 1695 and was not renewed by Parliament — which although it provided an impetus for a large number of new ventures (including the first daily in 1702, *The Daily Courant*) was not intended to signify any sudden softening of official attitudes. So long as Edward Lloyd (the coffeeman whose establishment was the forerunner of Lloyds of London) confined his *Lloyd's News,* begun in 1696, to matters of trade and shipping or items gleaned from new arrivals at the docks he published undisturbed. But when, in February 1697, he made brief mention of a Quaker petition presented to Parliament, he was summoned to the bar of the House of Lords and ordered to apologise. Rather than do that in print, he folded his paper.

Printers in England in the early 18th century (editors were not yet a distinctive breed — correspondence was usually published under the heading of 'letters to the printer') were on the whole cautiously inclined, unwilling deliberately to explore the limits of their supposed freedom. In America, too, cooperation with the authorities paid off handsomely: as one of the initial contractors for the new postal system, John Campbell successfully launched America's first authorised newspaper, *The Boston News-Letter,* in 1704 and charged himself no postal fees on mailed copies. In other colonies postmasters followed his example, rivalling the printers as the mainsprings of the early American press. But if prosecutions against papers were fewer in America than in Britain, it was not necessarily due to any slavish subservience on the part of the newsmen — rather that the sanctions of an administration thousands of miles away from London were harder to put into effect. When Peter Zenger, owner of *The New York Weekly Journal* was hauled up by the royal governor before a grand jury for seditious libel, his case was triumphantly dismissed by his fellow-Americans, much moved by Andrew Hamilton's eloquent pleas for liberty of the press.

Yet, in Britain, for all their caution the newspaper proprietors were rewarded only by the imposition of a stamp tax in 1712, with the express intention of suppressing libels. At the same time a crippling tax on the publication of advertisements was also levied. But, after a temporary recession that had Jonathan Swift for one mourning that 'Grub Street was dead and gone', the press revived and in spite of two further increases in the tax (in 1757 and 1776) new papers persisted in being born and stumbling along, somewhere between the breadline and bankruptcy, throughout the century. By the 1770s London could boast over fifty journals of varying frequencies, and a readership that had increased by more than ten-fold. Moreover in the battle against official interference, which had yet to be fought on a broad front, no aid was more valuable than the support of this greatly increased reading-public.

As long as it was left to government-appointed judges to rule what was libel and what was not, there was no safety for the press. Juries were called upon only to decide if it was the accused who had printed them. In the latter half of the 18th century this legal doctrine was

severely undermined by the assaults of Junius and John Wilkes. The letters of the former in *The Public Advertiser* (virulently attacking George III and his ministers) brought swift prosecution down on the head of the paper's printer, Henry Woodfall, but once only, for this first attempt was frustrated by the jury and never repeated. Junius kept his anonymity; Wilkes on the other hand became a popular hero, after issue number 45 of his paper *The North Briton* was seized for attacking the King and he himself was arrested on a general warrant in 1763. Since this legal device was highly questionable, Wilkes won his case. More than that, he retaliated by suing the Government official responsible for wrongful arrest, and winning. His name became synonymous with 'liberty' of the press and of the common man (who supported him faithfully in his repeated efforts to regain his seat in the Commons, and eventually elected him Lord Mayor of London).

His fame percolated even to the patriots of the American colonies. But when their own test came in 1765, their newspapers found champions of their own. It was in that year that a short-sighted British government, in contempt of the principle of 'no taxation without representation', voted to levy a stamp duty on colonial papers. In the face of concerted and spontaneous opposition (crystalised partly by the arguments set forth in John Dickinson's 'letters of a Pennsylvania farmer' in *The Pennsylvania Chronicle*) the stamps were never distributed and stamp-agents 'declined' to take up their duties. Some papers printed their own satirical stamps and published regardless: others retired temporarily but soon returned to the fray. After the Act was repealed in 1766, general opposition to British colonial rule naturally gravitated to the newspaper offices. The Boston tea-party was plotted in the back-room of Edes and Gill's *The Boston Gazette* ('Monday's dung-barge' as one loyalist described it), and Isaiah Thomas's *The Massachusetts Spy* was so provocative that it had to decamp to Worcester, bag and baggage, when the British army piled into Boston in 1775. Nor did the patriot editors have a monopoly on outspokenness. The tory proprietor of *The New York-Gazetteer*, James Rivington, took considerable personal risks in upholding the right to *support* the government as well, though the mob eventually drove him to flee for sanctuary in England. Before the Revolution there were 37 current newspapers in the colonies — and although the exigencies of wartime killed off a great many of them between 1775 and 1781, enough new shoots blossomed and survived for 35 going concerns to emerge at the end of the struggle.

So, in the infant republic the press was already a seasoned campaigner and duly reaped the rewards for its part in influencing the course of the revolution. A number of fledgling states specifically guaranteed its freedom in their new constitutions and, in time, Congress itself was persuaded to pass the First Amendment restraining it from 'abridging the freedom of speech or of the press'. Thus semi-institutionalised, as it were, over the next hundred years it was to play an influential role in the shaping of the new nation: partly by growing with it — as new frontier settlements sprang up, there was rarely an embryonic postal service and a pioneer printer with his portable press far behind; and partly by providing uninhibited (if ultra-partisan) platforms in the great cities to men whose ideas were shaping America's future. Until the 1830s the most potent newspapers and the greatest editors were the most committed: Benjamin Russell's *The Massachusetts Centinel* (1784), Noah Webster's *The American Minerva* (1793), Philip Freneau's *The National Gazette* (1791), William Coleman's *The New York Evening Post* (1801) and William Cobbett's brief and blustery *Porcupine's Gazette*.

But these productions, aimed as they were at the men of affairs who still comprised the bulk of the buying public, were inevitably more literary than journalistic. By the 1830s the Eastern cities — and New York in particular — had expanded enormously and were ripe for the entrepreneurial flair of Benjamin Day and his harbinger of popular American journalism, *The New York Sun* (1833), whose cohorts of newsboys hawking the papers in the streets fascinated the populace almost as much as the stunts and minutiae of city-life with which Day festooned his pages. Even more dramatic proved to be James Gordon Bennett's *The New York Herald*, founded in 1835, which was as similar to its rivals as a supermarket is to a family grocer's. Bennett's paper gave his readers a taste of *all* the news their bountiful city supplied each day, tremendous or trivial, sacred or sinful. In just over a year he was rewarded with a circulation of 40,000 and there was no newspaper in the world (except in London *The Times*) to touch him. New York was rapidly becoming the press capital of America. In 1841 Horace Greeley's *The New York Tribune* entered the lists, as idealistic and idiosyncratic as its proprietor. 1851 witnessed the birth of Henry Raymond's *The New York Times*, from the beginning as conscientious and enterprising a news gatherer as any to burst upon the field.

In Britain the press continued to labour beneath the burden of the stamp tax — offset however in certain sections by the iniquitous practices of accepting government subsidies (amounting to many hundreds of pounds a year) for printing the right news, and of suppression and contradiction fees from individuals who had been forewarned of certain damaging items (a custom even *The Times*, founded as *The Daily Universal Register* in 1785 by a prosperous coalmerchant, John Walter 1st, was not above participating in during its earliest years). Nevertheless the crusading banner of Wilkes was also carried into the 19th century by men like Leigh Hunt of *The Examiner*, whose attack on the excesses of the Prince Regent in 1813 earned him and his brother two years in prison (where they continued to edit the paper in modest comfort), and like William Cobbett. The *Porcupine's* activities in America had driven him back to England in 1800, but in no way taken away his taste for radical journalism. He too offended superior powers in his *Political Register* (1802) by exposing the brutal punishment inflicted on some soldiers who had mutinied at Ely in 1809. He had once been a soldier himself and willingly took up the cudgels against the army corruption he had come to loathe. The military fought back, however, and Cobbett found himself in Newgate for two years (where he too continued to pen furious diatribes against the government).

The government's final bout of legislation against the press came in 1819, with the passing of the infamous 'Six Acts' whose primary purpose was to stamp out the radical disorders that had been plaguing the country for several years, but whose shafts were pointedly aimed at the newspapers which were suspected in high places of fermenting the disaffection with their seditious libel. This legislation was indeed the death-knell for much of the cheap radical press, but the work of men on other papers, men like James Perry on *The Morning Chronicle* (founded in 1769) and Daniel Stuart on *The Morning Post* (1772), had shown that serious and responsible journalism was not invariably attended by financial disaster. Equally, Thomas Barnes coming to the editorial chair of *The Times* in 1817, proved that editorial independence in a newspaper was in fact distinguishable from irresponsibility. From the moment *The Times* unexpectedly opposed the King (George IV) in 1820 and supported Princess Caroline's claim to be Queen, the paper never lacked for

THE EXAMINER.

No. 257   SUNDAY, NOV. 29, 1812.

THE POLITICAL EXAMINER.

Party is the madness of many for the gain of a few. SWIFT

No. 248.

TO HIS ROYAL HIGHNESS THE PRINCE OF WALES, REGENT OF THE UNITED KINGDOM, &c. &c.

SIR,—In putting this letter into the hands of your ROYAL HIGHNESS, I am anxious, both from a sentiment of compassion and from a wish to have it properly read, that you should be relieved from a host of distressing anticipations which will come rushing upon you at the sight of it. I therefore inform you at once, that you need not hesitate to read what it *does* contain, for fear of what it *may*. A secrecy, implied if not enjoined, on some points,—a reservation of others,—a tenderness for one or two persons on another,—even a wish not to leave your ROYAL Highness destitute of all means of recovering yourself in the good opinion of his MAJESTY's subjects,—and, above all, a desire to have the great contest in which I am engaged kept as free as possible from petty advantages on my own side, and attractions to a mere vulgar curiosity on your's, —all these motives induce me to address you upon the broadest and most public grounds; and if I could find any likelier mode of engaging your attention than by letter, I would most certainly adopt it, for I am rather nice than otherwise in my correspondents, and would willingly keep my familiarity, as well as my style of writing, for those who know how to appreciate it. But your ROYAL Highness stands upon record (you know in what place) for your love of the epistolary; it has been a family passion ever since the example of the late Duke of CUMBERLAND; and if the present letter does not approach you under the usual advantages of vellum and perfume, with rampant honours on the outside, and secrets equally vivacious within, it has at least the merit of novelty, and by addressing you publicly instead of privately, may furnish your Household as well as yourself with a little original conversation for a week to come. The private mode, I am aware, has been much recommended of late by a noble and learned Lord, who, to the habitual exercise of his judgment as a dispenser of the law, has added a particular taste for advice in his quality of a Privy-Counsellor; but not to repeat the reasons just given for preferring the other, nor the natural doubts respecting the safe arrival of private letters at their journey's end, nor the question, equally natural, how far, in case of such arrival, attention would be paid to a packet of grievances humbly left at the door with a Minister's or Prince's footman, I wish to avoid every thing that might tend to confound me, in the smallest character of proceeding, with other journalists who have adopted this private

mode:—I wish to prove to your ROYAL HIGHNESS, if indeed you are not *abundantly* satisfied on that head already, that you must not form your opinion of every newspaper by what you know of *Heralds* and *Morning Posts*, of BATES and of BENJAFIELDS: my object is neither title nor pension nor compromise of any sort; I consider myself, in concert with my brother, as the representative of a great public question, which is about to be tried between the Licentiousness of a Court and the Voice of Public Virtue; and the least that I can do in justice to my cause, is to shew you, before all the world, that a true sense of it's dignity sets me at once above all the meannesses and the covert-ways of a conscious interestedness. In a word, Sir, in coming into contact, however rough, with the *Examiner*, you shall find that you have to do with a gentleman; and I could name many eminent persons, both male and female, not unknown to your ROYAL HIGHNESS, who would have blessed themselves at having such luck in their dealings.

Proceedings, it appears, have been revived against the paper on account of the alleged libel which appeared in a former number, expressing, it must be allowed, no unreserved difference of opinion with a panegyric on your ROYAL HIGHNESS's habits and accomplishments from the enamoured pen of the *Morning Post*. The composition of that alleged libel was the work of an instant; it was struck out in the heat of an honest indignation; yet it cost the late Mr. PERCEVAL, I am told, three good consultations in Downing-street, before he could make up his mind to a prosecution. The grave foreheads at Carlton-House can hardly have undergone less agony of deliberation; it must at least have taken your ROYAL HIGHNESS as much time to resolve upon venturing into the arena of a Court of Law, as to come to a determination upon joining a feast or a procession; and if so, the issue must be still unknown; the torture is not yet over; and I cannot but pity the situation of the Solicitor-General, who is not to know till the last moment, whether he is to muster up his usual professional hardihood, or whether he is once more to give way to his native bashfulness, and blushingly declare himself unable to proceed.

I shall not attempt therefore to anticipate, which of the two evils your ROYAL HIGHNESS shall eventually choose, whether for giving me a license in future which you may think I shall not otherwise take, or for a tenfold diffusion of the "libel," with all the comments of a pro and con arguing. Neither, in case of your resolving upon the latter, shall I waste my time in pointing out to you the *possibility* of an unfavourable verdict. Your ROYAL HIGHNESS will, of course, have weighed all the chances to which you commit yourself; you will have called to mind, that the trial was put off last term upon a pretence that the person

2

---

public support. Under Barnes and his successor in 1841, John Delane, the 'Thunderer' built up a near-monopoly in the first half of the 19th century, eventually outselling *all* its rivals put together.

In 1855, after bitter debates and with many misgivings, Parliament finally conceded the need for an unfettered press, and abolished the newspaper tax (or the 'tax on knowledge' as it had come to be called by its critics) and six years later removed the last vestiges of the duty on paper. Almost at once the stranglehold of *The Times* was broken for good (the major objective, it must be said, of some reformers at the time). A crop of 2d, soon 1d, papers sprouted in London and many provincial cities, with Colonel Sleigh's *The Daily Telegraph* in the van of the new, cheap and popular journalism. Founded on the day before the removal of the tax, it could soon boast a readership of over 200,000 and 'the greatest circulation in the world'. A multitude of other journals flourished in this more wholesome economic air: whereas in 1850 there had not been many more than 500 periodicals of any kind published in Britain, forty years later there were over 2,200 newspapers alone.

On both sides of the Atlantic the drawn-out battle for the right to print — to print at all in the first place, then unharrassed and independently — was accompanied by an even slower search for more efficient means of gathering and disseminating current news. With official suppression or the debtor's prison everlastingly staring them in the face, most newspapers of the 17th and 18th centuries were content to rely on government handouts or whatever they could glean from the occasional private letter or ship's captain. At the beginning of the 18th century it was not unknown for a paper to be up to a year behind in its news. Even a full century later it took nearly three weeks for the news of Nelson's victory at Trafalgar in 1805 to filter through to the London papers.

The first impetus to provide some kind of special coverage of foreign events in Britain was provided by the proximity of — and obvious public concern over — the French Revolution, which broke out in 1789. *The Times* scored heavily by running eye-witness accounts from its own correspondents of many important incidents during the revolution — one that stirred the public imagination in particular was the account of the execution of Marie Antoinette. Within a few years *The Times* had organised a network of European correspondents from St. Petersburg to Lisbon, which was to make its pre-eminence on Continental affairs the wonder of the world's press. During the Peninsular War in 1808 John Walter (now the 2nd) even dispatched his editor, Henry Crabb Robinson, to Corunna to act as a roving war correspondent. Robinson was not, however, the first war correspondent: he was anticipated at least by the energetic John Bell, editor of *The Oracle*, who travelled himself to Flanders to observe the fortunes of the British forces against the French in 1794/5. In America it was not until the Mexican War of 1846 that the more enterprising newspapers had the opportunity of organising their own battle accounts: on that occasion it was the New Orleans papers (who had done their damnedest to encourage the war) who were best placed to provide the most comprehensive coverage. Their reports were sold and republished by papers all over the continent. But the real baptism of fire for most of the American press came with the Civil War — about which there will be more later.

By the middle of the 19th century, then, papers both in America and Britain were poised on the edge of an era of enormous and thrilling expansion. The next half of the century was to be a period of unprecedented prosperity and dizzying technical improvements. The electric

THE SUN.

Number 1.] NEW YORK, TUESDAY, SEPTEMBER 3, 1833. [Price One Penny.

PUBLISHED DAILY,

AT 222 WILLIAM ST.............BENJ. H. DAY, PRINTER.

The object of this paper is to lay before the public, at a price within the means of every one, ALL THE NEWS OF THE DAY, and at the same time afford an advantageous medium for advertising. The sheet will be enlarged as soon as the increase of advertisements requires it—the price remaining the same.

Yearly advertisers, (without the paper,) Thirty Dollars per annum—Casual advertising, at the usual prices charged by the city papers.

☞ Subscriptions will be received, if paid in advance, at the rate of three dollars per annum.

FOR ALBANY—PASSAGE ONLY $1.

The large and commodious steamboat COMMERCE, Capt. R. H. Fitch, will leave the foot of Courtlandt street on Friday, at five o'clock, P. M. for Albany, stopping at the usual landing places to land and receive passengers. Passage $1. For particulars apply to the Captain on board.

REGULAR DAYS.

From New York, Mondays, Wednesdays, Fridays.
From Albany, Tuesdays, Thursdays, Saturdays. a29

FOR NEWPORT AND PROVIDENCE.

The splendid steamboat BENJAMIN FRANKLIN, Capt. E. S. Bunker, and the PRESIDENT, Capt. R. S. Bunker, will leave New York at 5 o'clock, P. M. and Providence at 12 o'clock, M. every Monday, Wednesday and Friday. For further information apply to the Captain on board, foot of Courtlandt-st. or at the office, 14 Broad st. s3

FOR HARTFORD—PASSAGE 1 DOLLAR.

Through by Daylight.

The splendid low-pressure steamboat WATER WITCH, Capt. Vanderbilt, leaves the foot of Catherine street every Tuesday, Thursday, and Saturday mornings, at 6 o'clock, and arrives in Hartford at 7 o'clock the same evening. Passage One Dollar—meals extra.

The above boat leaves Hartford on Mondays, Wednesdays, and Fridays, at the same hours. s2 tf

FOR LONDON—To sail 10th of Sept.—The new packet ship Montreal, Champlin, Master, will sail on the 10th inst. For freight or passage, having elegant accommodations, apply to the Captain, on board, Pine-st. wharf, or to
s2 JOHN GRISWOLD, Agent, 69 South st.

FOR LIVERPOOL.—The fast-sailing ship Tallahassee, S. Glover, Master, will be ready to receive cargo in a few days, and have despatch. She has excellent accommodations for both cabin and steerage passengers. For freight or passage, apply to
s2 WOOD & TRIMBLE, 157 Maiden-lane.

FOR HAVRE.—The Packet ship Formosa, Orne, master, will sail on the 8th Sept. For freight or passage apply to the captain on board, or to WM. WHITLOCK, Jr. 46 South st. s2

FOR LIVERPOOL.—Packet of the 8 Sept.—The packet ship Roscoe, J. C. Delano, master, is now in readiness to receive cargo. For freight or passage apply to the captain on board, foot of Maiden lane, or to
s2t10 FISH, GRINNELL & CO. 134 Front st.

FOR KINGSTON, JAM.—Packet 10th Sept. The elegant coppered ship Orbit will sail as above. For freight or passage, having splendid accommodations, with state rooms, apply to
s2 B. AYMAR & Co. 34 South st.

FOR NEW ORLEANS.—Packet of the 8th September, the very fast-sailing coppered ship, Nashville, Capt. Rathbone, will sail as above.—For freight or passage, having handsome accommodations, apply to E. K. COLLINS, 68 South st.
N. B. A lighter is in readiness to receive cargo at Pine street wharf. s2

FOR NEW ORLEANS—Packet of Sept. 15. The ship Tennessee, Capt. Sears, will sail as above. For freight or passage, having handsome accommodations, apply to
SILAS HOLMES & CO. 62 South st.
N B A lighter is in readiness to receive cargo. s2

AN IRISH CAPTAIN.

"These are as sweet a pair of pistols as any in the three kingdoms;" said an officer, showing a pair to a young student of his acquaintance, "and have done execution before now; at the slightest touch, off they go, as sweet as honey, without either recoiling or dipping. I never travel without them."

"I never heard of highwaymen in this part of the country."

"Nor I." replied the officer, "and if I had I should not trouble myself to carry the pistols on their account—Highwaymen are a species of sharks who are not fond of attacking us lobsters; they know we are a little too hard to crack. No, my dear sir, highwaymen know that soldiers have not much money, and what they have they fight for."

"Since that is the case, how come you to travel always with pistols?"

"Because," answered the officer, "I find them very useful in accommodating any little difference I may accidentally have with a friend, or which one friend may chance to have with another."

"Do you often settle differences in that way?"

"Why, I was twice out before I arrived at your age.—The first time was with a relation of my own, who said he would see my courage tried before he would contribute with the others towards the purchase of my first commission; so I sent him word that I would be happy to give him one proof the very next morning, and when we met, I touched him so smartly in the leg, that he has halted ever since. But all his doubts being now removed, he cheerfully contributed his quota with the rest of my relations, and we have been very good friends ever since."

"Pray what gave you occasion for the second?" said the young student.

"How it began originally is more than I can tell," answered the captain; all I know is, that a large company of us dined together; we sat long, and drank deep, and I went to bed rather in a state of forgetfulness, and was awaked in the morning from a profound sleep, by a gentleman who began a long story, how I had said something that required explanation; and also, that I had accidentally given him a blow, but he supposed I had no intention to affront him, and so he continued talking in a roundabout kind of way, without coming to any point. So I was under the necessity of interrupting him, "upon my conscience, Sir, (said I,) I am unable to declare, with certainty, whether I had any intention of affronting you or not, because my head is still a little confused, and I have no clear recollection of what passed, nor do I fully comprehend your drift at present, but I conjecture that you wish to have satisfaction; if so, I must beg you will be kind enough to say so at once, and I shall be at your service." Finding himself thus cut short, he named the place and the hour. I met him precisely at the time. His first pistol missed fire, but I hit him in the shoulder. At his second shot, the bullet passed pretty near me, but mine lodged in his hip, and then he declared he was quite satisfied. So as I had given a blow the preceding night, and two wounds that morning, upon declaring himself satisfied, I said I was contented."

"You would have been thought very hard to please, if you had made any difficulty."

"I thought so myself," rejoined the captain, "and so the affair ended, he being carried home in a coach, and I marching from the field of battle on foot."

"Pray, may I ask if you ever was in a battle?"

"No," replied the captain with a sigh, "I never was; I never had that good fortune, though I would give all the money I have in the world, and all the money I am owing, which is at least treble the sum, to be in one to-morrow."

"Provided you had a good cause;" replied the young student.

"I should not be squeamish respecting the cause, provided I had a good battle: that, my dear, is what is the most essential to a conscientious officer, who wishes to improve himself in his profession. I have much reason, therefore, to wish for a war; and at the present juncture, it would be much to the advantage of the nation in general, as it is dwindling into a country of ploughmen, manufacturers, and merchants. And you must know, too, that I am pretty fortunate, having already stood thirteen shots, and I never was hit but once."

"Thirteen! what, have you fought thirteen duels?"

"No, no!" replied the captain, "the last shot fired at me completed only my sixth duel."

Wonders of Littleness.—Pliny and Elian relate that Myrmecides wrought out of ivory a chariot, with four wheels and four horses, and a ship with all her tackling, both in so small a compass, that a bee could hide either with its wings. Nor should we doubt this, when we find it recorded in English history, on less questionable authority, that in the twentieth year of Queen Elizabeth's reign a blacksmith of London, of the name of Mark Scaliot, made a lock of iron, steel, and brass, of eleven pieces, and a pipe key, all of which only weighed one grain. Scaliot also made a chain of gold, of forty-three links, which he fastened to the lock and key, and put it round the neck of a flea, which drew the whole with perfect ease. The chain, key, lock, and flea, altogether weighed but one grain and a half!

Hadrianus Junis saw at Mechlin in Brabant, a cherry-stone cut into the form of a basket; in it were fourteen pair of dice distinct, the spots and numbers of which were easily to be discerned with a good eye.

But still more extraordinary than this basket of dice, or any thing we have yet mentioned, must have been a set of turnery shown at Rome, in the time of Pope Paul the Fifth, by one Shad of Mitelbrach, who had purchased it from the artist Oswaldus Norhingerus. It consisted of *sixteen hundred* dishes, which were all perfect and complete in every part, yet so small and slender that the whole could be easily enclosed in a case fabricated in a peppercorn of the ordinary size! The Pope is said to have himself counted them, but with the help of a pair of spectacles, for they were so very small as to be almost invisible to the naked eye. Although his holiness thus satisfied his own eyes of the fact, he did not, we are assured, require of those about him to subscribe to it on the credit of his infallibility; for he gave every one an opportunity of examining and judging for himself, and among the persons thus highly favored, particular reference is made to Gaspar Schioppins, Johannes Faber, a physician of Rome.

Turrianus, of whose skill so many wonderful things are related, is said to have fabricated iron mills, which moved of themselves, so minute in size, that a monk could carry one in his sleeve; and yet it was powerful enough to grind in a single day, grain enough for the consumption of eight men.

A Whistler.—A boy in Vermont, accustomed to working alone, was so prone to whistling, that, as soon as he was by himself, he unconsciously commenced. When asleep, the muscles of his mouth, chest, and lungs were so completely concatenated in the association, he whistled with astonishing shrillness. A pale countenance, loss of appetite, and almost total prostration of strength, convinced his mother it would end in death, if not speedily overcome; which was accomplished by placing him in the society of another boy, who had orders to give him a blow as soon as he began to whistle.

telegraph had already made its bow, between Washington and Baltimore in 1844, completely transforming the idea of 'news' from one of days to one of hours. The printing industry had already embarked on the series of technological developments which were soon to raise potential readerships from tens of thousands into millions. What the newspapers needed was news, and the men to find it.

From this point on this book is not concerned, except incidentally, with the internal history and development of the press. There are already a great many general and specialist studies available on the subject. What it is concerned with are the news stories as they appeared in the press. It is, if you like, an anthology of famous events from 1850 to the present day as seen through the newspapers themselves. For many of them I have attempted to provide the historical context and, so far as space allows, to show how attitudes and reactions differed from one country's press to the other, from one newspaper to another.

The selection is, of course, purely personal. I admit to having adopted journalistic criteria for my choices rather than historical ones – it seemed somehow more appropriate. If I appear to have given equal weight to, say, Valentino's funeral as to the declaration of a war – well, that is in the nature of daily journalism and sometimes how it looks in the papers themselves. Nor have I gone out of my way to present the press in a consistently good light: this collection includes its disasters as well as its triumphs, some of its obvious vices as well as its virtues. I would like to believe (indeed I do) that the newspapers concerned would not have it any other way. Certainly an institution which spends a great deal of its time concerned with other people's shortcomings should be robust and honest enough not to be over-sensitive about its own. Besides I personally believe that in the balance of history the good that newspapers have wrought far outweighs the bad, and I hope that in general this book reflects that.

Landmarks in the 19th and 20th centuries

NEW-YORK EVENING POST.

THE TIMES

THE SUNDAY TIMES

THE NEW YORK HERALD.

New-York Tribune.

The Times-Picayune.

1801 *The New York Evening Post* founded on funds raised by Alexander Hamilton and other federalists. Under distinguished editors as William Cullen Bryant and E. L. Godkin *The Post* became one of New York's most venerable and influential journals.

1817 Thomas Barnes appointed editor of *The Times* (founded 1788). Three years before the paper had revolutionised printing by inventing and installing the first steam press. This, combined with the flair of Barnes and his successor in 1841 (John Delane), gave *The Times* a near-monopoly in Britain for half a century.

1819 Parliament pass the 'Six Acts', the last serious attempt to enact repressive legislation against the press in Britain (analogous to the Sedition Act in America in 1798).

1822 Henry White founds *The Sunday Times* selling at 7d.

1827 *The Standard* founded as a London evening paper, becoming a morning paper in 1857 and one of the first journals in the country to sell at 1d. *The Morning Standard* folded in 1917, but its evening stablemate prospered and absorbed both *The St. James's Gazette* (1905) and *The Pall Mall Gazette* (1923).

1833 Benjamin Day starts *The New York Sun* the first penny daily to reach a popular audience.

1835 James Gordon Bennett launches *The New York Herald* as a popular, truly independent daily. His personal and enterprising brand of journalism — especially during the Civil War — was to give *The Herald* a pre-eminence among mid-Victorian newspapers.

1841 Horace Greeley, later to become a Presidential candidate, starts *The New York Tribune* a close competitor to *The Herald* in the circulation race but more crusading and idealistic than its rival. Under Greeley's successor, Whitelaw Reid, the paper gave its unswerving loyalty to the Republican party.

1846 *The Daily News* founded, with Charles Dickens as its first editor and dedicated to the cause of reform.
The New Orleans *Picayune*, and other newspapers from that city, pioneer organised war correspondence during the Mexican War.

The New-York Times.

Chicago Daily Tribune
THE WORLD'S GREATEST NEWSPAPER

The Daily Telegraph

San Francisco Chronicle
LEADING NEWSPAPER of the PACIFIC COAST

THE GUARDIAN

San Francisco Examiner
MONARCH OF THE DAILIES

 The **World**

1847 The Hoe Rotary Press is developed, heralding a rapid expansion in circulations.

1848 The Associated Press is formed by six New York newspapers.

1851 Henry Raymond founds *The New York Times* and establishes a tradition for comprehensive and energetic news-gathering which is still epitomised in the paper's slogan today — 'all the news that's fit to print'. Under the vigorous direction of its publisher (from 1895) Adolph Ochs, *The Times* gradually achieved the reputation as America's most respected paper.

1855 Stamp duty on all British newspapers abolished, followed six years later by the final repeal of duty on newsprint. Joseph Medill buys into *The Chicago Tribune* and founds a dynasty noted for its aggressive, patriotic yet parochial Republicanism.
The Daily Telegraph founded in London by Colonel Sleigh, the first in the newspaper boom following removal of the Stamp duty and pioneer of cheap journalism in Britain. It could very soon lay claim to possessing the 'biggest circulation in the world'.

1863 Stereotyping and web-perfecting presses begin to be used paving the way for circulations of a million and more.

1865 *The San Francisco Chronicle* started by the De Young brothers from a theatre programme sheet. With contributors such as Mark Twain and Bret Harte it was to dominate West Coast publishing for many years.

1872 C. P. Scott becomes editor of *The Manchester Guardian* (founded 1821). His reign, the longest in British journalism lasting 57 years, elevated this provincial paper to the leadership of liberal opinion in Britain.

1876 Victor Lawson buys *The Chicago Daily News* (founded the same year) and successfully devotes it to the cause of local reforms.

1878 E. W. Scripps launches *The Cleveland Press*, the foundation-stone of one of America's greatest newspaper chains.

1883 Joseph Pulitzer (already proprietor of *The St. Louis Post-Dispatch*) takes over the moribund *New York World* and transforms it — apart from a deplorable lapse at the turn of the century — into the successful leader of liberal opinion in the city.

1886 Linotype setting machines make their first appearance (at *The New York Tribune*), followed in 1897 by Monotype machines.

1887 William Randolph Hearst takes over as editor of his father's paper, *The San Francisco Examiner*, and revolutionises the concept of popular journalism.

1890 *The Daily Graphic* originated by an engraver, William Thomas, as London's first picture paper.

1894 Alfred Harmsworth, later Lord Northcliffe, buys *The Evening News* (founded 1881) — initiating the largest chain of newspapers the world has ever seen.

1896 Hearst founds *The New York Journal*, based on and in competition with Pulitzer's *World*, but with a more sensational bias. This ushers in the animated but widely-deprecated era of the 'yellow press'. Within a few years Hearst goes on to build up a chain that was to include newspapers in Boston, Washington, Detroit, Los Angeles, Wisconsin, Atlanta, Albany and many other American cities.

Daily Mail.

Daily Mirror

THE OBSERVER

DAILY SKETCH

Daily Express

SUNDAY·PICTORIAL
SALE MORE THAN DOUBLE THAT OF ANY OTHER SUNDAY PICTURE PAPER

News Chronicle

THE SUNDAY TIMES *magazine*

1897 Harmsworth founds *The Daily Mail* in London, which sells for ½d and is the pioneer of mass-circulation newspapers in Britain.
Halftone engraving process perfected, so making photographs in newspapers a practical proposition.

1901 Marconi transmits the first message by wireless-telegraphy across the Atlantic (from Cornwall to Newfoundland).

1904 *The Daily Mirror* inaugurated by Lord Northcliffe originally as a women's paper. After several months of gigantic financial loss, he transmutes it into an illustrated daily newspaper, and is immediately successful.

1908 J. L. Garvin is appointed editor of *The Observer* (founded 1791) and revitalises serious Sunday journalism in Britain during his long incumbency (–1942).

1909 *The Daily Sketch* founded by Sir Edward Hulton as a rival to *The Mirror*. It is later to absorb its other competitor, *The Graphic*, assuming its name for a period.

1912 *The Daily Herald* comes into existence as a national paper after its birth as a temporary strike sheet. Sustained through many vicissitudes by the political left and a levy from the trades unions, it was bought in 1929 by Odhams Press and, with heavy promotion, became the first British paper to reach a circulation of 2 million.

1915 Lord Beaverbrook buys *The Daily Express* (founded 1900) and, infusing it with his own vision of Imperial solidarity, builds it up to a prosperity based upon a very wide range of readership.
The Sunday Pictorial, Britain's first Sunday picture paper, founded in haste by Lord Rothermere to pre-empt the publication of *The Sunday Graphic*.

1919 Joseph Medill Patterson quits Chicago to found the tabloid *The New York Daily News* (based on Northcliffe's *Mirror*), leaving his brother Colonel Robert McCormick in sole charge of *The Chicago Tribune*. The success of *The Daily News*, which was to become America's largest-selling newspaper, inspires a rash of imitators including Hearst's *Mirror* and Bernard Macfadden's *The Evening Graphic*. The era of the New York tabloids was remarkable for its out-and-out sensation-seeking.

1924 Frank Munsey (the 'great high executioner' of newspapers) sells *The New York Herald* to *The Tribune*.

1930 Decease of the *World*, which is fossilised within the Scripps-Howard chain as *The World-Telegram*.

1930 *The News Chronicle* begins publication, an amalgam of *The Daily News* and *The Daily Chronicle* which are themselves hybrids of several other Liberal newspapers. In 1960 their reputable descendant, too, is summarily executed.

1933 *The Philadelphia Inquirer* is merged with *The Public Ledger* after the death of Cyrus H. K. Curtis and the disintegration of his chain of papers.

1937 *The Morning Post*, Britain's oldest surviving newspaper, is absorbed by *The Daily Telegraph*.

1953 Britain's Press Council meets for the first time.

1961 Royal Commission on the Press is set up in Britain.

1962 *The Sunday Times* issues the first colour supplement in Britain and, later, pioneers in-depth reporting with its 'Insight' column.

HEADLINES 1850-1880

THE WAR.

TELEGRAPHIC INTELLIGENCE.

AUSTRIA AND THE CONFERENCE.

BALLOON NEWS FROM PARIS.
THE BOMBARDMENT OF THE FORTS.

EFFECTS OF THE FIRE

The World

NEW YORK : SUNDAY, JANUARY 7, 1872.   PRICE FIVE CENTS.

VOL. XII. NO. 3795.

THE FARCE.

Prosecution of Fisk for Libel in the Yorkville Police Court.

FAIR HELEN IN TEARS.

Bixby and Beach Bewildered by Blubbering Beauty.

A WICKED HEART AND AN AFFECTING SCENE.

The Testimony of Stokes and Josie's Cousin.

TRAGEDY

Fisk, Jr., Assassinated by Edward S. Stokes.

THE INQUEST.

THE STANDARD, THURSDAY, SEPTEMBER 17, 1857.

THE MUTINIES IN INDIA.

THE OVERLAND MAIL.

THE DISTURBED PROVINCES.
DELHI.

THE PALL MALL GAZETTE

An Evening Newspaper and Review.

No. 3362.—VOL. XXII.   FRIDAY, NOVEMBER 26, 1875.   Price Twopence.

THE SUEZ CANAL.

RURAL MUNICIPALITIES.

The Globe
AND TRAVELLER.

MONDAY EVENING, DECEMBER 16, 1861.

DEATH OF THE PRINCE CONSORT.

The World

PRICE FOUR CENTS.

CUSTER KILLED.

DISASTROUS DEFEAT OF THE AMERICAN TROOPS BY THE INDIANS.

SLAUGHTER OF OUR BEST AND BRAVEST.

A WHOLE FAMILY OF HEROES SWEPT AWAY.

THREE HUNDRED AND FIFTEEN AMERICAN SOLDIERS KILLED AND THIRTY-ONE WOUNDED.

WASHINGTON.

JULY 6, 1876.

SENATOR MORRILL ACCEPTS THE TREASURY PORTFOLIO.

Whom shall we hang?

The Crimean War

THE NEW BARRACK-HOSPITAL, AT SCUTARI.

Illustrated London News.

There could be no arguments about the commercial success of a newspaper that sold more copies a day than all its competitors put together. Still less could there by any question about the political influence of *The Times* at the pinnacle of its splendour in the 1850s. What other journal in the world was consulted on policy by Prime Ministers? Or bribed (unsuccessfully) by Emperors? Which of its contemporaries would have dared to announce the repeal of the Corn Laws before the Cabinet had even given its decision to Parliament? From what other source could the Tsar in 1854 have learnt the terms of the British ultimatum to Russia — before it had been presented to him? There were times when the paper appeared better-informed on the country's policies than the Ministers concerned. Little wonder Lord John Russell should write peevishly to the Queen in 1854: 'The degree of information possessed by *The Times* with regard to the most secret affairs of State is mortifying, humiliating and incomprehensible'.

Mortifying it may have been to Russell, who more than once suffered from what he called the 'vile tyranny' and 'dangerous omnipotence' of *The Times*, but it should not have been incomprehensible. For under Thomas Barnes (editor from 1817–1841) and now John Delane *The Times* had consciously identified with the middle classes, not long enfranchised and still aspiring to political power; it had grown to be the spokesman for and barometer of this important section of the country, and a Prime Minister who neglected to assure himself of *The Times*' support did so at his own risk.

It was this sensitivity to the mood of the country that persuaded *The Times* in 1854 to support an aggressive policy against Russian opportunism in Eastern Europe. Deprived of it

for forty years, the British people had set their hearts on 'a good war' or so it seemed to Delane. And as the paper's proprietor, (the third) John Walter, said: 'When the country would go for war, it was not worth while to oppose it'. So, the decision made, *The Times* set out to provide its public with a ringside seat. The paper began marshalling its team of war correspondents as early as October 1853, but it was not until the following February that its most distinguished representative, a genial and enterprising Irishman called William Russell, was assigned to accompany the British force embarking for Malta. This was intended as no more than a show of strength by Britain — Russell fully expected to be home by Easter.

But Easter came and found Britain at war with Russia, and Russell at Gallipoli hanging grimly onto the shirt-tails of the army until the inevitable invasion of the Crimea began. For Russell to have got that far was something of a minor triumph: the days of official accreditation were yet to come and war correspondents were a novelty, at best tolerated by commanders on sufferance, often not at all. The man from *The Times* found himself denied rations, transport, even a tent until he scrounged one for himself through a sustained effort of blarney. When a brigadier discovered that Russell had pitched it within the lines, it was summarily dismantled and thrown outside. Even Delane's string-pulling among the Cabinet at home seemed to have little effect on the banks of the Alma.

Russell's own discomforts, however, were the least of his pre-occupations. Part of the army had contracted diseases in Malta, and many more since. Hospital facilities were pitifully inadequate, medical supplies virtually nonexistent. The lack of concern by senior officers seemed to Russell worse than criminal:

British soldiers were dying of muddle and mismanagement, before a shot was fired. For the sick there were no beds, barely one blanket each; food was contaminated, cholera rampant. The military bureaucracy, grown corpulent through long years of peace, had collapsed under its own weight. Russell's furious indictments — printed in full in *The Times* — came so thick and fast that in August Delane himself felt obliged to travel out to the Crimea and scrutinise the situation for himself. He had circulated Russell's private letters among the Cabinet, but he also had to have a firsthand answer to the puff's chorus who complained bitterly that the dispatches were giving information and encouragement to the enemy.

He observed for himself 'the sad traces of cholera and fever in the pale faces, lank forms and tottering steps of the men . . . the reduced giants looking hardly able to carry their own epaulets'. He returned to England to step up the campaign for the relief of this vanishing army. *The Times* somewhat tarnished its own ardour in October by mistakenly announcing the fall of Sebastopol, at a time when the generals were only beginning to contemplate an assault. Yet it was a tribute to the paper's impact on the public conscience when, after an editorial on the 12th appealing for a Relief Fund, *The Times* found itself inundated with donations. This fund, which the paper administered personally at the front ultimately topped £25,000 and enabled Florence Nightingale's pioneering nurses to minister to such famous effect in spite of a tight-fisted Treasury.

As winter approached Russell's reports took on a more urgent tone: 'These are hard truths but the people of England must hear them' he wrote on November 25. 'They must know that the wretched beggar who wanders the streets of London in the rain leads the life of a prince compared with the British soldiers who are fighting out here for their country and who, we are complacently assured by the home authorities, are the best appointed army in Europe'. Now, punctuating his unrelieved catalogue of misery, there came specific allegations against the military competence of the commanders. Russell had observed, on October 25, the futile misunderstandings which had sent the Light Brigade to certain annihilation at Balaclava. 'Lord Raglan is utterly incompetent to lead the army' he complained to Delane, and Delane duly translated this into the full flowering of political rhetoric, castigating a commander-in-chief who 'should survive alone on the heights of Sebastopol, decorated, ennobled, duly named in despatch after despatch . . . amid the bones of fifty thousand British soldiers' (December 30).

For a month his unrelenting campaign against the conduct of the war continued, until on January 25 he pronounced 'We wipe our hands of the war under the existing management'. But the existing management (in the persons of Prime Minister Aberdeen and Secretary for War Newcastle) were now under siege themselves. Anonymous pamphlets with ominous titles like 'Whom shall we hang?' were circulating and Parliament was getting touchy at the public outcry. On February 1 the Ministry resigned, in favour of Lord Palmerston, who was certainly no friend of *The Times*, but pledged to prosecute the war with vigour and therefore given the benefit of a probationary truce.

It did not last long, for Raglan inexplicably stayed on at his post, and on and on. The siege of Sebastopol lurched on through spring and into summer. Conditions in the army improved with the weather and the abundant supplies that now arrived from England (even from the government). In June Raglan died, 'killed by *The Times*' those less kindly disposed maintained. But *The Times* gave him an exemplary obituary, and looked forward to better things. Even then they were slow in coming: Sebastopol held out till September and the new commanders seemed more active in defending themselves against the press than in attacking the Russians. Their most frequent grumble was that Russell's detailed accounts of British movements, dispositions, intentions and morale were of inestimable benefit to the Russians – who pored over *The Times* in Moscow the day after publication. There may, to be fair, have been some substance in these allegations (although Russell was informed after the war by the commander of the Sebastopol garrison that, though he had very much enjoyed the articles, he had learnt nothing new from them).

The fault, if any existed, lay in the total absence of news-censorship. Until the coming of the telegraph and of specialist war correspondents like Russell none had been neccessary. Towards the end of the campaign feeble efforts had been made to introduce it, but the War Office proved as incompetent as to what to permit as the newspapers themselves. Against this must be balanced the inescapable conclusion that, alone and unaided, *The Times* had saved an army – and for many years it reaped the benefits of the widespread admiration it won in so doing. And just to rub the point in, *The Times* (via a correspondent in Vienna) received the news that the Russians had unconditionally accepted the British peace terms before even the government was informed. As an appeasing gesture Palmerston passed the official word from Moscow along to Delane the moment he received it. He was too late again – a special edition of *The Times* was already on the streets.

THE CAVALRY ACTION AT BALAKLAVA.

OCTOBER 25.

And now occurred the melancholy catastrophe which fills us all with sorrow. It appears that the Quartermaster-General, Brigadier Airey, thinking that the Light Cavalry had not gone far enough in front when the enemy's horse had fled, gave an order in writing to Captain Nolan, 15th Hussars, to take to Lord Lucan, directing his Lordship "to advance" his cavalry nearer to the enemy. A braver soldier than Captain Nolan the army did not possess. He was known to all his arm of the service for his entire devotion to his profession, and his name must be familiar to all who take interest in our cavalry for his excellent work, published a year ago, on our drill and system of remount and breaking horses. I had the pleasure of his acquaintance, and I know he entertained the most exalted opinions respecting the capabilities of the English horse soldier. Properly led, the British Hussar and Dragoon could in his mind break square, take batteries, ride over columns of infantry, and pierce any other cavalry in the world as if they were made of straw. He thought they had not had the opportunity of doing all that was in their power, and that they had missed even such chances as they had offered to them,—that, in fact, they were in some measure disgraced. A matchless horseman and a first-rate swordsman, he held in contempt, I am afraid, even grape and canister. He rode off with his orders to Lord Lucan. He is now dead and gone. God forbid I should cast a shade on the brightness of his honour, but I am bound to state what I am told occurred when he reached his Lordship. I should premise that as the Russian cavalry retired, their infantry fell back towards the head of the valley, leaving men in three of the redoubts they had taken, and abandoning the fourth. They had also placed some guns on the heights over their position, on the left of the gorge. Their cavalry joined the reserves, and drew up in six solid divisions, in an oblique line, across the entrance to the gorge. Six battalions of infantry were placed behind them, and about 30 guns were drawn up along their line, while masses of infantry were also collected on the hills behind the redoubts on our right. Our cavalry had moved up to the ridge across the valley, on our left, as the ground was broken in front, and had halted in the order I have already mentioned. When Lord Lucan received the order from Captain Nolan and had read it, he asked, we are told, "Where are we to advance to?" Captain Nolan pointed with his finger to the line of the Russians, and said, "There are the enemy, and there are the guns, sir, before them; it is your duty to take them," or words to that effect, according to the statements made since his death. Lord Lucan, with reluctance, gave the order to Lord Cardigan to advance upon the guns, conceiving that his orders compelled him to do so. The noble Earl, though he did not shrink, also saw the fearful odds against him. Don Quixote in his tilt against the windmill was not near so rash and reckless as the gallant fellows who prepared without a thought to rush on almost certain death. It is a maxim of war, that "cavalry never act without a support," that "infantry should be close at hand when cavalry carry guns, as the effect is only instantaneous," and that it is necessary to have on the flank of a line of cavalry some squadrons in column, the attack on the flank being most dangerous. The only support our light cavalry had was the reserve of heavy cavalry at a great distance behind them, the infantry and guns being far in the rear. There were no squadrons in column at all, and there was a plain to charge over, before the enemy's guns were reached, of a mile and a half in length. At 11 10 our Light Cavalry Brigade rushed to the front. They numbered as follows, as well as I can ascertain:—

	Men.
4th Light Dragoons	118
8th Irish Hussars	104
11th Prince Albert's Hussars	110
13th Light Dragoons	130
17th Lancers	145
Total	607 sabres.

The whole brigade scarcely made one effective regiment, according to the numbers of continental armies; and yet it was more than we could spare. As they passed towards the front, the Russians opened on them from the guns in the redoubt on the right, with volleys of musketry and rifles. They swept proudly past, glittering in the morning sun in all the pride and splendour of war. We could scarcely believe the evidence of our senses! Surely that handful of men are not going to charge an army in position? Alas! it was but too true—their desperate valour knew no bounds, and far indeed was it removed from its so-called better part—discretion. They advanced in two lines, quickening their pace as they closed towards the enemy. A more fearful spectacle was never witnessed than by those who, without the power to aid, beheld their heroic countrymen rushing to the arms of death. At the distance of 1,200 yards the whole line of the enemy belched forth, from 30 iron mouths, a flood of smoke and flame, through which hissed the deadly balls. Their flight was marked by instant gaps in our ranks, by dead men and horses, by steeds flying wounded or riderless across the plain. The first line is broken, it is joined by the second, they never halt or check their speed an instant; with diminished ranks, thinned by those 30 guns, which the Russians had laid with the most deadly accuracy, with a halo of flashing steel above their heads, and with a cheer which was many a noble fellow's death-cry, they flew into the smoke of the batteries, but ere they were lost from view the plain was strewed with their bodies and with the carcasses of horses. They were exposed to an oblique fire from the batteries on the hills on both sides, as well as to a direct fire of musketry. Through the clouds of smoke we could see their sabres flashing as they rode up to the guns and dashed between them, cutting down the gunners as they stood.

THE BRITISH EXPEDITION.

(FROM OUR SPECIAL CORRESPONDENT.)

CAMP BEFORE SEBASTOPOL, JAN. 2.

We have had rather a rough and dreary Christmas of it, and we have not had a very happy New-year, as yet, on these heights before Sebastopol. Where are our presents—our Christmas Boxes—the offerings of our kind countrymen and country-women, and the donations from our ducal parks? Where are the fat bucks which had, we were told, exhausted the conservative principles of a Gunter; the potted meats, which covered the decks and filled the holds of adventurous yachts; and the various worsted devices which had employed the fingers and emptied the crochet-boxes of our fair sympathizers at home? They may be all on the way, but they will arrive too late; and, whether they are knocking about among the Cyclades, or struggling against the storms of the Mediterranean, they are wanting to the army in its utmost need. While our friends at home are disputing about the exact mean degree of cold of the Crimean winter, and are preparing all kinds of warm clothing, which at some good time or other will come out to the men, our army is rapidly melting away—dissolved in rain. It is the rain and the melting snows we have to dread as yet more even than excessive cold. For two or three days at Christmas time there were cold dry winds and fine weather. On the heights there was hard frost at night, but the men did not suffer from the cold so much as they would have done from wet. On the contrary, they rather cheered up and became active and hopeful, when once they could move about on solid ground. But this change did not last long, for the rain began to fall once more; the roads and the fields, which had begun to dry up, were again turned into mud and slush, and disease and despondency assumed their sway with redoubled power. At the present date there are no less than 3,500 sick men in the British camp before Sebastopol, and it is not too much to say that their illness has, for the most part, been caused by hard work in bad weather, and by exposure to wet without any adequate protection. Think what a tent must be, pitched, as it were, at the bottom of a marsh, into which some 12 or 14 miserable creatures, drenched to the skin, have to creep for shelter after 12 hours of vigil in a trench like a canal, and then reflect what state these poor fellows must be in at the end of a night and day spent in such *shelter*, huddled together without any change of clothing, and lying packed up as close as they can stow in saturated blankets. But why are they in tents? Where are the huts which have been sent out to them? The huts are on board ships in the harbour of Balaklava, and are likely to stay there. Some of these huts, of which we have heard so much, I have seen floating about the beach; others have been landed, and now and then I have met a wretched pony, knee-deep in mud, struggling on beneath the weight of two thin deal planks, a small portion of one of these huts, which would be most probably converted into firewood after lying for some time in the camp, or be turned into stabling for officers' horses when enough of *disjecta membra* had been collected. As I write the rain is falling in torrents, and the floods of mud are flowing down the hill sides and roads so as to cut off supplies to the camp to a great extent. Now, if central depôts had been established, as Mr. Filder proposed, while the fine weather lasted, much, if not all, of the misery and suffering of the men and of the loss of horses would have been averted.

The Times.

Bohemians and Copperheads

The American Civil War

Washington, April 12 1861. 'The city was uncommonly quiet today' (telegraphed *The World's* correspondent) 'but the terrible reality came tonight in the midst of the lull which had been created by telegrams holding out the olive branch and proclaiming peace . . . About 6 o'clock tonight a dispatch stating that Fort Sumter had been fired on was received and bulletined. The excitement which followed is beyond all description . . .' All the same, the reporter manfully wrestled with his vocabulary to do justice to the ferment of carriages stampeding through the capital in the drenching rain, the crowds besieging hotel lobbies to read the news for themselves, the comings and goings of Congressmen through the night. Secessionists were said to be holding secret revels around the city. Informed of the bombardment the President was reported to have declared 'he did not like it'. No gloom or despondency was anywhere to be found, only anxiety 'that the dignity and honour of the government should be maintained'.

Thus, at last, it had come to war, inevitable for weeks and diligently prepared for by the press. The London *Times* had dispatched William Russell to America on the first day of March — a sure sign that war was to be expected for Russell's reputation as a war correspondent was a byword in the (formerly) United States.

Within days of the President's war declaration, Washington was inundated with hundreds of correspondents from Northern papers, 'the Bohemian Brigade' as the more adventurous of them came to be styled. 'You meet a newspaperman at every step' *The New York Times* reported. 'They block up the approaches to Headquarters; one of them is attached to the button of every officer'. The scramble for accreditation (such as there was to be had) was as undignified as it was very often fruitless. It availed Russell nothing that not many days previously he had been wined and dined, and effusively welcomed by the President: there was no pass for him (though, in his case no doubt, this was an official reaction of disapproval at *The Times*' strident support of the Southern cause). He returned to Britain a few months later having witnessed — sadly for his reputation in America — only the headlong stampede of the Union army after Bull Run.

It was, perhaps, inevitable that the whole campaign would be fraught with clashes between the press and the authorities. To the commanders in the field, the idea of trailing along a bevy of war correspondents like so many camp-followers was a novel and, for the most part, ridiculous one. There was barely a general in the Union army who did not, at one time or another during the war, banish newsmen

from his headquarters. The Administration had but a hazy conception of what was required in the way of censorship, and applied it often in arbitrary fashion, sometimes via the State Department, sometimes through the War Department. What made its task no easier was the humiliating fact that, as often as not, official sources were hours if not days behind the newspapers.

The newspapers, for their part, showed they had profited from the example of the New Orleans press — and *The Picayune* in particular — which had so successfully sent correspondents to cover the Mexican War of 1846. When the Civil War exploded, James Gordon Bennett plunged no less than 40 reporters into the fray for *The New York Herald* with explicit instructions to bring back the news first (in which they regularly succeeded, though the effort cost Bennett more than a quarter of a million dollars over four years). In the case of other papers the editor went along himself, notably Henry Raymond of *The New York Times*. Nor was it simply because lack of official information (or control) threw reporters back on their own initiative and enterprise that the scramble for news reached unprecedented cut-throat proportions. The spread of the railroads and, more important, of the electric telegraph alongside them was already revolutionising communica-

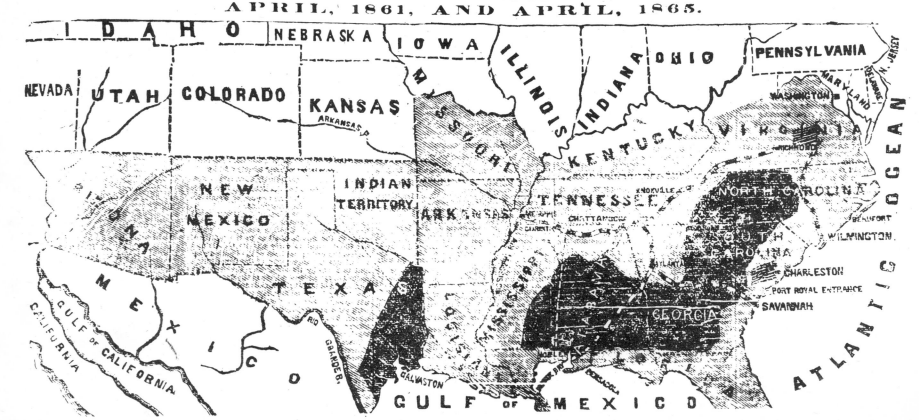

Left: The first report in the New York Times of the Battle of Bull Run.

tions. Gone were the days of the 'special's' long, purple and discursive analysis of events recollected in tranquility: the public that had once thought of news in terms of days, now felt cheated if it was not available in hours. The Civil War was the first modern war, not just in terms of weaponry and tactics, but also in the dissemination of information.

The exciting corollary, of course, was the vast and, as it turned out, permanent increase in circulations. Bennett's $\frac{1}{4}$ million was money well spent; his paper's superiority in war-coverage earned it a readership of considerably more than 100,000 by the end of the war, and other papers could point to increases equally dramatic. Then, as at no period in their history since pre-Revolution days the newspapers were a force in the land. During the Draft Riots of 1863 it was the newspaper offices that the various mobs set upon, particularly Horace Greeley's *The New York Tribune* (which continued to publish uninterruptedly, hurling its defiance the while). It was an over-optimistic, but not entirely facile, ambition that Bennett nursed when he declared his aim to make the newspaper press the great organ and pivot of government, society, commerce, finance, religion and all human civilisation'.

It cannot, however, be said that all the newspapers of the Civil War showed themselves equal to Bennett's ideal. The freedom with which the Press operated was not always matched by its sense of responsibility. Stories were not infrequently to be found bearing the headline 'Important, if True' — nor did it always transpire that the important news *was* true (as the spate of premature reports in New York of a great Union victory at Bull Run bore witness). One Baltimore paper unashamedly headlined one of its pieces 'Rumours and Speculations', which exhibited an honesty of sorts, to be sure.

One of the strangest aspects of the press 'freedom' of this period was the existence in several Northern cities of the 'copperhead' newspapers. These journals were not simply critical of the federal administration, of the President (or 'half-witted usurper' to descend to their phraseology) or the conduct of the war; they were vehemently pro-slavery and embraced the rebel cause with open arms. There were five such papers in New York alone, including *The Journal* and *The Daily News* (bearing no relation to their descendants) and one major one in Chicago, *The Times*. The response to these papers by the government was sometimes equally uninhibited, and a number of copperhead editors found themselves cooling their venom in prison. Nor could the President count absolutely on the support of all the 'patriotic' press, either. Lincoln had occasion

THE NEW YORK HERALD.

WHOLE NO. 8983.   SUNDAY MORNING, APRIL 14, 1861.   PRICE TWO CENTS.

THE WAR.

THE CONFLICT AT CHARLESTON

The Bombardment Fiercely Continued.

FORT SUMTER ON FIRE

Major Anderson's Men on Flotillas Dipping Water to Stop the Blaze.

The Men Fired Upon from the Forts.

The Surrender of Fort Sumter.

THE BOMBARDMENT CEASED.

THE FORT EVACUATED.

Major Anderson the Guest of General Beauregard.

NO ONE KILLED IN THE CONFLICT.

All the Federal Officers Unhurt.

Blockade of the Port of Charleston.

dense volume of smoke expanding. Major Anderson ceased to fire for about an hour. His flag is still up. It is thought the officers' quarters in Fort Sumter are on fire.

CHARLESTON, April 13—12 M.

The ships in the offing appear to be quietly at anchor. They have not fired a gun yet.

The entire roof of the barracks at Fort Sumter are in a vast sheet of flame.

Shells from Cumming's Point and Fort Moultrie are bursting in and over Fort Sumter in quick succession.

The federal flag still waves.

Major Anderson is only occupied in putting out fire.

Every shot on Fort Sumter now seems to tell heavily.

The people are anxiously looking for Major Anderson to strike his flag.

CHARLESTON, April 13—P. M.

Two of Major Anderson's magazines have exploded.

Only occasional shots are fired at him from Fort Moultrie.

The Morris Island Battery is doing heavy work.

It is thought that only the smaller magazines have exploded.

The greatest excitement prevails. The wharves, steeples and every available place are packed with people.

The United States ships are in the offing, but have not aided Major Anderson. It is too late now to come over the bar, as the tide is ebbing.

CHARLESTON, April 13—Evening.

Major Anderson has surrendered, after hard fighting, commencing at half past four o'clock yesterday morning, and continuing until five minutes to one to-day.

The American flag has given place to the palmetto flag of South Carolina.

You have received my previous despatches concerning the fire and the shooting away of the flagstaff. The latter event is due to Fort Moultrie, as well as the burning of the fort, which resulted from one of the hot shots fired

Topographical Sketch of Fort Sumter.

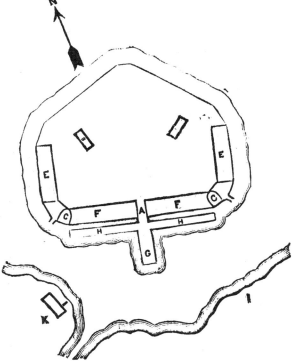

A Arched gateway in the southwest wall.
B Barracks for beating shot.
C Powder magazines.
D Daily ports.
E Barracks for the soldiers.
F Officers quarters.
G Wharf—depth of water on east side sixteen to eight feet.

H Principal landing—extending along the entire south-west wall.
I Morris Island Beach.
K Fort Johnson, on James Island.
We would mention that the position of Morris and James Islands, owing to the small size of the engraving, is not indicated to be considered as more than indicating their proximity to Fort Sumter.

Major Anderson expresses himself much | balls can be seen skipping over the water and

Three fire companies from Charleston are now on their way to Sumter to quell the fire before it reaches the magazine.

Fort Sumter has unconditionally surrendered.

Ex-Senator Chesnut, ex-Governor Manning and W. P. Miles have just landed and marched to Governor Pickens' residence, followed by a dense crowd, wild with joy.

It is reported that the federal flag was shot away by the Palmetto Guards at Morris Island.

In all two thousand shots have been fired. No Carolinians killed.

Major Anderson and his men, under guard, were conveyed to Morris Island.

The bells are ringing out a merry peal and our people are engaged in every demonstration of joy.

It is estimated that there are nine thousand men under arms on the islands and in the neighbourhood.

THE LATEST NEWS.

CHARLESTON, April 13, 1861.

I have seen W. Porcher Miles, who has just returned from a visit to Fort Sumter. He assured me that no one was killed at Fort Sumter. This is reliable, and puts at rest all previous reports about Sumter.

Major Anderson has reached the city, and is the guest of General Beauregard.

Our people sympathise with Major Anderson, but abhor those who were in the steamers off our bar and in sight of our people, and did not even attempt to reinforce him.

The Fairfield regiment, one thousand strong, has just passed the Courier office on their way to Morris Island.

There are now ten thousand men under arms in the harbor and on the coast.

Judge Magrath, who has just returned, reports that the wood work and officers' quarters at Fort Sumter are all burnt.

None of the officers were wounded.

The fort will be taken possession of to-night by the Confederate troops.

A boat from one of the vessels outside the harbor communicated with General Simons, in command of the forces on Morris Island.

bearing rebel despatches, were also sent. The Yankee left the port on Monday evening last, and the Uncle Ben on Tuesday night.

THE LANDING.

Nearly thirty of the boats—it is said are serviceable are most useful in effecting a landing of troops over shoal water, and for affording a discharging battery when covered with sand and gunny bags—have been taken out by the Powhatan and by the steam transports Atlantic, Baltic and Illinois.

RECAPITULATION.

Vessels.	Guns.	Men.
Sloop-of-war Powhatan	10	280
Sloop-of-war Pocahontas	11	215
Cutter Harriet Lane	5	96
Steam transport Atlantic	—	300
Steam transport Baltic	—	160
Steam transport Illinois	—	300
Steam tug Uncle Ben	—	ordinary crew
Steam tug Yankee	—	ordinary crew
Total number of vessels		8
Total number of guns (for naming sort of)		36
Total number of men and troops		1500

It is understood that several transports are to be also chartered and despatched to Charleston with troops and supplies.

THE NEWS FROM WASHINGTON.

WASHINGTON, April 13, 1861.

The capital continues in a frantic state of excitement. Business is half suspended in consequence of the intense excitement. The bombardment of Fort Sumter are gathered at the corners; the living spit offices, the White House and the War and Navy Departments are besieged by crowds of eager inquirers. The hotel lobbies and parlors were jammed with humanity all the morning.

The republicans are well in with indignation, and curse the rebels and clever Major Anderson most roundly.

The President and Cabinet have been in session nearly all the morning. A large number of prominent men of all parties repaired to the White House at an early hour to tender their services to the President, but none were admitted except the Virginia Committee of Inquiry, who had a conference with him from eight to nine o'clock.

An intense horror prevailed in the Washington most during the forenoon. Four hundred federal troops passed from New York by special train early this morning. About eighteen hundred regulars and volunteers are here here on or arms.

The President is calm and composed. The first question he asked a Western Senator last night was, "Will your State support me with military power?" He will doubtless receive a call for and to the several Governors of the republican States in the course of to-day.

A special session of the press is not likely to be convened. The voice of the North has been heard through telegraphic despatches from every free State, assuring the President of the entire hostile support of the government with men and money.

It is evident that the Union sentiment has been greatly strengthened here since the rebel attack have assumed the responsibility of inaugurating civil war.

Capt. Wm. R. St. Johns, of the Third infantry, having declined the command of his company when ordered to

VIRGINIA!

LEE SURRENDERS!

THE REBELLION ENDED!

OFFICIAL CORRESPONDENCE.

GEN. LEE DESIROUS OF "PEACE."

Manly and Patriotic Letter from General Grant.

The Rebel Leader Must Lay Down His Arms.

He Capitulates on Gen. Grant's Own Terms.

The Officers to be Paroled and Sent Home.

Official Dispatches.

WAR DEPARTMENT,
WASHINGTON, April 9, 1865, 9 o'clock p. m. }

To *Major-Gen.* DIX, *New-York:* This Department has received the official report of the surrender this day of Gen. Lee and his army to Lieut.-Gen. Grant on the terms proposed by Gen. Grant.

Details will be given as speedily as possible.

EDWIN M. STANTON, Secretary of War.

HDQRS. ARMIES OF THE UNITED STATES, }
April 9, 1865, 4:30 p. m. }

Hon. EDWIN M. STANTON, *Secretary of War:* Gen. Lee surrendered the army of Northern Virginia this afternoon upon the terms proposed by myself. The accompanying additional correspondence will show the conditions fully.

U. S. GRANT, Lieutenant-General.

APRIL 9, 1865.

GENERAL: I received your note of this morning on the picket-line, whither I had come to meet you and ascertain definitely what terms were embraced in your proposition of yesterday with reference to the surrender of this army.

I now request an interview in accordance with the offer contained in your letter of yesterday for that purpose.

Very respectfully, your obd't servant,

R. E. LEE, General.

---

in 1865 to remonstrate personally with *The Chicago Tribune's* proprietor, Joseph Medill, when that gentleman began to carp at his city's draft quota. The President was obliged to remind him quite forcibly that his newspaper had done as much as any to ferment the war in the first instance.

Never before and rarely since has a war been reported by eye-witnesses so vividly, unrestrainedly or comprehensively. The exploits of individual correspondents are now an established part of the romantic canon of journalism: of *The New York Tribune's* Albert Richardson, who travelled incognito through the South in 1861, was captured and escaped back to Union lines; the desperate odyssey of the same paper's Henry Wing through Confederate territory to bring news of the battle of the Wilderness (1864) to the capital; the brave, fever-ridden dash by steamer, cab and train of *The New York Herald's* George Townsend to be the first to cable news of the Seven Days Battle in 1862. Still memorable and moving is the account of Gettysburg by Sam Wilkeson of *The New York Times* who, touring the battlefield after the conflict, came across the body of his son: 'Who can write the history of a battle whose eyes are immovably fastened on a central figure of transcendingly absorbing interest — the dead body of an oldest son, crushed by a shell in a position where a battery should never have been set, and abandoned in a building where surgeons dared not to stay?' Sometimes it was hard to decide which had the more epic quality, the marathons endured by the reporters to bring home the stories, or the battlefield heroics contained in their reports.

There was another war being fought in the columns of the Union papers alongside that being resolved on the fields of Maryland and Georgia, one quite as bitter but by no means as heroic — against the British Press. Whether it was through pure ignorance of America and American issues, or more likely through self-centered concern over the lucrative trade with the South, the bulk of London newspaper opinion (led, it must be said, by *The Times*) set its face against the Union. Only *The Daily News* gave the North positive and unflinching support, but its voice was powerless against the confederate chorus. This editorial alignment with the lost cause soured trans-Atlantic relations for years to come — not least in recriminations over the long drawn-out claim for damages inflicted by the Alabama, a Southern privateer which had been allowed to escape from Liverpool and inflict heavy losses on Northern shipping.

Only one event in the whole unhappy period brought the presses of the two countries together, however temporarily. On April 14 1865 President Lincoln (whose moderating influence had done much to curb the American papers' hostility to Britain) was shot in his box at Ford's Theatre by the assassin John Wilkes Booth, even as the last Confederate armies were laying down their arms. *The Daily Telegraph* told its readers: 'From vulgar corruption, from factious hatred, from meanest jealousy and uncharitableness this great ruler was wholly free'. *The Times* wanted to assure 'the American people that, whatever difference of opinion may exist in this country as to the present war, there is but one feeling of sympathy with them at the loss of an honest and high-minded Magistrate'. And, just to show that this wasn't just standard obituary de mortuis nihil nisi bonum stuff, it went on to prove 'the extent to which his influence was estimated . . . has been shown by a fall of universal severity in all classes of securities'.

THE ASSASSINATION.

JEFF. DAVIS AN ACCOMPLICE.

$100,000 Reward Offered for His Capture!

PROCLAMATION BY THE PRESIDENT

Davis, Thompson, Clay, Tucker, Saunders and Cleary Charged with the President's Murder.

THE BRAND OF CAIN FIXED ON THEM.

WHEREABOUTS OF THE ARCH-TRAITOR.

He was at Yorkville, S. C., on the 28th Ultimo.

OUR FORCES PURSUING.

DAVIS ONE DAY AHEAD.

A Proclamation.

Whereas, It appears from evidence in the Bureau of Military Justice that the atrocious murder of the late President, Abraham Lincoln, and the attempted assassination of the Hon. W. H. Seward, Secretary of State, were incited, concerted, and procured by and between Jefferson Davis, late of Richmond, Va., and Jacob Thompson, Clement C. Clay, Beverley Tucker, George N. Sanders, W. C. Cleary, and other Rebels and traitors against the Government of the United States, harbored in Canada; now, therefore, to the end that justice may be done, I, Andrew Johnson, President of the United States, do offer and promise for the arrest of said persons, or either of them within the limits of the United States, so that they can be brought to trial, the following rewards: One hundred thousand dollars for the arrest of Jefferson Davis; twenty-five thousand dollars for the arrest of Clement C. Clay; twenty-five thousand dollars for the arrest of Jacob Thompson, late of Mississippi; twenty-five thousand dollars for the arrest of George N. Sanders; twenty-five thousand dollars for the arrest of Beverley Tucker, and ten thousand dollars for the arrest of William C. Cleary, late Clerk of Clement C. Clay.

The Provost-Marshal-General of the United States is directed to cause a description of said persons, with notice of the above rewards, to be published.

*New York Herald April 10, 1865 (left)
and April 22, 1865 (above).*

THE NATION MOURNS ITS LOSS.

The Philadelphia Inquirer.

PRICE TWO CENTS.   PHILADELPHIA, MONDAY, APRIL 17, 1865.   PRICE TWO CENTS.

THE GREAT TRAGEDY!

A Nation Mourns Its Honored President!

JOY CHANGED TO MOURNING!

The Great Martyr to Liberty!

MURDER OF THE PRESIDENT.

Full Details of the Assassination.

ACCOUNT OF A DISTINGUISHED EYE-WITNESS.

Mr. Lincoln's Death-bed Scenes

A NOBLE PATRIOT GONE TO REST!

Escape of the Dastard Assassin.

MR. SEWARD STILL ALIVE.

His Condition Is Favorable.

Andrew Johnson Inaugurated as President!

HIS INAUGURAL ADDRESS.

Views of the New President.

HE RETAINS THE OLD CABINET!

Official Gazette from Sec'y Stanton.

OUR SPECIAL DESPATCHES

THE GREAT NATIONAL TRAGEDY.

Special Despatch to the Inquirer.

WASHINGTON, April 16.

The monstrous crime of Friday night shocked this city with an agony unutterable. Yesterday morning men walked the streets and looked into each other's eyes, and found no words willing to leave their lips. Their hearts were surcharged with grief and a wrath inexpressible.

J. WILKES BOOTH, THE ASSASSIN.

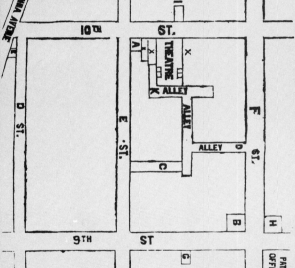

THE SCENE OF THE GREAT TRAGEDY.

E—Bank, formerly Savings Bank.
I—Restaurants.
H—Model House.
Most of the shops back to the alleys.
I—House taken to after the act.
K—The alley by which the murderer escaped.

A—Public School.
B—Herndon House Hotel.
C—The only exit not communicating with the alley.
D—The only alley outlet to F street.

FORD'S THEATRE.

The Locality and Description of the Edifice.

Ford's Theatre, the scene of the late terrible disaster, is situated on Tenth street, just above E street in Washington. It is a large edifice, constructed of brick, and of plain appearance.

In the Ring

The Breaking of the Tweed Ring

Thomas Nast's cartoon, The Tammany Tiger from Harper's Weekly.

New York City in 1870 was handsomely endowed with enterprising newspaper editors and proprietors. Some of the old giants were still around: the *Tribune's* Horace Greeley was shortly to be nominated as Democratic presidential candidate. James Gordon Bennett, it was true, had retired from *The Herald* but his son was busy putting even more ambitious projects to the test on the family paper. Edwin Lawrence Godkin, in due course *The Evening Post's* great editor, was still sharpening his teeth on *The Nation*. Charles Dana had just moved to *The Sun* and was in the process of 'making a newspaper out of it'. So it was slightly ironic, though wholly admirable, that it was *The New York Times* — still trying to come to terms with Henry Raymond's death the year before — that produced the greatest sensation in the city since the news of Lincoln's assassination.

George Jones, Raymond's partner and successor, was no hell-raising muckraker by nature. But he knew corruption when he smelt it. And he had perceived great wafts of it for some time emanating from Tammany Hall, the city's omnivorous Democratic administration. That the fruits of office, (mingled with a bit of political graft here and there) were enjoyed to the full by the city's bosses was no great secret even to the most myopic of newspapers — it was the extent of the civic plunder which was to stagger them. Republican to the core (Raymond had been one of the architects of the Grand Old Party) *The Times* had, perhaps, more incentive than many of its competitors to embark on a feud, but hadn't William Tweed, the Tammany Boss, publicly declared the price of Republican editors? 'Sometimes $5,000, sometimes $1,000, sometimes $500'. Within a year he was to come across one who couldn't be bought, even for $5 million.

Jones began his editorial sniping at the city officials early in the fall of 1870, taking as his prime targets Boss Tweed, the Mayor Oakey Hall, and the Controller Richard B. Connolly. What, he wanted to know, was the secret of Tweed's Croesus touch in view of the fact he had been a bankrupt only five years before. Why did Connolly persistently refuse to open the city accounts for public inspection? Why did they all surround themselves with gangs of hoodlums? The Ring replied in its own predictable way, by frightening off many of *The Times'* advertisers and setting its lawyers to grab the paper's real estate holdings. Less predictably, but on the eve of the city elections, it agreed to open the city accounts to a committee of respectable business. The committee took a cursory glance at the accounts and pronounced them in good working order. The Tammany candidates were re-elected lock, stock and barrel.

Rightly believing that the frauds were far more deep-seated than would be revealed by a hasty afternoon's book-keeping, *The Times* persisted with its campaign well into 1871. But although long on invective, it was desperately short on hard statistics, and this was a rough game being played. Already other papers, led by *The World* and *The Tribune*, were accusing *The Times* of political vindictiveness and there were rumours that the Ring were attempting to take over the paper by purchasing the shares belonging to Raymond's widow — emergency arrangements had to be made to pre-empt that move.

It was mid-summer before *The Times* got a break: more than a break in fact, a gift from the gods. A man named James O'Brien, a former sheriff and dedicated rival to Tweed within the Democratic party machine, walked into the paper's office bearing copies of carefully selected entries in Connolly's books. They made extraordinary reading: they showed that the administration had decorated, furnished and repaired 'armories' and 'drill-halls' all over the city till they were fit for several emperors to live in, and probably several kings as well. The armories and drill-halls in question proved to be at the addresses of a number of small shops, all in miserable condition. A new county courthouse had been 'plastered' at a cost approaching $3 million, and 'plumbed' for a mere $1 million by comparison. A carpenter appeared to have been paid for his 'alterations to county offices and buildings' at the princely rate of $27,000 per day. Plasterer, plumber, carpenter were all found to have quit the city when the news broke.

The Times began its series of revelations of 'secret accounts' on July 8 1871, modestly at first to give its readers an appetite for the feast. On July 12th there was an interruption from the city's Irish inhabitants who had chosen Orange Day to stage a Catholic-Protestant riot in which over 100 people were killed. But a week later the incredible swindle was unveiled once more. On the 22nd the copies of the accounts were published, with a further instalment on the 24th, and yet another the next day. A special supplement put out a few days later sold half a million copies on the spot: it contained *all* the figures that had come *The Times'* way so that the astonished city could add them up for themselves. They came to nearly $10,000,000 and were surely but a fraction of the total misappropriation (estimated later as between $50 and 200 million). During the pause occasioned by the Irish fisticuffs, Connolly had approached Jones with an offer of $5 million to call the whole thing off. Jones was not for sale at any price. His reward was to watch *The Tribune* and all the others eating their words. William Tweed was arrested in December after what could be found of the city's accounts had been fully investigated. He was sentenced to twelve years imprisonment in 1873, but escaped in 1875 to Spain. After only a few months in the Iberian sunshine he was recognised through, of all things, a cartoon drawn by Thomas Nast of *Harper's Weekly* who had joined *The Times* in its campaign in 1871. He was arrested and returned to Ludlow Street jail, where he died in his cell a few months later. Not a very luxurious place to conclude a prodigal life, unfurnished and unplastered. But then it was one of the civic buildings which had provided his percentage.

The New-York Times.

VOL. XX.......NO. 6189. NEW-YORK, SATURDAY, JULY 22, 1871. PRICE FOUR CENTS.

THE SECRET ACCOUNTS.

Proofs of Undoubted Frauds Brought to Light.

Warrants Signed by Hall and Connolly Under False Pretenses.

THE ACCOUNT OF INGERSOLL & CO.

The following accounts, copied with scrupulous fidelity from Controller CONNOLLY's books, require little explanation. They purport to show the amount paid during 1869 and 1870, for repairs and furniture for the New Court-house. It will be seen that the warrants are drawn in different names, but they were all indorsed to "INGERSOLL & CO."—otherwise, J. H. INGERSOLL, the agent of the Ring. Each warrant was signed by Controller CONNOLLY and Mayor HALL. What amount of money was actually paid to the persons in whose favor the warrants were *nominally* drawn, we have no means of knowing. On the face of these accounts, however, it is clear that the bulk of the money somehow or other got back to the Ring, or each warrant would not have been indorsed over to its agent.

We undertake to prove whenever we are afforded the opportunity, that the following account is copied literally from the Controller's books, and forms a part of the documents to which the public is entitled to have access.

The dates given for the work done are obviously fraudulent. For example: On July 2, 1869, a warrant was drawn for furniture supplied for County Courts and offices, from Oct. 18 to Nov. 23, 1868, for $42,560 64. On July 16—fourteen days afterward—another warrant was drawn for $94,038 13 for furniture supplied to the same offices from Nov. 7 to Dec. 31. That is to say, the bill was fully paid by the *first* of these two warrants down to Nov. 23. And yet a fortnight afterward another warrant was drawn paying the bill over again from Nov. 7. It is obvious that the fictitious dates were not remembered by the City authorities when those warrants were drawn. Many similar cases will be observed in the figures given below.

It will be seen that on one day furniture is supposed to have been supplied to the amount of $129,469 48—at least a warrant for that sum was signed by HALL and CONNOLLY in favor of C. D. BOLLAR & CO., and indorsed by INGERSOLL & CO.

1869. INGERSOLL & CO. 1869.

Date of Warrant.	*Character of Work. Date on Which Work was Supposed to be Done.*	*Amount Drawn.*
July 2.	—Paid for Furniture in County Courts and Offices from Oct. 18 to Nov. 23, 1868	$42,550 64
July 16.	—Paid for Furniture in County Offices from Nov. 7 to Dec. 31, 1868	94,038 13
Aug. 4.	—Paid for Furniture in County Offices July 19, 1868	53,206 75
Sept. 7.	—Paid for Furniture in County Offices Aug. 30, 1868	60,334 71
Sept. 8.	—Paid for Furniture in County Courts and Offices Sept. 23, 1868	42,901 47
Oct. 22.	—Paid for Iron Railing, Cases, Stairs, &c., Check in name of M. W. Davis, indorsed by Ingersoll & Co., July 29, '68	63,201 16
Oct. 23.	—Paid for Carpets, &c., in Co. Courts and Offices, Check in name of J. A. Smith, indorsed by Ingersoll & Co., Aug. 10, '68	27,154 55
Oct. 28.	—Paid for Furniture in County Courts and Offices Dec. 28, 1868	28,032 11
Nov. 5.	—Paid for Carpets, &c., in Co. Courts and Offices, Check in name of J. A. Smith, indorsed by Ingersoll & Co., April 6, '68.	36,422 10
Nov. 17.	—Paid for Carpets, &c., in Co. Courts and Offices, Check in name of J. A. Smith, indorsed by Ingersoll & Co., Jan. 26, '68.	32,617 13
Nov. 16.	—Paid for Carpets, &c., in Co. Courts and Offices, Check in name of J. A. Smith, indorsed by Ingersoll & Co., July 29, '68.	32,185 20
Nov. 19.	—Paid for Furniture, &c., in County Courts and Offices, Oct. 18, 1868	10,494 61
Nov. 24.	—Paid for Furniture, &c., in Co. Courts and Offices, Check in name of C. D. Bollar & Co., in'd. by Ingersoll & Co., Aug. 17, '68.	32,826 81
Dec. 3.	—Paid for Furniture, &c., in Co. Courts and Offices, Check in name of C. D. Bollar & Co., in'd. by Ingersoll & Co., Nov. 9, '68.	32,682 38
June 8.	—Paid for Furniture, &c., in Co. Courts and Offices, Check in name of C. D. Bollar & Co., in'd. by Ingersoll & Co., May 8, '69.	129,469 48
June 15.	—Paid for Carpets, &c., in New Court-House, Check in name of J. A. Smith, indorsed by Ingersoll & Co., April 16, 1869	72,605 97
June 8.	—Paid for Furniture, &c., in New Court-House to April 8, 1869	90,923 40
Dec. 16.	—Paid for Furniture, &c., in County Court-rooms and Offices, April 26, 1868,	54,243 57
Jan. 11.	—Paid for Furniture in Armories and Drill-rooms, Nov. 12, 1868	38,906 71
Jan. 19.	—Paid for Furniture in same, Dec. 3 and 22, 1868	31,801 95
Feb. 27.	—Paid for Furniture in same from Jan. 13, 1869, to Feb. 9, 1869	55,791 56
April 26.	—Paid for Furniture in same, March 11, 9186	39,844 68
June 5.	—Paid for Furniture in same, Nov. 17, 1868	26,325 26
Sept. 20.	—Paid for Furniture in same, May 26, 1869	30,116 26
Feb. 18.	—Paid for Shades, &c., Check in name of J. A. Smith, indorsed by Ingersoll & Co., Dec. 21, 1868	15,785 40
May 12.	—Paid for Shades, Curtains, Cornices, &c., Check in name of J. A. Smith, indorsed by Ingersoll & Co., April 6, 1869	19,163 65
June 7.	—Paid for Repairs, &c., Check in name of J. A. Smith, indorsed by Ingersoll & Co., March 13, 1869	22,496 33
May 12.	—Paid for Repairs, &c., Check in name of C. D. Bollar & Co., indorsed by Ingersoll & Co., April 9, 1869	21,969 13
June 5.	—Paid for Repairs, &c., Check in name of C. D. Bollar & Co., indorsed by Ingersoll & Co., to Feb. 3, 1869	38,907 43
Sept. 30.	—Paid for Fitting up Armories, Check in name of C. D. Bollar & Co., indorsed by Ingersoll & Co., Sept. 1, 1868	44,737 45
Sept. 20.	—Paid for Fitting up Armories, Check in name of C. D. Bollar & Co., indorsed by Ingersoll & Co., July 1, 1869	32,112 78

GEORGE S. MILLER, 1869—*All the Checks Indorsed by Ingersoll & Co.*

July 2.	—Paid for Repairs to Court of Common Pleas to Oct. 17, 1867	$905 51
July 2.	—Paid for Repairs to Courts and Offices from Aug. 1 to Oct. 20, 1868	6,089 24
July 28.	—Paid for Repairs to County Offices, Dec. 23, 1868	10,647 56
July 28.	—Paid for Repairs to County Offices and Courts, Nov. 20, 1868	11,349 54
Sept. 8.	—Paid for Carpenter-work, County Offices and Courts, from Nov. 12, 1868, to Dec. 12, 1868	48,833 23
Dec. 3.	—Paid for Repairs to County Offices and Buildings from Oct. 21 to Oct. 31, 1868	23,038 74
Dec. 29.	—Paid for Repairs and Alterations, County Offices and Buildings, July 21, 1868	27,885 04
Jan. 11.	—Paid for Repairs in Armories and Drill-rooms from Nov. 27 to Dec. 19, 1868	15,415 14
Jan. 19.	—Paid for Repairs in Armories and Drill-rooms from Oct. 23 to Dec. 4, 1868	14,691 78
Feb. 27.	—Paid for Repairs in Armories and Drill-rooms from Jan. 14 to Jan. 30, 1869	27,937 51
May 12.	—Paid for Carpenter-work in Various Armories from Jan. 30 to March 23, 1869	27,651 40
June 7.	—Paid for Carpenter-work in Various Armories from April 23 to May 18, 1869	38,676 50
June 7.	—Paid for Carpenter-work in Various Armories from March 30 to April 16, 1869	13,864 07
Sept. 20.	—Paid for Carpenter-work in Various Armories from May 25 to June 9, 1869	14,130 36
Oct. 11.	—Paid for Carpenter-work in Various Armories from May 25 to June 29, 1869	49,763 80

A. G. MILLER, 1869—*Checks Indorsed by Ingersoll & Co.*

Dec. 20.	—Paid for Repairs to County Offices and Buildings, March 8, 1868	$34,785 63
Dec. 20.	—Paid for Repairs to County Offices and Buildings, July 7, 1868	18,222 47
Sept. 28.	—Paid for Repairs to County Offices and Buildings, July 2, 1869	48,798 63

1870. INGERSOLL & CO. 1870.

Jan. 17.	—Paid for Furniture Furnished County Court-rooms and Offices, July 17, 1868	$20,655 72
Jan. 24.	—Paid for Furniture Furnished County Court-rooms and Offices, May 13, 1868	33,538 36
Feb. 7.	—Paid for Furniture Furnished County Court-rooms and Offices	11,186 92
Feb. 16.	—Paid for Furniture Furnished County Court-rooms and Offices, Aug. 21, 1869	29,404 48
Feb. 23.	—Paid for Furniture Furnished County Court-rooms and Offices, Sept. 23, 1869	51,813 77
Feb. 26.	—Paid for Furniture Furnished County Court-rooms and Offices, Oct. 6, 1869	26,981 90
Feb. 26.	—Paid for Furniture Furnished County Court-rooms and Offices, Sept. 3, 1869	33,037 15
May 6.	—Paid for Furniture Furnished County Court-house, Dec. 10, 1869	64,954 87
May 21.	—Paid for Cabinet-work County Court-house, July 23, 1869	70,117 59
May 21.	—Paid for Cabinet-work County Court-house, Oct. 17, 1869	64,984 82
May 28.	—Paid for Furniture County Court-house, Oct. 21, 1869	40,314 09
May 28.	—Paid for Furniture County Court-house, Nov. 3, 1869	39,844 19
May 30.	—Paid for Furniture County Court-house, Dec. 27, 1869	68,218 82
June 3.	—Paid for Furniture Furnished in County Buildings and Offices, Feb. 5, 1870	54,030 26
June 10.	—Paid for Furniture, Clocks, &c., Furnished in County Buildings and Offices, March 23, 1870	69,719 10
June 13.	—Paid for Furniture and Cabinet-work in County Court-house, April 18, 1870	98,259 07
June 20.	—Paid for Cabinet-work in County Court-house, Feb. 3, 1870	66,292 33
June 27.	—Paid for Cabinet-work and Furniture in Armories and Drill-rooms, Feb. 27, 1869	58,330 93
June 30.	—Paid for Cabinet-work and Furniture in Armories and Drill-rooms, Feb. 6, 1870	54,053 33
June 30.	—Paid for Cabinet-work and Furniture in Armories and Drill-rooms, March 26, 1870	29,129 99
Aug. 1.	—Paid for Furniture in Court-rooms and Offices, March 28, 1870	91,325 50
Mar. 14.	—Paid for Furniture in Armories and Drill-rooms, Nov. 3, 1869	58,937 60
April 16.	—Paid for Furniture in Armories and Drill-rooms, Sept. 11, 1869	28.608 68
Aug. 31.	—Paid for Fitting up District-Attorney's Office, Aug. 22, 1870	30,000 00
Aug. 30.	—Paid for Fitting up Commissioners of Taxes' and Receiver of Taxes' Offices, June 30, 1870	40,000 00
Aug. 30.	—Paid for Fitting up Register's Office, Aug. 3, 1870	10,000 00
Oct. 26.	—Paid for Fitting up Surrogate's Office, Sept. 3, 1870	12,000 00

C. D. BOLLAR & CO.—*Checks Indorsed by Ingersoll & Co.*

May 7.	—Paid for Furniture, &c., Furnished in County Court-house, Sept. 16, 1869	$39,260 17
May 7.	—Paid for Furniture, &c., Furnished in County Court-house, Oct. 18, 1869	35,114 08
May 13.	—Paid for Cabinet-work Furnished in County Court-house, July 18, 1869	89,379 00
May 21.	—Paid for Fitting up in County Court-house, March 6, 1870	39,950 18
May 21.	—Paid for Fitting up in County Court-house, Jan. 20, 1870	39,614 59
May 27.	—Paid for Cabinet-work Furnished in County Court-house, Aug. 23, 1869	125,830 56
June 10.	—Paid for Cabinet-work Furnished in County Court-house, April 16, 1870	67,487 21
June 30.	—Paid for Fitting up Armories and Drill-rooms, Jan. 7, 1870	49,208 14
June 30.	—Paid for Fitting up Armories and Drill-rooms, March 13, 1870	37,072 16
Aug. 1.	—Paid for Cabinet-work, &c., done in County Buildings and Offices, March 12, 1870	60,503 43

J. A. SMITH—*Checks Indorsed by Ingersoll & Co.*

May 6.	—Paid for Carpets Furnished in New Court-house, June 22, 1869	$34,082 25
May 7.	—Paid for Curtains and Shades Furnished in New Court-house, Sept. 23, 1869	36,083 80
May 21.	—Paid for Carpets and Shades Furnished in County Buildings and Offices, Feb. 21, 1870	34,515 73
May 28.	—Paid for Carpets and Shades Furnished in County Buildings and Offices, Feb. 21, 1870	73,602 46
June 3.	—Paid for Carpets and Shades Furnished in County Buildings and Offices, Dec. 27, 1869	63,175 51
June 6.	—Paid for Carpets &c., Furnished in County Court-house, Aug. 3, 1869	42,291 45
June 6.	—Paid for Carpets, &c., Furnished in County Buildings and Offices, June 21, 1869	44,259 23
June 6.	—Paid for Shades Furnished in County Buildings and Offices, Sept. 16, 1869	36,987 25
June 24.	—Paid for Carpets Furnished in Armories and Drill-rooms Dec. 22, 1869	36,441 42
June 30.	—Paid for Carpets Furnished in Armories and Drill-rooms, March 16, 1870	37,426 87
July 26.	—Paid for Carpets Furnished in County Court-house, April 17, 1870	72,819 81

GEORGE S. MILLER—*Checks Indorsed by Ingersoll & Co.*

Jan. 17.	—Paid for Carpenter-work in Court-rooms and Offices, Aug. 19, 1868, to Sept. 11, 1868	$20,291 44
Jan. 17.	—Paid for Repairs and Alterations in County Buildings, June 7, 1868	23,005 83
Jan. 24.	—Paid for Repairs and Alterations in County Offices, Aug. 5, 1868	26,952 99
Jan. 28.	—Paid for Repairs and Alterations in County Offices, Sept. 23, 1868	25,366 49
Mar. 21.	—Paid for Repairs and Alterations in County Offices, May 13, 1869	20,255 00
April 8.	—Paid for Repairs and Alterations in County Offices, Aug. 7, 1869	18,955 69
April 8.	—Paid for Repairs and Alterations in County Offices, July 23, 1869	29,494 74
April 8.	—Paid for Repairs and Alterations in County Offices, June 10, 1869	21,418 99
May 7.	—Paid for Carpenter-work in Court-house, May 13, 1869	42,126 47
May 13.	—Paid for Carpenter-work in Court-house, Sept. 29, 1869	38,902 22
May 21.	—Paid for Carpenter-work in Court-house, Dec. 15, 1869	34,990 66
May 28.	—Paid for Repairs in County Buildings and Offices, Aug. 31, 1869	39,361 21
June 3.	—Paid for Repairs in County Buildings and Offices, Sept. 22, 1869	37,326 02
June 6.	—Paid for Repairs in County Buildings and Offices, Dec. 18, 1869	32,381 73
June 6.	—Paid for Repairs in County Buildings and Offices, Oct. 25, 1869	35,663 82
June 10.	—Paid for Fitting up New Court-house, Jan. 12, 1870	44,474 30
June 17.	—Paid for Repairs in County Buildings and Offices, Jan. 25, 1870	48,768 21
June 20.	—Paid for Carpenter-work in Court-house, Feb. 9, 1870	40,965 41
June 27.	—Paid for Repairs in County Buildings and Offices, March 29, 1870	44,874 59
June 30.	—Paid for Repairs in Armories and Drill-rooms, Aug. 8, 1869	40,549 24
June 30.	—Paid for Repairs in Armories and Drill-rooms, Sept. 8, 1869	35,748 29
July 8.	—Paid for Repairs in Armories and Drill-rooms, Feb. 10, 1870	29,317 59
July 8.	—Paid for Repairs in Armories and Drill-rooms, March 2, 1870	46,947 32
July 26.	—Paid for Repairs in Armories and Drill-rooms, March 31, 1870	49,251 31
Aug. 9.	—Paid for Repairs in County Buildings, April 12, 1870	40,607 49
Aug. 12.	—Paid for Repairs in Armories and Drill-rooms, April 2, 1870	48.639 49
Aug. 12.	—Paid for Repairs in Carpenter-work in Court-house, March 28, 1870	46,343 45
Mar. 14.	—Paid for Repairs in Armories and Drill-rooms to Nov. 13, 1869	38,084 28
Mar. 31.	—Paid for Repairs and Carpenter-work in Armories and Drill-rooms, July 6 to July 31, 1869	45,266 04
April 16.	—Paid for Repairs and Alterations in Armories and Drill-rooms, Aug. 3 to Aug. 13, 1869	25,948 38
April 16.	—Paid for Repairs and Alterations in Armories and Drill-rooms	8,147 88

A. G. MILLER—*Checks Indorsed by Ingersoll & Co.*

June 24.	—Paid for Cabinet-work in Court-house, Jan. 9, 1870	$49,082 30
June 27.	—Paid for Cabinet-work in County Buildings and Offices, March 29, 1870	85,163 22
June 30.	—Paid for Cabinet-work in County Court-house, April 2, 1870	59,932 01
Aug. 1.	—Paid for Cabinet-work in County Court-house, Oct. 8, 1869	69,537 68
Aug. 9.	—Paid for Cabinet-work in Armories and Drill-rooms, April 16, 1870	77,949 58
Mar. 28.	—Paid for Repairs in Armories and Drill-rooms, Aug. 28, 1869	49,742 45
Mar. 31.	—Paid for Repairs in Armories and Drill-rooms, Oct. 20, 1869	38,818 84
April 16.	—Paid for Fitting up Armories and Drill-rooms, Oct. 2, 1869	22,6.2 10
	Grand Total	$5,663,646 83

WASHINGTON.

Clearing up a Muddle in the Revenue Department—Lively Work in the Pension Bureau—Imports of Australia—Immigration at New-York—Kuklux Investigation—National Bank Circulation.

Special Dispatch to the New-York Times.

WASHINGTON, July 21.—It will be remembered that over a year ago Congress tried to give an expression of its will concerning the reduction of a part of the income tax, but failed to find language to convey its purpose successfully in regard to the payment of certain income taxes for the last five months of 1870. Judge DOUGLAS, the acting Commissioner, had the question of how the law should be construed before him, and gave the Government the benefit of the doubt. Commissioner PLEASONTON reversed the decision, and the corporations paid their semi-annual interest without withholding the amount of the taxes, as they would otherwise have done. The Attorney-General in turn reversed PLEASONTON's decision, putting the case back where Judge DOUGLAS placed it, and now the corporations resist collection, on the ground that they acted on the instructions of an agent of the Government in neglecting to retain the amount of the tax, and that they are not liable to sustain loss because of the reversal of the decision on which they acted. Solicitor BANFIELD has been considering their plea, and today handed the Secretary of the Treasury his opinion as to the legality of action for the collection of these taxes. The opinion will be made public to-morrow, together with the Secretary's decision based upon it. This is another case which must make Commissioner PLEASONTON aware that he is one of the Secretary's subordinates, and that he is so regarded by the President.

BRISK WORK IN THE PENSION OFFICE.

A statement was not long ago published which showed that there were about 100,000 pension claims unexamined on the files of the Pension Office. Those who are anxiously looking for action upon applications will be glad to hear that the daily average work of the Pension Office under the new Commissioner, Gen. BAKER, has been already about doubled. Yesterday 188 certificates for pensions were issued, the largest number ever issued from the office in one day. The first week in June, which was the first week after Gen. BAKER came into the office, 423 certificates were issued. Since then there has been a general constant increase and last week 915 were issued. This week the number is expected to reach 1,100, and during July 4,000 are expected to be signed. At this rate the office will be gaining on its work instead of falling further behind, and an effort will be made to bring the work up to time as soon as possible with the limited force which can be employed.

SECRETARY DELANO.

Secretary DELANO has written that his return will be delayed till Tuesday next.

Dispatch to the Associated Press.

AUSTRALIA'S IMPORTATIONS.

A statement has been compiled at the Treasury Department from the latest statistics, showing the imports into Australia and New-Zealand, as follows: From Great Britain, £17,924,420; from the United States, £1,354,385; all other countries, £3,812,478. Stated by per centage, they are as follows: From Great Britain, 77 6-10; from the United States, 5 5-10; all other countries, 16 6-10. The Parliament of New-South Wales has recently voted a subsidy of $75,000 to a monthly line of American steamers between San Francisco and Sidney. The imports of Australia and New-Zealand being largely manufactured goods, it is believed that a very large and profitable commerce will spring up with our Western Coast.

IMMIGRATION AT NEW-YORK.

The official returns received at the Bureau of Statistics show that during the quarter ending June 30, 1871, the total number of passengers arrived at the port of New-York from foreign countries was 107,114, of whom 64,213 were males and 42,901 females. Of the total number arrived, 101,015 were actual immigrants—males, 60,082; females, 40,933. Ages—Under fifteen, 9,812; fifteen and under forty, 71,056; forty and upward, 10,147. The deaths on the voyage were 92, of whom 54 were males and 38 females. The principal nationalities of the immigrants were as follows: England, 17,845; Scotland, 4,613; Wales, 399; Ireland, 26,149; Great Britain, locality unknown, 6,672; Germany, 30,814; Austria, 1,983; Sweden, 5,727; Norway, 1,286; Denmark, 1,143; France, 849; Switzerland, 1,305; Spain, 104; Italy, 8,671; Holland, 409; Belgium, 78 Russia, 295; Poland, 183; Cuba, 43; Bermudas, 7.

THE KUKLUX INVESTIGATION.

The Kuklux Committee, today, examined a witness named MCBRIDE, who testified that while a teacher of a colored school in Chickasaw County, Mississippi, a band of disguised men seized and whipped him, and insisted he should leave the country. Other colored schools were broken up in that section. Three witnesses from North Carolina are in attendance, and will testify relative to the existence of Kuklux organizations in that State. A telegram was read in the Committee from a citizen of Macon, that he telegraphed on the 11th of July he was ready to report, but received the next day a telegram from the Sergeant-at-Arms of the Senate, telling him he need not come, as the Committee had not time for more witnesses. The Sergeant-at-Arms being out of town could not explain, but at the instance of the Democratic members this Georgian and six or more others were resummoned by telegraph to appear before the Committee.

NATIONAL BANK CIRCULATION.

The total circulation issued to the national banks to date is $318,686,999. The act of July 12, 1870, authorized the issue of $54,000,000 additional circulation, and the establishment of gold national banks, to which circulation can be issued upon the deposit of United States bonds, at the rate of eighty per cent. upon the par value thereof. Since the passage of the act, circulation has been issued to the following States: Virginia, $744,000; Illinois, $3,066; West Virginia, $950,000; Michigan, $1,166; Kentucky, $2,200,000; Indiana, $1,174,000; Wisconsin, $634,000; Ohio, $760,000; Tennessee, $1,300,000; Iowa, $1,076,000; Louisiana, $1,300,000; Minnesota, $380,000; Georgia, $561,000; Kansas, $176,100; North Carolina, $609,000; Missouri, $1,290,000; South Carolina, $258,000; Nebraska, $212,000; Texas, $145,000; Colorado, $61,000; New-Mexico, $155,000; Oregon, $137,000; Alabama, $260,000; California, $3,205. The law requires that one-half of the increased circulation shall be apportioned among the States not having an excess already, according to population, and one-half according to the existing banking capital resources and business of such State and Territory. The census returns of the valuation of property and banking capital have not yet been received, and the proportion of circulation for the States of Ohio, Indiana and Illinois cannot probably be ascertained with any accuracy until about the 1st of October. It is probable, however, that there will be sufficient circulation for all of the Southern and Western States when the full census returns are received. No additional circulation can be issued to the Eastern and Middle States.

THE ABUSED CAR-HORSES.

Inspection of Stables by Henry Bergh—Sickening Sights—Comparative Views.

Yesterday, Mr. BERGH and Mr. A. H. CAMPBELL, the President and Superintendent of the Society for the Prevention of Cruelty to Animals, accompanied by Dr. LIANTARD, of the New-York Veterinary College, and a TIMES reporter, made a tour of inspection of the principle car companies' stables to examine the horses, the condition of the stables, the quality of feed, and the general order of the homes of the best servants of mankind. The first stables inspected were those of the Fourth-avenue line. The Superintendent, Mr. MESSEROE, received his visitors very politely, and showed them over the premises. This line had lost eighteen out of ninety-four cases with the new disease. Ninety out of the ninety-four affected were mares, and the eighteen that died of the disease were mares. The hospital yesterday had sixty disabled horses in it. Only a very small portion, however, were down with the malady, the others being sick with sore feet, quittors, sore backs, and otherwise disabled. Some of the poor creatures had fearful wounds on the fetlocks, caused by their injuring themselves in the numerous switches on the line. This is reckoned the hardest road for horses of any in the City. The feed given the horses of this line is half oats and half corn. The condition of the stables is tolerable. The open windows of the stable in which the sick horses were, looked into a yard belonging to the proprietors of the Fourth-avenue stage line, and the filth and mud in this place was knee deep. The stench must be anything but conducive to the recovery of the sick horses. The feed was examined and found of medium quality.

The stables of Messrs. WILKINS & MARSHALL, the proprietors of the Fourth-avenue stage line, were next visited. The stables were three tiers deep, and the atmosphere of the lowest was very bad. The refuse besides ran through from the top to the lower stable, rendering it altogether quite unfit for the purpose, in addition to which it is quite underground, and excepting just at the entrances quite dark. In a dirty yard were fifteen horses turned out for exercise in course of recovery from the disease. The stock consisted of 330 horses. Eighty had been attacked, out of which number eleven mares had died. One of the proprietors drew Mr. BERGH's particular attention to one horse which had been kept from work two weeks simply because he had a sore back. Mr. WILKINS, one of the proprietors, said he felt certain that the disease was easily curable if attended to quickly. He said the first symptoms were swelling of the hind legs and running at the eyes, but Dr. LIANTARD did not at all agree with this view. The horses were fed on half corn and half oats.

The stables of the East Belt line, at Thirty-seventh-street and First-avenue, were next inspected. Here were found 400 horses, a great proportion of which were in appearance very unfit for the every day toil required of them. There were about seventy cripples in a deplorable condition, and many more with large sores and ulcers on the fetlocks. Superintendent TERRY was asked if the latter were worked, and replied that he was compelled to work such stock or he must stop the line; and besides, he thought such horses better working than standing idle. Mr. BERGH did not agree with him, and cautioned him not to use many of the suffering beasts which were noticed in the stalls. The horses go over eighteen miles every day, and the daily feed of each consisted of twelve pounds of meal and four and a half pounds of ground oats. The line had lost forty animals, principally mares, with the new disease. There were only six cases now under treatment.

Tee stables of the Second-avenue line were next overhauled. Mr. SHAW reported that they were now quite free of the disease, not having had a case for two weeks. They had lost eleven horses out of 135 stricken down with the malady. The stables were in pretty good condition, but there were no signs of bedding, and apparently the poor beasts, after toiling over sixteen miles every day, had nothing but the hard and damp boards to lie on at night. The stock consisted of 750 horses. Daily feed, ten pounds—half oats and half corn. The hospital had some twenty patients in, under the homeopathy treatment.

The stables of the Third-avenue line were visited. In them were 1,600 horses. In an extra stable were a number of "green horses," which the hard work of the road had crippled. In the hospital were several bad cases, the poor creatures being covered with blisters, and scars arising therefrom. Two or three appeared in a dying state. There were no signs of bedding in a large portion of the stables. The feed taken from some of the mangers was sour, and as poor as any that had been inspected. The stablemen stated that the animals did not like it, and no wonder.

The stables of the Sixth-avenue line were found in admirable order, or as Mr. BERGH said, they were "perfect models." Everything was in first-rate order—perfect system reigning throughout the establishment. The best of feed is supplied the horses, and their daily rations are seventeen pounds each horse. The night stock were all good, sound animals. They were lying in their stalls on clean bedding. Mr. BIDGOOD only reported four cases of the disease, all of which were slowly recovering. He said that the Company had decided not to use in future any kiln-dried corn. After being dried it was found to have lost its virtue, and when sown it would not grow. The horses of this line had seventeen pounds of feed per day supplied to each.

The stables of the Forty-second-street, or Cross-town line, which has of late given Mr. BERGH and his officers so much trouble, were next visited. The clerk was very civil, and called the stable-keeper, A. CHALMERS, to escort Mr. BERGH and his party over the premises, but CHALMERS recognized the visitors, kept out of the way, and was found only after great trouble. He said he had received strict orders from JOHN GREEN, the President, not to show any one over the stables, and especially Mr. BERGH nor any of his officers. The reason of this refusal was quite apparent, for a more filthy, dilapidated and unwholesome-looking place, even from the outside, is difficult to conceive of. The office is dirty, and a coke dealer would hardly deign to use it. The waiting-room is an inch deep in dirt, and the seats covered. Some half-dozen dirty-looking ruffians were squatting inside the shed, who were pointed out to our reporter as drivers and conductors of the "line." Mr. BERGH told CHALMERS he knew perfectly well the reason he was refused admittance, for he had gone over the cellars, called stables, a year ago, and had found them in an awful condition. CHALMERS denied that the stables were in a bad condition. It is strange that Mr. BERGH and his party should be so cordially received and treated so well at every other stable that was visited, and invited to call at any time and point out such horses as he might feel justified in ordering to be relieved of work, and yet be refused even admission to the "sheds" of the Green line. Mr. BERGH begged that CHALMERS would request Mr. GREEN to go over the Sixth-avenue stables, and then "go and do likewise."

DESTRUCTIVE FIRE.

Several Buildings in West Forty-Seventh and Forty-Sixth Streets Destroyed or Damaged.

Another destructive conflagration occurred last evening, which was discovered at about 9 o'clock, in the two-story saw and planing mill of KINNEY & CLARK, Nos. 628 and 630 West Forty-seventh-street, and which, being first seen in the boiler-room, probably originated from the furnace. The flames spread with extraordinary rapidity, and almost before the engines arrived the entire building was enveloped, and the fire communicated to adjacent property. The mill was entirely destroyed with all its contents and the loss will probably reach $15,000. Next west was the lumber yard of JOHN W. STEVENS & BRO., where stock to the amount of about $5,000 was destroyed. Next east was a five story building, Nos. 622, 624 and 626 West Forty-seventh-street, occupied as a morocco factory, by C. P. Buckin, the top floor of which was reached by the flames and the loss will probably exceed $5,000. The fire even reached across the street to the two story dwelling of THOS. ING, whose loss is $500; also to the building No. 627, owned by JOHN DARRAGH, and the lower floor of which was occupied as a stable and the upper portion as a tenement. The Twenty-second Precinct Police got out a great portion of the furniture of the tenants and the thirty horses in the stable, so that the loss was chiefly confined to the building, which will require $1,500 for repairs. No. 629 was occupied as a stable by HENRY BENKIN, whose loss is $500, and the slaughter-house of RICHARD DONOVAN, in the rear, was also slightly damaged. The fire also extended from the rear of the houses on the south side of the street to the raw-hide establishment of WM. CARR, Nos. 641 and 643 West Forty-sixth-street, whose loss is chiefly confined to the building, which is damaged $1,500. The fire at one time threatened to destroy the entire block, and that result would have undoubtedly followed, but for the great exertions of the firemen, ably directed by Chief Engineer PERLEY and the district engineers.

Meeting of the Riot Relief Fund Association.

A meeting of the Twelfth of July Relief Fund Association was held last evening at No. 295 Third-avenue, Dr. J. C. HANNAN presiding. The General Committee already appointed was authorized to begin the collection of subscriptions, and was authorized to name a subcommittee to investigate cases of distress arising out of the late riot. The election of a treasurer was deferred to the next meeting, each member of the Committee being ordered to report to the Secretary all collections made in the meantime. The name of JAS. H. GOODMAN, attorney-at-law, was added to the General Committee, which will meet at No. 204 East Twenty-first-street next Friday evening. Our reporter was informed that the subscriptions already promised amount to $700.

AFFAIRS IN EUROPE.

Mr. Gladstone's Sensational Flank Movement Against the Lords.

The Constitution Declared to be Violently Wrenched.

Parliament Brought into Contempt Before the People.

German Troops Ordered to be Withdrawn from Amiens and Rouen.

Formation of a Spanish Cabinet by Marshal Serrano.

Tumultuous Scene on the Adjournment of the Cortes.

GREAT BRITAIN.

The London Journals on the Recent Act of the Government—The Queen's Warrant Laid on the Table of the House of Commons—The New Castle Strikers.

LONDON, July 21.—The *Times* says the act of the Ministers abolishing the system of purchase of army commissions by royal warrant is a violent wrench of the Constitution, and a wanton setting aside of the will of the House of Lords. The *Times* regrets that this grave issue has been raised, but expresses the hope that the Lords will in their future action think of the effect upon the officers of the army rather than the indignity to their own privileges. The *Daily News* approves the conduct of the Government in making themselves the exponents of the popular will, and recommends that the Lords pass the bill abolishing the purchase of Army commissions. The *Telegraph* is exultant over the action of the Ministry, and says that Mr. GLADSTONE will be the more popular for vindicating the dignity of the House of Commons, in securing the harvest of its laborious session, and for reorganizing the defenses of the country and guarding the interests of the Army. The *Post* says the course of the Government has been somewhat unconstitutional, bringing, it believes, Parliament into contempt before the people. The *Standard* asserts that Mr. GLADSTONE has grossly violated the privileges of Parliament, wasting its time, and precipitating a constitutional crisis. In the House of Commons, this afternoon, Mr. CARDWELL, Secretary of State for War, laid on the table the Queen's warrant abolishing the system of purchase of army commissions.

The engineers on strike at Newcastle held a meeting today, and resolved to make no compromise with their employers.

FRANCE.

The Paris Elections To-Morrow—Rumored Resignation of the Orleans Princes—German Evacuation of the Northern Departments Ordered.

PARIS, July 21.—The Radicals are actively canvassing for the municipal elections to be held next Sunday. The contest grows more and more exciting. In the Assembly, today, Minister LAMBRECHT explained that the state of siege was still maintained in Paris, because the reorganization of the Police had not yet been completed. Notwithstanding the adverse report of the Committee of the Assembly, M. THIERS intends to defend his policy of protection before the Assembly. It is rumored that the Duke D'AUMALE and the Prince DE JOINVILLE have resigned their seats in the Assembly. President THIERS will shortly leave Paris for one of the watering-places. *Le Monde*, the ultra Catholic organ, demands that the Government support the Pope in the exercise of his temporal rights. Criminal proceedings have been commenced against the *Avenir Nationale* for calumniating the Government. The Prussian troops have received orders from Berlin to evacuate the Cities of Amiens and Rouen, and the Departments of the Somme, Lower Seine and Euse. Rouen will be evacuated to-morrow.

GENERAL EUROPEAN NEWS.

Serrano Forms a New Ministry in Spain—Adjournment of the Cortes—Alsace and Lorraine—A Fleet Preparing to Convey the Grand Duke Alexis to America.

MADRID, July 20.—Marshal SERRANO has been intrusted by King AMADEUS with the formation of a new Ministry, and has already designated the following members: Minister of Justice, Señor GOMEZ; Minister of Foreign Affairs, Señor CAUDAN; Minister of Marine, Admiral MALCAMPO; Minister of Finance, Señor CAMADIO. The Cortes has adjourned tumultuously amid the protests of the minority.

VIENNA, July 21.—Count AGENOR GOLUCHOWSKI has been appointed Governor of Galicia.

BERLIN, July 21.—Several decrees are published today, organizing Courts of law in Alsace and Lorraine.

LONDON, July 21.—The Grand Duke CONSTANTINE, of Russia, has arrived in England. A naval squadron is fitting out at Cronstadt to accompany the Grand Duke ALEXIS to America.

The "Reformed" Hackmen—Opposition to the Proposed New Regulations.

The Hackmen's Association met last evening in Apollo Hall, in Prince-street, with a very large attendance. JOHN MARRION, the President, occupied the chair, and J. PHILLIPS was Secretary. A dozen new members were elected, and $149 50 was received for dues and fees.

A resolution was passed to expel any member of the association who should take passengers with the Transfer Companies' tickets. The initiation fee was changed to $5 for owners, and $2 for drivers.

The Treasurer reported that the expenses for the past week had been $217, and the cash in hand, previous to the meeting, was $215.

The new regulations proposed by Mayor HALL did not meet the views of the hackmen. Several members spoke in opposition to them. They considered them as unjust and unconstitutional; they would drive the men out of their business, and the men who had new carriages would get all the business, while those who had second rate or middling carriages would have to go to the wall. They deemed the clause which prevents the hackmen from soliciting passengers as illegal, and they would contest it in Court if necessary. It was a job got up to benefit a few politicians who are engaged in the business, who wish to monopolize it and drive the poorer men out of it altogether. A committee was appointed to visit the Mayor and explain the view of the hackmen, and request him to modify it

The Road to Ujiji

Stanley and Livingstone

It could not be said of James Gordon Bennett Junior, who took over control of *The New York Herald* from his father in 1867, that he was an over-cautious man, nor given to undue reticence. Indeed, his parties were the talk of New York and he was not above supping his champagne from a chorus girl's slipper, when circumstances demanded. On one memorable occasion he had been horse-whipped in the street by a man whose sister he had insulted by, among other things, urinating into her fireplace. It had led, as these things do, to a duel but no-one was hurt. With the staff of his newspaper he was equally mercurial. After he had taken up permanent residence in Paris, it was his habit to summon editors across the Atlantic at a mere whim and, as often as not, forget about them. On being told that a certain employee could not be spared because he was indispensable, he cabled New York for a list of all his 'indispensable' employees, and fired the lot. He even banished one unfortunate music critic to St. Petersburg for refusing to get his hair cut.

But if he ruled *The New York Herald* like a despot, he also ran it with considerable journalistic flair. He was not content to find the news; he insisted on creating it — and in so doing broadened the whole canvas of foreign reporting. In the fall of 1869, while staying in his favourite Paris hotel, he was much moved by the concern shown in Britain over the fate of the missionary-explorer David Livingstone. Three years before the old gentleman had disappeared into the Central African bush to discover the source of the Nile for the Royal Geographical Society and had not been heard of since. Now over fifty, who knew what doom might have befallen him?

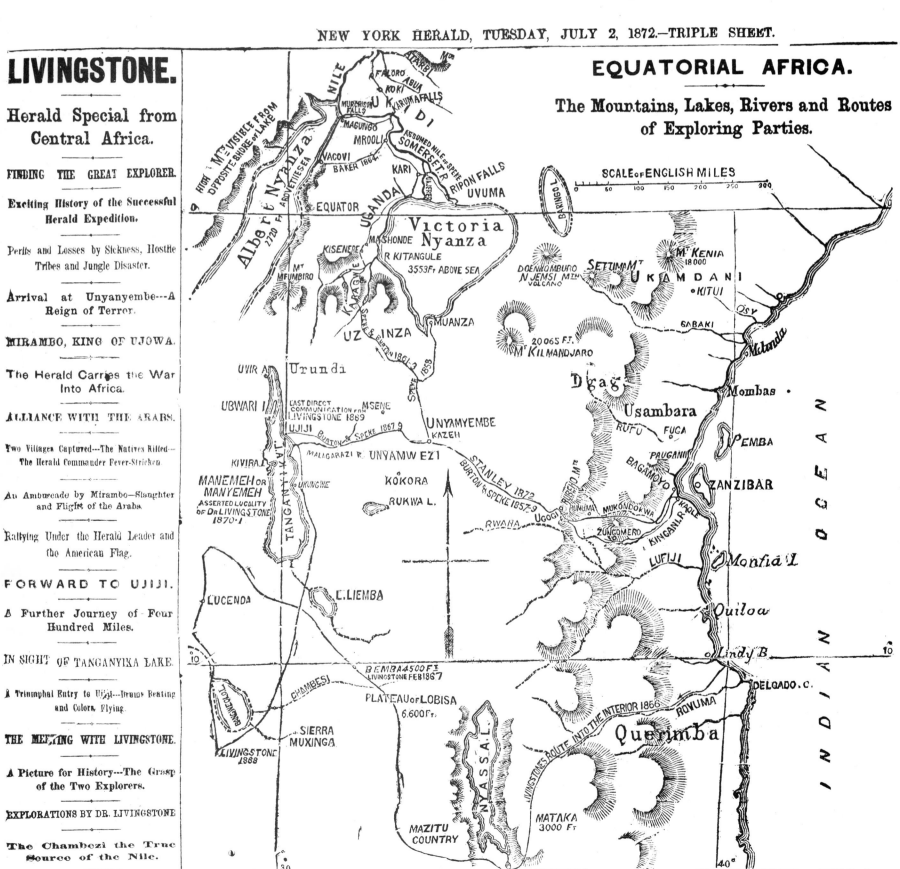

NEW YORK HERALD, TUESDAY, JULY 2, 1872.—TRIPLE SHEET.

LIVINGSTONE.

Herald Special from Central Africa.

FINDING THE GREAT EXPLORER.

Exciting History of the Successful Herald Expedition.

Perils and Losses by Sickness, Hostile Tribes and Jungle Disaster.

Arrival at Unyanyembe---A Reign of Terror.

MIRAMBO, KING OF UJOWA.

The Herald Carries the War Into Africa.

ALLIANCE WITH THE ARABS.

Two Villages Captured---The Natives Killed--- The Herald Commander Fever-Stricken.

An Ambuscade by Mirambo---Slaughter and Flight of the Arabs.

Rallying Under the Herald Leader and the American Flag.

FORWARD TO UJIJI.

A Further Journey of Four Hundred Miles.

IN SIGHT OF TANGANYIKA LAKE.

A Triumphal Entry to Ujiji---Drums Beating and Colors Flying.

THE MEETING WITH LIVINGSTONE.

A Picture for History---The Grasp of the Two Explorers.

EXPLORATIONS BY DR. LIVINGSTONE

The Chambezi the True Source of the Nile.

IT IS NOT SUPPLIED FROM TANGANYIKA.

The Great Doctor to Remain Two Years Longer.

EQUATORIAL AFRICA.

The Mountains, Lakes, Rivers and Routes of Exploring Parties.

they were in sufficient force to attack. The caravans that met at the various halting places threw every discouragement in the way, which tended to destroy the *morale* of the expedition. SPEEDY BOMBAY,

already occurred in which small bands of his soldiers had been beaten, several being killed. He had, therefore, declared to the traders that no caravan should pass to Ujiji except over his body. The Arabs hereupon held a council

with muskets, assegais (spears) and poisoned arrows, had suddenly burst upon the Arabs.

A TERRIFIC SLAUGHTER ENSUED, which ended in the rout of the Arabs, who took refuge in the jungle. The fourth day

tion of the presence of Dr. Livingstone in the province within a recent period, and accordingly preparations were made for

A TRIUMPHAL ENTRY INTO UJIJI. The pagazis who chanced to be unladen

LIVINGSTONE'S SAFETY.

Herald Special Report from London.

First Announcement of the Discovery of the Explorer as It Reached Zanzibar.

The Chief of the Herald Search Corps at Ujiji with the African Traveller.

Negroes Convey the Cheering Intelligence to the Coast.

"If Alive You Shall Hear What He Has to Say; If Dead I will Find and Bring His Bones to You."

English Confirmation of the Glorious News.

The Sultan of Zanzibar's Belief in and First Hope of a Herald Success.

Letter from Livingstone When at Bemba, Inner Africa.

TELEGRAMS TO THE NEW YORK HERALD.

The following special despatch to the HERALD has been received from our correspondent in the capital of Great Britain:—

LONDON, May 2, 1872.

Zanzibar advices, under date of April 29, have been received in the city.

The despatches bring the following report respecting Livingstone's safety additional to the news which was forwarded to the HERALD by telegram from Bombay and through the cable yesterday:—"A report is current here (Zanzibar) that Stanley, the commander of the NEW YORK HERALD expeditionary search corps in Africa, with Livingstone was at Ujiji in the month of January.

The report was brought down to the coast by negroes from the interior and is fully believed here.

English Confirmation of the Grand Fact—"Livingstone Safe with Stanley."

LONDON, May 2, 1872.

LIVINGSTONE'S RESCUE

Herald Special Report from London.

Rejoicing and Excitement in England Over the News.

The Herald's Despatches Republished in Full.

ABUNDANT THANKFULNESS OF ENGLAND.

Publishers and Picture-Takers After the Herald Correspondent.

He Must Write Them a Book and Sit for His Portrait.

The Mystery of Old Nile Considered Solved.

A Feeling of Shame Mingled with Joy at the Herald's Triumph.

The Work of England Left to a Foreign Newspaper.

TELEGRAM TO THE NEW YORK HERALD.

The following special despatch has been received from the HERALD correspondent in London:—

LONDON, July 3, 1872.

THE HERALD LIVINGSTONE SENSATION.

The copious information furnished by the NEW YORK HERALD regarding the safety of Doctor David Livingstone and the success of his explorations in Equatorial Africa is the great sensation of the day.

THE LONDON PRESS REPRINTING THE NEWS.

The HERALD's despatches have been quoted in all the evening papers published in the city. Large placards have been conspicuously posted in every quarter of London calling attention to the news of the great explorer. These are surrounded by the citizens, who discuss the HERALD's feat.

AT THE LONDON BUREAU.

The leading London publishers have thronged the London bureau of the NEW YORK HERALD in Fleet street. They profess the greatest anxiety to get into communication

LIVINGSTONE.

Stanley's Letters to the Herald Describing the Finding of the Great Traveller.

The Battles with Mirambo, King of Uyowa.

Cowardly Conduct of the Arabs in Deserting Stanley while Stricken with Fever.

MIRAMBO'S VENGEANCE.

Tabora, an Arab Town, Nearly Destroyed, Five Hundred Arabs and Five Soldiers of the Herald Expedition Killed.

STANLEY TO THE RESCUE.

The Journey Continued Through Hundreds of Miles Rarely Traversed Even by Arabs.

Terrible Sufferings of the Herald Expedition Party on Its March.

UJIJI AT LENGTH REACHED.

The Expedition Enters the Town Triumphantly Flying the American Flag.

Livingstone and Stanley Face to Face at Last.

STANLEY'S STORY OF FIVE YEARS.

Livingstone's Own Account of His Explorations as Related to the Herald Explorer.

A STORY MORE ROMANTIC THAN ROMANCE.

Stanley's Special Corps at the Service of the Doctor and the Start of the Travellers in Company.

Personal Loneliness and Destitution of Livingstone When Relieved by the Herald Search Corps.

DOCTOR LIVINGSTONE.

Grand Triumph for England and America.

The Flags of Both Countries United.

LIVINGSTONE SUCCESSFUL.

STANLEY SUCCESSFUL

Characteristic Letter from the Great Explorer to the Editor of the Herald.

Deeply Interesting Description of Five Hundred Miles Tramp.

"I Thought That I Was Dying on My Feet."

Deceived, Plundered, "a Mere Ruckle of Bones" and Almost Despairing at Ujiji.

The Inspiration of a Broken Photograph.

Plucking Courage from Superstition.

THE FIRST GLEAM OF HOPE.

Sighting the American Flag in the Distance.

SALUTATION TO THE GOOD SAMARITAN.

The Herald Commissioner's News.

THE NEW LIGHTS TO SCIENCE.

Bennett, however, decided he was merely lost and determined to find him. From Spain (where he was covering the Carlist wars) Bennett summoned a young Welshman who had impressed him in America with his reports from the Indian wars, Henry Morton Stanley. That was not his real name. He had been brought up as an orphan in a Welsh workhouse, worked his passage to the United States at the age of 15, and adopted the name of a kindly benefactor in New Orleans. He had fought (on both sides) in the Civil War, then drifted into freelance reporting since when he had wandered the world happily from Tombstone to Turkey. Money was no object, Bennett informed him, but he must find Livingstone if alive, or else his bones if he were dead.

It was March 1871 before Stanley was ready to plunge into the African interior, with 153 porters, a train of pack animals and a small army of local soldiers, for Bennett had given him other assignments to complete first. It proved an extremely hazardous journey. Numbers of his men died of smallpox or dysentery, and most of his animals perished. Stanley himself went down with fever, and found himself caught up in a war between Arab traders and Mirambo, king of Uyoma. At one stage he was forced to stand siege in the local Governor's house with the American flag flying defiantly over the roof. He was fleeced of half his supplies by a local sultan who demanded 'tribute', but Stanley pressed on until he reached Ujiji in November. Here he was alerted to the presence quite recently of a white man and, elated, he ordered the expedition to proceed to the shores of Lake Tanganyika with the flag at the head.

Livingstone was there, sure enough, 'a mere ruckle of bones' as he described himself, but otherwise healthy. He hadn't, it transpired, been lost at all — just going about his business — but he was delighted to see another white man (his last as it turned out). Stanley stayed on for Christmas, and the two men did a bit of exploring together. But Livingstone was not to be persuaded to return to civilization: he had two more years work ahead of him. So Stanley set off alone back to Zanzibar in March 1872.

News of his success went on ahead of him and reached the coast on April 29. On May 2 London papers carried the glorious news that The New York Herald correspondent had done the impossible. The New York Herald ran a surprisingly modest crop of headlines the next day, on receiving the news from London.

But Bennett was not one to hide a light under a bushel for long. As more and more fragments of news came in, he prepared a splash the ripples of which would wash over every newspaper in the continent. On July 1 Stanley's letters from Africa arrived in London. They were posted on, but The New York Herald's agent considered himself justified in spending a small fortune in cabling the substance of them to his proprietor. Next day in The New York Herald the headlines straggled more than halfway down the page.

There were, from the outset, a host of unbelievers. One paper was unkind enough to suggest that Stanley had never wandered further than the wilds of Central Park in his search for the lost traveller. The Boston Traveller sarcastically hoped Mr. Stanley wouldn't be seduced by 'the gayeties of that frivolous capital (Ujiji) so as to forget his mission'. In London a cynic wrote triumphantly to The Times pointing out that Stanley had claimed to have recognised the missionary amongst all the natives 'by his pale face'. Well, it couldn't be true then, because everyone knew Livingstone was dark, not fair!

Other newspapers began to get querulous as The New York Herald continued to flaunt its success. 'It is about time' muttered The Louisville Courier-Journal 'for The New York Herald to quit boasting of its correspondent's Livingston-

ian expedition. If the thing is kept up much longer we shall make it a point to hire Monsieur du Chaillu at fifty dollars a day to lose himself in the Wilds of Equatorial Africa and let one of our silver-plated correspondents to go in search of him.' But The New York Herald was not going to quit now. Its headlines grew longer still, until Bennett was ready to deliver the coup de grace to all his carping critics. On August 27 he proudly reproduced a facsimile of his personal letter from the Doctor. And what a nice thankyou letter it was, expressing deep gratitude for Bennett's great generosity and sending lots of news from the interior. Stanley was the hero of the year and had, incidentally, acquired a taste for exploration. After Livingstone's death in 1873, he assumed the great man's mantle and in the next few years crossed the African continent from east to west and traced the Congo river to its source, sending back his reports to The New York Herald and the London Daily Telegraph, which at that time commanded the highest circulation in the world (and had almost succeeded in seducing Stanley away from The New York Herald when he arrived back from Africa). Stanley's reports, in Britain particularly, were to play an important part in the opening-up of the new continent in the latter part of the century, which was quite an achievement for an orphan lad from North Wales.

CHIROGRAPHY FROM AFRICA.

Of Interest to Admirers of the Great Explorer.

A PROOF TO THE DOUBTING THOMASES.

The Carpers at Livingstone's Diction.

Brief Sketch of the Great Traveller's Life.

HIS THREE AFRICAN JOURNEYS.

THE OLD, OLD MYSTERY OF THE NILE.

Herodotus and Claudius Ptolemy as Nilotic Geographers.

GRADUAL LIFTING OF THE VEIL.

The Scotch Traveller Bruce Discovers the Sources of the Blue Nile.

Sir Samuel Baker's Explorations in Abyssinia and on the White Nile—The Albert Nyanza.

Captain Speke's Journey from Victoria Nyanza Down the Bahr el Abiad.

The Great Work Accomplished by Livingstone and the Work Before Him.

LIVINGSTONE'S SIGN MANUAL.

Fac Simile of Doctor David Livingstone's Letter of Thanks to the New York Herald.

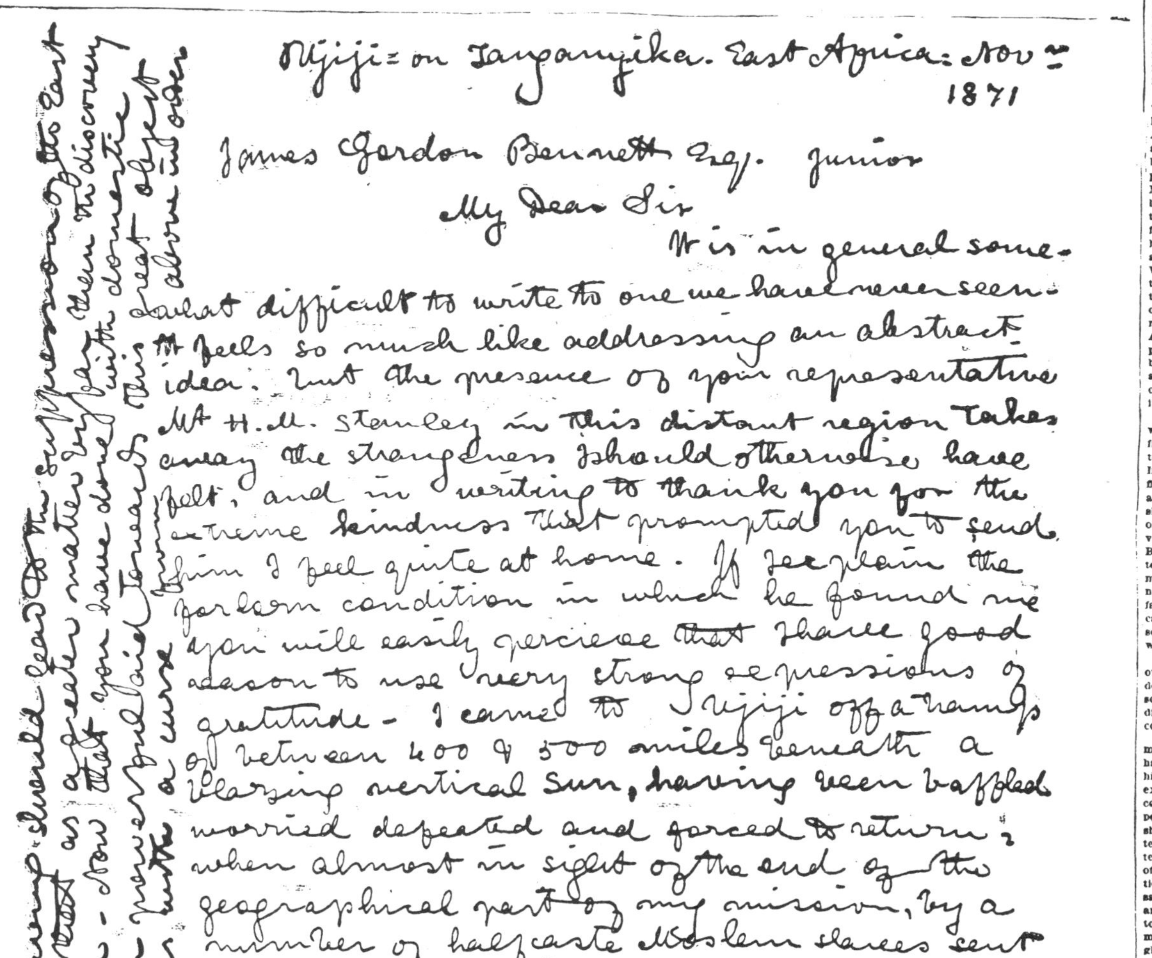

Ujiji on Tanganyika. East Africa. Nov. 1871

James Gordon Bennett Esq. junior

My Dear Sir

It is in general somewhat difficult to write to one we have never seen – it feels so much like addressing an abstract idea. But the presence of your representative Mr H. M. Stanley in this distant region takes away the strangeness I should otherwise have felt, and in writing to thank you for the extreme kindness that prompted you to send him I feel quite at home. If I explain the forlorn condition in which he found me you will easily perceive that I have good reason to use very strong expressions of gratitude. I came to Ujiji off a tramp of between 400 & 500 miles beneath a blazing vertical sun, having been baffled worried defeated and forced to return, when almost in sight of the end of the geographical part of my mission, by a number of halfcaste Moslem slaves sent to me from Zanzibar instead of men. The sore heart made still sorer by the truly woeful sights I had seen of man's inhumanity to man reacted on the bodily frame, and depressed it beyond measure. I thought that I was dying on my feet. It is not too much to say that almost every step of the weary sultry way was in pain, and I reached Ujiji a mere ruckle of bones. There I found that some £500 worth of goods I had ordered from Zanzibar had unaccountably been entrusted to a drunken halfcaste Moslem tailor who after squandering them for sixteen months in the way to Ujiji finished up by selling off all that remained for slaves and ivory for himself. He had divined on the Koran

regarding the trivial Ujijian slavery should lead to the suppression of the East coast slave trade I shall regard as a greater matter by far than the discovery of all the Nile sources together. Now that you have done with domestic slavery for ever lend us your powerful aid towards this great object. This fine country is blighted as with a curse from above in order

* * * * * * * * * * * * * * *

I conclude by again thanking you most cordially for your great generosity and am gratefully yours David Livingstone

On this page of the HERALD we present to our readers a *fac simile* of the opening page and the closing sentence of the first letter which Dr. David Livingstone addressed to the editor of this journal from Central Africa. In doing so a double object is achieved, which will in each part make its impression. The first lies in presenting to the public a specimen of how the great explorer writes in the wilds of Central Africa, with what firmness he grasps his pen and how he writes his mind without the afterthought visible in erasures and interpolations. The second is in exhibiting to the few doubting Thomases on this Continent, who may yet hold out against indisputable evidence, a sign whereby they can learn to enter the ranks of

THE MILLION OF TRUE BELIEVERS.

While it is the duty of a journal to make good its announcements of news by furnishing all reasonable corroboration of their truth when disputed, there is a certain limit to this at which a paper may reasonably rest from its task of convincing perverse incredulity. Long ago has that period been reached by the HERALD in the matter of its correspondent's search for and finding of Dr. Livingstone. The doubters first asked positive information from Mr. Stanley about Livingstone's movements during the last six years, his health, his appearance and where last seen. These points once satisfactorily covered, doubt shook its head; it wanted letters from Livingstone himself. From information received ahead these were promised by the HERALD and immediately upon their arrival in London were telegraphed through the cable to America. This even was unsatisfactory. The doubters knew better. The man who had "concocted" the story of the meeting with Livingstone in Central Africa might, with a similar display of what Miss Braddon calls "bold badness," forge a letter to the HERALD reciting in other words the story of Livingstone's travels and "so-called" discoveries. Nothing easier, they said. By and by news came to America of letters not only to the English Foreign Office, but to the family of the absent Livingstone. This was

A DIRECT ASSAULT UPON THE THOMASES.

But the certificates of Earl Granville and those of the explorer's family as to the genuineness of the letters completely tumbled over their fortresses, and brought even the high and Royal Geographical doubters down to signing a capitulation. It is, therefore, with but little regard to a further convincing of these individuals that we publish the accompanying *fac-simile*, yet its influence on them will result, if not in silencing them, at least in making their incredulities more deservedly ridiculous. To those who have long learned to admire the heroism of David Livingstone, which shone forth amid trying occasions, displaying perseverance, patience, dignity, self-control, benevolence and piety, as the times demanded or his heart dictated, this presentment of the tracing of his pen will be of high interest. The clear, running hand, which flowingly jots down thoughts that come from the mind like the current of the great river he has been following, will tell its own story of the nerve, even-mindedness and stamina of the man who sits down to write just as he "came to Ujiji off a tramp of between four hundred and five hundred miles, beneath a blazing vertical sun, having been baffled, worried, defeated and forced to return, when almost in sight of the end."

Every peculiarity of Doctor Livingstone's chirography has been faithfully followed in the *fac-simile*, even to the defects resulting from sluggish ink and such paper and pens as could be found in east longitude thirty degrees and south latitude five degrees on that November day last year. The disposition to save paper, which leads Livingstone, after filling the pages, to write upon every available square inch of margin, will be noticed too. In all civilized countries the preservation of scraps of handwriting of great men has been a sacred task long after the men had passed away. In the great libraries and museums of European countries such scraps arrest the attention of the student with an interest unsurpassed by the costliest or rarest tomes upon the shelves or among the carefully guarded archives of the State. The handwriting of Pope, with its frequent scorings out, corrections and interlineations; the sign manual of Milton, the remnants of the "Domesday Book," the Magna Charta, awake, perhaps, more interest in him who wanders around the spacious halls of the British Museum than the gorgeously illuminated missals that lie beside them in their sumptuous bindings and which cost so much constant, secluded toil to learned but forgotten monks in the Middle Ages. The truth is that the scraps bring the mind of the observer back by an intimate link to the men and times of the past, to which he has hitherto directed of the hero in one word, "action," and it is as a man of action the world first must look at the tireless explorer. From this standpoint it then can view his writing how it pleases; it will not affect his fame one iota. But apart from the rose-water few who think all great men should write with violet ink on scented paper, and phrase perspicuously as Cicero, Addison or Fénelon, the verdict of intelligence on Livingstone's letters will be that they are the clear, frank utterance of a man of kindly heart, unconquerable courage and of a gentleman above all. That he should come to Ujiji

"A MERE RUCKLE OF BONES"

is an unpardonable fact when told so graphically, but where he joins heart with Scotland's bard, and finds in Mid-Africa an application for one of the most nobly-sorrowful truths ever allied to melody of words—

> Man's inhumanity to man
> Makes countless thousands mourn—

the critics must pause in their fault finding. The brave words, however, which he addresses to humanity regarding the slave trade, doubtless knowing the peril in which they yet may place him among the slave traders of Ujiji, are those before which the phrase-splitter must hang his head, for they bespeak a loftiness of aim and an abnegation of self which the small-souled, pompous near Glasgow, about 1817. He is now, therefore, in his fifty-fifth or fifty-sixth year. His parents were poor, and his early life was passed working in a cotton mill, striving between the hours of labor and sleep to pick up the secrets of literary knowledge. As he grew older he longed to become a missionary, and, after he had studied medicine and theology for a few years, he was despatched by the London Missionary Society in 1840 to Port Natal, in South Africa. Long and faithfully did he labor among the wild natives of that hitherto unknown region, and there married the daughter of a fellow missionary, a Miss Moffatt, who accompanied him upon his travels until her untimely death from fever at Shupanga, in 1862. The extent of his explorations in South Africa will be imagined when it is stated that, during his absence of sixteen years until 1856, he marched 11,000 miles. In the last-named year he returned to England and published his first book, "Missionary Travels and Researches in South Africa." In March, 1858, he returned to Africa and undertook what is known as

THE ZAMBEZI EXPEDITION,

discovering Lake Nyassa. Here he lost and buried his faithful wife. In 1863 he returned to the coast, and thence proceeded to England, where he was received with increased favor. In 1865 he pub- deserter Moosa, startled England into sending an expedition, under the command of Mr. E. D. Young, to search for him or his remains. It may here be said that Moosa's cunning story, although doubted originally by many, was sufficiently disproved by this expedition, yet nothing definite of the great traveller's whereabouts was learned until March, 1869, when he was heard from at Ujiji. Two years of silence, doubt and misgiving passed, and no word came. This was the condition of things when, in 1871, the HERALD Search Expedition started its caravans under the command of Mr. Henry M. Stanley, the world already knows with what happy result. An interesting portion of Dr. Livingstone's letter is his reference to the sources of the mystic river which

HERODOTUS, THE FATHER OF HISTORY,

learned from the treasurer of the Temple of Minerva, on the island of Sais, in the delta of Egypt, 2,300 years ago. Misty, indeed, were the ideas of the time with regard to the great river source of Egypt's wealth, and Herodotus himself only corrects one absurd idea to account for the rise of the Nile to fall into another more ingeniously so. The treasurer of the temple aforesaid, while showing him over its marvels of ponderous architecture chatted the other, Mophi; that the sources of the Nile, which are bottomless, flow from between these mountains, and that

HALF OF THE WATER FLOWS OVER EGYPT

and to the north, the other half over Ethiopia and the South." In his travels Dr. Livingstone has heard repeatedly of such fountains, and while their position, as given by the registrar, is, of course, incorrect, the explorer has very little doubt of their existence, and that he is now, by the grace of God, preparing to clear up. The personal explorations of Herodotus reached no farther than the first cataract; his other information is admittedly hearsay. It speaks of long stretches of the river to the far country of the Automoli, and indicates a large lake to the south through which the Nile flows. While referring to Herodotus it may be worth while to point another possible coincidence between his history and an ethnological observation of Dr. Livingstone. The explorer says that he found a light-colored, handsome people in Rua, who worked copper mines, wove grass very finely and were otherwise more distinguished in appearance and customs than their neighbors. Herodotus recounts that two hundred and forty thousand Egyptian soldiers, being placed on frontier duty at Elephantine, as the troops of the Viceroy scour the same country expelling the former. They brought, he says, some civilization to the Ethiopians. Are the people of Rua their descendants? Another of the ancients, whose lights have been dimmed by intermediate ignorance and who comes like a seer from the past, is

CLAUDIUS PTOLEMY,

the Egyptian mathematician, astronomer and geographer, who flourished in the early part of the second century. In his universal geography he speaks of the Nile with certainty as rising far south in Africa and passing through a series of lakes, just as Livingstone describes it. Coming down to modern times it is curious to note how the "Holy Nile" has been won back, as it were, from the clouds of ignorance that dwarfed its length, rendering the mystery greater still of its 1,400 miles of unaided flow, its wonderful fertilizing rise of from twenty-four to thirty-six feet and its fall to the old level. In 1769

A SCOTCHMAN NAMED JAMES BRUCE,

with the old mystery at heart, left civilization behind him and the following year reached Gondar, in Abyssina. Two years' exploration followed, and he at last found three fountains, which he believed to be those of the true Nile, but which have since proved to be those of Bahr el Azrek or Blue Nile. The story of his travels was read by the youth of the generation with avidity for the curious views of savage and semi-savage life it furnished, but at which the wiseacres shook their heads, until later research justified him. Gradually the mists lifted from the mighty river, and the White Nile or Bahr el Abiad was declared to be the true Nile, while the Blue Nile was lessened to a tributary, ranking only above the Atbara, rising on the same Abyssinian plateau, and joining its rain flood to the Nile farther north near Berber. Again the Nile sources were lost, like the Hesperides of old. Many expeditions were undertaken both at the instance of the Egyptian government and of European governments. The first which claims attention, if not in its actual order, but in its collective importance, was that of

SIR SAMUEL W. BAKER,

who, accompanied by his lady, went up the Nile from Cairo and turned up the Atbara at Berber to solve finally the question of the annual rise. In one night he saw the dry bed of the Atbara filled with a roaring torrent, rushing perturbed and muddy down, and saw within a week the shrivelled trees and herbage put on new coats of green. After a complete survey of the various streams which join the Nile between Berber and Khartoum he bent his way to the latter city, and brought with him one-half of the mystery. It was this; that the extraordinary annual rise of the Nile is due to the prodigious rainfall on the elevated plateau of Abyssinia, which carries down in its headlong course the soft, black soil of the countries through which it channels its way to spread

THE THIN, BUT RICH MUD DEPOSIT

over the valley of the Nile, which makes it so wonderfully fertile. From Khartoum he proceeded south, and in about latitude three degrees north discovered the great Lake Albert Nyanza. The discoveries of

CAPTAIN JOHN H. SPEKE

must here be alluded to. In 1855 Captain Speke, having obtained a three years' furlough from his regiment, then stationed in India, joined an expedition to explore Central Africa under the command of Lieutenant R. H. Burton. This expedition rendezvoused at Berbera, on the African shore of the Gulf of Aden, and with Lieutenant Burton at its head started for the interior. With them were also two other military officers on furlough. A few days after the expedition got under way they were attacked by the savages. One of Speke's companions was killed, and he himself severely wounded. He now returned to England. His next expedition into Africa was more successful. The lake regions of the interior, so glowingly described by Doctors Krapf and Rebman upon information gathered from the natives, were the object of the journey which began at Zanzibar in June, 1857. They struck boldly forward, but met terrible obstacles in the way of sickness and desertion of their men. After a long and weary journey, broken by enforced, dispiriting halts, they came in sight of the great

TANGANYIKA LAKE,

at Ujiji. They were prevented by untoward circumstances from fully exploring the lake, and returned to Unyanyembe. Here they parted, Captain Speke taking a northerly trail, which led to his discovery of the Victoria Nyanza, and which he then

CONJECTURED TO BE THE TRUE SOURCE

of the Nile. On his return to England he prepared for the next voyage, which he undertook in company with Major Grant. They left the east coast in October, 1860, and marched for the Nyanza Lake. They skirted it on its western shore, and on the northern end of it discovered the effluents which they subsequently, after much worry and opposition from the native chieftains, succeeded in sufficiently tracing to the White Nile. On this journey, in February, 1863, they were met at Gondokoro by Sir Samuel Baker, who was then proceeding up the Nile. Thus the second line of drainage was brought to light by the proof that the Victoria Nyanza, at a point nearly under the Equator, flowed out into a stream which, through a series of falls, joined the Albert Lake, and thence went on to form the Nile. "At last the true Nile," the world cried in applause, but not yet was all the secret torn from old Africa's bosom. Lake Tanganyika, which lies to the south of Albert Lake, and which Richard F. Burton and Captain Speke had seen together before the latter set out for Victoria Nyanza, was suspected of being a link further south of the mighty river, and connecting with the Albert Nyanza. Alleged differences in altitude of these lakes befogged this question, and there it has since remained. Thus two great lines of drainage were secured. Dr. Barth, the German explorer; Mr. Petherick, the British Consul at Khartoum; Dr. Piaggia, the Italian, and Dr. Schweinfurth, another German traveller, had made extensive explorations of other confluents of the White Nile on the western bank. With these latter, through

THE BAHR EL GHAZAL

or Petherick's branch, Doctor Livingstone believes he will yet connect the third or great central line of drainage, which has cost him already six years of toil to trace from ten to four degrees south latitude. The great lacustrine river—the Lualaba—thus placed on the map, is not yet all explored; and, from the fact of the explorations being carried on from the South, the actual point of its confluence to the White Nile is unknown, although Dr. Livingstone feels assured that

HIS NEXT TWO YEARS' LABOR

will determine it. Here we must perforce leave the question. The savans of London, Paris and Berlin may see fit to doubt the conclusions of Dr. Livingstone, but they must look after all to him to resolve them. Whether, as Dr. Charles Beke imagines, the Lualaba flows into the Albert Nyanza by a bend to the eastward, or, as Dr. Livingstone believes, goes directly northward, through another great lake, into Petherick's Branch, we cannot say; but the glory of the discovery will be nowise dimmed around the great explorer's brow

WHATEVER WAY THE LUALABA RUNS.

His efforts in the cause of science will place him high upon the pedestal of fame. His quiet striving as a missionary among the benighted heathens will endear him to all lovers of the Gospel. His upright character as a man will preserve the balance between the two. These, making up as they do the bold outlines for a mind picture of him, who will deny him the place of honor which every such hero of the human kind deserves?

Of interest as forming a touching commentary on the epistle which we present in fac-simile form is

The Great Wild Animal Hoax

There was a sequel, of sorts, to *The New York Herald* correspondent's adventures in the darkest continent. Of course there is no evidence to show that Bennett's sinister imagination was fired directly by Stanley's thrilling dispatches from the jungle. It is quite possible he was just bored with the routine of life in New York (a city for which he never acquired any great taste). Anyway the disaster he conjured up in November 1874 was one he would have unquestionably relished taking a major, not to say heroic, part in himself.

On November 9 1874 readers of *The New York Herald* were arrested on page three by the bald and compelling headline announcing an 'Awful Calamity'. It all began, it seems, in the rhinoceros cage at the zoo in Central Park. Tormented beyond endurance by some foolish attendant, the huge beast broke out of its cage and ran amok around the zoo, breaking down other cages as it careered about. Within minutes all manner of ferocious animals were heading for Fifth Avenue, grizzly bears, lions, tigers, a puma, buffalo, cheetah, elephant and many others, leaving behind unutterable carnage in Central Park. The city authorities were caught totally unprepared: by the time the National Guard had been called out and armed policemen summoned dozens of citizens had been killed and hundreds more — women and children mainly — had been cruelly mauled.

It was of course, as a small paragraph at the very end of the report explained, a complete fiction, an elaborate hoax 'or whatever other epithet of utter untrustworthiness our readers may choose to apply to it'. Modern readers may think that the most valuable asset a newspaper has is its credibility, that to perpetrate such a monstrous fabrication would be nothing less than commercial suicide. But hoaxes were by no means unknown in the New York press in the nineteenth century. *The New York Sun* had got away for weeks with its Moon Hoax in 1835, reporting fantastic details of life on the moon as revealed by an amazing new telescope (the whereabouts of which was known only to *The Sun*). Somewhat tardily for such an ingenuous joke it was finally unmasked by its rival papers — but quite unrepentant it embarked on another in 1844. The Balloon hoax was the brainchild of Edgar Allan Poe: it reported a speed record to beat all speed records (right).

The Sun, this time, openly mocked its contemporaries for their inability to appreciate the pleasant satire'.

What distinguished *The Herald's* hoax was its meticulous mass of detail: names, places, times were all carefully worked out. Eye-witness accounts of thrilling incidents were suitably graphic: how Archbishop McCloskey was saved from the tiger's fangs by the sharpshooting of Governor Dix; how the rampaging rhinoceros met its end by charging into an Eleventh Avenue sewer excavation; how the anaconda tried to make a grisly meal of the giraffe; how a tiger wreaked havoc on a North River ferryboat. Indeed, viewed as a piece of pure fiction it was a remarkably fine piece of work, building up a vivid picture of mass hysteria at work.

The Herald, however, felt obliged the next day to justify its exercise as something more than that. In its editorial it reported (without apology) that 'the equilibrium of the public' had been disturbed by the previous day's fantasy,

then went on to ask what would happen 'if real beasts were substituted'. The writer recalled the panic created in Philadelphia by the escape of the tame elephant Columbus, and wondered whether the city fathers' in New York were prepared for such an emergency. Whether he really believed there should be some deeply-considered contingency plan to cope with escaped animals is a matter for conjecture. The one justification for the whole imaginative exercise which might have rung true — that the cages in Central Park were truly in dangerous condition — apparently didn't cross his mind. More likely he hadn't gone there to see.

*Right: The New York Herald November 9, 1874.
Below: The Great Balloon Hoax from The New York Sun April 14, 1844.*

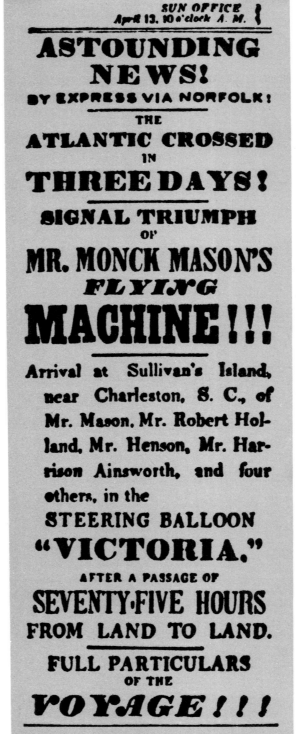

SUN OFFICE
April 13, 10 o'clock A. M.

ASTOUNDING NEWS!

BY EXPRESS VIA NORFOLK!

THE

ATLANTIC CROSSED

IN

THREE DAYS!

SIGNAL TRIUMPH

OF

MR. MONCK MASON'S

FLYING

MACHINE!!!

Arrival at Sullivan's Island, near Charleston, S. C., of Mr. Mason, Mr. Robert Holland, Mr. Henson, Mr. Harrison Ainsworth, and four others, in the

STEERING BALLOON

"VICTORIA."

AFTER A PASSAGE OF

SEVENTY-FIVE HOURS

FROM LAND TO LAND.

FULL PARTICULARS

OF THE

VOYAGE!!!

AWFUL CALAMITY.

The Wild Animals Broken Loose from Central Park.

TERRIBLE SCENES OF MUTILATION

A Shocking Sabbath Carnival of Death.

SAVAGE BRUTES AT LARGE

Awful Combats Between the Beasts and the Citizens.

THE KILLED AND WOUNDED

General Duryee's Magnificent Police Tactics.

BRAVERY AND PANIC

How the Catastrophe Was Brought About---Affrighting Incidents.

PROCLAMATION BY THE MAYOR

Governor Dix Shoots the Bengal Tiger in the Street.

CONSTERNATION IN THE CITY

Another Sunday of horror has been added to those already memorable in our city annals. The sad and appalling catastrophe of yesterday is a further illustration of the unforeseen perils to which large communities are exposed. Writing even at a late hour, without full details of the terrors of the evening and night, and with a necessarily incomplete list of the killed and mutilated, we may pause for a moment in the widespread sorrow of the hour to cast a hasty glance over what will be felt as a great calamity for many years. Few of the millions who have visited Central Park, and who, passing in through the entrance at East Sixty-fourth street, have stopped to examine the collection of birds and animals grouped around the old Arsenal building, could by any possibility have foreseen the source of such terrible danger

Unspeakable Turks

The Balkan Atrocities

The London *Daily News*, which in the summer of 1876 found itself embroiled in the affairs of a remote corner of Europe, was a very different paper from that which had driven its first editor, Charles Dickens, to the verge of a nervous breakdown in three weeks flat. That had been thirty years ago, when Joseph Paxton (shortly to give birth to his other, less enduring, memorial in the Crystal Palace) among others had boldly initiated a newspaper dedicated to the principles of 'progress and improvement, of education, civil and religious liberty and equal legislation'. Then it had mustered barely 4,000 readers for all its laudable aims; now, partly by reducing its price to 1d but equally through the swashbuckling reporting of its special correspondent Archibald Forbes in the Franco-Prussian War, it could claim more than 150,000. (It also had the distinction of having employed the first woman leader-writer on its staff, Harriet Martineau). In 1876 *The Daily News* was a journal of style and substance, even though the proprietor of *The Times* was popularly believed never to have so much as opened its pages.

On June 23 1876 *The Daily News* dropped a smouldering bombshell quietly into the laps of Mr. Disraeli's conservative ministry. The article on page five began somewhat melodramatically.

But it was not a report to be taken lightly. For one thing, it was from Sir Edwin Pears who had once been *The Times'* own correspondent in Turkey. He talked of 'trustworthy information' concerning 'the burning of forty or fifty Bulgarian girls in a stable and the massacre of upwards of a hundred children in the village school-house'. There was talk of 30,000 massacred, he said, and total censorship within the Turkish post-office. He reminded his readers of the breed of Turkish irregulars who were perpetrating these atrocities, the Bashi-Bazouks ('the dregs of the Turkish population . . . gipsies and gaolbirds let out for the purpose'). Veterans of the Crimean War would have remembered the name and shuddered over breakfast, no doubt.

For as long as anyone could remember — and certainly since Lord Byron had so romantically died for Greek independence fifty years before — the oppressed people of the Balkans had been of interest to Britain. Not so much (it had to be admitted) for their humiliating status within the now-derelict Ottoman Empire as for their value as a buttress against Russia's imperialistic ambitions. One of the ways of thwarting the Tsar was to bolster up Turkish sovereignty over the Balkans: that had been Aberdeen's policy, and now it was Disraeli's. There was also another solution which had been favoured once by Canning and now appealed to the Opposition leader, Gladstone: and that was to champion

the blossoming Serb, Croat and Slovak nationalism against the corrupt Ottomans and establish a string of sturdy independent buffer-states between Russia and the Mediterranean. Either way Britain's destiny to preserve the balance of power in Europe was undisputed.

In July 1875 that balance of power was rudely threatened. Mr. Disraeli notwithstanding, the Bosnian and Herzegovinians had taken it upon themselves to rebel against their Turkish overlords. Hence the presence of the uncouth Bashis. The massacres had begun in March 1876 but so efficient had been the Turkish censorship that *The Daily News'* report that Friday in June was the first whiff the British public had had of the stench being stirred up far away. Perhaps, under other circumstances, it would have contemplated the massacre of one set of unpronounceable aliens by another with equanimity. But in this instance the nation was profoundly moved, from the smoking-room of the Athenaeum to the pit of the Alhambra (where, when Russia threatened to intervene, the hit song of the year was 'We don't want to fight, But by Jingo if we do, We've got the men, we've got the ships, We've got the money too').

For it was more than an atrocity — it was a head-on confrontation between Disraeli and Gladstone. To the House of Commons, Disraeli contemptuously dismissed the report as 'coffee-house babble' and a piece of propaganda by the Russians. *The Daily News* was a Liberal newspaper, Mr. Gladstone was the Liberal leader; so naturally their policies coincided. The Turks themselves vigorously and officially denied the whole thing, and the Foreign Office soon announced that its man in Constantinople was unable to confirm the accusations. The onus was clearly on *The Daily News* to prove its charges or to climb down, to avert a new international crisis.

It chose the former course, announcing the appointment of a special investigator whose 'courage and daring . . : cool head and steady eye' would 'tell the impartial truth'. This hero turned out to be one Januarius Aloysius MacGahan, an occasional correspondent for *The New York Herald* from the court of St. Petersburg who by this time was operating freelance from Constantinople. There were several things to commend him: he was American and therefore presumably impartial, he had an excellent reputation, and he was a more single-minded reporter than his quaint name suggested. By the end of July he was on his way, hampered at first by an obstructive Turkish escort, but determined to see what there was to see for himself.

What he saw — and heard from survivors — almost defied description. For a week his

dispatches poured into *The Daily News* office compounding horror upon horror. He wrote of villages burnt wholesale and babies tossed casually into the flames, of women brutally raped and children with noses hacked off. One particularly graphic account was published in *The Daily News* on August 7.

For part of his journey MacGahan was accompanied by an artist from *The Graphic* who posted off his sketches as fast as his companion filed his stories. Appearing in print less than a after MacGahan's exposes, they fuelled the country's already white-hot indignation. 'If we are to go on bolstering up this tottering despotism' fulminated *The Daily News*, 'if we are to go on carrying this loathsome, vice-stricken leper about on our shoulders, let us do it with open eyes and a knowledge of the facts'.

There was no argument about the facts now. The Government admitted the incontrovertible, and belatedly acknowledged its debt to the gentlemen of the Press. Gladstone in his enthusiasm was almost fulsome in praise of *The Daily News*: 'it is even possible that but for . . . this single organ, we might even at this moment have remained in darkness'. Later, it was claimed that the ensuing Russo-Turkish war was the direct outcome of MacGahan's efforts. Be that as it may, the Tsar made haste to rescue his fellow-Christians in the Balkans from annihilation by the Moslem butchers; in six months he had mounted an invasion, and in another twelve had forced upon the Turks the terms of the Treaty of San Stefano, which among other things recognised the independence of Roumania, Montenegro and Serbia. MacGahan himself did not live long enough to see the whole Eastern Question 'solved' by the Western Powers at the Congress of Berlin; he died of typhoid in June 1878. His statue was erected in Sofia, and masses were said in his memory in churches throughout Bulgaria for many years to come.

The Daily News had justly left all its competitors standing — not least *The Times* whose pre-eminence in Europe was believed to be unassailable. But the sequel, at the Berlin Congress, was to provide some sweet revenge. On Saturday July 13 1878 Count Bismarck, who had been presiding for the past month over the secret machinations of statesmen which were going to produce 'peace with honour', received a telegram just before he sat down to append his signature to the momentous Treaty of Berlin. It informed him that in London *The Times* had that morning published the complete text of the as-yet unsigned treaty. The conspiratorial shroud which had enveloped the Congress had been stripped away, though too late to have any effect.

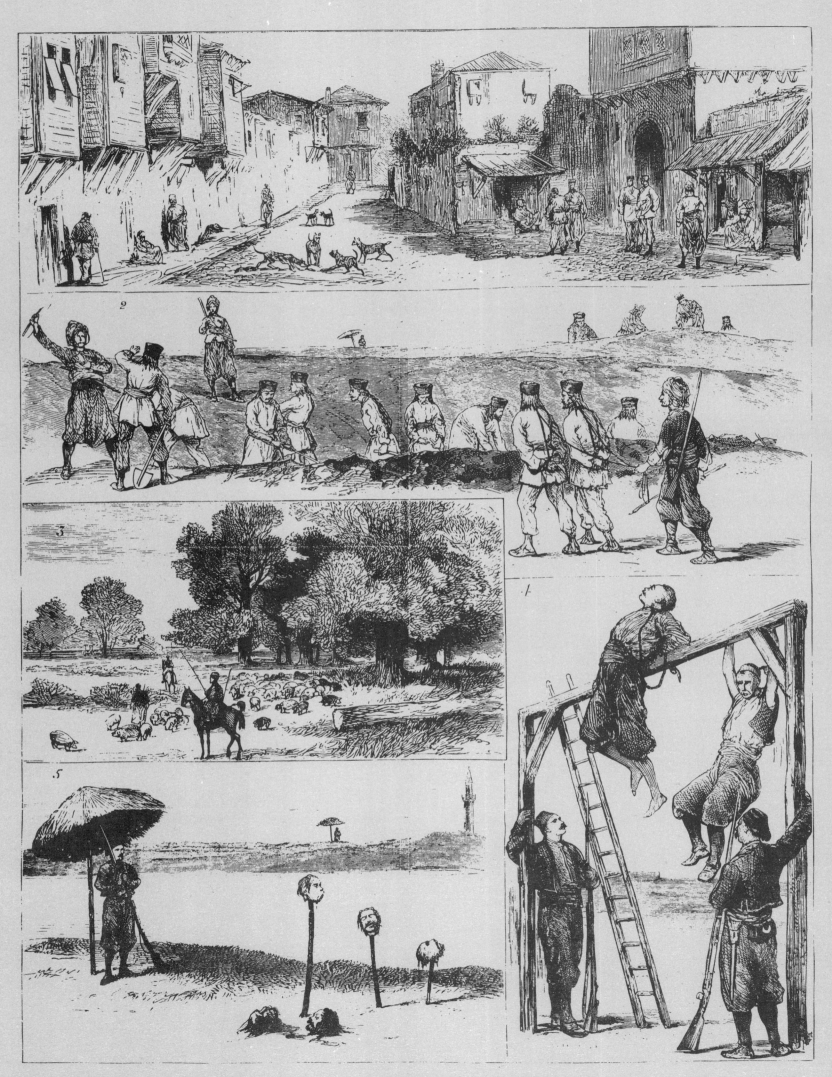

1. A Street in Widdin. — 2. Turks Driving Bulgarians to Work at the Fortifications. — 3. Servian Shepherd Sentinels Protecting their Flocks against the Bashi-Bazouks. — 4. The Gallows at Widdin. — 5. Insurgents' Heads Exposed in the Fortress, Widdin.

THE WAR IN THE EAST—SKETCHES BY OUR SPECIAL ARTIST

The Maiden Tribute of Modern Babylon

Child Prostitution in London

It was not in the nature of mid-Victorian journals to stir up trouble, any more than Thackeray's imaginary *Pall Mall Gazette* ('written for gentlemen by gentlemen') would have dreamed of disturbing the sensibilities of London's clubland 37 years earlier. But in 1885 the real *Pall Mall Gazette* was edited by a brave, zealous, grandiloquent non-conformist from Northumberland called William Stead. Under his predecessors the *Pall Mall Gazette*, in its short life, had achieved a political influence out of all proportion to its modest readership. Its more dedicated subscribers remembered how, in 1874, its editor had persuaded Mr. Disraeli to purchase shares in the Suez Canal and, more recently, had prevented the Royal Navy from falling into a state of irretrievable decrepitude by exposing 'The Truth about the Navy' to all the world. But not even its most ardent supporters were in the least prepared for the furore which Stead, newly-arrived in the editor's seat, calculatedly inspired in the summer of 1885.

In June that year Lord Salisbury had been obliged to form a minority Conservative Government, following the resignation of Gladstone over a hostile amendment to his budget. In its precarious position the new Ministry was reluctant to undertake any legislation for the time being, and least of all any contentious legislation. A number of impending Bills were accordingly postponed — some probably indefinitely, like the Criminal Law Amendment Bill. This admirable measure was designed to offer some protection to juveniles (and especially young girls) against exploitation and 'the white slave trade' as the enemies of child prostitution called it. There was no doubt that the situation in London and other large cities was a national reproach, partly because the existing law fixed the 'age of consent' at thirteen. Once past the age of twelve thousands of young girls could be — and were each year — 'purchased' from their unemployed and often starving parents by professional procurers for the casual pleasure of some flagging gentleman of means. The wholesale price was normally £5, rarely more than £10. Those who were lucky were deflowered overnight for the reward of 30/- and returned to their families. The less fortunate took to the streets after their degrading experience, or were earmarked for 'the foreign market'. Not only was this practice rampant among the working classes; there was nothing the law, as it stood, could do to stop it.

When the fate of the Bill became known, it was only natural that the Chamberlain of London (who was genuinely concerned about prostitution in his city) should approach the editor of the liberal and crusading *Pall Mall Gazette* for help. Stead was sympathetic, appalled, angry as any humanitarian would be; as a newspaperman he hesitated. He consulted General Booth,

leader of the Salvation Army who, if anyone did, knew what was going on in London's seediest quarters. He also inquired at Scotland Yard among senior police officers. It was worse than he ever dreamt; he realised that even the most moral members of Parliament could only be re-activated on the subject by an uncompromising exposure of the dreadful truth.

Before Stead set out to 'buy' his adolescent evidence, he took care to secure the support of bishops, social workers and other responsible citizens. He enlisted Booth's own son, as well as a reformed procuress by the name of Rebecca Jarrett, as his accomplices. He then sallied forth into London's West End in the guise of an indulgent, if discriminating, roué. He befriended and interviewed countless street-girls, and took down their pitiable stories verbatim. He tracked down their madames and pimps and won their confidence, too. Soon he had purchase options on more girls than he knew what to do with. According to accepted custom he was furnished with written 'agreements' from the girls offering themselves 'as presents' — though he discovered that none of them had the slightest idea what this entailed. All were examined by a doctor: those who proved to be virgins were given the customary certificate, the others were bundled off home by the procurers, clutching 5/- for their trouble.

By the beginning of July he was ready to reveal to the world the results of his Secret Commission, as he chose to call his little team of investigators. On the 4th he publicly warned those readers 'who prefer to live in a fool's paradise of imaginary innocence and purity, selfishly oblivious of the horrible realities which torment those whose lives are passed in the London Inferno' not to read *The Pall Mall Gazette* for the next four issues. On July 6 he began his sensational tale of young nursemaids abducted in London parks, of immature girls held down screaming to be seduced, of virgins inveigled into brothels with promises of fine clothes, of Mesdames X and Z who delivered in bulk to any address with two days' notice, of parents bartering their daughters' chastity for a few miserable shillings. It was a horrific narrative and the readers of the paper were duly horrified. In fact, there were so many readers that Stead ran out of newsprint trying to supply the demand.

The public reaction was not unexpected, except in the degree of its violence. The offices of *The Pall Mall Gazette* were mobbed; the paper was banned from many bookstalls; an MP suggested in Parliament that Stead be prosecuted for obscene libel. Advertisers and subscribers flocked to withdraw their patronage from this pornographic sheet. Yet still, as the revelations poured forth, *The Pall Mall Gazette* disappeared from the streets the moment it was re-printed. Initially the other London papers

kept grimly silent — until Stead himself in his columns needled them into some kind of reaction. *The Standard's* righteous outburst was typical of most: 'no other capital in Europe would tolerate for an hour the spectacle presented in the main thoroughfares of London at the present moment of men, women and children offering to men, women and children copies of a newspaper containing the most offensive, highly coloured and disgusting details concerning the vicious ways of a small section of the population . . . the sewer that runs underground may need cleansing; but the zeal that makes a handsome profit by turning it into the street will hardly be appreciated'.

But Stead was unmoved by the pontifications of his fellow editors: he continued to post extra platoons of newsboys and relays of advertising placards with each successive edition. It was not long before public meetings were being held in support of him, petitions sent to Parliament and appeals to the Queen; outside some houses of ill-repute vigils were kept, demanding the names of all men who entered them. Stead himself drummed up an impressive committee of prelates, lawyers and politicians to examine his statements and report to Parliament.

With unprecedented speed the Bill was exhumed, re-vivified and hustled through the Commons. It became known as Stead's Law — so it was an added irony when the first major defendant to be tried under the new provisions of the Amended Criminal Law was Stead himself. At the end of October he was charged at the Old Bailey with abducting Eliza Armstrong from her home in Charles Street. Eliza, or 'Lily' in the *Gazette's* story, was one of the girls signed away by her mother — a transaction arranged by Jarrett. Unknown to Stead at the time, she had omitted to get the father's consent, a blunder for which Stead took full responsibility. At the trial Mrs. Armstrong emerged as a drunken, hard-swearing lady but she stuck gamely to her story that she'd believed Eliza to be 'going into service' — though with whom and where, she had no idea. (What emerged after the trial, too late to save Stead, was that she was not married to Armstrong anyway — so making his consent legally unnecessary).

William Stead was sentenced to nine weeks in prison, which equipped with an armchair and a coal fire (thanks to the intervention of the Prime Minister) he bore manfully, composing vast screeds on the Christian morality of his crusade. 'In the slow but unceasing progress of mankind along the infinite ascent which God has fixed between the Actual and the Ideal' he wrote after the trial in his role of "Chief Director of the Secret Commission", 'the movement of this year marks a distinct advance'.

That was certainly not the impression one would have got from the majority of London papers after the event. Once again *The Standard* gave forth: 'Stead's offence is made to stand out plainly in all its almost cynical recklessness, divested of all moral disguises . . . the wonder grows that it should ever have been possible to conceal such atrocious proceedings under the mask of a holy purpose'. *The Daily Chronicle* was delighted that the offspring of even the poorest family had been saved from 'the experiments of busybodies; and *The Daily News* that 'libels upon the civilisation and credit of this country . . . are shown to be as fictitious as they are disgusting, resting upon the unsupported assertions of abandoned wretches' (ie. of Rebecca Jarrett). *The Observer* felt 'it is not the duty of a journalist to act as a literary knight-errant and to undertake a crusade for the redress of every wrong . . . Journalism, after all, is not a mission and editors are neither missionaries nor evangelists'. It was a long time before the newspapers — and the brothel-keepers — forgave Stead.

THE
PALL MALL GAZETTE

An Evening Newspaper and Review.

No. 6336.—Vol. XLII.   *MONDAY, JULY* 6, 1885.   *Price One Penny.*

"WE BID YOU BE OF HOPE."

THE Report of our Secret Commission will be read to-day with a shuddering horror that will thrill throughout the world. After this awful picture of the crimes at present committed as it were under the very ægis of the law has been fully unfolded before the eyes of the public, we need not doubt that the House of Commons will find time to raise the age during which English girls are protected from inexpiable wrong. The evidence which we shall publish this week leaves no room for doubt—first, as to the reality of the crimes against which the Amendment Bill is directed, and, secondly, as to the efficacy of the protection extended by raising the age of consent. When the report is published, the case for the bill will be complete, and we do not believe that members on the eve of a general election will refuse to consider the bill protecting the daughters of the poor, which even the House of Lords has in three consecutive years declared to be imperatively necessary.

This, however, is but one, and that one of the smallest, of the considerations which justify the publication of the Report. The good it will do is manifest. These revelations, which we begin to publish to-day, cannot fail to touch the heart and rouse the conscience of the English people. Terrible as is the exposure, the very horror of it is an inspiration. It speaks not of leaden despair, but with a joyful promise of better things to come. *Wir heissen euch hoffen!* "We bid you be of hope," CARLYLE'S last message to his country, the rhythmic word with which GOETHE closes his modern psalm—that is what we have to repeat to-day, for assuredly these horrors, like others against which the conscience of mankind has revolted, are not eternal. "Am I my sister's keeper?" that paraphrase of the excuse of CAIN, will not dull the fierce smart of pain which will be felt by every decent man who learns the kind of atrocities which are being perpetrated in cool blood in the very shadow of our churches and within a stone's throw of our courts. It is a veritable slave trade that is going on around us; but, as it takes place in the heart of London, it is a scandal—an outrage on public morality—even to allude to it. We have kept silence far too long. There are a few devoted workers who have been labouring for years endeavouring to save those who might well address GORDON'S homely reproach to the "majority of us: "While you are eating and drinking and "resting on good beds, we, and those with me, are watching by night and by day"—working against this great wrong—happy, indeed, if they escaped obloquy and abuse for endeavouring to remind us of our duty. No longer will good men be able with easy conscience to join in that indignant "Hush!" by which the evil-doers have hitherto silenced every attempt to make articulate the smothered wail that rises unceasing from the woeful under-world. There is now an end to that conspiracy of silence by which, after every inquiry, "the door was each time quickly closed upon "the question, as the stone lid used to be shut down, in the "Campo Santo of Naples, upon the mass of human corpses that "lay festering beneath." That "stone lid" is raised now, never again, we may hope, to be closed until something has been done. Under the ruthless compulsion of publicity even those but indifferent honest will do more good than many of the most virtuous when the evil could be hidden out of sight.

That much may be done, we have good ground for hoping, if only because so little has hitherto been attempted. A dull despair has unnerved the hearts of those who face this monstrous evil, and good men have sorrowfully turned to other fields where their exertions might expect a better return. But the magnitude of this misery ought to lead to the redoubling, not to the benumbing of our exertions. No one can say how much suffering and wrong is irremediable until the whole of the moral and religious forces of the country are brought to bear upon it. Yet, in dealing with this subject, the forces upon which we rely in dealing with other evils are almost all paralysed. The Home, the School, the Church, the Press are silent. The law is actually accessory to crime. Parents culpably neglect even to warn their children of the existence of dangers of which many learn the first time when they have become their prey. The Press, which reports verbatim all the scabrous details of the divorce courts, recoils in pious horror from the duty of shedding a flood of light upon these dark places, which indeed are full of the habitations of cruelty. But the failure of the Churches is, perhaps, the most conspicuous and the most complete. CHRIST'S mission was to restore man to a semblance of the Divine. The Child-Prostitute of our day is the image into which, with the tacit acquiescence of those who call themselves by His name, men have moulded the form once fashioned in the likeness of GOD.

If Chivalry is extinct and Christianity is effete, there is still another great enthusiasm to which we may with confidence appeal. The future belongs to the combined forces of Democracy and Socialism, which when united are irresistible. Divided on many points they will combine in protesting against the continued immo-lation of the daughters of the people as a sacrifice to the vices of the rich. Of the two, it is Socialism which will find the most powerful stimulus in this revelation of the extent to which under our present social system the wealthy are able to exercise all the worst abuses of power which disgraced the feudalism of the Middle Ages. Wealth is power, Poverty is weakness. The abuse of power leads directly to its destruction, and in all the annals of crime can there be found a more shameful abuse of the power of wealth than that by which in this nineteenth century of Christian civilization princes and dukes, and ministers and judges, and the rich of all classes, are purchasing for damnation, temporal if not eternal, the as yet uncorrupted daughters of the poor? It will be said they assent to their corruption. So did the female serfs from whom the seigneur exacted the *jus primæ noctis*. And do our wealthy think that the assent wrung by wealth from poverty to its own undoing will avert the vengeance and the doom?

If people can only be got to think seriously about this matter progress will be made in the right direction. Evils once as universal and apparently inevitable as prostitution have disappeared. Vices almost universal are now regarded with shuddering horror by the least moral of men. Slavery has gone. A slave trader is treated as *hostis humani generis*. Piracy has disappeared. Intestine war is now almost unknown. Torture has been abolished. May we not hope, therefore, that if we try to do our duty to our sisters and to ourselves, we may greatly reduce, even although we never entirely extirpate, the plague of prostitution? For let us remember that—

> Every hope which rises and grows broad
> In the world's heart, by ordered impulse streams
> From the great heart of GOD.

And if that ideal seems too blinding bright for human eyes, we can at least do much to save the innocent victims who unwillingly are swept into the maelstrom of vice. And who is there among us bearing the name of man who will dare to sit down any longer with folded hands in the presence of so great a wrong?

THE MAIDEN TRIBUTE OF MODERN BABYLON.—I.

THE REPORT OF OUR SECRET COMMISSION.

IN ancient times, if we may believe the myths of Hellas, Athens, after a disastrous campaign, was compelled by her conqueror to send once every nine years a tribute to Crete of seven youths and seven maidens. The doomed fourteen, who were selected by lot amid the lamentations of the citizens, returned no more. The vessel that bore them to Crete unfurled black sails as the symbol of despair, and on arrival her passengers were flung into the famous Labyrinth of Dædalus, there to wander about blindly until such time as they were devoured by the Minotaur, a frightful monster, half man, half bull, the foul product of an unnatural lust. "The "labyrinth was as large as a town and had countless courts and galleries. "Those who entered it could never find their way out again. If they "hurried from one to another of the numberless rooms looking for "the entrance door, it was all in vain. They only became more hopelessly "lost in the bewildering labyrinth, until at last they were devoured by "the Minotaur." Twice at each ninth year the Athenians paid the maiden tribute to King Minos, lamenting sorely the dire necessity of bowing to his iron law. When the third tribute came to be exacted, the distress of the city of the Violet Crown was insupportable. From the King's palace to the peasant's hamlet, everywhere were heard cries and groans and the choking sob of despair, until the whole air seemed to vibrate with the sorrow of an unutterable anguish. Then it was that the hero Theseus volunteered to be offered up among those who drew the black balls from the brazen urn of destiny, and the story of his self-sacrifice, his victory, and his triumphant return, is among the most familiar of the tales which since the childhood of the world have kindled

FOURTH EDITION.

A FRENCH POLITICAL AMNESTY.

(EXCHANGE TELEGRAPH COMPANY'S TELEGRAM.)

PARIS, Saturday.—It is reported that one of the first acts of the new Chamber when constituted will be to declare a general political amnesty. Many names are mentioned as likely to be included in this act of grace, but the most prominent are Louise Michel and Prince Krapotkin, the Nihilist.

THE ST. LOUIS MYSTERY.

(REUTER'S TELEGRAM.)

NEW YORK, Oct. 24.—The *New York Tribune* publishes a despatch from St. Louis stating that Mr. Samuel Brooks, of Hyde, has visited the prisoner Maxwell, who is charged with the murder of Mr. Preller, and has recognized him as his son Hugh.

THE ARMSTRONG CASE.

SECOND DAY'S PROCEEDINGS.

The knowledge of the difficulty in getting into the court prevented this morning anything in the nature of the crowd of yesterday, as depicted by our artist in the illustration below. And as a consequence, when the jury roll was called over at five minutes to ten o'clock, there were only the reporters, one or two barristers' clerks, one solitary barrister in a back seat, and two police constables in the dock awaiting the arrival of the defendants. In the five minutes that preceded the hour of commencing the counsel arrived,

tioning witness as to what took place at Wimbledon when her daughter was restored to her.

Cross-examined by Mr. Russell: There was considerable improvement in the child's appearance when she saw her at Wimbledon. It was at Mrs. Stead's suggestion that she saw her daughter alone. Mrs. Stead said that Mrs. Broughton was a very bad woman. When she wrote Mr. Booth asking him to return Eliza, and hoping that God would reward him for the trouble he had taken, she thought that he had been kind to the child and would return her. She did not say that she was satisfied with what the child had told her as to her not being outraged.

This answer was found not to be in accord with the witness's examination in chief before the magistrate. The question was repeated, and witness said it might be true that she said she was satisfied with what the child had told her.

You were a friend of Mrs. Broughton?—Yes.

How intimate?—Only as a neighbour.

To say good morning?—Yes, sir.

That was all?—Yes, sir.

No further intimacy?—No, sir.

MRS. ARMSTRONG.

You were not in the habit of going into each other's houses?—No, sir.

What her character or previous history had been you know nothing about?—No, sir.

And before Tuesday, the 2nd June, you had never seen the woman Mrs. Jarrett?—No, sir.

You did not even know, I think, what her name was?—No, sir.

You did not know till when?—Till the first letter, a week after the child left.

Up to that time had you asked Mrs. Broughton what the name of this strange person was?—Yes, sir; I did.

MRS. JARRETT ("Becky.")

MR. ARMSTRONG'S, 32, CHARLES-STREET.

MRS. BROUGHTON ("Nancy").

Above: Collage of Characters involved in Stead's trial as they appeared in the Pall Mall Gazette.

CHARLES ARMSTRONG.

ELIZA ARMSTRONG.

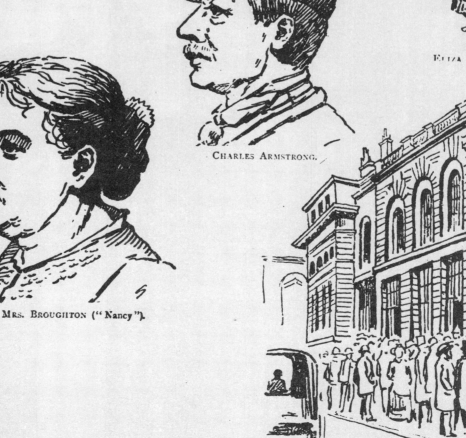

THE OLD BAILEY.

A HEADLINE AND PICTURE IN THE SUN, MAY 2, 1898

DEWEY WON
Our Glorious Naval Victory IN MANILA BAY.
Many of the Spanish

DAILY GRAPHIC, SATURDAY, APRIL 6, 1895.

THE QUEENSBERRY LIBEL CASE.
ABANDONMENT OF THE PROSECUTION.
ARREST OF WILDE.

THE CHINO-JAPANESE WAR.
THE ARMISTICE IN MANCHURIA.

STOP PRESS TELEGRAMS.
THE POPE AND ENGLAND.

OSCAR WILDE AT BOW-STREET.
PROCEEDINGS TO-DAY.
THE SCENE IN COURT.
ARREST OF TAYLOR.

VOL. XXII., No. 7257.
FIVE MINUTES WITH THE NEWS OF THE DAY.

THE PRESIDENT SHO—
A Chicago Lawyer Fires on Mr. Garfield Twice in the Washington Railroad Depot.
MADNESS, WITH MUCH METHOD.
"I Did It—I Want to be Arrested—I Am a Stalwart—Arthur is President Now."
LYING BETWEEN LIFE AND DEATH
Universal Sympathy with the Wounded Executive—Public Feeling as to the Results Should He Die.
THE PRESIDENT IMPROVING.

THE DAILY TELEGRAPH, FRIDAY, FEBRUARY 6, 1885.

KHARTOUM—THE MAHDI'S CAMP AND GORDON'S POSITION.

From The Philadelphia Inquirer of Wednesday, November 7, 1888

The Philadelphia Inquirer

VOL. 119—NO. 111.
PHILADELPHIA, WEDNESDAY, NOVEMBER 7, 1888.

HARRISON AND MORTON.
Chosen President and Vice President by Forty-seven College Majority.

NEW YORK CARRIED BY TEN TO FIFTEEN THOUS
Clean Sweep Made by the Republicans of the Entire Northern States.
Connecticut Redeemed.

AMERICAN INDUSTRIES ARE SAVED FROM WREC
No Free Trade Messages or Insulting Pension Vetoes During the Next Four Years—Latest Election Returns from the State and Nation.

FALL OF KHARTOUM THROUGH TREACHERY.
GORDON'S FATE UNKNOWN.
SIR CHARLES WILSON WRECKED.
OUR TROOPS AT KORTI, GAKDUL, AND METEMMEH SAFE.
LORD WOLSELEY'S DESPATCHES.
CABINET COUNCIL SUMMONED.
REINFORCEMENTS TO READY.
TRANSPORTS FOR T

BLIZZARD WAS KING
The Metropolis Helpless Under Snow.
HARDLY A WHEEL TURNS
Business Knocked Flat as if by a Panic.

BISMARCK AND THE DIARY OF THE EMPEROR.

LLOYD'S WEEKLY N
LARGEST CIRCULATION IN THE

No. 2,393.
LONDON: SUNDAY, SEPT. 30, 1888.

EXTRA SPECIAL SUNDAY EDITION.
LLOYD'S WEEKLY NEWSPAPER OFFICE, SUNDAY, NOON.
YESTERDAY'S TELEGRAMS.
THE AUSTRIAN EMPEROR IN DANGER.

MORE EAST-END TRAGEDIES
THIS (SUNDAY) MORNING.
ATROCIOUS MURDER OF A WOMAN IN ALDGATE,
THE VICTIM DISEMBOWELLED AND MUTILATED.
HORRIBLE MURDER IN COMMERCIAL ROAD EAST.

1887

Mr. Parnell's Letters

Irish Home Rule

In the second half of Queen Victoria's reign, it began to dawn on the incumbents of Printing House Square that *The Times* was not, perhaps, as secure in its exalted position as it had once been. The removal of the Stamp Duty on newspapers in 1855 had spawned a number of substantial competitors, not least *The Daily Telegraph* launched twenty-four hours before the ending of the tax and now in the vanguard of the New Journalism (or 'telegraphese' as some would have it). In the mid-80s *The Daily Telegraph* was claiming, and had, the largest circulation in the world; and there were several other relative upstarts (including *The Standard* and *The Daily News*) selling at 1d whose readership made *The Times* look meagre indeed.

The old Thunderer had its own answer to all this commercial opposition: ignore it. *The Times* had pride and confidence – and rightly so – in its tradition, its authority and independence, in the soundness and consistency of its policies. In short, in its uniqueness as an institution. It was in this spirit, too, that it pursued its undeviating opposition to Irish Home Rule, which since the General Election of 1885 had become the burning issue of the day. On more than one occasion *The Times* had shown itself sympathetic towards the sufferings of the Irish tenant farmers and had actively tried to alleviate the distress caused by the great famines. But, undeterred even by the recent attempt to blow up *The Times'* offices, it had denounced vehemently the terrorist outrages which had accompanied the struggle for Irish independence for decades. The culmination of these atrocities had come in 1882 when the new Irish Chief Secretary, Lord Frederick Cavendish, and his Under-Secretary had been murdered in cold blood on a stroll through Phoenix Park in Dublin. It had horrified nearly all shades of Irish opinion, including the moderate leader of the Home Rule party at Westminster, Charles Parnell.

Parnell knew, as well as anyone, that what would eventually bring about self-government was not political assassination, but political compromise. With 85 Irish members at his disposal he was well placed to achieve this, for he now held the balance of power between Liberals and Conservatives in Parliament. He accordingly courted first one party, then the other. At the end of 1885 he was pinning his hopes on Lord Salisbury's Conservative Government, but Christmas came and went without any sign of goodwill from the tory benches. In January he turned to the Liberals, and by so doing brought them to power. Gladstone the Liberal leader confessed himself a brand-new convert to the idea of Home Rule and in April duly introduced a Home Rule Bill for Ireland. But he failed to carry a sizeable portion of his own party: led by Joseph Chamberlain 93 Liberals trooped into the Opposition lobby and defeated the Bill at its second reading. Their continuing dissent also helped to bring the Conservatives back to power after the ensuing general election.

Thus Home Rule was temporarily deferred – but by no means doomed – when *The Times* embarked on its provocative series entitled 'Parnellism and Crime'. Its ostensible purpose was to aid the passage through Parliament of a drastic Irish Crimes Act, which had been introduced in January 1887, by showing (through juxtaposition) the connection between inflammatory Parnellite speeches and specific acts of terrorism. To be truthful, it was fairly innocuous stuff and Parnell studiously ignored it. But *The Times* had a trump card up its sleeve, which if played properly, could and should discredit the Home Rulers for good. It had obtained, at the end of the previous year, a series of letters bearing Parnell's signature which unmistakably implicated him in the appalling Phoenix Park murders. At the very least they showed he approved of them.

PARNELLISM AND CRIME.

MR. PARNELL AND THE PHŒNIX-PARK MURDERS.

In concluding our series of articles on "Parnellism and Crime" we intimated that, besides the damning facts which we there recorded, unpublished evidence existed which would bind still closer the links between the "constitutional" chiefs and the contrivers of murder and outrage. In view of the unblushing denials of Mr. Sexton and Mr. Healy on Friday night, we do not think it right to withhold any longer from public knowledge the fact that we possess and have had in our custody for some time documentary evidence which has a most serious bearing on the Parnellite conspiracy, and which, after a most careful and minute scrutiny, is, we are satisfied, quite authentic. We produce one document in facsimile to-day by a process the accuracy of which cannot be impugned, and we invite Mr. Parnell to explain how his signature has become attached to such a letter.

It is requisite to point out that the body of the manuscript is apparently not in Mr. Parnell's handwriting, but the signature and the "Yours very truly" unquestionably are so; and if any member of Parliament doubts the fact, he can easily satisfy himself on the matter by comparing the handwriting with that of Mr. Parnell in the book containing the signatures of members when they first take their seats in the House of Commons.

We particularly direct attention to the erasure in the manuscript as undesigned evidence of authenticity, and should any questions be raised as to the body of the letter being in another handwriting, we shall be prepared to adduce proof that this peculiarity is quite consistent with its genuine character.

The body of the letter occupies the whole of the first page of an ordinary sheet of stout white note-paper, leaving no room in the same page for the signature, which is placed on the fourth page near the top right-hand corner. It was an obvious precaution to sign upon the back instead of upon the second page, so that the half-sheet might if necessary be torn off, and the letter disclaimed.

It is right and necessary to explain that the "Dear Sir" is believed to be Egan and that the letter was addressed to him in order to pacify the wrath of his subordinate instruments in the Phœnix Park murders—then (on May 15, nine days after the tragedy) still at large and undetected. The anxiety of the writer to keep his address unknown will be noted, and is curious in connexion with a belief prevailing at the time that Mr. Parnell was so impressed by the danger he had incurred by denouncing the assassinations as to have applied for the protection of the police on the plea that his life was in peril.

Mr. Parnell in this letter describes Lord F. Cavendish's death as an "accident," but he "cannot refuse to admit that Burke got no more than his deserts." That is his language to the "Inner Circle," but before Parliament, yielding to what he considered "the only course," or as it stands amended in the text "our best policy," he spoke on Monday, May 8, two days after the murders, as follows :—

Mr. PARNELL said he wished to be permitted to express, on the part of his hon. friends, on his own part, and, he believed, on the part of every Irishman in whatever portion of the world he might live, their most unqualified detestation of the horrible crime which had been committed in Ireland. (Hear, hear.) He could not now refer to the steps which the Government proposed to take. He did not deny that it might be impossible for the Government to resist taking measures such as had been mentioned by the Prime Minister. But he wished to express his belief that the crime had been committed by men who absolutely detested the cause with which he had been associated (hear, hear), and who had devised that crime and carried it out as the deadliest blow in their power against his hopes and the new course which the Government had resolved upon.

Particular attention may now be drawn to the wicked suggestion here made that the Phœnix Park crimes had been the work of the enemies of Parnellism and the League, "devised and carried out as the deadliest blow in their power against his hopes and the new course which the Government had resolved upon." Has that infamous accusation ever been recalled or even qualified, and to what benevolent construction of motives is a public man now entitled who made such a charge at the very time when he was smoothing down the "anger" of Egan's "friends" for denouncing them as murderers in Parliament?

To the country at large Mr. Parnell, Mr. Dillon, and Mr. Davitt addressed on the day after the murder the following manifesto :—

To the People of Ireland.—On the eve of what seemed a bright future for our country, that evil destiny which has apparently pursued us for centuries has struck another blow at our hopes, which cannot be exaggerated in its disastrous consequences. In this hour of sorrowful gloom we venture to give an expression of our profoundest sympathy with the people of Ireland in the calamity that has befallen our cause, through a horrible deed, and to those who had determined at the last hour that a policy of conciliation should supplant that of terrorism and national distrust. We earnestly hope that the attitude and action of the whole Irish people will show the world that assassination such as has startled us almost to the abandonment of hope for our country's future is deeply and religiously abhorrent to their every feeling and instinct. We appeal to you to show by every manner of expression that almost universal feeling of horror which this assassination has excited. No people feels so intense a detestation of its atrocity, or so deep a sympathy for those whose hearts must be seared by it, as the nation upon whose prospects and reviving hopes it may entail consequences more ruinous than have fallen to the lot of unhappy Ireland during the present generation. We feel that no act has ever been perpetrated in our country during the exciting struggles for social and political rights of the past 50 years that has so stained the name of hospitable Ireland as this cowardly and unprovoked assassination of a friendly stranger, and that until the murderers of Lord Frederick Cavendish and Mr. Burke are brought to justice that stain will sully our country's name.

(Signed) CHARLES S. PARNELL. JOHN DILLON. MICHAEL DAVITT.

Here again the peculiar language employed will be noted. It is "the evil destiny which has apparently pursued us for centuries" which "has struck another blow at our hopes," &c.

Only a fortnight ago, on the first reading of the Crimes Bill, Mr. Parnell took occasion to refer to this manifesto in the House of Commons in the following remarkable terms :—

I do not believe you would ever have broken up that [the Invincible] conspiracy if it had not been for the denunciation of Mr. Michael Davitt, the member for East Mayo, and myself, issued after the crime in the Phœnix Park. It was the denunciation that shook that conspiracy and enabled the officers of the law in Ireland, by means of their secret inquiries and other agencies, to get under it and finally to break it up.

An interval of more than half a year elapsed between the Phœnix Park murders and the discovery of the perpetrators. In that interval, while "the stain on the name of hospitable Ireland," in spite of "the appeal" made in the manifesto, still adhered to it, Ireland's uncrowned king actually addressed to his trusted subordinate, the Treasurer of the Land League, Patrick Egan, the following extraordinary letter which tells its own significant tale.

In the facsimile which we place before our readers the paper lies open, the first page being to the right, and the fourth to the left.

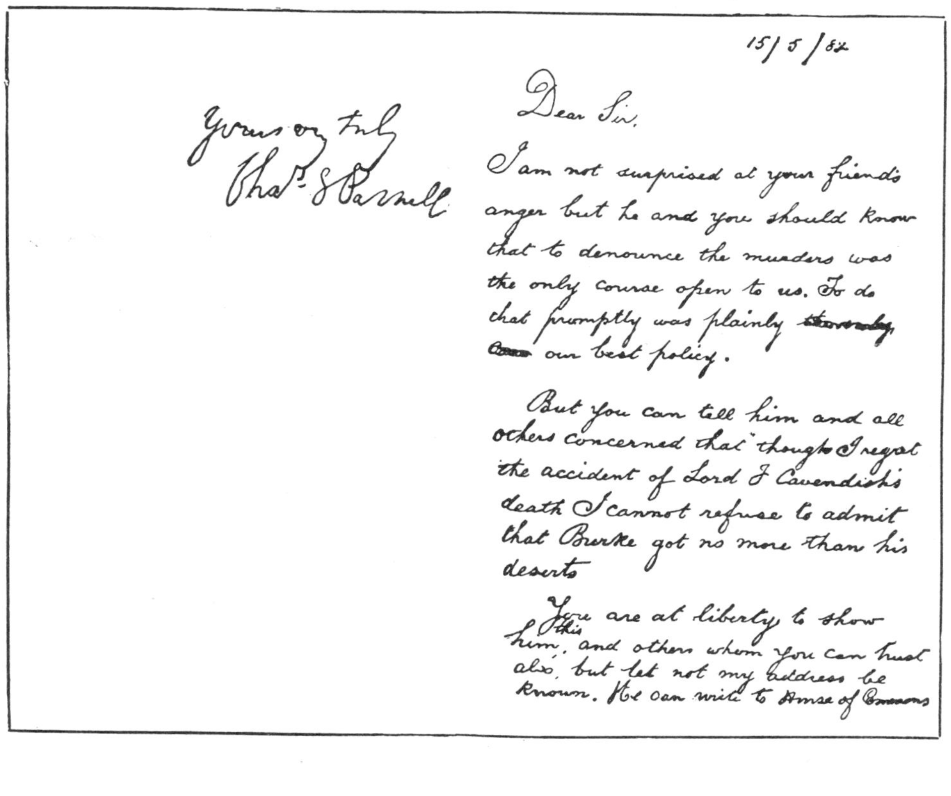
15/5/82

Dear Sir,

I am not surprised at your friend's anger but he and you should know that to denounce the murders was the only course open to us. To do that promptly was plainly our best policy.

But you can tell him and all others concerned that though I regret the accident of Lord F Cavendish's death I cannot refuse to admit that Burke got no more than his deserts.

You are at liberty to show him this, and others whom you can trust also, but let not my address be known. He can write to House of Commons.

Yours very truly
Chas. S. Parnell

The paper published the first of these letters on April 18 1887, marking the momentous occasion by breaking out into a two-column headline for the first time in its history. The letter read:

Dear Sir,

I am not surprised at your friend's anger but he and you should know that to denounce the murders was the only course open to us. To do that promptly was plainly our best policy.

But you can tell him, and all others concerned that though I regret the accident of Lord F Cavendish's death, I cannot refuse to admit that Burke got no more than his deserts.

You are at liberty to show him this, but let not my address be known. He can write to House of Commons.

The signature appeared on its own, on the fourth page of the letter (as folded). On the face of it these were seriously damaging sentiments, and more than one Home Ruler despaired of his cause at the breakfast table that morning. The same evening Parnell spoke in the House, rejecting the letters as a barefaced forgery and pointing out among other things that he had not written an S like that for ten years.

Reluctantly he was persuaded to begin a libel action against *The Times*, for £100,000 damages. In the meantime Parliament had set up a Special Commission of three eminent judges to examine not just the validity of the signature (which was what the Irish MPs demanded) but the charges as a whole. This, unfortunately for *The Times*, required the newspaper to prove every statement it had printed and at its own expense without any hope of legal redress. However, there was no backing-down now — even if the paper had wished to.

Inevitably the questions of how, and from whom, *The Times* had acquired the letters was soon going to become a matter of public scrutiny, so the proprietor (John Walter III) and the editor (George Earle Buckle) decided they would have to find out — for, amazingly, they had no idea. They had contented themselves only with an exhaustive handwriting examination. They had agreed with their 'contact' not to inquire into the history of the letters, nor indeed had they ever displayed much curiosity about it. Their contact had been one Edward Houston, the secretary of an Anti-Home Rule organisation and one-time contributor to *The Times*. He had seemed respectable enough, but now it was unwillingly drawn out of him that *his* source was anything but respectable. It turned out to be a Richard Pigott, known in seedy journalistic Dublin circles for being perpetually broke. During his 'search', on Houston's behalf, for evidence of Parnellite misdemeanours he had lived like a lord in hotels in America and on the Continent, and had eventually staged a cloak-and-dagger scene in a Paris hotel where two mysterious Irishmen, Brown and Murphy, had delivered the incriminating letters and waited downstairs while Houston handed Pigott £500.

And there the trail ended, since it was far too distasteful for *The Times* to descend any further into the murk of the under-world. In spite of Pigott's disappointing credentials, Walter and Buckle remained convinced of the authenticity of their letters — and to prove their conviction they published the complete series in facsimile on February 16 1889, even while their own Editorial Manager was testifying before the Commission. On February 21 Pigott was cross-examined by Parnell's counsel, Sir Charles Russell, who first of all requested him to write his name and a few words on a piece of paper, then proceeded with his questions. Had Pigott known the letters were going to be published? No. Then why had he written to the Archbishop of Dublin three days before publication warning

him. that the Irish party was going to come under attack? Was he not trying to play both ends against the middle?

The following day Russell produced copies of some letters written by Parnell to Pigott, which contained a strange feature. A number of identical phrases from them also appeared in *The Times'* letters. Only by the advent of lunch was Pigott spared more immediate embarrassment. Then in the afternoon Russell delivered his coup de grace. He drew Pigott's attention to his spelling of 'hesitancy' in court the previous day: it was spelt 'hesitency' — precisely the same mistake as in the so-called Parnell letter no. 1.

Pigott did not appear in court when it re-assembled three days later. Nor was he at his hotel where police had been sent to arrest him. He was, in fact, tracked down in a Madrid hotel room, where he shot himself before they could arrest him.

The previous weekend, however, he had made two confessions, one at the house of Henry Labouchere, the editor of an appropriately-named journal *Truth*, and the other in an affidavit to a Dublin solicitor. They differed considerably: the first admitted to the forgery of all the letters,

the second to only some of them. It was the first confession that was read out in court — and accepted, if only to avoid any more unpleasant complications. *The Times* naturally withdrew the letters, while the Commission ground on in rather more pedestrian fashion for the remainder of the year. It was deeply humiliating for *The Times* whose general charges against Parnell, however much they had acted in good faith over the letters (and few doubted that), could not now be viewed in anything but a sceptical light. It also proved extremely expensive, both in reputation and in money. Its once unimpeachable credibility had been seriously undermined, more by negligence than by malicious intent. But what was to have more enduring consequences was that its economy was shattered for many years to come. The costs of the Inquiry and the libel suit amounted to more than £200,000, and Walter gallantly refused all offers of a public subscription, insisting that *The Times* should pay its own debts. It was an honourable end to a not very honourable episode, but it meant *The Times* entered into one of the most strenuous periods in the history of journalism, virtually a cripple.

PENANCE!

"HIS HONOUR ROOTED IN DISHONOUR STOOD, AND FAITH UNFAITHFUL MADE HIM FALSELY TRUE."—TENNYSON.

Punch.

THE ALLEGED PARNELL LETTERS.

15/5/82

Yours very truly
Chas. S Parnell

Dear Sir,

I am not surprised at your friend's anger but he and you should know that to denounce the murders was the only course open to us. To do that promptly was plainly ~~the only~~ ~~course~~ our best policy.

But you can tell him and all others concerned that though I regret the accident of Lord F Cavendish's death I cannot refuse to admit that Burke got no more than his deserts.

You are at liberty to show him this, and others whom you can trust also, but let not my address be known. He can write to House of Commons.

9/1/82

Dear E.

What are these fellows waiting for? This inaction is inexcusable. our best men are in prison and nothing is being done.

Let there be an end of this hesitency Prompt action is called for.

your undertook to make it hot for old Foster and Co. Let us have some evidence of your power to do so.

My health is good. thanks

Yours very truly
Chas. S Parnell

Tuesday

Dear Sir,

Tell P to write to me direct.

Have not yet received the papers.

Yours very truly
Chas. S Parnell

Tuesday

Dear Sir,

I see no objection to your giving the amount asked for.

There is not the least likelihood of what you are apprehensive of happening

Yours Truly
Chas. S Parnell

Tuesday

Dear Sir,

Send full particulars What amount does he want?

Other letter to hand

Yours very truly
Chas. S Parnell

---

course we took. That is the truth. I can say no more.

Yours Very Truly
Chas. S Parnell

June. 16th 1882

Dear Sir

I am sure you will feel that I could not appear in Parliament in the face of this thing unless I condemned it. Our position there is always difficult to maintain; it would be untenable but for the

---

June. 16th 1882

Dear Sir, I shall always be anxious to have the good will of your friends but why do they impugn my motives! I could not consent to the conditions they would impose but I accept the entire responsibility for what we have done.

Yours Very Truly
Chas. S Parnell

37

1896

Brave Dr. Jim

The Jameson Raid

One morning late in November 1894 Alfred Harmsworth, publisher of *Marvel, Union Jack* and *Pluck Library* among other stirring weekly titles, sat down to breakfast at the Burlington with two real-life heroes. If Cecil Rhodes and Leander Starr Jameson hadn't read the latest episode of 'Death on the Zambesi', it was because truth was more exciting than fiction, and the King of the diamond mines and the Conqueror of the Matabeles had stories of their own as thrilling as any dreamed up by a writer of penny dreadfuls. It probably never crossed

their minds that among the empires they (and men like them) were helping to build was one of the greatest newspaper combines the world has even seen and that their host that morning was to become the most powerful press lord in the country. For such was the demand, in those golden days of Empire, for Mr. Harmsworth's stories of far-flung adventure and patriotic endeavour that only a few months ago he had been able to acquire an ailing London newspaper, *The Evening News*, on the proceeds. And here at the Burlington he was reaping the sweet rewards of his new status.

No doubt far more momentous subjects were discussed that morning than the possibility of Harmsworth buying some shares in Rhodes' South Africa Company (which he did the following year). For Alfred at that time was quite intoxicated with Rhodes' visions of the British Empire all-powerful (and all-prosperous) in Africa. Cecil Rhodes was the only statesman, Harmsworth's brother was to recall later, for whom he had ever heard him express unqualified admiration. It was that disciple-like faith in the great man's ideals which made him react in the way he did when the strange news of Starr Jameson reached London from Johannesburg on December 31 1895.

The booming, cosmopolitan town of Johannesburg, rapidly filling up with adventurers from all over the world attracted by the discovery of

gold in the Witwatersrand Hills, presented a marked contrast with the rest of the Transvaal inhabited and more or less run by dour, god-fearing Boer farmers. Paul Kruger, the Boer President, was reluctant to dignify the uitlanders, the foreign hotch-potch of Johannesburg (which included the English there) with the status of citizenship. Rhodes, for his part, was reluctant to watch all that gold lining Boer coffers unchallenged. As Prime Minister of the neighbouring Cape Colony, he determined to solve the problem in the way that had always worked against the Mashutos and the Matabeles — by force of arms. Unofficially he arranged for an insurrection in Johannesburg itself which would be supported by an invasion from the north by troops of his own South Africa Company. Jameson would be in command of the invasion.

It was a gimcrack scheme from the start. The insurrection was a mirage, and Jameson's armaments limited to half a dozen Maxims and one field-piece. Even Rhodes must have realised this at the last moment (much as he despised the fighting qualities of the Boers) for he telegraphed Jameson, poised on the frontier, to call it all off. Unfortunately he was too late, the little army had set off on December 29 and was marching as yet unopposed on Johannesburg. Predictably on January 2nd it was confronted and disarmed, with the loss of five men. The first details of Jameson's folly filtered through to London on New Year's Eve. It was totally obscure where or why he was marching: it was only clear that an act of armed aggression was being committed by a madcap doctor in the name of the British people.

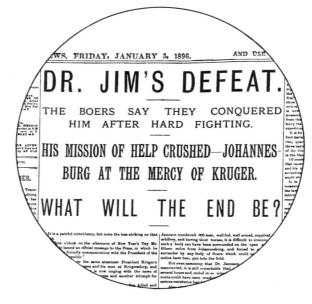

The Colonial Secretary, Joseph Chamberlain, immediately disowned the raid, as he was bound to, but there was undeniably a thrill of popular excitement on the streets at the thought of the

gallant little band advancing through the veld against the Boer tyrants. Most newspapers, for want of facts, remained non-committal. But not Harmsworth and *The Evening News*. For him, it was like a yarn from the pages of *Union Jack* come true, the ultimate test of Rhodes' imperial theories, though he did not know at the time

that he was behind it. On January 1 *The Evening News* burst forth into the biggest headlines ever seen in an English newspaper, it hailed Jameson (or Dr. Jim as it affectionately dubbed him) as a hero, it railed at Chamberlain for taking the Boers' part. The next day was most frustrating when no news whatever of Jameson's fate turned up. Undaunted, Harmsworth continued his paean by spreading brave Dr. Jim's portrait across three columns of his front page and exclaiming in the editorial: 'all English eyes are turned to "Dr. Jim" who, careless of self, went forth with his few brave followers to help our kinsmen in their hour of trouble. What a contrast to the red-taped weakness of the Colonial Office, which is ready

to sacrifice the freedom — nay, the very lives perhaps, of scores of thousands of our own English people — to the exigencies of the foreign politics of the hour, and the greed of renegade money-grubbers'.

How *The Evening News* knew anyone was in danger was not explained, but it did unearth a cable which had been delayed in transmission and which reported that the day before Jameson marched some Englishmen had insisted on singing God Save The Queen in a Johannesburg theatre (an invariable symptom of an Englishman in danger?). The next day (the 3rd) *The Evening News* was obliged to report Jameson's defeat, but with obvious disappointment that only five men had been killed — it was unwilling to believe that 'the gallant fellows who fought to such purpose against Lobengula were beaten in a fair and square battle without far heavier loss of life'. And to underline the point, it gave

The Evening News.

SPECIAL EDITION.

LONDON: THURSDAY, JANUARY 2, 1896.

MR. CHAMBERLAIN'S ACTION.   SEE PAGE 2.

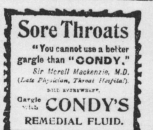

BRAVE DR. JIM:

Dr. Jameson, C.B. May his march to the relief of our brothers and sisters in the Transvaal be crowned with success!

---

some prominence to the events in the New Olympic theatre the night before. The cast had just finished the scene depicting Captain Wilson's last stand and massacre by the Matabeles, when a voice from the gallery cried out: 'That's the way an Englishman can die. To H*** with the Boers!' Whereupon the audience had demonstrated for a quarter of an hour.

On the 4th *The Evening News* was pleased to report that Dr. Jim had not been burnt alive, as one report affirmed, but it was far from pleased at the Kaiser who had sent a telegram to Kruger congratulating him on his victory. The Germans, of course, were Britain's closest competitors in the scramble for Africa, but this little affair was none of their business. Hands Off! thundered Harmsworth at the royal personage. When he later heard that German warships in Delagoa

Bay had been prepared to help Kruger, he was beside himself and launched into a sustained attack on German militarism — which he was to keep up unceasingly for the next 18 years (and which was to be vindicated in *The Daily Mail's* slogan during the First World War: The Paper that Persistently Forewarned the Public about the War).

Meanwhile, however, Rhodes had resigned the premiership of Cape Colony. *The Evening News* hastened to assure its readers it was not an admission of culpability — it chose rather to interpret it as an act of solidarity with his South Africa Company. Harmsworth himself was to be embarrassed by his purchase of shares in the South Africa Company, especially when it came in 1899 to outright war with the Boers whom he now did not 'reckon as possible

opponents of England in war however much their vanity may mislead them'. Seven years later he was to write: 'I was one of the fools, and still hold the shares but, in addition to the depreciation of their value, I have never received a dividend, and have been overwhelmed with abuse in Parliament and elsewhere, and quite rightly I think'. It was rumoured for many years that Alfred's new paper *The Daily Mail* (which he launched later in 1896) was partly financed with Rhodes' money. That has never been proved, and certainly the Harmsworth family by then had no need of hidden subsidies. For in spite of — or indeed because of — the Jameson debacle, *The Evening News* was flourishing, and if nothing else the events of that week in January had shown Harmsworth the way to attract attention.

39

1897

Gold!

The Klondike Gold Rush

Pearl King of the Pacific.
More wonderful than any of the stories of sudden wealth on the Klondyke. In the next :
SUNDAY EXAMINER.

The Examiner.

VOL. XLV.   SAN FRANCISCO; MONDAY MORNING, AUGUST 30, 1897.   NO. 61.   **SUNDAY EXAMINER.**

Most Picturesque of Pirates

LITTLE GOLD AND HARD-LUCK STORIES ON THE PORTLAND.

She Brought Out Less Than $100,000.

This Was Divided Among a Lucky Thirteen.

Last Man From Klondyke Tells Discouraging Tales.

Four Men Lost by the Capsizing of a Fishing Boat.

By Arthur H. Barendt.

Death for Two Who Made Fortunes.

Privations of Many in Search of Gold.

Beaching of the River Steamer Hamilton on the Yukon.

Soft-Muscled Clerks Soon Tired of a Hard Life.

By Edward H. Hamilton.

SCENES ALONG THE NEW WHITE PASS ROUTE TO THE GOLD FIELDS NEAR DAWSON.

BEAR FROM THE YUKON.

Peterson Tells of Those Who Did Not Succeed.

It was in the spring of 1897 that word first began to spread round San Francisco of vast gold-fields in the frozen wastes of Alaska. No more than rumours at first, sailing in on the first ships of the season to get through to the Pacific ports, stories matured and polished through long winter nights waiting for the seas to melt: stories of the Yukon which could make a millionaire out of a man inside a month, of the mountains and streams of the Klondike where gold was waiting to be picked up. In April some San Franciscans had already sold up, collected a year's supplies and taken the first boat north. Not many as yet: it was an expensive and perilous journey to Alaska, ships were scarce and there was many a veteran of the '47 rush ready to recall the hazards and disappointments of speculating on mere rumour. Gold never gave itself up that easily.

Then, in mid-July, a reporter from *The Seattle Post-Intelligencer* on board the steamer Portland telegraphed the news that more than a ton of solid gold was on its way. At the same time the Excelsior docked at San Francisco and disgorged more than a quarter of a million dollars-worth of dust and nuggets. Vagrants who had disappeared months ago, desperate and disreputable, now walked down the gang-plank wealthy and eminent citizens. Within hours it was the sensation of San Francisco — and no newspaper was better-equipped to do justice to a sensation than *The San Francisco Examiner.*

Until 1887 *The San Francisco Examiner* had been a moderately successful, worthy Democratic paper; in that year it had won its proprietor, George Hearst, a place in the Senate. Fully absorbed now by politics he appointed his son,

William Randolph, publisher — young though he was and brimful of ambitious ideas. Within five years it had outstripped all its rivals — not only in circulation but also in sensationalism: no human-interest story was unlikely enough for Hearst's columns, no stunt too adventurous or absurd. Others had done what he was doing, but never on so raucous (or riveting) a scale, whether it was sending eye-witness accounts of San Francisco by carrier-pigeon from a balloon floating above the city, campaigning against the Southern Pacific Railroad, or infiltrating a female reporter into the city's brothels. Indeed at times it seemed his reporters were less journalists than commandos, admitting themselves into lunatic asylums, falling off river-boats or collapsing in the streets in search of a story. 'News' Hearst was fond of saying 'has to be sent for' even to the Yukon if necessary.

The Gold Rush was *The San Francisco Examiner's* kind of story. The paper searched out prospectors from the Excelsior and the Portland and photographed their hoards. 'Eldorado in the Icy Yukon Fields' it announced on July 16. On the 18th there were more 'Reports from the Far-away Land where the Earth seems Lined with Gold' — and no modest little paragraphs at that, but pages full of them.. On the 20th it found a 'Happy Hunter of the Golden Fleece' who had found $60,000 in a month. Then on the 22nd (as if to examine the authenticity of the news it had created) *The San Francisco Examiner* announced its own Expedition to the Klondike, which would include, among others, a miner, a lady reporter appropriately named Dare, and a poet. The latter was, of course, essential if the true romance of the North-West was to be adequately retailed to the readers.

By now *The San Francisco Examiner* had helped to inspire an unparalleled gold-fever in the city. Every boat that floated (and many that didn't) was chartered to trundle a legion of prospectors northwards. Thousands more were setting out on the long and dangerous overland trail. On July 29 there were reportedly 25,000 people gathered at Mission Pier to wave farewell to *The San Francisco Examiner* Expedition. Even as the tug sailed into the sunset, more and more reports filtered back from the north. Day after day the paper regaled its stay-at-home readers — who must have been wondering if they were doing the right thing — with 'Tales of Wealth out of the Golden North' and 'More Millions coming from Klondike'. It seemed such a cheery place ('Good Order in the North ascribed to American Citizenship rather than to Fear of British Law') and the official poet was doing his stuff: 'But One Cry Heard, and That Gold!'

Even if few others had, *The San Francisco Examiner* had struck a rich vein. It even discovered more gold back home in California and precipitated another, minor rush. But as summer gave way to fall, and fall to early winter the visions of Eldorado faded to the inside pages and took on a new and ominous aspect. 'Little Gold and Hard Luck' came back the reports. 'Yukon miners may Famish and Freeze'. The Expedition gamely braved the rapids at White Horse, inched its way up the perpendicular trail at Chilcoot Pass and dossed down in the muck of Scagway and Dawson City. At the end it found not crystals glistening in sunlit streams, but winter setting in and a 'Mad Rush from the Klondike'. December came and there was nothing else to report but 'Men Swarm the Trail out of Dawson: Gold Hunters Fleeing from Starvation in the Arctic', and follow them like everyone else. Well, so what? Mr. Hearst was in New York by now and more concerned with his latest project, *The New York Journal*, and New Yorkers were too sophisticated for that sort of thing.

An Up-to-Date Pirate

With one of the most thrilling
histories ever published.
Read it in the next

Sunday Examiner.

The Examiner.

VOL. XLV.   SAN FRANCISCO, WEDNESDAY MORNING, JULY 21, 1897.   NO. 21.

Alaska! Alaska! Alaska!

Sunday Examiner.

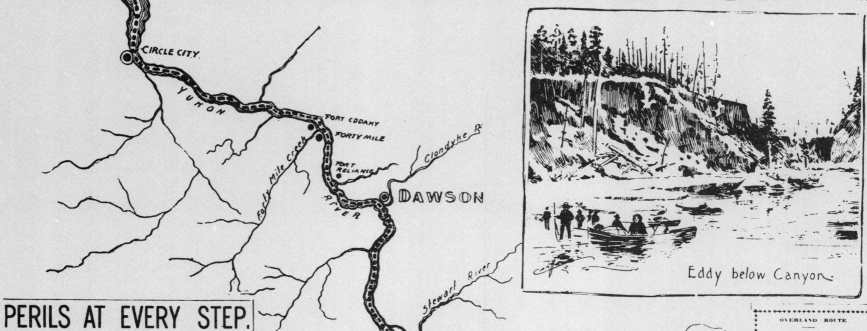

Eddy below Canyon.

PERILS AT EVERY STEP.

Over One Thousand Miles to Be Traversed Through a Desolate Region Before Reaching Klondyke.

Travelers Must Undertake Dangerous Mountain Climbs and Shoot Treacherous Rapids on the Journey From Juneau.

Supplies and Outfits Will Have to Be Carried Over Ice and Snow if Prospectors Hope to See Dawson City and Delve in Its Gravel Beds.

The daring miners who have returned fortune-laden from the frozen north have a story and a warning for those who think of emulating their example and seeking gold in the British Columbian ice fields. The road to the mines is a long one. Supplies are costly and dangers threaten at every step.

Those who penetrate into the ice and snow must be rugged and hardy. They must be able to endure the pains of dangerous travel and the chances that fortune brings. They must have money and courage, and even then they will take their lives in their hands as they travel over mountains, into canyons, across dreary wastes of snow and down treacherous streams to the mines. As one travels his perilous way he must carry his own outfit and provisions. If fortune does not favor the prospector he will find himself in a desolate region where those who have food to sell will sell only at fabulous prices for such.

There are two routes to the Klondyke mines. One is by water, and the other, after reaching Juneau, by land and water. The latter is by 2,000 miles the shorter, and, in a comparative sense, the safer of the two. The longer way is by steamer to St. Michaels, at the mouth of the Yukon river, and thence by the Yukon. The journey may begin at this city or from Tacoma or Seattle. It must be made at a time that will enable the traveler to reach the Yukon when the ice is breaking. But even under the most favorable conditions the journey is a slow one.

The route taken by 95 per cent of the prospectors is by steamer to Juneau and thence inland. When the miner leaves Juneau, a town of 3,000 inhabitants, he leaves everything but his own resources and self-reliance behind. He may purchase his outfit where he pleases, but if he buys it at Juneau it will cost him from $60 to $150. The fare from Juneau to Dyea, a distance of 100 miles, is from $6 to $10. The distance is made by steamer, the traveler passing Haines Mission, or Chilkat, on the way.

At Dyea, which is at the head of Chilkat inlet, the prospector leaves the last vestige of civilization behind. He shoulders his pack, hires his pack train and starts for the snow-covered mountains. Experience has proven that the best time to start is in the middle of March. It is then easier to move on sleighs or to go with the pack train of natives. The country is mountainous and hard to cross in the best of seasons. The ground is covered with brush and roads are unknown.

Those who know urge that prospectors go in parties of four or five, for in these numbers they may lighten their burdens and economize in materials that all may aid in common. This is of the greatest importance, for it costs fourteen cents a pound to hire natives to carry provisions from Dyea to the head of Lake Lindeman. This short journey is one of the worst stages of the route. The way is over a desolate and mountainous country to the summit of Chilcoot pass. Part of the journey may be made by canoe, but most of it is on foot or on sleigh. The distance between the two points is only twenty-three miles, but these days' one pass before it is traversed. At Lake Lindeman the way becomes comparatively easier although all stages of the

strength of the hardiest is taxed to the greatest degree.

At Lake Lindeman the journeying pros-

pectors must build a boat. The craft must be substantial, for the ice is breaking and death lurks at every point in the trip through the lake. It is for this reason that the miners are sure to remind inquirers that at least one member of the prospecting party must know something about practical boat building. Lake Lindeman is four miles long. When the end is reached the boat must be dragged on the resisting ground for over a mile to the next waterway, Lake Bennett.

At this point the prospectors must paddle their craft for many miles. Surveyors have not accurately calculated distances in this region of snow, but as far as figures go, the miners will travel on Lake Bennett for about twenty-five miles. When the foot of Lake Bennett has been reached the prospectors who are risking their lives for gold have traveled only 154 miles from Juneau. The boat is dragged from the water and lifted on a sleigh as the Indian pack train starts off for the Cariboo Crossing three miles away.

If the prospecting party has exhausted its supplies it can obtain no more. When Cariboo Crossing has been reached the travelers are only 158¼ miles from Juneau, and they cannot replenish their stock of food until they reach Forty-Mile post which is 728 miles from Juneau. The men who have brought fortunes with them from the North become eloquent when they attempt

40 Mile. North West Terr.

Big Eddy—Grand Canyon.

SCALE OF MILES.
25   50   75   100

OVERLAND ROUTE	
	Miles.
Juneau	0
Haines Mission (Chilkat)	80
Dyea	100
Head of canoe navigation	106
Summit of Chilcoot Pass	114.75
Head of Lake Lindeman	123.08
Foot of Lake Lindeman	127.50
Head of Lake Bennett	128.50
Foot of Lake Bennett	153.75
Cariboo Crossing	156.50
Foot of Tagish lake	173.25
Head of Lake Marsh	174.25
Foot of Lake Marsh	197.25
Head of Canyon	223
Foot of Canyon	223.75
Head of White Horse Rapids	225.25
Tahkeena river	240
Head of Lake Le Barge	268
Foot of Lake Le Barge	284
Hootalinqua river	316
Cassiar Bar	342
Big Salmon river	349
Little Salmon river	365.50
Five Fingers rapids	444
Rink Rapids	450
Pelly river	508.50
White river	590.50
Stewart river	609
Sixty-Mile Post	629
Fort Reliance	682.50
Forty-Mile Post	728
Fort Cudahy	728.75
Circle City	948
Klondyke	1,048

OCEAN ROUTE	
St. Michaels to confluence of White and Pelly rivers	2,044
Confluence of rivers to Klondyke	448.50

PERILOUS ROUTE TO THE KLONDYKE MINES.

The journey to the Klondyke mines is hazardous. While there are two routes prospectors may travel, that by land from Juneau is the one taken. Ninety-five per cent of the miners venturing into the frozen North choose it rather than the route to St. Michaels, at the mouth of the Yukon. It is a route up the Yukon that is 2,000 miles longer and may be said to be more dangerous than the route by land and the small lakes and rivers of the interior. This route is over mountains, into deep canyons, and across snow. At every stage of the journey it takes three days to make ten miles from Dyea to the head of Lake Lindeman, one having to climb to the summit of Chilcoot Pass.

THE BEGINNING OF THE OVERLAND ROUTE

JUNEAU

The Newspapers' War

The Spanish-American War

'Nothing so disgraceful as the behaviour of two of these newspapers this week has been known in the history of American Journalism' declared E. L. Godkin viewing the circulation battle between *The World* and *The Journal* from the impeccable heights of his own paper, *The New York Evening Post*. 'Gross misrepresentation of facts, deliberate invention of tales calculated to excite the public, and wanton recklessness in the construction of headlines which even outdid these inventions, have combined to make the issues of the most widely circulated newspapers firebrands scattered broadcast throughout the country. It is a crying shame that men should work such mischief simply in order to sell more papers'.

They were harsh words, even from so scathing a pen, but nothing less than the inglorious truth. In the early months of 1898 what came to be known as the era of the 'yellow press' reached its nadir. It was just over two years since Hearst, flushed with the success of his *Examiner* back West, arrived in New York intent on toppling Pulitzer's *New York World* from the pre-eminence it had achieved in just twelve years. Hearst certainly wasn't going to wait that long and, dissatisfied with the diet of sex, crime and scandal which was his daily fare, longed for a campaign which combining with these three essential ingredients would add an extra, epic dimension.

In 1896 there was one, ready-made for him, in the revolt of the oppressed Cubans against the tyranny of Spain. *The World* was already devoting a great deal of space to the excesses of the Spanish soldiers and the atrocities inflicted on women and children. Hearst responded by buying the services of the most celebrated foreign correspondent of the day, Richard Harding Davis, to report from Cuba for his *The Journal*. From then on, there was no respite from the two papers' efforts to out-sensationalise each other. The commander of the Spanish armies General Weyler was charac-

terised as 'The Butcher' and banished one of *The World's* reporters from the island. Undeterred, Pulitzer published the story of a massacre of 160 harmless civilians and claimed 200,000 people were dying of starvation (it was a wild and exaggerated guess).

The Journal meanwhile was specialising in human-interest stories, of a kind guaranteed to make every honest American's blood boil. Early in 1897 the best it could find was the suspected murder of a naturalised American dentist in his prison cell, but in August it discovered Evangelina Cisneros, 'the most beautiful girl in all Cuba'. She was also, as it happened, the niece of the rebels' President and had been charged with conspiring to murder one of the military governors. The truth of the matter, *The Journal* explained, was that this brute had made advances to her — and rallied hundreds of America's most prominent ladies to campaign on her behalf. *The Journal* did even better in October: it sent a reporter to rescue her, which he did. Through the courtesy of A.P. news of *The Journal's* initiative echoed the length and breadth of the United States.

But still the war, which Hearst sensed the public was psychologically ready for, did not come. Nonetheless when one of his artists asked to be withdrawn from Cuba, Hearst cabled back 'Please remain. You furnish the pictures and I'll furnish the war'. It would be extravagant to say that he made good his promise for there were many other war-like lobbies — political and financial — pressuring M'Kinley on the issue, but there is no doubt Hearst (and Pulitzer in his wake) was responsible for bringing the public at large up to fever-pitch.

Nor were the Spanish themselves any hindrance to him. In February 1898 a letter from the Spanish ambassador to a Madrid newspaper editor fell into the hands of *The Journal*. It denounced the New York newspaper but, better still it cast aspersions on the President as 'a weak and low politician catering to the rabble'. The letter was genuine enough and inflamed popular opinion still further — and Hearst didn't feel it necessary to point out that it had been a private letter, which had been stolen. No such scruples were involved, however, when a heaven-sent casus belli presented itself on the night of February 15.

That night the U.S. battleship Maine, which was standing by in Havana harbour to protect American citizens from the riots which were an almost daily occurrence in the city, exploded, killing 250 sailors. *The World* and *The Journal* at once concluded that it had been mined or torpedoed by the Spaniards. The U.S. official court of inquiry was inconveniently slow and objective (after six weeks it still was unwilling to point the finger at anyone) so *The World* appointed its own investigators to prove the point, while *The Journal* ferried its own team of Congressmen across to the island to see the appalling conditions for themselves (it had already assured its readers that 'The Warship Maine was Split in Two by an Enemy's Infernal Machine' complete with drawing to convince the sceptical).

In spite of the fact that *The Journal* reported that the Spanish navy was being completed for war, in Scotland, war was really the last thing Spain wanted. As a friendly gesture she sent a battleship on a goodwill visit to New York, but *The World* thoroughly frightened everybody by working out how much of Brooklyn could be raked by the ship's guns. War, promised, threatened or simply imagined (four weeks before it was declared *The Journal* was running colourful descriptions of 'Our flying squadron destroying the Spanish torpedo feet' for all the world as if it were a fact) seldom left the headlines. The Wall Street pacifists were cruelly abused, the patrons of a Harlem theatre

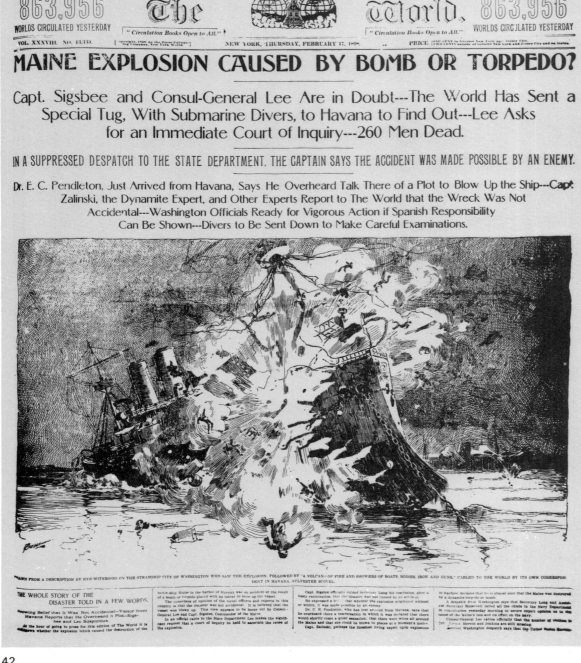

The Examiner.

VOL. LXV. SAN FRANCISCO, MONDAY MORNING, OCTOBER 11, 1897. NO. 103.

THE CIVILIZED WORLD APPROVES
THE RESCUE OF MISS CISNEROS.

EUROPE AND AMERICA JOIN IN PRAISING THE "EXAMINER-JOURNAL."

Governors, Senators, Priests and Laymen Commend the Deed as One Most Worthy.

MONS. MARTINELLI TO INFORM THE POPE.

Prominent Women of England Join Those of This Country in Extending Welcome to the Fair Cuban.

SCENE OF THE RESCUE OF THE FAIR CUBAN, MISS EVANGELINA CISNEROS.

This illustrates one of the most thrilling features in the story of the escape of the Cuban captive. Charles Duval of the "Examiner-Journal," with two aids in the persons of Joseph Hernandon and Harrison Mallory, scaled the walls of the Casa de Recogidas, in which the victim of the "Butcher's" vengeance was confined, and after reaching the bars of the cell, liberated the young woman and helped her to descend to the street over the roofs and down the walls by which they had come and out. In doing this there was a wide opening to be bridged between a wall and roof. Over a slender ladder the rescued and rescuers made a perilous journey, and then the descent to the street was comparatively easy. For fifteen months Miss Cisneros was kept "incomunicado," without a shadow of justification for her incarceration. Now, thanks to the energy and enterprise of the "Examiner-Journal" and the news men who undertook her rescue, she is breathing a freer air than she has ever known in her life before, for she is on her way to America, and will arrive to-day in New York City. The sketch is by an "Examiner" artist from the description by Charles Duval.

LATEST AFTERNOON EDITION

AN AMERICAN PAPER FOR THE AMERICAN PEOPLE

NEW YORK EVENING JOURNAL

LATEST AFTERNOON EDITION

NO. 5,611—P. M.
NEW YORK, MONDAY, MARCH 28, 1898.
PRICE ONE CENT.

PEACE! U. S. BACKS DOWN! NO WAR WITH SPAIN.

THE DONS ACCEPT M'KINLEY'S PLAN OF ARBITRATION TO END CUBAN WAR.

Armistice Will Be Declared Until After the Rainy Season.

EXTRA.
NO 10

CABINET

DISCUSSES

AGREEMENT

WITH SPAIN

43

$50,000 REWARD.—WHO DESTROYED THE MAINE?—$50,000 REWARD.

EDITION FOR GREATER NEW YORK.

NEW YORK JOURNAL

AND ADVERTISER.

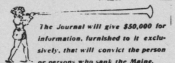

NO. 5,572.   Copyright, 1898, by W. R. Hearst.—NEW YORK, THURSDAY, FEBRUARY 17, 1898.—16 PAGES.   PRICE ONE CENT In Greater New York and Jersey City. TWO CENTS Elsewhere.

DESTRUCTION OF THE WAR SHIP MAINE WAS THE WORK OF AN ENEMY.

$50,000!

$50,000 REWARD!

For the Detection of the Perpetrator of the Maine Outrage!

The New York Journal hereby offers a reward of **$50,000 CASH** for information, **FURNISHED TO IT EXCLUSIVELY**, which shall lead to the detection and conviction of the person, persons or government criminally responsible for the explosion which resulted in the destruction, at Havana, of the United States war ship Maine and the loss of 258 lives of American sailors.

The **$50,000 CASH** offered for the above information is on deposit with Wells, Fargo & Co.

No one is barred, be he the humble but misguided seaman eking out a few miserable dollars by acting as a spy, or the attache of a government secret service, plotting, by any devilish means, to revenge fancied insults or cripple menacing countries.

This offer has been cabled to Europe and will be made public in every capital of the Continent and in London this morning.

The Journal believes that any man who can be bought to commit murder can also be bought to betray his comrades. **FOR THE PERPETRATOR OF THIS OUTRAGE HAD ACCOMPLICES.**

W. R. HEARST.

Assistant Secretary Roosevelt Convinced the Explosion of the War Ship Was Not an Accident.

—

The Journal Offers $50,000 Reward for the Conviction of the Criminals Who Sent 258 American Sailors to Their Death. Naval Officers Unanimous That the Ship Was Destroyed on Purpose.

$50,000!

$50,000 REWARD!

For the Detection of the Perpetrator of the Maine Outrage!

The New York Journal hereby offers a reward of **$50,000 CASH** for information, **FURNISHED TO IT EXCLUSIVELY**, for the detection and conviction of the person, persons or government criminally responsible for the explosions which resulted in the destruction, at Havana, of the United States war ship Maine and the loss of 258 lives of American sailors.

The **$50,000 CASH** offered for the above information is on deposit with Wells, Fargo & Co.

No one is barred, be he the humble, but misguided, seaman, eking out a few miserable dollars by acting as a spy, or the attache of a government secret service, plotting, by any devilish means, to revenge fancied insults or cripple menacing countries.

This offer has been cabled to Europe and will be made public in every capital of the Continent and in London this morning.

The Journal believes that any man who can be bought to commit murder can also be bought to betray his comrades. **FOR THE PERPETRATOR OF THIS OUTRAGE HAD ACCOMPLICES.**

W. R. HEARST.

POWDER MAGAZINE

NAVAL OFFICERS THINK THE MAINE WAS DESTROYED BY A SPANISH MINE.

George Eugene Bryson, the Journal's special correspondent at Havana, cables that it is the secret opinion of many Spaniards in the Cuban capital that the Maine was destroyed and 258 of her men killed by means of a submarine mine, or fixed torpedo. This is the opinion of several American naval authorities. The Spaniards, it is believed, arranged to have the Maine anchored over one of the harbor mines. Wires connected the mine with a powder magazine, and it is thought the explosion was caused by sending an electric current through the wire. If this can be proven, the brutal nature of the Spaniards will be shown by the fact that they waited to spring the mine until after all the men had retired for the night. The Maltese cross in the picture shows where the mine may have been fired.

Hidden Mine or a Sunken Torpedo Believed to Have Been the Weapon Used Against the American Man-of-War---Officers and Men Tell Thrilling Stories of Being Blown Into the Air Amid a Mass of Shattered Steel and Exploding Shells---Survivors Brought to Key West Scout the Idea of Accident---Spanish Officials Protest Too Much---Our Cabinet Orders a Searching Inquiry---Journal Sends Divers to Havana to Report Upon the Condition of the Wreck.

Was the Vessel Anchored Over a Mine?

BY CAPTAIN F. L. ZALINSKI, U. S. A.

(Captain Zalinski is the inventor of the famous dynamite gun, which would be the principal factor in our coast defence in case of war.)

Assistant Secretary of the Navy Theodore Roosevelt says he is convinced that the destruction of the Maine in Havana Harbor was not an accident.

The Journal offers a reward of $50,000 for exclusive evidence that will convict the person, persons or Government criminally responsible for the destruction of the American battle ship and the death of 258 of its crew.

The suspicion that the Maine was deliberately blown up grows stronger every hour. Not a single fact to the contrary has been produced.

Captain Sigsbee, of the Maine, and Consul-General Lee both urge that public opinion be suspended until they have completed their investigation. They are taking the course of tactful men who are convinced that there has been treachery.

Washington reports very late that Captain Sigsbee had feared some such event as a hidden mine. The English cipher code was used all day yesterday by the naval officers in cabling instead of the usual American code.

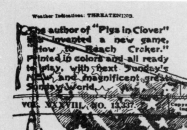

Weather Indications: THREATENING.

The author of "Pigs in Clover"
has invented a new game,
"How to Reach Croker."
Printed in colors and all ready
to play, with next Sunday's
new and magnificent great
Sunday World.

"Circulation Books Open to All."

The  World.

"Circulation Books Open to All."

VOL. XXXVIII., NO. 13,337.　　NEW YORK, THURSDAY, FEBRUARY 24, 1898.　　PRICE {ONE CENT in Greater New York and Jersey City.

Weather Indications: THREATENING.

This is a patriotic period.
The World prints next Sunday the words and music of
all the great national songs,
in sheet form. You MUST
have one!

EXPERTS AT HAVANA SAY SOME GREAT EXTERIOR FORCE RENT AND SUNK THE SHIP.

If the 10-Inch Magazine Had Let Go Its Store of Explosive Force, the Vessel Would Have Been Pulverized— Believed that the Forward Magazines Are Practically Intact.

(Copyright, 1898, by the Press Publishing Company, New York World.)

(Special Despatch from a World Staff Correspondent.)

[The following highly important despatch is sent by The World's staff correspondent in Havana by The World's despatch boat to Key West, and telegraphed hence to The World. He was not able to send this information before because of the strict censorship of matter sent by cable.]

HAVANA, Cuba, 10 A. M., by way of Key West, Fla., Feb. 23.—There is not one chance in a hundred but that the Maine was blown up deliberately.

Whether a mine detonating key was mistaken for a testing key or whether a mammoth contact torpedo broke its moorings by accident, the awful, astounding thing is that up to now there have been discovered fifty actual, positive physical proofs of the tragic fact.

Against it are only a few theories and suppositions.

Persons whose information and judgment command respect believe privately, though they may not say it openly, that the Maine was blown up through some outside agency.

They point to the fact that the only boilers which had steam up were in the part of the wreck which is intact now.

Spontaneous combustion, they say, was impossible in the bunkers, for the oldest coal in the exploded region had been aboard only three months.

The theory of spontaneous combustion in the magazines is disproved, these same experts say, for it would have influenced and exploded all the powder cases alike.

I shall not rush conclusions. I shall simply present the proof so far discovered on both sides, quoting naval expert testimony and allowing physical discoveries their just value.

I shall also give the arguments on the Spanish side and I shall state both as though I were under oath to the President of the United States in a case involving a national cataclysm or an international war.

It is now a hundred and eighty hours since the Maine's death throes shook Havana. Of these one hundred and thirty have been spent in examining the wreck and wreckage, the things found and the men who found them, and in subjecting each to experts.

Here are the results:

It seems absolutely certain—and it is exactly so unless the laws of nature changed Feb. 15— that the almost utter annihilation of the Maine cannot possibly have been caused by the explosion in any manner of even fifty times the amount of powder now conservatively known to have exploded in the Maine's interior.

It is well known that the rear group of big and little magazines is intact.

Those magazines did not explode. That portion of the Maine is practically uninjured.

Indeed the hull is not badly hurt for the length of forty feet forward of the after magazines. The heavy across-ship steel bulkhead between the two sets of boilers at this point is practically entire.

The only explosions in the Maine which could have broken her are much forward of this bulkhead.

The big ten-inch magazine—with a hundred and ninety service charges of two hundred and fifty pounds each—was forty-five feet from it.

Had its contents—or half of them—exploded, naval experts say the whole ship would have been pulverized. Yet forty-five feet from it the Maine is practically intact.

But the damage done is too great for the explosion of the small magazine adjoining the ten-inch magazine, and its shell room called the "reserve magazine."

Empty six-inch and ten-inch powder cases were stored there after the target practice, and it contained not over two thousand pounds of saluting powder.

It could not have caused one-tenth of the damage done even in the forty-foot space between the forward turret and the centre of the boilers mentioned.

A good deal is definitely known about the two other forward magazines. They were small.

One was immediately forward of the big magazine. It was called the "fixed ammunition magazine," and contained six-pound and one-pound loaded shells.

Inasmuch as the ten-inch shells in the big magazine, the shell room and the rear apartment— the vortex of the explosion—did not explode, the little ones surely are intact.

Or if they did explode they did comparatively little damage.

The only other forward magazine was the service six-inch powder and shell room immediately forward of the fixed ammunition magazine.

Nothing is known about it except that, being so far forward, in the opinion of experts its explosion would not have effected the total annihilation of the central portion of the Maine.

FIFTY PHYSICAL PROOFS THAT MAINE WAS BLOWN UP BY A MINE OR A TORPEDO.

World Correspondent Brings Out the Awful Truth---Fifty Times the Amount of Powder Which Is Known to Have Exploded Within the Maine Could Not Have Wrought the Dreadful Havoc.

However, these three little magazines play a small part in the Maine horror. They are described simply as a part of the forward explosives which might have aided in the wrecking of the ship.

All depends on the big magazine.

There have been raised from the forward part two apparently conflicting things:

One is a ten-inch powder case still loaded.

The other is an empty one, smashed and burned.

But as I am competently informed now that the empty ten-inch cases were piled after target practice in the reserve magazine instead of going back into their holes in the ten-inch magazine, this raised torn case seems to have been a spare or a used case, to which the explosion of the saluting powder in the reserve magazine, or any other explosives, may have given an exploded appearance.

Expert authority states that if the ruptured case had exploded its own iron handles would have blown off. They are on now.

Further inspection of day before yesterday's find of a six-inch case shows that its appearance might have been caused by fire and an outside explosive pressure.

A leading member of the Court of Inquiry thinks that neither the six nor the ten-inch empty case found was necessarily detonated. Both almost surely came from the reserve magazine, where both were stored.

But these are only weak negative proofs.

The recovering of a big ten-inch case with its cap sprung and the unexploded powder openly exposed is direct, absolute, positive proof that no great proportion of the twenty-five tons of the big magazine's powder exploded, and every expert, every man of common sense rejects the idea that even one charge of one-half pound or one hundred and twenty-five pounds of powder could explode in the closed magazine, holding 380 similar thin copper cylinders, each filled with red powder and each having its eight one-inch hexagons of quick-burning, black, detonating powder; without the explosion of all.

Had ten exploded, the explosion of all would have been absolutely assured under any and all possible conditions.

But there is one gaping case of powder which is filled and unexploded.

Even if ten big cases did go, and to them were added all the saluting powder and the rest of the forward explosives, the combined explosion could not have burst open the Maine from left to right, a full average of seventy feet away, or have done the actual, awful damage the divers find.

I have stated the worst possible case of an interior explosion.

The general idea of all experts is that none of th forward magazines, except the unimportant reserve one, has exploded, but that some great exterior force annihilated the ship.

Again let me say: Without the general explosion of the big forward magazine the damage to the Maine was impossible except from a big mine or a mammoth—a very mammoth—torpedo.

The big magazine did not explode, because everything on the wreck above and below the water has been hurled toward it. A movable object doesn't approach an explosion of twenty-five tons of powder.

In addition to the previous description of the main deck being curled over from the port side, while the magazine is on the starboard, and other things seen above water, I can now give more convincing proofs of the innocence of the magazine in the affair.

The divers find that ten-inch shells, which were in the exact centre of the ship, opposite the big magazine, are now partly on the starboard side, about the location of the magazine. They are unexploded and can be again used.

They were actually thrown against the shattered magazine. If that had gone pieces of ten-inch shells would have covered Havana's water front.

Another significant fact is that a grate bar from the boilers was found to-day in the forward part of the ship, near the magazine in question. It would have gone the other way had the magazine exploded.

This grate bar is strong proof of The World's original claim that in all probability the ship was destroyed beginning on the port side at the centre of the Maine.

Further proof is that no big magazine exploded is found in the fact that bodies are found close in and not burned, but only pierced by beams and debris.

Another proof is that three men who were sleeping twenty feet from the magazine in a cutter—their names were cabled to the World— were saved. So also were loaded cases and shells from the loading room above the magazine.

No ten-inch fragment was found on the steamer City of Washington or a here.

Moreover the main deck is curled toward the magazine instead of away from it.

Now that it is known that but few if any loaded cases were in the reserve magazine, the significance is taken from the discovery of the collapsed six-inch case found two days ago.

On the other hand, the place where the Maine lay was one where the ship seldom swung when moored to the Government buoy. It would seem to be the worst place to put a Government mine.

Besides, the time of night was ill chosen, if total loss was desired.

Furthermore, if war was desired, this was the worst way to bring it, for now revenge enters in.

Then the action was so fiendish as to be too much for even the Spanish Government. Probably it was done by a fanatic or a drunken attache or a man paid by the Cuban laborante, who want war.

SYLVESTER SCOVEL.

who had used the Spanish flag as a doormat were elevated to the rank of saints. Buffalo Bill declared he was 'ready to flay the Spanish'.

Selected front-page headlines from *The Journal* speak for themselves. March 22: War the Only End to the Crisis! March 28: War or Dishonour? March 29: Senate for War! April 1: War (it wasn't, of course). April 6: Moving for War! April 12: War Plan Adopted. April 13: Congress on the Verge of War! April 18: Deadlocked on the War. It must almost have seemed an anti-climax when on April 25 Congress actually did declare war, except to Pulitzer and Hearst whose circulations having already passed the million mark now leapt by several more hundred thousands.

Hearst flung his paper as energetically into the reporting of the war as he had into the stirring up of it. *The Journal* spent half a million dollars on covering the brief conflict, much of that going on a flotilla of tugs which hovered around the Navy at critical times, and a steamer equipped with printing press and composing room. Several *Journal* reporters

actually took part in the fighting, one of them, James Creelman, personally leading an infantry charge. Hearst himself, in be-ribboned Panama, landed in Cuba shortly after the first American troops, stumbled on some stranded Spanish sailors and took them prisoner. Naturally there were *Journal* photographers on hand to record the event.

The World, too, spent a fortune, which it could ill afford, to compete with its rival. Its outstanding correspondent was Stephen Crane — until he was unlucky enough to send in an honest report on what one regiment failed to do on San Juan Hill. 'Slurs on the Bravery of the Boys of the 71st!' thundered *The Journal*, and the poor Crane was recalled. *The New York Herald* was represented by Richard Harding Davis (who had defected from the Hearst camp in protest at the way his dispatches had been misinterpreted): it was to him that Teddy Roosevelt's Rough Riders owed their famous reputation, whenever he could restrain himself from joining in their charges.

By the end of July Spain had been duly

brought to her knees. On December 10 she ceded Cuba, Porto Rico, Guam and the Philippines — and so began the long period of agonizing introspection as to whether America was destined to become an imperial power or not. At the conclusion of the other struggle — the newspaper war — *The World* was forced into some critical self-analysis as well. Circulation had leapt upwards, certainly, but at what cost? *The World* had lost much of its reputation: many clubs and libraries wouldn't have it within their doors. Pulitzer was convinced he couldn't hold the figures; financially the paper was drained, physically he himself was chronically ill and almost blind. He relinquished the feud with Hearst, and set about building up a new respectability (and it may be said that by the time he died in 1911 he had succeeded handsomely). The real winner was Hearst, who went on to found his vast press empire. For him, at any rate, it had been (as he'd enthused to Creelman amid the bullets on Cuba) 'a splendid fight!'

THEY REMEMBERED THE MAINE!

The Chicago Daily Tribune.

THEY REMEMBERED THE MAINE!

VOLUME LVII.—NO. 122. MONDAY, MAY 2, 1898—TWELVE PAGES.

GREAT SEA VICTORY FOR AMERICA!

VENGEANCE FOR THE MAINE BEGUN!

SPAIN'S ASIATIC FLEET BURNED AND SUNK!

Washington Aflame with Joy Over the Reports of the Royal Victory Won by Commodore Dewey's Fleet.

NOTABLE COMPANY HEARS THE NEWS.

Additional Credence Lent to the Dispatches from Madrid Because They Emanated from Distinctively Spanish Sources.

THINK THE DEFEAT HAS BEEN DECISIVE.

General Rejoicing That the First Real Engagement of the War Should Have Been So Triumphant for the American Cause.

ENTHUSIASTIC COMMENT OF GUESTS OF PRESIDENT M'KINLEY.

Then conquer we must, when our cause it is just,
And this be our motto, "In God is our trust";
And the Star-Spangled Banner in triumph shall wave
O'er the land of the free and the home of the brave.

Washington, D. C., May 1.—[Special.]—Washington is aflame with joy at the splendid victory of Commodore Dewey and his fleet. From the President down nobody doubts the fact that the Spanish ships were routed and destroyed and that Manila is now practically at the mercy of our fleet.

President McKinley at midnight was still in the war chamber looking over the maps and charts and listening to the press dispatches as they were read to him.

Not a word of official information, of course, has reached Washington, and the President was exceedingly cautious in expressing an opinion, but after studying the dispatches he felt satisfied that Dewey's fleet had practically annihilated the Spanish ships.

Considering that the dispatches came from official Spanish sources, he was inclined to believe that our fleet had escaped with but slight injury, for the Spanish would be sure to magnify any American losses, and their reports do not lay stress on the injury to the American fleet.

With the President at the White House were Vice President Hobart, Justice McKenna, Attorney General Griggs, Secretaries Alger and Bliss, Senator Hanna, Chauncey M. Depew, Uncle Joe Cannon of Illinois, General Fitzgerald of New York, General Hastings, the President's old commander; Adjutant General Corbin, Assistant Adjutant General Heistand, and a number of ladies of the Cabinet.

All were wild with joy at the apparent completeness of the victory. The dispatches which spoke of the Americans having landed to dispose of their wounded caused some anxious moments, but on the whole the reports of the engagement created the most profound joy at the White House.

The President does not expect official dispatches before Tuesday, unless Dewey's forces land and seize the cable station. He explained that the commander of the fleet had the widest latitude of action and that he would land or not as circumstances seemed to dictate.

Wild with Joy Over Victory.

As the visitors retired from the White House they were interviewed by THE TRIBUNE correspondent, who obtained the following brief expressions of opinion:

Vice President Hobart—I have not expressed myself since war was declared, but I can hardly refrain from doing so now. Considering that our advices have come from Spanish sources, I think a great victory has been won by the American fleet.

Dr. Chauncey Depew—It looks as though they were wiped out. We might question the source of the news, but everything indicates, even though the dispatches come from Madrid, that Commodore Dewey has completely routed the enemy and that the Spaniards are trying to let themselves down as easily as possible.

Senator Hanna—Our squadron has won a great battle beyond any question. Commodore Dewey has demonstrated that Americans can fight when it is necessary to uphold the honor of the nation.

Secretary Alger—It is a great victory and indicates the strength of our naval forces. We have no official advices and therefore cannot make official announcement of the engagement. It must be taken into account that the dispatches received from Madrid by the Associated Press have undoubtedly been prepared under the supervision of Spanish officials.

Secretary Bliss—It was a wonderful victory; much greater than I expected.

Attorney General Griggs—Where were the Spaniards? We know where Commodore Dewey was.

Officers of the navy are fairly beside themselves with joy. They anticipated a fight at sea, but didn't imagine that Dewey would be able to run into the harbor so easily. Assistant Secretary Roosevelt was almost too happy to talk.

"It's glorious news," he said, "and we have won our first naval battle in a generation. The Spanish fleet is apparently wiped off the sea and Manila is ours. We could not ask for more, and the American navy has demonstrated its ability to stand up and fight with Spaniards or anybody else."

Commanders Hug Their Callers.

Commander Dickens and Captain Crowninshield of the Bureau of Navigation were ecstatic, and finally hugged their callers. The blockade in Cuba has been irksome to the navy, and the glorious news from the Philippines has compensated the sea dogs for the days of mere skirmish firing. The experts at the department figure out a victory even greater than is indicated by the Spanish advices.

The official statement that the American fleet sneaked into the harbor at dark Saturday night and commenced firing early Sunday morning is taken to mean that Commodore Dewey had the Spanish fleet bottled up in the harbor and sunk one ship after another.

The harbor of Manila is a big pocket, ten miles across at the mouth and thirty miles wide on the interior. At the mouth there are two channels, separated by Corregidor islands, the channels being known as Boca Chica and Boca Grande. They are deep sea straits.

The fleet apparently drove the Spanish ships ahead Saturday and after dark ran the batteries at the two edges of the entrance to the bay, Point Libones on the south and Cochinos Point on the north. As nearly as the navy experts can figure out the fleet spent Saturday night on the western side of the harbor and opened fire soon after daylight Sunday morning.

The powerful batteries in the harbor are those at Port Cavite, on the eastern shore of the bay, about three miles southwest of the City of Manila. It is believed that the Spanish ships were drawn up just off the Cavite batteries and that Dewey's squadron was able to fight in line of battle, engaging both the batteries and the Spanish fleet at the same time.

Dewey's Fleet the Stronger.

Considering the type of ships, Commodore Dewey's fleet is the heaviest armored in the American navy. The four protected cruisers, built of steel, with protective decks, carried no less than twenty-three six and eight inch breech loading rifles, and twenty of the famous five-inch rapid-fire guns peculiar to the American navy, and believed to be as effective guns as ever were put aboard ships. With the cruisers were the two steel gunboats, the Concord, of only 1,710, and the little Petrel, of only 892 tons, and yet the former carried six and the latter a quartet of the heavy six-inch rifles, each projectile from which weighs 100 pounds. One fire from all the main batteries of the four cruisers and two gunboats would have turned loose on the unfortunate Spaniards no less than fifty-three rifled projectiles of five, six, and eight inches in diameter. Each round of the guns means a hail of over 5,000 pounds of steel projectiles. The dispatches seem to show, as the Navy department figures it out, that the Spanish fleet was absolutely annihilated. The flagship, the Reina Christina, was the only ship in the fleet which could be classed as modern. It was built of steel and nominally mounted half a dozen six-inch Hontoria rifles, but there is good ground for the belief that they were not effective. The Reina Christina was apparently broken to bits, and so it naturally follows that the Castilla, which was an old wooden ship, bark rigged, was burned. The Don Juan de Austria and the Don Antonio de Ulloa were sister ships.

(Continued on third page.)

HERO OF THE BATTLE OF MANILA.

COMMODORE GEORGE DEWEY,
Commander of the Victorious Asiatic Fleet of the American Navy.

KNOWN CASUALTIES OF THE FIGHT.

Spanish cruiser REINA MARIA CHRISTINA, Admiral's flagship, burned.

Spanish cruiser CASTILLA, said to be completely burned.

Spanish cruiser DON JUAN DE AUSTRIA, blown up.

Several Spanish ships sunk.

Cadarzo, Captain of the Spanish flagship, and crew of 370, who perished with the vessel.

Commanders of the Spanish cruisers Castilla and Don Juan de Austria, with their crews of about 500 men all told.

American losses are unknown.

SUMMARY.

United States vessels lost (Madrid admission)	0
United States vessels damaged (from best information)	0
Spanish cruisers totally lost (Madrid admission)	3
Spanish gunboats damaged (Madrid admission)	2
Spanish Captains lost (commanding lost cruisers)	3

SHIPS THAT FOUGHT OFF MANILA.

UNITED STATES FLEET.	SPANISH FLEET.
OLYMPIA (flagship), first-class cruiser, Capt. C. N. Gridley.	REINA MERCEDES, cruiser.
BALTIMORE, protected cruiser, Capt. N. M. Dyer.	REINA CHRISTINA, cruiser.
BOSTON, protected cruiser, Capt. Frank Wildes.	ISLA DE CUBA, cruiser.
RALEIGH, protected cruiser, Capt. J. B. Coghlan.	ISLA DE LUZON, cruiser.
CONCORD, gunboat, Commander Asa Walker.	CASTILLA, cruiser.
PETREL, gunboat, Commander E. P. Wood.	DON ANTONIO DE ULLOA, cruiser.
M'CULLOCH, dispatch boat.	DON JUAN DE AUSTRIA, cruiser.
NANSHAN, collier.	VELASCO, cruiser.
ZAFIRO, collier.	ELCANO, gunboat.
	GENERAL LEZO, gunboat.
	MARQUIS DEL DUERO, gunboat.
	QUIROS, gunboat.
	VILLALOBOS, torpedo gunboat.
	GENERAL ALAVA, transport.
	CEBU, transport.
	MANILA, transport.
	ISLA DE MINDANAO, converted cruiser.

Commodore Dewey Crushes the Spanish Squadron in a Terrific Battle Off Cavite, Near the Capital of the Philippine Islands, Sunday Morning.

ONE OF THE GREAT NAVAL ENGAGEMENTS OF THE AGE.

Admiral Montejo's Flagship, the Reina Maria Christina, and the Cruiser Castilla Are Burned, While the Don Juan de Austria Is Blown Up.

OTHERS ARE SUNK TO SAVE THEM FROM BEING CAPTURED.

Captain Cadarzo Is Among the Killed on the Spanish Side, and the List of Fatalities Is a Large One, Though the Particulars on This Point Are Slow in Coming to Hand.

LOSS TO AMERICA'S WARSHIPS AND SAILORS IS NOT BELIEVED TO BE HEAVY.

Commodore Dewey's squadron won a decisive victory over the Spanish fleet yesterday.

The battle was fought off Cavite, ten miles southwest of Manila. It lasted for several hours and resulted in a crushing defeat for Spain.

The American squadron arrived off the Philippines on Saturday night, taking advantage of the darkness to gain a favorable position. The attack on the Spanish fleet began soon after daylight yesterday morning.

It was a terrific battle, undoubtedly one of the fiercest and most brilliant in the history of naval warfare. The nine ships of the American fleet were outnumbered by those of Spain, but the Americans were superior in armament.

The heavy fire from Commodore Dewey's guns was effective from the outset. Admiral Montejo's flagship, the Reina Maria Christina, was burned and its commander killed. The Don Juan de Austria was blown up and the Castilla was burned.

The Spanish sailors fought bravely, and refused to leave their burning ships when ordered to do so. Commander Cadarzo of the flagship went down with his vessel, and many of his crew perished with him.

Others of the Spanish fleet were badly damaged, and were sunk to prevent their falling into the hands of the Americans.

There was considerable loss of life on the Spanish side.

The American losses are not stated. As most of the news is sent by the Governor General of the Philippines it is certain that if Commodore Dewey's squadron was materially damaged the fact would not be minimized.

Admiral Montejo cabled to Madrid admitting the defeat of his squadron.

One Spanish report says that the American commander retired after an hour's fighting to land his wounded.

The battle took the form of a double engagement, according to the somewhat indefinite reports on this point. Presumably these reports are based on the maneuvers of the American squadron. The statement is made that Commodore Dewey's ships withdrew for a time and then returned to the attack. As the advantage was all on his side from the first, it is not believed that he at any period in the fight withdrew from action, though his ships may have changed positions.

The news of the Spanish defeat was fully confirmed in Lisbon last night, where the early reports gave Spain the victory.

Madrid officials profess to consider the battle a brilliant page in the nation's history, and the Minister of Marine telegraphed praise and congratulations to Admiral Montejo.

The feeling in London is that Commodore Dewey's job cannot be considered complete until he has captured Manila, and that he will be in an awkward position unless he succeeds in taking the city.

There was wild enthusiasm in Washington when the news of the victory arrived.

REINA MARIA CHRISTINA, SPANISH FLAGSHIP, BURNED.

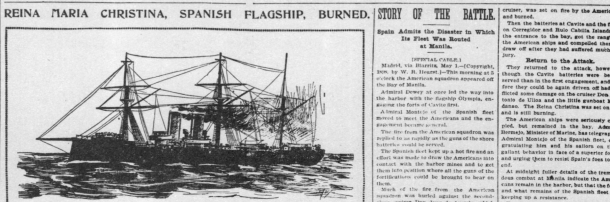

The Reina Christina was 280 feet in length, had a displacement of 3,090 tons, a natural speed of fourteen knots, and a crew of 370 men. Its armament consisted of six 6.2-inch Hontorias, two 2.7-inch, three 2.2-inch rapid fire guns, two 1-inch, six machine guns; hull, steel.

STORY OF THE BATTLE.

Spain Admits the Disaster in Which Its Fleet Was Routed at Manila.

[SPECIAL CABLE.]

Madrid, via Biarritz, May 1.—[Copyright, 1898, by W. R. Hearst.]—This morning at 5 o'clock the American squadron appeared off the Bay of Manila.

Admiral Dewey at once led the way into the harbor with the flagship Olympia, engaging the forts of Cavite first.

Admiral Montejo of the Spanish fleet moved to meet the Americans and the engagement became general.

The fire from the American squadron was replied to as rapidly as the guns of the shore batteries could be served.

The Spanish fleet kept up a hot fire and an effort was made to draw the Americans into contact with the harbor mines and to get them into position where all the guns of the fortifications could be brought to bear on them.

Much of the fire from the American squadron was hurled against the second-class cruiser Don Juan de Austria, which was severely damaged and its gallant commander killed. It then attempted to withdraw from the action, still firing, but the fire reached its magazine and it was destroyed by an explosion.

Another Spanish vessel, the Castilla, a cruiser, was set on fire by the Americans and burned.

Then the batteries at Cavite and the forts on Corregidor and Ruio Cabilla Islands, at the entrance to the bay, got the range of the American ships and compelled them to draw off after they had suffered much injury.

Return to the Attack.

They returned to the attack, however, though the Cavite batteries were better served than in the first engagement, and before they could be again driven off had inflicted some damage on the cruiser Don Antonio de Ulloa and the little gunboat Mindanao. The Reina Christina was set on fire and is still burning.

The American ships were seriously crippled, but remained in the bay. Admiral Bermejo, Minister of Marine, has telegraphed Admiral Montejo of the Spanish fleet, congratulating him and his sailors on their gallant behavior in face of a superior force, and urging them to resist Spain's foes to the end.

At midnight fuller details of the tremendous combat at Manila indicate the Americans remain in the harbor, but that the forts and what remains of the Spanish fleet are keeping up a resistance.

The insurgents have attacked from the land side of the city, but have been held in check.

The ministry admits severe Spanish losses in the fleet, but claims a virtual victory, as the City of Manila has not capitulated. It is insisted that the Americans were forced

HEADLINES 1900-1910

NEW ORLEANS, LA., TUESDAY, JULY 5, 1910.

RACE RIOTS FOLLOW THE RESULT OF THE FIGHT

VOL. LXXIV.   NO. 162

BLOODY CLASHES BETWEEN WHITES AND NEGROES.

Riots in Nearly All the Large Cities in the Country.

Fighting Immediately Followed the Result of Battle at Reno, Nev.

...le Cincinn

JOHNSON THE VICTOR IN THE FIFTEENTH ROUND.

James J. Jeffries Went Down to Defeat in the Ring at Reno.

Johnson Had the Best of It Almost From the Opening to the Close.

At No Time Did the Negro Champion Show Signs of Distress.

Jack London, the Famous Author, Graphically Describes the Great Battle—Story of the Fight by Rounds.

FACTS ABOUT THE BIG FIGHT.

...eated James J. Jeffries in their battle for
...mpionship at Reno, Nevada, yester-
...h round, when Johnson, after
...ked him to the floo

The Peers
...ave done

DECEMBER 1, 1909   THE WESTMINSTER GAZETTE.

FINANCE BILL REJECTED.

MOMENTOUS DECISION BY THE HOUSE OF LORDS.

THE GREAT PLUNGE.

IMPORTANT CABINET MEETING HELD TO-DAY.

...MONS' PROTEST.

MR. ASQUI ...HIS IMPORTANT

their demands and by those of the Free Churches to which
they belong. It is this fact that constitutes a debt of
honour. Those who put their hands to the plough must
not look back. To draw back is unthinkable. Not to press
forward with all our might would be to betray our faith,
our country, and those who had reposed confidence in us.

Political Duty of Free Churchmen.
Our challenge is addressed to Free Churchmen,
not to Free Churches. We do not desire to see
the Churches, as such, plunged into political strife.
We rejoice that the National Free Church Council
will repeat its action of four years ago at the
General Election. It cannot neglect its duty.

Reserve is, however, imposed upon us in the
Church, and this should, above all, be borne in
mind by preachers during the coming weeks...

EXIT HYPOCRIS

...RD ADVOCATE ON TH
...ND PLAIN ISS

MR
ON

NO. 1,066.

TO-DAY'S S

The weather forecast fer
Mild, mostly fair, southerly
easterly winds, freshening.
Lighting-up time, 7.9.

Tribune.

BIG FLEET OFF FOR PACIFIC.

PRICE THREE CENTS.

Copyright, 1907, by
The Tribune Association.

President Roosevelt Leads the First Stage of the Voyage to the West Coast.

RECEPTION ON THE MAYFLOWER.

...teen Battleships Pass Outside the Virginia Capes About Noon on Fourteen Thousand Mile Cruise.

New-York

VOL. LXVIII....No. 22,634.

NEW-YORK, WEDNESDAY, NOVEMBER 4, 1908.

TAFT AND SHERMAN SW

HUGHES'S BRILLIANT VICTORY

VERNOR

The

"Circulation Books Open to All."

Copyright, 1907, by the Press Publishing
Company, New York World.

NEW YORK, FRIDAY, OCTOBER 25, 1907.

SCARED DEPOSITORS WAITING IN LINE TO WITHDRAW THEIR MONEY FROM THE LINCOLN TRUST CO., AND SCENE AT AN UPTOWN B

...866.

ANDS!

37

advertise
r this year

The Imperial Year

The Boer War and The Boxer Rising

It wasn't quite the way Rudyard Kipling had written it:

> Take up the White Man's burden;
> Send forth your sturdy sons,
> And load them down with whiskey
> And testaments and guns.
> Throw in a few diseases
> To spread in tropic climes,
> For there the healthy niggers
> Are quite behind the times.

But it was what *The New York Times* thought of the militarist ambitions of the Anglo-American races as the old century gave way to the new. President M'Kinley had prayed to God for guidance on the question of annexing the Philippines, and it had come to him in the night: 'there was nothing left to do but take them all . . .' William Taft might call it Fraternity, but to the Democrats it was spelled Imperialism. In Britain, hadn't the Queen graciously lent an ear to the petitions of the South African uitlanders and tried in vain to reason with their Boer oppressor, Kruger? It was almost second nature for the Foreign Secretary, Joseph Chamberlain, to send in the infantry.

Only this time — for the first time since the Crimea War — it wasn't against chanting dervishes or ululating Zulus. It was against white men, men of Dutch and Huguenot descent with bibles in their pockets and keen sights on their (extremely efficient) rifles. The war in South Africa began in October 1899 — 'at tea-time' as *The Times* put it, implying it would all be over by bed-time. Yet, as the century drew to its close, the public were horrified to read that British troops were under siege in Kimberley, Ladysmith and Mafeking. The fact was that the War Office in London simply hadn't taken the whole thing seriously enough: the artillery, such as it was, was hopelessly inefficient, often pounding down on trenches the Boers had long evacuated; the infantry showed itself highly skilled in the military arts of twenty years ago, forming impressive squares and making brave frontal assaults on a mercurial enemy. The leaders were out of their depth, delivering stern little notes to their Boer counterparts about their uncivilised prosecution of the war.

Such was the state of affairs when the young special correspondent of the London *Morning Post*, Winston Churchill, began his assignment. He immediately undertook a campaign of his own to rally public opinion and speed up reinforcements — which he quickly appreciated would be required in vast numbers. Then, in the middle of November, he happened to be travelling on an armoured train reconnoitering towards Chieveley in Natal when it was derailed by a small Boer detatchment. Winston, so it was said, volunteered to lead a party to get the carriages back on the rails — in the teeth of enemy fire. He was wounded and captured. On November 20 it was headlines in *The Morning Post* (and *The New York World* which was also running Churchill's reports), though soon to be eclipsed by news of the black week in early December when three British armies were defeated at Stromberg, Magersfontein, and Colenso. The government began to see that Churchill had been right and hastened to appoint a new army commander — the hero of Kabul, Lord Roberts or Bobs as he was better known to caption-writers. He had only just received the news that his son had died winning a VC at Colenso. The public was deeply moved, but encouraged.

On December 22 a Russian newspaper, of all things, printed an odd little paragraph, saying that Winston Churchill had escaped from Pretoria but had been recaptured. It went on: 'It is feared his life is in danger. It is said that he decided to escape because his paper continues to pay him £1,000 per month, and he considered it obligatory to fulfil his duties as correspondent'. It was a wild exaggeration of Churchill's salary (though *The Post* did not choose to correct it) and, as it turned out, the correspondent was alive and well in Delagoa Bay. He had indeed escaped and the day after Boxing Day readers of *The Morning Post* were treated to Winston's own unadorned, but thrilling, account. He became a national hero overnight.

Thus enthroned, Churchill returned to his campaign. He likened the Boer government to Tammany Hall defended by Ironsides and warned 'it is a perilous policy to dribble out reinforcements and to fritter away armies . . . there is plenty of work here for a quarter of a million men'. 'Are the gentlemen of England all fox-hunting?' he wanted to know.

Under pressure from most of the newspapers now (the liberal *Daily Chronicle* continuing to oppose the war) the government was responding and preparing to embark another 100,000 men without delay. Many newspapers opened patriotic war funds, which met with generous response: *The Daily Telegraph's* reached £100,000 in January, *The Daily Mail's* by June. Mindful of a former triumph *The Times* sent out an MP to inspect hospital conditions and reported they were a disgrace (by the end of the war twice as many men had died of disease than had of wounds).

With the arrival of 'Bobs' British fortunes began to improve: Ladysmith was relieved in February by Redvers Buller (no longer known as Reverse) Bloemfontein captured in March.

SECOND EDITION.

MORNING POST, Dec. 27, 8.30 A.M.

THE WAR.

MR. WINSTON CHURCHILL.

HOW HE ESCAPED.

WANDERING FOR FIVE DAYS.

SIXTY HOURS OF MISERY.

We have received the following telegram from Mr. Winston Spencer Churchill, our War Correspondent who was taken prisoner by the Boers and escaped from Pretoria :

LOURENCO MARQUES, DEC. 21, 10 P.M.

I was concealed in a railway truck under great sacks.

I had a small store of good water with me.

I remained hidden, chancing discovery.

The Boers searched the train at Komati Poort, but did not search deep enough, so after sixty hours of misery I came safely here.

I am very weak, but I am free.

I have lost many pounds weight, but I am lighter in heart.

I shall also avail myself of every opportunity from this moment to urge with earnestness an unflinching and uncompromising prosecution of the war.

On the afternoon of the 12th the Transvaal Government's Secretary for War informed me that there was little chance of my release.

I therefore resolved to escape the same night, and left the State Schools Prison at Pretoria by climbing the wall when the sentries' backs were turned momentarily.

I walked through the streets of the town without any disguise, meeting many burghers, but I was not challenged in the crowd.

I got through the pickets of the Town Guard and struck the Delagoa Bay Railroad.

I walked along it, evading the watchers at the bridges and culverts.

I waited for a train beyond the first station.

The out 11.10 goods train from Pretoria arrived, and before it had reached full speed I boarded with great difficulty, and hid myself under coal sacks.

I jumped from the train before dawn, and sheltered during the day in a small wood in company with a huge vulture, who displayed a lively interest in me.

I walked on at dusk.

There were no more trains that night.

The danger of meeting the guards of the railway line continued, but I was obliged to follow it as I had no compass or map.

I had to make wide detours to avoid the bridges, stations, and huts.

My progress was very slow, and chocolate is not a satisfying food.

The outlook was gloomy, but I persevered with God's help for five days.

The food I had to have was very precarious.

I was lying up at daylight and walking on at night time, and meanwhile my escape had been discovered and my description telegraphed everywhere.

All the trains were searched.

Everyone was on the watch for me.

Four wrong people were arrested.

But on the sixth day I managed to board a train beyond Middelburg whence there is a direct service to Delagoa.

AT LAST! AT LAST!

BADEN-POWELL AND HIS MEN ARE FREE.

After Mafeking's Heroic Defence of Seven Months the Boers are Driven to Raise the Siege.

It is no news now, but every one is still repeating it with the same triumphant ring with which they shouted it forth last night when THE EVENING NEWS first announced it far and wide in London—

MAFEKING IS RELIEVED.

Although it did not possess the hall-mark of the War Office, the news was at once recognised as true, and "good old Kruger" was humorously thanked for allowing the news to come through, and thus saving us the additional suspense which would have resulted had we been forced to wait for the tardy message which is now on its way to the War Office

As Mr. Wyndham pointed out in the House of Commons, messages direct from Mafeking, having to come on horseback to the nearest telegraph point, may take from two to five days to get through, but last night's cable from Pretoria came in less than ten hours, and our thanks are due to the Boers for the early news.

The scenes in London when the news was made known beggared description. Every morning paper attempts the impossible in trying to picture the outburst of wild, mad enthusiasm. Those who took part in it need no description, and to those who did not no word painting would bring home the wonderful manifestations of delirious joy which made London last night one vast carnival. EVENING NEWS reporters who were present have attempted to describe the scene ; those who saw it know how far they have achieved the impossible.

THE BOER OFFICIAL MESSAGE.

PRETORIA, May 18 (11.35 a.m.).

It is officially announced that when the laagers and forts around Mafeking had been severely bombarded the siege was abandoned by the Boers. A British force advancing from the south then took possession of the town.—Reuter.

But still Mafeking and its plucky garrison under Baden-Powell was encircled. By now it had become the focal point of the whole Empire, the symbol of the unquenchable British spirit. When, after 211 days of siege, a Reuters telegram reached London at 9.00 in the evening of May 18 announcing that Mafeking had been relieved, there was doubt at first. There had been false alarms before, and this message did not carry the stamp of the War Office, who were unable to confirm it. Mr. Chamberlain, however, said he did not doubt the accuracy of Reuter's information — and London went berserk. (What had happened was that an enterprising Reuters man had wangled the news out of the Boers and, to beat any competition, had smuggled the bulletin out of Pretoria in a sandwich, if you please, and bribed a railwayman to get it across the border).

The papers the next morning were almost as full of London's antic mafficking as of details of the siege. As *The Star* aptly expressed it:

LONDON RELIEVED BY MAFEKING

There were flags everywhere, processions in every street and portraits of B.P. in every window. Down Piccadilly, staid old gentlemen were reported seen dancing in their clubs and spilling their whiskeys and soda. In Regent Street, *The Times* primly noted, feminine garments were displayed, of a kind 'usually only seen on a clothesline'. The comedian Dan Leno gave out the news from the stage of the London Pavilion then danced a jig. At Covent Garden, when the conductor could not be found, the Prince of Wales led the audience in God Save the Queen. In the streets, the police gave up trying to control the frenzy or rescue silk top hats. And so it went on for a night and a day, as the glorious news spread to the provinces. Only later did it emerge that the inhabitants of Newcastle mistaking a ship's siren for the pre-arranged signal of the news, had celebrated the relief of Mafeking 24 hours previously.

If the cheering populace imagined (as many of them did) that this was, to all intents and purposes, the end of the war, their celebrations were as premature as the city of Newcastle's. Two weeks later Pretoria was taken, yet the Boer farmers continued their guerrilla resistance till well into 1902. Nevertheless the headlines of war were to be usurped in the middle of June by news from a very different corner of the world.

The foreign communities in China at the turn of the century (predominantly British, American, Russian, German and French) could scarcely be called imperialist in the accepted sense. But to the leaders of the rapidly accelerating Chinese nationalism it was a fine distinction: thousands of Chinese were being converted yearly to western religion, and China's limitless market was being carved up by western powers at their pleasure. The answer according to I-ho Chuah (the Boxer fanatics) was simple: to kill all the foreign devils. They began with the Japanese chancellor in Peking on June 11 as he was making his way to the railway station to see if there was any news of the reinforcements the anxious legations had requested from Tientsin. He would have lived only to discover that the railway was destroyed and the telegraph cut: Peking was isolated. The German Ambassador was the next victim, on the 20th, shot in the street on his way to the Imperial Foreign Office.

There was no escape now, only retreat and some kind of resistance inside the Legation district. Every foreigner in the city made for there — missionaries, diplomats, some American scholars, a Russian banker, a Swiss hotel-keeper, an Austrian ship's captain, several hundred Chinese converts, and many others including an English journalist George Morrison, *The Times'* correspondent in China, facing the inside story of his life but with little prospect of ever filing it. To defend this cosmopolitan assembly stood a mile and a half of crude fortifications manned by an equally cosmopolitan corps of troops and marines — less than 500 against 50,000 implacable Boxers. Or was it 200,000, nobody could even guess.

Their plight was more desperate than they knew. A motley relief under Admiral Seymour had been turned back and Tientsin itself was cut off. Piecing together disjointed parts of the jigsaw which filtered through from the Shanghai office, the Press could only speculate on the fate of the besieged.

As the days went by the public, and the papers, were gripped in a fever of excitement. It was even more exciting than Mafeking, where B.P. had constantly been smuggling notes out that 'all was well'. All was self-evidently not well in Peking:

The Daily Mail, the youngest, most excitable but by far the most successful of the London papers, was perhaps over-eager to believe the worst when it came (though it did feel obliged to hedge its report on July 6):

Read right through the report displayed a few gnawings of doubt and ended with a classic fail-safe line: 'It may be, of course, that the massacre of all the Europeans at Peking has not taken place'. And that was how matters stood until the bombshell fell in the issue of July 16 (opposite):

The dates seemed a bit peculiar, but then the Chinese calendar was somewhat out of phase with the western one. Other papers published the terrible story, though none with the same panache as *The Daily Mail*.

Indeed on the 17th *The Times* published a glowing obituary to its China correspondent: 'No newspaper . . . ever had a more devoted, a more fearless and a more able servant than Dr. Morrison'.

But . . . there had been no massacre, and Dr. Morrison, though wounded, was very much alive. The gallant band had held out, day after day, and continued to hold out until August 14 when the flash of distant guns were seen on the night horizon, and a relief force later in the day burst through to the legations. Doubts had set in in Fleet Street on July 27:

On the 31st the error was finally exposed. Later the truth of those epic 55 days in Peking was discovered to be even more incredible than the fabrications (put about, it was thereafter assumed, by the Chinese for their own inscrutable reasons) which the papers had printed.

THE PEKIN MASSACRE.

ALL WHITE MEN, WOMEN, AND CHILDREN PUT TO THE SWORD.

AWFUL STORY OF THE 6TH & 7TH JULY.

HOW OUR PEOPLE DIED FIGHTING PRINCE TUAN'S HORDES.

FULL DETAILS FROM OUR SPECIAL CORRESPONDENT.

The complete account of the massacre at Pekin which we publish this morning was despatched from Shanghai last night (Sunday) at 8 p.m. (Chinese time), and marked "Urgent." This means that it travelled at the highest possible telegraphic cost, and reached us in almost record time, arriving at our offices at 7 p.m. (English time), Shanghai time being 7¾ hours ahead of ours.

It will be seen that the terrible story confirms in detail the Shanghai cablegram published exclusively in the "Daily Mail" on Friday last.

Ever since the first dread message suggesting the fate of the foreign colony in Pekin was flashed across the wires the whole civilised world has been hoping against hope that by some miraculous means some, at any rate, of the foreigners had survived to tell the tale.

But as the days crept by, days fraught with frightful anxiety to the relatives of the ill-fated prisoners in Pekin, the lamp of hope became dimmer and dimmer, and it is now unhappily extinguished.

A NIGHT OF AWFUL HORROR.

There can now no longer be any doubt about the date on which this, the greatest tragedy of the century, was consummated.

The news has been filtered through in exasperating driblets by that past-master in the art of duplicity, Sheng Taotai, of Shanghai.

He has now vouchsafed to the Consuls at Shanghai two telegrams, both of which name the morning of the 7th as that on which the British Legation was destroyed.

The Boxers had poisoned the Legation's sources of water supply. With famine staring them in the face, the gallant band of defenders appear to have made one desperate attempt to beat their enemies off.

Hundreds of Boxers were slain, and this so incensed the troops of Tung Fuh siang that orders were given to fire the guns which had been trained on the Legations.

Then the carnage commenced. All through the night, with pitiless insistency, the shells dropped in the compound, and by the morning of the 7th the destruction was complete, and every European, we are told, was put to the sword.

In confirmation—if it were needed—of the "Daily Mail" special cablegram we have the statement by Reuter's Shanghai correspondent that an official telegram has been received from the Governor of Shantung, who is the intermediary between the Pekin Government and Sheng Taotai, stating that all the foreigners at Pekin have been murdered.

And this, again, is confirmed by the special telegram from our St. Petersburg correspondent, who gives in brief an account of the awful news as it has reached the Czar of how all the white men, women, and children perished by the sword.

A Very Public Death

The Assassination of President M'Kinley

Weather Forecast: FAIR.

DO YOU READ THE
- - *Sunday World.*
America's Greatest Sunday Paper?
IT IS FOUR TIMES LARGER
THAN THIS ISSUE.

📖 See Auction Sales, page 14.

The ☽ World.

" *Circulation Books Open to All.* "   " *Circulation Books Open to All.* "

Weather Forecast: FAIR.

SEE the Photographs of Scenes and
Persons in the Buffalo Tragedy
in next *Sunday's World.*
ORDER IT OF THE NEWSDEALER AT
ONCE OR YOU WILL NOT GET ONE.

📖 See Auction Sales, page 14.

VOL. XLII. NO. 14,627.   Copyright, 1901, by the Press Publishing Company, New York World.   NEW YORK, SATURDAY, SEPTEMBER 7, 1901.   PRICE {TWO CENTS outside of Greater New York and Jersey City and on trains. ONE CENT in Greater New York and Jersey City.}

PRESIDENT M'KINLEY SHOT BY ANARCHIST; CONDITION CRITICAL

Weather Indications: FAIR.

Not Yesterday Alone,
but every day, as proved by the American
News Company, the New York City circulation of The World is tens of thousands
greater than that of any other paper.

The ☽ World.

" *Circulation Books Open to All.* "   " *Circulation Books Open to All.* "

Weather Indications: FAIR.

Not "Second in Command,"
but first in commanding the attention of the
public, is The World, with a regular paid
New York City circulation ten of thousands greater than that of any other paper.

VOL. XLII. NO. 14,628.   PRICE FIVE CENTS.   NEW YORK, SUNDAY, SEPTEMBER 8, 1901.   Copyright, 1901, by the Press Publishing Company, New York World.   52 PAGES   PRICE FIVE CENTS.

PRESIDENT'S CONDITION GRAVE; THE CRISIS COMES TO-DAY.

ACKNOWLEDGING CHEERS OF

WALKING TO STAND TO MAKE SPEECH.

LIFE OR DEATH VERDICT AT 4 TO-DAY, SAYS HANNA.

President's Life-Long Friend, While
Very Hopeful, Says No Definit
Opinion on the President's Condi-
on Can Be Given Until This (Sunday) Afternoon

NO SIGN OF PERITONITIS
AND PULSE NOT ALARMING.

(Special from a Staff Correspondent.)

BUFFALO, Sept. 7.—Senator Mark A. Hanna, after spending fifteen
minutes with Dr. Rixey early this evening gave to a World correspondent
a thorough review of President McKinley's case.

Senator Hanna, his face brightened by the same smile he wore when
the returns last November announced McKinley's re-election to the Presidency, expressed his confident belief that the President had passed the
crisis and that he would survive the murderous assault made upon him
yesterday.

"Your smile," said The World correspondent to Senator Hanna as the
President's closest friend left Mr. Milburn's home about 6.30 to-night,
"would seem to indicate that you have obtained encouraging news?"
Favorable Because Not Bad.

"Yes," Senator Hanna replied. "It is favorable news because it is not
unfavorable news.

"I have just had a fifteen-minute talk with Dr. Rixey, in which I have
thoroughly gone over the entire situation. I wanted to know just exactly
how matters stood.

M'KINLEY HOLDS HIS OWN, CONSCIOUS AND COURAGEOUS.

Peritonitis is the Chief Fear of the Sur-
geons, but if Patient is No Worse by
Noon They Will Be Hopeful of His
Recovery.

TWENTY-FOUR HOURS MORE
WILL MAKE THEM CONFIDENT

Seat of Government Is Temporarily Transferred to
Buffalo, Where the Members of the Cabinet
and Vice-President Roosevelt Are in Readiness
for an Emergency, and One Day's Official
Business Over the Wires Is Said to Have
Amounted to 100,000 Words.

LATEST ADVICES FROM HIGHEST SOURCES
ON PRESIDENT'S ACTUAL CONDITION.

" *If Mr. McKinley remains in his present condition
until to-morrow (Sunday) noon, his physicians
will begin to have definite hopes of his recovery.* "—From The World's Special Correspondent at
Buffalo.

PHOTOGRAPH OF PRESIDENT DELIVERING
HIS LAST SPEECH AT THE EXPOSITION.

If there was one thing President William M'Kinley excelled at, it was shaking hands. It was estimated he could shuffle through fifty guests a minute on a good day, and he was never happier than when in the thick of it. More than once his advisors had warned him of the dangers of unguarded hand-shaking; the President always replied that he had supreme confidence in the people.

Shortly after 4.00 pm on September 6 1901, in the Temple of Music at the Pan-American Exposition in Buffalo N.Y., a young Polish immigrant reached the head of a long line of visitors being greeted as warmly and tirelessly as ever by M'Kinley. The President reached to clasp the man's left hand, noticing that his right appeared to be bandaged with a handkerchief. But he never made that hand-shake. The 'wounded' hand shot forward and fired two shots at pointblank range into the body of the President. Amazingly M'Kinley was still conscious as he was carried to the Exposition Hospital, where an operation to discover the second bullet was carried out immediately (the first had glanced on the breast bone — or a button — and done little damage). The large Press corps which had followed the President to the exhibition waited anxiously for the first bulletin.

It came at 7.00 pm, not from the doctors but from the President's private secretary.

BULLETIN NO. 1.

7 P. M.—The President was shot about 4 o'clock; one bullet struck him on the upper portion of the breast bone, glancing and not penetrating; the second bullet penetrated the abdomen, five inches below the left nipple and one and one-half inches to the left of the median line. The abdomen was opened through the line of the bullet wound. It was found that the bullet had penetrated the stomach. The opening in the front wall of the stomach was carefully closed with silk sutures, after which a search was made for a hole in the back wall of the stomach.

This was found and also closed in the same way. The further course of the bullet could not be discovered, although careful search was made. The abdominal wound was closed without drainage. No injury to the intestines or other abdominal organ was discovered.

"The patient stood the operation well, pulse of good quality, rate of 130, condition at the conclusion of operation was gratifying. The result cannot be foretold. His condition at present justifies hope of recovery.

GEORGE B. CORTELYOU,
Secretary to the President.

From a layman, it was perhaps acceptable though it clearly begged a few questions. Why had the wound not been drained? Had the bullet track been cleaned? (It was also discovered later that, far from there being no other damage to abdominal organs, both the pancreas and kidney were affected). It was true that the surgeons had operated at speed and not under ideal conditions, but it appeared they had done little more than stitch the President up. At first sight the second bulletin, signed by a positive galaxy of doctors, was very reassuring.

THE SNAKE AT THE FIRESIDE

XS   Weather Forecast: FAIR, COOL.

That of The World over every other paper in regular paid New York City circulation is more than a million a month, every month in the year.

See Auction Sales, page 12.

The World.

"Circulation Books Open to All."

VOL. XLII. NO. 14,629.   Copyright, 1901, by the Press Publishing Company, New York World.

NEW YORK, MONDAY, SEPTEMBER 9, 1901.

2 + 2 Makes 4

Is no more certain than that the New York City circulation of The World is regularly tens of thousands a day greater than that of any other paper.

See Auction Sales, page 12.

"Circulation Books Open to All."

PRICE (TWO) CENTS outside of Greater New York and Jersey City.

PRESIDENT NO WORSE; EVEN CHANCES NOW FOR RECOVERY.

A PROFILE STUDY OF THE PRISONER IN POLICE SUPT'S OFFICE

CZOLGOSZ TRAPPED INTO DISCLOSING PLOT TO KILL.

Detective, Disguised as a Plumber, Said to Have Obtained Startling Admissions from Murderous Red.

I FELT IT MY DUTY TO KILL PRESIDENT MCKINLEY

DR. M'BURNEY SAYS SIGNS ARE ALL HOPEFUL NOW.

New York's Eminent Surgeon Tells The World that If Nothing Happens Within Forty-eight Hours He Will Feel Very Hopeful—Danger from Now Until Tuesday from Peritonitis --Latest Bulletin from Surgeon Non-Committal.

NO CONCLUSIVE VERDICT FOR NEXT 48 HOURS.

LATEST FROM THE MILBURN HOUSE.

STUDIED FROM SKETCHES BY HAYDON JONES AT POLICE HDQTS SAT SEPT. 7 BUFFALO N.Y.

THE CZOLGOSZ HOMESTEAD AT 306 FLEET ST.

LIFE-SKETCHES OF THE PRESIDENT'S ASSAILANT.

EMINENT SURGEONS WEIGH CONDITIONS AND HOPE FOR PRESIDENT'S RECOVERY.

At the Home Plate

The World.

"Circulation Books Open to All."

VOL. XLII. NO. 14,630.   Copyright, 1901, by the Press Publishing Company, New York World.

NEW YORK, TUESDAY, SEPTEMBER 10, 1901.

"Circulation Books Open to All."

Millions to Tell the Tale of The World's lead in New York City circulation every day, every week and every month.

See Auction Sales, page 12.

PRICE (TWO) CENTS outside of Greater New York and Jersey City and on trains.

ALMOST A CERTAINTY THAT PRESIDENT M'KINLEY WILL LIVE.

ANARCHY

MAY

DETROIT JOURNAL

STRANGLE IT RIGHT NOW.

55

PRESIDENT'S WOUND REOPENED; SLIGHT CHANGE FOR WORSE

EMMA GOLDMAN IN JAIL CHARGED WITH CONSPIRACY.

Caught Hiding in a Chicago Flat and Taken to Police Headquarters—A Warrant Is Served Formally Accusing Her of Plotting to Murder President McKinley.

VEHEMENTLY DENIES THAT SHE INSPIRED CZOLGOSZ.

Anarchist Queen Declares She Met Him Only Once and Then Only for a Moment—Makes a Detailed Statement Covering Her Movements for the Last Two Months.

STORY OF THE ARREST OF ANARCHIST QUEEN.

DR. CHARLES M'BURNEY DISCUSSING THE PRESIDENT'S CASE IMMEDIATELY AFTER COMING FROM THE MILBURN HOUSE.

Surgeons Remove Several Stitches Because of Slight Irritation from the Presence of a Fragment of Mr. McKinley's Coat, Carried Into the Wound by the Bullet, but They Declare Patient's Condition Is Unchanged in All Important Particulars.

PATIENT TAKES FOOD FOR THE FIRST TIME.

Dr. McBurney Had Planned to Leave for New York Last Night, but He Postpones His Departure and Takes Part in a Consultation of Surgeons that Lasts for Two Hours—Latest Operation Will Delay Healing of Wound.

LATEST OFFICIAL BULLETIN.

MILBURN HOUSE, BUFFALO, Sept. 10—10.30 P. M.—The condition of the President is unchanged in all IMPORTANT particulars. His temperature is 100.6; pulse, 114; respiration, 28.

When the operation was done on Friday last it was noted that the bullet had carried with it a short distance beneath the skin a fragment of the President's coat. This foreign material was, of course, removed, BUT A SLIGHT IRRITATION OF THE TISSUES WAS PRODUCED, THE EVIDENCE OF WHICH HAS APPEARED ONLY TO-NIGHT.

It has been necessary on account of this slight disturbance to remove a few stitches and partially open the skin wound.

This incident cannot give rise to other complications, but it is communicated to the public, as the surgeons in attendance wish to make their bulletins entirely frank.

In consequence of this separation of the edges of the surface wound the healing of the same will be somewhat delayed.

The President is now well enough to begin to take nourishment by the mouth in the form of pure beef juice.

(Signed)
P. H. RIXEY,
M. D. MANN,
ROSWELL PARK,
HERMAN MYNTER,
CHARLES McBURNEY.
GEORGE B. CORTELYOU,
Secretary to the President.

PROF. MAZZONI, THE POPE'S SURGEON, THINKS SECOND BULLET WILL HAVE TO BE REMOVED.

But no newspaper pointed out (at the time) that Dr. Mann, who performed the operation, was in fact a gynecologist; that Dr. Rixey, the President's physician, had not been present for most of it; that Mynter and Wanbin (both well-known surgeons) had only assisted, and that Dr. Park who was by far the best-qualified to operate had arrived half way through and, for reasons of medical etiquette, had let Dr. Mann get on with it. Later the best man in the U.S. Charles McBurney from New York was called in as consultant, and it was he who, hounded at all hours to prognosticate on the patient's chances, set the tone of cheery optimism which the Press wanted to hear. He had not yet, of course, viewed the President's insides.

For seven days and nights M'Kinley hovered between life and death, while the Press presented the public with the greatest real-life cliffhanger of their lives. Anyone whose opinion could be remotely called authoritative was interrogated as to whether he thought M'Kinley would live — the Pope's surgeon, Edward VII's, even the Kaiser's personal physician, who wanted to know (with good reason) whether the bowels had been injured in any way. No answer was forthcoming, but Senator Hanna, who seemed to know most about the case vouchsafed the opinion that when a man like the President said he would not die 'even the Old Man himself could not knock him out', which was certainly heartening news.

Indeed, so intensive was the coverage of the President's abdomen, temperature, pulse, respiration, bowels and general demeanour hour by hour and day by day, that the man on the tramcar could talk almost as knowledgeably as the doctors themselves. Never before — and probably never since — had a medical case-history been exposed so completely to the glare of publicity. Even the contents of the President's trouser pockets made front-page news (it was noted, somewhat soberly, that had he died among strangers they would have furnished no clue as to the identity of the President of the United States).

The euphoria persisted for five days. Even a minor operation, to remove from the wound part of M'Kinley's jacket which had unaccountably remained within, passed off without incident.

McBurney went home, relatives drifted away, Senator Hanna's face grew 'complacent' and Mrs. M'Kinley was bearing up 'like an American

Gentlewoman'. There was still, however, the question of the assailant.

His name was Leon Czolgosz and no-one was unduly surprised when, with a name like that, he pronounced himself an anarchist (except the Anarchists). Several newspapers immediately dug out their cuttings on the assassination of King Humbert of Italy the year before (that, too, had been the work of an anarchist). A Secret Service Chief was uncovered who claimed to have exposed an anarchist conspiracy in Paterson N.J. back in 1898 to murder both Humbert and M'Kinley. Reporters flocked to New Jersey and found — a nest of (harmless) anarchists.

'Red' haunts throughout the country were raided, providing meaty copy for paragraphs on the whiskey-sodden orgies of celebration which had allegedly gone on there (one of them down a coal-mine, it was said). From his hotel suite in New York, Senator Platt called for lynch law, and the populace of Memphis concurred.

At the centre of the national witch-hunt was the Queen of Anarchists, Emma Goldman. She had been seen in Buffalo earlier in the week, and hadn't Czolgosz admitted her words had inspired him? She was soon hunted down in a Chicago lodging house and promptly charged with conspiracy, on no evidence whatsoever (The World's reporter felt bound to say that he had found her 'anything but bloodthirsty'). The evidence for a conspiracy was, at best, thin. Czolgosz himself had repeatedly denied any accomplices, even under third degree. He had only hinted at a plot to a plumber who had come to mend the sanitation in his cell (a detective, of course, in disguise). The only fact to be forthcoming from the prisoner was that he'd considered it his duty, not believing that 'one man should have so much service and another man should have none'. And for that he was electrocuted in October, having made no defence and filed no appeal.

Meanwhile the President continued to improve. On the 11th the surgeons warned the public to be on its guard against rumours as to sudden changes in the President's condition. On the morning of the 12th they fed him some chicken broth, toast saturated in beef juice and some coffee. Before long it was clear he was in a bad way. Heroic quantities of physic, castor oil, colomel and enemas were pumped into him — but the next day the papers had no option but to report a sudden change in the President's condition. Dr. McBurney on the long distance telephone from Albany was 'not alarmed' of course, but by the early hours of the 13th the men on the spot were, in spite of the comforting headlines they read in the papers.

That was the President's last day. He spent it, if the newspapers were to be entirely trusted (which by this time they were frankly not), reciting verses from Nearer My God To Thee. In the long evening, in one of his diminishing periods of consciousness he spoke some words. Someone near him thought it might have been 'Goodbye all. Goodbye. It is God's will. Let his will, not ours, be done'. With the deference due to famous last words The World printed three different versions of it in the space of a page.

So occurred the very public death of a public man. Afterwards there were those who wished it had not been quite so public: the autopsy revealed that the inside of M'Kinley's wound, and all the organs surrounding it, were in an advanced gangrenous state. The stomach just was not functioning at all. The vice-President, Theodore Roosevelt, hurriedly returned from a climbing expedition to be sworn in as successor, but there was a hitch. Nobody could remember the correct procedure. The dilemma was finally solved — by consulting an old newspaper report of President Garfield's death.

Weather Forecast: FAIR.

The World.

Weather Forecast: FAIR.

"Circulation Books Open to All."

"Circulation Books Open to All."

VOL. XLII. NO. 14,634. ★ Copyright, 1901, by the Press Publishing Company, New York World. NEW YORK, SATURDAY, SEPTEMBER 14, 1901. PRICE [illegible] outside of Greater New York and Jersey City and on trains. [illegible] in Greater New York and Jersey City.

THE END COMES AT 2.15; PRESIDENT M'KINLEY IS DEAD.

LAST FAREWELL OF WIFE AND HER LOVER-HUSBAND.

As She Was Led In to His Bedside, He Clasped Her Hand and Whispered Words of Comfort and Affection.

THEN HE SANK INTO COMA AND SHE WAS LED AWAY.

Mrs. McKinley Wholly Overcome—Close Friends Dread the Effect Her Husband's Death Will Have on the Wife, Whose Well-Being Depended Upon Him Constantly.

(Special from a Staff Correspondent.)

BUFFALO, Sept. 13.—When the President asked for his wife they went to the room across the hall, where she sat with Mrs. McWilliams.

She was helped into her husband's room by Mrs. McWilliams, but Mr. McKinley had again fallen into unconsciousness.

After waiting a few moments she obeyed the suggestion of those about and went back to her room, leaving the doctors free to resume their efforts.

And now, one by one, those in the house, the President's brother, Abner, Secretary Root, Secretary Wilson, Secretary Hitchcock, Mrs. McKinley's sisters and the others went into the room of death for the last look.

Each looked at the form on the bed—some went no further than the doorway—and turned away. The sight of that brave face looking so like death caused them to weep. Not one person, man or woman, who came back downstairs was not weeping, and some of the men were sobbing almost hysterically.

About 3 o'clock Mr. McKinley recovered consciousness and again whispered Mrs. McKinley's name. Once more they led her in and placed her in a chair beside the bed.

They saw that he was conscious and then tured away—all except the nurse and one doctor.

She took his hand. His eyes opened. He spoke several sentences. Those near caught only one:

"Good-by, good-by. It is God's will. Let his will, not ours, be done."

It was a long leave-taking, and finally they carried her half fainting to her room. They are watching over her anxiously. They fear the effect of the severing of bonds which were so close and upon which she was so dependent.

News of what was happening went downstairs and out into the street. It was received everywhere with tears.

"They are saying good-by to each other," people whispered in the streets all along those crowded blocks near the house.

Every one was thinking of what their life had been, of the intense, beautiful devotion each to the other, of what a tender, chivalrous lover-husband he was.

It was impossible to think of this and then of the scene in that room upon which the thoughts of the whole world were centred without feeling the eyes hot under the lids and a lump in the throat.

In that room it was, for the moment, not the head of the mightiest nation on earth who was dying—it was a husband and lover standing by the dark river and giving the last look of love to that sad, lonely, invalid woman to whom his smile and cheerful words were literally the breath of life.

MRS M'KINLEY AT DYING BED BRAVE THROUGH ALL.

(From a Staff Correspondent.)

BUFFALO, Sept. 13.—Mrs. McKinley was with the President much of the time to-day. Gently as he could, Dr. Rixey broke the bitter news to her early in the morning.

The physicians decided during the night that she should not be awakened. But with the morning, when hope was all but gone, Dr. Rixey went into Mrs. McKinley's room and told her the truth.

No one knew how strong she could be. Mrs. McKinley braced herself visibly and asked to see the President. [illegible]

She was there but a moment. Mr. McKinley was very weak, but conscious. They smiled at each other for a moment, and Mrs. McKinley bent over the bed to whisper a few words.

Then she walked away. During the morning Mrs. Lafayette McWilliams called and had a few words with her cousin. The afternoon drive was omitted, though Mrs. McKinley was perfectly composed.

"We did not wish to let Mrs. McKinley leave the house at this stage," said Secretary Cortelyou.

During the afternoon all the women members of the McKinley family arrived at the Milburn house. They were Mrs. McWilliams, Mrs. [illegible], Mrs. Barber, Miss Mary Barber, Miss Helen McKinley, Mrs. [illegible] and Mrs. Abner McKinley.

When hope fell with the eventide Mrs. McKinley was once more summoned to the bedside of her husband. Dr. Rixey told her about all there was [illegible]. She bore up bravely, but those about her feared that the effort was supreme.

Again, at 8.30 P. M., the President asked for her. He had been [illegible] for a long time, but for the moment he was himself again.

The nurse led Mrs. McKinley in. Then the attendant withdrew with Dr. McBurney, who had been there for nearly an hour.

"It's the last flickering of the lamp before the light goes out," he whispered, shutting the door silently.

A moment later husband and wife were speaking softly together. Mr. McKinley was very sad and weak then, but Mrs. McKinley was very brave.

[illegible] had she left the room when the President lapsed [illegible] Mrs. McKinley was [illegible] of this.

"No [illegible] have been given [illegible]," said Mr. Cortelyou. "She knows the truth, just [illegible]"

[illegible]

Direct to Exposition Grounds. [illegible]

COPYRIGHT·1900·BY·G·G·ROCKWOOD·N·Y.

THEODORE ROOSEVELT,

who in the event of President McKinley's death will become the twenty-sixth President of the United States.

PLANS FOR FUNERAL WILL DEPEND ON FAMILY.

(Special to The World.)

WASHINGTON, Sept. [illegible]

When the Cabinet is fully advised it will be expected [illegible]. These arrangements will probably be made in Buffalo.

The general opinion here is that the President's body should be [illegible] to Washington for a state funeral, and that it should lie in state [illegible]. These are the only suggestions yet made [illegible].

It is stated that the wishes of the President's family will be [illegible] to any [illegible].

[illegible] Mrs. McKinley [illegible] consulted about every detail. Mrs. McKinley's [illegible] responsibility.

[illegible]

VICE-PRESIDENTS PROMOTED BY DEATH OF PRESIDENTS.

Vice-Presidents.	Presidents.	Cause of Death.
TYLER.	HARRISON.	NATURAL.
FILLMORE.	TAYLOR.	NATURAL.
JOHNSON.	LINCOLN.	ASSASSINATION.
ARTHUR.	GARFIELD.	ASSASSINATION.

THE LAST WORDS OF WILLIAM M'KINLEY.

"Good-By. All Good-By. It Is God's Way. His Will Be Done," He Whispered as He Sank into Unconsciousness—Had Chanted from "Nearer, My God, to Thee."

Buffalo, Sept. 13.

"Good-by all, good-by. It is God's will. Let His will, not ours, be done." These were the last words spoken by President McKinley.

His last words addressed directly to his wife were:

"God's will, not ours be done."

[illegible] unconsciousness he murmured lines from the hymn "Nearer, My God, to Thee."

Finally he said:

[illegible]

Just after he was shot [illegible] in the Emergency Hospital he was [illegible] words before he sank [illegible] unconsciousness [illegible] the influence of anaesthetics were:

"Thy kingdom come, Thy will be done."

Lingers in Unconsciousness for Many Hours After All Resources of Medical Science Are Exhausted and Fails to Respond to the Strongest Stimulants, Even Oxygen Being Given Without Effect.

MRS. M'KINLEY'S FAREWELL A LONG AND MOURNFUL ONE.

President, Aware of His Approaching End, Is Calm and Resigned, and Tells Those About Him that He Acquiesces Cheerfully in the Divine Will and Is Sure It Is Ordered for the Best.

(Special from a Staff Correspondent.)

MILBURN HOUSE, BUFFALO, N. Y., Sept. 14.—President McKinley passed away at 2.15 A. M.

In one of his conscious moments, when the administration of oxygen brought him back for a moment to knowledge of his surroundings, he feebly asked to see Mrs. McKinley. She was brought into the room, but the President again lapsed into a stupor. A little later he again revived, and this time was able to recognize his wife.

Their farewell was long and unutterably sad.

After Mrs. McKinley was led from the room the members of the Cabinet were admitted one by one for a last look at their chief.

Some went no further than the door.

Senator Hanna knelt beside the President's bed in an agony of grief and begged in vain for a sign of recognition. In the rooms below awaiting the dread summons were Mrs. Barber and Mrs. Duncan, the President's sisters; Miss Mary Barber, Mrs. McWilliams, Mrs. McKinley's cousin; John G. Milburn, John N. Scatcherd, Harry Hamlin, Secretary Cortelyou and a number of others.

As the night passed and the President still lived his vitality astonished the physicians. All that science could do for the patient had been done, and at last even oxygen failed to have perceptible effect. Yet the fluttering heart-beats told that life was present.

At one time when the President's mind wandered he begged the physicians to let him die. Then he lapsed into unconsciousness that bid fair to continue until the end.

At 1 A. M. President McKinley was barely alive. His breathing was scarcely discernible. His pulse had practically stopped and his extremities were cold. But he was still alive and the doctors were not able to say whether minutes or hours would mark the continuance of his period on earth. He had been unconscious since about [illegible] P. M.

Dr. Mann and Dr. Janeway, the heart specialist, who arrived at midnight from New York, were with him.

Dr. Janeway concurred with the other doctors that there was no hope. Whether artificial restoratives were still being administered could not be learned.

At 1.30 an attendant came from the house and said the President's pulse had shown practically no activity in four hours. There was only a slight heart beat. All the doctors were still upstairs, near at hand to the patient.

BUFFALO, Sept. 13.—The last stage was in two parts, from 3 P. M. yesterday until 2 P. M. to-day, and from 5 P. M. to-day onward.

Yesterday morning, with the full consent of all the doctors in attendance, a considerable quantity of food was given to the President, including a cup of coffee and a piece of toast that had been dipped in chicken broth.

About 3 o'clock the President complained of a feeling of uneasiness in the stomach and his pulse and temperature began to disturb the doctors. The unsatisfactory conditions steadily but very slowly increased until all the doctors saw that they had made a grave blunder in giving him food.

There was nothing to do but get rid of it, as it would not digest, but would lie and undergo chemical changes that would certainly kill him. So a cathartic was administered, one of the most powerful of cathartics, a mixture of oil and calomel.

Feared Result of Desperate Methods.

For several hours the doctors hardly dared to contemplate the consequences. But presently Mr. McKinley began to revive and the improvement continued hour after hour until they began to congratulate themselves that the error which they had committed as physicians to the imperilment of their splendid achievements as surgeons would not have serious results.

This hope continued until Mr. McKinley fell asleep, and all at the Milburn house settled for the night.

At 2 o'clock came a rude awakening.

The President's heart, which had been a river of strength from the beginning, suddenly collapsed. The nurse on the watch suddenly saw him begin to gasp for breath in what seemed to her to be a death struggle.

She called the doctors in wild alarm and almost a panic ensued.

It was evident to the doctors that Mr. McKinley was actually dying.

The most powerful restoratives were applied and all the skill of the doctors was used to meet this attack from a wholly unexpected quarter, for it was without any warning whatever that the enemy suddenly transferred his assault from the digestive organs to the heart.

After a long battle the physicians were at last able to take a breathing spell. Mr. McKinley rallied, and after a period of exhausted consciousness fell into a deep sleep which lasted several hours.

The question now arose: Was this heart failure the result of the coffee and toast and the cathartic, or was it evidence of a new and dangerous complication?

While this question was under debate the afternoon was wearing on, and on several trains several eminent physicians were speeding toward Buffalo.

Conditions Better than Expected.

The President seemed to be doing fairly well, far better than the alarmed doctors had hoped. [illegible] readings of pulse and temperature went they were [illegible] favorable [illegible] the experiment with coffee and dipped toast. A few hopeful bulletins were issued, and men coming away from the Milburn house said:

"He has a fighting chance and he is a brave man."

Then came another [illegible]. Toward 5 o'clock the enemy savagely attacked in a new quarter, the lungs. Mr. McKinley suddenly began to breathe sharply.

The physicians were instantly on the alert. But before they had time to do anything his respiration had risen until he was lying gasping like a

The San Francisco Earthquake

At 5.13 on the morning of April 18 1906 the earth beneath San Francisco shuddered. Its first violent fit of rage lasted 48 seconds. Then it quietened, only to tremble in spasms throughout the day that dawned over a city in ruins. Within minutes of the first upheaval, conflagrations were spreading over more than eight square miles of the most densely-built land in the world, indiscriminate and unstoppable. The city's water supply had disintegrated, the city's fire chief lay dying beside his wife amid the wreckage of his home. A nightmare had begun: cemeteries opened up their graves, lunatic asylums disgorged their inmates into the night, the streets filled with stunned and helpless families. As the fires took hold, landmarks disappeared and melted in the furnace: the ruins of City Hall, the Grand Opera House, Union Square, the *Call's* skyscraper building, the Palace Hotel and on inexorably towards Nob Hill where money, for once, was as impotent as the muddy trickle that oozed out of the fire-hydrants. The

fire was no respecter of property or persons: actor John Barrymore mingled with the poorest inhabitant of Chinatown, as did novelist Jack London and Enrico Caruso (insofar as an opera star could mingle). William James observed the panic — and the selflessness — with philosophic detachment. After the first day the American papers conservatively estimated the death-toll at over 1,000 (an exaggeration, as it turned out). For three days the fires raged, seemingly oblivious to the puny explosions that demolished miles of streets in an effort to contain them. Then on the evening of the 20th the blaze came under control at the foot of Telegraph Hill, and the city gasped back to life. As a sign of the unquenchability of San Francisco's spirit, the city's devastated newspapers had contrived to re-publish as early as the 19th — an extraordinary four-page bulletin entitled *The Call-Chronicle-Examiner*. And for once it had some *really* sensational news to report.

Weather Forecast: FAIR.

An Industrious Incubator!
3,968 WORLD WANTS YESTERDAY.
More Than same 1,511 Day Last Year.
907 More Than Any Other New York Newspaper.
WATCH WORLD WANTS WORK WONDERS WHILE YOU WAIT.

The World.

"Circulation Books Open to All."   "Circulation Books Open to All."

Weather Forecast: FAIR.

"His Fortune."
A Story in a Picture.
FREE
With Next Sunday's World.
ANOTHER CHARLES DANA GIBSON DRAWING.

VOL. XLVI. NO. 16,313.   Copyright, 1906, by the Press Publishing Company, New York World.   NEW YORK, FRIDAY, APRIL 20, 1906.   PRICE ONE CENT in Greater New York and Jersey City. TWO CENTS outside of Greater New York and Jersey City and on trains.

GENERAL VIEW OF THE RANGE OF THE EARTHQUAKE AND VIEWS AND BUILDINGS IN THE PRINCIPAL TOWNS.

GOLDEN GATE PARK, WHERE TENTS WILL BE PITCHED FOR THE HOMELESS.

HOTEL DEL MONTE, MONTEREY.

VIEW FROM CITY HALL at SAN JOSE.

SAN LUIS OBISPO.

SANTA MARIA.

HALL OF RECORDS, OAKLAND.

COURT HOUSE at STOCKTON.

SANTA BARBARA CHANNEL.

HOTEL POTTER, Santa Barbara.

CAPITOL BUILDING AT SACRAMENTO.

50 MILES

FIRES YET RAGING LAY ALMOST ALL THE CITY OF SAN FRANCISCO IN ASHES.

Flames Sweep Into the Wealthy Residence District, Destroying the Magnificent Mansions on Nob Hill, but It Is Believed the Worst Has Now Been Seen.

GREATEST DANGER THREATENING IS FROM THE LACK OF PROVISIONS.

Miles of Houses Dynamited in an Attempt to Check the Fire—300,000 Persons Made Homeless—Property Damage Estimated at $250,000,000—Hosts Camp in the Parks and Unoccupied Districts, and Many Flee the City—Loss of Life May Exceed 1,000.

The situation at 3 A. M. to-day is as follows:

1. San Francisco is a heap of ashes.
2. The property loss is placed at from $250,000,000 to $300,000,000.
3. A conservative estimate places the loss of life at 1,000, but this number may be increased, in fact, the present estimate is mere guess work.
4. More than twenty cities and towns other than San Francisco have been destroyed in part or in whole.
5. The property loss in outside places is estimated at $30,000,000.
6. The loss of life in outside places is estimated at 800.
7. The people made homeless exceed 300,000.
8. The only public or semi-public building standing in San Francisco is the United States Mint.
9. A slight tremor shook the Pacific coast yesterday from San Francisco to Los Angeles without doing great damage.
10. Measures for relief were undertaken by the nation, States and cities. More than $3,000,000 was raised.

(Special to The World.)

SAN FRANCISCO, April 19.—While the entire business section of this city is in ashes, and the best part of the residence district destroyed, the belief grew strong to-night that the worst had been seen. The fires that had devastated the city were believed to be burning themselves out.

Three distinct areas of fire were still raging at 10 P. M., but they were growing feebler. One was in the territory that extends from Nob Hill easterly toward the water front. It was travelling slowly northerly toward the Telegraph Hill section, and it was thought would die out from lack of material, or be turned toward the extreme water front.

The second centre was in the Mission district. Here the fire had reached Eighteenth street, but was making little headway toward the hillsides to the west, where thousands of people were camped.

The Most Dangerous Fire.

The third and most dangerous fire was that threatening the western part of the city. This was a continuation of the Nob Hill fire. It was wedge shape, with the apex pointing toward the west. This was the blaze against which the firemen bent their greatest efforts. Dynamite was used for back firing, but not with marked success.

Many blocks will be blown up, and the hope was strong that this fire might be checked.

The greatest danger now menacing the 300,000 homeless people is the lack of provisions. The water supply is also scant. It was announced to-night, however, that to-morrow there would begin a daily delivery of 10,000,000 gallons of water.

To-night, for the first time since the earthquake, direct telegraphic communication was re-established between San Francisco and the outside world. By the most energetic efforts in the face of great obstacles, the Postal Telegraph Company succeeded in restoring one of its shattered lines, and its managers were hopeful of bringing back its service to normal in a day or two.

The fire spread everywhere to-day, borne by an ever-changing wind. The section of the city west of Van Ness avenue, which contains the homes of the wealthy, was fired at 6 o'clock to-night. The district was soon surrounded by flames and could not be saved.

From noon until 6 o'clock soldiers, police and firemen demolished the splendid homes on the easterly side of the broad avenue with dynamite and black powder.

They carried the devastation for a distance of one mile, under orders from Mayor Schmitz and the Council and Gen. Funston.

Buildings were still toppling under the dynamite when the flames leaped across the area of destruction, and the district that a million dollars' worth of property had been destroyed to save was doomed.

300,000 Are Now Homeless.

The Deputy Chief of the San Francisco Fire Department got out the following bulletin:

"At 7.30 to-night the fire was still under headway, gathering force

PANIC IN LOS ANGELES FOLLOWS TWO SLIGHT EARTHQUAKE SHOCKS.

Men, Women and Children Ran to the Parks Fearing the Buildings Would Fall—Business Abandoned and the City in Anxiety Fearing Fate That Befell San Francisco.

(Special to The World.)

LOS ANGELES, Cal., April 19.—Two slight shocks of earthquake were felt here soon after noon to-day. Tall buildings swayed a little, windows rattled and chandeliers moved. No damage was done. At any other time little attention would have been paid to such a disturbance, but owing to the San Francisco disaster people became terror-stricken and for one hour the city was in a panic.

The shocks came about six minutes apart and lasted only a few seconds. They were followed by occasional faint tremors that died away after an hour.

So great is the fright that business was suspended generally for the remainder of the day. In every home to-night there is fear and trembling. Many people are remaining out of doors, apprehending a renewal of the shocks during the night.

Fled in a Wild Panic.

When the quaking began at noon large crowds were gathered around bulletin-boards eagerly reading the news from San Francisco. As the ground trembled beneath their feet they were paralyzed with terror for a moment. Then panic seized the throngs. Men, women and children ran blindly about, fearing that tall buildings would fall on them. From stores, office buildings, factories and homes thousands more fled toward open spaces and parks.

When it was found that the earth had quieted and no damage had been done there was a cautious return. Every nerve of the city is on edge, and the slightest disturbance would be the signal for another panic.

G. E. Franklin, head of the United States Weather Bureau in this city, in his report of the earthquake, ten minutes after it occurred, said:

"There was nothing at all unusual in the shock. It was hardly sufficient

(Continued on Third Page.)

More Than $3,000,000 Raised Yesterday for Relief Fund.

More than $3,000,000 cash was raised throughout the nation yesterday for the San Francisco sufferers. The principal contributors in this city and elsewhere were:

John D. Rockefeller	100,000	Florence Roberts	1,000
New York Stock Exchange	100,000	Bartlett, Frazer & Carrington	1,000
Clarence H. Mackay	100,000	Standard Oil Co.	
Ladenburg, Thalmann & Co., the United Railways Investment Company, Patrick Calhoun, Sydney Shepard, and Ford, Bacon & Davis	50,000	United States Steel Corporation	
Carnegie Hero Fund	25,000	Nixon, of Nevada, stopping in	
Morris K. Jesup	25,000	Dick Bros. & Co.	1,000
Brown Bros. & Co.	10,000	John A. Drake	1,000
August Belmont	10,000	E. Seligsberg & Co.	1,000
J. & W. Seligman & Co.	10,000	A. Cammann & Co.	1,000
J. Henry Smith	10,000	Flatbush Trust Company	1,000
H. E. Huntington	10,000	Richard Lounsbery	1,000
H. G. Otis	10,000	Representative W. S. Greenfield (Illinois)	1,000
Robbins Dry Goods Company	10,000	Nathaniel Wheeler	1,000
Members of local councils of Knights of Columbus		Bridgeport of Columbus Trust Company, Long Island	
W. J. Rothschild & Bro., Los Angeles, through amusement business	10,000	Johnston, North & Co.	1,000
		Carter Commission Co.	1,000
		Senator Stephen B. Elkins	1,000
Mrs. Phœbe Hearst	5,000	John M. Chapman Co.	1,000
Mrs. Collis P. Huntington	5,000	Carl C. Hoadley & Co.	1,000
W. K. Hearst	5,000	Congress appropriation	1,000,000
Charles M. Schwab	5,000	Chicago is pledged to raise	1,000,000
George J. Gould	5,000	Sacramento	
North British and Mercantile Insurance Company	5,000	Providence, R. I.	15,000
Mrs. John W. Mackay	5,000	Trenton, N. J.	5,000
H. H. Macy & Co.	5,000	Sioux City, Iowa	
C. A. Canfield	5,000	Pittsburg, Pa.	30,000
Consolidated Stock and Petroleum Exchange	5,000	Portland, Ore.	80,000
Bliss, Fabyan & Co.	5,000	Tacoma, Wash. 50 tons of supplies and	
Cornelius B. Bliss	5,000	Seattle, Wash.	
Charles Stewart Smith	5,000	Indianapolis, Ind.	
New York National Exchange Bank	5,000	Boston, Mass.	
Austin, Nichols & Co.	5,000	Philadelphia, Pa.	
Wolf Bros. & Co.	5,000	Detroit, Mich.	
J. E. Hagan	5,000	Oakland, Cal.	
Dowager Duchess of Marlborough, formerly Mrs. Hammersley	5,000	Syracuse, N. Y.	
Harman Ridder	5,000	Atlanta, Ga.	
Enoch Morgan's Sons	5,000	Claus Spreckels	25,000
Steinway & Sons	5,000	Rudolph Spreckels	25,000
Sutro Bros.	5,000	Harry Tevis	
Vice-President Fairbanks		L. J. Flood	
		Commercial Club of Montgomery, Ala.	
Harper Bros.		French Ambassador	
		Atlantic City	
		J. & W. Seligman & Co.	
B. F. Baruch			

Disaster Cost 1,845 Lives and $283,180,000 in Property.

In the following list of California cities, towns and villages blighted by earthquake and fire the casualties and damages reported as to each are estimated from the most conservative reports:

City, Town or Village.	Population.	Damage.	Casualties.
San Francisco	345,000	$250,000,000	1,000 +
Oakland	70,000	500,000	5 +
Alameda	17,000	400,000	?
San Jose	35,000	3,000,000	50 +
Agnew (State Hospital for Insane)	800	400,000	275 +
Palo Alto (Stanford University)	5,000	5,000,000	3 +
Napa	3,000	2,000,000	None
Suisun	5,500	250,000	?
Hollister	1,500	200,000	?
Vallejo	8,000	40,000	?
Sacramento	30,000	25,000	?
Redwood City	1,800	30,000	?
Port Richmond (Terminal of Santa Fe RR.)	400	?	?
Suisun	1,000	50,000	?
Santa Rosa	7,000	800,000	500 +
Watsonville	3,000	70,000	?
Monterey	2,500	25,000	?
Loma Prieta	300	?	4 +
Stockton	18,000	40,000	?
Brawley	500	100,000	?
Santa Cruz	7,000	150,000	Conflict'g
Gilroy	2,500	100,000	?
*Healdsburg	1,900	Reports conflicting.	
*Cloverdale	1,000	Reports conflicting.	
*Geyserville	500	Reports conflicting.	
*Hopland	600	Reports conflicting.	
*Ukiah (State Hospital for Insane)	2,000	Reports conflicting.	
Totals		$283,180,000	1,845 +

*Indicates probable greater loss of life.
*Note—The last five towns are reported wiped out; $20,000,000 would not cover property loss.

SOUTHERN PACIFIC TRAINS RUNNING.

The Southern Pacific Railroad Company received information at its New York offices yesterday afternoon that trains were running from San Francisco down the peninsula toward San Jose. Refugees were being handled as speedily as possible.

The company's station at Third and Townsend streets, San Francisco, while damaged, was not destroyed, and was

being used as a terminus.

A despatch from Sacramento said that the Southern Pacific repaired its tracks and telegraph lines south of San Francisco yesterday and resumed traffic in the afternoon between Sacramento and Oakland.

1.25 P. M. Saturday Special to Atlantic City.
April 21 and 28, via Pennsylvania Railroad Buffet parlor cars and coaches. Special train of parlor cars and dining car on coaches leaves Atlas or City for New York at 4.30 P. M. Sundays, April 22 and 29. Stop at Newark in each direction.

Trustbusted

The Anti-Soap Trust Campaign

Once he had been persuaded that sufficient women in Britain had become sufficiently cultured to read a newspaper, Alfred Harmsworth decided in the summer of 1903 to reward them with one of their own, to be called *The Daily Mirror*. It emerged from Carmelite House, in a haze of lavender water, on November 2. By the following February Harmsworth was obliged to inform his public: 'Some people say that a woman never knows what she really wants. It is certain she knew what she didn't want. She didn't want *The Daily Mirror*'. Yet he was not too downcast, for in the meantime he had conducted his own Night of the Long Tweezers, sending his female newsmen home in hysterics and transforming the paper into a *Daily Illustrated Mirror*, with photographs on the front page and a considerably more virile constitution. In the first month it put on well over 100,000 in circulation. Its senior stablemate, *The Daily Mail*, continued to be the wonder of the Half-penny Press galloping from one campaign to the next, from Mixed Bathing to the Export of Horses for Sausagemeat. No-one was surprised when later in 1904 Alfred was translated into Sir Alfred (and eighteen months later into Lord Northcliffe).

But even for a Baron good campaigns were hard to come by. On the other side of the Atlantic, it was well-known that the new American President was running a jolly exciting campaign of his own against the monopolistic combines which appeared to be flouting the Anti-Trust Laws. He had already had notable success against the Railroads and the Meat Packers and was about to pit his Administration against the might of Standard Oil and American Tobacco. The newspapers, riding in the wake of the Muckraking era, were getting a great deal of footage out of it all. In Britain Northcliffe searched hopefully for signs of 'this most odious form of modern tyranny'. He believed he detected them in *The Times*' new Book Club; he thought he caught a scent of an incipient Cocoa Trust; but he would stake his fortune there was a Soap Trust brewing. He very nearly did.

Maybe Soap wasn't in the same class as Oil or Railways, but a trust was a trust, and there was a highly suitable villain of the piece in William Lever whose rise had been as meteoric as Northcliffe's. He had started, as *The Daily Mirror* delighted in pointing out, as a grocer and in 1886 had turned his attention to soap manufacturing. The success of his many brands (including Lux and Vim) was epitomised in the new and beautiful garden city he had just laid out at Port Sunlight — dedicated to his top-seller. At the fifth attempt he had succeeded in becoming an MP, and was by no means an inconsiderable man to pick a quarrel with.

Northcliffe, of course, did not hesitate. Lever was up to something, gathering other manu-

The Daily Mirror

THE MORNING JOURNAL WITH THE SECOND LARGEST NET SALE.

No. 933.   Registered at the G.P.O. as a Newspaper.   SATURDAY, OCTOBER 27, 1906.   One Halfpenny.

THE SOAP KING, MR. WILLIAM HESKETH LEVER, M.P.

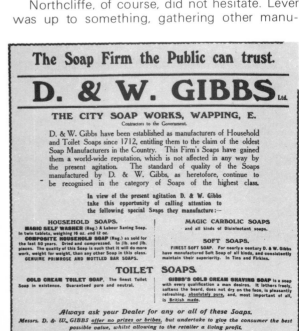

SOAP BUBBLES.
CARTOONISTS' VIEWS OF THE "SHORT WEIGHT TRUST."

POOR WOMAN: Please, Mr. Soap Trust, isn't this pound an ounce short?
MR. SOAP TRUST: Well, what are you going to do about it? You may think yourself lucky I let you live. I'm boss of the situation, and no one else can make soap except me, and I'll put as few ounces in the pound as I like and raise the price to what I like, and if you don't get out I'll call the police.

[From the "Daily Mirror."]

YANKEE BRAND—"WON'T WASH."
UNCLE SAM: "Bravo, Sonny! That's a boy after my own heart."
JOHN BULL: "Well he's not after mine, and I hope his bubble 'll burst."

[By special permission of the Proprietors of "Punch."]

THE GREEDY SOAP TRUST.
The greedy Soap Trust begins its operations by taking one ounce from every pound of soap, threatening to raise prices and discharging its employees. Its next move should include a further reduction in the weight of its pound, a lowering of wages, and an attack on the profits of the retailer.

[From the "Daily Mirror."]

SIGNOR SOAPO TRUSTI, THE CLUMSY MAGICIAN.
"Ladies and gentlemen.—This is the most wonderful trick in the world! I take this pound of soap, weighing sixteen ounces, and remove two ounces without you noticing the difference. I also raise the price and you don't know it, as I do it so cleverly. Then again—" (Loud cries of "Fake!" "Cheat!" "Robber!" "Give us our money back!" etc., etc.)

[From the "Daily Mirror."]

2¼ lbs. made
by the "Trust"
for 8½ d.

not made by
the "Trust"
2½ lbs. for 8d.

BEST PRIMROSE
J. J. NORMAN, MT RADFORD.

Grocers are displaying various ingenious devices in their windows warning their customers not to buy trust soap. The above is shown in Exeter, bearing the legend : "2¼lb., made by the trust, for 8½d." ; "Not made by the trust, 2½lb. for 8d."

In Alexandra-street, the principal thoroughfare of Southend-on-Sea, a grocer aroused great interest by displaying boxes of "15oz. Sunlight Soap," with a notice that it was refused and was "going back to Lever."

facturers around him as a 'protection' against the recent rise in the price of raw materials and to cut down on costs. But that in itself did not constitute a Trust. And when, in September, Lever and others began to cut down drastically on Press advertising, Northcliffe might not like it but he had to lump it. But when (as an alternative to raising the price of a 1lb. bar of soap to 8½d) the 'trust' firms began selling 15 oz bars for the old price of 8d, Northcliffe waded in with all his papers. He printed lists of 'Non-Trust' soap firms and enjoined his readers to buy only from them; his leaders inveighed against this American 'revival of feudalism', this American disease; even his news items fulminated against 'trust arithmetic', for what were such fine distinctions between fact and comment when the nation's economic soul was at stake?

THROTTLING THE SOAP TRUST.

Traders All Over the Country Refuse to Sell Trust Goods —More Dismissals from "Port Moonshine."

In ringing tones *The Daily Mirror* and *The Daily Mail* conscripted small shopkeepers up and down the country to their cause, asking to be kept informed of all short-weight brands, issuing propaganda placards (post free) and recording the retailers' righteous indignation in endless interviews. To be sure one or two of them pointed out that Lever Bros had originally informed shopkeepers of what they were doing and had printed the fact on the inside of their cartons (so as not to disturb the design, it was said), but many were carried away on the tide of conspicuous public-spiritedness, and awoke in the morning to find their window displays featured in *The Daily Mirror*.

Non-Trust firms made a virtue out of their predicament by inserting large advertisements on the front page of the *Daily Mail* very much in keeping with that paper's tone. But it still rankled with Northcliffe that so much other revenue had gone down the sink — he is said to have approached Lever unofficially offering a truce in return for the restoration of advertising. Lever, naturally enough, refused. The next day *The Daily Mirror* uncovered a dastardly plot:

SOAP TRUST'S SINISTER METHODS.

Latest Move Is to Buy the Press by Vast Advertising Campaign—"Notorious, London."

For two solid weeks readers were regaled with the cartoonists' visions of the hell-pit that was 'Port Moonshine', with predictions of huge redundancies,

WORKLESS THROUGH THE SOAP TRUST.

"25 Per Cent. More Profit" May Throw Out 3,000 Workers.

"CHEERFUL, LONDON."

and with the slightly alarming news that soap was bad for you anyway:

HOW TO WASH WITHOUT SOAP.

Methods of Disregarding Soap Trust's Influence Described.

SODA BATHS.

Before long, they had discovered brands selling 2 even 2½ oz below the pound and grabbed them by the throat unmercifully:

WATSON'S "MATCHLESS BLUFF."

Trust Soap Tablets Are Now 2½oz. Short of the Pound —Lever's and Watson and Co. Still United.

The whole thing was getting rather out of hand. Anonymous letters (in *The Evening News*) were being printed without a thought for the consequences; any news, from anywhere, which supported the Anti-Trust Campaign was bundled into the paper — including the earth-shattering item that The West Wales Lunatic Asylum had decided not to ask for any tenders from any trust firm.

After two unrelenting weeks Trust firm sales (not surprisingly) had dived so disastrously, along with their shares, that the restoration of the 16 oz bar was publicly announced, *as well as* a reduction in price. And that should have been an end of the matter, except that for *The Daily Mail* this was just another example of:

SOAP TRUST EFFRONTERY.

PLOT TO PURCHASE THE PRESS.

IMMENSE FALL IN TRUST SALES.

NEW TRUST CIRCULAR.

TEMPORARY CUT IN PRICES.

GREAT LONDON MEETING.

The price-cuts, it believed, would be only temporary — it was a well-known gambit of American Trusts and not to be taken seriously. And so the campaign continued. In due course, the soap manufacturers' combine disbanded itself, to the trumpeting of *The Daily Mirror* proclaiming a triumph of the British Lion over the Greedy Soap Trust, and most people in the country soon forgot which brand they were not supposed to have bought in the bad old days.

But the reckoning was still to come. In July 1907 Mr. Lever's libel suit against *The Daily Mail* and *The Evening News* came up at the Liverpool Assizes. The case got only as far as the third day and the cross-examination of William Lever, before the newspapers' own counsel threw in the towel. Commenting on the settlement of damages at £50,000 the judge couldn't refrain from adding 'if I had been called upon to deal with these articles, and there had been nothing more to justify them than what appeared from the cross-examination of Mr. Lever, I should have felt it my duty to express myself in no measured or hesitating language as to the character of these articles'. By the time all the claims of other aggrieved firms had been settled *The Daily Mail* and *The Evening News* (*The Daily Mirror's* case had not yet come to court) had paid out nearly a quarter of a million pounds. If nothing else it was a tribute to their immense resources.

The Race to the Pole

Commander Peary at the North Pole

The New York Herald had been thinking. It was nearly two years since the world had heard from Dr. Frederick Cook and over a year since there had been any news of Commander Robert Peary. Both of them were bent on the same goal, the undiscovered North Pole, though their declared routes were as different as the men themselves. Dr. Cook, a seasoned ice explorer but flamboyant and impulsive, was determined to make the dash for the Pole (that laborious, tortured slog over the ice-tops was invariably a 'dash' to the newspapers) in the middle of the black Arctic winter — unprecedented in polar exploration, but typical of the man's devil-may-care attitude. As for Peary, he was the veteran of the Arctic. No man alive knew more about those desolate regions than he. Seven times he had tried for the Pole and failed, but each attempt had brought him closer to his life's ambition and prepared him more thoroughly for his next assault. He had planned to batter his way by boat to Cape Sheridan and 'dash' from there before the summer ice-floes made the journey impossible.

It was now the end of August 1909, and both men had been away from their permanent bases longer than either had thought necessary to attain their objectives. So it seemed a reasonable question to ask: 'Have America's Explorers Discovered the North Pole?' as *The New York Herald* enquired on Sunday the 29th. There was not long to wait for an answer, it turned out. Three days later a cable from Cook in the Shetland Islands arrived in *The New York Herald's* office announcing that he had 'indeed reached the top of the world. It was especially pleasing to *The New York Herald* that it should have been Cook, for the paper had $20,000 invested in the exclusive serial rights to his story. At once it cleared its front page in anticipation of Cook's fuller account which he'd left with the Danish Consul at Lerwick, but it left room for an injured paragraph complaining at other newspapers' attempts to steal its scoop and to issue dire threats against anyone who succeeded.

However what *The New York Herald*, in its hour of triumph, had no control over was the wave of scepticism which greeted its news on September 2. The English Press in particular was most unfriendly.

Philip Gibbs, the London *Daily Chronicle's* roving reporter, actually sneaked an interview with the explorer before he reached Copenhagen and returned from it astonished at Cook's vagueness and dissatisfied with the few facts he had elicited. On the other hand there were more than enough eminent authorities quite ready to take the Doctor at his word, not least the Danish Establishment who, after all, knew a bit about Polar exploration and were giving Cook a hero's welcome. What if he was being a little laggard in publishing his papers? There were plenty more front pages for that.

Through all this *The New York Times* had been frightfully sporting, considering they held the rights on Peary's story: they devoted no less than three pages to Cook's achievement. Only in its editorial was a note of doubt allowed to creep in — 'Has Man Reached The Pole?' it wondered rather less than ingenuously. On September 6, though, *The New York Times* got its consolation prize: a cable from Peary at Indian Harbour in Labrador. It said 'I have the Pole April 6 (1909)'. Together with another sporting cable from Cook who had been told the news at a reception in Copenhagen ('Glad Peary did it. Two records are better than one') it splashed the good tidings over (almost) all its front page on the 7th. It was gratifying, too, to be able to report that Peary's version had been instantly accepted all over the world.

But there was a bigger sensation to follow. That same week *The New York Times* received a confidential message from Peary saying

THE NEW YORK HERALD.

NEW YORK, WEDNESDAY, SEPTEMBER 22, 1909.—TWENTY-EIGHT PAGES.—BY THE NEW YORK HERALD COMPANY.

DR. COOK IS WELCOMED HOME BY A HUNDRED THOUSAND VOICES AND A CLAMOR FROM THE WAR SHIPS OF MANY NATIONS

HERE IS THE NORTH POLE AS IT WAS PHOTOGRAPHED BY DR. COOK, ITS DISCOVERER—PROBABLY THE MOST REMARKABLE PICTURE EVER TAKEN.

AT THE POLE APRIL 21ST, 1908, DR. COOK PHOTOGRAPHED HIS ESKIMO COMPANIONS STANDING ON EITHER SIDE OF THE STARS AND STRIPES

OLD GLORY FARTHEST NORTH APRIL 21ST 1908

Mighty Throng Shouts Its Belief in Achievement of Returning Explorer

Greeted First by His Wife and Children, Who Were Taken on a Special Tug to Meet the Steamship Oscar II.

LIFTED BY EAGER HANDS TO EXCURSION BOAT, WHERE HE IS FORMALLY WELCOMED

Progress Up the Bay to Pier in Williamsburg Marked by Deafening Greeting from Vessels and the Multitudes on Shore.

POLICE UNABLE TO HANDLE CROWD IN BROOKLYN

HE who first stood upon the apex of the world, Dr. Frederick Albert Cook, was welcomed home yesterday amid a demonstration of popular confidence and enthusiasm without a parallel in the history of this city.

Hundreds of thousands acclaimed him as the Hero of the North from the moment he left the deck of the steamship Oscar II, on which he arrived from Copenhagen, until he had completed his triumphal journey through streets filled for miles by cheering throngs.

For him a flotilla of peace shrilled stentorian salutes and from the waters of the rock walled Hudson the sirens of a foreign fleet of war sounded in noisy greeting.

He came back from the conquest of the north, this simple, unaffected man of science, to find himself the central figure of an ovation, yet he bore his honors with such modesty and dignity, with such an absence of rancor against the one who had publicly attacked his claims, that the good opinion of his fellow citizens was enhanced tenfold.

He announced that he had brought with him irrefutable proof of his right to the title of the discoverer of the North Pole, that he was ready to meet Commander Peary at any time, and that he would give his data and observations to the scientific world as soon as they could be properly classified and arranged.

His quiet and earnest manner, his complete sinking of self in his joy at once more being with his family and friends and his generous backer, Mr. John R. Bradley, contrasted strangely with the record of daring achievement which has crowned him with the laurel of victory. Over his shoulders his admirers had thrown a wreath of white roses, which he wore throughout the rush of ceremonies in his honor. He carried the decoration shyly, almost awkwardly, at first, and soon forgot it in his pleasure in the many signs of esteem and affection with which he was surrounded.

Those who knew him best found him little changed. He is a trifle thinner than he was when he went away two years ago on his search for the goal of the explorers, but the rest of the last month has almost restored him to his abounding health and vitality.

His face is bronzed by the glare of the sun on ice and sea, with a ruddiness beneath the skin which comes and goes. He was attired in a plain suit of black of a distinctively foreign cut and he wore a black derby hat.

His manner was easy and confident and so free from anything which even suggested the theatric that it is not until one calls to mind how this man won the fight which resulted in the loss of so many noble lives amid the Arctic floes that the full significance of the achievement of Dr. Frederick A. Cook is recognized.

The multitudes who followed him yesterday or crowded together to hear the sound of his voice beheld in him a realized ideal, for he stood for American pluck and endurance and for manly dignity. His praises were heard everywhere throughout the city and his exploits were upon every tongue.

In the Upper Bay Dr. Cook was transferred to the tug John K. Gilkinson, which had come to meet him with his wife and children and his kin from whom he had been so long separated. After the reunion he was claimed by the public and from the deck of the tug was the focus of scores of cameras and the target of half a hundred interviewers.

Then came the steamboat Grand Republic with the delegation of the Arctic Club of America, to which he was taken to be hailed by the survivors of many an expedition within the Arctic circle and their friends.

Here, on behalf of the city and of Brooklyn, the returning explorer was hailed by the president of the transport of the borough, Mr. Bird S. Coler. One wreath was flung over his shoulders and others were ready if he could have stood their weight, and then followed a prolonged period of greeting and of handshaking, from which the hardy toiler among the Arctic snows emerged with fingers cramped and benumbed.

After that came the trip up the Hudson River, named for an intrepid explorer whose fate the frozen North has ever held. Every craft in the harbor voiced a welcome as the stream was ascended to Claremont and the staccato greetings came from the men of war lying at anchor awaiting the Hudson-Fulton celebration.

Around the Battery, close to the Brooklyn shore, the enthusiasm of the masters of vessels found expression in a diapason of sound which sent the echoes flying to Hell Gate.

Brooklyn next turned host, and her citizens by the thousands crowded about the landing at South Fifth street as the discoverer of the pole disembarked and was whirled in an automobile through the streets he knew so well, followed by several hundred flag decked cars.

It was in his home borough, where he had toiled to success over many obstacles, that the regard and affection of those who knew him best found expression in every form. Men, women and children for more than four miles had pressed to the curb for hours. Thousands of boys and girls of the public schools, with eager faces upturned and eyes kindling with enthusiasm hailed the man who had planted the Stars and Stripes at the spot where east and west and north ceased to be.

It was for these especially that Dr. Cook had hearty greetings and kindly smiles. He bowed and waved his hands and the children repeated his name in their shrill voices and cheered until long after he had disappeared from view.

Festoons of banners hung upon a homely little building which to those who know the history of Frederick A. Cook is as a fane to the early struggles through which he started on his road to achievement. It was the milk store in Red Hook avenue which, in his youth, the man who passed it yesterday, crowned with international honors, established to forward his efforts to obtain an education. Here he had had a milk route which took his time in the early hours of the morning, and from its profits he was able to pay for instruction which brought him his medical degree.

From medicine his attention was turned to other forms of science and then to exploration in strange lands and in polar seas.

And beyond, in Bushwick avenue, was another mark in the life journey of Dr. Cook, the house where he lived and where he had his office as a physician. It was decked with the national colors, and in front of it was a triumphal arch bearing upon it scenes from the polar regions and topped with a terrestrial globe. Or it the legend "We believe in Cook" expressed the faith which Brooklyn has always had in the explorer who for years has dwelt within her gates.

To bring to a close the crowded day was the reception at the Bushwick Club, surrounded at all hours by thousands; a dinner in the evening and at last the return to Dr. Cook's Manhattan headquarters, the Waldorf-Astoria.

Brings Proof That Will Convince Every One of His Discovery, He Says

Data and Observations Will Be Submitted to the Scientific World as Soon as They Can Be Classified.

HOLDS HIMSELF READY TO REFUTE THE CHARGES OF COMMANDER PEARY AT ANY TIME

Was the Lion on Board Ship During the Voyage Home and Won All on Board by His Frank and Sincere Attitude.

MRS. COOK GETS HER SHARE OF THE CHEERS

DR. COOK AMAZED AT STRENGTH OF THRONG WHICH WELCOMED HIM HOME

Two Hundred Thousand Persons Line Route of Automobile Parade and the Change from Arctic Solitude Is Almost Overwhelming

Vivid impressions of the sight of hundreds of thousands of faces seen in the course of the reception to him last night filled the mind of Dr. Frederick A. Cook at the conclusion of his day of welcome. To one accustomed to polar solitudes the change was almost overwhelming, and as he spoke of the experience he referred to the faces as an ever changing sea.

It is not often in this world that such a reception has been tendered to one man. There were two hundred thousand persons along the line over which travelled the automobile in which Dr. Cook and his family were seated. Bedford, Bushwick and Willoughby avenues were traversed for a distance of more than four miles, and every block was thronged with friends and admirers of the distinguished explorer. They had come not to see a pageant, for the automobiles which followed were merely the escort, and the gaze of the people was concentrated on the second conveyance in the line, in which sat Dr. Cook.

Small boys surrounded it, and only once in a while did the police escort disperse them, and not then until after they had

LONDON APPLAUDS PEARY'S EXPLOIT

Instant Acceptance of His Report a Contrast to Skepticism Toward Dr. Cook.

HAD AWAITED HIS VERDICT

Admiral Nares Thinks It Peculiar That the Announcements Should Come So Close Together.

Special Cable to THE 'EW YORK TIMES.

LONDON, Sept. 6.- The news that Commander Robert L. Peary had reached the north pole was made known throughout London by late editions of the evening papers, which displayed the brief announcement under headlines which suggested none of the reservations with which the reports of the discovery by Dr. Cook have been received.

In marked contrast with the skepticism with which Dr. Cook's reports were printed is the immediate and whole-hearted acceptance of Peary's dispatch. Nothing could snow this better than a comparison of headlines upon the two announcements.

A Difference in Headlines.

"North pole reached by Peary. Official news that the American flag was hoisted April 6, 1909." That is the way in which Commander Peary's dispatch is presented to its readers by a London paper which headed Dr. Cook's report as follows: "The north pole reported discovered. American explorer's statement."

With the general public a similar readiness to accept Commander Peary's statement is strikingly apparent and bears out the saying frequently heard here recently to the effect that had it been Commander Peary instead of Dr. Cook who had come forward with a bare announcement of the discovery of the pole not a single voice would have been raised in question. It is a testimony to Commander Peary's high reputation as a man and an explorer that the world accents his word without a shadow of hesitation.

Had Awaited Peary's Testimony

Mr. Peary's announcement is hailed with peculiar satisfaction, because, throughout the controversy that has been raging in the last few days, it has been stated again and again that Mr. Peary's testimony would settle the question definitely. "Peary will know the truth," it was said. Thus, Peary is the witness for whom the whole world is waiting. There was a consensus of opinion among the people with whom I talked to-night that if Commander Peary contests the claims put forward by Dr. Cook, the latter will find it an extremely difficult task to establish his pretensions to be the discoverer of the pole, even should the "proofs" which he is now withholding prove to be as good as he says they are.

Cook Expects Confirmation.

Dr. Cook, on being informed in Copenhagen to-night of the news from Mr. Peary, said:

"I hope it is true, for Peary's reports will confirm all my claims."

An arctic explorer to whom to-night I showed Mr. Peary's message to THE NEW YORK TIMES, saying, "I have the pole," made the comment that Mr. Peary, by implication, denied any other claim to the honor of discovering the pole, and that, consequently, it was to be inferred that the confirmation which Dr. Cook expects from Mr. Peary is hardly likely to be forthcoming.

Peculiar Coincidence, Says Nares.

Sir George Nares, who led the arctic expedition of 1875-6, when interviewed to-night with regard to Commander Peary's message announcing the discovery, said:

"It is difficult to avoid the conclusion that Commander Peary's Eskimos at Etah must have known that Dr. Cook had crossed Smith's Sound and passed Etah last Winter to reach Ellsmere Land. Dr. Cook, then," continued the Admiral, "gets down from his Eskimo headquarters at Annotook to Upernavik by a Greenland route never before traversed, passing all the sea glaciers in Baffin Bay just in time to catch a Danish Government vessel which leaves Upernavik early in the year before the whaling vessels are due.

"My first impression was that Dr. Cook had got hold of Commander Peary's Eskimos in some way or other and ought to have communicated either with Commander Peary or with the Eskimos at Etah.

"The question now arises how it comes about that Cook and Peary announce at practically the same time the discovery of the north pole. Is it not a peculiar fact that this coincidence takes place, in view of the possibility of news having reached Etah of the success of one or the other of the men?"

Capt. Scott of the exploring ship Discovery stated to-night that Commander Peary's message put it beyond doubt that the Stars and Stripes was the first flag to fly at the north pole.

The Proper Witness Arrives.

"Just at the very moment when men were saying that only the evidence of an independent witness who had himself visited the north pole could estab-

Continued on Page 2.

GREAT BEAR SPRING WATER.
10c. per case of 6 glass stoppered bottles.—Adv.

In order not to miss The New York Times of to-morrow, in which will be printed exclusively Lieut. Peary's own story of his discovery of the North Pole, order a copy from your newsdealer early to-day.

COOK GLAD PEARY REACHED THE POLE

Unmoved When, Wreathed with Flowers at Banquet, He Hears the News.

HOPE NOW FOR OTHERS

Believes More Expeditions Will Reach the Pole Within the Next Ten Years.

COPENHAGEN, Sept. 6.—Copenhagen was electrified to-night by the report of Commander Peary's announcement that he had reached the north pole. Dr. Cook was immensely interested and said:

"That is good news. I hope Peary did get to the pole. His observations and reports on that region will confirm mine."

Asked if there was any probability of Peary's having found the tube containing his records, Dr. Cook replied:

"I hope so, but that is doubtful on account of the drift. Commander Peary would have reached the pole this year, probably, while I was there last year. His route was several hundred miles east of mine. We are rivals, of course, but the pole is good enough for two.

"The fact of two men having reached the pole along different paths," continued the explorer, "should furnish large additions to scientific knowledge. Probably other parties will reach it in the next ten years, since every explorer is helped by the experience of his predecessors, just as Sverdrup's observations and reports were of immeasurable help to me.

"I can say nothing m̶o̶re concerning Commander Peary's success without knowing further details, than that I am glad of it."

While Dr. Cook was conversing casually this morning with some friends, a possibility of the dénouement which electrified the world to-day was laughingly suggested. Dr. Cook remarked:

"It is quite possible that Peary will turn up now. He is about due to get back if he carries out his plans."

Those who have had the best opportunities to become acquainted with Dr. Cook here believe that he is not likely to enter into a controversy with Commander Peary.

It is doubtful if history furnishes a more dramatic episode than the breaking of the news to Dr. Cook that Peary had realized the goal of his life's ambition and repeated struggles. Dr. Cook was seated at a dinner, surrounded by explorers and correspondents, in the gilded ballroom of the Tivoli Casino. Around his neck was hung a garland of pink roses, according to the Scandinavian method of honoring heroes, which the explorer wore blushingly and with visible embarrassment. Several speeches, acclaiming him, had been given and repeated toasts to him drunk with clamorous cheers.

Amid this scene a whisper went around that Peary had planted the Stars and Stripes at the pole. Cook was perfectly cool and unmoved. He made a striking speech, in which he paid high tribute to the work of Sverdrup, who sat near, to whose discoveries he largely owed his success; to John R. Bradley, who had financed the expedition; to "the intelligence, endurance, and faithfulness" of the Eskimos who had assisted in the preparations, and those who had accompanied him. The whole story of the expedition, he said, has not come out, and will not come out for some time, nor will it come out in installments, but only when it is completed.

Dr. Cook did not permit the whispers which came to his ear of Peary's success to move him in the least, but when he had finished he was surrounded by correspondents who looked for some sign of emotion, but the explorer said smilingly: "I am glad."

Nothing but arctic exploration has been thought of here for the last few days. The people at first refused to believe that such a report as that telling of Peary's success had been received. They thought it must be a canard or a practical joke. The Danish news agency, which received the telegram from London, feared that it had been imposed upon and cabled to London for confirmation before it would circulate the report.

Minister Egan characterized it as one of the most dramatic events of history. The rumor spread that Peary was returning by way of Denmark, and this made an immense sensation. Some questioned the authority of the Peary telegram on the ground that it was improbable that a scientific man would use such dramatic language.

After the dinner to-night Dr. Cook stood about talking with Sverdrup and the other guests in a most unconcerned manner. Later, with the roses still decorating his shoulders, his hosts led him through the Casino grounds to an automobile. A crowd of several hundred, half of the number being women, surrounded and followed him, cheering, but the people were not able to get near enough to shake hands, because of a cordon of police.

View Hudson-Fulton water pageants from DAY LINE Steamers. Send for schedule.—Adv.

PEARY DISCOVERS THE NORTH POLE AFTER EIGHT TRIALS IN 23 YEARS

Notifies The New York Times That He Reached It on April 6, 1909.

HE WIRES FROM LABRADOR

Returning on the Roosevelt, Which He Reports to Bridgman Is Safe.

IS NEARING NEWFOUNDLAND

Expects to Reach Chateau Bay To-day, When He Will Send Full Particulars.

McMILLAN SENDS WORD

Explorer's Companion Telegraphs Sister: "We Have the Pole on Board."

SEVEN VAIN EXPEDITIONS

Many Years Consumed in Learning the Feasible Route—Picked Men Were His Assistants.

Commander Robert E. Peary, U. S. N., has discovered the north pole. Following the report of Dr F. A. Cook that he had reached the top of the world comes the certain announcement from Mr. Peary, the hero of eight polar expeditions, covering a period of twenty-three years, that at last his ambition has been realized, and from all over the world comes full acknowledgment of Peary's feat and congratulations on his success.

The first announcement of Peary's exploit was received in the following message to THE NEW YORK TIMES:

> Indian Harbor, Labrador, via Cape Ray, N. F., Sept. 6.
> THE NEW YORK TIMES, New York:
> I have the pole, April sixth. Expect arrive Chateau Bay, September seventh. Secure control wire for me there and arrange expedite transmission big story. PEARY.

Following the receipt of Commander Peary's message to THE NEW YORK TIMES several other messages were received in this city from the explorer to the same effect.

Soon afterward The Associated Press received the following:

> INDIAN HARBOR, Via Cape Ray, N. F., Sept. 6.—To Associated Press, New York.
> Stars and Stripes nailed to the pole.
> PEARY.

To Herbert L. Bridgman, Secretary of the Peary Arctic Club, he telegraphed as follows:

> Herbert L. Bridgman, Brooklyn, N. Y.:
> Pole reached. Roosevelt safe.
> PEARY.

This message was received at the New York Yacht Club in West Forty-fourth Street:

> INDIAN HARBOR, Via Cape Ray, N. F., Sept. 6.—George A. Carmack, Secretary New York Yacht Club:
> Steam yacht Roosevelt, flying club burgee, has enabled me to add north pole to club's other trophies.
> (Signed) PEARY.

Cipher Shows Authenticity.

The telegram to Mr. Bridgman was sent in cipher. The cipher used was a private one and indicated clearly that the dispatch was undoubtedly from Commander Peary.

Commander Peary also sent a message to his wife at South Harpswell, Me., where she has been spending the Summer.

"Have made good at last," said the explorer to his wife. "I have the old pole. Am well. Love. Will wire again from Chateau."

The message was signed simply "Bert," an abbreviation of Robert, Commander Peary's first name. Mrs. Peary sent a wife's characteristic reply, with love and a blessing and a request for him to "hurry home."

By a strange coincidence, Mrs. Frederick A. Cook, too, was in South Harpswell, Me., when she received the first news from her husband.

Peary's Companion Reports.

Two messages were received in this country also from Donald B. McMillan, who accompanied Peary. Mr. McMillan was an instructor in mathematics and physical training at the academy in Worcester, Mass., until the close of school last year, when he obtained a leave of absence of two years to go on the Peary expedition.

In addition to his message to Dr. D. L. Abercrombie, Principal of the academy, Mr. McMillan sent the following to Mrs. W. C. Fogg, his sister, who is Postmistress at Freeport, Me.:

> Indian Harbor, Sept. 6, 1909.
> Mrs. W. C. Fogg, Freeport, Me.:
> Arrived safe. Pole on board. Best year of my life. BEN.

Follows Cook's Report Quickly.

These messages, flashed from the coast of Labrador to New York and thence to the four corners of the globe while Dr. Frederick A. Cook is being acclaimed by the crowned heads of Europe and the world at large as the discoverer of the north pole, added a remarkable chapter to the story of an achievement that has held the civilized world up to the highest pitch of interest since Sept. 1, when Dr. Cook's claim to having reached the "top of the world" was first telegraphed from the Shetland Islands.

The two explorers, Dr. Frederick A. Cook and Commander Robert E. Peary, both Americans, had been in the arctic seeking the goal of centuries, the impossible north pole, whose attainment has at times seemed beyond the reach of man. Both were determined and courageous, and both had started expressing the belief that their efforts would be crowned with success.

Peary the Better Known.

Peary was well known to both scientists and the general public as a persistent striver for the honor of reaching the "farthest north." Dr. Cook, on the other hand, had held the public attention to a lesser degree. He made his departure quietly and his purpose was hardly known except to those keenly interested in polar research.

Then suddenly, and with no word of warning, a steamer touched at Lerwick, in the Shetland Islands, and Dr. Cook's claim to having succeeded where expedition after expedition of the hardiest explorers of the world had failed was made known. Dr. Cook's announcement was that he had reached the pole on April 21, 1908.

Three days later Dr. Cook arrived at Copenhagen and received a welcome such as no explorer had ever received before.

Peary Announces Success.

Five days after the receipt of the Lerwick message, almost to the hour, came the sensational statement from Indian Harbor, Labrador, that Commander Peary also had been successful on his third expedition to the coveted goal, the date being April 6, 1909.

He filed his brief messages and continued on his way to the south, leaving the world to marvel at a dramatic situation such as has seldom been recorded —the double achievement of a purpose that for almost ten centuries had baffled the endeavor of man and had taken many an explorer to his death in the frozen north.

It is almost certain that Commander Peary did not know of Dr. Cook's announcement when he sent his messages from Indian Harbor.

Under ordinary circumstances Commander Peary's announcement would have evoked world-wide interest, but the existing conditions conspired to add many times to the importance of his communication.

According to Dr. Cook's account of his expedition, he buried the American flag at the pole in a metal tube; Peary's words would indicate that the Stars and Stripes were raised by him and left standing.

How the News Came.

The message from Commander Peary to THE NEW YORK TIMES was received in New York at 12:39 yesterday through the Postal Telegraph Company. It was handed in at Indian Harbor, Labrador, and was sent from there by wireless telegraph to Cape Ray, Newfoundland, and from Cape Ray to Port aux Basques by the Newfoundland Government land lines; thence to Canso, Nova Scotia, by cable, and to New York from there over the lines of the Commercial Cable Company.

PEARY REPORTS TO THE TIMES

ANNOUNCES HIS DISCOVERY OF THE POLE AND WILL SEND A FULL AND EXCLUSIVE ACCOUNT TO-DAY.

Indian Harbor, Labrador, via Cape Ray, N. F., Sept. 6.

The New York Times, New York:

I have the pole, April sixth. Expect arrive Chateau Bay September seventh. Secure control wire for me there and arrange expedite transmission big story.

PEARY.

PEARY'S MESSAGE TO HIS WIFE.

SOUTH HARPSWELL, Me., Sept. 6.—Commander Robert E. Peary announced his success in discovering the North Pole to his wife, who is summering at Eagle Island here, as follows:

> INDIAN HARBOR, via Cape Ray, Sept. 6, 1909.
> Mrs. R. E. Peary, South Harpswell, Me.:
> Have made good at last. I have the old Pole. Am well. Love. Will wire again from Chateau.
> (Signed) BERT.

In replying Mrs. Peary sent the following dispatch:

> SOUTH HARPSWELL, Me., Sept. 6, 1909.
> To Commander R. E. Peary, Steamer Roosevelt, Chateau Bay:
> All well. Best love. God bless you. Hurry home.
> (Signed) JO.

CONFIRMED BY FELLOW-VOYAGER.

> INDIAN HARBOR, Labrador, Sept. 6, 1909.
> Dr. D. W. Abercrombie, Worcester Academy, Worcester, Mass.:
> Top of the earth reached at last. Greetings to Faculty and boys.
> (Signed) D. B. McMILLAN.

DR. COOK CABLES THE TIMES.

To the Editor of The New York Times:

COPENHAGEN, Sept. 6.

Glad Peary did it. Two records are better than one, and the work over a more easterly route has added value.

COOK.

WASHINGTON CREDITS PEARY.

Believes Cook, Too, but Has Said That He Must Produce Records.

Special to The New York Times.

WASHINGTON, Sept. 6.—There was instant acceptance among the geographers in Washington of the assertion in Commander Peary's laconic cable message that he had discovered the north pole. And there was just as ready rejoicing for Peary is popular with the scientific men in the National capitol, and they are ready to take his word at its face value without examination or delay.

In the manner of their acceptance of this announcement of a second discovery of the point that has baffled discovery for so many years there is a sharp contrast to the attitude of the same men toward the announcement from Dr. Cook. Most of them, indeed, accept Cook's assertion, and announce their belief that the Brooklyn man actually did reach the north pole in April, 1908. But there

New York Times September 7, 1909.

COOK'S BEWILDERED STORY OF RETREAT

Miracles of Killing Bears and Birds and of a Hitherto Unmentioned Boat.

ZIGZAGGING FOR MONTHS

Sounded Like a Fairy Dream — Lectures Before Geographical Society and Gets a Gold Medal.

PEARY FOUND NO TRACE OF COOK AT POLE

Members of Crew Surprised When Informed of the Former's Claim.

HIS STEAMER IS DELAYED

Bad Weather Prevents Peary from Reaching Telegraph Lines Till To-day.

RECOGNITION IN LONDON

President of Royal Geographical Society Promptly Cables Congratulations.

BRIDGMAN STARTS NORTH

Will Meet Peary at Sydney, N. S.— Resigns from Committee to Arrange Dinner to Dr. Cook.

PEARY ON COOK.

THE LIE DIRECT.

"NOT OUT OF SIGHT OF LAND."

DR. COOK'S CHANGED PLANS.

THE CASE AGAINST HIS CLAIM.

AMERICAN SCEPTICISM.

As press reports grew more sceptical (left: New York Times, above: Daily Mail), Cooks claims grew even more extravagant (far left The New York Times).

'Cook's story should not be taken too seriously. The Eskimos that accompanied him say he went no distance north. He did not get out of sight of land'. The paper refrained from publishing this, but it did run another one to Peary's wife: 'Don't let Cook story worry you. I have him nailed'. Now it was *The New York Times'* turn to threaten — but fail to obtain — the heavy hand of the Law on poachers. Hearing an injunction to restrain *The World* and *The New York Sun* from publishing Peary's account a New York judge ruled against *The New York Times*, on the basis that the story was in the public interest, that news could not very well be copyrighted and, anyway, Peary had spent a great deal of his own money on the expedition. *The Philadelphia Times* pointed out 'the cornering of the Peary story has served not only to suppress it in considerable measure by limiting the extent of its circulation, but it appears to have aroused considerable hostility towards the explorer himself, who is put in the ungracious position of speculating on the results of his expedition'. *The New York Herald* too couldn't resist adding that its rival had had no compunction in lifting Cook's copyrighted cablegram.

But if the newspapers' incestuous quarrel was getting bitter, so too was the controversy between the two explorers. Peary continued to insist that Cook had been nowhere near the Pole: Cook plaintively demanded to know why every other great explorer's word was believed

except his own. The whole of America began lining up in one camp or the other. When *The Toledo Blade* held a poll on who had discovered the Pole, Cook won hands down 550–10. His arrival back in New York on September 21 was greeted by a hundred thousand cheering fans and a deafening fanfare from every boat on the Hudson River. Declaring he was about to submit data to the scientific world which would convince everyone, he was feted everywhere he went, and obligingly embroidered on his earlier descriptions.

Indeed Peary's stock began to sink pretty low at this point. *The Buffalo Commercial* was of the opinion that 'Dr. Cook is behaving like a man under great provocation: Commander Peary like a very angry and ill-bred child'. It was recalled that he had taken only a black man as companion on his final march because 'he wanted the glory for himself', and that like a bounder he had refused to bring back some of Cook's belongings from the Frozen North. Even his arrival in New York was inauspicious on October 1. He found himself eclipsed entirely by a grand naval parade being held to celebrate the Hudson-Fulton Exposition and, worse still, his brave and battered ship broke down in the middle of it all.

But time was on Peary's side. As the weeks passed nothing materialised to support Cook's claim, no eskimo companions who if they had ever existed had disappeared back into their fastnesses, no mysterious cache of documents

supposedly deposited at somewhere called Annootok. *The New York Times* exhumed Cook's earlier 'discovery' of Mount McKinley and doubted if he'd ever got to the top of that either. Some strange discrepancies in his 'North Pole' photographs were found under closer scrutiny, and a great many unanswered questions about his quoted dates, times and distances. The final discredit came in December when the University of Copenhagen, to whom Cook had submitted his 'papers', rejected them in no uncertain terms and withdrew the honorary degree it had previously presented him. When Cook returned from Denmark after this denouement in December, there were no hordes of supporters waiting to greet him this time, only his relatives. He warranted just three inches in *The New York Herald*, who quoted him as saying he had come back 'solely for the purpose of rehabilitating myself and my family by setting matters right with my countrymen'.

Commander Peary, who had never lacked the support of the scientific world, whatever the general public may have thought of him, in due course had his records fully endorsed by the National Geographical Society. He pronounced himself satisfied, but he might have been forgiven for wondering who in the end had gained most from his discovery, science, himself or the newspapers?

Aeroplane Mania

The Early Aviators

Virginian-Pilot.

VOL. XIX. NO. 68.   NORFOLK, VA., FRIDAY DECEMBER 18, 1903. TWELVE PAGES.   THREE CENTS PER COPY.

FLYING MACHINE SOARS 3 MILES IN TEETH OF HIGH WIND OVER SAND HILLS AND WAVES AT KITTY HAWK ON CAROLINA COAST

Sometimes even the greatest newspapers can be handed a sensational story and fail to recognise it. When, on December 17 1903, Orville Wright pointed his heavier-than-air machine into the wind, took off under his own power and stayed aloft for fifty-nine seconds on the coast of North Carolina, news editors all over America greeted the events with almost universal indifference. Only one paper, *The Norfolk Virginian-Pilot* (the name was a pure coincidence), took the trouble to headline it on the front page. Eight days later *The New York Times* deigned to report that the Wright Brothers wanted to sell what it unflatteringly called their 'box kite machine' to the Government – but without any noticeable enthusiasm. After all, hadn't the assembled Press recently watched Samuel Langley's 'flying machine' dive ignominiously into the Potomac before their very eyes?

Over the next two years Orville and Wilbur steadily improved their performances, yet so unobtrusively that when Santos Dumont bounced a mere 250 yards at Paris in November 1906, the European Press was wildly excited. Lord Northcliffe was especially impressed and upbraided his *Daily Mail* for according the feat only four lines. On the spot he offered a princely £10,000 to the first man to fly from London to Manchester (*The Star* also liked a good joke and offered £10 million to anyone who flew just five miles – which was very rash of it considering the Wright brothers had already done it). After the French aviator Henry Farman had succeeded in flying a circular kilometre in January 1908 – albeit without rising more than 25 feet above the ground – France became the magnet for all aspiring aeronauts. The Wrights transferred their headquarters to Le Mans, and by the end of the year Wilbur had modestly flown nearly 100 miles in one outing. In 1909 the talk was all of the new French monoplane: in June M. Hubert Latham set a new record by flying for over an hour in one; the following month Louis Bleriot won the French Aero Club's prize for flying a monoplane across country in a straight line for 25 miles.

But Lord Northcliffe now thoroughly enthused (he'd even written to the War Minister suggesting he investigate this amazing phenomenon) had a much more spectacular idea. He offered a £1000 for the first flight across the English Channel. On July 19 Hubert Latham made the attempt – only to come down in the sea a few miles off the French coast. He informed the watching world he would try again in a week's time. At 4.30 am on July 25 Latham's mechanic who had been instructed to watch for a break

in the weather saw, to his amazement, a monoplane flying in the direction of Dover. It was Bleriot. Half an hour later he had landed in Northfall meadow near Dover and was announcing to a few half-asleep, astonished locals that now he would like some breakfast. When someone finally dared wake Latham and tell him the news, the poor fellow broke down and sobbed like a child.

In spite of the fact that Bleriot's dawn flight had caught all his reporters asleep, Northcliffe was thrilled and immediately held a celebration dinner at the Savoy. The impulsive Frenchman with his drooping ginger moustache had captured the imagination of the public and – perhaps more to the point – publishers on both sides of the Atlantic. Joseph Pulitzer who had already announced that *The World* was offering $10,000 to the first man to fly from New York to Albany now gave notice that *The Post-Dispatch* would reward the first flight to St. Louis with no less than $30,000. *The New York Herald* sponsored a 'Gordon-Bennett' air speed race, while Hearst's *Journal* attempted to outdo everyone by backing a Paris-Berlin-London jaunt. When *The Daily Mail's* London to Manchester prize was finally won, by yet another Frenchman, in April 1910, Northcliffe immediately slapped another £10,000 in the kitty for a round-Britain race.

There seemed no end to it. For two years the daring, often foolhardy, stunts of the plucky aviators were automatic front-page news. The crowds that flocked to airfields in their thousands gasped at the feats being performed at speeds in excess of forty miles an hour! Or covered their eyes as the flimsy contraptions disintegrated in the herculean effort to get airborne. But for those not lucky enough to see these wonders for themselves, no thrilling detail was omitted from the morning papers; every telegraph pole cleared by fractions of an inch, every modest disclaimer uttered by the flyer as he lurched from his machine to the strains of his national anthem. When the American ace Glenn Curtiss embarked on his attempt for the New York–Albany prize, *The New York Times* hired a special train to convey reporters and cameramen along the aeroplane's route and drop off progress-reports at each station (it was extremely galling for *The World* – who were giving the prize – when the railroad company refused to allow them to hire another special to follow in the wake of *The New York Times*: races in the sky were all very well, but trains were too dignified for that sort of thing). The next day *The New York Times* devoted no less than seven pages to their triumph (and Mr. Curtiss's). When the day dawned for *The New*

York Times' own air-race, from New York to Philadelphia, the newspaper went to endless pains to ensure that the tables weren't turned on them.

It was an expensive form of promotion, but worth every penny. Those papers who couldn't afford such lavish prizes just made do the best they could. The London *Daily Graphic* determined to write another page in the annals of the rather more gentle art of ballooning, by assaulting the world long-distance record. But somehow the gods of the air just weren't on their side (perhaps they were bored by mere balloons). At the first attempt, on March 18 1910, the skies opened up and snowed the whole endeavour under. At the second, on April 20, an enormous hole was discovered in the balloon. When, at the third attempt in November, *The Daily Graphic* balloon sailed proudly into the ether, it was only to descend 12,000 feet in three minutes in a Bavarian pine-forest.

Equally ill-omened was *The Chicago Record-Herald's* attempt to cross the Atlantic in the dirigible *America*, in October 1910. Although the airship was making history by being in radio contact with *The New York Times* (who were sharing the 'story' rights) a passing ship reported that the *America* had been seen depositing something in the sea. Imagining it to be a message-in-a-bottle, or some such thing, *The New York Times* wired its enquiries. It turned out, in fact, that the airship's cat had jumped overboard and had had to be fished out of the ocean. Nevertheless it was the crew themselves who had to be rescued the next day by a passing steamer.

Editors' enthusiasm for aeroplanes remained more or less undimmed, right up to the outbreak of war, though their headlines never quite recaptured that ingenuous excitement of those pioneering years 1909–10. Prizes continued to be put up for every conceivable means of testing man and machine; endurance, navigation, speed, altitude. In 1913 a race around Manhattan was organised to celebrate the tenth anniversary of the Wright Brothers' first flight. The race was won at well under a mile a minute. Even if the newspaper kings had only considered aviation as a circulation booster or little more than a rather dangerous sport (Northcliffe after one experiment promised his mother he would never again go up in a flying machine without her consent) they had stimulated a staggering technical advance. A few of them were even to appreciate the military significance of their munificence a little later on.

HOW I FLEW ACROSS THE CHANNEL: BY M. BLERIOT. (See Page 7.)

No. 6122.—Vol. LXXIX.

LONDON: MONDAY, JULY 26, 1909.

Registered as a Newspaper.

BRAVO BLERIOT!

M. BLERIOT AND HIS MONOPLANE, IN WHICH HE YESTERDAY ACCOMPLISHED THE FIRST CROSS CHANNEL FLIGHT BY A "HEAVIER-THAN-AIR" MACHINE.—THE FLIGHT FROM BARAQUES, NEAR CALAIS, TO DOVER OCCUPIED TWENTY-THREE MINUTES.

315

THE ENVELOPE PARTIALLY INFLATED.—IT CONTAINED 3,000 CUBIC FEET OF GAS WHEN THE PICTURE WAS TAKEN.
YESTERDAY'S PREPARATIONS AT THE CRYSTAL PALACE FOR THE START WHICH, AT THE ELEVENTH HOUR, HAD TO BE POSTPONED. OWING TO THE UNFORTUNATE CHANGE IN THE WEATHER.

SCENES AT THE CRYSTAL PALACE YESTERDAY WHEN, OWING TO A DEFECT IN THE ENVELOPE, THE GREAT BALLOON COULD NOT BE INFLATED.

THRILLING END OF THE "DAILY GRAPHIC" BALLOON EXPEDITION.

THE BALLOON ALIGHTING ON THE TREE-TOPS OF THE PINE FOREST NEAR MUHLHAUSEN, BAVARIA, AFTER DESCENDING 12,000 FEET IN THREE MINUTES. (See pages 9 and 10.)

The Daily Graphic's three ill-fated attempts on the World Ballooning Record in March (top) April (centre) and November (left) 1910.

MR. MOISANT, AMERICAN, WINS STATUE OF LIBERTY FLIGHT BY 43 SECONDS; THREE AERIAL RACERS SOAR OVER BAY

(A) ROUTE FOLLOWED BY COMTE DE LESSEPS AND J.B. MOISANT
(B) ROUTE FOLLOWED BY C. GRAHAME-WHITE

J.B. MOISANT'S BLERIOT IN COLLISION WITH CLIFFORD B. HARMON'S BIPLANE.

COUNT JACQUES DE LESSEPS JUST AFTER HIS FLIGHT.

CORTLANDT F. BISHOP AND CLAUDE GRAHAME-WHITE

MISS LOUISE MOISANT, JOHN B. MOISANT AND MISS TILLIE MOISANT.

Triumph Over English Racer in Face of Seeming Defeat

In Bleriot Monoplane, Purchased for $10,000 When His Own Is Smashed, Daring Aviator Gains the Prize by Narrow Margin.

PLAUDITS OF 75,000 RESOUND AT BELMONT

Aeroplane Battle for Supremacy Witnessed by a Million Persons, Who See Winged Competitors Fly Over the City and the Harbor.

RESULTS OF CONTESTS AT BELMONT

Statue of Liberty Flight.—Won by Moisant, 34:38.84; Grahame-White, second, 35:21.30; De Lesseps, third, 41:56.25.

Hourly Distance.—Won by Latham, 33 laps; Moisant, second, 28 laps; McCurdy, third, 19 laps.

Hourly Altitude.—Won by Simon, 950 feet; Barrier, second, 932 feet; Radley, third, 614 feet.

Special Hourly Altitude.—Won by Latham.

Monoplane Race (10 laps).—Won by Grahame-White, 14:56.60; second, Simon, 16:34.80; third, Aubrun, 16:37.05.

Cross Country Flight (20 miles).—Won by Radley, 20:05.60; Aubrun, second, 21:52.40.

Belmont Park rocked and roared yesterday with an outburst of wild, unconfined enthusiasm that made the memory of its maddest hours on Decoration Day, 1906, seem tame, for Mr. John B. Moisant, American, had won the Statue of Liberty flight after it had passed hopelessly to all appearances to Mr. Claude Grahame-White.

At the last hour, with every chance of an American winning apparently gone, Mr. Moisant climbed into the chassis of a machine he had never entered before, bought for him by his brother from Mons. Alfred Leblanc, and dashing off past the first pylon shot away on a trip that was to end in a demonstration that has never been equalled anywhere in aviation.

The spectacle that followed Mr. Moisant's return and the announcement that he had beaten Mr. Grahame-White by a bare forty-three seconds after covering a distance of seventeen miles across Queens county, Brooklyn, and the harbor of New York and seventeen miles back to Belmont Park, was most dramatic.

Seemed Victory for Briton.

Earlier in the afternoon Mr. Grahame-White had made the thirty-four miles in his 100-horse power Blériot, winning easily over Comte Jacques de Lesseps in his 50-horse power Blériot. The superiority of the 100-horse power motor over the 50-horse power engine had dashed the hopes of all Americans and apparently had given the victory to Mr. Grahame-White beyond chance of loss. There was only one other 100-horse power motor on the field, that belonging to Mons. Hubert Latham, and this had been shown to be hopelessly slow in the huge, boat-bodied Antoinette. The 110-horse

power motor in the biplane of Mr. Charles K. Hamilton was still in the hospital, with no chance of recovery for weeks.

The great crowd of 75,000 persons greeted Mr. Grahame-White with the generous sportsmanlike spirit which marks the American. He was cheered and applauded. The band played "God Save the King," and the officials gave to him cordial greeting in the grand stand.

It was all over in all appearances.

Comte Jacques de Lesseps had started at 5 minutes and 46.95 seconds after 3 o'clock. Mr. Grahame-White had started after him at 8 minutes 47.60 seconds after 3 o'clock. Mr. Grahame-White dashed over the finish line at 44 minutes and 8.9 seconds after 3 o'clock, while Comte de Lesseps followed him in a little more than half a minute, at 44 minutes 48.2 seconds after 3 o'clock. The elapsed time of Mr. Grahame-White was 35m. 21.3s. That of Comte de Lesseps, 41m. 56 1-4s.

Count De Lesseps had taken the direct line across Brooklyn. Mr. Grahame-White had flown over Coney Island. The greater power of his motor had given him the victory over Comte De Lesseps, although he had flown the greater distance.

So far the contest was over. The 100-horse power motor was king.

Grand Climax Thrilling.

Then came the grand, crashing climax, and it was a thing to stir the blood of any man, for this great race in the air must take its place with the greatest classics in the history of sport.

Snatching victory from hopeless defeat, as did Mr. John B. Moisant, will continue to be a theme for the novelist and the dramatist rather than an actuality of every day life.

Nobody had ever thought of the game little aviator from Chicago, who since his trip from Paris to London has held the attention of an entire world. Early in the day his newly built racer, patched from the wreck caused by his fall ten days ago, had been smashed again by a collision with the biplane of Mr. Clifford B. Harmon, and the Chicagoan was apparently hopelessly out of the conflict.

And then from the hangars dashed out a flat plane racin Blériot bearing the number 21 on tail and lower plane, and the bulletin board announced that Mr. Moisant

was about to make the Statue of Liberty flight. It was not satisfying to the crowd, even though the battle seemed hopeless, and when he finished the sheer reaction turned 75,000 men and women into shouting cheering enthusiasts for many minutes.

To the man who was there the recollection of those minutes will come as the taste of rare Falernian wine upon his lips in the days when his blood has chilled and he no longer cares to spend a keen, sparkling autumn day watching a great sport.

Winning of Forlorn Hope.

The story of the great victory and the winning of a forlorn hope by an American after an English racer had been admitted really began early in the afternoon.

Mr. Moisant had been entered as a contestant in the Statue of Liberty flight early in the aviation meet and the morning was spent by him in getting into shape the racing Blériot which had been rebuilt for him by the Lovelace-Thompson Company. When it was apparently in perfect shape and ready for a flight he rolled it out, mounted into his seat and set his whirring Gnome motor in motion.

In the infield, in front of the Moisant hangar and far inside the red flags marking the field, lay the great, wide winged Farman biplane of Mr. Harmon. It had been used by Mr. Grahame-White and having suffered some trifling damage had been left there for the workmen to repair, instead of being wheeled into the hangar, as the rules of the field required.

When Mr. Moisant gave the word his Blériot shot forward, but, fortunately for him, did not leave the ground. The rudder jammed, and, dragged forward by the swiftly revolving Gnome motor and its propeller, the monoplane whirled off in a wide half circle and, striking the biplane, ripped the port wing and part of the tail off the Harmon machine and tore away a part of the port wing of the monoplane.

By anybody else on the field the accident might have been accepted with hopeless resignation, but Mr. Moisant does not resign himself easily to misfortune. The racing Blériot he had brought with him had been smashed before the meeting opened and the passenger carrying Blériot with which he had made his trip from Paris to London had had its wings broken off on Sunday a week ago when he had gamely tried to get into the air at a time when the wind was blowing thirty-five miles an hour. Mr. Moisant is not the sort of man who accepts a mishap as a defeat.

Offer to Buy Machine.

As Mr. Moisant jumped from his machine to the ground his brother, Mr. Alfred J. Moisant, ran to meet him.

"I'll buy you another machine if you can find one, no matter what it costs, Johnny," he cried. "You find a machine we can buy, and I've got a check book and a fountain pen."

Mr. Alfred J. Moisant owns a bank in Central America and a few gold mines and things of that sort. He wears a gold nugget as big as an egg and a long string of gold nuggets as big as filberts for a watch chain and there isn't a dollar

in his possession that his little brother can't have for the asking.

"Crank her up, Fred. I know where I can get a machine," said Mr. Moisant, of Chicago, as he climbed into his brother's automobile, and in true Chicago fashion he dashed off to the hangar of Mons. Leblanc.

"Fill those tanks with gasolene," he said to the French mechanicians, "and paint 21 on the tail and lower plane of that machine. Tune it up and have it ready when I get back."

"But, monsieur," cried the mechanicians in chorus, "it is the aeroplane of Mons. Leblanc."

"But it won't be in twenty minutes," said Mr. Moisant, the elder, "for Mons. Leblanc is going to sell it to me for my brother."

With wondering looks the mechanicians set to work filling the oil tanks and painting the Moisant number on the Leblanc Blériot, a new machine just out of the factory, while the Moisant brothers dashed off across the field to the grand stand.

There Mr. Alfred Moisant called Mr. Leblanc from his bed in the Knickerbocker Hotel, where he had been ordered by his physician to remain in order to recover from injuries suffered the day before when he knocked a section out of a telegraph pole in his splendid attempt to win the international trophy. Mr. Leblanc could hardly grasp the proposal that was being put up to him by the Moisant brothers.

$10,000 to Win for America.

"Fifty thousand francs outright for the machine and a bonus if we win," cried Mr. Alfred Moisant into the telephone. It was a large offer, for Blériots of this type sell in France for $7,000, and to Mons. Leblanc was being offered $10,000.

"Make it stronger if he wants it," said Mr. John B. Moisant. "I think I can win back the $10,000 and we'll pay the remainder for the privilege of winning for America."

And a short time after he had won the $10,000 prize and had paid for the machine within three hours after its delivery to him, which is really one of the best parts of the story.

Mons. Leblanc permitted himself to be persuaded into parting with his Blériot, but not until after Mr. Moisant assured him that no other French aviator had a chance to win.

Long before Mons. Leblanc reached Belmont Park the great race for the $10,000 prize offered by Mr. Thomas Fortune Ryan was on. Comte de Lesseps rolled his 50-horse power Blériot out from its hangar, took the air and circled around the field and passed between pylon No. 4 and the judges' stand. Then he dashed off around pylon No. 5 and straightened out on the long trip to the Statue of Liberty.

The great crowd watched as though fascinated the man who was about to undertake a feat never before attempted. The history of aviation has not so far furnished an instance of a flyer crossing over a town of any size, and the danger of flying above a city like Brooklyn is regarded by aviators as almost beyond the bounds of recklessness. A fall means almost certain death.

Almost straight into the west flew the swift winged aeroplane, heading a quarter of a point north. This was the line a straight edge laid on a map would make, and Comte de Lesseps held to it, knew that in following this course lay his only hope of victory.

He went up at five minutes past three o'clock with certain very finely divided seconds added. Three minutes later the Blériot of Mr. De Lesseps, double the power of Mr. De Lesseps machine, shot up into the air. Past pylon No. 1, along the field and around pylon No. 5, on the course that must be followed on the field, he passed the grand stand after turning and headed away after his rival.

His course was not the same, however. Mr. Grahame-White was evidently bound off on the longer course that took him

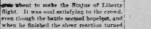

CLAUDE GRAHAME-WHITE ROUNDING THE STATUE OF LIBERTY.

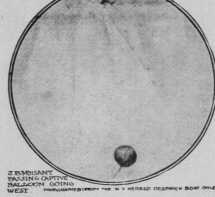

J.B. MOISANT PASSING CAPTIVE BALLOON GOING WEST. PHOTOGRAPHED FROM THE N.Y. HERALD DESPATCH BOAT OWLET.

away from Brooklyn and over Coney Island.

Disappears from Sight.

Quickly the broad wings dwindled into mere patches, then grew smaller and smaller until only the keenest eye could follow and hold them in sight, and then they disappeared against the background of fleecy clouds.

Then the grandstand waited as the hangars waited even less patiently, for the folks around the hangars have the same interest that jockeys and stablemen have in a contest, an interest that is razor edged in its keenness, for it is personal.

Slowly the minutes drifted by as the crowd waited. Gruesome possibilities flocked in the wake of the two racing Blériots, and the crowd did not know whether the next announcement would tell of the rounding of the Statue of Liberty or of the death of the contestants by a frightful fall from the great heights to which they had attained, for both were flying above the two thousand foot line.

A few "supper acts" were put on to keep the crowd entertained, but the tension was growing greater every moment, when suddenly Mr. Peter Prunty, the official announcer, through his megaphone, sent the announcement booming across the crowded grand stand and lawn:—

"The New York Herald reports aeroplane No. 6 and No. 9 as having rounded the Statue of Liberty."

Cheers for the Herald.

The crowd greeted the announcement with loud, resounding shouts and cheers for the HERALD, and then waited expectantly. A few moments later came the announcement:—

"The New York Herald reports aeroplane No. 6 of the Statue of Liberty, headed back to Belmont Park at 3:31."

Then followed a wait of hardly more than eight minutes, and far off to the

southwest Mr. Grahame-White's machine was sighted, headed in, a small speck in the sky. Almost at the same moment the machine of Comte de Lesseps was sighted heading in from the west.

There was no cheering. All eyes were fastened on watches or on the two Blériots racing home. Comte de Lesseps had started first by three minutes, and all were awaiting to see where he would finish.

The agony was not prolonged. Flashing through the air like an arrow, with the swiftly whirring propeller making a silvery blur over the nose of the machine, came Mr. Grahame-White and, greeted by shouts, his Blériot shot across the southwest corner of the old Turf and Field Club, house and across the finish line, high in the air.

A bare thirty-five seconds behind followed the machine of Comte de Lesseps, and on the bulletin board appeared the figures:—

	Grahame-White.	De Lesseps.
Started	3.08 47.60	3.05 46.95
Finished	3.44 08.90	3.44 43.26
Elapsed time	35m. 21.s.	Elapsed time, 41m. 56.45s.

Mr. Grahame-White had done much better than a mile a minute in his one hundred horse power machine, for he had flown more than thirty-five miles in taking the southerly course. He had set a mark apparently impossible for any other aviator at Belmont Park to reach.

Honor English Racer.

The official automobile raced out onto the field as the two machines descended and Mr. Grahame-White in his brown aviator's costume and Comte de Lesseps in his "rompers" of blue jeans were taken into the car and escorted back to the judges' stand. As Mr. Grahame-White was taken up into the stand the band played "God Save the King," and Mr. Grahame-White removed his leather helmet and bowed to all sides.

"He may be an Englishman, but you've got to hand it to him," was the good natured cry that went up from one megaphone voiced man, and the crowd cheered wildly. Mr. Grahame-White never received a greater demonstration or more applause.

"We'd rather have seen an American win,

Speed of Mile a Minute Kept Up for Entire Course

Mr. Grahame-White, Flying Over Coney Island, Covers Longer Route Than Victor in Thrilling Contest.

COMTE DE LESSEPS IN GALLANT STRUGGLE

His Fifty Horse Power Machine Unable to Cope with Rival's —New Record Is Made in Hourly Distance Contest of the Tournament.

PROGRAMME AT BELMONT TO-DAY

1:30 to 3:30 P. M.—Aero Club distance event. Prizes—First, $2,000; second, $1,000; third, $500.

3:30 P. M.—Special altitude prizes. For ascending more than four thousand feet, $500; for making new record for present meet, $500; for making new world's record, $1,000.

5 P. M.—Grand speed prize contests; two sections. First between Messrs. Grahame-White and McCurdy, and second between Messrs. Aubrun and Mars; $1,000 to first and second in each event.

Other special events and prizes contingent upon weather conditions.

HEADLINES 1910-1920

DUBLIN: REBEL BASE BESIEGED.

LONDON: SATURDAY, APRIL 29, 1916.

ONE HALFPENNY.

OVER 100 PEOPLE KILLED AND "HANDS UP!"

THE MUDDLE—

EDUCATIONAL

tunities of all kinds are best sold gh the Classified Advertising Col of San Francisco's best newspaper

HE CHRONICLE

San Francisco Chronicle

LEADING NEWSPAPER of the PACIFIC COAST

SAN FRANCISCO, CAL., THURSDAY, MARCH 16, 1916

XXXX

UNDED 1865

J. S. ARMY BEGINS ITS CAMPAIGN IN M

egimental Colors

Villa Bullets Head Invadin

ALL MERCHANDISE ADVER-TISED IN THE TRIBUNE IS GUARANTEED

New York

HIS BANDIT STAFF

...with his lieutenants are

GENERA

USSIANS RESCUE

Va. LXXIX No. 26,509

Vickers 'Plane Speeds Overseas for I

First to Last — the Truth: News · Editorials · Advertisements

Tri

(Copyright, 1919, New York Tribune Inc.)

SUNDAY, JUNE 15, 1919—NINE PARTS—80 PAGES—PARTS I AND I

BESIEGED BRITISH

British Flyers Ten Hours Out, but Sen

IN MESOPOTAMI

Entente Begins W

Allies Will

Iungary, Frend

The Tragedy of the Antarctic.

Board to End All Building Trade Wars

Clear Sky Wind A

DAILY SKETCH.

ESDAY, FEBRUARY 11, 1913.

THE PREMIER PICTURE PAPER.

[Registered as a Newspaper.] ONE HALFPENNY.

ement With Various ciations of Employ s Announced by ration of Labor

mpath...

The Men

SCOTT AND PARTY PERISH AFTER GAINING THE POLE.

THE NEW YORK HERALD.

NEW YORK, TUESDAY, MAY 16, 1911.—TWENTY-SIX PAGES.—BY THE NEW YORK HERALD COMPANY.

(COPYRIGHT, 1911, BY THE NEW YORK HERALD COMPANY.)

PRICE THREE CEN

STANDARD OIL COMPANY A CONSPIRACY AND COMBINATION IN RESTRAINT OF TRADE, FEDERAL SUPREME COURT DECIDES; EAT TRUST MUST FULLY REORGANIZE WITHIN SIX MONTI

Record in Case Cover Than Twelve Th

THE MORNING POST, TUESDAY, MAY 2, 1916.

MESOPOTAMIA.

TURKISH FLANK MENACED.

IMPORTANT RUSSIAN SUCCESS.

VERDUN BATTLES.

GERMAN EMPEROR AND AMERICA.

The heroic nature of General Townshend's resistance at Kut-el-Amara has met with chivalrous acknowledgment on the part of Veili Pasha, the Turkish Commander-in-Chief, who has allowed him to retain his sword.

Turkish accounts of the surrender, whilst throwing some light upon the privations endured...

Petrograd.

GERMANS HELD IN WOLHYNIA.

Yesterday's communiqué:

Western Front.—In the region of Pulkarn, south-east of Riga, our artillery successfully bombarded an enemy battery. German artillery bombarded the neighbourhood of the railway station and bridgehead of Ükskull.

In one sector of the Dvinsk positions our artillery fire caused a fire in the enemy trenches.

South-west of Lake Naroteh the Germans attempted to debouch from their trenches, but were met by our fire, and were obliged to return immediately.

South-east of the Olyka railway station, on the railway from Rowno to Kovel, the enemy three times attempted to surround and attack the village of Khromiakovo, but were each time repulsed by our artillery, rifle, and machine-gun fire.—Reuter.

Berlin.

THE MORT HOMME BATTLE.

"Western theatre of war.—The situation generally is unchanged. Again yesterday there was vigorous fighting at the height of Mort Homme. Our aeroplane squadrons abundantly bombarded enemy troop quarters west of Verdun and magazines to the south of the town. In an air fight a French biplane was shot down east of Noyon. The occupants were dead."—Reuter.

Turkish Campaign.

RUSSIAN ADVANCE.

TURKS ROUTED WEST OF BAGHDAD.

GUNS CAPTURED.

An official report issued to-day states:

PETROGRAD, May 1.

On the front towards Diarbekr our Cossacks energetically drove back the Turks towards the west.

In the direction of Baghdad we throw back an important enemy detachment towards the west and captured a portion of his artillery and a number of ammunition waggons.—Reuter.

GENERAL TOWNSHEND.

PERMISSION TO KEEP HIS SWORD.

Reports from Constantinople state that the booty taken at Kut has not yet been counted. Amongst the prisoners taken are four Generals, 240 British officers, and 270 Indian officers. The Turkish Chief-in-Command...

United States.

PEACE WITH AMERICA.

THE EMPEROR'S REPORTED DESIRE.

DIRECT APPEAL TO BE MADE.

(FROM OUR OWN CORRESPONDENT.)

WASHINGTON, May 1.

Count Bernstorff has told his friends that the German Emperor will make a direct appeal to the President not to break the traditional friendship existing between the two nations; that, should the United States become a belligerent, it would not hasten the termination of the war now drawing to an end, but would only prolong it; and that the Emperor requested the presence of Mr. Gerard at General Headquarters for that reason, and so that he might outline his views before sending his appeal to President Wilson.

While Count Bernstorff always makes much of the extreme difficulty he has in communicating with his Government because the cable is denied him, it is noteworthy that he always knows, or at least professes to know, what Berlin is doing. Usually his predictions have been sustained, and he has a...

DUBLIN REVOLT ENDED.

AN UNCONDITIONAL SURRENDER.

ANARCHY'S BRIEF REIGN.

A THOUSAND PRISONERS.

WANTON DESTRUCTION BY FIRE.

COUNTRY REBEL COLLAPSE.

OFFER TO SACRIFICE LEADERS.

ful as on any other bright Sund were ringing on all sides, and women hurried through the rid prayer books in their hands. T into the outer world was to chur

NOTABLE BUILDINGS I Not until this morning—save d to the Viceregal Lodge by a circ Friday afternoon—were the ac spondents who came to see anyth morning permitted to see anyth sieged districts. Indeed, with tl this journey to be received by th could not leave their hotel at No. two miles from the centre of Dub information I include in the follo of damage done is the first hand observation.

Sackville-street is an extraordin of wanton ruins The heart of it ha out. Yet the area of the fire smaller than one, after watching housetop a mile away, would have b night, is a wall roofless shell. T massive portico is still upright, w pillars pitted with rifle bullets. H between the Post Office and the bri with bricks and charred wood...

In the Name of the Law

The Hunt for Dr. Crippen

Even in more frivolous times, very likely, that news-vacuum brought about by the approach of high summer which we know as 'the silly season' was a perennial headache for newspaper editors. But in July 1910 the prospects looked even bleaker than usual: in England there was a limit to the microscopic detail that could be spooned out on the new King's daily routine, and that had been reached; in America, national indignation over Johnson's defeat of white heavyweight Jeffries could not be fuelled indefinitely. The summer's staple diet from sportsmen, suffragettes and socialites looked utterly predictable. But into this hiatus stepped unpredictable fate, as fate obligingly does, with gruesome news from Hilldrop Crescent, London.

Number 39 was the residence of an American 'doctor', Hawley Harvey Crippen whose designation apparently covered a variety of activities from dentistry to theatrical management. On July 11 detectives from Scotland Yard called at the house to question Crippen further about his claim that his second wife Cora — better known to the cognoscenti of the music-halls as Belle Elmore — had travelled to America in February and died there in March. Crippen had disappeared: so too had his 'typewriter' (as one paper insisted on designating her) and mistress, Ethel le Neve. But apart from the revolver found in a wardrobe, the house seemed innocent enough. Chief-Inspector Dew, however, was not satisfied. For two days he and his sergeant took the building apart. On the 13th, they reached the coal-cellar. Some of the floor bricks were a little loose, Dew thought, and determined to have the floor up. After four shovelfuls, they reached the quicklime and very soon were digging up neat chunks of dissolving human flesh. By the end they had uncovered much of a body, expertly dismembered: but no pelvis, no limbs or skull, no bones in fact of any description. Nothing that would give a clue to the sex of the victim, so Dr. Pepper the pathologist said. But who could doubt that

these were the mortal remains of Belle Elmore, what was left of her?

Immediately a hue and cry was raised for Crippen and his accomplice. Photographs were published in the press, very ancient ones to be sure but Crippen's drooping Walrus moustache and beady eyes were recognisable anywhere. And they were, of course, recognised everywhere, from Vernet-les-Bains in Southern France where a moustachioed gentleman had suspiciously left a meal unfinished and slipped across the Spanish frontier, to Chicago where the suspect was arrested and had no little trouble in persuading the police he really was Albert C. Rickward. The fugitives, who by now were the leading topic in every popular European paper, were observed all over the continent, including Andorra which had omitted to conclude any extradition treaty with Britain. Miss Le Neve was reported to have committed suicide in Bourges, on the same day as she booked into a hotel in Brussels. William Laird, bearing no resemblance whatever to the alleged murderer, was interrogated for hours by New York police until he succeeded in convincing them he genuinely was an Episcopalean pastor from Birmingham, Pa.

In London, Crippen was spotted purchasing ladies' underwear in a West End women's shop; Le Neve was recognised entering a gents' lavatory in Fulham. The two of them were reported to have taken off in a balloon from a small town on the south coast. For a full week the press joined in the national sport of Hunt Crippen with relish. Enthusiasm was just beginning to wane when, on the 23rd, the captain of a liner in mid-Atlantic sent a momentous radio message to London. He had, he said, seen a photo of Crippen in the *Daily Mail* and he was certain the suspects were on board.

Since Scotland Yard refused at this point to divulge which liner it was, the papers were free to exercise their powers of detection still further. *The New York World* divined it was the Marrion,

bound for Quebec from Antwerp. *The Daily Graphic* insisted it was the Sardinian from Le Havre to Montreal and produced an 'exclusive' account of how Crippen's false eyebrows had come unstuck and exposed his disguise as the Reverend Robinson. *The New York Tribune* favoured the Montrose, sailing from Antwerp to Montreal. And correctly, as it soon became known. Then began a cliff-hanging Atlantic chase, as Inspector Dew boarded the first fast steamer out of Liverpool (the Laurentic) in pursuit of the Montrose.

For a week Crippen's nemesis slowly overtook him unawares, with all the fateful inevitability of a Greek tragedy. To the spellbound publics of two continents the press acted as Chorus interpreting, glorifying and speculating on the events in the drama unfolding in mid-ocean. On July 25, Dew was still 285 miles behind, on board the Laurentic. By the 29th both ships had entered the Gulf of St Lawrence, with Dew just in the lead! Would he get on board the Montrose without arousing the suspects' suspicions (no-one, clearly, was prepared to trust the Canadian Mounties with such a delicate operation, and the arrest had to be made before the boat berthed at Montreal — if only because literally hundreds of reporters were already assembling there).

How was he going to do it? On the 31st the Montrose pulled into the quay at Father Point, Quebec, to take on the pilot — and Dew's cunning strategem was revealed. The pilot in his gold-buttoned uniform, cocking a wise weather-eye at the sky was none other than — Chief Inspector Dew. The decks of the Montrose were curiously empty. At the captain's orders all passengers had been sent below: except one, who had been invited onto the bridge.

Inspector Dew stepped up briskly. All over the world the public held its breath. He tapped Crippen lightly on his right shoulder. 'In the name of the law' he said gravely.

MONDAY   NEW YORK EVENING JOURNAL, AUGUST 1, 1910.   MONDAY

How Inspector Dew of Scotland Yard Proved the Nemesis of Dr. Crippen

| Inspector Dew questions Dr. Crippen in London home. | Inspector Dew's men find body of woman in cellar. | Top—Dew boards Laurentic. Bottom—Dew leaving Laurentic. | Captain of the Montrose reports by wireless that he first noticed disguised girl pressing the hand of Crippen. | Inspector Dew, on board the Montrose, with officers disguised as pilots, identifies the suspects as Dr. Crippen and his stenographer, and orders the Canadian police officials who went with him to arrest the alleged wife slayer and Ethel Le Neve. |

The Daily Mirror

THE MORNING JOURNAL WITH THE SECOND LARGEST NET SALE

No. 2,104.   Registered at the G.P.O. as a Newspaper.   MONDAY, JULY 25, 1910   One Halfpenny.

INSPECTOR DEW'S PURSUIT OF "DR." CRIPPEN AND MISS LE NEVE, WHO, SCOTLAND YARD BELIEVE, ARE FLYING TO CANADA.

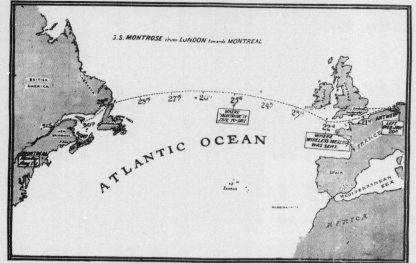

S.S. MONTROSE from LONDON towards MONTREAL

ATLANTIC OCEAN

Chart showing the course of the Montrose from Antwerp to Montreal, with her position day by day.

Inspector Dew.   "Dr." Crippen.   Miss Le Neve.   Sir M. Macnaghten.—(Elliott and Fry.)

So convinced are Scotland Yard that "Dr." Crippen and Miss Le Neve are on board the Canadian Pacific steamer Montrose, bound from Antwerp to Montreal, that Inspector Dew has been despatched post haste to Canada to bring the fugitives back. He left Liverpool on Saturday by the Laurentic. Crippen is said to have entered his name as "Mr. Robinson," while Miss Le Neve was disguised as his son. It was at first thought that the fugitives were on board the Allan liner Sardinian, which left Havre on July 18, and is due to arrive at Montreal on July 29. Sir Melville Macnaghten, whose portrait appears above, is Assistant Commissioner of the Metropolitan Police.

The Daily Mirror

THE MORNING JOURNAL WITH THE SECOND LARGEST NET SALE

No. 2,108.   Registered at the G.P.O. as a Newspaper.   FRIDAY, JULY 29, 1910   One Halfpenny.

"CRIPPEN BEYOND A DOUBT"—YESTERDAY'S WIRELESS MESSAGE FROM CAPTAIN KENDALL, OF THE STEAMER MONTROSE.

Inspector Dew, who will bring back the fugitives.   Captain Kendall, of the steamer Montrose.

Mr. Llewellyn Jones, Marconi operator on the Montrose.   The steamer Montrose, on board which are Crippen and Miss Le Neve.

Miss Le Neve, who accompanies "Dr." Crippen dressed as a boy.   Chart showing the positions of the Montrose and the Laurentic.   "Dr." Crippen, who is now definitely said to be on the Montrose.

A wireless message was received yesterday from Captain Kendall, of the steamer Montrose, which stated that the identity of the suspected passengers on the ship had been established "beyond a doubt." It will be remembered that two passengers who entered their names on embarking on the Montrose at Antwerp as "Mr. Robinson and son" were suspected as being "Dr." Crippen and Miss Le Neve, for whom a world-wide search was being made; and as a result of a wireless message from the captain Inspector Dew, of Scotland Yard, was sent to overtake the suspects on the faster steamer Laurentic.

The Daily Mirror

THE MORNING JOURNAL WITH THE SECOND LARGEST NET SALE

No. 2,109.   Registered at the G.P.O. as a Newspaper.   SATURDAY, JULY 30, 1910   One Halfpenny.

"I AM STILL CONFIDENT CRIPPEN AND LE NEVE ON BOARD": CAPTAIN KENDALL'S WIRELESS TELEGRAM FROM THE MONTROSE.

Programme

VIO & MOTZKI'S
AMERICAN
Bright Lights Company
From the Principal American Theatres.

MACKA MOTZKI

FUN, MUSIC & VARIETY.

Stage Manager .... H. CLARKE
Acting Manager .... H. H. CRIPPEN
Agent in Advance .... C. LUDLOW
Musical Director .... SAVILLE HOWARD
General Manager and Sole Director .... SANDRO VIO

Two photographs of Mrs. Crippen as she appeared on the stage.

Chart showing how the Laurentic has beaten the Montrose.

Cover of a programme with Mrs. Crippen's portrait in the centre.

The programme was issued on the occasion of Mrs. Crippen's first appearance on the stage in England, when, under the name of Miss Macka Motzki, she appeared at Balham in a sketch entitled "An Unknown Quantity." The acting manager, it will be noticed, was H. H. Crippen.

Two points of interest are seen on the above chart. They are Father Point, where the formal arrest of the couple, believed to be Crippen and Le Neve, will take place, and Amour Point, to which was sent the wireless message in which Captain Kendall, master of the Montrose, stated definitely that the suspects were on board his vessel.

The Daily Mirror

THE MORNING JOURNAL WITH THE SECOND LARGEST NET SALE

No. 2,110.   Registered at the G.P.O. as a Newspaper.   MONDAY, AUGUST 1, 1910   One Halfpenny.

END OF THE ATLANTIC CHASE: "DR." CRIPPEN, WHO WAS ARRESTED AT FATHER POINT, CANADA, YESTERDAY.

Yesterday "Dr." H. H. Crippen and Miss Le Neve were arrested at Father Point, Canada, thus bringing to an end the great chase across the ocean, which has provided a detective romance more amazing and more dramatic than ever came from the pen of a Gaboriau. Their capture is a great triumph for wireless telegraphy, which has demonstrated in a new direction its wonderful utility in the service of man. Whatever the outcome of the present case, it has proved the immense potentialities of the invention, which in future will undoubtedly prove a powerful weapon in the armoury of the detective, and a terror to the fugitive from justice. Above is a recent photograph of Crippen, who is alleged to have murdered his wife, Belle Elmore, at 39, Hilldrop-crescent, Holloway.

The Unsinkable Sinks

The Titanic Disaster

April 11, 1912 THE DAILY MIRROR

NARROW ESCAPE OF THE TITANIC, THE LARGEST SHIP IN THE WORLD.

R.M.S. Titanic, the largest ship in the world, came perilously near to being involved in a collision when she left Southampton on her maiden voyage to New York yesterday. As the new White Star liner came abreast of the steamer New York, the ropes which were holding that vessel to the quay began to strain and then snapped. The stern of the New York began to drift round, and a collision seemed inevitable, a few feet only separating the two vessels. (1) A tug going to the assistance of the New York. The Titanic is the vessel with four funnels. (2) An innovation on the Titanic: the interior of the Parisian café. (3) Another innovation: the private promenade deck in connection with a suite of apartments, the charge for which is £850.—(Daily Mirror photographs.)

There was, perhaps, some excuse for American news editors to be frankly sceptical of the A.P. bulletin which landed on their desks at the ungodly hour of 1.00 am on the morning of April 15 1912. It said that the pride of the White Star Line, the liner Titanic, had struck an iceberg at 10.25 and had put out a general call for assistance. After all, several other liners had recently had brushes with the ice-fields floating abnormally far south for the time of the year, and they had all reached port safely. Besides, it was generally agreed that the Titanic, with its well-publicised safety compartments, was unsinkable. And the White Star office in New York was doggedly clinging to that fact, in spite of the SOS and then an ominous silence.

In Britain the day was almost dawning and the last pages had been printed hours ago, but in New York there was still time to catch the final edition — just. But what with? An unconfirmed report that the unsinkable was sinking? The New York Sun decided to dismiss the idea entirely; most other newspapers contented themselves with publishing the bulletin alongside palliatives about the great ship's invulnerability. Alone, in splendid isolation, The New York Times grasped the nettle in both hands by categorically affirming the liner had sunk.

It had been a bold decision, taken by the paper's managing editor Carr Van Anda. For most of that day (Monday) it began to look even bolder than perhaps he'd bargained for,

for a mass of confused and contradictory reports about the liner's fate emerged from the ether. One announced that the Parisian and the Carpathia were in attendance on the stricken ship; another that all the passengers had been safely transhipped; yet another that the Virginian had taken the Titanic in tow. A later message at 4.31 pm (British time) reported that the Titanic was making for the shoal water near Cape Race with the intention of beaching her. And throughout, total silence from the Titanic's wireless.

The White Star Company was hardly more communicative. Just after breakfast in New York it categorically refuted the idea that its ship had foundered. At lunchtime it conceded that all the passengers had been transferred, but there was no information about the extent of damage to the boat. Only that night did it announce that The New York Times had been correct, and indeed that the disaster was worse than anyone had dared fear. The Titanic had sunk at 2.20 am in water two miles deep. The only ship to pick up survivors was the Carpathia, which reported only 866 on board (in fact, there were 706) — that meant that over 1,500 passengers and crew had gone down.

That night's editions carried only a partial list of survivors (and those all first-class). It was difficult to pick out everything the Carpathia's operator was communicating, but it certainly looked as if Colonel Jacob Astor was missing, as was W. T. Stead the former editor of The Pall Mall Gazette (see page 31). There was no news of Millet, the French artist, nor of Major Butt, President Taft's military aide. The true story would not be known until the Carpathia docked in New York on Thursday evening — for since her initial dispatches she had been strangely reticent in forwarding any further information.

Van Anda was determined The New York Times would be there at the dockside in force, to cap Monday's now world-famous coup. He deployed his forces with military precision, reporters to cover every conceivable angle on the great arrival, chauffeurs to ferry men and copy and photographs, telephone operators to hold countless lines open. He hired a complete floor of a nearby hotel as a headquarters, and arranged every conceivable facility to get the stories through by that evening's deadline.

The biggest stumbling-block was that no reporters would be allowed on board until the last survivors had disembarked, and he dearly wanted to interview the Titanic's wireless operator, if he was still alive. There was only one man who could accomplish that: Marconi, the man who had invented wireless in the first place and who still employed all ships' wireless operators at that time. They would surely allow him on board. Van Anda knew Marconi, and prevailed on him to set off for the pier-head at once, to jostle his way through 30,000 frantic sight-seers and to confront the police barrier with the full majesty of his name. Very well, the police reluctantly agreed, Signor Marconi might proceed, but only accompanied by his business manager. It was perhaps as well that business managers were not a distinctive breed, for the man who in fact accompanied Marconi that evening was one of The New York Times' leading reporters, Jim Speers. His story, along with the distillation of many thousands of words filed that night by Times reporters, adorned nearly the whole of the next day's The New York Times. It was all there — the exclusive story of Harold Bride, the ship's one surviving radio operator, and eye-witness accounts of the sinking, of the band lined up on deck playing as she went under, and of the fated passengers singing the Episcopal hymn. With good reason, it was remembered for years after as a most moving account and a journalistic triumph.

The New York Times.

THE WEATHER.
Unsettled Tuesday; Wednesday,
fair, cooler; moderate southerly
winds, becoming variable.
☞ For full weather report: see Page 73.

VOL. LXI...NO. 19,986.　　NEW YORK, TUESDAY, APRIL 16, 1912.—TWENTY-FOUR PAGES,　　ONE CENT In Greater New York, | Elsewhere, Jersey City, and Newark. | TWO CENTS

TITANIC SINKS FOUR HOURS AFTER HITTING ICEBERG; 866 RESCUED BY CARPATHIA, PROBABLY 1250 PERISH; ISMAY SAFE, MRS. ASTOR MAYBE, NOTED NAMES MISSING

Col. Astor and Bride, Isidor Straus and Wife, and Maj. Butt Aboard.

"RULE OF SEA" FOLLOWED

Women and Children Put Over in Lifeboats and Are Supposed to be Safe on Carpathia.

PICKED UP AFTER 8 HOURS

Vincent Astor Calls at White Star Office for News of His Father and Leaves Weeping.

FRANKLIN HOPEFUL ALL DAY

Manager of the Line Insisted Titanic Was Unsinkable Even After She Had Gone Down.

HEAD OF THE LINE ABOARD

J. Bruce Ismay Making First Trip on Gigantic Ship That Was to Surpass All Others.

The admission that the Titanic, the biggest steamship in the world, had been sunk by an iceberg and had gone to the bottom of the Atlantic probably carrying more than 1,400 of her passengers and crew with her, was made at the White Star Line offices, 9 Broadway, at 8:20 o'clock last night. Then P. A. S. Franklin, Vice President and General Manager of the International Mercantile Marine, conceded that probably only those passengers who were picked up by the Cunarder Carpathia had been saved. Advices received early this morning tended to increase the number of survivors by 200.

The admission followed a day in which the White Star Line officials had been optimistic in the extreme. At no time was the admission made that every one aboard the huge steamer was not safe. The ship itself, it was confidently asserted, was unsinkable, and, inquirers were informed that she would reach port, under her own steam probably, but surely with the help of the Allan liner Virginian, which was reported to be towing her.

As the day passed, however, with no new authentic reports from the Titanic or any of the ships which were known to have responded to her distress call for help, it became apparent that authentic news of the disaster probably could only come from the Titanic's sister ship, the Olympic. The wireless range of the Olympic is 500 miles. That of the Carpathia, the Parisian, and the Virginian is much less, and as they neared the position of the Titanic they drew further and further out of shore range. From the Titanic's position at the time of the disaster it is doubtful if any of the ships except the Olympic could establish communication with shore.

Titanic Sank at 2:20 A. M. Monday.

In the White Star offices the hope was held out all day that the Parisian or the Virginian had taken off some of the Titanic's passengers, and efforts were made to get into communication with these liners. Until such communication was established the White Star officials refused to recognize the possibility that there were none of the Titanic's passengers aboard them.

But by nightfall came the message from Capt. Haddock of the Olympic to Cape Race, Newfoundland, telling of the foundering of the Titanic and the rescue of 655 of her passengers by the Cunarder Carpathia, which, the wireless message said, reached the position of the Titanic at daybreak. All they found there, however, was lifeboats and wreckage. The biggest ship in the world had sunk at 2:20 o'clock yesterday morning.

Mr. Franklin admitted late last night that the Parisian and the Virginian, though they were among the first to answer the Titanic's calls for help, could not have reached the scene before 10 o'clock yesterday morning, seven and a half hours after the big Titanic buried her nose beneath the waves and pitched downward out of sight. The Carpathia, so the wireless dispatch from Capt. Haddock to Cape Race announced, reached the scene of the Titanic's foundering at daybreak, several

POLAND WATER preserves Health. Avoids contagion by drinking purest water in world. O.I. 1,189 B'way. Tel. Mad. Sq. 4168.—Adv.

hours before the expected arrival of the Virginian and the Parisian.

It is unbelievable, so White Star Line officials were compelled to concede finally, that the Carpathia should have failed to pick up every lifeboat which still floated on the waves. If they failed to pick up more than 655 passengers, it was because the others of the ship's complement had gone with her to the bottom.

But it was not until nearly nightfall that the extent of the disaster was realized. Before that the reassuring nature of the bulletins issued by the White Star line was sufficient to quiet the fears of those who had relatives or friends aboard the unfortunate ship. Until such reports spread belief in a serious disaster.

Capt. Haddock's message from the Olympic, which is printed in another column of THE TIMES, strongly indicated that none of the 655 taken from life boats by the Carpathia had been saved. This message was re-

First Reported Titanic in Tow.

Throughout the day there had been reassurances that the Titanic was being towed to port by the Virginian.

CHTA CREME HAND SOAP. Instantly removes stains. Large Can 15c. —Adv.

layed immediately to the White Star offices, but Mr. Franklin positively declined to make the text of the message public. He offered still the hope that passengers were aboard the Parisian and the Virginian, and even when the admission was wrung from him that there seemed little hope of the saving of any others than the 655 aboard the Carpathia, he clung to the hope that in some unexplained way there were other passengers aboard the two Allan liners.

Fears Serious Loss of Life.

We have asked for that report from Capt. Haddock, and we are expecting a reply at any time. The Carpathia

GREAT BEAR SPRING WATER. Noted for ease of 6 glass-stoppered bottles. —Adv.

several hundred passengers of the Titanic, is now en route to New York. At 9 o'clock, however, he modified this statement, declaring.

As far as we know the situation, there have been rumors from Halifax that three steamers were at the scene of the Titanic's sinking, namely, the Virginian, the Parisian, and the Carpathia. We have heard from Capt. Haddock of the Olympic, who says that the Titanic sank at 2:20 o'clock this morning. Haddock also informs us that the Carpathia has 675 survivors on board. It is very difficult to say whether the Virginian and the Parisian have any survivors on board until we can get a report from those vessels.

Capt. Haddock of the Olympic sends a wireless message to the White Star offices here that the Titanic had sunk, and that all the passengers and crew had been lowered to life boats and transferred to the Virginian. The steamship Carpathia, with

THE PROBABLE LOSS.

Number Aboard.

First cabin	330
Second cabin	320
Steerage	750
Crew, (estimated)	900
Total	2,100
Saved.	
By the Carpathia	868
Probably drowned	1,254

The Lost Titanic Being Towed Out of Belfast Harbor.

CAPT. E. J. SMITH,
Commander of the Titanic.

PARTIAL LIST OF THE SAVED.

Includes Bruce Ismay, Mrs. Widener, Mrs. H. B. Harris, and an Incomplete Name, suggesting Mrs. Astor's.

Special to The New York Times.

CAPE RACE, N. F., Tuesday, April 16.—Following is a partial list of survivors among the first-class passengers of the Titanic, received by the Marconi wireless station this morning from the Carpathia, via the steamship Olympic:

Mrs. JACOB P. ————— and maid.
Mr. HARRY ANDERSON.
Mrs. ED. W. APPLETON.
Mrs. ROSE ABBOTT.
Miss G. M. BURNS.
Miss D. D. CASSEBERE.
Mrs. WM. M. CLARKE.
Mrs. B. CHIBINACE.
Miss E. G. CROSSBIE.
Miss H. ROEBIE.
Miss JEAN HIPACK.
Mrs. HY. B. HARRIS.
Miss ALEX. HALVERSON.
Miss MARGARET BAYS.
Mr. BRUCE ISMAY.
Mr. and Mrs. ED. KIMBERLEY.
Mr. F. A. KENNYMAN.
Miss EMILE KENCPEN.
Miss G. F. LONGLEY.
Mrs. A. F. LEADER.
Miss BERTHA LAVORY.
Mrs. ERNEST LIVES.
Miss MARY CLINES.
Miss SINGRID LINDSTROM.
Mr. GUSTAVE J. LESNEUR.
Miss GIORGETTA A. MADILL.
Mme. MELICARD.
Mrs. TUCKER and maid.
Mr. J. B. THAYER.
Mr. J. B. THAYER, Jr.
Mr. HENRY WOOLNER.
Miss ANNA WARD.
Mr. RICHARD N. WILLIAMS.
Miss HELEN A. WILSON.
Miss WILLARD.
Miss MARY WICKS.
Mrs. GEO. D. WIDENER and maid.
Mrs. J. STEWART WHITE.
Miss MARIE YOUNG.
Mrs. THOMAS POTTER, Jr.
Mrs. EDNA S. ROBERTS.
Countess of ROTHES.

Mr. C. ROLMANE.
Mrs. SUSAN P. ROGERSON. (Probably Ryerson).
Miss EMILY P. ROGERSON.
Mrs. ARTHUR ROGERSON.
Master ALLISON and nurse.
Miss K. T. ANDREWS.
Miss NINETTE PANHART.
Miss E. W. ALLEN.
Mr. and Mrs. D. BISHOP.
Mr. H. BLANK.
Miss A. BASSINA.
Mrs. JAMES BAXTER.
Mr. GEORGE A. BATT————
Miss C. BONNELL.
Mrs. J. M. BROWN.
Miss G. C. BOWEN.
Mr. and Mrs. R L. BECKW————
Miss RUTH TAUSSIG.
Miss ELLA THOR.
Mr. and Mrs. E. Z. TAYLOR.
GILBERT M. TUCKER.
Mr. J. B. THAYER.
Mr. JOHN B. ROGERSON.
Mrs. M. ROTHSCHILD.
Miss MADELEINE NEWELL.
Mrs. MARJORIE NEWELL.
HELEN W. NEWSOM.
Mr. FIENNAD OMOND.
E. C. OSTBY.
Miss HELEN R. OSTBY.
Mrs. MAMAN J. RENAGO.
Mlle. OLIVIA.
Mrs. D. W. MERVIN.
Mr. PHILIP EMOCK.
Mr. JAMES GOOGHT.
Miss RUBERTA MAIMY.
Mr. PIERRE MARECHAL.
Mrs. W. E. MINEHAN.
Miss APPIE RANELT.
Major ARTUR PEUCHEN.
Mr. KARL H. BEHR.
Miss DESSETTE.

Mrs. WILLIAM BUCKNELL.
Mrs. O. M. BARKWORTH.
Mrs. H. B. STEFFASON.
Mrs. ELSIE BOWERMAN.

The Marconi station reports that it missed the word after " Mrs. Jacob P." In a list received by the Associated Press this morning this name appeared well down, but in THE TIMES list it is first, suggesting that the name of Mrs. John Jacob Astor is intended. This supposition is strengthened by the fact that, except for Mrs. H. J. Allison, Mrs. Astor is the only lady in the " A " column of the ship's passenger list attended by a maid.

NAMES PICKED UP AT BOSTON.

BOSTON, April 15.—Among the names of survivors of the Titanic picked up by wireless from the steamer Carpathia here to-night were the following:

Mr. and Mrs. L. HENRY.
Mrs. W. A. HOOPER.
Mr. MILE.
Mr. J. FLYNN.
Miss ALICE FORTUNE.
Mrs. ROBERT DOUGLAS.
Miss HILDA SLATTER.
Mrs. P. SMITH.
Mr. BRAHAM.
Miss LUCILLE CARTER.
Mr. WILLIAM CARTER.
Miss CUMMINGS.
Mrs. FLORENCE MARE.
Mrs. ALICE PHILLIPS.
Mrs. PAULA MUNGE.
Mrs. JANE.
Miss PHYLLIS O. ————
HOWARD B. CASE.
Miss MINEHAN.
Miss BERTHA ————

Biggest Liner Plunges to the Bottom at 2:20 A. M.

RESCUERS THERE TOO LATE

Except to Pick Up the Few Hundreds Who Took to the Lifeboats.

WOMEN AND CHILDREN FIRST

Cunarder Carpathia Rushing to New York with the Survivors.

SEA SEARCH FOR OTHERS

The California Stands By on Chance of Picking Up Other Boats or Rafts.

OLYMPIC SENDS THE NEWS

Only Ship to Flash Wireless Messages to Shore After the Disaster.

LATER REPORT SAVES 866.

BOSTON, April 15.—A wireless message picked up late to-night, relayed from the Olympic, says that the Carpathia is on her way to New York with 866 passengers from the steamer Titanic aboard. They are mostly women and children, the message said, and it concluded: "Grave fears are felt for the safety of the balance of the passengers and crew."

Special to The New York Times.

CAPE RACE, N. F., April 15. —The White Star liner Olympic reports by wireless this evening that the Cunarder Carpathia reached, at daybreak this morning, the position from which wireless calls for help were sent out last night by the Titanic after her collision with an iceberg. The Carpathia found only the lifeboats and the wreckage of what had been the biggest steamship afloat.

The Titanic had foundered at about 2:20 A. M., in latitude 41:46 north and longitude 50:14 west. This is about 30 minutes of latitude, or about 34 miles, due south of the position at which she struck the iceberg. All her boats are accounted for and about 655 souls have been saved of the crew and passengers, most of the latter presumably women and children.

There were about 2,100 persons aboard the Titanic.

The Leyland liner California is remaining and searching the position of the disaster, while the Carpathia is returning to New York with the survivors.

It can be positively stated that up to 11 o'clock to-night nothing whatever had been received at or heard by the Marconi station here to the effect that the Parisian, Virginian or any other ships had picked up any survivors, other than those picked up by the Carpathia.

First News of the Disaster.

The first news of the disaster to the Titanic was received by the Marconi wireless station here at 10:25 o'clock last night [as told in yesterday's New York Times.] The Titanic was first heard giving the distress signal "C. Q. D.," which was answered by a number of ships, including the Carpathia.

is proceeding to New York direct. We very much fear that there has been serious loss of life, but it is impossible for us to say definitely concerning the sad part of the situation until we are able to reassure ourselves whether or not any of the Titanic's passengers are aboard the Allan liners.

We are hopeful that the rumors which have reached us by telegraph from Halifax that there are passengers aboard the Virginian and the Parisian will prove to be true, and that these vessels will turn up with some of the passengers. It is the loss of life that makes this thing so awful. We can replace the 'money loss,' but not the lives of those who went down.

Another version of the message from the Olympic was current last night and included the sentence: "Loss likely total 1,800 souls." This sentence was not in the message received by THE TIMES from Cape Race nor in that sent to the White Star line offices.

Continued on Page 2.

The New York Times.

THE WEATHER.
Cloudy Friday; Saturday, fair; moderate to brisk west winds.
☞ For full weather report see Page 22.

VOL. LXI...NO. 19,809. • • •   NEW YORK, FRIDAY, APRIL 19, 1912.—TWENTY-FOUR PAGES.   ONE CENT   In Greater New York, Jersey City, and Newark. Elsewhere TWO CENTS

745 SAW TITANIC SINK WITH 1,595, HER BAND PLAYING; HIT ICEBERG AT 21 KNOTS AND TORE HER BOTTOM OUT; 'I'LL FOLLOW THE SHIP,' LAST WORDS OF CAPT. SMITH. MANY WOMEN STAYED TO PERISH WITH HUSBANDS

Rescue Ship Arrives— Thousands Gather At the Pier.

FOUR BODIES BROUGHT IN

206 of the Crew and 4 Officers Are Among Those Rescued.

THREE LIFEBOATS LOST

Two Filled with Women Were Drawn Under and One Was Swamped.

SURVIVORS HURRIED AWAY

Many Among Them Ill as a Result of Long Hours Spent in Open Boats.

HOW BRUCE ISMAY ESCAPED

Several Versions of This—One Is That He Was Persuaded by Women in a Lifeboat to Go.

The Cunard liner Carpathia, not only a rescue ship, but a hospital ship as well, steamed slowly up the harbor last night and to the Cunard piers at the foot of Fourteenth Street and North River at 9:25 o'clock. She brought with her the first definite, authentic news which has been received since Monday of the sinking early on that morning of the giant White Star Liner Titanic, the biggest steamship afloat.

For hours the pier to which she made fast echoed with the shrieks of women and even of men, who seemed driven temporarily insane by their experiences of the last few days. But finally these facts were learned from the rescue ship:

The sinking Titanic went down to death 1,595 persons.

Those who were rescued number just 745.

More than this number were picked up from the Titanic's boats and from pieces of wreckage to which they clung, but four died of exposure after having been transferred to the Carpathia and were buried at sea.

Of the 745 who reached here last night 210 were members of the crew, most of these stewards and firemen. Only four officers were saved.

Two Versions of Ismay's Escape.

A great deal of interest among the crowds awaiting to greet survivors centred in how J. Bruce Ismay left the Titanic. Various tales of his going were told, one having it that he was a passenger in Lifeboat 1.

In this boat also were Sir Cosmo and Lady Duff Gordon, and only nine other persons, and some of the survivors spoke of it last night as "The Millionaires' Special." It was said that Mr. Ismay later had the crew of this boat photographed aboard the Carpathia and that he liberally rewarded them.

Another version, according to a statement said to have been made by T. D. M. Cardeza of Philadelphia in the lobby of the Ritz-Carlton last night, was that Mr. Ismay had been persuaded to enter one of the lifeboats by the women who had already embarked in it.

The hardships of those who were rescued were extreme. Dozens of women were taken from the Carpathia last night, ill and almost deranged for the moment.

Band Played As Titanic Sank.

Survivors said that the lifeboats in which they floated for hours were not stocked with either water and that this added greatly to the hardship which the escaped ones had to undergo. Two of the boats which put off from the Titanic were sucked beneath the waves by the sinking of the giant liner. Another landed, as were the other two, with passengers, mostly women, was swamped as she tried to get away from the Titanic.

Many persons were picked up by the lifeboats after the Titanic had sunk.

The big steamship went down with her band playing "Autumn." Every soul remaining aboard the vessel had already perished when

Continued on Page 5.

THRILLING STORY BY TITANIC'S SURVIVING WIRELESS MAN

Bride Tells How He and Phillips Worked and How He Finished a Stoker Who Tried to Steal Phillips's Life Belt—Ship Sank to Tune of "Autumn"

BY HAROLD BRIDE, SURVIVING WIRELESS OPERATOR OF THE TITANIC.

(This statement was dictated by Mr. Bride to a reporter for THE NEW YORK TIMES, who visited him with Mr. Marconi in the wireless cabin of the Carpathia a few minutes after the steamship touched her pier.)
(Copyright, 1912, by The New York Times Company.)

In the first place, the public should not blame anybody because more wireless messages about the disaster to the Titanic did not reach shore from the Carpathia. I positively refused to send press dispatches because the bulk of personal messages with touching words of grief was so large. The wireless operators aboard the Chester got all they asked for. And they were wretched operators.

They knew American Morse but not Continental Morse sufficiently to be worth while. They taxed our endurance to the limit. I had to cut them out at last, they were so insufferably slow, and go ahead with our messages of grief to relatives. We sent 119 personal messages to-day, and 50 yesterday.

When I was dragged aboard the Carpathia I went to the hospital at first. I stayed there for ten hours. Then somebody brought word that the Carpathia's wireless operator was "getting queer" from the work.

They asked me if I could go up and help. I could not walk. Both my feet were broken or something, I don't know what. I went up on crutches with somebody helping me.

I took the key and I never left the wireless cabin after that. Our meals were brought to us. We kept the wireless working all the time. The navy operators were a great nuisance. I advise them all to learn the Continental Morse and learn to speed up in it if they ever expect to be worth their salt. The Chester's man thought he knew it, but he was as slow as Christmas coming.

We worked all the time. Nothing went wrong. Sometimes the Carpathia man sent and sometimes I sent. There was a bed in the wireless cabin. I could sit on it and rest my feet while sending sometimes.

To begin at the beginning, I joined the Titanic at Belfast. I was born at Nunhead, England, 22 years ago, and joined the Marconi forces last July. I first worked on the Haverford, and then on the Lusitania. I joined the Titanic at Belfast.

Asleep When Crash Came.

I didn't have much to do aboard the Titanic except to relieve Phillips from midnight until some time in the morning, when he should be through sleeping. On the night of the accident, I was not sending, but was asleep. I was due to be up and relieve Phillips earlier than usual. And that reminds me—if it hadn't been for a lucky thing, we never could have sent any call for help.

The lucky thing was that the wireless broke down early enough for us to fix it before the accident. We noticed something wrong on Sunday and Phillips and I worked seven hours to find it. We found a "secretary" burned out, at last,

and repaired it just a few hours before the iceberg was struck.

Phillips said to me as he took the night-shift, "You turn in, boy, and get some sleep, and go up as soon as you can and give me a chance. I'm all done for with this work of making repairs."

There were three rooms in the wireless cabin. One was a sleeping room, one a dynamo room, and one an operating room. I took off my clothes and went to sleep in bed. Then I was conscious of waking up and hearing Phillips sending to Cape Race. I remembered how tired he was and I got out of bed without my clothes on to relieve him. I didn't even feel the shock. I hardly knew it had happened after the Captain had come to us. There was no jolt whatever.

I was standing by Phillips telling him to go to bed when the Captain put his head in the cabin.

"We've struck an iceberg," the Captain said, "and I'm having an inspection made to tell what it has done for us. You better get ready to send out a call for assistance. But don't send it until I tell you."

The Captain went away and in 10 minutes, I should estimate the time, he came back. We could hear a terrible commotion. I noticed as I came back from one trip that they were putting off women and children in lifeboats. I noticed that the list forward was increasing.

Phillips told me the wireless was growing weaker. The Captain came and told us our engine rooms were taking water and that the dynamos might not last much longer. We sent that word to the Carpathia.

I went out on deck and looked around. The water was pretty close up to the boat deck. There was a great scramble aft, and how poor Phillips worked through it I don't know.

He was a brave man. I learned to love him that night and I suddenly felt for him a great reverence to see him standing there sticking to his work while everybody else was raging about. I will never live to forget the work of Phillips for the last awful fifteen minutes.

I thought it was about time to look about and see if there was anything detached that would float. I remembered that every member of the crew had a special life belt and ought to know where it was. I remembered mine was under my bunk. I went and got it. Then I thought how cold the water was.

I remembered I had some boots and I put those on, and an extra jacket and I put that on. I saw Phillips standing out there still sending away, giving the Carpathia details of just how we were doing.

We picked up the Olympic and told her we were sinking by the head and were about all down. As Phillips was sending the message I strapped his life belt to his back. I had already put on his overcoat.

I wondered if I could get him into his boots. He suggested with a sort of laugh that I look out and see if all the people were in the boats, or if any boats were left. On my way out I saw the captain giving orders through the megaphone to the crowd.

The Last Boat Left.

I saw a collapsible boat near a

Great Scramble on Deck.

Our Captain had left us at this time and Phillips told me to run and tell him what the Carpathia had answered. I did so, and I went through an awful mass of people to his cabin. The decks were full of scrambling men and women. I saw no fighting, but I heard tell of it.

I came back and heard Phillips giving the Carpathia fuller directions. Phillips told me to put on my clothes. Until that moment I forgot that I was not dressed. I went to my cabin and dressed. I brought an overcoat to Phillips. It was very cold. I slipped the overcoat upon him while he worked.

Every few minutes Phillips would send me to the Captain with little messages. They were merely telling how the Carpathia was coming our way and gave her speed.

I noticed as I came back from one trip that they were putting off women and children in lifeboats. I noticed that the list forward was increasing.

Phillips told me the wireless was growing weaker. The Captain came and told us our engine rooms were taking water and that the dynamos might not last much longer. We sent that word to the Carpathia.

I went out on deck and looked around. The water was pretty close up to the boat deck. There was a great scramble aft, and how poor Phillips worked through it I don't know.

He was a brave man. I learned to love him that night and I suddenly felt for him a great reverence to see him standing there sticking to his work while everybody else was raging about. I will never live to forget the work of Phillips for the last awful fifteen minutes.

Band Plays in Rag-Time.

From aft came the tunes of the band. It was a rag-time tune, I don't know what. Then there was "Autumn." Phillips ran aft and that was the last I ever saw of him alive.

I went to the place I had seen the collapsible boat on the boat deck, and to my surprise I saw the boat and the men still trying to push it off. I guess there wasn't a sailor in the crowd. They couldn't do it. I went up to them and was just lending a hand when a large wave came awash of the deck.

The big wave carried the boat off. I had hold of an oarlock and I went off with it. The next I knew I was in the boat.

But that was not all. I was in the boat and the boat was upside down and I was under it. And I remember realizing I was wet through, and that whatever happened I must not breathe, for I was under water.

I knew I had to fight for it and I did. How I got out from under the boat I do not know, but I felt a breath of air at last.

There were men all around me—hundreds of them. The sea was dotted with them, all depending on

Joked at Distress Call.

We joked that way while he flashed signals for about five minutes. Then the Captain came back.

"What are you sending?" he asked.

"C. Q. D.," Phillips replied.

The humor of the situation appealed to me. I cut in with a little remark that made us all laugh, including the Captain.

"Send 'S. O. S.,'" I said. "It's the new call, and it may be your last chance to send it."

Phillips with a laugh changed the signal to "S. O. S." The Captain told us we had been struck amidships, or just back of amidships. It was ten minutes, Phillips told me, after he had noticed the iceberg, that the slight jolt that was the collision's only signal to us occurred. We thought we were a good distance away.

We said lots of funny things to each other in the next few minutes. We picked up first the steamship Frankfurt. We gave her our position and said we had struck an iceberg and needed assistance. The Frankfurt operator went away to tell his Captain. He came back and we told him that time we could observe a distinct list forward.

The Carpathia answered our

their life belts. I felt I simply had to get away from the ship. She was a beautiful sight then.

Smoke and sparks were rushing out of her funnel. There must have been an explosion, but we had heard none. We only saw the big stream of sparks. The ship was gradually turning on her nose—just like a duck does that goes down for a dive. I had only one thing on my mind—to get away from the suction. The band was still playing. I guess all of the band went down.

They were playing "Autumn" then. I swam with all my might. I suppose I was 150 feet away when the Titanic, on her nose, with her after-quarter sticking straight up in the air, began to settle—slowly.

Pulled Into a Boat.

When at last the waves washed over her rudder there wasn't the least bit of suction I could feel. She must have kept going just so slowly as she had been.

I forgot to mention that, besides the Olympic and Carpathia we spoke some German boat, I don't know which, and told them how we were. We also spoke the Baltic. I remembered those things as I began to figure what ships would be coming toward us.

I felt, after a little while, like sinking. I was very cold. I saw a boat of some kind near me and put all my strength into an effort to swim to it. It was hard work. I was all done when a hand reached out from the boat and pulled me aboard. It was our same collapsible. The same crowd was on it.

There was just room for me to roll on the edge. I lay there not caring what happened. Somebody sat on my legs. They were wedged in between slats and were being wrenched. I had not the heart left to ask the man to move. It was a terrible sight all around—men swimming and sinking.

I lay where I was, letting the man wrench my feet out of shape. Others came near. Nobody gave them a hand. The bottom-up boat already had more men than it would hold and it was sinking.

At first the larger waves splashed over my clothing. Then they began to splash over my head and I had to breathe when I could.

As we floated around on our capsized boat and I kept straining my eyes for a ship's lights, somebody said, "Don't the rest of you think we ought to pray?" The man who made the suggestion asked what the religion of the others was. Each man called out his religion. One was a Catholic, one a Methodist, one a Presbyterian.

It was decided the most appropriate prayer for all was the Lord's Prayer. We spoke it over in chorus with the man who first suggested that we pray as the leader.

Some splendid people saved us. They had a right-side-up boat, and it was full to its capacity. Yet they came to us and loaded us all into it. I saw some lights off in the distance and knew a steamship was coming to our aid.

I didn't care what happened. I just lay and gasped when I could and felt the pain in my feet. At last the Carpathia was alongside and the people were being taken up a rope ladder. Our boat drew near and one by one the men were taken off of it.

One Dead on the Raft.

One man was dead. I passed him and went to the ladder, al-

Continued on Page 2.

Col. Astor Went Down Waving Farewells to His Bride.

SOME STORIES OF PANIC

Others Say Order Was Maintained—Mrs. Straus Clung to Husband's Side.

SHOCK CALLED "SLIGHT JAR"

Card Playing Continued in the Cabin and None Realized the End Was Near.

SOME HEARD SHOTS FIRED

A False Rumor of Captain's Suicide and of Shooting of Men Rushing for Boats.

MEN LEAPED INTO THE SEA

Col. Gracie Saved Another with Himself—Says Titanic Did Not Blow Up.

In a clear starlit night that showed a clear, deep, blue sea for miles and miles, the Titanic, an hour after she had struck a submerged iceberg at full speed and head on, sank slowly to her open grave. The bottom of the big ship had been ripped open. Her band, lined on deck, was playing pleasant music as she sank in full view of the boatloads of her wretched survivors, and those left of her passengers and crew—fully two-thirds—stood quietly and resigned on deck, awaiting the final plunge.

The bow went under first and then the huge hulk slowly settled until she stood nearly upright, with 15 feet showing out of water. There she hung, a fascinating but fearful spectacle, and then dropped slowly out of sight.

Capt. Smith Refused to Be Rescued.

Capt. Smith died a hero's death. The unwritten law of the sea, which holds with tradition's force all the men who go down to the sea in ships, had cast its spell about him while the great craft was plunging to her doom.

It was left to a fireman of the Titanic to tell the story of the death of Capt. Smith and the last message he sent behind him. This man had gone down with the vessel and was clinging to a piece of wreckage about half an hour before he finally joined several members of the Titanic's company on the bottom of a boat which was floating among other wreckage.

Harry Senior, the fireman, with eight or nine companions in distress, had just managed to get a firm hold on the upturned boat, when they saw the Titanic reeling preparatory to her final plunge. At that moment, according to the fireman's story, Capt. Smith jumped into the sea from the promenade deck of the Titanic with an infant clutched tenderly in his arms.

It took only a few strokes to bring him to the upturned life boat, where a dozen hands were stretched out to take the little child from his arms and free him to safety.

"I will follow the ship," said the fireman, "said Capt. Smith was dragged on the upturned boat," and he had on a life buoy and a life preserver. He clung there a moment and then he swung dragged from the sea from the promenade deck of the Titanic with an infant clutched tenderly in his arms.

He took off his life preserver, tossed the life buoy on the inky waters, and slipped into the water again with the words: "I will follow the ship."

At that time there was only a circle of troubled water and some wreckage to show the spot where the biggest of all ocean steamers had sunk out of sight.

Among those who remained on the ship were at least six women, passengers to go into the lifeboats, had resolutely refused, preferring to meet death hand in hand with the husbands who could not accompany them and share life with them more.

On deck, leaning over the rail and waving his hand to his bride of but many months ago, stood John Jacob Astor. His wife arrived here safely last night and is at her home, 840 Fifth Avenue.

While utterly exhausted from her experiences, she was declared by Nicholas Biddle, a Trustee of the Astor estate, to be in no danger. Her phy-

---

1,595 Went to Death on the Titanic.

NUMBER ABOARD		THE SAVED	
First Class	330	First Class	210
Second Class	320	Second Class	125
Third Class	750	Third Class	200
Officers and Crew	940	Officers and Crew	210
Total	2,340	Total	745

Of the members of the crew saved, 4 were officers, 39 seamen, 96 stewards, and 71 firemen.

The Suffragettes

Throughout the Edwardian era in Britain riots and disturbances by those demanding women's suffrage in or around the sacred precincts of Parliament were dependable fare for the newspapers. The spectacle of brick-heaving, slogan-waving feminists never ceased to amaze and baffle most sections of the press. *The Daily Mail* might not approve of the guerrilla tactics of these suffragettes (as it christened them) but it could be relied upon not to miss one single mail-box burning or public horse-whipping of a politician. Only *The Daily Herald* (from 1912 on) consistently approved their goings-on: other newspapers ranged from mild sarcasm to outraged chauvinism like *The Westminster Gazette* which found the whole thing 'too painful' even to comment on. After the Commons rejected the women's franchise bill in March 1912, however, the issue became yet more painful as the suffragettes militated from chaining themselves to the railings of Downing Street to a more aggressive policy. In February 1913 Lloyd George's new country-house was bombed (though only one of the bombs succeeded in going off). It was, said Mrs Pankhurst, 'to wake him up'. The following June a militant lady flung herself beneath the King's horse in the Derby, with terrible consequences. In March 1914 Miss Mary Richardson strolled into the National Gallery and set about Velasquez' painting of the Rokeby Venus with a chopper. Art-loving editors and philistines were united in denouncing this act of vandalism against the nation's precious heritage, and ensured (if it weren't already a foregone conclusion) that the House of Lords would throw out yet another enfranchisement bill a few weeks later. Only the war brought a truce to these sexual hostilities — and soon ladies were permitted, indeed encouraged, to dig potatoes and drive ambulances with the best of men. By the time it was all over, public places were thick with women with bobbed or shingled hair, brazenly smoking cigarettes if you please, and the battle of 1914 was as good as won.

DAILY SKETCH.

No. 1,223.—THURSDAY, JUNE 5, 1913.   London: 46-47, Shoe-lane, E.C.   Manchester: Withy-grove.   ONE HALFPENNY.
Telephones—Editorial and Publishing: 6670 Holborn.   Advertisements: 10,782 Central.   [Registered as a Newspaper.]

HISTORY'S MOST WONDERFUL DERBY: FIRST HORSE DISQUALIFIED: A 100 TO 1 CHANCE WINS: SUFFRAGETTE NEARLY KILLED BY THE KING'S COLT.

The Daily Mirror

THE MORNING JOURNAL WITH THE SECOND LARGEST NET SALE.

No. 2,919.   THURSDAY, FEBRUARY 20, 1913.   One Halfpenny.

THE LATEST POLITICAL ARGUMENT: MR. LLOYD GEORGE'S NEW COUNTRY HOUSE WRECKED BY A BOMB.

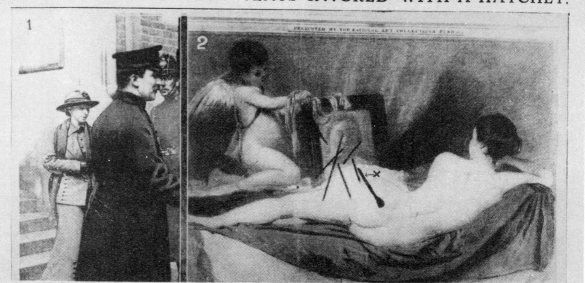

SUFFRAGETTE DESPAIR: VENUS INVOKED WITH A HATCHET.

The Road-Hogs of Europe

World War I

HEIR TO AUSTRIAN THRONE MURDERED.

ARCHDUKE AND HIS WIFE SHOT DEAD IN THE STREET.

DETERMINED PLOT.

BOMB FIRST THROWN AT THEIR CAR.

SECOND ATTEMPT WITHIN AN HOUR.

BOY ASSASSIN.

DUCHESS TRIES IN VAIN TO SAVE HER HUSBAND.

DEATH IN EACH OTHER'S ARMS.

There was more than enough in the headlines, that summer of 1914, to divert the public's attention from Europe's troubles: the uneasy prospect of civil war in Ireland if Ulster persisted in opposing Home Rule, not to mention the spine-tingling issue of whether Paris would really get away with those daring slit skirts.' There was Commander Shackleton's forthcoming assault on the South Pole, and those suffragettes' endless assaults on the police. Then there were those rumours from America of a deliciously wanton new dance called the Tango . . .

If anyone had penetrated as far as the small strap-line which proclaimed that the 'Outlook for the Shooting Season' was good, he no doubt took it as an omen for the pheasants, rather than for generals and politicians. Even when on June 29 his Monday morning papers informed him that the heir to the Austrian throne and his wife had been slain in Sarajevo by an assassin's bullets, he would have been more likely to ask 'what does morganatic mean?' than to ponder on how this would affect the Balance of Power, or what the implications were for the Entente. Concerning the ramifications of high diplomacy he probably knew little, and cared less — and as events of July drew him inexorably closer to war, the newspapers gave him virtually no sign. For this the papers themselves were hardly to blame: there was no official Austro-Hungarian reaction against Serbia until July 23, and few could have divined beforehand that the terms of its ultimatum would be so calculatedly harsh. It was true there had been warning-signals of an impending crisis, if any editor had cared to heed them; the stock-exchanges of Europe were dropping hell-for-leather, and the Austrian Press had been even more vituperative than usual. But at least the German Press was sure that the Kaiser wanted no war.

Serbia did its best to meet Austria's humiliating conditions, agreeing to eight out of the ten demands. It wasn't enough: on July 28 Austria declared war on Serbia and thus set in train the whole irreversible machinery of Europe's treaties and alliances. The British left their offices on Friday evening, the 30th, for the weekend troubled at the local difficulties in the Balkans, but uncomprehending. By the time they returned to work after the Bank holiday, nearly the whole of Europe was marching. Russia had mobilised to come to Serbia's aid — France, too, to honour her obligations to the Tsar. Germany had sent an ultimatum to Moscow, signed a treaty with Turkey, declared war on Russia, occupied Luxembourg and issued an ultimatum to Belgium, to allow her troops a clear passage to France.

It had all happened so quickly. Almost plaintively The Times, issuing an extraordinary Sunday edition, remarked: 'War has come upon Europe so swiftly that few understand how and why . . . for weeks past efforts have been made to hide and confuse the cause at stake'. It was still far from clear what Britain's role in the coming conflict would be. There seemed to be a moral obligation to stand by France, though according to the Government there were no binding signatures to that effect. The Cabinet itself was reported to be divided, Prime Minister Asquith, the Foreign Secretary Sir Edward Grey and Churchill all inclined towards involvement; Lloyd George, Sir John Simon, Lord Morley amongst others favouring neutrality.

The Press, too, was divided though most papers, like The Observer (speaking with the weighty voice of J. L. Garvin) were eloquent for war: if the Government failed in its duty 'we shall have been false to those who trusted us — false to moral engagements as sacred as written bonds'. Alone of the Sunday papers Reynolds' News pleaded 'We must keep out of it. In this land the voice of the mafficker is silent, and the whole people has its face set against war'. Probably it would have been truer to say that, now as rarely before, the whole people looked to the Press for enlightenment and guidance. Lord Northcliffe had never skimped on the latter: for years his Daily Mail had fulminated against the threat of German imperialism. Now all his papers (and that included The Times and The Evening News) were adamant that Britain should not stand aloof.

Among the dailies The Manchester Guardian was under no illusions about 'the abomination which The Times and its attendant satellites are attempting to drag us into'. Other Liberal papers were non-committal, except the Daily News which denounced what it called 'the rabble of Jingo journalism' and hinted at a conspiracy between certain forces and the Yellow Press to fill the streets of every town with starving men, women and children. It accused The Times and the Mail of 'paving the way for this stupendous catastrophe by years of anti-German propaganda'.

All this internecine warfare was rendered academic on the Monday (August 3) when the Kaiser's divisions invaded Belgium willy-nilly. Britain was pledged to protect Belgian neutrality, and the waverers in the Cabinet were carried on the wave of righteous indignation at the rape of a near-defenceless democracy. An ultimatum was speedily dispatched to the German Government requiring it to guarantee Belgian integrity — with no expectation of a contrite answer. None came, and a state of war was declared from 11.00 pm, with the country united in a way that had seemed impossible days earlier.

The newspapers immediately marshalled their own forces in readiness for the struggle; but the first antagonist they encountered was not the fire-eating hun, but the dampening Press Bureau. From the outset a severe, impossibly severe, censorship was imposed by both French and British authorities. At first no correspondents were accredited, later only a mere handful; reporters were barred from the front, so that news of the retreat from Mons and even the battlefields of the Marne only dribbled in piecemeal to Fleet Street; all letters, all dispatches from the front were scrutinised and often discarded. Gone were the days of the flamboyant correspondent, wielding his colourful rhetoric like a sabre to cut through inefficiency and red tape to get at the truth. In defence of the Realm now only good news was official news. At the risk of prison — or the closure of his paper — did an editor defy the new stringency (one journal, The Globe, was actually suppressed for a time in 1915 for spreading rumours about Lord Kitchener's resignation).

As a result press reports of actions in the early stages of the war were often wildly confusing. Heavy defeats became 'strategic withdrawals'. When a frank dispatch about the Mons retreat was (amazingly) passed by the censor and published in The Times, Asquith inveighed against it in Parliament on the grounds that it would 'spread alarm and confusion'. Frequently, the public was informed in great detail about the re-capture by British troops of positions the papers had been forbidden to mention had been lost in the first place. The general impression was, not surprisingly, that the war was a push-over; little wonder there was so much talk of 'it all being over by Christmas'.

'We shall lose this war by secrecy' Lord Roberts felt obliged to remark to Northcliffe,

Evening Standard
and
St. James's Gazette

LARGER DAILY CIRCULATION THAN THAT OF <u>ANY TWO</u> OTHER PENNY EVENING PAPERS.

No. 28,099.

LONDON, TUESDAY, AUGUST 4, 1914.

ONE PENNY.

ENGLAND TAKES ACTION TO-DAY.

ULTIMATUM

SENT BY ENGLAND TO GERMANY TO-DAY.

EXPIRES AT MIDNIGHT.

DEMAND FOR THE NEUTRALITY OF BELGIUM.

MOMENTOUS DECLARATION.

The English Government has sent an ultimatum to Germany to respect the neutrality of Belgium.

A satisfactory reply is demanded by midnight.

The King has called up the Army Reserves and the Territorials.

This momentous announcement was made by the Prime Minister in the House of Commons this afternoon.

Before sending the Ultimatum, the Government received the following message from the German Government:—

"Please dispel any distrust that may exist on part of British Government with regard to our intentions by repeating most positively the formal assurance that even in case of armed conflict with Belgium, Germany will not, under any pretence whatever, annex Belgian territory."

Belgium has indignantly refused to obey the second ultimatum sent to her by Germany. She declares she will fight to save her independence.

Following representations made by Germany to Italy to-day to the effect that acts of French hostility on the German frontier imposed on Italy the duty of abandoning her neutrality and come to the defence of her German ally, the Italian Government has reaffirmed to Germany her attitude of neutrality.

Belgium.
BELGIUM TO FIGHT

STIRRING SCENES IN THE CHAMBER.

THE KING'S APPEAL.

Exchange Special.

BRUSSELS, Tuesday.

King Albert to-day presided over a combined sitting of the Chamber and the Senate.

In the course of his address to the assembly his Majesty said that never since the year 1830 had the situation been more grave. It was imperative, he said, that to prevent Belgium being violated every Belgian must accomplish his duty and resign himself to all the sacrifices that it may be necessary for him to make. He went on:—

"The Fatherland is in danger. Let me make an appeal to you, my brothers. At this supreme hour the entire nation must be of one mind. I have called together. Parliament, where now there is but one party, so that it may support the Government in declaring that we will maintain untarnished the sacred patriotism of our fathers." (General cries of "Yes, Yes.")

King Albert concluded his speech with the words: "Long live independent Belgium!" A prolonged and stirring scene of enthusiasm ensued, all the deputies rising to their feet cheering and crying, "Belgium will do her duty!" His Majesty then withdrew.

Premier's Statement.

Baron de Broqueville, Premier and Minister for War, made a statement regarding the German ultimatum and Belgium's reply. He declared with emphasis that the Government would not sacrifice the nation's honour. The country would resist by every means in her power all encroachment upon her rights. The German Government, he announced, had replied to them that she would employ force to attain her objects. "The word is, therefore, 'To arms,'" said the Premier. "Upon this land of ours we shall not weaken. Even if we are conquered, we will never submit. (Cries of "Long live Belgium!") Union makes for strength, and Belgium, supported by the energy of her sons, will not perish."

When the Premier had finished, the members again made a long and enthusias-

Continued on Next Page.)

BRITAIN'S ACTION.

PROVOKED BY GERMAN ATTACK ON BELGIUM.

THE ULTIMATUM.

PREMIER'S STATEMENT THIS AFTERNOON.

THRILLING SCENE

From Our Parliamentary Representative.

In a crowded House this afternoon the Prime Minister said that, in conformity with the policy laid down by the Foreign Secretary yesterday, a telegram was sent early this morning by him to our Ambassador at Berlin as follows:—

The King of the Belgians has made an appeal to his Majesty the King for diplomatic intervention on behalf of Belgium.

His Majesty's Government are also informed that the German Government has delivered to the Belgian Government a note proposing friendly neutrality in the event of free passage through the Belgian territory, and promising to maintain the independence and integrity of the King and his possessions on the conclusion of peace, and threatening, in case of refusal, to treat Belgium as an enemy, and requiring an answer within twelve hours.

We also understand that Belgium categorically refuses this as a flagrant violation of the laws of nations.

His Majesty's Government is bound to protest against this violation of treaty in which Germany is a party in common with others, and must request an assurance that the demand made upon Belgium will not be proceeded with, and that her neutrality will be respected by Germany.

We ask for an immediate reply.

Germany's Threat.

Mr. Asquith continued: We received this morning from our Minister in Brussels the following telegram:—

"The German Minister has this morning addressed a Note to the Belgian Minister for Foreign Affairs, stating that the Belgian Government, having declined the well-intentioned proposals submitted to them by the Imperial Government, the latter, deeply to their regret, will be compelled to carry out

Continued on Next Page.)

ULTIMATUM EXPIRES.

EXPLANATIONS DEMANDED FROM RUSSIA AND FRANCE.

THE KING INTERVENES.

HIS MAJESTY'S MESSAGE TO THE CZAR OF RUSSIA.

KAISER'S WARLIKE SPEECH.

"THE SWORD IS BEING FORCED INTO OUR HANDS."

---

words deliberately calculated to stir the Press Lord to the bottom of his heart. In the spring of 1915 Northcliffe came to believe, with justification, that the war was indeed being lost through secrecy. For some reason, the army was being starved of high-explosive shells.

After the war *The Daily Mail* produced a Golden Peace Number (printed throughout in gold), in which one of the articles was a summary of the achievements of the newspaper towards winning the war. In it the writer explained *'The Daily Mail* had been privately familiar with the facts about the lamentable shortage of high-explosive shells — and all forms of shells — for several months; in fact since the first battle of Ypres. It remained silent on the point because, like Lord French, it hoped against hope that the Government and the War Office would grapple with the situation and make good the deficiencies which were causing our brave men to die needlessly in heaps'. The crisis came to a head in March, when the bombardment at Neuve Chapelle fell silent after two hours for want of ammunition, and when the artillery barrage at Gallipoli spluttered out in an ineffectual hail of shrapnel. From his conversations with repatriated wounded Northcliffe knew the effect of this on the troops' morale, and laid the blame firmly at the door of the Secretary for War Lord Kitchener (for whose appointment *The Daily Mail* had been taking credit only a few months before). But in this, as in all things, Northcliffe's hands were tied by by the censor.

Advertisement from the Daily News July 30, 1914.

"THE DAILY NEWS & LEADER"
Football Annual
NOW READY.
1d. everywhere.

Daily News & Leader

4.30 EDN.

BRAND'S ESSENCE OF BEEF AND OF CHICKEN
For Exhaustion and Weak Digestion.
OF CHEMISTS AND GROCERS.

No. 21,343. LONDON & MANCHESTER, WEDNESDAY, AUGUST 5, 1914. ONE HALF-PENNY.

GREAT BRITAIN & GERMANY AT WAR.

AT WAR!

Fateful Decision Last Evening.

KING'S MESSAGE TO NAVY.

"The Sure Shield of England and Empire."

FIRING IN THE NORTH SEA.

It was officially announced early this morning that war was declared between Great Britain and Germany last night.

This declaration followed a British ultimatum to which an answer was demanded by midnight.

The British action followed Germany's declaration of war on France and Belgium and the receipt of official news during the forenoon of the invasion of Belgian territory.

Germany is now at war with Great Britain, France, Russia and Belgium.

The Premier, in announcing the Government's momentous action to the House of Commons, stated that early yesterday morning Germany was asked for an assurance that her demand upon Belgium would not be proceeded with, and that her neutrality should be respected.

An immediate reply was asked for, and a message was received from the German Foreign Secretary to the effect that no Belgian territory would be annexed, but that Germany was compelled to disregard Belgian neutrality owing to fears of a French attack through that country.

News also reached London that the German Army was marching into Belgium.

Thereupon the British Government repeated its request for an assurance of Belgian neutrality on the same lines as that given by France, demanding that a satisfactory reply should reach London before midnight.

This grave announcement was received with loud cheers.

First news of Germany's declaration of war on Belgium reached London yesterday in a telegram from Mr. Ernest W. Smith, the special correspondent of "The Daily News" at Brussels. The German action was a reply to Belgium's firm refusal to allow the Kaiser's troops to cross her frontiers.

Great Britain is prepared for war. The Navy is mobilised and at sea; the Army is being mobilised. Men and youths are flocking to the colours, and crowds besiege the recruiting offices.

Admiral Jellicoe has been appointed to the supreme command of the Home Fleet, with Rear-Admiral Madden as his Chief of Staff. Sir John French has been reappointed to his former post as Inspector-General of the Forces.

The Admiralty has made a notable addition to the British Navy by the seizure of two battleships and two scouts, building in English yards. The battleships belonged to Turkey and the scouts to Chile.

The Lobby Correspondent of "The Daily News" says that Lord Haldane, the Lord Chancellor, is acting as Assistant Secretary for War, Mr. Asquith retaining the office of Secretary. Lord Kitchener's services, it is believed, will be available in this country.

The British railways have been taken over by the Government for military purposes, and it is notified that the ordinary services may be dislocated for some time.

Public fears as to food supply are groundless. An official statement by the Cabinet (See Page 5) shows that our supplies of corn and meat are ample, and that there is no justification for a rise in prices.

FIGHTING IN BELGIUM.

Germans Driven Back Near the Frontier.

BRUSSELS, Tuesday.

According to a wireless telegram received here, an engagement is said to have taken place near Liége between Belgian and German troops.

The Germans were driven back. Numbers of Belgians were wounded, and will be brought to Brussels.—Reuter.

GERMANS TAKE VISE.

AMSTERDAM, Tuesday Night.

Visé has been taken by the Germans.

The Belgian engineers have blown up the bridge over the Meuse, and the Germans are building a new bridge.

A state of siege has been proclaimed at Limbourg. Belgian engineers have blown up the bridges over the Ambleve.—Central News.

MOVING INTO FRANCE.

Three Columns Pressing Forward from Luxemburg.

BRUSSELS, Tuesday.

The German forces are advancing from Luxemburg in three columns, one towards Longwy, another towards Villerupt, and the third towards Thionville.

A telegram from Givet states that the French and German troops are blowing up the French and German frontier stations. --Central News.

[Villerupt is a French village situated eight miles east-south-east of Longwy. Thionville (German, Diedenhofen) is situated in Alsace-Lorraine, 16 miles north of Metz on the Moselle.]

NEAR MARS-LA-TOUR.

PARIS, Tuesday.

A German company is reported to be in French territory near Mars-la-Tour, the scene of one of the most sanguinary battles of the war of 1870.—Reuter.

[Mars-la-Tour lies close to the German frontier, south-west of Metz.]

THE DECLARATION

BRITISH DEMANDS REJECTED.

OFFICIAL MESSAGE.

AMBASSADOR HANDED HIS PASSPORTS.

The following statement was issued from the Foreign Office at 12.15 a.m. to-day:

Owing to the summary rejection by the German Government of the request made by his Majesty's Government for assurances that the neutrality of Belgium would be respected, his Majesty's Ambassador in Berlin has received his passports, and his Majesty's Government has declared to the German Government that a state of war exists between Great Britain and Germany as from 11 p.m. on August 4.

There was some confusion in earlier messages, the first being to the effect that Germany had declared war, while a second stated that Great Britain had taken the fateful step.

From the above official announcement it appears that Germany committed the act of war in rejecting the British ultimatum, while Great Britain, on receipt of this decision, declared the state of war.

WILD SCENES.

How News of Declaration was Received.

In anticipation of the receipt of Germany's reply, huge crowds gathered in Whitehall and outside Buckingham Palace, and extraordinary scenes of enthusiasm were witnessed.

had been intended to hold a midnight Council at the Palace, but owing to Germany's summary rejection of our ultimatum this gathering took place earlier.

It was preceded by a concentration of Ministers at 10, Downing-street, and each was loudly cheered as he entered the Premier's official residence.

Not for years—since Mafeking night—have such crowds been seen in London, and Whitehall, the Mall, and Trafalgar-square were all packed with excited throngs.

AT THE PALACE.

The enthusiasm culminated outside Buckingham Palace when it became known that war had been declared. The word was passed round by the police that silence was necessary, inasmuch as the King was holding a Council for the signing of necessary proclamations.

A lady came out of the Palace and announced that war had been declared.

This was received with tremendous cheering, which grew into a deafening roar when King George, Queen Mary, and the Prince of Wales appeared on the balcony shortly after eleven o'clock.

They looked down upon an extraordinary scene—a dense mass of excited people, many of whom had clambered on to the Victoria Memorial.

THE NATIONAL ANTHEM.

As if by general accord, the cheers gave way to the singing of the National Anthem, which was taken up lustily by the whole throng.

For fully five minutes the Royal Party remained on the balcony. They retired amidst a perfect storm of cheering, and although the crowd subsequently began to melt away, thousands remained.

They grew gradually less demonstrative, and it was noticeable that the news of the actual state of war had a sobering effect on many. Mafficking gave way to distinct seriousness.

THE GERMAN FLEET.

Bombardments in Baltic and Mediterranean.

An official message issued by the French Embassy informs Reuter that the German cruiser Breslau bombarded the town of Bona, in Algeria, at four o'clock yesterday morning, and afterwards steamed off at full speed in a westerly direction.

A Central News message from Flushing (received yesterday by an indirect route) makes the statement that several of the German warships were lying off that port.

A German cruiser has bombarded the Russian port Libau. According to a Russian official communiqué cabled by Reuter, one shot hit the naval hospital, and two struck private houses. The material damage was very small, and there were no casualties.

There is no confirmation of the report that German warships have seized the Aland Islands.

The "Daily News" War Telegrams arriving during the day will be published in "The Star."

A MAP OF THE NORTH SEA, SHOWING THE GERMAN NAVAL BASES.

GERMANS SINK BRITISH SHIP.

Reported Loss of a Mine-Layer.

Late last night we received the following:

The Press Association learns that there is no truth in the report of a naval engagement in the North Sea.

It is understood that the British Government has received intimation of the sinking of a British mine-layer by the German Fleet.

KING'S MESSAGE TO ADMIRAL JELLICOE.

The Navy, the Sure Shield of the Empire.

The following message has been addressed by his Majesty the King to Admiral Sir John Jellicoe:

At this grave moment in our national history I send to you, and through you to the officers and men of the fleets of which you have assumed command, the assurance of my confidence that under your direction they will revive and renew the old glories of the Royal Navy, and prove once again the sure shield of Britain and of her Empire in the hour of trial.

GEORGE, R.I.

The above message has been communicated to the senior naval officers on all stations outside of home waters.

NEW HEADS OF NAVY AND ARMY.

Admiral Jellicoe to Command the Fleet.

It was announced officially yesterday that Vice-Admiral Sir John Jellicoe has been appointed to the supreme command of the Home Fleet.

Field-Marshal Sir John French has been reappointed to his former position of Inspector-General of the Forces, which he resigned some time ago in connection with the General Gough incident in Ulster.

Sir John Jellicoe has been Second Sea Lord since December, 1912, and it was known several months ago that he had been selected to succeed Admiral Callaghan He has had a most distinguished career, having served in the Egyptian war and in China. He was wrecked in 1893 in the Victoria, but was saved after sinking, and severely wounded at Peitsang. Among his many decorations is one conferred by the Kaiser. He is 55, and has been described as the Roberts and the Kitchener of the Navy.

Rear-Admiral Chas. E. Madden has been appointed Chief of Staff to Admiral Jellicoe. He has been Rear-Admiral Commanding the Third Cruiser Squadron since 1912; prior to that he commanded the Home Fleet, and he has also been Fourth Sea Lord.

GERMAN ADVANCE.

Guns Heard Ten Miles Within the Belgian Frontier.

BRUSSELS, Tuesday.

It was reported last night that the 6th German Army Corps had encamped in the territory of Moresnet, and was continuing its advance, massing between Moresnet and Eupen.

All Germans have been expelled from Liege and Namur.

Artillery fire has been heard at Aywaille.

Dutch Limburg, in North Brabant, is defended by a strong contingent of Dutch soldiers.

It seems probable that the Germans are desirous of reaching the Meuse, and following the course of that river.—Reuter.

[Moresnet is between the province of Liége and the Prussian Rhine province. Eupen is in the Rhine province, just on the Belgian frontier. Aywaille is in Belgium, on the Ambléve, in the province of Liége, about ten miles from the German frontier. It is less than sixty miles east of the field of Waterloo.]

WAR DECLARED ON BELGIUM.

German Army Enters Her Territory.

KING'S SPEECH IN THE BELGIAN CHAMBER.

From Our Special Correspondent, ERNEST W. SMITH.

BRUSSELS, Tuesday.

I learn officially at the Ministry of War that Germany has declared war upon Belgium this morning.

M. de Broqueville, the Prime Minister, has announced in the Chamber that Belgian territory has been invaded at Verviers. He read the German reply to the Belgian Note, which said that Germany would take by force of arms the measures of security demanded by the situation.

I feel it my duty to pay a tribute to the splendid calm and restraint of the population in the days which preceded Germany's ultimatum with its tragic sequel—a state of war. Their attitude has been unprovocative and fired by the sole desire to defend the independence of the country. This little people has emulated the splendid calm reigning in Paris up to the time I left there.

I wired last night that events were moving quickly, but I confess I was unprepared for the dramatic turn which things took this morning. Thousands of people collected around the Royal Palace to cheer the King on his way to open Parliament, and when the news that Germany was at war with Belgium was known it spread like wildfire. I called at the Ministry of War, where I received confirmation, and thence to the Chamber, where M. de Broqueville, the Premier and Minister of War, was making a long declaration.

M. de Broqueville read almost textually Sir Edward Grey's statement made in the House last night describing Germany's demand and Belgium's answer. "We have waited till this morning for Germany's reply to the Belgian Note," said the Minister. "Germany has replied that she will take the measures which the situation imposes by force of arms." A murmur of incredulous astonishment ran through the Chamber. "This reply is beyond comment," added M. de Broqueville. "La parole est donc aux armes. We will do our duty, our whole duty. We may be beaten, but we shall never be cast down. The Belgian people will not fail to do their duty; of that I am convinced."

Later the Premier announced that Belgian territory had been violated. Great cheering greeted the announcement that M. Vandervelde, the Socialist leader, had been nominated Minister of State. Immense crowds ovated King Albert on his return to the Palace, and then promenaded the centre of the city amid tremendous scenes of enthusiasm and cries of "Vive Belgique, France, Angleterre."

This afternoon the aspect is almost normal except that many groups are discussing the situation.

KING GEORGE'S MESSAGE.

King George, before the rupture with Germany, sent a telegram to King Albert assuring him of his support and determination to respect and make respect (respecter et de faire respecter) the independence, integrity, and neutrality of Belgium.

The British Minister has arranged for a special dispatch of letters for England on Saturday morning.

KING ALBERT'S CALL.

Every Citizen Required to Do His Duty.

BRUSSELS, Tuesday.

The King delivered the following speech to the deputies:

"Never since 1830 has a graver hour sounded for Belgium. The strength of our right and the need of Europe for our autonomous existence make us still hope that the dreaded events will not occur. If it is necessary for us to resist an invasion of our soil, however, that duty will find us armed and ready to make the greatest sacrifices. Our young men have already come forward to defend the Fatherland in danger. One duty alone is imposed upon us, namely, the maintenance of a stubborn resistance, courage, and union. Our bravery is proved by our faultless mobilisation and by the multitude of voluntary engagements.

"This is the moment for action. I have called you together to-day in order to allow the Chambers to participate in the enthusiasm of the country. You will know how to adopt with urgency all necessary measures. Are you decided to maintain inviolate the sacred patrimony of our ancestors?

"No one will fail in his duty, and the army is capable of performing its task. The Government and I are fully confident. The Government is aware of its responsibilities, and will carry them out to the end to guard the supreme welfare of the country. God will be with us."—Reuter.

SEIZED FOR THE BRITISH NAVY.

Turkish Battleships and Chilian Scouts.

The Government have taken over the two battleships, one completed, and the other shortly due for completion, which had been ordered in this country by the Turkish Government.

The two destroyer scouts ordered by Chile have also been seized.

The battleships will be named Agincourt and Erin, and the scouts will be called Faulkner and Broke, after two famous naval officers.

ADMIRALTY TAKES OVER LINERS

MONTREAL, Tuesday.

The Canadian Pacific Railway Company announces that its liners, Empress of Russia, Empress of Japan, and Empress of Asia have been taken over by the Admiralty.—Central News.

CABINET & THE WAR.

Lord Haldane Assisting at War Office.

(By Our Lobby Correspondent.)

War has been declared, and the German Ambassador, Prince Lichnowsky, will call at the Foreign Office at 10.30 this morning, as a preliminary to leaving the country. It has been arranged that the United States will take over the affairs of the German Embassy.

Lord Haldane is acting in effect as Assistant Secretary of State at the War Office, and is in daily attendance there. This fact will be generally welcomed, since it is obvious that the Prime Minister requires the ablest assistance in his double duties, and the great reputation which Lord Haldane won at the War Office is fresh in everyone's memory.

Lord Kitchener's invaluable services will, there is reason to believe, be available in this country, but the suggestion which has been put forward in irresponsible quarters that he should be appointed Secretary of State was not very happy. Parliamentary experience is peculiarly necessary in a Minister of State at this juncture.

LIBERAL AND LABOUR FEELING.

The feeling among the Liberal rank and file yesterday was more solidly behind the Government in the course which events have inevitably thrust upon them. The German declaration of war against Belgium is resented by the Liberal Members who attended the meeting at which Mr. Ponsonby presided on Monday.

The Labour Party are now divided in feeling. Some hold that the Government must be supported in view of the accomplished fact. If an attitude of direct antagonism to the Government were adopted the party would not have a general support from the Labour Party in the country.

The Labour Conference which has been summoned for to-day will probably give its chief consideration to the steps which must be taken for the relief of distress if unemployment results. But there will also be a peace propaganda.

CABINET RESIGNATIONS.

Lord Morley and Mr. John Burns have tendered their resignations. It is not believed that Lord Morley will withdraw his resignation, but whether Mr. Burns will reconsider his position was in doubt last night. Mr. Trevelyan, Secretary to the Board of Education, has also tendered his resignation. No official announcements have yet been made, but neither Lord Morley nor Mr. Burns attended the Cabinet meeting yesterday.

About 60 members of the Opposition and 30 Ministerialists in the House of Commons are called up to the Army and the Reserves.

Mr. Balfour's contemptuous reference to Liberals who in this crisis have been wrestling with their conscience, as the "lees and dregs," when these Liberals included some of the most respected members of the party, is much resented. The less we have of Mr. Balfour in these high matters the better it will be for the country, which has not forgotten how he mismanaged a war.

THE SESSION AND HOME RULE.

It is rumoured that the session will be prorogued on Saturday. A new session could be begun and adjourned to keep Parliament in being if necessary. A prorogation instead of an adjournment is vital to the Government's position, since the Home Rule Bill must go formally on the Statute Book. Otherwise the situation in Ireland would be hopelessly prejudiced, and the effect of Mr. Redmond's fine speech nullified. The Government count on the patriotism of the Opposition to recognise this, and it is believed the Opposition leaders conferred on the subject yesterday.

The Arms Proclamation, it is stated, is about to be revoked in Ireland.

A. P. N.

STEPS WHICH LED TO THE WAR.

King of the Belgians' Appeal.

Mr. Asquith in the House of Commons yesterday made the momentous announcement that an ultimatum, expiring at midnight, had been presented to Germany in respect to the neutrality of Belgium.

Received with general cheers, the Premier said:

"In conformity with the statement of policy which was made by my right hon. friend the Foreign Secretary yesterday, a telegram was sent early this morning by him to our Ambassador in Berlin. It was to this effect:

The King of the Belgians has made an appeal to his Majesty the King for diplomatic intervention on behalf of Belgium. His Majesty's Government are also informed that the German Government has delivered to the Belgian Government a Note proposing friendly neutrality for maintaining a free passage through Belgian territory, and promising to maintain the independence and integrity of the kingdom and its possessions at the conclusion of peace, but threatening in case of refusal to treat Belgium as an enemy. An answer was requested within twelve hours. We also understand Belgium has categorically refused this as a flagrant violation of the law of nations. His Majesty's Government are bound to protest against this violation of a treaty to which Germany is a party in common with us, and must request an assurance that the demand made upon Belgium will not be proceeded with and that her neutrality shall be respected by Germany. (Cheers.)

We asked for an immediate reply. (Renewed cheers.)

BELGIUM INVADED.

"We received this morning from our Minister at Brussels the following telegram:

The German Minister has this morning addressed a Note to the Belgian Minister for Foreign Affairs stating that, as the Belgian Government had declined the well-intentioned proposals submitted to them by the Imperial Government, the latter, deeply to their regret, is compelled to carry out, if necessary by force of arms, the measures considered indispensable in view of the French menace.

"Simultaneously, or almost immediately afterwards, we received from the Belgian Legation here in London the following telegram from the Belgian Minister for Foreign Affairs:

General Staff announce that territory has been violated at Gemmenich, near Aix-la-Chapelle. Subsequent information tends to show the German force has penetrated still further into Belgian territory.

THE GERMAN REPLY.

"We also received this morning from the German Ambassador here a telegram sent to him by the German Foreign Secretary, and communicated by the Ambassador to us, which is in these terms:

Please dispel any mistrust that may subsist on the part of the British Government with regard to our intention by repeating most positively the formal assurance that even in the case of armed conflict with Belgium, Germany will under no pretence whatever annex Belgian territory. (Laughter.) The sincerity of this declaration is borne out by the fact that we have solemnly pledged our word to Holland strictly to respect her neutrality. It is obvious we could not profitably annex Belgian territory without making at the same time territorial acquisitions at the expense of Holland. (Laughter.)

Please impress upon Sir Edward Grey that the German army could not be exposed to French attack across Belgium, which was the plan, according to absolutely unimpeachable information. Germany has consequently to disregard Belgian neutrality, it being to her a question of life and death to prevent the French advance.

That is the end of the communication. I have to add this on behalf of his Majesty's Government:

We cannot regard this as in any sense a satisfactory communication. (Cheers.) We have in reply to it repeated the request we made last week to the German Government that they should give us the same assurance in regard to Belgian neutrality as was given to us and to Belgium by France last week—(cheers)—and we have asked that the reply to that request—a satisfactory answer to the telegram of this morning which I have read to the House—should be given before midnight. (Loud cheers.)

TO-DAY'S WEATHER.

London and Channel Forecast.—Southerly and south-easterly winds, shifting later to the westward or north-westward; rainy at first, then fair; remaining cool.

Lighting-up time, 8.42.

WHY MR. CHURCHILL RESIGNS.

SINGLE MEN FIRST.

JUSTIFICATION OF "THE DAILY MAIL."

EFFECT OF THE PLEDGE TO THE MARRIED.

RECRUITING RUSH EXPECTED.

RUSSIAN GAIN IN MARSHES.

GEN. RUSSKI'S ADVANCE ON HINDENBURG.

GERMANS THROWN BACK NEAR RIGA.

The great duel between General Russki and Hindenburg on the Riga-Dvinsk front is steadily turning to the advantage of the Russian leader. Hindenburg on Thursday blamed the weather for a withdrawal west of Riga, but the absurdity of this is proved by the news that the Russians after eleven days' severe

MR. CHURCHILL RESIGNS.

ONE OF THE 22 BUT NOT OF THE 5.

NOT ENOUGH WORK TO JUSTIFY £4,000 A YEAR.

BACK TO HIS REGIMENT IN FRANCE.

LATE WAR NEWS.

GREAT ARTILLERY DUEL.

FROM BELGIUM TO THE MEUSE.

FRENCH OFFICIAL.

Paris, Friday, 11 p.m.
Particularly violent artillery duels were reported during the day in Belgium in the region of Boesinghe, in Artois, in the sector of the Somme near Dompierre, between the Oise and the Moselle, and in the forest of Apremont. There was no infantry action.—Reuter.

SERBS HEAVILY ENGAGED.

MOUNTAIN BATTLE WITH GERMANS.

FRENCH CAPTURE TWO VILLAGES.

A TURK ON GERMAN AIMS.

The Serbians report that on Wednesday they were heavily engaged with the Germans south and east of Kraljevo, just south of which the high mountain ridges of Central Serbia begin. Here our Allies

---

PEEPS AT THE TRUTH.

GALLIPOLI GAMBLE.

MR. CHURCHILL'S EXPLANATION.

I did not receive from Lord Fisher the clear guidance or firm support I might have expected.

WHAT NAVAL EXPERTS SAID.

THE ANTWERP FIASCO.

MIDNIGHT DISTRESS OF THE CABINET.

SIR E. CARSON.

FLAT DENIAL OF SIR EDWARD GREY.

A DECISION: "TOO LATE TO HELP SERBIA."

THE MEMORANDUMS BY MR. BONAR LAW & MR. LLOYD GEORGE.

Sir Edward Carson made his important speech last night in the middle of the general debate on the Vote of Credit. It was a reply to Sir Edward Grey's speech last week.
"In my opinion," said Sir E. Carson, "Sir E. Grey's statement is inaccurate, in my opinion it is misleading, in my opinion it does a great injustice to myself."

BULGAR VILLAGE TAKEN.

FRENCH SUCCESS.

ENEMY'S NEW ROUTE TO MONASTIR.

GERMAN "PURSUIT EVERYWHERE."

The French by their capture of the Bulgarian frontier heights, reported yesterday, have succeeded in taking a village in Bulgarian territory five miles south of Strumnitsa town, which is not to be confused with the station of the same name to the west in Serbia.
It is officially stated at Salonica that the Bulgarians, who have failed to force

ALLIES' DEMANDS OF GREECE.

SOMETHING MORE THAN ARMED NEUTRALITY.

IMPORTANT TELEGRAM.

FROM OUR OWN CORRESPONDENT.

Athens, Monday.
It having been decided by the Entente Powers to create an entirely new front in the Balkans entailing the presence of a very considerable number of troops, it has been considered necessary to obtain from the Greek Government something more definite in the way of a guarantee for the forces' security than mere promises of benevolent armed neutrality.
The nature of these guarantees has not yet been declared, but I am informed in high diplomatic and military quarters that they will be in no way incon-

SINGLE MEN FIRST.

MR. ASQUITH'S REPLY.

NO COMPULSION WITHOUT THE CONSENT OF PARLIAMENT.

Mr. Whitehouse asked the Prime Minister in Parliament yesterday whether, in view of the statement issued by Lord Derby through the Press Bureau, it had been decided to apply conscription to all unmarried men of military age without the assent of the House of Commons.
Mr. Asquith said he would like to defer saying anything till today. He need not say that no attempt would be made to apply compulsion in any shape or form without the consent of Parliament. (Cheers.)

ARMLETS THIS WEEK.

NOT FOR THE REJECTED AT

U.S.A. AND THE WAR.

COLONEL ROOSEVELT'S SYMPATHIES.

THE EX-PRESIDENT IN A MINORITY.

INTERESTING INTERVIEW.

FROM OUR SPECIAL CORRESPONDENT, SYDNEY BROOKS.

New York, Monday.
I had on Saturday a long talk with Colonel Roosevelt at his country home. The ex-President's friends in England will be glad to know that he is as fit and full of fight as ever, and that he is doing all he can, first, to uphold the cause of the

---

UNDOING THE DARDANELLES BLUNDER.

SUVLA AND ANZAC EVACUATED.

GREAT ARMY WITHDRAWN WITHOUT TURKS KNOWING.

MOVE TO ANOTHER SPHERE.

CASUALTIES INSIGNIFICANT: FINE NAVAL SUPPORT.

YPRES HEAVILY SHELLED.

VIGOROUS BRITISH REPLY.

44 AIR FIGHTS.

BIG FRENCH BOMBARDMENT

BRITISH OFFICIAL.

General Headquarters, France, Monday, 9.3 p.m.
To-day, opposite the southern portion and centre of our line, we bombarded several portions of the enemy's trenches.
Hostile artillery heavily shelled Ypres and St. Jean this afternoon, and were also active against our front line and support trenches north-east of Ypres during the day.
We replied, shelling the enemy's front

GREEK KING'S CHANGED MIND.

LIGHTNING EFFECT OF ALLIES' DECISION.

BERLIN BLUFF FAILS.

NEW GREEK MOVE ON FRONTIER.

BRUSH WITH BULGARS.

Greek troops are reported to have occupied Doiran Station and town. The importance of this, if true, is that they are thus interposed between the enemy and the Allies' lines in Macedonia.

Bulgarian and Greek troops have had a brush in Albanian territory in which men of both sides were wounded. An in-

ber of submarines offered was exactly equivalent to all the submarines Germany, by a reasonable calculation, had in the world.
This evidence of the great strain is sufficiently impressive. Furthermore, Germany had promised that four fresh irresistible army corps would appear on the frontier round about November 20. The enemy submarines have been active, and their failure to produce an armada or legions has given the King his first insight into the great sham.
The halting of the Germano-Bulgarian army on the threshold of Greece is sufficient proof that, at least at present, a sufficient number of German troops is lacking and the arrival of our reinforcements is regular, so that this factor is favourable and may be said to endure.

BERLIN RIOTS' EFFECT.

The other permanent factors that have influenced Greece are the news received from the Greek Minister in Berlin, which

"TOO LATE."

MR. LLOYD GEORGE WARNS THE GOVERNMENT AND LABOUR.

THE SHELL SCANDAL IN MAY.

Germans' 250,000 a Day : British 2,500 a Day.

"You can only talk of over-ordering when we have as much as the enemy."

However, when *The Times'* correspondent in May somehow escaped the censor's pencil and disclosed that we had failed in the battle of Festubert because 'the want of an unlimited supply of high explosive was a fatal bar to our success', Northcliffe threw all caution to the winds. *The Daily Mail* weighed into the Government for its lack of foresight, and on May 21 in a withering editorial it exposed Kitchener's 'tragic blunder' and the 'scandal of the shells'. Retrospectively it claimed this was the most famous leading article it had ever published . . . 'it did its work. It told the nation what it was entitled to know'. This judgement may be coloured by the fact that within five days of the editorial the old war Cabinet had ceased to exist and a brand-new Coalition had taken its place, and that the following month a ministry of munitions had been set up with

Lloyd George at its head (this, too, had been a recurring theme at *The Daily Mail*). Nevertheless, it was a brave move: *The Daily Mail's* circulation fell immediately by over a quarter of a million, while advertisers withdrew their advertising in bulk. Copies of both *The Daily Mail* and *The Times* were burnt ceremoniously on the Stock Exchange, and ostracised from London Clubs. Yet the campaign continued, in spite of suggestions within the Cabinet that *The Times* be taken over by the Government.

Among its other war-time triumphs the Golden Number recalled in tranquility was its campaign for compulsory recruitment (though many other papers could claim the same) and its ceaseless demands for more aeroplanes. It also took a great delight in repeating its damning verdict on Asquith published the day he resigned: '. . . the destroying touch of his

feeble hand has been felt in every field of the war. The monument of his inactivity is in Gallipoli, at Kut, in western Belgium, in ruined Serbia, in hapless Rumania. For him history has repeated itself, but without teaching him anything' . . . 'Declaring he would "stick at nothing", he stuck at everything, and only moved when pushed'. For this Northcliffe had incurred the implacable wrath of the Liberal papers (though themselves disenchanted with Asquith by then). His reward was later to be offered a post in the Government as Air Minister by the new Prime Minister Lloyd George. He declined rather more publicly than the situation warranted. It was, perhaps, his first signal to Lloyd George that Northcliffe believed press lords were more important than mere ministers of state.

THE DAILY MIRROR, Saturday, November 13, 1915.

ANOTHER ENLARGED ISSUE OF "SUNDAY PICTORIAL" TO-MORROW

The Daily Mirror

CERTIFIED CIRCULATION LARGER THAN ANY OTHER PICTURE PAPER IN THE WORLD

No. 3,762. | Registered at the G.P.O. as a Newspaper. | SATURDAY, NOVEMBER 13, 1915 | One Halfpenny.

WHICH? WILL YOU BE A VOLUNTEER OR A CONSCRIPT? HOW THEY DEALT WITH "FETCHED" MEN.

There were no posters and no meetings in Trafalgar-square in the old days. The press gang had its own peculiar methods of filling up any vacancies which occurred, and this picture illustrates the "send-off" of a recruit. It is by Gillray, and is entitled "The Liberty of the Subject." Gilray lived between 1757 and 1815.

In August, 1914, men struggled to enlist—

—and mounted police were necessary to regulate the crowds outside the recruiting stations.

"If young men medically fit and not indispensable to any business of national importance, or to any business conducted for the general good of the community, do not come forward voluntarily before November 30, the Government will after that date take the necessary steps to redeem the pledge made on November 2." The pledge means "other compulsory means would be taken before the married men were called upon to fulfil their engagement to serve." Great Britain has not always had the voluntary system. Rough-and-ready means were taken to fill up the ranks, and the press gang did not stop to listen to any objections which might be put forth.

Play in your own Back Yard

America in World War I

The overture to Europe's war was as baffling to American newspapers as it was brief. On the same day that *The New York Times* concluded that a general war was 'unthinkable . . . beyond the realm of possibility' Austria declared war on Serbia: within a week the whole continent was at war. Perhaps from the remoteness of America a certain proper sense of perspective could be gained. Perhaps what it did all boil down to (in the memorable words of a local Iowa newspaper) was 'blood-mad monarchs preparing dread sacrifice . . . and wreaking ruin on fated lands'. But whatever regal folly had wrought across the ocean, once war broke out in earnest *The New York World* summed up the fervent attitude of America when it warned: 'If Europe insists on committing suicide, Europe must furnish the corpse for Europe's funeral'. Or as *The San Francisco Chronicle* put it bluntly to all protagonists: 'Play in your own back yard'.

In declaring America's neutrality President Wilson had stressed the importance of being 'neutral in fact as well as in name . . . in thought as well as in act'. Which were honourable sentiments, but hard for an outspoken press to live up to. The aggressive neutrality of *The New York Journal* (and of all Hearst's newspapers) became extremely unpopular in many quarters for appearing pro-German. *The New York Times*, on the other hand, never entirely shook off the suspicion (totally unfounded in fact) that it was somehow being controlled by mysterious British interests. But apart from the inclinations of individual editors and proprietors, there was another factor that governed the flow of war news throughout America. That was the fact that direct communications between Germany and America were cut, and most correspondents were accredited to the Allies (if only to ensure their copy got through quickly). Many papers also found it convenient to make reciprocal arrangements with the London press.

At different times in 1915 and 1916 both British and German Governments outraged public opinion by seeming to exploit, nibble away at, or openly flout American neutrality. Britain, with her superiority on the seas, tended to interpret maritime law to suit her own ends: what constituted contraband cargo was conveniently defined in Whitehall and seized from neutral ships accordingly; the blockade of Germany was rigorously enforced to the inconvenience of many non-combatants; a blacklist was issued against eighty US firms suspected of trading with the enemy. The American flag was frequently hoisted by British ships seeking to escape the U-Boats, while American mail was constantly intercepted and examined. Wilson expended a great deal of ink, formally protesting against these practices – but no action was ever taken, for these were only offences against American property (which after all were always fully compensated) or, at worst, against American pride.

The same could not be said of the Kaiser, however. His saboteurs and submarines not only took an immense toll on U.S. property, but increasingly, as the war ground on, on American lives as well. On land repeated efforts were made to disrupt the American supply of munitions to Britain by bomb plots in factories, steel plants and docks. Many were discovered, some were successful – but almost any domestic catastrophe not immediately attributable to the due processes of nature was readily ascribed by

The "warning" which appeared in several New York papers the week before the Lusitania sailed.

sections of the Press to the insidious presence of German saboteurs.

On the high seas, German atrocities were still more blatant. In the early stages of the war American ships were fired on, with earnest German apologies ricocheting to and fro after the event. Far more serious were the U-Boat attacks on civilian liners, often carrying American passengers. The Germans suspected (sometimes correctly) these boats were armed or carrying munitions – though rarely did a submarine captain wait long enough to find out. On May 7 1915 the British liner Lusitania was sunk by a German torpedo off the coast of Ireland: 1,198 people lost their lives, including 124 American citizens. The nation was incensed. 'Premeditated slaughter' *The New York Herald* called it; and *The New York American* – 'wholesale murder'. *The New York Tribune* was not far from the mark when its headline emotively recalled America's last great naval insult, the sinking of the Maine. In England, *The Daily Mail* happily fuelled the fires of indignation by publishing a piteous photograph of American babies 'murdered by the Kaiser'. A reminder that, on the morning the Lusitania sailed, an advert (supposedly inserted by the German Embassy) had appeared in major New York papers, warning Americans not to travel in it, served only to convince people further of the Huns' evil intent.

Against the rising tide for intervention Hearst's *New York Journal*, while admitting this was reminiscent 'of the days of ocean piracy', still saw this as no reason to get warlike: 'it should be the determination of the U.S. to KEEP OUT OF THE WAR. We, at least, did not begin this war; we are not responsible for it; we don't *want* it'. Nor yet did President Wilson, who contented himself with a salvo of stern diplomatic notes and a stiff demand for indemnity. Nor was he inclined to change his pen for a sword (or his typewriter for tanks) when yet more Americans were torpedoed on the Arabic in August and on the Sussex the following March – but neither did he forbid American citizens to travel on belligerent vessels, which would have been the reaction of a more dedicated neutralist.

Then in the summer of 1916 much of the fund of good will towards Britain which had been accumulating in America was dissipated by news of the summary vengeance exacted by the British Government on the Irish rebels who had risen in revolt on Easter Monday. In particular there was much resentment at the execution of Sir Roger Casement who had landed in Ireland from a German submarine in the course of the rising. In vain did George Bernard Shaw write in *The Manchester Guardian* that 'Casement should be treated as a prisoner of war. I believe this is the view that will be taken in the neutral countries, whose good opinion is much more important to us than the satisfaction of our resentment'. In America Randolph Hearst thundered that 'England faces Eternal Infamy' in putting Casement to death, and instructed all his papers to pen furious editorials. *The New York Journal* did more: it even printed Hearst's letter to the editor. It began: 'Please write an editorial on Sir Roger Casement's speech. It seems to me a wonderful effort and tells a fundamental truth about the attitude of Englishmen toward Irishmen and, in fact, toward everybody except Englishmen.' And it ended: 'Of course Englishmen cannot understand or

New York Tribune

First to Last—the Truth: News - Editorials - Advertisements

Vol. LXXV.... No. 25,010.

[Copyright, 1915,
By The Tribune Association.]

SATURDAY, MAY 8, 1915.

PRICE ONE CENT In City of New York, Newark, Jersey City and Hoboken, ELSEWHERE TWO CENTS.

WEATHER
FAIR TO-DAY AND TO-MORROW;
SOUTHWEST TO WEST WINDS.
Yesterday's Temperatures:
High, 64; Low, 55.
Full report on Page 13.

GUARANTEE
Your Money Back
If You Want It.
See Editorial Page, First Column.

900 Die as Lusitania Goes to Bottom; 400 Americans on Board Torpedoed Ship; Washington Stirred as When Maine Sank

CAPITAL AROUSED, SITUATION GRAVEST YET FACED IN WAR

Washington Determined That Germany Shall Not Be Allowed to Shirk Responsibility for Deaths.

GREATLY FEARS LOSS OF AMERICANS

President Shows Nervousness as Bulletins of Disaster Come In—Strongest Protest Yet Made Planned Even if No U. S. Citizens Were Lost

[From The Tribune Bureau.]

Washington, May 7.—The news of the heavy loss of life on the Lusitania stirred Washington as it has not been stirred since the sinking of the Maine. The earlier reports that both passengers and crew had been landed safely had quieted apprehensions of an immediate crisis in the relations of the United States and Germany. But when it became clear that Americans—undoubtedly a considerable number of them—were to be counted among the victims of German savagery at sea the full significance of the tragedy off Queenstown struck home.

President Wilson made little effort to conceal his feelings. At 8 o'clock to-night the President received the following dispatch from the United States Consul at Cork:

"Lusitania sank at 2:30 o'clock. Probably many survivors. Rescue work proceeding favorably. Shall I send you list of survivors?"

As soon as he read it he put on his hat and walked out of the White House without the knowledge of the Secret Service men who are guarding him. The President walked up Sixteenth Street to Corcoran Street, crossed over to Fifteenth Street and back to the White House, where he went into his study to await further information and to turn over in his mind the message that it is expected he will send to the German Foreign Office as soon as all the details of the disaster are known.

Cabinet To Be Called Together.

The President will probably call the Cabinet together to-morrow to discuss what action this government may take.

In reply to the inquiry from Consul Frost, at Queenstown, as to whether he should send a list of survivors, the State Department instructed him to send a list of all Americans dead, injured or missing.

That State Department officials feared the sinking of the Lusitania or some other large passenger-carrying vessel was indicated a few days ago, when Secretary Bryan issued a statement saying that no passports would be issued to persons going abroad for pleasure.

High officials in the administration declined to-night to discuss the possibility of this country being drawn into the war because of the loss of American lives. They insisted upon taking an optimistic view of the situation and asserted that when the list of survivors was finally made up few would be found to be missing.

That the situation will be acute when loss of American lives is proved is admitted on all sides. No action will be taken by this government until all the details of the torpedoing of the Lusitania are received. There is one thing certain, however, and that it that Germany will not be allowed to shirk any responsibility for the disaster, should investigation show that the act was performed by a German submarine.

The possibility of the Lusitania having struck a mine was discounted here by the receipt of news that the British Admiralty had given assurances that there were no mines in the neighborhood in which the vessel was blown up.

Protest Will Be Vigorous.

Even if no American lives had been lost, the sinking of the Cunard liner by a German torpedo would have been made a part of the most vigorous protest that the American government had yet transmitted to the German Foreign Office. This is the belief of officials high in the administration to-night.

The United States has repeatedly asserted that it recognizes the right of belligerents to visit and search only, and that it will hold the German government to strict accountability for the loss of any American lives through the undersea warfare of the German government.

The United States has no concern over the sinking of the Lusitania itself, but it is gravely concerned over the probable loss of the lives of American citizens through the activity of German submarines in the war zone. In the note of the American government to the German Foreign Office on February 10 it was declared that this country would take any steps it might think necessary to safeguard American lives and property and to secure to American citizens the full enjoyment of their

Continued on page 2, column 8

LONDON SEES VITAL QUESTION FOR U. S.

America Is 'Bound to Defend Lives of Its Subjects,' Declares 'Daily News.'

[By Cable to The Tribune.]

London, May 8.—The "Daily Chronicle" says editorially to-day:

"To destroy by deliberate aim one of the great floating towns which traverse the Atlantic without something like 2,000 lives in their keeping, is to attempt in cold blood such a massacre o fnon-combatants as even the most ferocious conquerers have seldom perpetrated save in heat.

"When, last October, the Germans began to sow floating mines in the Atlantic, a shudder went through the civilised world on realizing that the Olympic had come near to striking one. But nobody at the time, in Germany or elsewhere, ventured to suggest that the sailors of a civilized power would actually aim a torpedo to bring about such a catastrophe. Step by step then the German admiralty, like the German General Staff, has progressed from infamy to infamy.

"From the notice circulated last week by the German embassy in the United States, it is plain that this final crime was not the work of a particular submarine officer over-tempted by an opportunity, but that it was done on express orders of Berlin.

"The sowing of illegal mines, the submarining of merchantmen, the butchery of fishermen, the Falaba case, the Lusitania case—it is a long and terrible list. On land, the sacking of towns, the massacre of non-combatants, the use of explosive bullets and asphyxiating gas, the poisoning of wells with arsenic and with disease'—all develop a hideous parallel.

"We have said before, and repeat now, that the United States of Germany's making war in this way is to render it absolutely impossible for the Allies to conclude such a peace with her as they might otherwise have concluded. The policy of the Allies in consequence of those atrocities cannot be what it would have been if they had not occurred. It would be a disastrous day to mankind and for civilization if the Allied statesmen ever thought it could. A more drastic surgery will be needed for the cancer of German militarism than any wise prophet could have predicted last August."

Raises Question for United States.

"The Daily News," in its editorial this morning on the sinking of the Lusitania, says:

"Nothing the Germans have done will

Continued on page 3, column 1

THE LUSITANIA, SUNK BY GERMAN TORPEDO, WITH HEAVY LOSS OF LIFE.

GERMANS TOAST 'VICTORY' AMID 'HOCHS' IN CAFES

Steins Clink as Celebrators Predict Downfall of Britain's Sea Power.

OFFICERS GAY IN CLUBHOUSE

Restaurants Thronged and Entire Families Out to Cheer Kaiser and His Submarines.

"Deutschland, Deutschland, Ueber Alles" resounded last night wherever Germans met to discuss and to toast "the day" which, to their mond, sealed the fate of British world dominion on the seas. In the fashionable German Club, headquarters of the Teutonic élite and camping ground of German military officers unable to join the colors, the sinking of the Lusitania was the principal topic of animated conversation. Everything else was forgotten in the blow struck at Britain, the "arch enemy," through the torpedoing of the Lusitania.

"This is a masterstroke, which will curb transatlantic travelling and isolate Great Britain more effectively than a whole fleet of super-dreadnoughts could possibly accomplish," said a stalwart captain of cavalry. "It's the doom of Great Britain."

And then followed the toasts to the Kaiser, to von Tirpitz and to the U boat heroes.

At Luebow's, in Fourteenth Street, the show of patriotism was exuberant, for ruthlessly sinking a merchant ship for ruthlessly sinking a merchant ship to play only patriotic songs, and these were sung with a vim by the Germans, who packed the premises to suffocation. With wives and children they had come to celebrate the "victory."

The orchestra had been instructed to play only patriotic songs, and these were sung with a vim by the Germans, who packed the premises to suffocation. With wives and children they had come to celebrate the "victory." The goblet and stein were raised often to the Kaiser last night at the Hofbrau Haus, Broadway and Thirtieth Street, and at the Kaiserhof, 1416 Broadway. There was little noise at either place, but there was a marked feeling of good cheer and camaraderie in the news that the Lusitania had been sunk by a German submarine.

"A thousand dollars is a fortune to me," shouted the cashier at the Hofbrau Haus, "but I'd willingly lose it for the sake of hearing the greatest bit of news in many a day. Just watch poor Britain sneaking back with a scorched tail."

Victims Were Warned.

"They were warned!" exclaimed a sober enthusiast, as he ordered a round of drinks for all present. "They were told that if they sailed they ran chances of being torpedoed. Now they've got it good and plenty."

One young man explained that $5,000,000 worth of war munitions had

Continued on page 3, column 4

U. S. OWES IT TO SELF-RESPECT TO ACT, SAYS ROOSEVELT; 'PIRACY ON VAST SCALE'

[From a Staff Correspondent of The Tribune.]

Syracuse, May 7.—After the appalling details of the Lusitania disaster had been told to Colonel Roosevelt late to-night he said: "It seems inconceivable that we should refrain from taking action on this matter, for we owe it not only to humanity but to our own national self-respect.

"This represents not merely piracy, but piracy on a vaster scale of murder than any oldtime pirate ever practiced. This is the warfare which destroyed Louvain and Dinant and hundreds of men, women and children in Belgium; warfare to innocent men, women and children travelling on the ocean, to our own fellow country men and country women who are among the sufferers."

ACT OF BARBARITY, SAYS F. R. COUDERT

Lawyer Insists Sinking of the Lusitania Is Without Justification.

"An act of barbarity without justification," was the expression of Frederic R. Coudert, of the law firm of Coudert Brothers, in referring to the torpedoing of the Lusitania.

"I make that statement on the supposition that lives of citizens of the United States, a neutral nation, were destroyed by the sinking of the vessel," he added. "Until it is known definitely what the results of the explosion are it is impossible to hint at the stand this government may take.

"There is no justification, however, for ruthlessly sinking a merchant ship in the open seas when that vessel is not engaged in any manner as a belligerent vessel and when the lives of noncombatants depend upon its safety.

"Of course, a great deal depends upon whether the Lusitania was sunk with the loss of American life. If that was done, however, it would seem to be time for the government of this country to determine whether it will sit idly by and accept explanations that Americans were warned to keep off the steamer or take a definite stand upon the rights of our citizens on the seas. To deliberately sink a passenger-carrying ship without warning or allowing opportunity for the passengers to leave is an act that cannot be condoned. It is a serious matter when it is considered that no consideration was given the lives of people of this country when the attempt was made to send them to the ocean's bottom as they lay asleep in the cabins."

FIRST SURVIVORS' NAMES RECEIVED

The first names of survivors of the Lusitania disaster received here are as follows:

Lassiger, General, and son, first cabin.
Bretherton, Mrs., second cabin.
Smith, George A., New York, wine merchant.
Smith, Mrs. J. T., Braceville, Ohio.

SOUTH COAST OF IRELAND.
Showing where the Lusitania was attacked and the points where survivors of the passengers and crew were landed.

MANY NOTED NEW YORKERS ON LUSITANIA

Alfred G. Vanderbilt Was on Way to England on Business Trip.

N. J. REPRESENTED ON FIRST CABIN LIST

Charles Frohman, Lindon Bates, Jr., Charles Klein and Justus Miles Forman Aboard.

The first cabin list of the Lusitania's first cabin list was composed of New Yorkers.

Alfred G. Vanderbilt was necessarily a prominent figure among the passengers. His brother, Cornelius, was, like many others, skeptical when he heard the first rumors about the Cunarder's fate. Captain George C. Day and Commander F. L. Sawyer, both United States naval officers, who are working with Mr. Vanderbilt on the plans for the reception of the Atlantic fleet, were incredulous, too. But when Mr. Vanderbilt learned through The Tribune that the news had been confirmed, he asked the newspaper for ten-minute bulletins.

His brother Alfred expected to be gone for four or five weeks on a business trip. Had it not been for the war, Mrs. Vanderbilt would have accompanied her husband on the Lusitania.

Major F. Warren Pearl and Mrs. Pearl, who sailed with their children, are well known in New York. Both had intended to do war aid work. Major Pearl, who is a surgeon, was to be attached to a field hospital for the Allies in Belgium, while Mrs. Pearl hoped to assist the wounded. She is the daughter of Mrs. J. P. Duncan and sister of Mrs. Ottomar H. Van Norden and Mrs. George D. Dunscombe.

Another woman passenger who went over on the Lusitania to do relief work for Belgium was Mrs. O. H. Hammond, who accompanied her husband, a member of Frank & DeBois, insurance brokers, at 80 Maiden Lane. The Jammonds live at 30 East Seventieth Street. Before her marriage Mrs. Hammond was a Miss Stevens, a member of the well known Castle Point family.

Charles Frohman was on his annual business tour intending to look over his foreign interests and to pick up some plays. He was accompanied by Justus Miles Forman, the author, whose first play, "The Hyphen," a war drama, was produced in New York a few weeks ago. Edgar Gorer, the London and New York art dealer, who has a connection here through Dreicer & Co., and who is now bringing a $575,000 slander suit against Joseph J. and Henry J. Duveen, was also a passenger.

Charles F. Fowles, who was accom-

Continued on page 8, column 1

Dying and Injured Brought in with Other Survivors to Queenstown—Some Landed at Kinsale and Clonakilty.

TWO TORPEDOES FIRED, SAYS STEWARD

Attack Made About Eight Miles from Irish Coast in Broad Daylight and in Fine Weather—Survivor Tells of Bravery of Cunard Officers.

[By Cable to The Tribune.]

London, May 8, 3 a. m.—At least 900 lives were lost when the Lusitania was torpedoed without warning in broad daylight yesterday afternoon by a German submarine, according to estimates by survivors. The estimate of First Officer Jones puts the total nearer 1,500.

Of the dead more than two hundred are supposed to be Americans, as it is believed there were about 400 on board.

A dispatch from Queenstown sent out at midnight says:

"Up to the present 520 passengers from the Lusitania had been landed here from boats. Ten or eleven boatloads came ashore, and others are expected."

The motor boat Elizabeth has arrived at Kinsale and reports that at 3:30 p. m. she picked up two lifeboats containing 63 and 16 survivors of the Lusitania, respectively. A Cork tug took the rescued to Queenstown. They were mostly women and children.

The Lusitania could not launch many of her lifeboats.

The tiny hospitals at Kinsale and Clonakilty, and the institutions at Cork and Queenstown are jammed with survivors from the ocean horror, those not actually wounded suffering terribly from shock. The giant Cunarder now rests on the bottom of the ocean, about eight miles off Kinsale Head and twenty miles from the entrance to Queenstown Harbor.

ADMIRALTY GIVES OUT NEWS.

Telegrams have been filtering into London last night and early this morning stating that the rescued are being brought to Queenstown by three steamers. The Admiralty says between five and six hundred have already been landed at Clonakilty and Kinsale, coming into the latter port in a string of boats towed by a Greek steamer. Motor fishing boats hovered near the scene of the wreck, picking up what boats they could and turning them over to the powerful ocean going tug Stormcock.

Huge crowds fill Cockspur Street near the Haymarket, storming the Cunard offices for news. The women, who had been weeping so bitterly, paused for a moment when an agent of the line bellowed through a megaphone the following dispatch:

"Our Liverpool office says First Officer Jones wires from Queenstown he thinks between five hundred and six hundred have been saved. This includes passengers and crew, and is only an estimate."

A steward in the first boat which landed at Kinsale said he feared that 900 lives had been lost.

THE PASSENGERS WERE AT LUNCHEON.

The tug Stormcock returned to Queenstown, bringing about one hundred and fifty survivors, principally passengers, among whom were many women, several of the crew and one steward.

Describing the experience of the Lusitania, the steward said: "The passengers were at luncheon, when a submarine came up and fired two torpedoes, which struck the Lusitania on the starboard side, one forward and the other in the engine room. They caused terrific explosions.

"Captain Turner immediately ordered the boats out. The ship began to list badly immediately.

"Ten boats were put into the water, and between four hundred and five hundred passengers entered them. The boat in which I was approached the land with three other boats, and we were picked up shortly after 4 o'clock by the Stormcock.

"I fear that few of the officers were saved. They acted bravely."

WENT DOWN BY BOW.

"There were only fifteen minutes from the time the ship was struck until she foundered, going down bow foremost. It was a dreadful sight."

More dispatches brought word that the hotel and lodging houses are being canvassed in an effort to obtain more or less authoritative lists of the survivors.

One of the first persons landed from the ship by a boat which reached Kinsale Head was General H. B. Lassetter, late commander of an Australian Light Horse Brigade. His wife and he were returning from a trip to Los Angeles. George A. Kessaler, the New York wine agent, and Mrs. J. T. Smith, of Braceville, Ohio, were also reported among the saved.

The Admiralty gave out the official news about midnight that the attack was made in broad daylight and with absolutely no warning.

A Queenstown dispatch to "The Daily Chronicle" says that seven torpedoes were discharged from the German craft and that one of them struck the Lusitania amidships.

There is no question in anyone's mind here that it was a submarine which caused the disaster. There is information at hand

Little Girl's Dime May Build A Warship to Guard America

Child, Tired of Funds for Foreigners, Starts One for Own Nation.

A little girl sent a dime to The Tribune yesterday. With it was the following letter:

"369 St. John's Place, Brooklyn,
February 2, 1916.
"To the Editor of The Tribune.

"Dear sir: I read in your paper every morning a lot about preparedness. My grandpa and greatgrandpa were soldiers. If I was a boy I would be a soldier, too. But I am not, so I want to do what I can to help. Mama gives me a dime every week for helping her. I am sending you this week's dime to help build a battleship for Uncle Sam. I know a lot of other kids who would give their errand money if you would start a fund. I am thirteen years old and go to Public School 9, Brooklyn. Truly yours,

"MARJORIE STERRETT.

"I am true blue American and I want to see Uncle Sam prepared to lick all creation like John Paul Jones did.

"P. S.—Please call the battleship America."

Only a little girl's letter, but to the editor, weary of spies and hyphenated citizens and the complications of literary diplomacy, it seemed to speak the heart of America itself. There must be thousands of children like her, wholesome, ardent little patriots. Why not let them speak for their country?

Marjorie was embarrassed, but plucky. It never occurred to her when she wrote the letter to The Tribune that it would mean expounding her views on patriotism and preparedness for publication. However, if her country needed her——

"I just got tired of all these funds for Belgium and everything," she said, "and when it came to America, nothing doing."

She sat on the edge of the library

Marjorie Sterrett and her baby sister, Ruth.

table, twisting her long curls bashfully, and only now and then favoring the reporter with a peep at her true blue American eyes.

"I just wrote the letter because I thought maybe other children would like to give money if they knew where to send it. I am going to get the other girls in my class to give their dimes to-morrow. We all know about the Revolution and the War of 1812 and John Paul Jones, because we had them in our history class. Most of the girls are foreigners, but they ought to be proud of America, too."

"Would you be able to tell them

Continued on page 6, column 4

---

appreciated these facts at this time. They learn, like the dull boy at school, only through the application of the rod. Nor was Mr. Hearst averse to applying it. But then, on this occasion, even *The New York Times* agreed that the execution of the Irish leaders was 'incredibly stupid'.

Since the outbreak of the war there had been an escalating debate within America concerning the best way to preserve the country's neutrality inviolate. Wilson himself — possibly looking forward to a role of blameless peacemaker when hostilities ceased — had always resisted any pressure towards armament. In this he was stoutly supported by leading pacifists like Secretary of State Bryan and Henry Ford (whose contribution had been a much-derided scheme to send a Peace Ship to Europe at the end of 1915, with the declared intention of 'getting the boys out of the trenches before Christmas'). Against them stood Theodore Roosevelt, who was constantly composing urgent philippics on the inadequacy of national defence and was the leading proponent of the policy of 'Preparedness'. As the war brought more and more challenges to American rights on the sea, Wilson too began to incline towards a measure of Preparedness. By the beginning of 1916 he had embarked on a cautious campaign, which many newspapers were delighted to reflect in their columns.

The New York Tribune was only one of them, but its crusade found a touch of originality which ignited the imaginations of ordinary folk all over the continent. The idea came by chance — more accurately, it came through the post one morning in February 1916. In a letter to the editor a little girl from Brooklyn who had 'read in your paper every morning a lot about preparedness' enclosed a dime to help build 'a battleship for Uncle Sam. (P.S. Would they call the battleship 'America'?)'. When a reporter went round to see Marjorie Sterrett in Brooklyn she explained she had 'got tired of all these funds for Belgium and everything — and when it came to America, nothing doing'. The next day *The New York Tribune* ran her picture and her letter on the front page. Well, why not? If everyone in America gave a dime, perhaps she'd get her battleship.

So, on a dime, 'Marjorie's Battleship' Fund was launched. Three days later Theodore Roosevelt sent Marjorie ten dimes, 'four for his four grandchildren' and six more for the future grandchildren the ex-President hoped to have some day. Now *The New York Tribune* knew it was on a winner: from then on Marjorie never

THEODORE ROOSEVELT TO MARJORIE STERRETT

SAGAMORE HILL Feb 5th 1916

Dear little Miss Marjorie,

On behalf of my four grandchildren I join in the effort to help you and your schoolfellows put our country in shape to "Fear God, and Take Her Own Part".

I enclose a dollar. Forty cents — a dime apiece — are for:—

Gracie Roosevelt
Richard Derby II
Theodore Roosevelt III
Cornelius Van Schaak Roosevelt

Cornelius is the youngest. He is only about two months old. He isn't as long as his name. But he will grow up to it. He is named after his great-great-grandfather, who when I was very small, over fifty years ago, helped teach me a Dutch baby-song. Little Richard is the eighth Richard Derby, from father to son, born here in America. He loves the bulldog — a nice, friendly, almost toothless bulldog. Little Ted is really Theodore IV; for my father was

Theodore Roosevelt. He was the best man I ever knew; strong, fearless, gentle. He "feared God and took his own part"! Gracie is four. The other day her mother was giving her one of her first bible lessons.

Her mother said "Now, Gracie, remember that God made everything."

Gracie (much impressed) "Did He make everything?"

Her mother (with emphasis) "Yes; everything!"

Gracie (after a pause) "Well, He didn't make my leggings fit very well; but I'm sure He meant to, so I won't say anything about it!"

The other sixty cents are for my other six grandchildren. They are not born yet. If they are girls I think some of them will be named Edith, Alice, Ethel, Eleanor and Belle. If they are boys some of them will be

named Kermit, Archie, Quentin and Jonathan Edwards. Jonathan Edwards was an ancestor of their grandmother's, who lived in colonial times. He was a great preacher and a strong and good man. I don't agree with all his theology; but his life teaches the two lessons which are more important than all others for the Americans of today; for he always acted in accordance with the strongest sense of duty, and there wasn't a touch of the mollycoddle about him.

Your friend
Theodore Roosevelt

BATTLESHIP GIFT A JERSEY BULL

Connecticut Breeder Sends Four-Legged Dime to Help Preparedness.

DREADNOUGHT NEVER TOO PROUD TO FIGHT

Contribution Accepted, and Plans Are Under Way to Add Him to Fund.

left the front page. She became a national celebrity overnight, making public appearances, attending gala charity performances, appealing cutely but convincingly for more and more dimes. In under two weeks the fund had topped $1,000 in dimes and soon larger donations and gifts (including a Jersey Bull) were pouring in from every State. Marjorie failed to collect enough to build her battleship (even a pocket one), but by the beginning of 1917 that was irrelevant anyway, for a $500 million naval construction project was well under way. Which was just as well, because in January two events occurred which were to drag America inexorably into the war. In the middle of the month a coded cable was received by the German ambassador in Mexico from his Foreign Minister Zimmermann, advising him to seek an alliance with America's troublesome neighbour in the event of a war between Germany and the U.S. It so happened that the infamous 'Zimmermann telegram' had been intercepted by British Intelligence, who were keeping it in cold storage until America was psychologically prepared to receive it. That wasn't long. On January 31 Germany — convinced that America would soon be in the war anyway — announced its policy of unrestricted naval warfare.

Neutrality was now a dead letter. On February 3 the U.S. broke off diplomatic relations. On the 25th Britain revealed the contents of the Zimmermann telegram, which coupled with news of a number of American ships sunk without warning fanned the embers of indignation to the burning pitch of war fever. On April 2 the President confronted Congress and solemnly called on America to throw in its lot with the Allies. 'It is a fearful thing' the public read next morning that he had told the House 'to lead this great peaceful people into war, into the most terrible and disastrous of all wars, civilization itself seeming to be in the balance. But the right is more precious than peace, and we shall fight for the things which we have always carried nearest our hearts — for democracy, for the right of all those who submit to authority to have a voice in their own Governments . . .' Congress cheered him hoarse. Four days later America was at war.

New York Tribune

First to Last — the Truth: News · Editorials · Advertisements

Vol. LXXVI No. 25,645   The Trib.   **THURSDAY, FEBRUARY 1, 1917**   ··   ONE CENT In New York City, Newark, Jersey City and Hoboken

Berlin Orders Ruthless U-Boat War; Puts Rigid Limit on American Ships; Washington Fears Break Will Follow

U. S. CLOSES NEW YORK HARBOR TO ALL SHIPPING

Destroyers Bar Incoming and Outgoing Craft at Quarantine

URGE NOBEL PEACE PRIZE FOR KAISER

Berlin, Jan. 31.—The legal and literary faculties of Stamboul University, says a despatch from Constantinople, on being asked to suggest a candidate for the Nobel Peace Prize, have named the German Emperor as the "fore-fighter for the peace idea."

MALONE GUARDS PORT NEUTRALITY

Several Vessels, Including Towboats, Turned Back by Warships

The United States destroyers Henly and Burroughs, on guard off Quarantine, held the gates of New York

BRITAIN READY FOR NEW PERIL

TEXT OF GERMAN WARNING

Submarine Pledge to the United States Repudiated

Washington, Jan. 31.—Ambassador von Bernstorff presented the following memorandum from the German Government to Secretary of State Lansing to-day:

Washington, Jan. 31, 1917.

Mr. Secretary of State.

Your Excellency was good enough to transmit to the Imperial Government a copy of the message which the President of the United States of America addressed to the Senate on the 22d inst. The Imperial Government has given it the earnest consideration which the President's statements deserve, inspired, as they are, by a deep sentiment of responsibility.

It is highly gratifying to the Imperial Government to ascertain that the main tendencies of this important statement correspond largely to the desires and principles professed by Germany. These principles especially include self-government and equality of rights for all nations.

Germany would be sincerely glad if in recognition of this principle countries like Ireland and India, which

After attempts to come to an understanding with the Entente powers have been answered by the latter with the announcement of an intensified continuation of the war, the Imperial Government—to serve the welfare of mankind in a higher sense and not to wrong its own people—**is now compelled to continue the fight for existence, again forced upon it, with the full employment of all the weapons which are at its disposal.**

Sincerely trusting that the people and the government of the United States will understand the motives for this decision and its necessity, the Imperial Government hopes that the United States may view the new situation from the lofty heights of impartiality and assist on their part to prevent further misery and unavoidable sacrifice of human life.

Enclosing two memoranda regarding the details of the contemplated military measures at sea, I remain, etc.
(Signed.)   J. BERNSTORFF.

Germany Tells America Where and How Her Ships May Sail

U. S. ON "VERGE OF WAR" IF WILSON BACKS NOTES

Diplomats See No Peaceful Way Out Under Sussex Case Ultimatum to Germany

OFFICIALS ARE STUNNED; BLOCKADE BEGINS TO-DAY

President Reads Kaiser's Message Until Late at Night—Teutons Believed to Have Between 300 and 500 U-Boats Ready

ALL THE NEWS THAT'S FIT TO PRINT

THE NEW YORK HERALD.

IT SHINES FOR ALL

PART II. NEW YORK, THURSDAY, MARCH 1, 1917.—[COPYRIGHT, 1917, BY THE NEW YORK HERALD COMPANY.] PRICE ONE CENT

JAPAN AND MEXICO ASKED BY PRUSSIANS TO JOIN THEM AND MAKE WAR ON AMERICA; DARING PLOT LONG KNOWN TO MR. WILSON

ARMED NEUTRALITY MEASURE IN MOST DRASTIC FORM IS CERTAIN TO BE PASSED AT THIS SESSION

publican Opposition to the Authorization of Action by the President Is Dispelled and the Proposed Filibuster by Senator La Follette Is Expected To Be Killed by Weight of Numbers.

HOUSE COMMITTEE ELIMINATES PROVISION GRANTING BROAD POWER TO THE EXECUTIVE

Retention of the Clause by the Senate Is Believed to Meet the Wishes of a Majority of the Lawmakers—$100,000,000 Bond Issue Approved.

William Eva, Civil War Veteran of 74, Lost with the Laconia

William Eva, who was lost when the steamship Laconia was torpedoed off the Irish coast Sunday night, was an American citizen, according to an announcement by Cunard line officials here last night. He was seventy-four years old and lived in California, where he was interested in mining properties. He served in the civil war as a marine on the Union side, it was said.

HERALD BUREAU,
No. 1,502 H STREET, N. W.,
Washington, Thursday.

Crumbling republican opposition in Congress to President Wilson's request for unlimited power to use the armed forces of the United States against the Prussian submarines makes the enactment of the armed neutrality bill in its most drastic form now almost a certainty within a few days.

Although Senator La Follette, of Wisconsin, progressive republican and pacifics, apparently is preparing to wage a determined filibuster against the bill, it seems likely that, in the last few days of the session, he will be overwhelmed by the rapidly solidifying forces of both the democratic and republican parties favoring drastic operations against the Prussians.

By the action yesterday of the Committee on Foreign Affairs of the House the issue over granting unlimited powers to the President was squarely joined. The committee voted 17 to 4 to order a favorable report on the Armed Neutrality bill, authorizing the President to arm merchant vessels for defence but eliminating the authority "to employ such other instrumentalities and methods as in his judgment and discretion seem necessary and adequate." But the Senate Committee on Foreign Relations has agreed upon a bill which retains this authorization to employ unlimited means, and is even more drastic than the original recommendations of President Wilson.

Forecast in Senate Action.

The significant fact in the much muddled situation is that the Senate committee is made up of leaders of both parties, and its action, therefore, is a forecast of what a majority of the Senate will do, whereas, on the other band, the House committee is not a representative body of men and its action yesterday is not regarded as foreshadowing the vote in the House when the bill comes up for consideration. It seems certain that the drastic armed neutrality bill as drafted by the Senate committee and reported fully in the HERALD yesterday morning will be enacted by Congress.

Senator La Follette began a single handed filibuster against the bill when the Senate reconvened at five minutes to one o'clock this morning, after a recess of ten minutes following passage of the Revenue bill.

Prompt objection to the consideration of the Neutrality bill came from Senator La Follette, who insisted upon consuming time reading the Journal of previous days, over the vigorous objection of Senators Fall and Poindexter, republicans.

Senator Stone, chairman of the Foreign Relations Committee, had sought unanimous consent to dispense with parliamentary formalities in order to get the measure before the Senate.

Finally the Wisconsin Senator was induced to withdraw his objection on condition that there should be no attempt to pass the bill before Friday. When democratic leaders agreed to that the committee presented the bill with a favorable report and Senator Stone asked that it go over until Friday.

The Senate then adjourned until ten o'clock this morning, the majority abandoning arrangements for taking up the Naval Appropriation bill.

Representative Flood, of Virginia, chairman of the House Foreign Affairs Committee, yesterday told the members that he had been assured by two Cabinet officers—Mr. McAdoo, Secretary of the Treasury, and Mr. Burlson, Postmaster General—that the amended House bill would be acceptable to the administration. Other prominent democrats in the House assert that the President is not willing to accept the limit on his power. It is certain that vigorous efforts will be made to retain the language which the committee killed and that administration leaders will aid in the effort.

Fight Over Munition Ships.

A hard fight was made in the committee by Representative Cooper, ranking republican, of Wisconsin, and Representative Porter, republican, of Pennsylvania, to prevent ships carrying munitions of war or contraband of war from being armed. Amendments offered for that purpose were defeated.

The meeting was secret, but it is understood that the following members voted for the amendment denying arms to ships carrying munitions:—Democrats, Representatives Huddleston, Alabama; Smith, New York; Ragsdale, South Carolina; Thompson, Oklahoma, and Shackleford, Missouri. Republicans, Representatives Cooper, Wisconsin, and Porter, Pennsylvania.

As a concession to the members opposing arms for munition ships, an

(CONTINUED ON PAGE TEN, COLUMNS SIX AND SEVEN.)

THE PIFFLE STEAMS UNDER ORDERS FROM WILHELMSTRASSE.

ARMING OF AMERICAN VESSELS MEANS FIGHT AND CERTAIN WAR

[By Cable to the Associated Press.]

AMSTERDAM, via LONDON, Wednesday.

Referring to President Wilson's statement to Congress, in asking for power to arm American ships, that the overt act had not yet occurred, the Cologne Volks Zeitung, a copy of which has been received here, says:—

"It is only due to a lucky accident that American ships have not been sent to the bottom, and unless American ships avoid the danger zone the overt act is bound to come. There is no doubt that the arming of American merchantmen will mean a fight between submarines and American vessels, which necessarily will produce a state of war."

KINSMAN OF AMERICAN WOMEN LOST WITH THE LACONIA MAKES APPEAL

Austin Y. Hoy, Whose Mother and Sister Perished, Cables to President Wilson Demanding Revenge for "Foul Murder"—Four American Consular Officers Held as Hostages by Germans—Fact Kept Secret by State Department.

HERALD BUREAU,
No. 1,502 H STREET, N. W.,
WASHINGTON, D. C., Wednesday.

Crowning the damning evidence received concerning the lawless attack on the steamship Laconia, of the Cunard line, President Wilson to-day received from Austin Y. Hoy, the son and brother of the two American women "foully murdered" in the submarine attack, an appeal to avenge their deaths and to spare other Americans from such grief by upholding American rights. Here is Mr. Hoy's cable message to the President:—

"I am an American citizen representing the Sullivan Machinery Company, of Chicago, living abroad not as an expatriate, but for the promotion of American trade. I love the flag, believing in its significance. My beloved mother and sister, passengers on the Laconia, have been foully murdered on the high seas.

"As an American citizen outraged and as such fully within my rights, and as an American citizen and brother bereaved, I call upon my government to preserve its citizens' self-respect and save others of my countrymen from such deep grief as I now feel. I am of military age, able to fight. If my country can use me against these brutal assassins I am at its call. If it stultifies my manhood and my nation's by remaining passive under outrage I shall seek a man's chance under another flag."

Four Consular Officers Held.

In addition to the continued detention as prisoners of war of the American seamen from the Yarrowdale Germany is now holding four American consular officers as hostages for the safe conduct of German consular officers to Central and South American stations, a matter with which the United States has no concern at all.

The American consular officers being held as hostages in Germany are Henry C. A. Damm, Consul at Aachen, ordered to Harput, Turkey; John Q. Wood, Consul at Chemnitz, ordered to Messina; C. Inness Brown, Vice Consul at Mannheim, ordered to Constantinople, and W. Bruce Wallace, Vice Consul at Madgeburg, ordered to Constantinople.

While the submarine issue remained suspended in expectation of the overt act against American life and vital interests this matter of the detention of American officials and citizens by the German government was purposely "played down" by the administration. There was fear that attention might be diverted from the main issue—the submarine menace.

But the sinking of the Laconia has afforded the evidence to establish incontrovertibly the violation of American vital rights by the submarine operations; hence this corollary issue of the detention of Americans by Germany is now bared.

The United States government has ordered four of its consular officers to proceed from their posts in Germany to posts in Turkey and Italy, and the German government has officially notified the United States government that they will not be allowed to proceed nor to leave Germany.

The reason assigned is that Germany is in fear that German consular officers ordered from the United States to Central and South American posts may not safely reach their posts.

The Case of Mr. Mueller.

The one specific case cited by Germany is that of Wilhelm Mueller, formerly Acting German Consul at Atlanta, Ga., ordered to Quito, Ecuador, who cabled his government from Havana that he had been detained there.

Mr. Mueller, it has been ascertained here, was detained at Havana because of his failure to obtain passports from the Ecuadorean government. These have since been obtained and he left Havana several days ago. But the United States government had nothing and could have had nothing to do with Mr. Mueller's detention in Havana in any case. Germany appears to hold the United States responsible, by means of holding its representatives as hostages, for the safe conduct of German Consuls across the seas to their posts in foreign lands. As a matter of fact American responsibility stops when they leave American soil. The detention of American consular officers by Germany, therefore, is an unwarranted affront to the United States.

Added to this are the several false statements of the Gereman Foreign Office that the American seamen of the Yarrowdale crew have been released. While the German Foreign Office has stated to the Spanish Ambassador in Berlin, in charge of American interests, that these men were released on the 16th, the semi-official Overseas News Agency sent out despatches, passed by the German offi in.

CONTINUED ON PAGE 10, COLUMN 4.

INVASION OF UNITED STATES BY MEXICO A PART OF GERMAN SCHEME TO CONQUER WORLD

Instructions Sent from Berlin to Kaiser's Minister at Mexico City Reveal Plot to Win Japan from Her Allies and Crush England with Aid of Ruthless Submarine War.

MONEY OFFERED TO CARRANZA FOR FIGHT TO REGAIN "LOST PROVINCES" ACROSS BORDER

"First Chief" Suggested as Mediator in Negotiations with Tokio Government—Details of Conspiracy Known to the President Since Break in Relations.

At twenty minutes past ten o'clock last night the Associated Press sent the following note to editors:—

"NEW YORK, Feb. 28.—An important war story, probably two thousand words, will be sent about eleven o'clock, Eastern time.

"THE ASSOCIATED PRESS."

At fifteen minutes past eleven o'clock the following was sent to all editors:—

"WASHINGTON, Feb. 27.—Editors:—Very sensational and fully authenticated story following immediately, 1,500 up.

"THE ASSOCIATED PRESS."

Following is the despatch of which notice was sent:—

WASHINGTON, D. C., Wednesday.

The Associated Press is enabled to reveal that Germany, in arranging for unrestricted submarine warfare and counting its consequences, proposed an alliance with Mexico and Japan to make war on the United States if this country should not remain neutral.

Japan, through Mexican mediation, was to be used to abandon her allies and join in the attack on the United States.

Mexico, for her reward, was to receive general financial support from Germany, reconquer Texas, New Mexico and Arizona—lost provinces—and share in the victorious peace terms Germany contemplated.

Details were left to the German Minister at Mexico City, Herr von Eckhardt, who, by instructions signed by Dr. Zimmermann, the German Foreign Minister at Berlin, January 19, 1917, was directed to propose the alliance with Mexico to General Carranza and suggest that Mexico seek to bring Japan into the plot.

Those instructions were transmitted to Von Eckhardt through Count von Bernstorff, formerly German Ambassador here, now on his way home to Germany under a safe conduct obtained from his enemies by the country against which he was plotting war.

World Domination the Dream.

Germany pictured to Mexico, by broad intimation, England and the Entente Allied defeated; Germany and her allies triumphant and in world domination by the instrument of unrestricted submarine warfare.

A copy of Dr. Zimmermann's instructions to Von Eckhardt, sent through Count von Bernstorff, is in possession of the United States government. It is as follows:—

"Berlin, January 19, 1917.

"On the first of February we intend to begin submarine warfare unrestricted. In spite of this it is our intention to endeavor to keep neutral the United States of America.

"If this attempt is not successful, we propose an alliance on the following basis with Mexico:—That we shall make war together and together make peace. We shall give general financial support and it is understood that Mexico is to reconquer the lost territory in New Mexico, Texas and Arizona. The details are left to you for settlement.

"You are instructed to inform the President of Mexico of the above in the greatest confidence as soon as it is certain that there will be an outbreak of war with the United States and suggest that the President of Mexico, on his own initiative, should communicate with Japan suggesting adherence at once to this plan. At the same time offer to mediate between Germany and Japan.

"Please call to the attention of the President of Mexico that the employment of ruthless submarine warfare now promises to compel England to make peace in a few months.

(Signed) "ZIMMERMANN."

Kept Secret by the President.

The document has been in the hands of the government since President Wilson broke off diplomatic relations with Germany. It has been kept secret while the President has been asking Congress for full authority to deal with Germany and while Congress has been hesitating. It was in the President's hands while the Imperial Chancellor, Dr. von Bethmann-Hollweg, was declaring that the United States had placed an interpretation on the submarine declaration "never intended by Germany" and that Germany had promoted and honored friendly relations with the United States "as an heirloom from Frederick the Great."

Of itself, if there were no other, it is considered a sufficient answer to the German Chancellor's plaint that the United States "brusquely" broke off relations without giving "authentic" reasons for its action.

The document supplies the missing link to many separate chains of circumstances which until now have seemed to lead to no definite point. It sheds new light upon the frequently reported but indefinite movements of the Mexican government to couple its situation with the friction between the United States and Japan. It adds another chapter to the celebrated report of Jules Cambon, French Ambassador in Berlin before the war, of Germany's world wide scheme for stirring strife on every continent where it might aid her in the struggle for world domination, which she dreamed was close at hand. It adds a climax to the operations of Count von Bernstorff and the German Embassy in this country, which have been colored with passport frauds, charges of dynamite plots and intrigue, the full extent of which never has been published.

U-Boat Bases in Mexico?

It gives new credibility to persistent reports of submarine bases on Mexican territory in the Gulf of Mexico. It takes cognizance of a fact long recognized by American army chiefs, that if Japan ever undertook to invade the United States it probably would be through Mexico, over the border and into the Mississippi Valley, to split the country in two. It recalls that Count von Bernstorff, when he received his passports, was very reluctant to return to Germany, but expressed a preference for asylum in Cuba. In

(CONTINUED ON PAGE TEN, COLUMNS ONE AND TWO.)

THE DAILY MIRROR, Thursday, August 16, 1917.

HAIG STRIKES BIG BLOW NORTH OF LENS

The Daily Mirror

CERTIFIED CIRCULATION LARGER THAN THAT OF ANY OTHER DAILY PICTURE PAPER

No. 4,309. | Registered at the G.P.O. as a Newspaper. | THURSDAY, AUGUST 16, 1917 | One Penny.

LONDON'S GREAT WELCOME TO OUR AMERICAN ALLIES.

The King and Queen Alexandra watching the march past from Buckingham Palace. Behind them, and standing at attention, is Lord French.

Watchers of the procession. Left to right:—Lord French, Queen Alexandra, the King and Mr. Lloyd George.

The procession passing through Trafalgar Square. Teeming crowds lined the roadways.

London had a chance yesterday of expressing its enthusiasm over America's entry into the war. It availed itself of that chance to the fullest extent. A contingent of United States troops marched through the streets and past the King at Buckingham Palace.

They passed along avenues lined by cheering crowds, while the Stars and Stripes floated from countless mastheads. Four thousand men—all American railway engineers—took part in the march. The procession included one American band

Open Covenants

The Versailles Treaty

The war had begun with one man tearing up 'a scrap of paper'. In the streets of New York it ended — four days early — with the sidewalks littered inches deep with millions of scraps of paper, the debris of tape-machines and waste-baskets tossed from office windows in an orgy of celebration. On the afternoon of November 7 1918 (Paris time) the president of United Press, Roy Howard, had obtained what he believed to be official confirmation from the U.S. Naval Commander in Brest that the armistice terms had been signed by Germany. It was the beat every newsman in France had stayed awake for days to prise out of the tight-lipped censors, and that afternoon it had been handed to Howard on a plate! His cable reached New York in time for UP triumphantly to flash it to all the afternoon papers in time for their deadline. Some editors simply didn't believe it: the State Department could not and would not confirm, and rival news agencies immediately put out sceptical bulletins reporting a deafening silence on the subject from their own correspondents.

All the same, papers in Boston and New York rushed out special editions carrying the unofficial tidings and provoking a hysteria of excitement in their wake up and down the East Coast. In New York impromptu processions marched up and down Fifth Avenue; church bells in Pittsburgh rang out all over the city; in Philadelphia the official celebration programme was declared open by the credulous mayor. In Washington a huge throng gathered outside the White House causing a slightly puzzled President Wilson to appear on the balcony and good-humouredly wave his white hankie at them. Not even an official denial from the State Department in mid-afternoon could stem the tide of delirium, which by that time had spread to Chicago and the mid-West. The truth was that negotiations with the Germans had barely begun. UP belatedly retracted its story, and a furious Marshal Foch banned all reporters from his headquarters. The next day the papers were full of bitter recriminations, even those who had not been duped by the UP report: *The New York Tribune* called it somewhat unfairly 'one of the greatest hoaxes in newspaper history'.

When peace finally came, at the eleventh hour of the eleventh day of the eleventh month, if there was any sense of anti-climax in America there was none in Britain. London witnessed the whole gamut of emotions, from pious relief to the strains of 'Home Sweet Home' by a military band outside Buckingham Palace, to the facetious vindictiveness of parades bearing the Kaiser hung in effigy. On the prevailing wave of unassuaged resentment against the enemy of the past four years, Lloyd George's Coalition was swept back into office at the general election a month later. 'Make Germany Pay' was the universal sentiment, 'Squeeze them till the Pips Squeak' the most popular election slogan and echoed in varying degrees by much of the press. When Germany complained that the continued Allied blockade was causing millions of civilians to starve, *The Daily Mail's* headline comment was: 'Hun Food Snivel' which was no more than an accurate reflection of the spirit of the day. Even Lloyd George could offer no resistance and more or less pledged himself to remorseless demands at the forthcoming peace conference.

Indeed the only principal at the Versailles Conference, when it convened in mid-January 1919, who could be said to have come armed with ideals, rather than demands, was the American President Woodrow Wilson. When he had set off from New York in November in a liner full of assistants and advisors he had been roundly criticised in some quarters for being the first President to leave American soil during his term of office — but since it was his vision, and his alone, that was going to fashion the destiny of Europe and render honest democracies secure for honest men to live in, this was overlooked.

His Fourteen Points, which were intended to provide a framework for a just peace, had been unveiled before Congress in January 1918 and made a deep impression on the American people. In spite of a Republican backlash in the election early in November, Wilson sailed for Europe sustained by a deep reservoir of goodwill towards his principles of self-determination of independent nations and global alliance in a League of Nations. Initially, he went also with the best wishes of the Press, who liked the sound of the first of his fourteen points: open covenants, openly arrived at.

Paris, however, was never a city renowned for the openness of its diplomacy. After the first session on the 18th, where all participating countries attended, the decisions of the conference were appropriated by a Council of Ten which was in turn whittled down to an even more exclusive Council of Four: Wilson, Lloyd George, Clemenceau of France and Orlando of Italy. And one of the first decisions was to exclude the Press from all meetings and to keep all agreements secret until ready for ratification. It was true that some delegations condescended to give daily press-briefings — totally inadequate and often fallacious — but it was a rare occasion indeed when any of the leading figures would consent to be interrogated. They were, it soon became clear, having difficulties enough communicating with one another in private, without having to justify themselves to the Press at the same time.

For one thing, Wilson's moderate proposals and generalised idealism had nothing in common with Clemenceau's ruthless pragmatism. France's uncompromising object was to reduce Germany to a state where she would never again be a military (and, hopefully, economic) threat. This was to be achieved by advancing France's frontier to the Rhine, by parcelling out the relics of the old Austro-Hungarian Empire and redrawing the map of Europe generally, and above all by extracting gigantic reparations from the last drop of German sweat for a generation or more. (All French estimates, and many British ones, in fact set a minimum figure, the interest on which alone would have permanently crippled the German economy).

Lloyd George consequently found himself in the role of mediator between Wilson and Clemenceau, at the same time having to placate his vengeful electors at home. In April he was 'summoned' back by a telegram from over 200

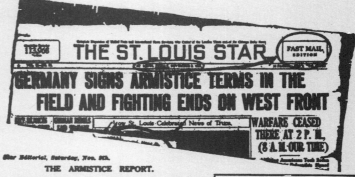

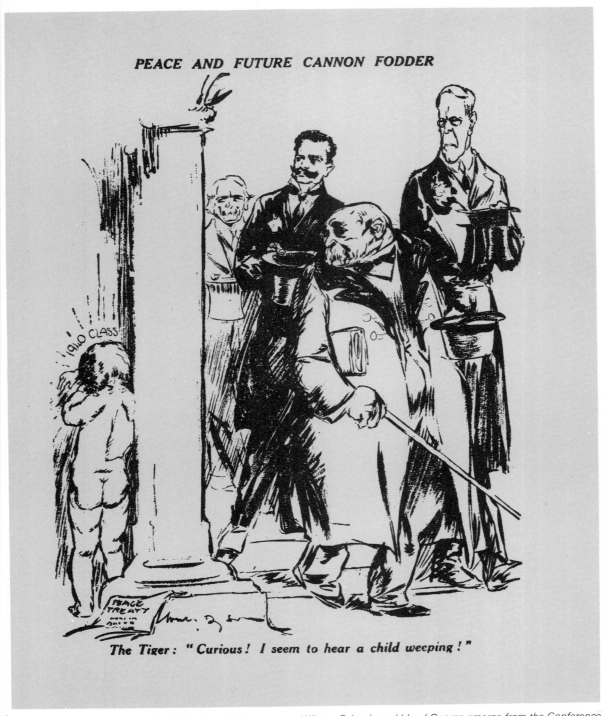

PEACE AND FUTURE CANNON FODDER

1920 CLASS

PEACE TREATY

The Tiger: "Curious! I seem to hear a child weeping!"

Dysons famous cartoon from The Daily Herald. Clemenceau, Wilson, Orlando and Lloyd George emerge from the Conference to hear the prophetic wailing of the next generation.

Conservative MPs wanting to know if, under all the tough talk, he was going soft on the Germans. These back-bench murmurings were echoed — if not actively fostered — by Northcliffe's *Daily Mail* which for weeks had been regaling its readers with The Warning: 'They will cheat you yet, those Junkers! Having won half the world by bloody murder, they are going to win the other half with tears in their eyes, crying for mercy'. *The Daily Mail* was by no means the only paper baying for German blood (*The Daily Express* had no compunction in dismissing Germany's mitigating pleas as a mixture of 'arrogance, bluff, hypocrisy and subterfuge'), but in fairness it was not the spokesman of all the British Press. Geoffrey Dawson, editor of Northcliffe's other national paper *The Times*, parted company with his proprietor largely on this very issue, and *The Manchester Guardian* especially approved of the Wilson terms and was their chief spokesman in Britain (*The Guardian's* great editor, C. P. Scott, was the only non-official with whom Wilson consented to confer on his brief visit to England before the conference).

Lloyd George returned to London to deal with his dissident supporters, in his finest fighting form. What, he inquired of the MP who had organised the telegram, was their anxiety based on? An interview published in *The Westminster Gazette*, it turned out. But that was anonymous. Who implied *he* had given it? the Prime Minister wanted to know. No, he would answer that himself — and embarked on a sustained and withering attack on Northcliffe and his newspaper battalions. 'I am prepared to make some allowances — even great newspaper proprietors will forgive me for saying so — but when a man is labouring under a keen sense of disappointment . . . he is always apt to think the world is badly run . . . But let me say that when that kind of diseased vanity is carried to the point of sowing dissension between great Allies whose unity is essential to the peace and happiness of the world . . . then I say not even that kind of a disease is a justification for so black a crime against humanity'.

Such was the Welsh eloquence which was to serve him well in due course when the final terms of the Treaty came to be ratified by Parliament. Wilson, on the other hand, was not so well-placed. He, too, was being made aware of a rapidly growing opposition to his aims, both in the Senate and in the Press. In order to preserve his longest suit — the League of Nations — in the four-handed poker game at Versailles, he had been gradually forced to discard, at least to modify, a number of his cherished principles. True, he had succeeded in introducing a certain moderation into the proceedings, but only at the price of repeated concessions and commitments (for which there was no guarantee of approval in Washington). In April an overwhelming majority of newspaper editors in a poll had declared themselves generally in favour of the League: the significant exception was Randolph Hearst and his Empire, who had seen no virtue in America getting embroiled in Europe's war and saw none now in becoming guarantor for her peace. As the protracted negotiations dragged on into the summer virtually all the Republican press began carping. In the Senate Henry Cabot Lodge was building up a voluble and decisive Republican lobby whose concept of the League — if there had to be one at all — coincided hardly at all with the President's and certainly did not embrace involving America in any 'entangling alliances'.

Wilson found himself trapped by a situation of his own making. He had isolated himself from American opinion by going to Paris, and by isolating himself from American correspondents in Paris he had forfeited the chance to inform and persuade opinion. The only channels of

THE CHICAGO DAILY TRIBUNE: TUESDAY, JUNE 10, 1919.

What Treaty Looks Like and Facsimiles of Opening Pages

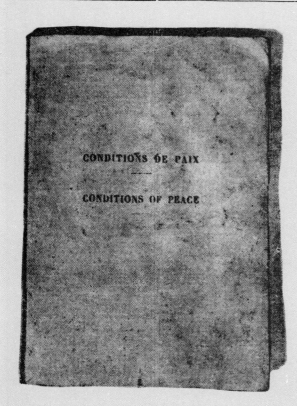

communication left were 'informed speculation' and the 'leak'. Since Wilson, at first, stubbornly refused to use these channels himself, it necessarily meant they were used to convey unfavourable information. The contentious Article X of the League covenant (which could have pledged America to go to war at the bidding of foreign powers) was illicitly brought to the public's attention by a UP correspondent, who apparently walked into an empty office late one night and copied the article out of a draft that had been left lying around.

So much for his open covenants. However he did conclude that if anything was going to be leaked, it had better be leaked to the right source. Since *The New York World* remained his most faithful — and one of his few — supporters, it was not entirely surprising that it should have been the first paper to obtain the first summary of the revised Covenant early in April. Such tactics

only served to alienate other papers still further, and to initiate a headlong scramble for more Parisian tit-bits. On June 9 *The Chicago Tribune* played the winning hand: a complete copy in English of the final Treaty, before even the Senate had set eyes on one. Without bothering to indulge in any false modesty it informed its readers of 'one of the greatest news beats of the generation' and patriotically handed the copy over to the Senate before revealing to all America the details of the terms.

At last the world could read in full the humiliating document which the Germans, in spite of all their protests, were going to have to sign. In spite of Wilson's moderation, the final text showed that Germany was required to admit a war-guilt clause, accepting unlimited liability in the matter of reparations, which Clemenceau rightly regarded as a victory, even if Lloyd George preferred to regard it only as a

deferment of the problem. So far as America was concerned, the salient point was that the League was inextricably bound up with the Treaty and its attendant obligations. In July the President returned to Washington to defend his mission in person and to secure ratification as swiftly as possible. But the Republicans were not to be hurried: Senator Lodge alone took up a fortnight reading aloud every word of the Treaty to the Senate, more usually to thin air. With every day that passed, Wilson's shining goal drifted further out of his reach. The tide of public opinion, caring little now for the glories of moral world leadership, swung against him: Wilson himself fell desperately ill while on a passionate, nation-wide tour to appeal directly to the people. It was all in vain. In March 1920 the Senate finally rejected the Treaty, having already voted not to join the League less than a week after it came into being.

The Klean-up

The Ku Klux Klan

It is one of the more satisfying ironies of history that the Ku Klux Klan — which prospered greatly during the Reconstruction through the support of many Southern papers and which was re-animated after the First War largely by the efforts of an ex-newspaperman — should ultimately have been rendered more or less impotent by the courage of the Press itself. The original Klan, the masked terror of negroes and carpet-baggers alike in the 1860s and 1870s, had been bitterly attacked at the time by Greeley's *The New York Tribune* among others. In due course the 'fraternity' formally dissolved itself and those who refused to be dissolved quickly lost influence. Its successor was the inspiration of one Colonel William Joseph Simmons ('colonel' only by virtue of having once led a Woodmen's drill squad). On Thanksgiving night 1915 he and a few friends re-enacted one of the old Klan's weird and arcane initiation ceremonies, beneath a fiery cross on top of Stone Mountain, Georgia.

Except in its love of ritual mumbo-jumbo and fixation with white, Anglo-Saxon supremacy, the new Klan bore little resemblance to its predecessor. Nor in its first five years did it seem to have the same appeal, mustering probably less than 5,000 members by 1920. But then in June of that year Simmons 'hired' (in reality handed over the entire operation to) two press agents, Edward Young Clarke a former newsman and patriotic fund-raiser, and Elizabeth Tyler his — well, that was never properly determined. They immediately set about re-organizing the Klan into a more hierarchical structure: states were divided into Domains run by Grand Goblins and into Realms headed by King Kleagles. Klanmen were to be recruited by Kleagles into Klaverns (local units) on payment of their Klecktoken. As boss of this Invisible Empire Clarke was naturally Imperial Kleagle, and by some unfathomable logic Simmons was Imperial Wizard.

Clarke and Tyler were in it for the money only; they took three dollars for each new member and untold royalties from the manufacture of regalia (not to mention from the 'initiation water' from the Chattahoochee River at ten dollars a quart). In return Clarke gave his members nothing, except something to believe in: the 'American way of life'. And since Simmons had been somewhat woolly on this subject, Clarke made it quite explicit that pure Americanism, in his book, did not embrace Negroes, Jews, Catholics and other such troublesome minorities, like labor unions. Thus under the masquerade of defending Christian 'values', the Klan was fed on hatred and encouraged to acquire local (and soon national) power by any means at its disposal, and those included traditional favourites like tarring and feathering or lynching, where boycotting and character-smearing failed.

So successful was Clarke's recruiting that in the early summer of 1921 his activities came to the attention of Herbert Bayard Swope, once one of *The World's* star foreign correspondents, now its managing editor. *The World* had performed creditably after Pulitzer's death under his sons though, as America withdrew from the outside world, it was finding it increasingly difficult to sustain its leadership of liberal opinion and, as sensational tabloids like *The Daily News* began to sprout in New York, its circulation. In the 20s Swope engaged the paper on a series of effective campaigns on domestic issues, of which the Ku Klux Klan exposure was one of the first and most

memorable. A senior reporter, Roland Thomas, was detailed exclusively to the investigation and although some of his findings, as he was to admit afterwards, were based on hearsay, at the end of three months he had amassed a formidable dossier of compromising documents that was to enable *The World* to publish fresh and damning evidence each day for three uninterrupted weeks.

On September 6 1921 it launched the series in fearless style, in headlines three-deep across the whole of the front page. In the days that followed readers of *The World* were to learn of the fraudulent methods of recruitment used by the Klan (using the New York Army and Navy Club as a phoney box number), how Clarke and Tyler were building up a fortune through gullible subscribers and Simmons was living in an Atlanta palace costing over a million dollars. They read of the racial, and racist, tests imposed on aspiring Klansmen (Q. Are you a Gentile or a Jew? Q. Do you believe in the principle of a PURE Americanism?) and, perversely, how the Klan's mail-order machine had inadvertently invited Negroes to become members. They also read some of the vile anti-Catholic propaganda leaflets published by the Klan (sample: Do you know — that the Pope controls the daily and magazine press — that our war industries were placed exclusively in Roman Catholic hands, etc.). They learnt, on September 19, a few unsavoury facts about the leaders of the Klan themselves: how Clarke and Tyler, the self-appointed guardians of the nation's morals,

the super-prohibitionists, had been 'arrested at midnight and in their sleeping garments in a notorious underworld resort' for disturbing the peace in October 1919, and how they had been charged with having whiskey on the premises.

Perhaps the biggest eye-opener of all was the list compiled by *The World* of all known Klan violence over the last twelve months. Under the heading '152 Valid Objections to the Revival of the Ku Kluxing Spirit' it detailed 4 killings, 1 case of irreparable mutilation, 1 case of branding with acid, 41 floggings, 27 tar and feather parties, 5 kidnappings, 43 threats to individuals, 14 threats to communities by poster or advertisement, and 16 parades' of masked Klansmen displaying warning placards. It went on to list all the known public condemnations of the Klan by authorities, all the arrests, Grand Jury investigations and parades officially forbidden — and a pitiable testimonial to public weakness it was. Under the headings of 'trials and convictions' there were no entries whatsoever.

The World's exposure was an immediate sensation, and in due course the paper was awarded the Pulitzer Prize for its investigation. But what was equally important was that the series was published simultaneously by 17 other newspapers throughout the States, from *The Boston Globe* to *The Seattle Times*, for by that time the Klan claimed representation in all but three States. Particularly impressive was the fact that so many Southern newspapers agreed to run the series, papers like *The New Orleans*

Times-Picayune and *The Dallas News*, for their areas being strongholds of the Klan they had much to lose — whether it was from intimidation or cancellation of advertising. Such tactics were to become familiar weapons of the Klan against local editors — one Indiana editor was severely beaten up for joining in the campaign and later 'framed' (there was sweet revenge for the Press when *The Indianapolis Times* later succeeded in having the Grand Dragon of the State convicted of second-degree murder).

It has been claimed that *The World's* revelations did more good than harm to the Klan, that it boosted recruiting enormously, and gave Clarke more publicity than he could ever have dreamed of. Possibly so, for in the next five years the Klan claimed to reach a membership of six million and to have acquired a subterranean influence in Congress and courts everywhere. But *The World* had unquestionably brought to public notice the nature of the enemy, and it certainly inspired a great many newspapers to wage a ceaseless war of attrition on the organisation. One of the immediate results of the exposures — apart from the enforced retirement of the Imperial Wizard — was a Congressional Inquiry into the Ku Klux Klan which, however inconclusive its findings, at least continued the necessary process of shining a little light on the Klan's darkness. The saddest footnote of all was that *The World* was destined to disappear from sight (in 1930) before the last vestiges of Klanism did.

KU KLUX KLAN USED ARMY AND NAVY CLUB ADDRESS TO PEDDLE MEMBERSHIPS IN CAMPAIGN BY MAIL; THE WORLD REPRODUCES "GRAND GOBLIN" DOCUMENTS

HOW KU KLUX KLAN USED ARMY AND NAVY CLUB ADDRESS.

FRATERNAL ORGANIZATION
MEN WANTED
Splendid Opportunity

High class, remunerative work; organization and propagation of a Fraternal Order to which real Americans are flocking.. Applicants must have a clean record and must be native born Gentile Protestant Americans. Some Eastern territory still open.

Write giving full particulars about yourself to —

Box 36, 18 Gramercy Park, ---- New York City

ADVERTISEMENT IN *The SEARCHLIGHT* for SALESMEN of K.K.K. MEMBERSHIPS and ENTRY in CITY DIRECTORY SHOWING THE ADDRESS AS THAT of ARMY and NAVY CLUB

CONFIDENTIAL

If you are a 100%, true red-blooded American, believing in the tenets of the Christian religion and in the separation of church and state, and know yourself to be qualified as a real man, of good moral character, and are seriously interested in the principles as set forth in the enclosed literature, you may have the opportunity to meet with a representative by filling out the enclosed questionnaire and returning it to Box 36, #18 Gramercy Park, New York City. Proper attention will be given you.

W.K.G.
K.K.O.I.S.

"APPROACH" LETTER SENT OUT from ARMY and NAVY CLUB at OLD LOCATION

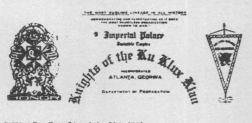

Knights of the Ku Klux Klan
INCORPORATED
ATLANTA, GEORGIA
DEPARTMENT OF PROPAGATION

DATED AT New York City, July 11th, 1921.

SEND REPLY TO (Use enclosed envelope)

Dear Sir,-

CONFIDENTIAL.

A personal friend of yours has asked us to send you the enclosed literature regarding the Invisible Empire, Knights of the Ku Klux Klan.

From his representation we believe you to be a REAL 100% AMERICAN, and as such we extend to you an invitation to become one of the charter members of the First Brooklyn Klan which is now being formed.

If you can measure up to the requirements in every way and are interested, fill out the enclosed questionnaire, mail it to Box 6 #112 Central Park South, and you will be accorded an interview with a representative of the order who is now in the eastern territory.

A.K.K.
K.O.I.S.

(Enc)

IN THE NAME OF OUR FATHERS—FOR OUR COUNTRY, OUR HOMES AND EACH OTHER

INVITATION to JOIN BROOKLYN KLAN SENT from ARMY and NAVY CLUB at PRESENT LOCATION

MONROE DOCTRINE IS RAISED BY CHILI AS BAR TO LEAGUE

Cannot Meddle in Her Dispute With Bolivia Over Tacna-Arica, Republic's Protest Says.

By Lincoln Eyre.
Copyright, 1921, by the Press Publishing Co. (The New York World.)
(Special cable Despatch to The World.)

GENEVA, Sept. 7.—There was staged in the Assembly this morning the first act of a diplomatic drama the outcome of which may have a vital bearing upon the future of the League of Nations.

The spectacle in question was the

WHITE HOUSE GETS STORM OF PROTEST AGAINST THE KLAN

Letters Urging President to Act Are Turned Over to Department of Justice.

(Special to The World.)

WASHINGTON, Sept. 7.—Showers of protests against the Ku Klux Klan, accompanied by demands for Government action to check the menacing movement, began to pour in on Government officials to-day. The World story, exposing the secrets of the money-hungry organization, is being read by United

Steady Stream of Anonymous Correspondence Moves for Months In and Out of Gramercy Park and Central Park South Club Houses by Means of Fictitious Box Maintained for Sending Out Propaganda.

"GRAND GOBLIN" HOOPER, DISTRICT AGENT, IN CHARGE OF ACTIVITIES IN THIS SECTION.

"Confidential" Missive, Illustrated With Groups of Masked and Robed Men Bearing Fiery Crosses, Is Invitation to Join—Editorial by Kaufman, Who Could Not Qualify Under Questionnaire, Circulated and One Appeal by Mistake Goes to Negro.

Copyright, 1921, by the Press Publishing Co. (The New York World.)

WHAT IS THE KU KLUX KLAN?

How has it grown from a nucleus of thirty-four charter members to a membership of more than 500,000 within five years?

How have its "domains" and "realms" and "klans" been extended until they embrace every State in the Union but Montana, Utah and New Hampshire?

What are the possibilities of an order that preaches racial and religious hatred of the Jew and the Roman Catholic, of the negro and the foreign-born citizen?

What are the possibilities of a secret organization that practises censorship of private conduct behind the midnight anonymity of mask and robe and with the weapons of whips and tar and feathers?

What ought to be done about an order whose members are not initiated but "naturalized," whose oaths bind them to obedience to an "Emperor" chosen for life?

What ought to be done about an organization with such objects and methods when the salesmen of memberships in it work first among officers of the courts and Police Departments, following this with especial attention to officers on the reserve lists of the military and naval forces of the United States?

At the end of months of inquiry throughout the country and in the performance of what it sincerely believes to be a public service, The World this morning continues the publication of a series of articles in which answers to these questions will be offered, set out against the vivid background of as extraordinary a movement as is to be found in recent history.

Because of its exposure of the Klan and its methods, The World continues to receive many anonymous threats.

ARTICLE III.

The Army and Navy Club in this city has been used as headquarters of agents of the Ku Klux Klan in their drive to secure new members at $10 apiece.

As was stated yesterday in the second article of this series, one of the

KU KLUX KLAN'S INVISIBLE EMPIRE OF HATE SCORED BY ARMY OFFICER WHO ABANDONS IT; DEPARTMENT OF JUSTICE TO MAKE INQUIRY

COMMISSION OF KLEAGLE IN KU KLUX KLAN.

KLEAGLE'S CREDENTIALS

IMPERIAL PALACE
INVISIBLE EMPIRE

Knights of the Ku Klux Klan
(INCORPORATED)

TO THE LOVERS OF LAW AND ORDER. PEACE AND JUSTICE, AND TO ALL TO WHOM OF RIGHT IT MAY CONCERN, GREETING:

Know ye that I have this day appointed and, as evidenced by this document, do commission Mr ——————H. P. FRY——————whose address is ——————KNOXVILLE, TENNESSEE—————— a KLEAGLE OF THE INVISIBLE EMPIRE, KNIGHTS OF THE KU KLUX KLAN, for the term ending December 31st, 19 31 or until same is by me revoked.

By this

=== **Commission** ===

HE IS AUTHORIZED as a representative of this Society to secure charter members, collect required "Kontributions", administer the Oath of Allegiance, organize Klans, instruct Klansmen and to assist generally in the work of promoting the organization of this Society, in strict accordance with the Constitution, Laws, Usages and Imperial Authority and instructions of same.

HE IS NOT AUTHORIZED to make or incur any debts for which the Knights of the Ku Klux Klan, or either of the undersigned shall be held in any way responsible, unless he has specific written authority to do so prior to incuring such debts.

Witness my hand and the Seal of this Society in the City of Atlanta, Georgia, this the 7th day of ——APRIL—— 1931

By Imperial Authority, —

William Joseph Simmons
Imperial Wizard, Invisible Empire, Knights of the Ku Klux Klan

Countersigned by *Edward Jay Clarke*
Imperial KLeagle

Jimm Arthur
King KLeagle

Realm of TENNESSEE.

Capt. Henry P. Fry, Southerner, Disillusioned After Serving as Kleagle of Order, Resigns Membership in Letter Denouncing "Ugly Structure and Nefarious Potentialities" as Demanding Quietus by Government.

CONDEMNS OUTRAGES PERPETRATED BY USE OF WHIP, TAR AND FEATHERS.

In Defiance of Threats of "Dishonor, Disgrace and Death," He Denounces Ritualistic Work as Hypocritical Cloak for Gain Under Pretense of Piety and Warns That Malicious and Inflammatory Teachings Threaten Bloodshed and Revolution in This Country.

WHAT IS THE KU KLUX KLAN?

How has it grown from a nucleus of thirty-four charter members to a membership of more than 500,000 within five years?

How have its "domains" and "realms" and "Klans" been extended until they embrace every State in the Union but Montana, Utah and New Hampshire?

What are the possibilities of an order that preaches racial and religious hatred of the Jew and the Roman Catholic, of the negro and the foreign-born citizen?

What are the possibilities of a secret organization that practises censorship of private conduct behind the midnight anonymity of mask and robe and with the weapons of whips and tar and feathers?

What ought to be done about an order whose members are not initiated but "naturalized," whose oaths bind them to obedience to an "Emperor" chosen for life?

What ought to be done about an organization with such objects when the salesmen of memberships in it work first among officers of the courts and Police Departments, following then with the officers on the reserve lists of the military and naval forces?

At the end of months of inquiry throughout the United States and in the performance of what it sincerely believes to be a public service, The World this morning continues the publication of a series of articles in which answers to these questions will be offered, set out against the vivid background of as extraordinary a movement as is to be found in recent history.

ARTICLE II.

More than once in their investigation of Ku Kluxism as incorporated and put on a strictly business basis by "Imperial Wizard" Simmons, financial wizard Clarke and their associate, Mrs. Elizabeth Tyler, the representatives of The World have come across Klansmen from whose eyes the scales of false romance and patriotic bombast had dropped. They saw the Klan as what it really was, a grotesque menace and anachronism in free America.

They bitterly repented having yielded to the lures and persuasions of its glib-tongued membership peddlers and wished the investigators all success in showing the vicious enterprise up. But when it was suggested that their inside knowledge of its workings gave them special fitness to aid in the fight against its further insidious spread, they held back from active participation in the attack. They were still Klansmen. They had taken the oaths of the order and felt that, bad as it was, the obligations thus assumed compelled them to keep the secrets they had learned.

To this attitude, however, there has been one exception. One member of the Klan, who also served its business managers as a successful organizer, was so outraged by the realities and potentialities which came under his observation in the course of his regular work as a salesman for Simmons and Clarke that he not only gave up his position as a "Kleagle" of the order, but in a blistering letter withdrew wholly from the order and notified its head that he repudiated its oath as conflicting with a higher obligation he had previously assumed as an officer in the Reserve Corps of the United States Army.

Capt. Fry Branded the Klan as Dangerous Public Menace

NEW YORKERS HAIL EXPOSURE OF KLAN; PRAISE THE WORLD

Leaders in Many Lines of City's Activities Denounce Venomous Society and Secret Methods.

New Yorkers hailed with approbation yesterday the opening chapter

---

Burns to Investigate Klan; House and Senate Inquiries Promised

Attorney General Daugherty Aroused by Revelations in The World—Official Washington Amazed and Congressmen Demand Prompt Action

(Special to The World.)

WASHINGTON, Sept. 6.—As a result of The World's story on the activities of the Ku Klux Klan, the Department of Justice will make a thorough investigation of the organization. It is believed its officers can be reached under Federal statutes. Chief William J. Burns of the Bureau of Investigation will be asked to

Major Bruce Craven, former Grand Dragon of North Carolina, had said on quitting his job and the organization that one of the reasons he joined the Ku Klux Klan was that he had been informed Mr. Daugherty belonged to it, the Attorney General said, "I was never asked to join and never in any way authorized or con-

Red Letter Day

The Zinoviev Letter

Just four days to go before the British general election, and the Prime Minister was trying to snatch a few hours sleep in his Welsh constituency of Aberavon after a punishing week of whistle-stop speeches all over the country. For Ramsay MacDonald, who had led Britain's first-ever Labour Government for the last nine nerve-wracking months, it was a crucial contest. Would the voters endorse his (by socialist standards) utterly respectable administration, or leave him in the wilderness? It had not been an easy reign. The Labour party had held no majority in the House of Commons, except by uneasy alliance with the Liberals. Now the Liberals were growing restless, particularly about his current trade negotiations with Russia. He felt himself rapidly becoming the scapegoat for the country's deep-seated terror of communism: if the Tory Press was to be believed, there were Reds behind every riot, Bolsheviks under every bed — and Mr. MacDonald egging them on.

Red scares were nothing new, of course. Within months of the Great War ending *The Daily Express* had been quite explicit about the new enemy facing Britain.

And so it had continued, right up to October 8 1924 when the Conservatives had seduced the Liberals into censuring the government for dropping a prosecution against the communist newspaper *Workers' Weekly*. The charge should never have been brought, as MacDonald had been pointing out all that week, but that hadn't stopped *The Daily Mail* from insisting that 'The Bolsheviks are taking a hand in the election for the Socialists . . . the Moscow tyrants hope, by co-ercing the British voter and terrorising the old and feeble, to get the Socialists here back into power'. The editorial also quoted Zinoviev (the President of the Third International in Russia) as saying that the strength of the Bolsheviks was being concentrated in Britain. That, if nothing else, should have alerted the Prime Minister there was a leak at hand — but he was too exhausted to notice.

The next day MacDonald awoke in Aberavon to read chilling headlines in every newspaper he opened. The Foreign Office had released to the papers a letter from Zinoviev to the British Communist Party calling on it to 'stir up the masses of the British proletariat', hinting at 'armed insurrection' and recommending agit-prop cells in all the units of the army. The very thought was ludicrous — the British Communist Party could barely scrape together 3,500 card-carrying members. But Mr. MacDonald was agitated, not because of the contents of the letter (the Intelligence Service files were full of such missives), but because he had not authorised publication nor had he finalised his protest note to the Russian Ambassador. That, too, had been released to the papers.

His Cabinet colleagues were dumbfounded at the disclosure; they had not even known of the letter's existence but they appreciated, far quicker than their leader, the damage it would do to their election chances. In the immortal words of the Colonial Secretary they were 'bunkered'. When they telephoned the Premier in Aberavon, he explained he didn't know if the letter (which the Foreign Office had sent him ten days before) was genuine and he had merely instructed the civil servants to find out. He had drafted a protest note, just in case it did turn out to be authentic. Someone had gone behind his back. He would make enquiries.

That day was Saturday, and in his scheduled speeches MacDonald made no reference to the letter whatsoever. Nor again on Sunday. By now the Tory Press was approaching a climax of 'Bolshie' hysteria, led by *The Daily Mail* which claimed to have discovered the plot. Now his silence was interpreted, out of hand, as complicity. When he did finally break his silence he failed, unaccountably, to denounce the thing outright as a forgery, whether it was or not. In any case it was too late: polling day was tomorrow and *The Daily Express* had already printed its banner headline in dramatic red:

DO NOT VOTE 'RED' TODAY!

No editorial effort was spared to send the voter to the booths with visions of imminent Siberian horrors which awaited him if he chose wrong. Alone among all the dailies *The Daily Herald* sprang to the government's defence and did what all the other papers should have done, as a matter of course, before jumping to conclusions: it examined the letter. At short notice they made out a fairly convincing case that, textually, the document was a pretty feeble forgery. But it was a lost cause — not only did the Tory Press command ten times as many readers, had not *The Daily Herald* itself three years before been exposed for accepting Russian subsidies?

The Manchester Guardian, too, had doubts about the letter's authenticity and mentioned in passing that Tory Central Office had been in possession of it before it had been officially released. But nothing was made of that strange fact. Nor of the fact that Zinoviev had not been in Moscow on the day he was supposed to have signed it (well, would a subverter admit his subversion?). Nor of the fact that the leader of the British Communists, Arthur MacManus (who had also signed the letter) *had* been in Moscow at the time, and could very easily have brought it to England himself without risking interception. Nor of the fact that to have sent such a letter at such a juncture Zinoviev would have had to have been, as one intelligence man put it later, a 'blithering idiot'.

For the predictable happened; it was a landslide victory for the Conservatives, Labour losing 40 seats. But the real loser was the Liberal Party, whose representation in Parliament was reduced from 158 to 40. It never recovered, nor for many years did Anglo-Russian relations. By the time a Labour Government next came to power in 1929, Stalin had already won his ideological victory at the All-Union Congress.

For some time after the election *The Daily Herald* kept up its offensive against the machinations of Whitehall, and rather strangely Moscow brought one of the 'forgers' to trial some years later, but in Britain neither an official enquiry in 1925 nor another in 1928 provided convincing answers to important questions. Why had the Foreign Office been in such a hurry to authenticate and release the letter? How had a copy reached *The Daily Mail* before the official publication? Above all, had the letter been genuine or not? It was to be another forty years before these mysteries were to be satisfactorily cleared up.

Daily ✦ Express

LATE EDITION

NO. 5.875. LONDON, FRIDAY, FEBRUARY 7, 1919. ONE PENNY.

Bolshevist Plot to Seize Power in Great Britain.

NOT MERELY STRIKES BUT A GREAT PLOT AGAINST THE STATE.

EXPOSURE OF THE SINISTER PLOT HATCHED BY BOLSHEVISTS.

RAILWAY STRIKE SETTLED LAST NIGHT.

TRAIN AND TUBE SERVICES MAY BE RESUMED TO-DAY.

ELECTRICIANS COME OUT.

CONFERENCES AT WHITEHALL.

CABINET IN CLOSE TOUCH WITH THE MEN.

MANY MEETINGS.

FIRST WINNERS IN £1,000 FOOTBALL CONTEST

SEE PAGE 2

The Daily Mirror

NET SALE MUCH THE LARGEST OF ANY DAILY PICTURE NEWSPAPER

No. 6,543 | Registered at the G.P.O. as a Newspaper. | SATURDAY, OCTOBER 25, 1924 | One Penny

RUSSIAN CALL FOR BRITISH REVOLT

M. Zinoviev, the Russian leader, who has written an astounding letter calling for a revolutionary rising in Britain.

M. Rakovsky, the Soviet Chargé d'Affaires in London, who has just returned after explaining in Moscow the terms of the Russian Treaty.

Mr. Arthur Henderson.   Mr. Ramsay MacDonald

Is it correct that Mr. MacDonald and Mr. Henderson have been in possession of the Zinoviev letter for some weeks? If so, will they kindly explain why publication was delayed until to-day.

Mr. J. D. Gregory, of the Foreign Office, who signed the letter of protest to Russia.

Amazing revelations are made in our news columns of the plans made by the Russian Reds to bring off a coup d'état in Great Britain. We publish a copy of a letter marked " very secret," written by M. Zinoviev, president of the Third Communist International, to British Communists, instructing them to stir up sedition to enlist the military on the side of the Communist party, to get Red sympathisers into munition and military depots, and to make other preparations to subvert the State. Above we publish photo-graphs of M. Zinoviev and M. Rakovsky, the Soviet Chargé d'Affaires, and of Mr. Gregory, the Foreign Office official who, in the absence in his constituency of the Socialist Secretary of State for Foreign Affairs (the Prime Minister), has signed the firm letter to Moscow protesting against this breach of international comity. This was communi-cated through M. Rakovsky, Soviet Chargé d'Affaires in London. Electors will ask why M. Rakovsky is not recalled at once.

In December 1966 it came to light in an official publication of government documents that an important paper in the Zinoviev file was missing. *The Sunday Times*, which was in the process of building up a formidable reputation for in-depth reporting, became interested. It examined some newly-discovered documents and interviewed some of the survivors who, now that many of the principals were dead, were readier to talk. Their conclusions were these: the letter had indeed been forged, in Berlin by a group of Russian emigrés who had devoted their lives to harassing the Bolshevik regime, and had been planted in the Polish Intelligence network (a far more credible source than a bunch of dissident exiles). From there it had reached the Foreign Office, senior members of which (though supposed to be politically neutral) were inclined by nature to be hard-line anti-Bolsheviks. MacDonald, as Foreign Secretary, should of course have had the last word, but during an election campaign communication with Whitehall had been reduced almost to nil.

The complicating factor in the affair was that the existence of the letter had been revealed to an ex-M15 agent called Donald im Thurn (very English in spite of his name). He had, it seems, been approached by a mysterious X (very likely a senior Polish agent) on October 13 and told of the contents of the letter, and had patriotically decided it should be published. Through his former colleagues it had been easy for im Thurn to spread the word around various branches of the Secret Service – and Tory Central Office (who were subsequently shown to have paid out large sums of money for this titivating news). There followed a period of inter-departmental confusion which culminated in the letter being officially circulated around Whitehall, which was tantamount to authenticating the document. At that point im Thurn felt safe in revealing the existence of the letter to *The Times*.

But someone had beaten him to it, at *The Daily Mail*. On the evening of October 23 – the night that *The Mail* was composing its kite-flying Bolshie editorial – the editor Thomas Marlowe was actually presented with a copy of the document. He never revealed who passed it on but, speculatively, it was via the upper echelons of the overseas secret service. Marlowe immediately had the letter set up in proof and, in a burst of public-spiritedness, the next day had the proofs distributed to all other newspapers. Officially, the Foreign Office still maintains that its haste in publishing the letter and the Protest Note was because of *The Daily Mail's* action: it wanted to pre-empt the charge that MacDonald had deliberately hushed up the affair. But there is evidence to show that, convinced that the agent who originally forwarded the letter 'had never made a mistake', it would have acted anyway. After that, naturally, it had no control over how the papers would treat the revelation – and few of them could claim very much credit for the events that followed.

MOSCOW ORDERS TO OUR REDS.

GREAT PLOT DISCLOSED YESTERDAY.

"PARALYSE THE ARMY AND NAVY."

AND MR. MACDONALD WOULD LEND RUSSIA OUR MONEY!

DOCUMENT ISSUED BY FOREIGN OFFICE

AFTER "DAILY MAIL" HAD SPREAD THE NEWS.

A "very secret" letter of instruction from Moscow, which we publish below, discloses a great Bolshevik plot to paralyse the British Army and Navy and to plunge the country into civil war.

The letter is addressed by the Bolsheviks of Moscow to the Soviet Government's servants in Great Britain, the Communist Party, who in turn are the masters of Mr. Ramsay MacDonald's Government, which has signed a treaty with Moscow whereby the Soviet is to be guaranteed a "loan" of millions of British money.

The letter is signed by Zinoviev, the Dictator of Petrograd, President of the Third (Moscow) International, and is addressed to A. McManus, the British representative on the executive of this International, who returned from Moscow to London on October 18 to take part in the general election campaign.

Our information is that official copies of the letter, which is dated September 15, were delivered to the Foreign Secretary, Mr. Ramsay MacDonald, and the Home Secretary, Mr. Arthur Henderson, immediately after it was received some weeks ago. On Wednesday afternoon copies were officially circulated by the Executive authorities to high officers of the Army and Navy.

A copy of the document came into the possession of *The Daily Mail*, and we felt it our duty to make it public. We circulated printed copies to other London morning newspapers yesterday afternoon. Later on the Foreign Office decided to issue it, together with a protest, dated yesterday, which the British Government has sent to M. Rakovski, the Bolshevik Chargé d'Affaires in London.

The salient passages of Moscow's plot letter are:

Armed warfare must be preceded by a struggle against the inclinations to compromise which are embedded among the majority of British workmen, against the ideas of evolution and peaceful extermination of capitalism.

Only then will it be possible to count on complete success of an armed insurrection.

From your last report it is evident that agitation-propaganda work in the Army is weak and the Navy a very little better. . . . It would be desirable to have [propaganda-agitation] cells in all the units of the troops, among factories working on munitions and at military store depots.

The military section of the British Communist Party further suffers from a lack of specialists, the future directors of the British Red Army . . . . . It is time you thought of forming such a group.

The British protest is signed, in the absence of the Foreign Secretary, Mr. MacDonald, by Mr. J. D. Gregory, Permanent Assistant Secretary of the Foreign Office. It requests a reply "without delay."

The text of this protest is in another column.

THE BRITISH RED ARMY.

OUR COMMUNISTS TOLD TO FIND GENERAL STAFF.

The text of the civil war document is:

VERY SECRET.

EXECUTIVE COMMITTEE
THIRD
COMMUNIST INTERNATIONAL.
PRESIDIUM.
Sept. 15th, 1924.
MOSCOW.

TO THE CENTRAL COMMITTEE
BRITISH COMMUNIST PARTY.

Dear Comrades,

The time is approaching for the Parliament of England to consider the Treaty concluded between the Governments of Great Britain and the S.S.S.R. for the purpose of ratification. The fierce campaign raised by the British bourgeoisie around the question shows that the majority of the same, together with reactionary circles, are against the Treaty for the purpose of breaking off an agreement consolidating the ties between the proletariats of the two countries leading to the restoration of normal relations between England and the S.S.S.R.

The proletariat of Great Britain, which pronounced its weighty word when danger threatened of a break-off of the past negotiations, and compelled the Government of MacDonald to conclude the Treaty, [illegible] possible energy in the further struggle for paign of disclosure of the foreign policy of MacDonald.

ARMED INSURRECTION.

The IKKI [Executive Committee, third (Communist) International] will willingly place at your disposal the wide material in its possession regarding the activities of British imperialism in the Middle and Far East. In the meanwhile, however, strain every nerve in the struggle for the ratification of the Treaty, in favour of a continuation of negotiations regarding the regulation of relations between the S.S.S.R. and England. A settlement of relations between the two countries will assist in the revolutionising of the international and British proletariat not less than a successful rising in any of the working districts of England, as the establishment of close contact between the British and Russian proletariat, the exchange of delegations and workers, etc., will make it possible for us to extend and develop the propaganda of ideas of Leninism in England and the Colonies. Armed warfare must be preceded by a struggle against the inclinations to compromise which are embedded among the majority of British workmen, against the ideas of evolution and peaceful extermination of capitalism. Only then will it be possible to count upon complete success of an armed

Zinoviev, whose real name is Apfelbaum.

insurrection. In Ireland and the Colonies the case is different; there there is a national question, and this represents too great a factor for success for us to waste time on a prolonged preparation of the working class.

But even in England, as in other countries where the workers are politically developed, events themselves may more rapidly revolutionise the working masses than propaganda. For instance, a strike movement, repressions by the Government, etc.

From your last report it is evident that agitation - propaganda work in the Army is weak, in the Navy a very little better. Your explanation that the quality of the members attracted justifies the quantity is right in principle, nevertheless it would be desirable to have cells in all the units of the troops, particularly among those quartered in the large centres of the country, and also among factories working on munitions and at military store depots. We request that the most particular attention be paid to these latter.

A CLASS WAR.

In the event of danger of war, with the aid of the latter and in contact with the transport workers, it is possible to paralyse all the military preparations of the bourgeoisie, and make a start in turning an imperialist war into a class war. Now more than ever we should be on our guard. Attempts at intervention in China show that world imperialism is still full of vigour and is once more making endeavours to restore its shaken position and cause a new war, which as its final objective is to bring about the break-up of the Russian proletariat and the suppression of the budding world revolution, and further would lead to the enslavement of the colonial peoples. "Danger of War," "The Bourgeoisie seeks War; Capital fresh Markets"—these are the slogans which you must familiarise the masses with, with which you must go to work into the mass of the proletariat. These slogans will open to you the doors of comprehension of the masses, will help you to capture them and march under the banner of Communism.

The Military Section of the British Communist Party, so far as we are aware, further suffers from a lack of specialists, the future directors of the British Red Army.

It is time you thought of forming letariat and desire in the future to direct not the blind mechanical forces in the service of the bourgeoisie but a national army.

Form a directing operative head of the Military Section.

Do not put this off to a future moment, which may be pregnant with events and catch you unprepared.

Desiring you all success, both in organisation and in your struggle,

With Communist Greetings,
President of the Presidium
of the IKKI.
ZINOVIEV.

Member of the Presidium,
McManus,
Secretary, KUUSINEN.

FOREIGN OFFICE PROTEST.

REPLY WITHOUT DELAY REQUESTED.

The following is the text of the letter sent yesterday by Mr. J. D. Gregory to M. Rakovski, the Chargé d'Affaires in London of the Soviet Union:—

FOREIGN OFFICE.
October 24, 1924

Sir,—I have the honour to invite your attention to the enclosed copy of a letter which has been received by the Central Committee of the British Communist Party from the Presidium of the Executive Committee of the Communist International, over the signature of Monsieur Zinoviev, its president, dated September 15.

The letter contains instructions to British subjects to work for the violent overthrow of existing institutions in this country, and for the subversion of his Majesty's armed forces as a means to that end.

2. It is my duty to inform you that his Majesty's Government cannot allow this propaganda and must regard it as a direct interference from outside in British domestic affairs.

3. No one who understands the constitution and the relationships of the Communist International will doubt its intimate connection and contact with the Soviet Government. No Government will ever tolerate an arrangement with a foreign Government by which the latter is in formal diplomatic relations of a correct kind with it, while at the same time a propagandist body organically connected with that foreign Government encourages and even orders subjects of the former to plot and plan revolutions for its overthrow.

Such conduct is not only a grave departure from the rules of international comity, but a violation of specific and solemn undertakings repeatedly given to his Majesty's Government.

4. So recently as June 4 of last year the Soviet Government made the following solemn agreement with his Majesty's Government:—

The Soviet Government undertakes not to support with funds or in any other form persons or bodies or agencies

McManus

or institutions whose aim is to spread discontent or to foment rebellion in any part of the British Empire . . . and to impress upon its officers and officials the full and continuous observance of these conditions.

5. Moreover, in the Treaty which his Majesty's Government recently concluded with your Government, still further provision was made for the faithful execution of an analogous undertaking which is essential to the existence of good and friendly relations between the two countries.

His Majesty's Government mean that these undertakings shall be carried o[illegible], both in the letter and in the spirit, and it cannot accept the contention that while the Soviet Government undertakes obligations, a political body, as powerful as itself, is to be allowed to conduct a propaganda and support it with money,

Continued in Next Column.

LATEST NEWS

SPEAKER'S DEATH AT MEETING.

When concluding a speech in sup-

The Daily Mail.

LATE LONDON EDITION

DAILY HERALD

No. 2,725 (No. 1,732—New Series) LONDON, MONDAY, OCTOBER 27, 1924 ONE PENNY

HOW THAT "RED PLOT" WAS WORKED

ATTACK ON PRIME MINISTER COLLAPSES

Incident a Proof of the Govt.'s Determination to Insist on Keeping of Agreements

"ZINOVIEFF LETTER" A CLUMSY FORGERY

The Zinovieff letter "bombshell" has turned out a damp squib.

The Tories have tried frantically to use the "Red Plot" scare to damage Mr. MacDonald and the Government. Their efforts have failed, and nothing is left of their uproar except proof of the Labour Government's firm resolve to insist that agreements shall be kept.

Moreover, the "Red Plot" itself has vanished. For the alleged letter from the Communist International to the Communist Party of Great Britain is now seen to be a demonstrable forgery.

The question remains, however, how did such an obvious forgery come to be "planted" upon the Foreign Office, and how did the experts come to accept it?

Past experience has shown how much harm can be done by such documents, which have proved on other occasions to be the work of Russian "Whites" in touch with the British Secret Service.

RUSSIAN "WHITES" AT WORK AGAIN

By Our Political Correspondent

The publication of the alleged letter from Mr. Zinovieff to the Communist Party of Great Britain and of the Foreign Office Note in reply was rapturously hailed by the Tory and Liberal Press as a "bombshell" which would win the election.

Yesterday their enthusiasm waned. Mr. Rakovsky's reply denouncing the Zinovieff letter as a clumsy forgery was damping. The attempt to damage the Prime Minister's reputation had collapsed.

The Tories realised that, whether the Zinovieff letter were genuine or a forgery, all that they had succeeded in doing was to prove beyond a doubt the intention of the Government to hold the Russians strictly to their agreement not to engage in subversive propaganda.

They changed their tactics. They began to talk of a "mystery." Why, they asked, had the document not been published before? The Cabinet, they said, had known of it on October 9, and had done nothing until the "Daily Mail" threat of publication forced its hands. And so on.

TISSUE OF NONSENSE

This is a tissue of nonsense. The facts are simple, so far as the Foreign Office action is concerned.

The "letter" was received and considered in the usual way by the experts. The usual routine in such cases was followed.

The statement made during the week-end that the document had been considered by the Cabinet is absolutely false.

It was not a Cabinet matter, but a Foreign Office matter. And as soon as the experts had convinced themselves—albeit wrongly—of the authenticity of the document, action was taken without delay.

A draft Note was prepared, for use, first, as the basis for a friendly request for an explanation from Mr. Rakovsky, in accordance with normal diplomatic procedure.

During Mr. MacDonald's absence in South Wales, that Note was completed, sent to Mr. Rakovsky by Mr. Gregory, and issued to the Press.

This action was taken "as a routine matter," without consultation either with Mr. MacDonald or Mr. Ponsonby, who was also away in his constituency.

Those are the simple facts about which so much "mystery" has been made.

A CLUMSY FORGERY

Internal Evidence Enough to Expose It

I now come to the question of the authenticity of the alleged letter from the Communist International.

Mr. Rakovsky, in a reply to the Gregory Note (the full text of which will be found on Page Two), at once declared it to be a "gross forgery."

I understand that he has now received a telegram from Moscow confirming this.

But these denials were scarcely needed. The internal evidence is quite enough.

If the original document in the possession of the Foreign Office were available for scrutiny, one could, of course, examine the signatures, the paper, the typing, and so forth. In its absence one can only examine the wording.

Even this is sufficient to convince me that there is not a shadow of doubt that the document is a forgery, and a clumsy forgery at that.

Take first the signatures.

They run:—

"President of the Presidium of the IKKI, Zinovieff.

Member of the Presidium, McManus.

Secretary, Kuusinen."

Now, as has already been pointed out, Mr. Zinovieff is not "President of the Presidium of the IKKI," but "President of the IKKI." It is inconceivable that he would sign himself as "President of the Presidium." Nor in an English letter would he be likely to use the Russian initials IKKI in place of the English "Executive Committee."

And he signs, not "Zinovieff" but "G. Zinovieff."

Mr. McManus is certainly a "member of the Presidium." But he signs himself either "A. McManus" or "Arthur McManus"—not, as in the "document," "McManus."

Moreover, we have his word that he never saw or heard of the letter he is alleged to have signed.

Nor is Mr. Kuusinen secretary of the Executive Committee, or entitled so to sign himself. The secretary is Mr. Kolaroff. Mr. Kuusinen, as a subordinate member of the secretariat, signs—as a genuine document before me shows—not "Secretary," but "For the Secretariat."

And—he does *not* sign "Kuusinen," but "O. W. Kuusinen."

THREE MORE BLUNDERS

Things No Genuine Document Would Contain

So much for the signatures. Now turn to the heading.

The Foreign Office document is headed:—

"Executive Committee
Third
Communist International
Presidium."
Sept. 15, 1924. Moscow.

I have in front of me, by the courtesy of the Communist Party, an actual letter of instruction from the Presidium.

It is headed:—

Workers of all countries unite.
THE EXECUTIVE COMMITTEE OF THE COMMUNIST INTERNATIONAL.
Address, Mokhovaia 16. Address for telegrams, International, Moscow. Telephone No., 2-24-12, 56-71, suppl. 26.
No. 194. Moscow, Sept. 15, 1924.

The two, it will be seen, are absolutely different. It is plain that the "document" is not written on genuine Communist International paper.

Apart from that, it uses the phrase "Third Communist International"—an absurdity of which no Communist, let alone Mr. Zinovieff, would be guilty.

Now we come to the address.

The "document" is addressed to "The Central Committee, British Communist Party."

Again a blunder. The official title of the British "C.P." is "Communist Party of Great Britain." That is the phrase used in all genuine official Communist documents.

In every detail, then, in heading, in address, and in signature, the alleged letter contains those blunders of detail by which the forger always betrays himself.

Nor—to anyone familiar with Communist literature—is the body of the letter one whit more convincing. It is plainly the work of a Russian, whose English is, to say the least of it, clumsy. The English documents of the Communist International are, on the other hand, now always written in excellent English, and are evidently either drafted or revised by British members of the staff.

It is the work of a Russian ignorant of British conditions—so ignorant of the British Communist movement that he believes that the British Party has a "military section" and "military cells."

And it is the work of a Russian whose main concern has been to frighten public opinion here by suggesting that the army is infected with Communism, and to create prejudice against the Treaties by suggesting that their ratification will "make it possible to extend and develop propaganda."

In fact, this amiable Russian puts into the mouth of Zinovieff the very points upon which Tory speakers and Tory writers have been laying such stress in their campaign.

There can, then, be no question, to my mind, that the document is one of that long series of "White" forgeries which have played such a part in European politics since 1917.

But how came it that this forgery passed into the hands of the British Foreign Office and was accepted by the "experts" as genuine?

Unhappily one has to admit that these "experts" are singularly inexpert. This is not the first time, by a long way, that they have "fallen for" White forgeries.

SIR BASIL GOES

It should suffice to recall Lord Curzon's famous Note of September 7, 1921, in which most serious allegations were made against the Soviet Government on the strength of certain documents. These documents were obtained from a set of German private detectives who, in default of genuine information, supplied their clients with "fakes." And they were full of the most obvious absurdities.

Nevertheless, the "experts" accepted them as genuine. They were solemnly given to the world. The Russian reply was humiliating. The Foreign Office became the laughing-stock of Europe, and Sir Basil Thomson resigned.

I suspect that the history of the "Zinovieff" letter is much the same.

SECRET SERVICE

Is It the Same Department as Made 1921 Mess?

The story that it was intercepted in the post, photographed and then delivered, may be dismissed at once. There is no truth in it.

I am inclined to believe that the document came through that same Secret Service department which has been responsible for many "gaffes" besides that one of the 1921 Note.

Through the Secret Service, and from ——?

The authorship, as I have said, is clearly Russian.

And there has been close contact between the British Secret Service and the heads of the "White" Russian counter-revolutionary organisations.

In this connection, let me recall the famous DAILY HERALD exposure of the "Pravda" affair, when we proved that the Secret Service had assisted the "Whites" in the preparation of forged documents for use in Russia.

There is, then, ground for believing that the real genesis of the Zinovieff letter is that it was concocted by one of the "White" organisations, communicated by them to the Secret Service, passed on to the Foreign Office, and there accepted by the experts, without adequate critical examination.

That, I believe, is probably the solution of the "mystery" of the origin of the document. The other mystery—how the existence of such a document in a Government office, and apparently the contents of the document itself, came to be communicated to the heads of the Tory Party and to the Tory Press, is a matter which can only be cleared up by searching examination.

TORIES' S O S TO LIBERALS

Votes That Would be Used for Tariffs

A PRETTY PLOT

Candidate Explains His "Open Mind"

There is real alarm in the Tory camp. The generals have been reviewing the battlefield, and their optimistic visions of a Tory majority are now very much blurred.

Word has, therefore, gone forth for a special effort to capture the Liberal vote, not only where the "pact" operates, but even in constituencies where there is a Liberal candidate. Fate, however, is against them.

In "pact" constituencies where the Tory has a straight fight with Labour, as the DAILY HERALD has already pointed out, there has been a big movement of the Liberal rank and file towards Labour. This is bound to continue.

Nor are the Tories likely to have any better luck in weaning Liberal votes elsewhere.

For the blunt fact is that the electors with Radical traditions are realising that a vote for a Tory in any constituency is a vote that would be used for Protection.

When Mr. Baldwin dissolved Parliament a year ago he declared that unemployment was the most urgent problem before the country, and that he regarded Protection as essential if that problem was to be solved.

Mr. Baldwin has not altered his view about Protection, and he still urges that unemployment must be solved.

If he were returned to power pressure upon him to deal with unemployment would, therefore, result in the production of measures of Protection.

That is not merely a logical deduction from his views: his followers are confirming it.

For illustration, consider what is happening in North St. Pancras, one of the London constituencies.

The late Labour member, Mr. James Marley, is opposed by Capt. Fraser (Tory) and Mr. Roome (Lib.).

Capt. Fraser is making special appeals to the Liberals, by circular and speech, not to waste their votes on Mr. Roome, who has no chance, but to help to defeat Labour.

TORY MIND OPENED

An elector asked him on Saturday night for his views on Protection. His answer killed his chances of any Free Traders' votes.

Protection was not an issue at this election, he said, but he had an open mind on the subject. How "open" it is he proceeded to show.

He recalled that Mr. Asquith, Mr. Lloyd George, and Sir John Simon had supported measures of Protection, and he ridiculed the idea of absolute Free Trade.

He thought some British industries needed protection, so he would consider it his duty to examine the position and would feel free to advocate tariffs where he thought them necessary to help any industry.

In other words, the candidate is naively asking Liberals to vote for Protection in so far as the Tories thought it desirable!

That is the position of the Tory Party in general, and if there were no other reason the Liberal rank and file will look to Labour rather than to Toryism for their political expression.

Many Liberal Free Traders will vote for Labour in spite of having a Liberal candidate, for even though the Liberal leaders had clean hands on the subject of tariffs (and, as Captain Fraser recalled, they have not), they are parties to a pact which makes them vassals of the Tory Party.

TO-MORROW!
OUR
EVE OF THE POLL
SPECIAL
Another Budget of Splendid Ammunition
GET IT AND SELL IT
We Want a Million Sale Order from Newsagents NOW

LATE NEWS

THE SOVIET REPLY

The Soviet's Note in reply to Britain declares the letter to be a proved forgery, demands an apology for the use of this forgery in an official document, and urgently demands that the matter be referred to arbitration.

KNOCKED INTO A COCKED HAT!

Fate of Anti-Labs. This Week, Says Premier

"Labour is going to knock the other parties into a cocked hat on Wednesday!" said the Prime Minister at Swansea on Saturday.

"It is sheer humbug, hypocrisy, and impertinence," he went on, "for the men responsible for sowing seed of the harvest of poverty to use their tongues in condemnation of the Government which happens to be in power at the time the harvest they sowed is being reaped!"

The only business Government, according to those who knew, that had been in office in this country for the last generation was the Labour Government.

There was no Party in the State that was a more certain bulwark against unconstitutional practice than the Labour Party, especially to-day.

"The Party, in the years which followed the war, that kept its head and neither talked nonsense about peace, as was done at Paris, or nonsense about revolution, as at Moscow, was not the Liberal or the Tory Party, but the Labour Party!" (Cheers.)

Referring to unemployment, the Prime Minister said: "I am bound to confess that there is some mystery about the South Wales figures. I would really like to inquire why all these pits are being closed. I would like to get at the root of why the steel works and iron works are being closed. Is it for a fortnight?" he asked, amidst great applause. He would like to know as he was not at all satisfied.

The man responsible for unemployment was Mr. Lloyd George, whose action as Prime Minister when peace was being arranged was now bearing its fruit of unemployment, trade depression and poverty in his own native land.

The Prime Minister was the guest of Mr. J. D. Morgan at Rhubina, the picturesque suburb of Cardiff, over the week-end.

He spent yesterday resting, and in the evening joined in the family home circle.

Old Welsh hymns, which the Premier said he knew when he was a boy, were sung. Altogether, it was a homely and restful week-end.

Members of the Locksmiths' Society are solid in support of Mr. David B. Williams, Labour candidate at East Wolverhampton. Miners, too, are likely to poll heavily in his favour.

MEASURES THAT WORKERS WANT

Stop Profiteering and Give Widows Pensions

THE WRECKERS' AIM

Mr. Parkinson Drives Home the Truth

The tremendous importance of the present election to the workers of this country is emphasised by Mr. J. Allen Parkinson, Comptroller of the King's Household, Labour candidate for Wigan.

All the Labour Government Bills before Parliament are now stopped, Mr. Parkinson points out.

They include the Factory Acts Amendment Bill, the Bill to prevent profiteering in building materials, and the Forty-Eight Hours Bill.

Preparation of the Bill to provide pensions for widowed mothers with children had reached an advanced stage, and was to have been introduced next session.

Other measures in course of preparation include nationalisation of mines, adequate protection for tenants, a drastic dealing with the Poor Law system, taxation of land values, reorganisation in the national interest of electricity and transport undertakings, prevention of profiteering, substantial improvements of Workmen's Compensation Acts, anti-sweating measures.

The question Mr. Parkinson puts to the workers is: Will you permit this work to be interrupted? This is what the Liberals and Tories have combined to stop.

BUILT UNDER WHEATLEY

Houses for Workers in Otley Area

"Opponents of Labour are saying that no houses have been built under the Wheatley scheme," writes Mr. H. Bambridge, chairman of Otley Housing Committee. "Here we have some houses with the roofs on under Wheatley's Act. It is true that they were begun under the Chamberlain scheme, the scheme being sent forward to the Ministry in February, with the proviso that if the Labour Government gave better terms to local authorities we should come under it.

"The Wheatley Bill was passed on August 7, and on September 8 my Council, which has a majority of non-Labour members, agreed, without a dissenting vote, to change over to the Wheatley scheme."

WRONGLY INFORMED

Mr. D. G. Somerville, the Tory candidate at Barrow, has admitted that he was not correct in his statement that there was no Russian work at Barrow. "I acknowledge that I had wrong information," he says.

To-day's Weather

Wind variable to southerly. Mainly fair; risk of rain later; some mist. Moderate temperature.

NATIONAL UNION OF PRINTING, BOOKBINDING, MACHINE RULING, AND PAPER WORKERS.

Fellow Members,

The greatest and most momentous fight in the history of the Working Class Movement is now nearing its close. The forces of reaction and privilege have waged a war of the most despicable and unscrupulous character to prevent Labour being returned to power. They know only too well that Labour in power means the end of class domination, monopoly and exploitation of the worker.

We, therefore, earnestly appeal to every one of our members, irrespective of sex, to vote for the Labour Candidates on Wednesday next, and thus assist in securing a victory that will establish a new social order that will mean

PEACE AMONG NATIONS AND SOCIAL JUSTICE AT HOME.

GEO. HARRAWAY, General President.
T. G. NEWLAND, General Secretary.

The Discovery of Tutankhamen's Tomb

No. 15,548. — Register-15; a Newspaper. — FRIDAY, FEBRUARY 16, 1923. — 16 PAGES—ONE PENNY.

PUTTING THE CLOCK BACK 3,300 YEARS IN EGYPT.

The treasure from Tutankhamen's tomb have been stored in the empty tomb of Seti II., near by. On the table on the left are fragments of the Pharaoh's decayed robe, which experts are trying to reconstruct. Beyond is the seat of the throne, which is lying on its back.
"The Times" World Copyright, by arrangement with the Earl of Carnarvon.

Seti's tomb has been turned into a laboratory, where, besides restoring the decayed, two experts are preserving the intact from decay by chemical treatment. One of the staff, Mr. Lucas, at work with a paint brush.
"The Times" World Copyright, by arrangement with the Earl of Carnarvon.

Lady Evelyn Herbert, Lord Carnarvon's 21-year-old daughter, enjoying a cigarette beside the entrance of Tutankhamen's tomb. A maiden of 1923 meditating among the tombs of the Pharaohs!

Mr. Mace, one of the expert staff, treating fragments of a roll of linen from the tomb—linen 3,300 years old.
"The Times" World Copyright, by arrangement with the Earl of Carnarvon.

Above: The Daily Sketch. Right: The Times.

Any news editor could have told you that the pedestrian pursuits of the archaeologist were hardly the raw material of front-page news. But in November 1922, in the wilderness outside Luxor, after 16 years of sustaining the newsmen's thesis by fruitless digging, a dedicated excavator called Howard Carter was about to prove them wrong. On November 30 *The Times* broke to the world the sensational story of Carter's discovery of Tutankhamen's 3,000 year-old burial-place — beneath the fittingly archaic dateline 'Valley of the Kings (by runner to Luxor)'. From that moment the boy-king of Egypt hit, and hogged, the headlines. Week after week the public marvelled at the procession of gold carvings, precious stones, ivory, alabaster vases and royal furnishings that emerged from the inner darkness of the tomb, and speculated like inveterate egyptologists on the contents of the mysterious, still unopened third chamber. Like the cliffhangers at the new silent cinemas the denouement came eventually, on February 16 the following year. It was the Pharaoh himself, entombed in an awesome golden sarcophagus and surrounded by a veritable treasure-house of unimaginable wealth and beauty. Fabulous King Tut became a household name, a brief antidote to the otherwise depressing pageant of stampeding currencies, strikes and hunger marches. The 'Pharaoh Look' even found its way that season into ladies' fashion, and the more enterprising designers found it extremely profitable, for a time, to encourage a short-lived craze for egyptian design. Even the hit song of the year, predictably enough, was entitled 'Tutankhamen in the Valley of the Kings'. Once resurrected Tutankhamen was never permitted to return to oblivion — at least not by those Sunday papers who perceived the 'curse of the tomb' at work each time one of the unfortunate archaeologists passed away.

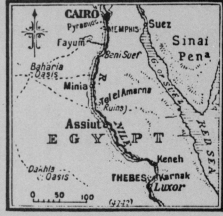

The Monkey Trial

Dayton's Evolution Trial

The New Orleans Times Picayune July 11, 1925.

FARMER JURY WILL HEAR BRYAN, DARROW BATTLE ON TENNESSEE 'APE LAW'

"G.H.Q."

The Richard Rogers home in Dayton, William J. Bryan's home while he is in Dayton, has been termed "Fundamentalist Headquarters" by the special writers who remember the days of the World war when "General Headquarters" was the cynosure of all eyes overseas.

Bernard Shaw in Fiery Fling at Bryanites

Scores Fundamentalists, Warns Tennessee to Rally to Duty

The Jury:

(By The Associated Press)

Dayton, Tenn., July 10.—The jury to try John T. Scopes is composed of nine farmers, one school teacher and farmer; one fruit-grower and one shipping clerk. Eleven of the jurors are church members. They are:

W. F. Robinson, farmer; J. W. Dogley, farmer; Jim Riley, farmer; W. B. Taylor, farmer; R. L. Gentry, farmer and school teacher; J. A. Thompson, fruit grower and former United States marshal;

Talesmen Selected to Decide Merits of Anti-Evolution Statute Violated by Youthful Teacher

NEW INDICTMENT ELIMINATES DOUBT

Grand Jurors Waste No Time in Finding True Bill and Counsel Stage First Clash of Trial

(By The Associated Press)

Dayton, Tenn., July 10.—Evolution was written into the records of a court here today as a legal issue when John Thomas Scopes was placed on trial on a charge of violating the Tennessee law prohibiting the teaching of theories of evolution in the public schools of the state.

The first day of the trial moved swiftly on its way, bringing into the open of the courtroom the first legal battle to be fought Monday, the question of admission of scientific testimony in regard to evolution. The twelve seats in the jury box were filled at the afternoon session of the court with little effort.

Twelve of the twenty prospective jurors examined became jurors in fact after being passed in the main without questions from the state. The

At 8.30 on Friday morning, July 10 1925, it was already hot in Dayton, Tennessee, promising yet another day in the 100s by noon. That was nothing unusual for this sleepy farming community in the back of nowhere: what was unusual was the extraordinary spectacle of frenzied activity which presented itself along Market Street, buntinged and bannered as for a carnival. Outside Rhea County courthouse a phalanx of motion picture cameras encircled the building, each one manœuvering hopelessly for a clear view through any open door or window. In a store-room at the back of the grocer's, 22 Western Union telegraphers cursed and sweated over their apparatus, and fell over each other. More than 100 journalists, not counting the staffs of four rival press associations, bustled in and out and about. H. L. Mencken was observed progressing down the street, button-holing anyone who looked like a native.

The newsmen were up early, of course. But soon waggon-loads of Tennessee farmers began to roll into town, alongside an army of hot-dog vendors, strolling musicians, organ grinders, beggars, bums and revivalist preachers. One, Deerk Çarter 'the bible champion' who claimed to be the first human since Joan of Arc to talk directly with God, had already hung his advertising placards on the gates of the very courthouse. Soon there were hymns and harangues echoing from every street corner. For a few cents you could experiment futilely with one of the new-fangled slot-machines which had blossomed overnight. Or else you could purchase a medallion carved with a hideous grinning ape and inscribed with the legend 'Dayton 1925' — a more permanent memento of your presence at the opening of the already world-famous Monkey Trial.

More accurately, of course, it was the trial of a local teacher John Thomas Scopes for contravening a recent State law which forbade the teaching of evolution ('or any theory that denies the story of the Divine creation of man as taught in the Bible') in schools supported by State funds. But Scopes was the least of the defendants: he was already, as *The New Orleans Times-Picayune* put it, 'a convicted man unless a miracle happens and the Lord speaks in a way that the devout hill folk of Tennessee do not expect'. No, for modernists all over America this was to be the trial and laying-bare of Fundamentalism, the great reactionary stumbling-block to progress and the march of science. Likewise to the fundamentalists it was Modernism that was on trial, those new and evil scientific ideas which were spreading atheism and agnosticism over the land, and even encouraging young and impressionable clergymen to challenge orthodoxies like the Virgin Birth.

It should not be supposed that the citizens of Dayton (85 per cent fundamentalists, though they were, according to the newspaper polls) had altruistically emerged as champions of God's literal Word. They had seen this as an opportunity of putting their little township on the map — some said Scope had even been put up to it. But if the setting for this drama was modest, the leading characters were giants. For the defence there appeared (largely through the persuasion of Mencken) Clarence Darrow, the most famous criminal lawyer in America, a radical and an agnostic. As prosecutor stood William Jennings Bryan, three times a Presidential candidate, former Secretary of State, a fire-breathing Presbyterian and as formidable an opponent of modernism as he was of that other scourge, liquor. He had already, two years before, skirmished with Darrow on the Evolution issue in the columns of *The Chicago Tribune*.

At 9.00 am the trial opened with a stirring reading of the first chapter of Genesis from Judge Raulston, the presentation to Bryan of a caricature of himself as an ape (Mr. Bryan said he did not regard it as a 'perfect likeness') and the selection of twelve good men and true. One by one the jurors trooped in, admitting variously that they'd never heard of evolution or that they'd only read about it in the papers (probably intrigued by *The Chattanooga Daily Times'* memorable headline 'Well, What Is This Here Evolution?') or that they couldn't read or write anyway. It didn't seem to matter, for everyone wanted the battle to commence. 'If you can find anyone round here who believes in evolution' Darrow, in his lavender braces, told the prosecution, 'you are welcome to challenge him'.

On Monday the 13th the contest began in earnest, with Darrow in full satirical flood. Now sinking to a whisper, now rising to a towering rage he fulminated: 'This is as brazen and bold an attempt to destroy liberty as was ever seen in the Middle Ages'. But H. L. Mencken in his report to the Baltimore *Sun* was despondent at the court's apathetic response: Darrow might just as well have 'bawled up a rainspout in the interior of Afghanistan', he concluded. The Judge said he would sleep on whether he would admit the evidence of scientists. On the Wednesday, the modernist Dr. Potter opened the proceedings with a prayer to God 'for whom there are many names' and infuriated the fundamentalists but, unruffled, the prosecution proceeded to put on the stand two boys from the class whose prospects of eternal salvation Scopes had seriously impaired. In fact they were little help: one could barely remember what his teacher *had* said, the other did but was confident, no sir, it hadn't hurt him any. In the afternoon the jury was excused while the Judge admitted one scientist to the stand to define evolution'. There were audible whisperings of disgust from the folks of Rhea Country (or 'yokels' as Mencken was in the habit of calling them before they threatened to run him out of town) when he pitched the Cambrian Age as being 600,000,000 years ago.

On the Thursday (16th) the prosecution made its sustained attack on the evidence of scientists, and whatever resemblance to a trial there was left was utterly dissipated. In passionate appeal Attorney-General Stewart lifted his hands and face to heaven and cried 'Would they have me believe that I was once a worm and writhed in the dust? I want to go beyond this world to where there is eternal happiness for me and others'. Indeed he went so far that by his religious fervor, in the opinion of *The New York Times* 'he quite eclipsed Mr. Bryan's long-awaited invective.

The next day the Judge dropped a bombshell on the defence's case by barring the testimony of scientists, at which Darrow stormed that the court was a mockery and risked a charge of contempt by glaring his defiance at the Judge. However by Monday he had recovered enough to hit on the idea of putting Bryan himself on the stand as a defence witness to prove that the Bible need not be taken literally. At last, here it came — the great confrontation. So stifling was the courtroom that day that the Judge ordered everyone onto the lawn where, more than ever, the affair took on the aspect of an open-air concert party. Launching into his weird cross-examination Darrow inquired whether Bryan believed a whale really had swallowed Jonah. Certainly, or at least a big fish had. Had the sun truly stopped for Joshua? Of course.

No, Mr. Bryan had no idea how old Egyptian civilization was but, yes, he was certain nothing went back to before the Flood; and just as certain that before the Tower of Babel 4155 years ago everything had spoken the same language. As the debate went on it was patently obvious that Darrow and Bryan were not speaking the same language. Bryan believed implicitly that Eve was created out of Adam's rib and he was quite content, he told his questioner, to let the agnostics work out where Cain got *his* wife. The exchanges became bitter: Darrow railed at Bryan's 'fool religion' Bryan inveighed against Darrow's 'slur at the Bible'. It was brought to an end by the Judge mercifully calling an adjournment, and refusing the next day to let it go on.

Scopes was duly convicted on the Tuesday and fined $100, but the real antagonists had got their hackles up. Bryan promised to continue the debate in the press — a promise he never fulfilled for within a week he was dead, called to his Maker, if the London *Star's* verdict carried any weight, to answer for his credulity. The gem of the proceedings, said *The Star*, was 'Mr. Bryan's reply to the evidence of the rector of the Episcopal Church in Tennessee, who held that when the Bible says the little hills skipped like young rams no-one is expected to accept the statement literally. But it would take more than that to daunt the credulity of Mr. Bryan, for had he not heard of earthquakes and landslides? Mr. Bryan's faith might not move mountains, but it is quite sufficient to shake the flimsy foundations of a shack in Tennessee . . . One more example of what Mr. Bryan can swallow and the arboreal instincts of the natives will reassert themselves. They will take to the trees'.

Never before had the public — not just in America, but in Europe, Russia, Japan, even China — been so intimately informed of the minutiae of a trial, from the changing expressions on the stolid jurymen's faces to the offer from a Circus to lend their tame monkey to the defense as 'the missing link'. *The New York Times* estimated two million words had been telegraphed from Dayton in just over a week, in spite of violent electrical storms that frequently blacked out the lines. *The Times'* correspondents themselves had telegraphed 120,000 words fit to print. Somehow or other in all that verbiage it missed the comment that if you gave a monkey a typewriter, in a million years it might accidently tap out the complete works of Shakespeare — or, come to that, the complete speeches of William Jennings Bryan.

MAN AND MONKEY LINKED IN DEFENSE OF TEACHER

"I OBJECT TO PRAYER!"

Spectators in the Dayton courtroom were aghast when Clarence Darrow, chief of Scopes defense counsel, cried out, "I object to prayer!" in his fight against having court opened daily by invocation. Photo shows Darrow in characteristic attitude, coatless, hair ruffled.

Zoologist Describes Evolution as Battle of Scopes Counsel Begins in Dayton Courtroom

MOTION TO QUASH DENIED BY JUDGE

Scientist Declares His Colleagues All Are Opposed to Belief Fundamentalists on Creation

(By The Associated Press)

Dayton, Tenn., July 15.—Argument as to the competency of scientific testimony in the Scopes case will be made in the courtroom here tomorrow, a development eagerly anticipated by participants and lookers-on in Dayton.

The state had rested its case and one scientific witness, Dr. Maynard M. Metcalf, former professor of zoology at Oberlin College, Ohio, was on the witness stand for the defense when court adjourned late today.

DAYTON CRIES FOR LIGHT AS SCIENCE PLEA RINGS

THE PREACHER

When William Jennings Bryan yesterday trumpeted his challenge to science in the Dayton courtroom his mein was far from that of Sunday when he occupied the pulpit in a Dayton church. Photo shows the shirt-sleeved Commoner in the pulpit at the beginning of his sermon.

Scopes Defender Drives Out Effect of Bryan's Wrathful Tirade and "Sells" Modernism to Tennesseeans

WAVES OF APPLAUSE DRAWN BY ADDRESS

Stern Fundamentalists Join in Ringing Ovation for Man Who Would Open New Book of Revelations

Dayton, Tenn., July 16.—"Shall the parents have a right to say that no teacher paid by their money shall rob their children of faith in God and send them back to their homes, skeptical, infidels, agnostics, or atheists?"

Thus William Jennings Bryan set forth the case for the prosecution in the Scopes trial today.

"Close no doors of knowledge from them. Let science and theology both be loved, but let them not be confused."

Thus Dudley Field Malone put the case for enlightenment.

BY PHILIP KINSLEY
(Special to The Times-Picayune)

Dayton, Tenn., July 16.—Dayton began to read a new Book of Revelations today.

If God spoke, at this climax of the Scopes trial, on this day of days in Tennessee, it was in a strange tongue, in favor of science, rather than through the lips of William Jennings Bryan.

An All American funeral

The Death of Rudolph Valentino

SECOND-EXTRA-SECOND

Your Newspaper
With no private axes to grind, no selfish personal interests to serve and no financial strings leading to any other source of power or influence.

Los Angeles Record

CITY EDITION 2 CENTS

Thirty-first Year — Entered as second-class matter, April 1, 1896, at the postoffice at Los Angeles, California, under the Act of March 3, 1879. — LOS ANGELES, MONDAY, AUGUST 23, 1926 — Published Daily Except Sunday at Record Building, 612 Wall Street — Number 9837

VALENTINO DEAD

HOLLYWOOD MOURNS FILM 'SHEIK'S' DEATH

By JIMMY STARR

RUDOLPH VALENTINO, the screen's greatest lover, died this morning, and Hollywood is silent, having waited all night long to hear the latest report of the famous screen sheik's condition.

This morning, as the news came over the wire, Hollywood bowed its head once more for one of its famous ones.

Five years ago "Rudy" started the national wave of the Argentine tango when he appeared in "The Four Horsemen" for Metro, but he came into real popularity when he appeared as the leading man with Agnes Ayres in "The Sheik."

So fine was his performance in that picture that he automatically became a star in his own right when the film was released.

Rudy's famous role as the sheik started the whole world imitating.

* * *

EVERY youth in the country copied Rudy's Argentine peon trousers which he had worn in "The Four Horsemen." Then in the role of "The Sheik" he made bronze complexions and sleek hair even more popular.

Rudy was born in the Italian village of Castellaneta, on May 6, 1895 (31 years ago). He was christened Rudolpho Alfonso Raffaelo Pierre Filiberto Guglielmi di Valentina d'Antonguolla.

Rudy first appeared and received screen credit seven years ago under the direction of James Young. His name at that time was Rudolpho de Valentino.

It was in "Roads to Romance," which Young directed with Earle Williams, for Vitagraph, that Valentino was enlisted to do an Apache dance. So clever were his terpsichorean steps that he was given three days' work at $15 a day.

* * *

THIS $45 was Valentino's Hollywood fortune. Later on he appeared with Universal as a villain in a film starring Carmel Myers. He also won a small role with Clara Kimball Young in "Eyes of Youth."

Each part grew until he was finally selected for the leading male role in "The Four Horsemen," which Rex Ingram was directing for Metro studios.

June Mathis, scenarist, is credited with having first "discovered" the young screen sheik. However, James Young, who directed Rudy for Vitagraph, was the first to go on record as having said Valentino would be a great star some day.

Valentino received not more than $250 per week while making "The Four Horsemen." His estimated salary at the time of his death was between $8000 and $10,00 per week.

After appearing in the Ingram feature, Rudy was engaged to appear opposite Alice Lake in "The Uncharted Sea." This part attracted the attention, as did "The Four Horsemen" role, of Nazimova, who selected him immediately for the part of Armand Duval in her version of "Camille."

* * *

NATACHA RAMBOVA, who later became Mrs. Rudolph Valentino the second, was art director for Nazimova. It is believed that Valentino's association with Rambova while making the Nazimova film resulted in their marriage, which took place two years later.

After "Camille" Valentino was continued under Ingram's direction in "The Conquering Power," once more appearing with Alice Terry (Mrs. Rex Ingram) who won national fame as his leading woman.

When June Mathis departed from the scenario staff of Metro studios and joined the Famous Players Lasky corporation, she immediately thought of Valentino and saw that he was engaged for "The Sheik."

After this Rudy played opposite Dorothy Dalton in "Moran of the Lady Letty" and opposite Gloria Swanson in "Beyond the Rocks."

Then came Fred Niblo's version of "Blood and Sand," which placed Valentino, after a series of mediocre films, back into the limelight once more.

Studio trouble resulted over the small salary he was receiving, and Valentino started suit to break his contract with the Lasky organization.

* * *

AFTER many weeks of discussion, a new company, the Rudolph Valentino Productions was organized by J. B. Williams. Valetino completed "The Young Rajah" for Lasky and then went directly to New York, fighting his case and also making public appearances and fulfilling a dancing engagement in Chicago's largest ballroom.

Upon his return to Hollywood, with most of his accumulated fortune wasted upon lawyers in New York, Rudolph was heartsick and discouraged. His new company, which wanted to produce "Cobra," brought only trouble to Rudy's mind. His affairs at home were in turmoil and Rambova is blamed for part of the friction at the studio, which arose between Valentino and his company.

Valentino's small fortune was now practically gone and he was in dire need of funds, once more as he had been four years before.

After considerable trouble, both with his company and his wife, Rudolph decided to disband his organization and signed with Joseph M. Schenck, head of United Artists corporation, who had offered him a long term contract at a huge figure and a percentage interest in his pictures.

* * *

THE friendship between Valentino and Schenck began when the latter aranged $5000 bail after Valentino had been arrested for bigamy and was lodged in the county jail.

It was this move of Schenck's, who had never met the screen idol, personally, which gave Valentino implicit faith in the producer.

Valentino's first picture under the Schenck management was "The Eagle," directed by Clarence Brown and marked a decided departure from any of his other productions.

It was hailed for bringing back a new Rudolph. Then came the sequel to "The Sheik," entitled "Son of the Sheik," for the opening of which Rudolph went to New York when an operation became necessary.

New York meant much to Rudolph, who had once been an apprentice landscape gardener in Central park. This was long before Rudolph had talked himself into a short vaudeville engagement with Bonnie Glass, and it was this act which drew the attention of Joan Sawyer, one of Broadway's famous dancers, who asked Rudolph to form a dancing partnership with her, which after weeks of severe training, resulted into one of the most famous of dancing teams.

* * *

RUDOLPH claimed at that time that he did not want to be a dancer and with a little money he worked his way to San Francisco where he danced for several months, then later coming to Hollywood with only a hope that he could really crash the studio gate.

Rudolph's dream after he became a star was to play "Romeo and Juliet" opposite Norma Talmadge, who was outside his door at the hospital when he passed away. Mrs. Schenck had promised Rudolph a chance to

[CONTINUED ON NEXT PAGE]

LAST ROLE PLAYED

RUDOLPH VALENTINO

* * *

Here's 'Official' Life of 'Sheik'

Here's the official biography of Rudolph Valentino as kept in the files of United Artists' Corporation:

RUDOLPH Alfonzo Raffaelo Pierre Filibert Guglielmi di Valentina d'Antonguolla was born in the little village of Castellaneta, Italy, May 6, 1895. His mother was the daughter of a learned Parisian doctor, Pierre Filibert Barbin. His father, Giovanni Guglielmi, was in his youth a captain of Italian cavalry and later a veterinary doctor.

When Valentino was 11, his father died. He was sent to Dante Alighieri college, where he finished the course at 13. Then he went to a military college where he is said to have been more interested in romantic novels than in studies. It is recorded he was once sent home because he broke out of a room in which he was confined for discipline in order to see the king, a visitor to the school.

* * *

VALENTINO next enrolled in the Royal Academy of Agriculture to learn to be a scientific farmer; he was graduated with highest honors in his class. Several months of life in Paris and Monte Carlo followed. When the prodigal returned to his home it was decided by his family that if he were going to continue the reckless life he had pursued in France, it were better he be shipped to America.

* * *

SO RUDOLPH VALENTINO arrived in New York December 23, 1913. Although most of his money was spent in cafes, he did learn one thing that was to prove invaluable to him,—how to dance. His money gone, he had to seek a job and his first position was as superintendent of the Long Island estate of Cornelius Bliss, Jr.

His next position was as an apprentice landscape gardner in Central Park, New York. At the Civil Service bureau, he was told he was ineligible for a regular position there.

Quite penniless and literally homeless, this phase of the future star's dramatic career was best summarized by the statement that he took any little odd jobs he could get,—shining brass on cars, sweeping out, what not.

Finally the head waiter at Maxim's employed him as a dancer, and so his professional career began. As dancing partner to Bonnie Glass and later with Joan Sawyer, he attained same reputation.

But the Italian scientific farmer cherished hopes of forsaking the dancing profession, which was never close to his heart, to become a farmer in California. Toward this end he joined a musical comedy troupe headed for the coast, which organization pleased Fate by stranding in San Francisco.

* * *

VALENTINO was advised by a friend he had known in the east, Norman Kerry, to try motion pictures, and on the bounty of Kerry he traveled to Los Angeles, where he did not get a job in the movies.

For a long time, Valentino could not even secure the most menial form of studio employment. One day

[CONTINUED ON NEXT PAGE]

Last Conscious Word Uttered at 3 O'clock

BULLETIN

By United Press.

NEW YORK, Aug. 23.—Rudolph Valentino, who came to this country as an emigrant and rose to the heights of fame as an actor, died at the Polyclinic hospital here today.

Humbly born, the son of a farmer in Italy, he died with four skilled physicians at his bedside and with the country waiting each word from his sick room almost as it waits for a word from the sick room of a president.

Death came at 12:10 P. M.

Dr. Harold Meeker, one of the attending physicians who was with the actor throughout the night and morning, said he believed the last conscious words were spoken at 3:30 a. m.

At that time, Valentino, still thinking he was to recover from an operation for appendicitis and gastric ulcers, spoke of the days he would spend in recuperation and asked the doctor about trout fishing.

"Do you have plenty of rods and hooks?" the actor asked Dr. Meeker.

At 4 a. m. Valentino became irrational and talked mostly in Italian.

Two hours later he was semi-conscious and lapsed into a coma at 8. From then on he occasionally opened his eyes when his name was called. He died without pain. The cause of death, in medical parlance was "septic pneumonia and septic endocarditis."

Scientists considered a blood transfusion and Edward Day, engineer at the hospital, volunteered a pint of his blood. It was decided, however, that the actor was too weakened to stand the extra strain on his heart.

The corps of physicians then ordered an X-ray. It was found that the pleurisy, which brought about a relapse Saturday when Valentino seemed on the road to recovery, had been followed by septoendocarditis (poisoning of the wall of the heart).

The last official bulletin was issued shortly before noon, when it was admitted that the actor was "rapidly failing."

His temperature had mounted to 105. His pulse was hammering at the rate of 140 strokes to the minute. His respiration was 30 to the minute.

In a few moments the actor was dead.

The operation was performed a week ago Sunday. Valentino had been in New York in connection with the release of one of his pictures, "The Son of the Sheik." He had attended several parties and was in a gay mood most of the week preceding his illness.

After he had been stricken by acute appendicitis he was taken to the hospital.

The ulcerous condition was said to be more of a menace to his health than the appendicitis.

At first it was believed the operation had been completely successful. On Tuesday it was known that peritonitis had developed, but physicians said it was localized.

The hospital, meanwhile, was besieged by personal and telephone calls from thousands of those whose hours had been made happier by Valentino's screen appearance.

Once there was a report of his death, and extra girls were assigned to telephone duty at the Polyclinic.

"Mr. Valentino is alive and his condition is the same," intoned the operators to the callers and a gasp of relief followed.

Father Congodo administered the last rites of the Catholic church to the dying man shortly after 10 a. m. today. Just before Valentino died, Father Bennon, of the Church of St. Malachi, known as the Actors' church, in Forty-ninth street, arrived in the sickroom.

Joseph M. Schenck announced Valentino's death. He came downstairs at 12:15 and read the brief bulletin signed by Drs. Paul E. Durham, G. Randolph Manning and Howard D. Meeker.

The relapse came Saturday. Valentino still showed a remarkable constitution and physicians took hope from his courage. However, the disease traveled slowly but certainly toward the heart and death could not be denied.

After news of his death came today, the telephone girls were immediately beseiged once more.

By Thursday of last week Valentino was in better spirits and hopes were high that his recovery would be complete. He even consented to an interview, through George Ullman his personal manager.

Valentino had lost consciousness shortly before the end.

* * *

Pola Faints at News of Death

Unconscious and hysterical by turns, crying out her grief over the death of Rudolph Valentino, Pola Negri, reported fiancee of the dead film star, was under the care of two physicians in her Ambassador hotel bungalow today.

The Polish film star's grief was touching.

Informed of Valentino's death by newspapermen, Miss Negri fainted.

Frantically her maid, crying out for aid, summoned th hotel house physician. A few moments later the star's pr vate doctor arrived. Restoratives returning her to conscious ness, Miss Negri wept bitterly. The star was completely unnerved. A few moments later and her grief turned to hysteria.

In her dialect of mixed English and Polish, Miss Negri screamed again and again the name of Valentino.

Again physicians quieted her.

As news reached the studio where she had been working night and day on her new picture, "Hotel Imperial," in an effort to finish her work in order that she might rush to her lover's bedside, officials dispatched messengers, hoping to be able to reach the actress before she had heard the story from other sources.

They were too late.

Mr. and Mrs. Charles Eyton, close personal friends of the star, were the only ones admitted to her hotel bungalow.

Mrs. Eyton remained with Miss Negri, seeking to comfort her.

The star's hysterical condition prevented her from issuing any statement. It could not be learned if she plans to go to New York, should the funerel be held there.

All work on Miss Negri's picture was abandoned.

At her bungalow home none could say whether the star will rush to New York or not.

At the Famous Players studio flags were lowered to half-mast immediately upon receipt of the news.

Work on all stages was abandoned, the film players assembling in groups. It was the same at other studios in Hollywood and Culver City. There too the flags were lowered.

As the news spread through the great stages on the Famous Player-Lasky "lot" and at United Artists, directors shouted their commands of "cut," and cameras stopped clicking.

Film players rushed to executive offices and grouped about asking for further news after the first bare announcement of the star's death.

Women film stars wept. Many of the male players made no effort to hide their tears. The genuine affection with which Valentino was held by his film world was clearly evident.

Rudolph Valentino died ('with a smile as his lips touched the priest's crucifix' — *The New York Daily News*) on Monday afternoon August 23 1926 of a ruptured gastric ulcer and peritonitis, and with an overdraft of truly spectacular proportions. That night the laboratories at United Artists began feverishly producing extra prints of The Son of the Sheik — though whether they would repay the lavish millions expended on the Prince of Lovers depended on whether there was, in that day and age, life after death. And that in turn depended on the newspapers.

The first glimmer of life appeared when as day dawned on the 24th hundreds of people were found to be besieging Campbell's Funeral Parlour on Broadway, some of them brandishing *The New York Journal* whose front page announced that Rudy had wished for his body to be viewed. Inside, everything that the embalmer's art could accomplish was being done to make that very body viewable. Evening wear had been decided upon, and scented candles, with discreet lighting and a single red rose. *Very* tasteful, and more than could be said of the behaviour of the 10,000 mourners who had gathered outside by lunchtime. They fought, screamed, resisted the futile police baton-charges, and with a final surge burst through the plate-glass window of the mortuary. Before order was restored the Final Resting-Place was a shambles, stripped bare of all decorations, and hundreds wounded in the stampede.

Eventually a moderately docile procession was got going past the body — or at least past the tailor's dummy that had now been made to look passably like the film star (it was a wise precaution, since every now and then a crazed girl would insist on flinging herself on the catafalque and pressing her lips to the glass). It began to look as if the undertaker's press agent was at last getting things together: a guard of honour from the Fascisti League of America arrived on cue, with a wreath that purported to be from Mussolini; advance photographs of everything were distributed to the Press (one of them — of the funeral cortège — was later said to have appeared in one newspaper on the streets an hour before the funeral procession started); an official physician, one Dr. Wyman, was appointed in the event of any more riots.

In the days that followed there was more than enough to keep the papers at full stretch. There were the continuing riots:

FIGHT TO SEE DEAD FILM HERO
20,000 Struggle to View Valentino Lying-in-State: Baton Charges by Police
DAILY SKETCH PICTURE BY RADIO-PHOTOGRAPHY

though over in Britain *The Daily Sketch* was clearly in two minds which was more important — Rudy's death or the radio-photograph they had obtained of his lying-in-state and which

VALENTINO LYING IN STATE: *By Wireless*

This exclusive picture of Rudolph Valentino lying in state was transmitted by wireless from New York to London in less than an hour. It is reproduced just as it was received. The body, dressed in a dinner suit, is here seen behind glass, under a strong top light. By arrangement with the Radio Corporation of America and the Marconi Telegraph Company in London, special operators were retained in New York and in London to expedite the transmission of the photograph.

The Daily Sketch.

adorned the front page in spite of being virtually indecipherable.

Then there was the progress of the grief-maddened Miss Pola Negri across the continent from Hollywood and her arrival in New York. She and Valentino were to have been married, a, fusion of great talents amply borne out by her dramatic performance at the bier on August 30. she even moved the hardbitten reporter from *The Daily News* ('. . . she prayed, wept and collapsed and gave to the public all of the spectacle of grief that the greatest of dramatic writers had pictured in song, story and opera from the beginning of things theatrical'.) Not that she forgot herself so far as not to oblige a photographer who complained the light wasn't right.

Soon came the intriguing news from England of the tragic girl who had committed suicide out of genuine grief for Valentino (below, this page).

How many more like her would there be? But equally disturbing were the rumours that lurked everywhere. Was Rudy poisoned? *The Daily News* had come out with the theory at the very beginning. It was not clear how, or by whom, but the motive was either revenge or

jealousy, or both. *The Chicago Tribune* spread the idea further across the continent, but it was left to *The New York Graphic* which had already reported contact with Rudy in the Other World and had published a 'composograph' of Valentino meeting up with Caruso in the Elysian Fields, to give divine substance to the rumours.

On the strength of this *The New York Graphic* instituted a full-scale investigation which uncovered precisely nothing, but was worth every minute of it.

The Los Angeles Examiner revealed a posthumous confession by the Great Lover that he was a failure at love. Dr. Wyman, the official physician, was unmasked as a con-man, a former convict cashing in on the credulous.

And one sensation followed another until the controversial body was finally convoyed across America and interred in Hollywood Cemetery, and left in peace. But where the ballyhoo left off, the box-office took over. Such was the impetus of that frantic week in New York that the posthumous royalties from Valentino's films turned that colossal overdraft into a balance of $600,000 in no time at all. *The New York Graphic* never said how the ghost of Rudy reacted to that.

Nine Days in May

The General Strike

Few people in Britain were entirely surprised when a General Strike was called by the Trades Union Congress at midnight on May 3 1926, nor totally unprepared for it either. The determination of the coalminers faced with longer hours and lower wages, and the intransigence of the mineowners confronted with rising costs and falling profits suggested throughout 1925 no other possible outcome. The soft-pedalling, if not semi-paralysis, of the Government over industrial disputes matched by the willingness, if not enthusiasm, of the TUC to test its new-found solidarity guaranteed a nation-wide trial of strength. For some time before the coal-owners finally locked out the miners on May 1 1926, it was no secret that both sides were busily drawing up their contingency plans. The Unions organised their 'front line' of workers in the transport, railway, building, utility, printing and heavy industries, who were to take to the trenches at the commencement of hostilities. In defence the Government disinterred and revamped an ancient emergency transport system and appointed civil commissioners throughout England to keep essential services going.

The shot that ended the uneasy truce came, perhaps not surprisingly, from *The Daily Mail* whose columns had incessantly howled at the spectre of an imminent red revolution. On May 2 many newspapers had been asked to print an appeal by the Government for volunteers: the printers objected to setting enemy propaganda. Most papers broke the deadlock by calling it an advertisement, but Thomas Marlowe the editor of *The Daily Mail* decided to fling down the gauntlet by endorsing it in an inflammatory editorial entitled 'King and Country' which denounced the idea of a general strike as 'a revolutionary movement' that could only succeed 'by destroying the Government and subverting the rights and liberty of the people'. The London compositors, many of whom had unquestioningly served their King and Country through four years of war, couldn't take this, and walked out (although the editorial was printed in the Manchester and Paris editions of *The Daily Mail*).

Such negotiations as had been proceeding during the day were suspended at once. On the 4th Britain woke up to discover what a general strike meant on its first morning: no milk, no papers, no trams or trains to work, telephone lines jammed, groups of pickets outside the local factory. It was certainly inconvenient, but jolly good-humoured that day and in the days that followed: pickets played football with police and, sometimes, strike committees would help out with emergency distribution. Banks continued to pay workers their strike-pay and chaps from Oxford had lots of fun driving steam-engines. The strike did not last long enough for these cordial relations to turn very sour — there was indeed remarkably little violence: barely 1000 disruptors of the peace convicted during or after the crisis. Hardly worthy of what many foreigners believed to be the final great struggle in a class war, nor quite up to *Pravda's* headline (as quoted in *The Times*) 'Baldwin Preparing a Bloody Bath for

the Proletariat'. Still, there must have been some consolation for the Russian press in 'Bourgeoisie Panic Stricken by Cancellation of Race Meetings and the Appearance of *The Times* as a Small Typewritten Sheet of Paper'. Really the record of those nine days in May, as it appeared in the various makeshift papers that struggled out, reads more like a huge impromptu social experiment than a do-or-die industrial Armageddon.

FOR KING AND COUNTRY.

The miners after weeks of negotiation have declined the proposals made to them and the coal mines of Britain are idle.

The Council of the Trades Union Congress, which represents all the other trade unions, has determined to support the miners by going to the extreme of ordering a general strike.

This determination alters the whole position. The coal industry, which might have been organised with good will on both sides, seeing that some " give and take " is plainly needed to restore it to prosperity, has now become the subject of a great political struggle, which the nation has no choice but to face with the utmost coolness and the utmost firmness.

We do not wish to say anything hard about the miners themselves. As to their leaders all we need say at this moment is that some of them are (and have openly declared themselves) under the influence of people who mean no good to this country.

A general strike is not an industrial dispute. It is a revolutionary movement intended to inflict suffering upon the great mass of innocent persons in the community and thereby to put forcible constraint upon the Government.

It is a movement which can only succeed by destroying the Government and subverting the rights and liberties of the people.

This being the case, it cannot be tolerated by any civilised Government and it must be dealt with by every resource at the disposal of the community.

A state of emergency and national danger has been proclaimed to resist the attack.

We call upon all law-abiding men and women to hold themselves at the service of King and country.

Day One (Tuesday 4th): 2½ to 3 million workers reported to be out on strike. 30,000 'volunteers' have offered to take over their work. Streets of London jammed with limousines and 'coughing relics of pre-war motoring' as everyone makes the trek to work as best they can — one 'silk-hatted habitué of Throgmorton Street' seen jolting to the City on the tailboard of a dustcart. Such democratic times! The Prince of Wales hurried back from Biarritz. Sir W. Joynson-Hicks ('Jix') announced new emergency regulations in the Commons and left early to be sure of getting home. Newspapers badly hit today, but Winston Churchill has taken over the offices of the *Morning Post* (where else?) to issue an official government newspaper. The TUC in their turn have moved into the *Daily Herald* and will keep the workers' presses rolling.

Day Two (Wednesday 5th): Churchill's *British Gazette* out on the streets, but very hard to find and missing pages 2 and 3. Nevertheless Zoo Notes and Radio Programmes on 2LO are there — also the news that Alderman Edwin Pease (a mineowner from Darlington) has left £295,213 in his will. After lunch the TUC's *British Worker* makes its debut, no less than 8 pages of exhortatory news. Many London papers appeared in a ghastly variety of shapes, sizes and typefaces — typewritten, roneo'd or (like *The Daily Express*) laboriously pulled as single proof-copies. The *Daily Mail* comes out the best of all, having flown in thousands of copies of its Continental edition from Paris.

Hyde Park has turned into a sprawling ram-shackle city of huts, the nerve-centre of Britain's distribution system. The Australian cricket tour continues undisturbed (Gregory 120 n.o.).

Day Three (Thursday 6th): the Government have won a by-election in Yorkshire handsomely and the communist MP from North Battersea is sentenced to two months in prison for making a seditious speech. *The British Worker* reports its offices were raided by police the previous night, while a crowd outside sang the Red Flag, and that the import of strawberries 'for the wealthy classes' has been stopped.

Day Four (Friday 7th): *The Daily Mirror* today claims to be the first strikebound paper to appear with photographs of the strike. It has been produced in a furtive flat in a secluded part of London ('from out of that secluded flat men came with suitcases and kitbags, entered high-powered cars and vanished into the night'!) Neighbours have reported suspicious goings-on to Scotland Yard. Armoured cars are appearing on the streets accompanying food convoys, even in the absence of anything to protect them from. London taxi-drivers have joined the strike. The Archbishop of Canterbury today issued a plea for peace, but the BBC has refused to broadcast it.

Day Five (Saturday 8th): the first strike edition of *The Daily Graphic* out today — it shows Lady Mountbatten cooking sausages at Marble Arch. At Marylebone police court a newsvendor is charged with advertising false news ('Great public revolution. Army has refused to fight') and claims in his defence 'It's a free country — I'll say what I like'. Lloyd George is said to be making strenuous efforts to persuade *The Daily News* (which has not appeared during the strike) to combine with the *Chronicle* and *Westminster Gazette* to form one great Liberal strike paper, which would lay responsibility for the strike equally on the TUC and the Government.

Day Six (Sunday 9th): *The Sunday Times* has appeared in virile form, roundly castigating 'a junta of trade union officials' for overruling Parliament, and complaining 'we become the victims of a rapacious tyranny'. No *British Gazette* today, but *The British Worker* is indignant that the humblest of special constables is being paid more than a pit-worker was offered. The headmaster of Eton and fifty of his assistant masters have signed on as special constables. An Oxford rowing blue is driving a train from Bristol to Gloucester. During the weekend the stubborn siege at London docks was peacefully broken by the 1st battalion of the Grenadier Guards, and bags of flour emerged through the gates guarded by men of the Tank Corps.

Day Seven (Monday 10th): The TUC has been studying Lord Samuel's memorandum on a new way of implementing the proposals in his Commission on the Coal Industry, and today shows it to the miners' leaders. They reject it utterly, but the TUC clearly wants to end the strike. *The Times* editorial is very moderate: 'no-one suggests for a moment that any considerable number of men on strike are animated by revolutionary motives', but *The British Worker* stoutly denies that any union

THE
BRITISH WORKER
OFFICIAL STRIKE NEWS BULLETIN
Published by The General Council of the Trades Union Congress

No. 4.   SATURDAY EVENING, MAY 8, 1926.   PRICE ONE PENNY

PEACE CALL SILENCED

Plan of Churches Not Broadcast

IS IT FAIR?

The Churches, under a sense of moral responsibility, have offered some leadership in this national crisis, and have put forward their view as to the basis of a possible concordat; but their voice has been officially silenced by the B.B.C., which is thus shown once more to be the instrument of the Government.

The General Council, without necessarily endorsing the terms of the Concordat, calls the attention of the public to the grave significance of the Government's attitude to such peace efforts.

This morning Mr. E. L. Poulton, the chairman of the Publicity Committee of the General Council, received a letter from the Rev. Henry Carter, general secretary, Wesleyan Social Welfare Department, and the Rev. P. T. R. Kirk, Vicar of Christ Church, Westminster, and director of Industrial Christian Fellowship, referring to an important pronouncement by the Archbishops of Canterbury and York asking for a resumption of negotiations with a view to the early settlement of the present crisis.

"The terms of this pronouncement," the letter says, "were settled after full conference between the Archbishop and leaders of the Christian Churches of the country.

"The Archbishop of Canterbury sent the message to the British Broadcasting Company on Friday night to be broadcast from 2LO.

Definite Refusal

"The British Broadcasting Company officially and definitely refused to broadcast the appeal.

"In view of this refusal, the Archbishop sent the message to 'The Times' and the news agencies. As far as we are aware it has been published in 'The Times' only.

"We are anxious to secure the widest publicity for the message at this juncture."

Accordingly we print the message in full :

"Representatives of the Christian Churches in England are convinced that a real settlement will only be achieved in a spirit of fellowship and co-operation for the
Continued on Page Four, Col. Three

WEATHER

Northerly winds, moderate or fresh; local showers of rain or hail cold.

MISLEADING THE NATION

Our Reply to Sir John Simon's Innuendos and Charges

In his speech in the House of Commons on Thursday Sir John Simon made much play with the statement that in ceasing to work on Monday night certain workers had broken their contracts with their employers. He went on to argue that this proved that a general stoppage differed essentially from a stoppage in a single industry. He concluded by saying that " the attack on the community" had "deprived the miners of a great deal of the sympathy they thoroughly deserved." The same speech was broadcast this morning.

There is, as far as the Trade Union Movement is concerned, no " attack on the community." There is no "attempt to set up a rival Government." There is no " challenge to the Constitution." The workers have exercised their legal and long-established right of withholding their labour, in order to protect the miners against a degradation of their standard of life, which is a menace to the whole world of labour.

If, in the exercise of that right, contracts have, in certain instances, been broken, that incident, as Sir John Simon must be well aware, cannot, with any show of reason, be used to give to the present struggle the sinister character which he has chosen to ascribe to it.

On the contrary, as has repeatedly been explained by the General Council, its origin and its object are both purely industrial.

It began because the Government first refused to secure the suspension of the mineowners' notices, in order that discussions might continue free from the threat of a lock-out, and then abruptly broke off negotiations on the pretext of an incident of which the Trade Union representatives had no knowledge. It will continue until the Government is willing to resume negotiations for an honourable termination of the Mining Dispute.

Sir John Simon spoke of the " sympathy " which the miners " thoroughly deserved." His sympathy would have been appreciated better if it had been given at a somewhat earlier date, and if it were not confined to words.

Had the Trade Union Movement not responded to their appeal for assistance, the miners would have been condemned to struggle unaided against the monstrous terms imposed by the mineowners. The sympathy which counts has found expression in the spontaneous movement of generous indignation which has rallied the workers to their defence throughout the length and breadth of the country.

SILENT ARSENAL AT WOOLWICH

"Not One Case of Blacklegging Reported "

50,000 OUT

From Our Special Correspondent

The silent strike holds sway in Woolwich. The great Arsenal and Dockyard are like an industrial mausoleum. No sound of a hammer breaks the stillness throughout the hundreds of shops and not a wheel is turning.

The eight to ten thousand workers who in normal times inhabit during working hours this vast hive of metalworking are either at home, attending to their picket duties, playing cards or billiards at one of the many Labour clubs in the district, or chatting in the street with comrades.

I was told stories of naval ratings and troops, as guards within the Arsenal and dockyards, but force is futile

LEVY YOURSELVES IF AT WORK!

The General Council requires that all workers who are still in service or employment shall contribute 5 per cent. of their wages to the Strike Fund.

This levy should be remitted to the General Council through the Headquarters of the Unions concerned.

Other contributions should be sent to X2, Trades Union Congress, 32, Eccleston-square, London, S.W.1.

to make the wheels go round. The O.M.S. has not been able to provide the skilled and technical workers that can work metal with accuracy and precision, nor do the heavy manual tasks normally performed within the great establishment.

Outside, not a tram, bus, or other public conveyance is to be seen. The dock gates all the way to London are closed. Loyalty to the call of the General Council is complete, and order and good humour prevail.

Workers at one big glass works gave a percentage of their last week's wages towards the strike funds, 410 joined the union, formed a new branch and threw in their lot with the strike, refusing the offer of the management of 2s. per hour and a three months' bonus.

Not one case of blacklegging has been discovered; the local Committee has the situation in complete and orderly control.

Published for the General Council of the Trades Union Congress by Victoria House Printing Company, 2, Carmelite-street, London, E.C.4. Telephone (8 lines): 6210 City.

DAILY GRAPHIC

No. 11,344   Registered Newspaper   SATURDAY, MAY 8, 1926   ONE PENNY

THE SPIRIT OF GOOD WILL.

ENROLLING VOLUNTEERS IN THE WOMAN'S AUXILIARY SERVICE FOR TRANSPORT AND WELFARE WORK.

THE RIGHT SPIRIT. A POLICE CONSTABLE AND AN AMATEUR DRIVER IN CHARGE OF AN L.G.O.C. MOTOR OMNIBUS.

LADY LOUIS MOUNTBATTEN (RIGHT) ... SAUSAGES AT MARBLE ARCH.

GETTING TO WORK. THE STRIKE DID NOT TROUBLE THIS SMILING LOT OF YOUNG PEOPLE GOING TO WORK.

members were returning to work. Five passenger trains, driven by 'blackleg labour', involved in accidents.

Day Eight (Tuesday 11th): *The British Worker* announces that from tomorrow the 'second line' will go into action, principally the engineers and shipbuilders. *The British Gazette* now insists that supplies and transport everywhere were improving: today, 850 omnibuses on the streets of London. *The Daily Express* reports a large number of employees applying for reinstatement, *The Daily Mirror* says theirs should apply in writing.

Day Nine (Wednesday 12th): shortly after 12.00 the TUC chiefs arrive at Downing Street asking to see the Prime Minister. They are told he will not see them until the strike is called off: they explain that is why they are there (though the miners' leaders were conspicuously absent). In a very few minutes the General Strike was over. That evening the King broadcast to the nation calling on it to 'forget whatever elements of bitterness the events of the past few days may have created' and to look forward to a lasting peace. Alas, at the same moment the miners were announcing 'The decision of the TUC has nothing to do with us. Our stoppage may continue for an indefinite period.'

It did in fact last until November 19, when the men were finally driven back to work by starvation. They won nothing from their efforts, being forced to accept conditions worse than when they started. The newspapers themselves were back to normal within a week. *The British Gazette* then bowed out on Thursday 13th with the announcement that in eight issues it had reached a circulation of 2,209,000 — 'an unexampled achievement in journalism'. And in a sense this was true, though there had scarcely been any serious competition. *The British Worker* reached 713,000 in spite of suffering from an acute paper shortage.

For all the national papers the strike had been a time of intense excitement. Some like *The Daily Herald*, which since its presses were otherwise occupied had appeared with the same news and a different dateline each day, were content just to keep going in some form. Others like *The Times*, which amongst other things had to contend with an attempt at arson, took up the challenge with gusto. After it was all over, there was not a paper without some stirring exploit to recount — of proprietors working in their shirtsleeves in the foundry, of volunteer printers more accustomed to setting menus laying out the news like the table d'hote, of delivery cars averaging 57 mph for six hours down the A1. But perhaps the most exciting thing of all — to the proprietors anyway — was the subsequent agreement with the unions that never again would there be 'interference with the contents of newspapers'.

PLEASE PASS ON THIS COPY OR DISPLAY IT

The British Gazette

Published by His Majesty's Stationery Office.

No. 7. LONDON, WEDNESDAY, MAY 12, 1926. ONE PENNY.

ORDER AND QUIET THROUGH THE LAND.

Growing Dissatisfaction Among The Strikers.

INCREASING NUMBERS OF MEN RETURNING TO WORK.

850 Omnibuses In The Streets Of London.

MORE AND MORE TRAINS.

OFFICIAL COMMUNIQUE.

WHITEHALL, May 11.

The situation throughout the country shows a further improvement.

The distribution of food supplies gives no cause whatever for apprehension. There have been a few reports of temporary local shortages in particular commodities, but on investigation it has been found that in the majority of these the reports are inaccurate, and in the remaining cases the necessary steps have been at once taken to make the position secure. Especially large supplies of sugar were distributed yesterday.

The situation at the ports is entirely satisfactory, and there is a growing confidence among traders as to their ability to move goods consigned to them without the direct assistance of the Government.

The distribution of petrol is proceeding more rapidly than at any previous period of the General Strike.

There has been no interruption of the power services, and traffic on the railways is continuously increasing. Apart from the surprisingly good service on the London Underground railways, over 4,000 trains were run on the four main systems yesterday, and more than 4,500 will be run to-day. A great increase in the number of goods trains is reported, and the railway companies are concentrating on a further improvement in this class of traffic.

Seven hundred omnibuses were working in London yesterday, and this number will be increased to-day to 850. The public are urged to avail themselves freely of the traffic facilities.

SHARP SENTENCES.

Order and quiet reign throughout the whole island, and practically no attempts at sabotage have been brought to the notice of the authorities. Sharp sentences have been imposed by the local magistrates on a number of persons who were arrested last week for disorder and intimidation.

The recruitment of special constables proceeds apace. The numbers enrolled are already 200,000 in the Provinces and over 40,000 in London, in addition to a very satisfactory intake as a result of the first day's enlistment for the new Civil Constabulary Reserve.

As regards the strike position generally, it can be said that the number of individuals returning to work is increasing, and in some cases considerable bodies of strikers have applied for reinstatement. On the other hand, there is as yet little sign of a general collapse of the strike, and the Trade Union Committee is believed to be making efforts to call out certain trades still at work.

It can be, however, definitely stated that there is a growing dissatisfaction among the strikers with the policy of a General Strike, and considerable uneasiness as to its ultimate results.

CIVIL CONSTABULARY RESERVE.

Pay of Officers and Men.

Recruiting for the Civil Constabulary Reserve is well under way in the drill halls of the City of London and County of London Territorial Associations.

The Reserve is a paid whole-time force organised in units. The men will wear plain clothes, but will be supplied with armlets, steel helmets and truncheons.

All able-bodied men who are either officers or men in the Territorial Army, or are in a senior contingent of the Officers Training Corps, including those already serving as special constables when their services can be spared, are eligible if they are under 50 years of age.

Ex-military men who can be vouched for at the headquarters of Territorial Army units will also be eligible.

Army rations, or special subsistence allowance will be given to every man and accommodation will be provided when necessary.

A special allowance of 5s. a week will be given to cover incidentals.

Cases of personal injury will be dealt with under the "Special Constables Order."

Pay will be as follows:—Commander, 10s. a day; inspector, 7s. 6d. a day; sergeant, 6s. a day; constables, 5s. a day.

CANADIAN FOOD SUPPLIES.

(From Our Own Correspondent.)

TORONTO, May 11.

Canadian shippers of bacon are continuing their shipments to British ports as if conditions were normal. They will continue to do so until advised by their agents to suspend shipments, but up to the present their reports from England are encouraging.

The millers here are offering flour daily, and are shipping to British ports as in normal times. They will continue to do so.'

OFFICERS ON LEAVE.

Permitted To Accept Any Employment.

The War Office announces that officers at home on leave from abroad are permitted to accept any form of employment in the present emergency that will not interfere with the military obligations of their return to their units at the end of their leave.

THE SOUL OF ENGLAND.

A nation yet, the rulers and
the ruled—
Some sense of duty, something of a faith,
Some reverence for the laws
ourselves have made,
Some patient force to change
them when we will,
Some civic manhood, firm
against the crowd.

TENNYSON.

WORK AS USUAL.

Tour Through Agricultural England.

FOOD FOR THE TOWNS.

(By a "British Gazette" Representative.)

A dash by road through the Eastern Counties of England brings home something of the magnitude of the task which has to be faced in feeding London. All through the day the rumble of great lorries is heard in this peaceful agricultural area, including the Counties of Norfolk, Suffolk, Cambridgeshire, Huntingdonshire and Essex, to feed the millions in the cities. In the evening the stream is reversed and this time the empty vehicles are radiating steadily from London to pick up more of their precious freight, and so it goes on.

In a run from London, via Cambridge and Ely to Hunstanton, I did not see a single breakdown or lorry held up for an accident, and considering the volume of traffic this is a remarkable achievement on the part of the drivers. It was a testimony to the remarkably high standard of driving. The lorries were, without exception, handled with great skill, and their drivers were always courteous in making way for faster traffic, so that the overtaking of a group of a dozen or more of these heavy vehicles held no terrors for the drivers of lighter and faster cars.

BUSY MARKET TOWNS.

The agricultural people of the district were carrying on their work in a normal manner, and everywhere I heard the opinion expressed that the trouble would soon be over. In Norfolk great droves of cattle were being driven along the roads to the nearest markets and the herds would gradually mingle, until at times one had to pick one's way through half a mile of them. The only visible signs of the strike were at the railway stations or the frequent level crossings, where a few striking railwaymen listlessly watched the stream of lorries as they passed.

All the market towns were busy with buying, selling, and the loading up of lorries. The shops were doing a good trade. There were few private cars on the roads and nearly every vehicle was labelled "Food only," but as I came back on to the Great North Road, at Baldock, the evening stream of returning London workers began to thicken.

As an example of the determination of the public I gave a lift to a commercial traveller from near Hatfield to London. He had been making his rounds as usual. Undeterred by the difficulties of transport he had visited all his customary Hertfordshire towns by taking lifts when he could get them, using the restricted train service and walking a little. He was tired, but satisfied with his day's work.

INCREASE OF WAGES LOST.

Iron Miners Hit by Strike.

The price of Cumberland hematite pig iron, which has been steadily decreasing during the past two years, recently advanced by 13s. 4d. a ton. The iron ore miners at Hodbarrow, the largest iron mine in England, would therefore after a long series of reductions have had their wages slightly increased. In view of the strike, however, the mine managers announce that they must close the mines this week.

CHARGE OF SEDITION.

Communist Sentenced to Three Months' Hard Labour.

John Frederick Hedley, 41, Communist, was charged at Liverpool with sedition. It was alleged that, addressing an open air meeting, he stated that the Welsh Guards were confined to Chelsea Barracks for refusing to entrain for a mining area; that Aldershot troops had also refused to go to a mining area; and that all transport in the East End of London had been stopped by the workers in spite of repeated baton charges by mounted police.

Hedley was remanded, but later in the day he was again before the Stipendiary Magistrate on the charge of sedition and was sentenced to three months' imprisonment with hard labour.

AUSTRALIAN CRICKETERS.

The Australian cricketers have accepted an invitation to be present at the evening performance of "No, No, Nanette" at the Palace Theatre on Saturday. The team will be entertained at supper afterwards at the Howard Hotel, Norfolk-street.

WEDNESDAY'S CRICKET

Lord's.—Middlesex v. Somerset.
Oval.—Surrey v. Gloucestershire.
Southampton.—Hampshire v. Australians.
Worcester.—Worcestershire v. Yorkshire.
Oxford.—University v. Kent.
Cambridge.—University v. Sussex.
Nottingham.—Notts v. Essex.
Hinckley.—Leicestershire v. Warwickshire.
Cardiff.—Glamorgan v. Lancashire.

TO-DAY'S CARTOON.

By BERNARD PARTRIDGE.

UNDER WHICH FLAG?

JOHN BULL: ONE OF THESE TWO FLAGS HAS GOT TO COME DOWN—AND IT WON'T BE MINE.

(By Courtesy of the Proprietors of "Punch.")

FOOD CARGOES.

Dutch Sailings to London Bi-Weekly.

ROTTERDAM, May 10.

The Batavier steamer which is leaving to-night for London is taking only passengers, but the boat to-morrow evening is taking a cargo of foodstuffs, including butter, margarine, eggs, cheese and bacon. The Kersten Hudig Company have been informed by the British Government that their vessels, with consignments of foodstuffs, which make a bi-weekly service between Rotterdam and London, can be discharged and the service will consequently be resumed on Wednesday.—*Reuter.*

TO ALL WORKERS IN ALL TRADES.

Additional Guarantees. Official.

Every man who does his duty by the country and remains at work or returns to work during the present crisis will be protected by the State from loss of trade union benefits, superannuation allowances, or pension. His Majesty's Government will take whatever steps are necessary in Parliament or otherwise for this purpose.

STANLEY BALDWIN.

BANKING CONDITIONS.

The usual statement of monthly averages of the Clearing Banks for the month of April shows most of the movements to be of a normal character. As is customary during the month of April, deposits rose—after their previous depletion—by nearly £8,000,000, while the rather large rise of £7,300,000 in cash and money at call suggests that precautionary measures were taken in view of the outlook. Similarly, there was a renewal of the sales of investments which have been a feature of the banking figures for some time past, the total for the month of April showing a further decline of £2,000,000.

DEALING IN POTASH BONDS.

The Stock Exchange Committee held their regular weekly meeting on Monday and it may be of some interest to state that the question of closing the Stock Exchange, in view of the strike, has not come officially before the attention of the Committee. Permission has been given by the Committee to deal in the fresh issue of German Potash Syndicate Bonds for £3,000,000 placed privately a week or two ago.

T.U.C. FOOD "PERMITS."

The Government's View.

No Co-operation With Strikers.

The following official statement was issued from the T.U.C. Headquarters, Eccleston-square:—

"The General Council offered to assist in the distribution of food supplies in a letter sent to the Prime Minister before the strike was declared. Its offer was ignored, not even an acknowledgment being sent to the Council, but several local bodies made arrangements with local strike committees, and the latter issued permits. It has now to be reported that the Government has ordered such permits to be withdrawn in many places. In order to avoid any conflict between the authorities and men on strike, the Council felt it necessary to withdraw its permits in those cases."

His Majesty's Government, with reference to the above, took the view that no one has the right to interfere with the food supplies of the country, and that the Government are responsible for overcoming all such difficulties and for assuring all citizens that their rights and freedom under the law will not be invaded.

The offer of the Trades Union Council to assist in distributing supplies after having previously called a general strike was an attempt to usurp the duties of the Government and of Parliament. It was, in fact, an act of constitutional presumption.

The Government have, therefore, throughout steadily refused to accept any form of co-operation with the Trades Union Council, and have consistently enjoined the same course of action upon all local authorities and private people.

All persons who have felt constrained to accept the so-called T.U.C. permits should realise that they are failing to show due confidence in the strength of their country.

TRAWLERS AT WORK.

Several vessels of the Scarborough fishing fleet have resumed operations, and fish is being conveyed to York, Leeds, and other inland towns by motor-vans. The steam trawler "Ben Hope" brought in a good catch yesterday, which met with a fair market. This was in direct contrast to Saturday, when a quantity of small plaice was practically given away.

ANOTHER FALSE RUMOUR.

The *South London Worker* states that all workers employed by the London brewers, Messrs. Barclay, Perkins, and Co., Ltd., have ceased work and are taking their stand with all workers in support of the miners. The firm in question informs us that the facts are that no less than 99 per cent. of their workpeople are carrying on as usual.

LEGAL ISSUE OF THE STRIKE.

Sir H. Slesser against Discussion.

THE TRADE DISPUTES ACT.

WESTMINSTER, Monday.

On the motion for the adjournment of the House of Commons, the legal aspect of the General Strike was raised.

Sir H. SLESSER referred to the speech made by Sir J. Simon, on Thursday evening last, on the subject of the law as it applied to trade disputes. He said that the legislature had decided that where a trade dispute existed, the procurement of a breach of contract was not in itself an illegal matter. Whether the act was lawful or unlawful must depend on whether the trade dispute came within the definition of the Trade Disputes Act.

That was a matter to be decided by a court of law. Under the existing law, in the case of every trade union, no member could recover benefits at present.

He thought that it was most unfortunate that the legal question had been introduced at all at this juncture. He desired that the settlement, which he hoped would soon be achieved in this matter, should not be prejudiced by anything that might ultimately be decided by a court of law.

Sir GODFREY COLLINS regretted that Sir H. Slesser had not given notice to Sir J. Simon that he intended to raise this matter so that he could be present.

A SIGNAL CONTRIBUTION.

Sir DOUGLAS HOGG (the Attorney-General), who said he had only been given two minutes notice that the matter was to be raised, did not agree that it was unfortunate Sir J. Simon should have made the speech he did. His view was that Sir John's speech was a signal contribution to the knowledge of the public as to the true facts surrounding the present dispute, and that he did a great public service in stating in clear and unequivocal language what in his view was the law on the subject.

It would not be right, however, for him (Sir Douglas), holding the post he did, to say just what he believed to be the lew in regard to the present position. It was his responsibility to advise the Government, and he did not think it would be useful from any point of view that he should state his views now.

Sir Douglas Hogg declared that any court would restrain, by injunction, any attempt to expel a member from a trade union for disobeying an illegal order or to deprive him of legal benefits. He repeated the Government's guarantee that no expulsion or deprivation of benefits would be permitted as a result of refusal to take part in the strike.

ILLEGAL STRIKES.

An important corollary.

The following appeared in the *Manchester Guardian* on Monday:—

"It may be doubted whether full importance of the statement of law authoritatively made by Sir John Simon in the House of Commons on Thursday is even yet fully appreciated. It amounts to this. The lightning strike being itself illegal no instructions given by the Trade Unions to enforce it will hold good in law. No member of the trade unions disregarding them therefore and continuing to remain at work can be deprived in consequence of any of his union benefits. He is exactly as free as if no instructions had been given him. Trade Unionists may or may not desire to act on this liberty, but having been called out without being consulted it may naturally and properly influence their decision."

FORGED NOTES TRIAL.

BUDAPEST, May 10.

Raba, one of the prisoners in the Hungarian note forgery case, whose evidence was heard to-day, created a sensation by stating that Count Bethlen and Count Paul Teleki both supported the franc forgery, intending to proceed by its help to recover Upper Hungary. Prince Windischgrätz, the police here believe, told Raba this to allay his fears.

INSURANCE.

Motor Vehicles and Cargoes.

Notice is given that the Government has arranged with insurance companies throughout the country for insurance against sabotage risks to be available in respect of:—

(a) Commercial motor-vehicles,

(b) Goods carried in motor vehicles,

and that this insurance is available at reasonable rates, whether for short or extended periods.

Comprehensive policies covering private motor cars will, on application to the companies concerned, be extended to cover sabotage risks free, provided such applications are made immediately.

AMONG THE MINERS.

Uneventful Days in Yorkshire.

MEN ANXIOUS TO RETURN.

No Trouble Expected.

(By a "British Gazette" Special Representative.)

I have just returned to London after a week spent in Barnsley—the centre of the mining industry in the West Riding of Yorkshire and the headquarters of the Yorkshire Miners' Association.

I left London hastily by the first train after the declaration of the strike on May 1, anticipating trouble in this district: but it has been entirely uneventful—a week spent in the midst of people who are sorely distressed at the upheaval, but are anxious to preserve order and to return, as soon as possible, to normal working conditions.

The train by which I travelled north was well filled with people who were leaving for their homes at the first hint of trouble; but there was no panic. Barnsley was spending a quiet week-end: it took the inhabitants some days to realise that a strike had been proclaimed, and they wandered happily enough about the town, filling the picture theatres, and looking for the football results more eagerly than for the strike news.

At first there was a certain air of excitement throughout the town. The men were beginning to realise that there was little hope of a general settlement, and large crowds of them congregated in the streets, while some abortive strike meetings were held in the squares. The men listened apathetically to the speakers and wandered away when the orations were finished.

EVERYTHING QUIET.

I made various short tours of the coalfields in the surrounding district during the week and paid some visits to Sheffield. I talked to miners and mine owners. On all sides the same story was to be heard: "Everything quiet." The pit ponies were brought above ground and were allowed to graze in quiet comfort—the only creatures who have anything to gain by the strike; the men played football at the pitheads.

There were various slight outbreaks of ill-temper in the district, but they were not serious. The people who overturned 'buses were mostly callow youths, glad of some escape from inactivity; they cannot be regarded as representative of the general community.

I called daily on the superintendents of police and the head of the local Territorials, who were standing by at the Drill Hall: on the officials at the Public Hall, where volunteers were being enrolled. They replied unanimously to my inquiries, "There is no trouble so far and we do not expect it. The men are loyal and anxious to return to work as soon as possible."

I spent one evening with the proprietors of a large paper mill, which was straining every nerve to keep the local newspapers supplied with paper. One of the heads of the firm had motored up from London, and he, together with a few faithful employees, worked from midnight until dawn in loading the lorries with huge rolls of paper. They were dispatched quietly to Sheffield and Leeds in order to keep the presses at work.

MINERS AND THE PRESS.

The officers of the Yorkshire Miners' Association, after two or three hectic days, lapsed into a state of pleasant somnolence. They made one statement only to the Press; after this they informed us that they no longer recognised our official existence and refused to give any further news. They state that they have sufficient funds to keep their members for four weeks at the rate of strike pay which they intend to distribute.

My journey back to London was uneventful. I motored from Barnsley to Doncaster, which is the principal railway centre of the district. Several trains are now running regularly, and I found a train which had been unexpectedly placed on the schedule ready to leave for London. It was not unpleasantly crowded and a restaurant car was attached. We accomplished the journey in little more than normal time.

WESTMINSTER GAZETTE Emergency Edition

10233 Thursday: 6th May, 1926 ONE PENNY

GENERAL POSITION.- Strike still in full swing. Government sending up transport. No discussions in prospect. Miners' Executive met yesterday, but adjourned without announcing any decisions.

YESTERDAY'S COMMONS.- Home Secretary announced he had declared supply of electricity, maintenance of electric plant of Port of London, transport of petrol, and continuance of railway services to be vital under emergency regulations. He asked public to enrol in large numbers as special constables. Mr. Henderson said it was duty of all sections to try to get back to position they were in last Monday to see if they could not settle by reason. Mr. Lloyd George strongly supported.

DISORDERLY INCIDENTS.- Police charged London crowd who attempted to hold up delivery of British Gazette, Government's newspaper. Casualties in baton charge in East London. Lorry fired and fire engine held up. Newcastle bus drivers driven away from buses. Motors smashed at Chester-le-street and Wallsend. 2,000 Hull tram-men refuse to return uniforms. Army ... train driver left Engine near Portsmouth. ... cars attacked by

The Times

4263. London Wednesday May 5. 1926 Price 2d.

WEATHER FORECAST. Wind N.E.; fair to dull; risk of local rain.

THE GENERAL STRIKE.

...e response was made yesterday ...out the country to the call of ...nions which had been ordered by ...C. to bring out their members. ...workers stopped generally, though ...railway clerks are reported to ...med duty, confining themselves ...ordinary work, and protested ...the strike. Commercial road ...was only partially suspended. ...the tramways and the L.G.O.C. ...ere stopped. The printing in... practically at a standstill, ...aphers have not been with... compositors in London have ...d instructions to strike. ...s of building operatives, ...those working on housing ...

Liverpool, Leeds, Northampton, Cardiff, Portsmouth, Dover, N.Derbyshire and Monmouthshire.

Evening papers appeared at Bristol, Southampton, several Lancashire towns and Edinburgh, and typescript issues at Manchester, Birmingham and Aberdeen.

The Atlantic Fleet did not sail on its summer cruise at Portsmouth yesterday. The men went on shore duty.

Road & Rail Transport:- There was no railway passenger transport in London yesterday except a few suburban trains. Every available form of private transport was used. A few independent omnibuses were running, but by the evening the railway companies, except the District and Tubes, had ...

...ervice. ...y will ...ylebone ...ester; ... 9 a.m ...oss to ...erbor... ...King's ...tween ... will ...n all ...y ex... ...good ...a.m. ...ain... ...tine ...veen ...ol... ...ord ...v... ...be ...f

BISHOPS AND JUSTICE FOR MINERS (See Page Seven)

DAILY HERALD

To-Day's Weather: Wind between E. and N.E., fair to cloudy; moderate temperature.

No. 3,205 (No. 2,212—NEW SERIES) LONDON, MONDAY, MAY 17, 1926. ONE PENNY

Bishops Call For Justice, Mercy & Humanity

BISHOPS' PLEA FOR MINERS — Stirring Reply ... Criti... — FURTHER ... — Call for ... "Ju...

THE CRISIS RUSHED — Subvention Should be ...

SWIFT AID FROM OVERSEAS — International Transport Workers Move

NO PRIVATE FIREARMS! — Does Ban Cover the Fascists? — The Government is taking elaborate precautions to see that no ... of the public retain posses...

"DEAD" SOLDIER SON ALIVE! — Strange Letter: Is It True or a Cruel Hoax? — After mourning for eight years a son officially reported to have been killed in the war, a family, living at Scunthorpe, Lincolnshire, have just ... letter announcing that he

"STEERING FOR THE RAPIDS" — J.R.M. on Coalowners Before the Strike — Writing prior to the declaration of a general strike in the May issue of the *Socialist Review*, Mr. Ramsay MacDonald states that the coalowners had been encouraged in their attitude by two political con...

In a letter to ... on the coal cr... Winchester an... saying that w... turbed in their ... to the dispute ... pared to assi... side alone, a... pear to do i... on Saturday ... The rema... letter is as ... "From ... view every ... that the p... industry i... the other ... not an o... very back... trial. I... granting ... Governm... responsi... fare of t... repudia... "It ... industr... and it ... subsid... lapse ... least c... full a... const...

BISHOPS AND JUSTICE FOR MINERS (See Page Seven)

DAILY HERALD

To-Day's Weather: Wind between E. and N.E., fair to cloudy; moderate temperature.

No. 3,195 (No. 2,202—NEW SERIES) LONDON, WEDNESDAY, MAY 5, 1926. ONE PENNY

Bishops Call For Justice, Mercy & Humanity

BISHOPS' PLEA FOR MINERS

Stirring Reply to "Times" Criticism

FURTHER SUBSIDY

Call for Government "Justice"

In a letter to the *Times* yesterday, on the coal crisis, the Bishops of Winchester and Southwark write saying that while profoundly disturbed in their consciences in regard to the dispute, they "are not prepared to assign the blame to one side alone, as you (the *Times*) appear to do in your leading article on Saturday."

The remainder of the Bishops' letter is as follows:—

"From the economic point of view every one is, of course, agreed that the principle of a subsidised industry is thoroughly bad. On the other hand, the coal industry is not an ordinary industry, but the very backbone of the body industrial. Further, the nation, in granting the subsidy through its Government, has taken upon itself responsibility in regard to the welfare of the industry which it cannot repudiate at a blow.

"It is common ground that the industry has to be reconstructed, and it would seem natural that the subsidy which prevented its collapse nine months ago should at least continue, not necessarily in its full amount, until a part of that reconstruction is effected.

SUBSIDY CONTINUANCE

"Whether this could best be done ...y a long-distance loan or other...ise it is not for us to say, but ordinary citizens like ourselves would seem commonsense that subsidy, instead of being ab...tly terminated, should continue the present, though lessening *passu* with the process of re...truction, until by that means ...ndustry can once ...

THE CRISIS RUSHED

Subvention Should be Continued

"It must be obvious that in view of the complexity and the detailed character of the issues raised by the Coal Commission's Report a settlement based on agreement could only be the outcome of unhurried and well-considered negotiations.

"We feel strongly that sufficient time has not been allowed and that negotiations ought to be carried further. These involve a temporary continuance of the financial assistance from the Government, a price we believe the public will be prepared to pay.

"The proposals so far put before the men seem to involve an immediate and definite sacrifice on their part in return for a prospective and uncertain reorganisation.

"To correct this inequality it seems to us essential that the Government should not only undertake unconditionally to carry out that part of the Report which calls for action on its part, but should declare forthwith its intention to take whatever measures may be necessary to ensure the effective enforcement of the full proposals for the reorganisation of the industry as outlined by the Commission."

The above appeared in a letter, signed by M. E. Sadler, A. D. Lindsay, Gilbert Murray, A. J. Carlyle, G. N. Clark, and G. D. H. Cole in yesterday morning's *Times*.

"G.B.S.'" VIEW

"Nothing But Crisis Till Coal is Nationalised"

"There will be nothing but coal crisis until a special branch of the Civil Service is created to manage the coal mines as a national concern. The fact that the Commission was afraid to say so, and gave a ridiculous reason for not saying so, places on the Government the obligation to have a little more courage and a good deal more financial intelligence," wrote Mr. George B. Shaw in ...

SWIFT AID FROM OVERSEAS

International Transport Workers Move

NO FOREIGN COAL

Foreigners Will Not Man British Ships

From Our Own Correspondent

AMSTERDAM, Monday Night.—The International Transport Workers' Federation has lost no time in throwing the weight of its powerful organisation into the scale on the side of the British miners.

An emergency meeting of the management committee was held this morning from which telegrams were sent immediately to transport workers' unions in France, Holland, Belgium, and Germany calling upon them to prevent the export of coal to Great Britain, and to prevent all bunkering of British ships in Continental harbours and non-British seamen from joining British ships.

To the Dutch Central Transport Workers' Union belongs the honour of being the first Continental union to take action on behalf of the British miners.

READY FOR ACTION

Anticipating that a call for help would be issued comrades in Brautigau worked on Saturday and Sunday to prepare a manifesto which was actually printed, and distributed on the docks at Rotterdam and other places this morning.

"Not a ton of coal must be shipped to England," it stated.

Dockers and seamen who belong to the main union are called upon to give all possible support to the British workers. Dockers are specifically instructed to refuse to work on vessels shipping for England, and to refuse to bunker coal on vessels ... narily bunk...

NO PRIVATE FIREARMS!

Does Ban Cover the Fascists?

The Government is taking elaborate precautions to see that no members of the public retain possession of any firearms.

Notices have already gone out to members of the Territorial Force ordering them to return rifles to their respective headquarters at once.

Following is the notice issued to members of the 47th (2nd Lon.) Divisional Engineers: "All rifles and bayonets are required at H.Q. for inspection. You will therefore arrange to return the rifle and bayonet in your charge to these H.Q. on Monday evening, May 3, without fail."

But what of the members of the Fascisti? Have they been required to surrender any firearms in their possession?

It would appear that instead of this being the case the members of the Fascisti, with the help of the organisation, are busy gaining knowledge on how to use a rifle.

STUDENTS' ACTIVITY

This view is prompted by the experience of a responsible London trade union official, who writes that during the past three days he has noticed no fewer than five young men, between the ages of 19 and 21, all wearing the badge of the British Fascisti in their coat lapels, who have been studying the "Small Arms Training Manual."

"In one instance," he says, "I observed a letter on the inside of one of these manuals from a branch of this organisation.

"It would appear from my experience that the whole of the energies of this ...

"DEAD" SOLDIER SON ALIVE!

Strange Letter: Is It True or a Cruel Hoax?

After mourning for eight years a son officially reported to have been killed in the war, a family, living at Scunthorpe, Lincolnshire, have just received a letter announcing that he is alive.

The circumstances in which the news was received have, however, caused them considerable anxiety.

Mr. Bunyon, a Scunthorpe boot repairer, received a letter purporting to have been written by "Gunner Frank Bunyon," from Camp No. 30, Larkhill, Salisbury Plain, in which the writer says he is alive, and, after mentioning his brothers and sisters, adds that he may be expected home very shortly.

Frank Bunyon, who joined the Leicester Regiment, was officially recorded as killed with the Essex Regiment on April 23, 1918. So far as his parents knew he was never attached to the artillery.

In this rather surprising letter, the writer said his best "pal" was a young man named Graves, from Broughton, a village a few miles from Scunthorpe.

Mr. Bunyon and one of his other sons at once went over to see Mrs. Graves, who verified the fact that she had a son a gunner at Larkhill. Even young Graves, in a recent letter home, said he had picked up a friendship with a Scunthorpe man, but he did not mention the latter's name.

Mr. and Mrs. Bunyon, anxious to know whether the son mourned as dead so long is really alive or whether the letter is a heartless hoax, have communicated with the commanding officer at the camp and are awaiting a reply.

Only the other week, as he ... the custom of ...

"STEERING FOR THE RAPIDS"

J.R.M. on Coalowners Before the Strike

Writing prior to the declaration of a general strike in the May issue of the *Socialist Review*, Mr. Ramsay MacDonald states that the coalowners had been encouraged in their attitude by two political considerations.

"First of all, they know that in the Cabinet there is a group of die-hards (an unfortunate word that seems to be passing into ordinary use) who will, all things considered, welcome a fight, would like to see the O.M.S. driving lorries on the roads under the pretence that their country needs them, and who believe that in the irrationality that could be created on the outbreak of such a dispute the merits will be swamped in a flood of fear and prejudice, and that such lies as that the miners are holding the country to ransom will pass as truth," writes the ex-Premier.

TWO CALCULATIONS

"They calculate that we shall have people who never lifted their little finger to fill the empty cupboards or coal-scuttles of their fellow-citizens of the working class, whining, when their own are depleted, that the community is being attacked, that there are men in authority who would like to strut for a week or so in the glory of strong heroes, and that, in addi... to these, thous...

SUNDAY TIMES MAY 9, 1926

> "This England never did, and never shall, lie at the proud foot of a conqueror."
> Shakespeare.

Sunday Times

Established 1822. and SUNDAY SPECIAL. 103rd Year of Issue.

> "We desire at the earliest moment the resumption of negotiations to bring peace and reconstruction to our coalfields. But the anti-social weapon, which has been so unadvisedly drawn, must first be sheathed." Oxford & Asquith.

No. 5378 [POSTAGE OF THIS ISSUE ABROAD, 2½ INLAND, CANADA AND NEWFOUNDLAND, 1½] LONDON, MAY 9, 1926 PRICE TWOPENCE

SIXTH DAY OF THE STRIKE.

SITUATION IMPROVING EVERYWHERE.

HOSTS OF VOLUNTEERS.

ESSENTIAL SERVICES BEING MAINTAINED.

HOME SECRETARY'S MESSAGE.

To-day the sixth day of the strike and, in the words of the Home Secretary, in a special message to the "*Sunday Times*," the news is good. The essential services are improving everywhere.

Reports from all parts of the country are highly satisfactory.

Food supplies are everywhere normal, mails are being well maintained, and reports from the police show that apart from isolated instances, good order is generally prevailing.

There has been no recurrence of intimidation at petrol depots.

THE RAILWAYS.

On the railways, there are steadily improving services, and good progress is being made with the clearance of food stuffs at ports, sidings and depots.

Road transport, moreover, is generally satisfactory.

The organisation of medical and surgical supplies has been extended and as an example, it may be mentioned that one ton of insulin was sent to Scotland by motor cars within four hours of the request for it.

VOLUNTEERS.

Recruiting in London and the Home Counties has reached the striking figure of 92,000 men and women. Similar encouraging figures are to hand from various parts of the country.

THE CABINET.

The Cabinet held another meeting yesterday, and it is understood that the legal position of those taking part in the General Strike was under consideration. The uncompromising opinion expressed by Sir John Simon, K.C., M.P., recognised as a great authority on Trade Union law, that the General Strike is illegal and that the leaders and the men are liable for damages, has created a profound impression.

There is reason to believe, too, that the Government's declaration that members of trades unions who remain or return to work will be given the full protection of the State is having a marked effect. From all parts of the country news has come of men returning to work.

FOOD SUPPLIES.

SAFEGU,ARD MEASURES.

It was officially announced yesterday that Mr. Walter Runciman, M.P., has been appointed chairman of the Shipping Emergency Commission which will sit daily and all day, and will work in conjunction with the Board of Trade and the Food Supply Department.

The prime duty of the Commission is to provide for grain, meat, and other supplies being brought to this country and distributed through the ports.

TRANSPORT WORKERS' UNION.

The Transport Workers' Union has ordered men engaged in the flour milling industry to cease work at Liverpool, Birkenhead, Seacombe, and Ellesmere Port. The delivery question will be dealt with by the Union area officers.

There are large stocks at Seacombe Mills, but motor lorries arriving there were sent away empty. Steps are to be taken to get the flour mills open.

COMMUNISTS' CLUB ARRESTS.

Seven men and one woman were remanded at Bradford yesterday on the charge of a breach of the emergency regulations order. Defendants were arrested following a visit by police officers to the Communist Club, Gallows Hill, Shipley, on Wednesday.

At Doncaster yesterday, Henry Huckerby, a miner, was sentenced to two months' imprisonment for a breach of the Emergency Regulations. It was stated that he interfered with a railway porter at Arksey Station, and told him if he did not leave work he would be taken by force. The porter was the same night thrown out of his lodgings, and the Railway Company had had to transfer him to another district.

TO-DAY'S WEATHER.

The forecast: Light North to N.W. winds; occasional showers of rain or hail. Considerable bright intervals. Generally cold with ground frost at night.

The Spanish Government has ordered that all British steamers in Spanish ports shall be given every facility for obtaining coal supplies.

FOOD PRICES NORMAL

GOVERNMENT'S WARNING AGAINST HOARDING

In official circles, it was learned yesterday that according to reports from different parts of the country, food prices generally are remaining normal. A few slight increases in price are reported, chiefly due to the extra cost of handling.

The public is again urged by the Government not to buy more than usual quantities of food stuffs. Such action can only only create artificial shortage.

MINERS REPORT NO CHANGE.

The executive of the Miners' Federation held a meeting at Russell Square yesterday afternoon and received reports on the situation. Mr. Herbert Smith and Mr. A. J. Cook were in consultation with the T.U.C. General Council all the morning, Mr. Ramsay MacDonald being also present at the conference.

Mr. Cook informed a Press representative that there had been "absolutely no change" in the situation, and that there were no signs at present of any peace moves. He said the position had been "considerably strengthened" from the trade union and the miners' point of view. He did not anticipate any developments over the week-end and there was not likely, he added, to be any new phase in the general situation earlier than Monday.

WHITEHALL SENTRIES IN SERVICE DRESS.

Whitehall, particularly in the neighbourhood of New Scotland Yard, was the the scene of considerable activity this the scene of considerable activity yesterday. Coningents of special conemerging from the police headquarters and marching westwards attracting much public attention.

The Horse Guards wore a very business-like appearance. The mounted sentries, who in their full dress, are the objects of constant public attention have been replaced by dismounted men of the Life Guards in service dress, bearing rifles.

A similar change was made at Buckingham Palace, and the various Royal residences where the Guards post sentries. All were in service khaki. The change is not intended to be provocative, but it demonstrates the fact that the posting of the sentries is not a merely ceremonial observance.

CRICKET.

Oval.—Surrey v. AAustralians. Australians, 119 for 3.

Lords.—Middlesex v. Essex. Essex 98 for 2.

Worcester.—Worcester v. Somerset. Worcester 137 for 5.

Ilkeston.—Derby v. Yorks. Yorks 122 for 5.

Birmingham.—Warwick v. Hants. Warwick, 126 for 6.

Nottingham.—Notts v. Sussex. Notts. 112 for 4.

Gloucester.—Gloucester v. Lancs. Lancs, all out 145.

Leicester.—Leicester v. Glamorgan. Leicester 110 for 3.

NEWSPAPERS CARRY ON.

STRIKE UNPOPULAR.

MANY PRINTERS OFFER TO RETURN TO WORK.

A large number of newspapers are carrying on. Not only are more papers being published, but they are appearing in larger form.

In the provinces the strike is proving thoroughly unpopular in the printing trade. Large numbers of men are offering to return to work. A similar movement is beginning to show itself in London.

"Imperative that members come out," was the message received by the Grimsby branch of the Typographical Association. The T.A. members of the Grimsby "Telegraph" sent the following reply:—

"Your communication has been put before the members of the Chapel, and I am asked to state that having given the firm an undertaking that they will abide by the national wages and hours agreement, they intend to do so."

The entire clerical staff of the "*Daily Mail*" (Manchester), has asked to be allowed to return to work tomorrow, unconditionally.

The "*Financial Times*" was the only London paper to appear in its ordinary form on Wednesday, and has appeared in that form ever since.

The "*Daily Graphic*" was published yesterday with a page of pictures.

The "*Western Mail*," Cardiff, which has been published each day since the strike, was on sale in London at 8.30 a.m. yesterday, containing eight pages of its usual size.

The "*North Mail and Newcastle Chronicle*" and the "*Newcastle Evening Chronicle*" have appeared each day in their usual form, the former being brought to London by air.

The "*Sheffield Daily Telegraph*" and "*Yorkshire Telegraph and Star*" have also appeared in their usual form, the "*Sheffield Daily Telegraph*" being conveyed to London by air.

In Glasgow [illegible] have combined to publish the "*Glasgow Emergency Press.*"

MORE GLASGOW RIOTS.

There was a renwal on Friday night of the scenes which have marked the East end of Glasgow since Wednesday. Up till midnight forty-eight arrests had been made following upon a series of baton charges by the place.

So alarming became the situation that the police reserves as well as the mounted constabulary were called out. According to the police, rowdy gangs assembled in several main streets and attempted to hold up all vehicular traffic. The bread vans were special objects of attack. No sooner was one gang broken up than another renewed the fray in adjoining thoroughfares. These were speedily dispersed, but not before the batons were drawn.

ALLEGED SEDITIOUS DOCUMENTS CASE.

At Old Street Police Court yesterday, Albert James Frost, 35, secretary, and Arthur Nelson, 34, flower seller, were charged with having on premises at 204, Goswell Road, Finsbury, documents calculated or likely to cause sedition or disaffection among the civil population.

A detective-inspector stated that outside the address were displayed some type-written documents. One stated under the heading of "soldiers" "we hear on good authority that soldiers of the Grenadier and Coldstream Guards refused to parade this morning and have been confined in the Birdcage Walk Barracks. Another stated "Five hundred Royal Aircraftsmen, who are trade unionists, ceased work last night." Frost said he got the information from the General Council bulletin.

Accused was remanded on bail.

NEWSVENDOR CHARGED.

General Sir George Milne gave evidence at the Marylebone Police Court, yesterday, when George William Green, 36, newsvendor, was charged with committing an act likely to cause disaffection among the civil population by shouting "Great public revolution—Army has refused to fight." Green was remanded in custody.

Sir George Milne said he heard the accused man shout the words in Lower Berkeley Street, W., and gave him in charge.

Police Constable Poll said that when arrested the accused said, "I will say what I like. It is my country. I have fought for it."

The accused said that all he said was, "Latest Strike News."

The Magistrate (Mr. Bingley), in remanding the accused, pointed out that there was no definite clause dealing with the crying of false news in the Emergency Regulations.

JOURNALISTS' UNION.

The National Executive Committee of the National Union of Journalists have passed the following resolution:—

"That it is permissible for our members to work on makeshift papers which are being produced by labour which cannot permanently displace men who are out on strike."

TRAIN STONED.

A Berwick to Newcastle train was stoned by a crowd on either side of a level crossing on Friday night.

Home Secretary's Message.

TO THE EDITOR, "SUNDAY TIMES."

I am delighted you are going to publish to-morrow.

Sunday without its "Sunday Times" would be a sad day.

Please tell the loyal people of our Country to keep a good heart and a stiff upper lip.

The news to-day is good. The first convoy from the London docks came out this morning and was received with cheers, while the Guards who marched down yesterday afternoon to Dockland had a perfect ovation.

One of the battalions, by the way, was the one which the lying bulletins stated had mutinied.

Tell your readers to believe no news that is not official.

England wins to a certainty.

W. JOYNSON-HICKS.

GUARANTEE TO ALL WORKERS.

PRIME MINISTER'S PLEDGE.

The Prime Minister last night broadcast the following message:—

"Every man who does his duty by the country and remains at work or returns to work during the present crisis will be protected by the State from loss of trade-union benefit, superannuation allowances, pensions. His Majesty's Government will take whatever steps are necessary in Parliament or otherwise for this purpose.

STANLEY BALDWIN."

STRIKE ITEMS FROM ALL PARTS.

REDUCED HOURS FOR PUBLIC HOUSES.

Edinburgh public houses were closed yesterday from 3 p.m.

In a letter to Mr. J. H. Thomas, M.P., the Bishop of London offers Fulham Palace as a neutral meeting place for future negotiations.

The executive of the Typographical Association of South Africa warns its members against interfering in the British strike and against wrecking the agreement which has worked satisfactorily in the printing trade in South Africa.

Three large liners, whose accommodation is fully booked up, are sailing from Capetown for England. Among the passengers are Lord Kitchener and his son, Viscount Broome.

Staff of Kingston on Thames Corporation Electricity Works struck yesterday. Volunteers are carrying on.

The Royal Tournament has been postponed from May 20 to July 8.

A military guard was posted yesterday at Temple Mills, one of the principal locomotive departments of the L. and N.E. Railway.

Labour Party orders to newsagents to sell newspapers in the Alfreton mining district of Derbyshire are being ignored. Supplies of newspapers are, instead, increasing daily.

RIGHT TO WORK.

MAGISTRATES AND THE NATION'S DETERMINATION.

There were only twelve charges before the West London magistrate yesterday compared with over twenty on Friday and over 40 on Thursday. Mr. Ratcliffe Cousins (the magistrate), said: "I think the neighbourhood may feel some sense of congratulation that there are so few charges. It shows that in this district, and, indeed, throughout the whole country, the great bulk of the people are determined to see that the right of every Briton to work, when and how he will, so long as he observes the law of the country, shall be maintained. He owes obedience to no-one else."

George Thomas Dowdswell, 42, pump attendant at Fulham Electricity Works, was charged at West London, with inciting persons to commit acts calculated to prevent the proper use and working of the Fulham borough electrical generating station.

Alexander Murdoch, superintendent of the works, said that he saw Dowdswell go up to a turbine driver and a switch-board attendant, and immediately afterwards all the switches and the steam valves were disconnected. As a result, the borough's electric supply was cut off for an hour.

Dowdswell was remanded on bail in £100.

VICTORIA PARK TAKEN OVER.

Victoria Park, London, has been taken over by the Military Authorities, and yesterday it was closed to the public, and is now being utilised as a military encampment.

MORE TRAINS RUN.

12,000 MEN AT WORK ON THE SOUTHERN.

Reports from all railways show improved passenger and goods services. On the Southern over 12,000 men are on duty. Many more railwaymen are anxious to return to work.

On Friday 2,574 train were run by the four main line railway groups. This was excluding trains run on the Underground and Metropolitan lines, which would bring the total to well over 3,000.

Lord Ashfield, in a message to those who are helping to re-establish the Underground services, says: "We are proud of you, just as you are of yourselves. Be assured of our complete support in the great work you are performing in this crisis in the history of our beloved country."

SOUTHERN.—12,014 men of all grades have remained loyal or have returned to work, in spite of their union's instructions. 56 per cent. of the Southern's supervisory and clerical staff are at work, and there are indications that a large number of men of various grades on various parts of the line desire to return to duty.

Many goods trains containing food and other important supplies are running, and the main line expresses are gradually returning to normal.

L.M.S.—Up to 8 a.m. yesterday 2,813 milk churns were dealt with at Euston and St. Pancras.

This week a day service will run from Euston to Glasgow, leaving London at 8.30 a.m., and leaving Glasgow at 7.30 a.m. for Euston.

GREAT WESTERN.—No disorders reported throughout the system. Many strikers have applied to return to work. Dissatisfaction expressed at being called out without a ballot being taken according to union rules.

Early yesterday, 3,000 churns of milk were received in London alone. Daily perishable and fruit trains are now running from the West of England. Fish trains reached London from South Wales.

L.N.E.R.—Services continue to improve steadily. Additional services in all districts yesterday. Total number of trains yesterday, 700, compared with 702 on Friday. London suburban ser- train from Stafford arrived at King's Cross on Friday night with 1,068 churns.

METROPOLITAN.—Two additional trains will be run to-day (Sunday), to and from Aylesbury as follows: from Baker Street, 9.30 a.m., and 3.30 p.m.; From Aylesbury 12.55 p.m., and 5.55 p.m.

75 TUBE STATIONS OPEN.

Seventy-five stations on the Underground Railways are now open, including South Kensington, West Kensington, and Knightsbridge. Trains between Acton Town and Hounslow on the District Railway, and on the Highgate branch of the Hampstead tube began running at mid-day yesterday.

The London General Omnibus Co. are now operating over 300 'buses on four routes:—No. 1, Ealing Broadway, Oxford Street, Piccadilly, Kensington, Hammersmith, Brentford; No. 2, Richmond, Turnham Green, Putney, Chelsea, Piccadilly, Vauxhall, Clapham Common; No. 3, Hendon, Cricklewood, Kilburn, Marylebone, Piccadilly, Oxford Circus, Marble Arch; No. 4, Harlesden, Marylebone High Road, Euston Road, Liverpool Street, Bank, Holborn, Oxford Street, and Holland Park.

Fourteen hundred men have now been trained as 'bus drivers and conductors, and a large number of men are in training for duty as soon as additional routes are opened up.

TRAMWAYMEN DISMISSED.

The Reading Corporation tramcars resumed running yesterday with the aid of a volunteer service, and under the protection of the police. The Tramways Committee has notified their employees that unless they returned to duty yesterday morning, they must consider themselves dismissed. They refused to return.

Middlesex County Council tramcars were running yesterday for the first time since the strike began. Most of them carried two or three conductors, and a similar number of volunteers on the driver's platform. The service links up northern suburbs with Golders Green, and the London tubes.

Fulham Electric Light Company's men having struck work, the plant is being run by members of the higher staff and volunteers.

Princess Ena, Southern Railway steamer, leaves St. Malo with perishable goods to-day.

WAGES FORFEITED.

RAILWAY COMPANIES' PRONOUNCEMENT.

It was stated by a high official that under no circumstances would railwaymen be able to claim wages which were due when they withdrew their labour.

"It was the settled policy of the companies," he added "that a man on strike and who left work without notice should forfeit his wages."

FRENCH DEBT TO BRITAIN.

M. Parmentier, the French financial expert flew from Paris to London on Friday evening to resume discussions with the British Treasury on the subject of the French debt to Britain.

MR. ORMSBY GORE'S RETURN.

Mr. Ormsby Gore, Under-Secretary for the Colonies, with Mr. W. C. Rhys, M.P., and others, who has been making an official tour of British possessions in West Africa, landed at Plymouth yesterday. The journey to London was made by road.

T. U. C. AND SIR JOHN SIMON.

"NO ATTACK ON THE CONSTITUTION."

At the Press Conference last evening at the headquarters of the T.U.C., it was stated, in regard to the general tenour of the situation, that "reports which covered the greater part of the country went to show that solidarity is maintained and, if possible, increased. The second line of defence men are coming out steadily."

Referring to the recent speech of Sir John Simon, the T.U.C. repudiated the allegation that the Congress was engaged in an attack on the Constitution, and emphatically repeated that they did not attempt to overthrow the Government.

Mr. Poulton (of the T.U.C. Council) said it was inevitable that in any general stoppage contracts might in certain instances be broken. "The struggle," he said, "is being carried on as an industrial one, and the Government and the mine-owners are responsible for the national stoppage."

The following official statement was also issued by the T.U.C. General Council last night: "An attempt is being made to confuse and prejudice the position of the Trade Union movement by an allegation that we have received money from Moscow. This morning a cheque arrived from the All Russian Central Council of Trade Unions, Palace of Labour, Moscow. It ran into some thousands. We fully considered the matter and decided to send a courteous reply expressing our appreciation but our inability to accept the cheque and and it has been returned.

CABINET MEETS LAST NIGHT.

A fully attended meeting of the Cabinet was held at 10, Downing Street at o'clock last evening when further emergency measures were considered. About the time the Cabinet was assembling the Earl of Balfour and the Marquess of Londonderry called at No. 10, and Lord Balfour remained while the Cabinet meeting was in progress.

ITEMS.

A Liverpool telegram says that 3,500 men were working yesterday at the docks unloading foodstuffs from 25 steamers.

At Walthamstow two hours after the opening of a recruiting centre for voluntary workers a hostile crowd surrounded the place. A few persons froced their way in, but with the arrival of the police the situation was soon under control.

A number of telegraph wires between Newcastle and Hexham on the railway and about twenty Post Office wires were discovered cut yesterday.

A passenger train on the London and North Eastern Railway from Grimsby to Sheffield was held up on Friday night for an hour by strikers at Worksop. The men refused to budge at the level crossing until dispersed by the police.

The Duke of Connaught arrived in England yesterday from Paris. He journeyed from the coast to London by motor car.

The death occurred yesterday of Lieut.-Colonel Matthew Gerald Edward Bell, aged 54, the owner of Bourne Park, the famous Kent estate. He was a grandson of the first Lord St. Leonards.

The "Sheffield Telegraph" published a 32 column newspaper yesterday, and had a circulation of 175,000.

There has been a great rush of volunteers in response to Messrs. Lyons' appeal, and a new permanent staff is being assemblede at Cadby Hall. With the exception of a few positions in skilled trade departments. The personnel will be complete by tomorrow morning.

TRAMWAYMENS' RETURN.

Tramwaymen returend to work at Grimsby yesterday, and a full service was running. There is plenty of voluntary labour. On the docks perishable goods are being landed and loaded on motor lorries from the midlands. Twenty-nine trawlers arrived yesterday and 28 went to sea. Since yesterday fish is being sent all over the country by motor lorries.

THE RIGHT SPIRIT

An effort to bring out the employees of the Oxford and District Omnibus Company yesterday proved futile. A meeting of the men was called by the Council of speakers and the meeting ended with the singing of "Land of Hope and Glory."

CLERGY PLEA FOR PEACE

The Bishop of Birmingham was one of 150 clergymen who passed a resolution at Birmingham yesterday calling upon the Government to resume negotiations for a settlement on condition that the general strike is called off, the lock-out notices at the mines cancelled and a subsidy from public funds promised for a longer or shorter period as required.

LINERS SAIL.

With approximately 1,000 passengers on board, the Canadian Pacific liners Montroyal left Liverpool at 6 p.m. on Friday, and the Metagama sailed from Glasgow shortly before midnight for Quebec and Montreal. Whilst the majority of the passengers were settlers for Canada, there were also a number of returning Canadians and Americans.

PEOPLE STRONG AND QUIET,

LATEST OFFICIAL REPORTS.

DEALING WITH ATTACKS ON TRANSPORT.

Home Office, Saturday night.

In the main, reports from all quarters continue to tell the same story of a strong, quiet and good-tempered people.

The Civil Commissioner announces that the enrolment of special constables will continue in London throughout to-morrow. Special constables may join for the duration of the emergency or for a period of one or three years. Special constables injured while on duty will receive compensation on the same basis as the regular police.

There have been no further developments during the day. Isolated attacks on transport vehicles are being dealt with everywhere. Special measures have been taken by the Government to ensure the transport of food from the London docks. Over 700 tons of sugar were shifted from the docks yesterday—470 tons from Silvertown and 300 from Plaistow.

BALLOT BEFORE STRIKE.

MR. HAVELOCK WILSON'S MESSAGE

The following cable from Mr. Havelock Wilson general President of the Seamen's Union, has been wirelessed to masters of all ships of the British Mercantile Marine:—

orised persons are calling seamen out on strike, they say, on instructions from the T.U.C. They have no authority to do so. The Council of your Union is the only body which has power to do so, and then only after members of the Council have been ballotted. I am out for the right of the seamen to decide such questions as strike for themselves.

"A ballot has not yet been completed because of difficulties of the postal services. I hope to have the ballot completed by Thursday or Friday of next week.

"If the ballot declares in favour of a strike, it is my duty to inform you that the Courts of Law will declare that no strike money can be paid from Union funds for a sympathetic strike. It would be helpful if you could cable whether the crew of your ship endorses my view of ballot before strike."

METROPOLITAN RAILWAY.

SUNDAY SERVICE.

The train service on the Metropolitan Railway to-day is as follows:—

Baker Street to Harrow (all stations) ½-hourly service; first train, 9.0 a.m.; last train, 7.0 p.m.

Harrow to Baker Street (all stations) ½-hourly service; first train, 9.20 a.m.; last train, 7.20 p.m.

Baker Street to Uxbridge (all stations), ½-hourly service; first train, 9.0 a.m.; last train, 6 p.m.

Uxbridge to Baker Street (all stations), hourly service; firstt rain, 10.0 a.m.; last train 7.0 p.m.

Baker Street to Rickmansworth (all stations), hourly service; first train, 9.30 a.m.; last train, †.30 p.m.

Rickmansworth to Baker Street (all stations), hourly service; first train, 10.30 a.m.; last train 6.30 p.m.

Baker Street to Aylesbury, 9.30 a.m. and 3.30 p.m.

Aylesbury to Baker Street, 12.55 a.m. and 5.55 p.m.

The train services on the following sections of the Metropolitan Railway—Inner Circle, Hammersmith to Paddington, Moorgate to Finsbury Park, will not run to-day.

UNDERGROUND RAILWAYS

The Underground Railways announce that to-day there will be no buses running, but Underground trains will run on all lines from twelve noon to eight p.m.

Two new tramway services were opened to-day, one, of the Metropolitan Electric Tramways, operated between Finchley and Golders Green, Hendon and Willesden via Cricklewood; another, of the London United Tramways, between Hampton Hampton Wick, Twickenham, and Hampton Court. There will be no Sunday services [illegible] on the above systems. The tramway services operated on Friday were continued yesterday, an increased number of cars being run.

1927

Lindbergh's Atlantic Flight

At 7.52 on the morning of May 20 1927 Charles Lindbergh's monoplane, The Spirit of St. Louis, juddered down the runway of Roosevelt Field, Long Island. Observers watched it rise a few feet, fall, stagger into the air, fall again, and with but a few yards left finally lurch itself into the sky with one last desperate effort. Ahead lay the 3,800 solitary miles to Paris. It was not the first trans-Atlantic flight (Alcock and Brown had crossed from Newfoundland to Ireland in June 1919) but no-one had yet flown direct from New York–Paris, least of all alone and at the tender age of 25. Far more experienced flyers, like Commander Byrd of North Pole fame, had scanned the clouds that morning and called off their attempt: even as he prepared for his flight, few people were inclined to give 'the flying fool' the ghost of a chance. The exclusive rights to his story (if he were successful) had gone for a song to The New York Times, with its uncanny knack for picking a winner, and The St Louis Globe-Democrat. Yet no sooner was Lindbergh airborne than it became clear they had invested in a goldmine: the man with the boyish grin gripped the imagination of America spontaneously. 40,000 boxing fans at the Yankee Stadium prayed in silence for his safety that evening: newspaper offices were overwhelmed with anxious enquiries. For 37 hours it seemed as if the entire country existed in a state of suspended animation; when it was announced that he had landed at Le Bourget to the rapturous applause of 100,000 Frenchmen, the nation let out its breath and went berserk. Women wept in the streets, gales of paper were tossed out of New York offices while planes looped the loop over the city. Film offers, military titles and medals were showered on him: the President sent the navy to France to bring him back to America, where his arrival was greeted by celebrations and triumphal processions unparalleled even on Armistice Day. The press was unanimous in its acclamation of the hero, not least for his patent and disarming modesty: the more so since, in the months and years that followed, his very name was guaranteed to put tens of thousands on their circulations.

The Execution of Sacco and Vanzetti

The execution of the Boston shoemaker Nicola Sacco and fish-seller Bartolomeo Vanzetti half an hour after midnight on August 23 1927 marked the culmination of nearly seven years' bitter controversy in the columns of the American press. Their crime, which at the time had warranted not even a single paragraph outside the local papers, was the alleged murder of a pay-roll guard in South Braintree, Massachusetts, in April 1920. Of all the flimsy evidence which was adduced at the time, that which counted most was the discovery of 'radical' anti-Government leaflets in the car in which the two suspects were picked up (these were the days when America lived in daily expectation of the Red Revolution). If it hadn't been for a series of violent attacks on American property in European capitals by crowds protesting against their conviction the two 'anarchists' might well have been executed then and

there. As it was, appeals dragged the case out for more than six years while many liberal American papers grew more and more uneasy at the summariness of 'Massachusetts justice'. The villain of the piece appeared to be Judge Thayer who had refused the last appeal of what he was alleged to have described as 'those anarchistic bastards'. In 1927 public opinion obliged Governor Fuller of Massachusetts to refer the case to a civil committee of respected citizens. They, too, upheld Thayer's decision — but the press persisted in its censure, including such reputable state newspapers as *The Springfield Republican* which riposted to criticism of its 'disloyalty' to the home legislature with the editorial comment: 'What constitutes loyalty to Massachusetts? Must one flout his own intelligence and conscience in order to support blindly certain official conclusions involving human lives?' *The Boston*

Herald, which had been awarded the Pulitzer prize for its outspoken editorials on the subject in 1926, appeared at the last moment to be wavering — thus incurring the wrath of *The St Louis Post-Dispatch* which two days later addressed an appeal to the President to intervene. None of it did any good: no amount of eleventh-hour dashes by the defence in search of fresh judges availed anything. Sacco and Vanzetti went to the chair, the latter mouthing as his last words (according to the A.P. correspondent, if no-one else) 'long live anarchy'. Some days before the execution Heywood Broun, columnist of *The New York World*, had written 'From now on, I want to know, will the institutions of learning in Cambridge which once we called Harvard be known as Hangman's House?' That was the end of his column on *The New York World*, but a thought that lingered on in many a mind.

Sacco and Vanzetti Must Die, Says Fuller; Decision Is Backed by His Inquiry Committee

VOL. LXVIII. NO. 24,080—DAILY. Copyright Press Publishing Company (New York World) 1927 ★ NEW YORK, THURSDAY, AUGUST 4, 1927. IN TWO SECTIONS SECTION ONE ••• TWO CENTS In Greater New York | Within 200 Miles | Elsewhere

OFFICIAL WEATHER FORECAST. Fair to-day and to-morrow, with slowly rising temperatures; moderate to fresh southwest winds. TEMPERATURE YESTERDAY Highest 71, 5 P. M.; lowest 58, 4 A. M.,

THE BOSTON HERALD

FAMOUS STORY SERIES See Page 14
FUNNY POEM SERIES See Page 14

PARTLY CLOUDY BOSTON AND VICINITY: Partly cloudy today; Tuesday showers. NEW ENGLAND: Partly cloudy to-day, followed by showers tonight or Tuesday. Full report on page 2.

VOL. CLXII, NO. 53 MONDAY MORNING, AUGUST 22, 1927—TWENTY-TWO PAGES •••• TWO CENTS

RUSSIAN LABOR FARES BETTER UNDER SOVIET

Many Improvements, But Land Not Workers' Paradise

BENEFITS LIMITED TO UNION MEMBERS

Unemployed Total 1,100,000 —Living Very Expensive

This is the fifth of a series of daily articles on Russia by Robert Choate, Washington correspondent of The Boston Herald. Mr. Choate went to Russia to investigate conditions at first hand. For fear that his stories might be censored, he wrote nothing until he had returned to Berlin. He has treated the whole subject in a spirit of impartial inquiry. These articles will answer in an authoritative way the scores of questions which Americans have been asking in regard to the economic, industrial, military and social conditions of Russia.

By ROBERT CHOATE

BERLIN, Aug. 14—The Union of Socialist Soviet Republics, although run for workers and peasants, is not yet a paradise for either. That both classes

THREE DEAD, SEVEN LOST, $300,000 SPENT, TOLL OF PACIFIC RACE

Stunt-Flying; Not Practical with Land Planes, Says Ernest Smith

DOLE DID NOT PLAN ANY SUCH CONTEST

Expected Properly Equipped Expedition — No Trace of Missing

SAN FRANCISCO, Aug. 21 (AP)—The first transoceanic air race in history has taken a high toll in men and money. To date, the record shows three killed, seven missing and more than $300,000 spent to win $35,000 in prizes and fame.

The only contribution to the development of commercial aviation made by the flight, according to aviation experts, is that a professional aviator starting on a flight over a 2400-mile course to Honolulu has the odds four to one against his getting there. Originally there were 13 starters in the race who obtained planes. Three were killed on the way to the take-off place; one never got far away from his home hangar and

Rumored as Successor of Bishop Anderson

(Photo by Keystone)
RT. REV. JOHN G. MURRAY
Prelate who is reported to have been chosen to come to Boston to take up the work of the late bishop

Digs Out of Cave After Six Days

Ashley Weak and Dazed, But Says He Has Not Suffered

SHELLMOUND, Tenn., Aug. 21 (AP) —Trapped six days in Nick-A-Jack cave, Lawrence S. Ashley geologist who entered the cave last Monday on an exploring trip, dug his way out today. Ashley said that he had been trapped by falling earth as he crawled through a narrow passage while trying to reach a large underground cavern believed to be connected with the cave.

Although weak and dazed, Ashley said he had not suffered from his confinement. He had previously cached food at a point near where he was caught, and had not suffered from hunger. He used a small shovel he carried in digging his way to the surface.

Ashley, who had given more than two years to the exploration of the famed Nick-A-Jack cave, went in Monday to examine a new cavern, leaving a message that, if he did not return by Tuesday, the government should be notified. When he failed to return on schedule time a party was organized and began the quest.

After days of fruitless effort, it was concluded that Ashley had met his death in the cavern. Ashley, who had leased the cave for 50 years. It has a large number of sub-caverns, some of which have never been explored. For a mile and a half from the entrance the "River of Darkness" runs

RESPITE ENDS TONIGHT; NIGHT DASH TO MAINE MADE FOR SACCO STAY; BRANDEIS DENIES PLEA

TURNS DOWN SACCO PLEA AT CHATHAM HOME

"Personal Relations with Some Interested in Case" Given as Reason

BRANDEIS'S REFUSAL COMES SPEEDILY

Justice Chats with Party on Other Subjects at

ROUTES TAKEN BY SACCO COUNSEL

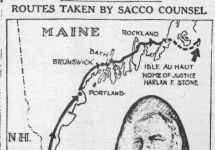

JUSTICE STONE NEW HOPE OF SACCO COUNSEL

Race to Jurist's Home on Isle Au Haut, off Rockland, Maine

FACE 35-MILE RIDE IN POWER BOAT

Are Due to Reach Summer Residence Shortly Before

The World October 25, 1929

Market in Panic as Stocks Are Dumped in 12,894,600 Share Day; Bankers Halt It

Federal Reserve Board Meets, With Secretary Mellon Sitting In, but Announces No Action—Rumors of Rate Cut

TREASURY, HOWEVER, FINDS BASIC CONDITIONS SOUND

Senators Renew Cries in Chorus for Sweeping Investigation of Wall Street Tactics

By Elliott Thurston
Special Despatch to The World

WASHINGTON, Oct. 24.—Reassurances from the Treasury that underlying business conditions are sound, an extended but unproductive meeting of the Federal Reserve Board attended by Secretary of the Treasury Mellon, and renewed cries from Capitol Hill for a sweeping investigation of Wall Street, came rapidly in the wake of the stock market debacle.

There were signs that when Secretary Mellon did the rather unusual thing of sitting in with the Federal Reserve Board at a meeting that began when the market closed and lasted for nearly two hours, some sort of statement was to be issued. Gov. Young emerged at the end of the meeting holding what seemed to be the statement, but if it was it had been vetoed. Nothing was said or intimated. The board kept its customary complete silence.

Rumors of Rate Cut

Rumors were going around that the rediscount rate might be cut back to 5 per cent., after the sudden full point advance that was intended but failed to halt the upward march of the market. Another rumor was that the board might announce credit would be available at tight points, if needed. This was meant to give a reassuring psychological effect like that produced in Florida by a similar announcement that halted the closing of banks there.

The Treasury preserved an unshaken front of confidence, ascribed the latest cyclonic effects to technicalities, which appeared to include bear raiding, and heavily stressed the point that business is sound, and that even the worst

Outside J. P. Morgan & Co.'s

By World Staff Photographer

Scene at Broad and Wall Streets During Stock Market Excitement. Insets Show **THOMAS W. LAMONT**, Morgan Partner (Left), and **CHARLES E. MITCHELL**, National City Chairman (Right), Who Turned the Tide of Selling

BUSINESS IS SAFE, FINANCIERS ASSERT

Leaders See No Economic Basis in Securities Panic

MEN ON EXCHANGE KEEP THEIR NERVE

In Face of Disaster, They Joke Amid Violent Scene

Richard Whitney's Cry of "205 for Steel" Halts Decline in Record Day's Disorder on Stock Exchange

EXPERTS TERM COLLAPSE SPECULATIVE PHENOMENON

Effect Is Felt on the Curb and Throughout Nation—Financial District Goes Wild

By Laurence Stern

The stock markets of the country tottered on the brink of panic yesterday as a prosperous people, gone suddenly hysterical with fear, attempted simultaneously to sell a record-breaking volume of securities for whatever they would bring.

The result was a financial nightmare, comparable to nothing ever before experienced in Wall Street. It rocked the financial district to its foundations, hopelessly overwhelmed its mechanical facilities, chilled its blood with terror.

In a society built largely on confidence, with real wealth expressed more or less inaccurately by pieces of paper, the entire fabric of economic stability threatened to come toppling down.

Into the frantic hands of a thousand brokers on the floor of the New York Stock Exchange poured the selling orders of the world. It was sell, sell, sell—hour after desperate hour until 1.30 P. M.

The Tide Is Turned

Then, in as dramatic a manoeuvre as financial history has ever known, the tide was magically turned by the organized power of the city's largest banking interests.

With prices at their worst and a buzz of rumors turning ordinarily sane men silly, a quiet group of financiers gathered in the austere offices of J. P. Morgan & Co., at Wall and Broad Streets. They included Thomas W. Lamont, Thomas Cochrane and other Morgan partners; Charles E. Mitchell, Chairman of the National City Bank; Albert H. Wiggin, Chairman of the Chase National Bank; W. C. Potter,

Anyone wishing to test the strength of the newsman's unwritten assertion that Good News is No News could do a lot worse than to examine the front pages of the American press in the fall of 1929. So long as the stock markets continued to climb from summit to summit — and there seemed no end to the high summer of national prosperity — it was to the financial pages that millions of small investors had to turn to see what giddy advances their nest-eggs had made overnight. There, sure enough, were acres of reading-matter, most of it bullish and confident. Here were documented the amazing careers of General Motors, Radio Corporation, Montgomery Ward and all the rest of the new giants who had reached unheard-of levels on the crest of Coolidge prosperity. Here were the reassuring predictions, the mergers and rumours of mergers, the split-share issues and all the other paraphernalia of high finance.

But affluence was a fact, not front-page news. Even on September 3, when the Dow-Jones index reached its most glittering peak in a glittering year, you would never have persuaded an editor to make a headline out of it: for one thing, there were more demanding calls on his space; and for another, there was no reason to suppose the big Bull wouldn't go bellowing onwards and upwards. Even those prophets (and there were a few) who were troubled by the high-flying trends expressed themselves in un-newsworthy utterances like 'possible movement to lower levels' or 'potential readjustment' — for nothing brings on a Depression faster than being depressing. Similarly when the market slipped in early September, steadied and slipped again in October there were plenty of perpetual optimists ready to analyse it as only 'an intermediate movement'. This sort of thing had happened in June 1928, and hadn't prices recovered and soared to a new plateau? Soon it would be time to buy.

But it wasn't an intermediate movement, as some of the more cautious brokers began to appreciate. The first headline 'news' came on October 24 after a torrent of liquidation the day before.

It happened so fast and unexpectedly, said *The World*, that it 'caught the public in a blue funk' and wiped out all the laborious 1929 gains at a stroke. *The Wall Street Journal* was inclined to blame it on the London Exchange where the fortnightly settlement had just occurred after being postponed for some weeks after the collapse of the Hatry finance group. But, astonishingly, the general consensus in Wall Street was reported as looking on it as the long-overdue 'shake-out'.

It was, however, only the first rumblings of the volcano that erupted the next day. Within an hour of opening the ticker tape bringing the fearful news to the outside world was way behind dealings on the floor of the Exchange. Stock quotations fell at a dizzying rate, quite unprecedented even in the memory of the oldest member. *The New York Times* reported 'Weird Roar Surges From Exchange Floor During Trading in a Record Smashing Day' and identified this singular cacophony as the death-rattle of those whose paper fortunes were evaporating in front of their eyes. Not that anyone had the slightest idea of where the market stood at any one moment; those within were as blind as the vast crowd that was

The World October 24, 1929.

Stocks Off 5 Billion; Crash Is the Worst In Wall St. History

The New York Times October 25, 1929.

STOCKS GAIN AS MARKET IS STEADIED; BANKERS PLEDGE CONTINUED SUPPORT; HOOVER SAYS BUSINESS BASIS IS SOUND

The World October 25, 1929.

Gigantic Bank Pool Pledged To Avert Disaster as Second Big Crash Stuns Wall Street

The New York Times October 30, 1929.

STOCKS COLLAPSE IN 16,410,030-SHARE DAY, BUT RALLY AT CLOSE CHEERS BROKERS; BANKERS OPTIMISTIC, TO CONTINUE AID

The World October 31, 1929.

Buying Strong, Stocks Rise; Rockefellers Join in Move; Exchange to Close Two Days

gathering along Wall Street. Movie cameramen were rushed to the vicinity to capture for posterity this moment of a million personal tragedies. Rumours of suicides spread through the crowd like wildfire. Dazed old-timers reminisced, to anyone who could be bothered to listen, about what it was like in the 'panic year' 1907.

One wonders if the truth had sunk in yet. When the closing gong sounded at 3.00 pm, *The New York Times* observed, 'tired brokers, their faces streaming with perspiration, their collars torn, leaned against the posts . . . others laughed and jumped about, while handfuls of torn paper or memorandum pads were thrown in the air'. 'It's all due to Mitchellism' growled Senator Glass, scoring the President of the National City Bank for defying Washington by advancing Reserve credit to support the market. In fact Charles Mitchell was once more attempting to stop the rot, huddled in the offices of J. P. Morgan with a clique of other leading bankers. Shortly after lunch they had dispatched Richard Whitney with $240 million to put some backbone into the 'demoralized market' as the unflappable *Wall Street Journal* described it (refusing, crisis or no crisis, to deviate one printer's em from its normal headlines).

The desperate expedient worked, for a time. Prices rallied and, for the most part, held. The following day (26th) the papers were peppered with hopeful salves to Wall Street's wounds, from the President downwards. Only towards the end of Saturday's trading did prices begin to totter once more. All through the weekend the lights burned in Wall Street and Broad Street as brokers tried to catch up with their paperwork and issued calls to their clients for more margin. The results were immediately apparent on the Monday (28th): there were no hysterics this time, no jumpings up and down in brokerage houses around the city, just grim and silent faces watching the ticker spell out a landslide, in a 'camaraderie of fellow-suffering' (*NY Times*). It wasn't the small investor being plundered now, it was the rich and powerful, the one-time millionaires. Such was the force of this second, unexpected stampede that at the end of the day no-one, but no-one, couldn't believe but it had finally run itself into the ground.

Yet it hadn't. It was unabated — worse even — on the Tuesday. Hardly had the echoes of the opening gong died away than the phone lines were jammed. Cable companies reported heavier pressure than even in war-time, as more than 16 million shares changed hands. Now the human casualty-lists began to jostle for space in the papers in place of endless — and meaningless — figures. In Providence R.I. a businessman fell down dead at his ticker . . . a bank clerk from the Bronx admitted stealing $6,000 for speculation on the stock market . . . police were searching for the partner in a Fifth Avenue brokerage firm accused of grand larceny . . . a Kansas City insurance man fired two shots into his chest, gasping 'Tell the boys I can't pay them' . . .

Then on Wednesday (30th) the prayed-for rally arrived, materially assisted by John D. Rockefeller who let it be known he was taking advantage of the slump to pick up a few bargains, by the Steel Corporation which declared an extra dividend, and by Richard Whitney who announced that the Exchange was closing for two days at the end of the week. You could tell things were improving from the fact that his announcement was greeted, not by another wave of panic-selling, but by cheers of relief. In fact, on the Friday, stocks which had been frantically dumped a few days before were not at all easy to buy back.

But although after the market reopened on November 4 the fever had gone, the patient was still critically ill. Too many people began trading on the hopes of recovery and, although at 1.37 pm the ticker caught up with business for

On November 1 the World reported a rally . . .

Public Stampedes to Buy, Sending Stocks Up Sharply; Rediscount Rate Cut to 5

. . . which barely survived the re-opening of the Exchange on the 4th.

10 Billion Decline In Stocks Cancels Rally After Crash

In the weeks that followed more tragedies were announced . . .

J. J. Riordan, County Trust Co. Head, Suicide; Health Blamed; Officials Say Bank Is Sound

. . . and further unbelievable losses, until . . .

Stocks Crumble To Lowest Levels On Forced Sales

. . . on November 13 prices reached rock bottom.

Mellon Announces Tax Cut; Million Shares Standard Oil Bid at 50 as Stocks Plunge

Floor of the Stock Exchange During the Panic as Seen by a World Staff Artist

SAMUEL CAHAN
STOCK EXCHANGE

In the Foreground the Pandemonium Around Post No. 2 Where Steel Stocks Are Traded Is Shown. Back of It Is No. 4, the General Motors Post

Above: An artist's impression from The World October 25, 1929, and left: a sad advertisement in the same paper 2 days later.

the first time since 11.17 am on October 23, the bottom of the graph was still to come. For the next few days — in curiously muted two-column headlines — the papers continued to report stock diving by the billion, utterly bewildered. They could not explain it, nor could anyone else, unless it was God's retribution on man's greed (why, even the Vatican was reported to have lost a fortune). The all-time low was reached on November 13 and very sorry reading it made: General Motors which at the beginning of September was quoted at $73\frac{1}{4}$ points, now stood at 36; the Radio Corporation had slumped from 101 to 28; Montgomery Ward from 137 to $49\frac{1}{4}$. In 71 days $30 billion dollars had disappeared into thin air.

HEADLINES 1930-1945

The New York Times.

Section **1** "All the News That's Fit to Print."

Copyright, 1933, by The New York Times Company.

NEW YORK, SUNDAY, MARCH 5, 1933.

Including Rotogravure Picture, Magazine and Book Sections.

TEN CENT

F

VOL. LXXXII....No. 27,434.

Entered as Second-Class Matter, Postoffice, New York, N. Y.

ROOSEVELT INAUGURATED, ACTS TO E
THE NATIONAL BANKING CRISIS QUIC
WILL ASK WAR-TIME POWERS IF N

PLAN TO USE SCRII

Bankers Ready to
Clearing House P
at End of Holid

WILL MEET WOODIN

Daily Express

ONE PENNY.

TO-DAY'S WEATHER: CLOUDY; BRIGHT INTERVALS.

TUESDAY, FEBRUARY 28, 1933.

NO. 10,237.

THE REICHSTAG IN FLAMES LAST NIGH

Daily Herald

ONE PENNY

THURSDAY, OCTOBER 3, 1935.

No. 6126

50,000 ITALIANS INVADE
ABYSSINIA: EMPEROR CABLES GENEVA
OUNCIL SUMMONED
ORROW

2,066,000
MAJORITY
FOR
SANCTIONS

Labour Party
ds By

6 A.M. EXTRA PANIC SWEEPS U.S.
AS RADIO STAGES MARS RAID

Dramatized Wa
Believed Real

News Chronicle

No. 26,742

LONDON

PO-TAGE: in U.K., 1d.; Canada, 1d.; Abroad, 1½d.

MONDAY, JANUARY 4, 1932

MANCHESTER

ONE PENNY

GANDHI ARRESTED THIS MORN
VICEROY'S SWIFT ACTION
CONGRESS PRESID

tes of the
Day

n ishes to see the parable
e beam and the mote
ed by modern examples.
hardly do better than
a batch of French
Italian and American
s and read what they
about the present state
ld.

News Chronicle
£500 FIRE
INSURAN

Surren
sau
a
in

WE TRAP 3
WOP DIVNS

RAF Regt. take
Daba drome
FIRST TIME
IN ACTION

THREE Italian divisions—the Trento, Brescia and Folgore, probably totalling about 40,000 men—have been trapped by British forces in the southern teeter of the Alamein front.

Large numbers of prisoners are being rounded up, including 3,000 Italians who surrendered in a lunch.

NOV 7

Daily Mirror
MIRROR, Saturday, November 7, 1942.

Herald

MARCH 1, 1933

ONE PENNY

Holbrook's
Worcestershire SAUCE
PIQUANT,
PLEASING,
PALATABLE

HITLER'S DEATH
DECREE FOR GERMANY

Story of Wholesale
Massacre
Next Week-End

250,000 NAZIS TO SWOOP
ON BIG CITIES

PRESIDENT VON HINDENBURG, under pressure from Hitler, signed a decree last night crushing every form of personal liberty in Germany. The death penalty will be imposed for breaches of the peace; what is virtually martial law will be declared.

VON HINDENBURG

P.C. SHOT DEAD
IN BELFAST

A POLICEMAN, John Ryan, was shot dead at midnight last the Lon...

jomery, G.O.C.
...id yesterday:—
...mplete and abso-
...y and the enemy is
...tely smashed.
...che is finished in
North Africa
this is the reason—

There will be a
Second Front
—Stalin

Gib. fleet
sails—Axis

Penetrate German Line

EXTRA

Journal
New York
American

No. 18,891—DAILY MONDAY, SEPTEMBER 4, 1939

FINAL
COMPLETE
EXTRA

FRENCH GUNS OPEN UP!

VE-Day
TUESDAY,
8, 1945

Evening Standard

FINAL NIGHT EXTRA
MOON: Sets 4.51 pm; Rises 5.43 am.
LIGHTING-UP TIME: 10.33 pm.
ONE PENNY

VE-Day
VICTORY
EDITION

DOED

hurchill: Hostilities cease at 12.1 a.m.

ADVANCE
BRITANNIA

'Brief rejoicing—then Japan'

an historic broadcast at three o'clock this afternoon Mr. Ch...
British people the news they had waited...
German war is at an end...

German artillery opened a tre-
...ith 1,460 including 310 Amer-
...overnment charged the ship
...erman 'big push' in Poland.

Artillery Duel
Raging at Nazi
Western Wall

By KENNETH T. DOWNS
International News Service Staff Correspondent.
PARIS, Sept. 4.—The gigantic military...

1930

The Jake Lingle Story

A Chicago Murder

After ten years the 'great social and economic experiment' that was Prohibition was still going strong. So, on the other hand, was drinking. True, you couldn't just walk into a saloon and order a cocktail; there were no saloons and, officially, no cocktails. But you *could* walk round the corner to the speakeasy for a tarted-up bottle of corn whiskey; you might even get a 'prescription' from the doctor, as thousands did. If you knew the right people you could get it delivered to the door; if you didn't you could brew it yourself in the bath-tub, or take a boat-trip to outside territorial waters and back again. The profits of this bootlegging trade, of course, were enormous and the men who ran it went to great lengths to protect their investment. By 1930 it was estimated by federal agents that Al Capone controlled a booze empire worth more than $60 million a year from his inviolate Chicago suburb of Cicero. And to that had to be added an equivalent income from all his spin-off rackets, gaming, dog-tracks, brothels . . . and protection.

For Mr. Capone certainly offered protection. The O'Bannion boys had learnt that in a back-street garage only last Valentine's Day – which was a summary warning to all the other roughnecks and hoodlums who operated in Chicago; Greasy Thumb Gusick, Dutch Vogel, Mike de Pike Heitler, Potatoes Kaufmann and all the rest of them. Scarface Al's activities were by no means unknown to the Press – indeed they occupied a pretty considerable number of column inches and inspired some good censorious editorialising at times. Mr. Capone didn't mind that. The boys, after all, was only doin' their job, and it was as well to be on good terms with policemen and reporters. The Press and the profiteers lived, on the whole, in a state of comfortable co-existence. That way a hard-working newsman could always count on an underworld exclusive from time to time.

Alfred J. Lingle, police reporter of *The Chicago Tribune*, was such a man. In his 17 years with the paper he had a creditable score of scoops, perhaps better than most. So when, one afternoon in early June 1930, 'Jake' Lingle was murdered in a busy underpass, shot in the head by a ·38, it went against all the canons of accepted criminal procedure. The Chicago press took it as a personal affront, a brazen challenge from the racketeers to their integrity and

THE CHICAGO DAILY NEWS, THURSDAY, JUNE 12, 1930.

CITY'S LEADERS JOIN IN TRIBUTE AT LINGLE BIER

Thousands in Procession as Slain Reporter Goes to His Grave.

City county and state officials, judges, civic and business leaders, legionnaires, former associates and friends by the thousand from varied walks of life paid final tribute today to the memory of Alfred Lingle, Chicago Tribune reporter, slain by gangsters Monday. From 15,000 to 20,000 persons joined in the funeral procession or stood along the line of march.

The funeral conducted with military rites, was held from the home of his wfie's parents, Mr. and Mrs. M. J. Sullivan, at 125 North Austin avenue to Our Lady of Sorrows church, 3121 West Jackson boulevard.

Long before the hour set for the cortege to move to the church hundreds called at the house to file in line before the bier and to offer their condolences to the family. As the hour neared the crowd before the house was so great that a detail of policemen was assigned to handle the traffic.

Inside the house was packed with floral tributes which almost filled the living room, where the casket lay, and overflowed into the hall and the dining room. To them were attached such names at those of Arthur Cutten, Attorney General Oscar Carlstrom, Commissioner of Police William P. Russell, Corporation Counsel Samuel A. Ettelson and Assessor Charles Krutchkoff.

Messages Pour In.

Telegrams of condolence from friends in other cities and newspaper

CROWDS AT MILITARY FUNERAL FOR SLAIN NEWSPAPER REPORTER

GUSICK AND EIGHT CHICAGO GUNMEN

ILLNESS DELAYS WEDDING OF KIN

HIT BANK ROLLS AND END GANGS, LEADERS URGE

[illegible] gangster's money [illegible] is now able to use effectively [illegible] section purposes.

"There is no doubt [illegible] police department [illegible] through the [illegible] enforcement of the law [illegible] police and [illegible] liquor and gambling places which are now operating in violation of the law and in that way cut off the revenue upon which the gangster thrives, and without which he cannot exist.

"Immediate action on the part of the police," Mr. Healy concluded, "will be accepted as evidence of good faith."

High Cost of Beer.

Frank J. Loesch, president of the Chicago crime commission and a member of President Hoover's law-enforcement commission, used a few figures on barreled beer as an introduction to his diagnosis of the revenue problem.

"I understand that beer now is selling at about $60 a barrel, and that the cost of making it is about $3," he said. "Let us say that the cost of distribution is $6. Perhaps $20 more goes for protection to corrupt police and peace officers and public officials; it goes to 'grease the roads' by bribery from the point of manufacture to the beer's destination. That leaves about $30 as net profit on one barrel of beer.

"The profits thus are enormous, despite the heavy protection the gangsters pay; they are thirty times as high as the old-time brewers expected to make."

Stop Sources of Profit.

After stating that gambling and prostitution seemingly are not the problems here that they were not long ago, Mr. Loesch continued:

"This gang situation could be met if you could strike at the places where

independence – and leader of the chorus of denunciation was *The Chicago Tribune's* own imperious proprietor, Colonel Robert McCormick, who personally took charge of an all-out, no-holds-barred investigation. '*The Chicago Tribune* accepts this challenge. It is war' he thundered from the editorial on June 11. 'There will be casualties but that is to be expected, it being war. *The Chicago Tribune* has the support of all the other Chicago newspapers . . . Justice will make a fight of it or it will abdicate'. The Colonel was a warrior by profession, and when he said it was war, he meant it.

The Chicago Tribune immediately offered $30,000 reward for the conviction of the killer (it was not a cent too little, either, there being upwards of 500 totally unsolved gangland slayings on the police files at that very moment). *The Chicago Herald & Examiner* also put up $25,000. At a meeting of the Chicago Newspaper Publishers' Association a newspaper truce was called and every local paper agreed to co-operate in a special investigation committee. Even *The Chicago Tribune's* bitterest rival, *The Chicago Daily News* plastered the Resolution over its front page the next day:

> '. . . *the undersigned interpret that murder as an especially significant challenge to the millions of decent citizens who have suffered the vicious activities of some paltry hundreds of criminal vagrants known as gangsters*'.

And it was signed by a list of journals calculated to wring the withers of any but the most insensitive racketeer:

The Chicago Daily Illustrated Times
The Chicago Daily News
The Chicago Evening American
The Chicago Evening Post
The Chicago Herald & Examiner
The Chicago Journal of Commerce
The Chicago Tribune

The same day all the papers carried pictures of the grand military funeral accorded the slain newspaper reporter, and the streets of Chicago were crowded with people honouring the City's hero.

The police department also set to with a will, causing unusual ripples round normally placid hideouts. The murder gun, discarded after the killing, was traced to a member of the Moran gang, Frank Forster (alias Frost). He was out of town at the moment. For ten days the investigation seemed to be going swimmingly. Suddenly it turned sour. It had been common knowledge that Lingle had lived well and not always too wisely (when he was killed he had over $1,000 in his wallet and was wearing a belt-buckle encrusted with diamonds), but he was also known as a hard-betting man. And he'd always claimed his father had left him $50,000. Now it was discovered his father had left but a few hundred dollars – and the diamond belt was a gift from none other than Al Capone.

More disquieting facts tumbled out: his bank deposits recorded entries of over $60,000 in the past 18 months – in spite of his having lost some $80,000 in the stock-market crash. One of his joint accounts was shared with the city's Police Commissioner William F. Russell (who resigned on the spot). *The Chicago Tribune's* competitors quite understandably forgot their truce and dug deeper. *The Chicago Daily News* linked Lingle's name with an unsuccessful dog-racing fix. *The Chicago Herald & Examiner* talked darkly of gambling connections. But whatever it was, it was certain the reporter had been operating a vast-scale racket, unsuspected by even his closest colleagues. On June 30 *The Chicago Tribune* was bound to admit 'Alfred Lingle now takes on a different character, one in which he was unknown to the management of the Tribune when he was alive . . . He was not and could not have been a great reporter' it added. To its credit, *The Chicago Tribune* never attempted to play down the sordid revelations. It matched its rivals, headline for headline – and it continued with the search for the killer. It was not long before one was found, a gunslinger by the name of Leo Brothers, though it was widely believed he was a sacrifice from gangland to get the heat off everybody else.

Confidence in the press, for the time being, was profoundly shaken; nor was it helped by the bout of back-biting among the newspapers themselves after the Lingle murder. They started investigating one another. As one paper put it, editors were getting 'cross eyed from looking behind them'. The only result was a crop of threatened libel actions. Reporters from *The St Louis Star* and *The Post-Dispatch* (whose circulation areas overlapped with the Chicago papers') began to sniff around the Windy City, and came up with some sensational accusations – all of which collapsed on serious investigation. The climax of *The St Louis Star's* exposure came when its reporter, Harry Brundidge, actually penetrated to Capone's inner sanctum in Miami Beach. His account read for all the world as if he had sneaked an advance look at a 1940s screenplay:

> 'It was 1 o'clock in the morning and the beams of a tropical moon danced on the waters of Biscayne Bay. For more than three hours this writer had communed with Alphonse Capone on a divan chatting about Chicago, its underworld, the assassination of 'Jake' Lingle, and the activities of some other Chicago newspaper men. Suddenly the big beer and bullet baron leaned over, put his left arm around my shoulders and with typical Latin effusiveness squeezed me and said: "Listen Harry. I like your face. Let me give you a hot tip. Lay off Chicago and the money-hungry reporters . . . You can't buck it, not even with the backing of your newspaper, because it's too big a proposition. So lay off".'

But then Jake had been a good friend' of Al's.

End of the R101

'Well, Tiny, everything is all right'. Jack Hastings, engineer of the airship R101 on its maiden voyage, had just finished duty and was handing over his watch for the night to Victor Savory. Elsewhere the vast floating palace was quiet, except for the throbbing of the engines. It was 2.00 am, Sunday October 5 1930, somewhere over Beauvais in the North of France. The last of the distinguished passengers, including Lord Thomson Britain's Secretary of State for Air, had left the luxurious dining-room ('after enjoying a number of cigars' as the last chatty wireless to the control-tower at Le Bourget had confided), strolled along the wide promenade deck to their roomy, white and gold staterooms, and settled down to sleep until it was time for a sunny breakfast over the South of France.

This was an important flight. This voyage, to Karachi and back, would put Britain in the forefront of the world's airship pioneers. The R101, the world's most splendid — and safest — airliner, would be a worthy challenger to Germany's Graf Zeppelin which only a year before had triumphantly completed her round-the-world flight in a blaze of welcoming searchlights. 'I've promised the P.M. to be back on October 20' Lord Thomson had laughed as he'd embarked six and a half hours earlier. Why, five years ago such a remark would have been sheer madness. At the controls the second pilot, H. J. Leech, felt the wind rise and whirl round the cabin, and stepped up the power of the motors.

In a wood a few miles outside Beauvais Georges Rabouille was laying snares for the rabbits. He was poaching, but there was no-one anywhere near — so he was startled when he caught the sound of a motor approaching. Then the huge illuminated monster appeared in the sky over the village of Allonne. Fascinated, he watched it come nearer, dipping and dipping still until as it passed over the wood, he could make out every detail. He noticed the nose was pointing downwards . . .

'Well, Tiny, everything is all right' Hastings reported to Savory. No sooner had he said it than both men were hurled to the ground by a violent shock, followed in a split second by a gigantic explosion. Savory saw at once the ship was engulfed in a sheet of flame, managed to clamber over the top of the car, the flames scorching his face and hands, and jumped. By the sheerest luck he landed not on burning debris, but on grass. In the crew quarters two of his fellow-engineers, Bell and Binks, thought they were being killed when the water ballast tank burst over their heads. That drenching saved their lives.

For Leech, it was his third airship wreck in fourteen years. He hurled himself against the cabin partition and frantically tore away a space barely large enough to squeeze through. Then he heard a voice crying out; it was Disley the wireless operator. He plunged back in and dragged the man to safety. Disley remembered afterwards seeing another man run out of the control room towards the crew quarters shouting 'We are down!' He was never seen again. Another survivor's last glimpse of the wreck was Flight-Lieutenant Irwin standing at his post quietly giving orders. He was still there when the flames enveloped him.

The news reached London at 3.05 am, an hour after the crash — too late for most papers but not the The Sunday Pictorial which continued to publish the latest news, and pictures, of the disaster until late in the day. The News Chronicle, without hesitating to count the cost, chartered an airliner which flew over the disaster area and returned with the most striking aerial shot of the grotesque iron skeleton. Many papers were nearly side-tracked by a potential mystery: the French authorities announced they had recovered 47 bodies, there were eight survivors but the passenger and crew lists amounted to only 54. Had there been a stowaway? No question of it, said the Air Ministry, and the whole thing turned out to be a mistake. So the papers at once addressed themselves to the burning question: what had caused the tragedy?

Everything from the weather to the use of hydrogen gas instead of helium was blamed. The Daily Express was ominously prophetic on its front page the day after the crash when it recalled that the airship had been in difficulties from leaky gas bags during its trial flight in June. But it was left to an unknown local paper The Bedford Record to make the most sensational allegations of the week (it was, of course, the newspaper based nearest to the R101's permanent home at Cardington). Under the heading 'The Indictment', its editorial asked: 'Why did they let her go? They knew she was dipping at the nose . . . they knew that she had not been tested properly: and they knew that one engine at least was out of order. They knew she was heavy to begin with, and they knew the climatic conditions were against them. And yet they let her go'. The Record concluded 'our brave men and our wonderful ship were sacrificed to improvidence if not even to improvisation'.

The official inquiry the following month substantiated The Record's worst fears. The trial flight had indeed been conducted on one engine, so that a totally unproved machine had been sent on its maiden voyage because Lord Thomson had insisted on it being ready by the end of September, as 'he had made his plans accordingly'. In retrospect the engines had proved to be many tons heavier than anticipated. There was deep suspicion that the altimeter had been faulty, and that the elevator cable-controls had snapped. Worst of all, the ship had knowingly been allowed to take off riddled with thousands of actual or potential gas leaks. When asked if he would have given a certificate of air-worthiness for the flight, the inspector in charge replied: 'I'm afraid I should not'. The one man who could not be called to the Inquiry was the R101's designer. For he had been burnt to death in his sleep in the holocaust of his own leviathan.

News Chronicle

No. 26,355.   MONDAY, OCTOBER 6, 1930.   ONE PENNY.

5 A.M. EDITION.

HOW R 101 WAS WRECKED
Collision with Hilltop : 46 Dead, 8 Saved.

The terrible disaster to Britain's great airship R 101 yesterday in France, with the loss of 46 lives, is vividly told in this remarkable picture, taken yesterday afternoon from the air.

Lord Thomson at the lift of the mooring mast at Cardington.

Miss Winifred Spooner and Sir Sefton Brancker photographed just before the R 101 took off.

TWO PICTURE PAGES.

Special 'News-Chronicle' Air Liner.

In view of the wide national interest in the R 101 disaster the "News-Chronicle" to-day contains two picture pages illustrating the appalling tragedy—Pages 3 and 16.

Immediately news of the wreck reached London the "News-Chronicle" chartered a twin-engined Air Liner to bring pictures of the disaster from France to London.

LATE NEWS

A ROARING FURNACE.

TRAIL OF OIL IN THE FIELDS.

BRITAIN'S great passenger airship R 101 was wrecked with a loss of 46 lives yesterday. Among the dead are the Air Minister (Lord Thomson) and the Director of Civil Aviation (Sir Sefton Brancker). There are eight survivors. The bodies are to be brought back to England in a warship.

The disaster occurred near Beauvais, 40 miles north of Paris, at 2.5 a.m.

A Startling Report.

Early this morning the Central News sent a startling message that the fields over which the R 101 had passed bore traces of oil and that this discovery had changed the whole line of inquiry.

R 101, the most spacious airship ever built, left Cardington (Bedfordshire) on Saturday night at 7.36 for India via Egypt. She roared her way over London between 9 and 9.30 p.m. in driving rain and a rising gale.

The last message from her came at 1.50 a.m. She reported by wireless her position just north of Beauvais. Apparently all was well. She was battling her way through wind and rain and flying rather low. There was no hint of the coming disaster.

The sender of the message indicated that he was going off to bed.

Fifteen minutes later the stately air liner was a mass of burning wreckage.

It was five minutes past two. All on board were preparing for bed except the pilot and the night-watch—twelve men all told.

A Whirlwind Gust.

A terrific gust of whirlwind force suddenly struck the airship and drove her downwards. The engineer states that the tail broke. The airship collided with the top of a 700 feet hill at Allonne. Flames shot out. There was a loud explosion. R 101 collapsed and became a roaring furnace.

The airship met her fate only 6½ hours after the start of her voyage. Her captain, Flight-Lieut. H. C. Irwin, was last seen at his post with the flames around him.

A PUBLIC INQUIRY.

AIR MINISTRY AND THE CAUSE.

It was stated officially last night that a public inquiry into the disaster would be held in this country.

An official communication issued from the Air Ministry stated: "There is no evidence to show whether the vessel caught fire or broke her back while in mid-air."

Sir John Salmond has returned from Beauvais, but feels, in view of the fact that all the circumstances of the accident must be closely inquired into, that it would be inadvisable for him to give his own personal impressions as to what happened at the present stage.

Air Commodore Holt, Director of Technical Development, flew to Beauvais with Sir John, and is remaining in France.

If the French Government wishes to hold an official inquiry, which they are entitled to do under International Regulations, the British Government will do everything to co-operate with them.

TIME-TABLE OF THE VOYAGE.

Extracts from R 101's Messages.

SATURDAY.

7.36 p.m.—Left Cardington.

9 p.m.—Over London. Airship wirelessed: "Intend to proceed via Paris, Tours, Toulouse and Narbonne."

9.30 p.m.—Seen over South-East London.

10.35 p.m.—Near Hastings. Airship wirelessed: "It is raining hard and there is a strong S.W. wind. Engines running well at cruising speed 54.2 knots. Ship behaving well."

11.38 p.m.—Reached French coast near Point St. Quentin.

12 midnight.—15 miles S.W. of Abbeville.

SUNDAY.

12.12 a.m.—Croydon aerodrome received wireless from airship saying: "Thanks for valuable assistance. Will not require you further to-night."

1.23 a.m.—Croydon replied: "Still remaining on watch."

1.43 a.m.—Le Bourget aerodrome (Paris), in wireless communication with R 101 and gave her her position.

1.50 a.m.—Last message from R 101, received at Le Bourget. According to Reuter it said: "At the moment passengers after an excellent meal and after enjoying a number of cigars are getting ready to go to bed."

2.5 a.m.—Airship destroyed.

3.5 a.m.—Reports of accident reached London.

3.16 a.m.—Le Bourget sent out wireless message that R 101 "has taken fire."

THE MAN IN CONTROL.

HIS OWN ACCOUNT OF WHAT HAPPENED.

From GEORGE RENWICK,
The "News-Chronicle" Paris Correspondent who was on the spot soon after the disaster.

BEAUVAIS, Sunday.

MR. H. J. LEECH, foreman engineer, Royal Airship Works, who acted as second pilot, was at his post in the control cabin when the disaster happened to R 101.

He was taken by surprise by a sudden dip of the airship and the explosion which followed its collision with the hillside. Let me give his account of what happened in his own words:

"Just before we reached Beauvais," he said, "we ran into a tremendous storm. Wind and rain whirled round the cabin and made the entire structure quiver. Confident in the solidity of the R 101, I continued to keep the ship towards Paris.

"Just over Beauvais I felt the front end drop—a danger signal.

"We went on slowly, feeling our way as it were, but steadily.

Altitude Unknown.

"At 1.48 Le Bourget told me our position and I sought for a calm spot in the atmosphere, still ignorant of our precise altitude.

"I increased the strength of the motors in the teeth of the wind, but heavy rain settled on the ship's bulk and weighted us down. At this point the motors seemed to respond badly, so I put on more power.

"**Then abruptly, unexpectedly, and devastatingly, came catastrophe.**

"The ship's nose, after two hesitating dips, struck the earth violently on the top of a slight rise in the ground. A terrible explosion occurred, and everything burst into flames.

"I threw myself against the partition of the cabin and tore away at everything I could in order to make a way of escape for myself. I managed to burst open a space large enough for me to get out head first. Then I dashed through and out of the flames, badly burned, but safe.

"The most dramatic rescue was that of my two comrades, Binks and Bell. They thought they were being killed when the water ballast tank burst over their heads. They were soaked through and then thrown out of their cabins without being very badly burned."

Mr. Victor Savory, one of the engineers, who escaped with severe burns about the face and hands, said: "I rose at 1.45 to take over duty. It is some distance from the sleeping cabins in the centre to our respective machine cabins, and mine was right starboard amidships.

"I was just inside when the catastrophe took place. I was relieving poor Jack Hastings and he told me as I entered 'Well, Tiny, everything is all right.' Then, suddenly, I was hurled down by the shock and the explosion.

"I was dizzy and when I got up I put my hands over my eyes, wondering what had happened. I then saw that the airship was surrounded by flames, I thought 'I must get out of this.'

"I managed to climb outside and over the top of the car. It was then that the flames burned me on the face and hands and I fell off to the ground. By an extraordinary chance I did not fall into the burning debris. I was unhurt and managed to walk a little distance when I saw a man who took me to a motor-car."

I asked Mr. Savory if everybody, except some members of the crew, was asleep at the time of the accident.

"As far as I can tell," he replied, "everybody, with the exception of the officers and men on duty, must have been asleep. All those who were in

Continued on Page Two, Col. One.

LATE NEWS.

EIGHT SURVIVORS.

THEIR CONDITION THIS MORNING.

At two o'clock this morning the "News-Chronicle" ascertained by telephone from Beauvais that the injured were progressing satisfactorily. Their condition was described earlier by the Air Ministry as follows:—

SERIOUS.

W. G. Radcliffe, rigger.

FAIRLY SERIOUS.

S. Church, rigger.

NOT DANGEROUS.

A. V. Bell, engineer.
J. H. Binks, engineer.
A. J. Cook, engineer.
V. Savory, engineer.
A. Disley, wireless operator.

NOT SERIOUS.

H. J. Leech, foreman engineer.

Seven are members of the crew and one, Mr. Leech, an official at Cardington.

Mr. Binks's home is at Thornwell Bank, Luxley, Sheffield; Mr. Radcliffe lives at Bedford. All the other survivors are from Cardington.

Engineer Bell had been chaffed because he had been allotted bunk No. 13.

Are Airships Worth it? By Commander Kenworthy—Page Eight.

A DISCREPANCY.

HOW MANY WERE ON BOARD?

While the Air Ministry gave the casualty list as 46 dead and eight injured, messages from Beauvais stated that 47 bodies had been recovered.

A Reuter message spoke of "very positive statements" by survivors that 58 people were on board.

An Air Ministry official stated late last night that it would be impossible to explain the discrepancy until further inquiries had been made to-day.

TO-DAY'S WEATHER.

Squally; occasional rain; bright intervals.

THE EIGHT SURVIVORS.   Left to right: A. J. Cook, A. Disley, W. G. Radcliffe, V. Savory, H. J. Leech, J. H. Binks, A. O. Bell, S. Church.

Bruno Hauptmann: The Lindbergh Kidnapping

NEW YORK
Herald Tribune

LATE CITY EDITION

THE WEATHER
Today: Rain, somewhat warmer; strong northeast winds. Tomorrow: Fair
Temperatures yesterday: Max. 60 Min. 48
Detailed report on Page 25

Vol. XCII No. 31,225 — (Copyright, 1932, New York Tribune Inc.) — FRIDAY, MAY 13, 1932 — ★★★★ — TWO CENTS In Greater New York | THREE CENTS Within 200 Miles | FOUR CENTS Elsewhere

Lindbergh Baby Is Found Slain Near Hopewell;
Killed Soon After Kidnaping, Flung Into Thicket

Taxicab Broker Admits $26,535 Gift to Walker

J. A. Sisto Tells Seabury He Declared Mayor in on Stock Pool at Time of Control Board Plans

Acted on the 'Hints' Of Friends, He Says

'Will Explain This Testimony When the Time Comes,' Says City Executive of Disclosures

Mayor James J. Walker in November, 1929, accepted a $26,535.51 payment in bonds from a broker who was engaged in financing the large taxicab company which had most at stake in the Mayor's taxicab regulation program, put in motion soon thereafter with the company's enthusiastic approval.

J. A. Sisto, the broker, told Samuel Seabury and the Hofstadter legislative committee yesterday that on his first social meeting with the Mayor his admiration for that public figure, urged on by hints of the Mayor's friends, prompted him to the generosity of declaring Mr. Walker in on 1,000 shares of a Cosden Oil stock pool.

Says Mayor Invested Nothing

The Mayor invested no money, but Mr. Sisto said that the $26,500 bonds were paid to Mr. Walker as profits on the stock transaction. The securities included ten convertible bonds in the Parmelee Transportation Company, which, in association with the Yellow and Checker companies, composes the city's largest taxicab interest.

Mr. Sisto refused to waive immunity to criminal prosecution before he testified, and so also did the Mayor's intimate friend, John J. McKeon, who received immunity and was forced to tell about his delivery of the bonds to Mr. Walker.

Subway Flood Puts Thousands In 2-Hr. Tie-Up

Rush Hour Crowds Delayed as Water Main Break Stalls West Side I. R. T.

A break in a water main in Varick Street, between King and West Houston Streets, tied up the Seventh Avenue subway for two hours last night, delaying tens of thousands of homeward-bound passengers. Southbound service was held up from 4:45 until 6:45 p. m., while northbound trains were running again at 6:15.

The tie-up in the heaviest part of the rush hours congested the stations south of Forty-second to Chambers Street, and the confusion among the passengers was increased by the rain, through which many had to walk to change to the elevated lines.

The main twelve-inch main broke

Plan of Relief Is Proposed By President

Compromise Program Calls for 1½ Billions in Loans to States and for Job-Providing Projects

Money To Be Lent By Dawes Board

Announcement Follows Meeting With Republicans of Bank Group

By Theodore C. Wallen
WASHINGTON, May 12.—At the end of a White House conference with the Republican members of the Senate Banking Committee tonight, following an earlier meeting between President Hoover and his financial advisers, on the one hand, and Senator Joseph T. Robinson, Democratic leader of the Senate, on the other hand, the President publicly offered a compromise plan of unemployment relief on a mammoth scale through the Reconstruction Finance Corporation.

The President did not announce that any agreement had been reached although, in the statement issued, he set forth his proposal as a "program for united action." Even among the Republican group which met with Mr. Hoover tonight there were signs that harmony was not complete.

The program, embodying in effect a substantial part of the relief proposals made yesterday by Senator Robinson, with the backing of prominent leaders of his party, enlarges the borrowing powers of the Reconstruction Corporation; he increased the amount of $1,500,000,000 for use in making loans to states for relief purposes and in underwriting loans for self-sustaining enterprises undertaken either by public bodies or by private enterprises.

The grant of new authority to borrow money would increase the borrowing authorization of the Reconstruction Corporation to the total amount of $3,000,000,000. It already has authority to issue $1,500,000,000 in debentures and has an additional subscription of $500,000,000 from the Treasury. The new plan would call for the sale of the corporation's securities in the same

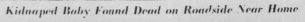
Kidnaped Baby Found Dead on Roadside Near Home

Charles Augustus Lindbergh jr. — Paramount News – Associated Press

Police Call Condon and Curtis In Hunt for Baby's Kidnapers

Hope 'Jafsie' and Norfolk Man Can Reveal New Data as Forces of Law Are Freed of Restraint Shown in Fear for Child's Safety

The first move of the police freed by the discovery of the body of Charles A. Lindbergh jr. of the restraint imposed by fear that undue activity might cause harm or death to the child, was to summon John F. Condon, of New York, and John Hughes Curtis, of Norfolk, Va., volunteer intermediaries in dealings with the "kidnapers."

The two men, Colonel H. Norman Schwarzkopf, head of the New Jersey State Police, announced early this morning, "will be at these headquarters in a few minutes" for questioning in connection with this case and will

Entire Nation Joined Search For Lost Child

Citizens by Thousands and Underworld Joined Police in 10-Week Hunt

Probably no crime committed in the United States ever aroused such a feverish search for a solution as the kidnaping of Charles A. Lindbergh jr. In every quarter of the nation police agencies, from the Federal Secret Service to the constable in the humblest hamlet, worked day and night, and the detective zeal of thousands of private citizens was unprecedented.

As the people throughout the nation sympathized with Colonel and

U.S. Redoubles Efforts to Find Killers of Baby

Covered by Leaves, Skull Fractured

Body Found by Negro Truck Helper Identified by Shirt, Flannel Band, Hair, Teeth, Overlapping Toes

News Finds Colonel Absent on Vain Lead

Tragic Denouement of 72-Day Hunt Around World Comes Five Miles From Nursery Where It Began

Charles A. Lindbergh jr., kidnaped on the night of March 1 from the crib in his parents' Sourland Mountain home near Hopewell, N. J., was found dead at 3:15 o'clock yesterday afternoon in a thicket at Mount Rose, N. J., just off the Hopewell-Princeton highway and approximately five miles southeast of the Lindbergh estate.

The child had been murdered and abandoned to the elements soon after the kidnaping, it was announced last night after an autopsy at an undertaking establishment in Trenton, to which the body was taken from the thicket. Death was attributed to a fractured skull due to external violence.

Parents Accept the Identification

Identification of the body was stated as a fact by Colonel H. Norman Schwarzkopf, Superintendent of the New Jersey State Police, who has been in charge of the kidnaping investigation, and Dr. Charles A. Mitchell, County Physician, who performed the autopsy. No direct word was forthcoming from the parents, but Colonel Schwarzkopf indicated they had no doubt of the correctness of the identification, concerning which they had been informed in detail.

The identification was based on certain physical characteristics of the Lindbergh child and on the garments worn by the baby at the time of the kidnaping. Despite the decomposition of the body resulting from exposure to the weather, Dr. Mitchell said the autopsy had disclosed positively that the body was that of the Lindbergh baby.

Confirmation of the identification came early this morning from Dr. Philip Van Ingen, of New York, who examined the body at Trenton. Dr. Van Ingen, who was accompanied

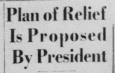
Herald Tribune photo—Steffen
J. A. Sisto

If only through his frantic efforts to shun publicity since his epic transatlantic flight in 1927, Lindbergh had contrived to hold the admiration and curiosity of all America. Forced to honeymoon in secret, build a retreat in the middle of a large estate in New Jersey, even to disguise himself sometimes in public, he had succeeded in winning a measure of privacy for his new family by the beginning of 1932. But on the evening of March 1 that year a tragedy struck which moved the Western world to the core, and which was to expose the Lindberghs once more to the cruel glare of public scrutiny. Their twenty month-old baby was kidnapped. Against his window leaned a rickety, homemade ladder: on the sill had been left an ill-spelt ransom note. Amid an avalanche of well-intentioned but entirely misleading information, two positive leads emerged in the search for the kidnapper. A Norfolk shipbuilder, John Hughes Curtis, came forward on March 9 with a complex story of his 'negotiations' with the kidnappers (who appeared to have sailed off into mid-ocean) and had a hundred ships and planes combing the Atlantic for a week. He later admitted his despicable hoax. A lecturer from

the Bronx on the other hand, a Dr. 'Jafsie' Condon, who had for some reason advertised his services as a go-between in the local paper, really did seem to have contacted the kidnapper (a mysterious Germanic-sounding 'John'). To Lindbergh he conveyed further ransom notes identical to the one left on the window-sill. On April 2 $50,000 was paid to 'John': at a Bronx cemetery in return for the information that the baby was to be found on a boat at Martha's Vineyard. Lindbergh and the police searched the island in vain. Then on May 12, the tragedy was completed: the baby was discovered, dead, near a road just a few miles from the Lindbergh house. The child had clearly been dead for a long time. Twenty-eight months later, on September 19 1934 Bruno Hauptmann was arrested in the Bronx after passing one of the ransom bills. On January 2 1935 he was brought to trial for the murder of the Lindbergh baby. Even before the evidence was paraded before the world, Hauptmann's cards were stacked against him: he had a criminal record, he was a lavish spender with no visible means of support, he was an illegal immigrant into the United States. During the

trial and for long afterwards it was argued that Hauptmann had been tried, convicted and sentenced for the crime by sections of the press before he even came to court. There was, regrettably, a great deal of truth in this accusation: there were times when the actual trial seemed a mere formality to some papers (as a few random headlines suggest January 4: 'Ann's Story on Stand puts Bruno Near Chair'. January 12: 'Hauptmann signed Own Death Warrant in Ransom Notes', January 9: Bruno's Calm a Triumph of Art – or Innocence, February 11: Bruno's Acquittal Hopes Fading'). Every newspaper reader in America was invited to be his own juror. Every word, every shred of evidence was recounted by the popular press – analyses of Bruno's handwriting, reconstructions of witnesses' testimony, close-ups of the ladder which had clearly been constructed from Hauptmann's floor-boards. The trial could not have been more public if it had been filmed. The evidence was indeed damning and, in spite of The New York Journal's 'sidewalk jury' (who voted 7–4 not guilty, early in the trial) Hauptmann was duly convicted, and executed on April 4.

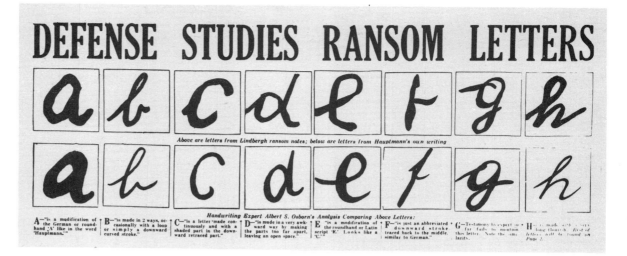

DEFENSE STUDIES RANSOM LETTERS

A Gentlemen's Agreement

The Abdication Crisis

CINDERELLA UP TO DATE

Above: cartoon from the Chicago Tribune. Below: US headlines

On October 28 1936 several London papers carried a modest little item on how Mrs. Wallis Warfield Simpson had the previous day, at the Ipswich Assizes, been granted a decree nisi from her second husband, an insurance agent, on the grounds of his adultery.

The more eagle-eyed members of London society whose pastime it was to scour the divorce notices no doubt read the routine account with more than passing interest — that is, if they recognised this Mrs. Simpson as the same dark-haired lady who had accompanied the King on his Mediterranean cruise that summer, and who gave such witty dinner-parties at Bryanston Court. At those leisurely breakfast tables a few knowing eyebrows were certainly raised: but the great bulk of the British public that morning drank its tea and went to work sublimely ignorant of the momentous implications of those few innocent paragraphs.

That Mrs. Simpson's divorce should have rated such discreet treatment in the press was, of course, no oversight on the part of the editors. On the contrary, it was the result of remarkable voluntary restraint, unanimously agreed upon at a private meeting on October 16. No-one in Fleet Street was in any doubt that there was a constitutional crisis looming: if the King was determined, as he certainly appeared to be, to marry Mrs. Simpson (now twice divorced) he would be forced to abdicate. It was not that the lady was a commoner, not even that she was American — public opinion (at least as interpreted by the Prime Minister, Mr. Baldwin) was liberal enough to have welcomed that. But it was not so liberal, nor was the Cabinet, as to suffer a Queen who was a divorcee, nor a King's wife who was not a Queen. The future of the monarchy, no less, was at stake. There were no illusions in the press about the gravity of the situation.

Yet for two months not one single hint of the royal romance crept into their columns, in deference to the King ('a gentlemen's agreement', the King later called it. 'The British Press kept its word, and for that I shall always be grateful'). Sitting on such a hot story proved to be an increasingly uncomfortable process — particularly as the newsmen themselves were so intimately involved in the delicate negotiations. The Editor of *The Times* and pillar of the Establishment, Geoffrey Dawson, was on the phone to Baldwin quite as frequently as the King was consulting Beaverbrook of *The Daily Express* (on one occasion even summoning him back from America for his advice) and Rothermere of *The Daily Mail*. Already the newspapers were taking up their positions in readiness for the battle which was brewing.

The blanket of silence which persisted throughout November was as sackcloth and ashes to British journalists as they observed the abandon with which their American colleagues, unshackled by constitutional delicacies, speculated and gossiped on the great British love affair. From the moment news of an impending divorce action broke the story never left America's front pages. On October 15 Wallis's home-town newspaper *The Baltimore Sun* announced 'Mrs. Simpson, King's Friend, Asks Divorce' and mentioned her flat was a mere 10 minutes away from Buckingham Palace. 'Weigh Chance of Mrs. Simpson Marrying King' ruminated *The Chicago Tribune* the next day and announced the odds on King Edward's coronation taking place on schedule the following May had dropped from 20—1 to 5—1 (which was exceedingly strange). Over the next few weeks no irrelevant detail was overlooked. *The New York Sunday News* spoke darkly of 'suppressed rage in the Royal Household' at the mortifying prospect of a scandal. Other papers reported that the King had been seen buying up large quantities of ladies' underwear in Vienna, that he had presented Wally with an emerald

THE DAILY MIRROR, Saturday, December 5, 1936.

Daily Mirror

THE DAILY PICTURE   NEWSPAPER WITH THE LARGEST NET SALE

SATURDAY
Dec. 5 No. 10301
ONE PENNY
Registered at the G.P.O. as a newspaper

GOD SAVE THE KING!

TELL US THE FACTS, MR. BALDWIN!

"Suggestions have appeared that if the King decided to marry, his wife need not become Queen. These ideas are without any constitutional foundation.

"There is no such thing as what is called a morganatic marriage known to our law. The Royal Marriages Act of 1772 has no application to the Sovereign himself . . .

"This Act, therefore, has nothing to do with the present case. The King himself requires no consent from any other authority to make his marriage legal, but, as I have said, the lady whom he marries by the fact of her marriage to the King necessarily becomes Queen.

"She herself therefore enjoys all the status, rights, and privileges which, both by positive law and by custom, attach to that position . . . . and her children would be in the direct line of succession to the throne.

"The only possible way in which this result could be avoided would be by legislation dealing with a particular case. His Majesty's Government are not prepared to introduce such legislation.

"Such a change could not be effective without the consent of all the Dominions. I am satisfied from inquiries I have made that this assent would not be forthcoming."
—MR. BALDWIN IN PARLIAMENT YESTERDAY.

THE NATION INSISTS ON KNOWING THE KING'S FULL DEMANDS AND CONDITIONS

The Country Will Give You the Verdict

necklace worth $125,000, that the police were moving people on from Mrs. Simpson's flat because it was now 'Crown Property'. *The Daily News* at one point even decided the whole thing was off: 'King Edward VIII will marry a hand-picked Princess and not Mrs. Wallis Simpson, after all . . . London believes that Edward was breaking the news tonight to his American sweetheart at a rustic rendezvous far from Buckingham Palace. It will be a marriage of convenience, a concession to the Victorian temper of modern England'.

Sadly for 'Victorian' England there was no means of gauging its temper as yet. Even when on December 1 Bishop Blunt of Bradford (as good as his name) regretted publicly to his Diocesan conference that the King hadn't shown 'more political awareness of the need for Divine guidance in the discharge of his high office', the public thought the bishop meant the King ought to go to church more often. That, in fact, was precisely what he did mean, but the press was by now too pent-up with private knowledge to interpret the obvious. Reporting the episcopal address the next day the *Yorkshire Post* made reference to the rumours 'published of late in the more sensational American newspapers'. *The Manchester Guardian* talked of a controversy that had sprung up between the King and the government.

The collusion of silence in the Press was breaking up irretrievably, as *The New York Times* appreciated when it plunged into its lead story on December 3:
EDWARD MAY ABDICATE THRONE TODAY REFUSING TO BREAK WITH MRS. SIMPSON BRITAIN IS ASTOUNDED BY THE CRISIS
Britain, in point of fact, was more confused than astounded that particular morning. Clearly from the tortured prose of the leader-writers there was some sort of crisis and 'grave issues' at stake. *The Times'* first leader was explicitly concerned with 'King and Monarchy' and the excitement brought on by 'transatlantic journalism', but nowhere did it mention Mrs. Simpson's name. Nor did any of the other national dailies — until *The Daily Mirror*, never the most retiring of papers, dived in headfirst in its last (and very late) edition. The next day (the 4th) every paper exploded with all the hurricane force of their bottled-up frustration: they scoured the Empire for official reactions, drummed up all their feature material on Mrs. Simpson (much of it already set up in type) and documented in minutest detail every statement, comment, coming and going, every theory, constitutional alternative, every flush on Mrs. Simpson's cheeks.

Over the next dramatic week they were unstinting in their advice to the King, unpalatable or not. As the Establishment closed its ranks *The Times* soberly followed the Cabinet's intractable line, renunciation of Mrs. Simpson or abdication. It hastened to point out 'this is no crisis precipitated by a Government of Mrs. Grundies or snobs' and that there was no way out by inventing special legislation. It urged a quick end to the matter. *The Daily Mirror* on the other hand counselled patience and, through the voice of its columnist Cassandra, accused 'the Prime Minister and his Government of manoeuvring, with smooth and matchless guile to a desperate situation where humiliation is the only answer'. *The Daily Telegraph* had no doubts that the King's private feelings should 'yield to his sense of public duty to the Realm'. And if he didn't *The Daily Sketch* ominously predicted that 'never again could every English man be a "King's man" as all of us were without exception under George V'. Even the trades union paper *The Daily Herald* appeared to be glumly on the government's side for a change: 'Is the King bound to accept the advice of his popularly elected Ministers in matters which are clearly of national welfare and are capable of great national influence? However harsh the personal consequences only one reply is possible. Either the King accepts his Ministers' advice, or else the British democratic Constitution ceases to work'.

Unequivocally still King's men, apart from *The Daily Mirror*, were *The News Chronicle* which oddly for a liberal non-conformist paper pronounced itself in favour of morganatic marriage, *The Daily Express* ('No Government can stand in the King's way if he is resolved to walk that way . . .') and *The Daily Mail* ('Abdication is out of the question, because its possibilities of mischief are endless'). The newspapers of the Empire were guarded in their editorials, looking either to the people of Britain to decide, like *The Cape Times* of South Africa, or to the King's own sense of honour, like *The Times of India*. European papers maintained a respectful sense of neutrality: in Germany the Ministry of Propaganda put out a curt statement to the effect that the matter was one which did not concern the Germans. A few of the world's remaining crowned heads suppressed any mention of the crisis in their own countries, notably Egypt, Yugoslavia and Rumania.

On December 10 the King sadly announced that he believed he had no alternative but to renounce his throne and follow Mrs. Simpson into self-imposed exile. The same day he signed the instrument of abdication and bade farewell to his former subjects the next. So far as the public, at least, were concerned the storm was over as swiftly as it had apparently arisen. The whole of the United States (in the words of Sinclair Lewis's open letter to 'Mr. David Windsor' in *The New York Evening Post*) was 'so excited that you have become a human being instead of King of England. We believe it is more important to the British Empire that a young man in England should be completely loyal to the girl he loves than to the British mirage'. .

A great many other American papers were infused with Mr. Lewis's romantic and republican sentiments, as well. But of all the world's press it was left to *The New York Times* to pose the $64,000 question about that Gentlemen's Agreement, even if its answer was open to question: 'The curious voluntary censorship in Britain of the past few weeks is dissolving and revealing what appears to be a really major crisis in the history of the British Crown. This conspiracy of silence tended only to stiffen headstrong wills and moral prejudices that might otherwise have been less intransigent'. But *The New York Times*, even if it didn't underrate the inherent streak of puritanism left in the British, undoubtedly misjudged Mr. Baldwin's sense of timing.

GOD SAVE THE KING

Daily Mirror

Registered at the G.P.O. as a newspaper.   No. 10302 Mon. Dec. 7, 1936 One Penny

45,000,000 DEMAND TO KNOW—

1. **What, justly stated and in detail, is the King's request to his Cabinet?**

2. **What steps were taken to ascertain the views of the people of the Dominions and to explain to them the issues involved in this great crisis?**

3. **Is the British Cabinet prepared to approach the Governments of the Dominions with a frank request that they should reconsider their verdict against the King and consent to a marriage even if it involved new legislation?**

4. **Is the British Cabinet sure beyond doubt that the abdication of Edward VIII would not strike a terrible blow at the greatest institution in the world—our monarchy—and thereby cause irreparable harm?**

5. **Would the abdication of our King mean that he would be EXILED not only from Great Britain but also from every country in his Empire?**

—and Then They Will Judge!

Evening Standard

To-morrow's Weather—
Colder. SEE PAGE THREE.

Lighting-up Time
To-day 4.21 p.m.

No. 35,030   LONDON, THURSDAY, DECEMBER 3, 1936   ONE PENNY

THE KING: PREMIER ASKS M.P.s NOT TO QUESTION HIM YET

"No Constitutional Difficulty at Present"

MRS. SIMPSON REPORTED TO BE GOING ABROAD TO-NIGHT

Duke and Duchess of York, Duke of Kent Cancel Engagements

MR. BALDWIN was questioned in the House of Commons this afternoon about the issues which have arisen between the King and his Ministers concerning the King's desire to marry Mrs. Ernest Simpson.

Mr. Attlee, the Opposition Socialist leader, asked:

"May I ask the Prime Minister a question of which I have given him a private notice—whether any constitutional difficulties have arisen and whether he has any statement to make?"

Mr. Baldwin replied:

"I have no statement to make to-day. While there does not at present exist any constitutional difficulty, the situation is of such a nature as to make it inexpedient that I should be questioned about it at this stage."

Mr. Attlee.—May I ask the Prime Minister whether, in view of the anxiety reports on this matter are causing in the minds of many people, he can assure the House that he will make a statement at the earliest possible time that statement can be made?

Mr. Baldwin.—I have all that the right honourable gentleman says very much in mind.

MR. CHURCHILL.—WOULD MY RIGHT HONOURABLE FRIEND GIVE US AN ASSURANCE THAT NO IRREVOCABLE STEP WILL BE TAKEN BEFORE A FORMAL STATEMENT HAS BEEN MADE TO PARLIAMENT?

The House broke into cheers as Mr. Churchill asked this question.

Mr. Baldwin replied: "I have nothing to add to the statement that I have made at this present moment. I will consider and examine the question that my right honourable friend has asked."

Mrs. Simpson's Plans

THE London headquarters of a leading American news agency has been informed on good authority that Mrs. Simpson has decided to go abroad for a stay of some months.

It is understood that she will be leaving London to-night.

The King to-day was at Fort Belvedere. He drove there last night after Mr. Baldwin had called at Buckingham Palace.

In the morning he summoned three members of his entourage to Fort Belvedere—Major Ulick Alexander, Keeper of the Privy Purse; the Hon. Piers Legh, his Equerry; and Sir Godfrey Thomas, his assistant private secretary.

They were with the King for an hour and a half and then left by car for London.

The Duke and Duchess of York returned to London from Edinburgh

MRS. ERNEST SIMPSON—a new portrait.   (By Fayer)

to-day. They arrived at Euston at 7.30 a.m. During the morning they called at Marlborough House and saw Queen Mary.

The Duke and Duchess had engagements in London in the afternoon and evening. All were cancelled. The Duke of Kent cancelled a dinner

(Continued on PAGE FOUR)

LEADING ARTICLE—"CROWN AND CABINET"—PAGE SIX.
MRS. SIMPSON AND THE KING—PAGE SIXTEEN.
THE CONSTITUTIONAL POSITION ANALYSED—PAGE SEVEN.
PRESS COMMENT—PAGE TWO.

News Chronicle

No. 28,273   ONE PENNY   **TUESDAY, DECEMBER 8, 1936**

POSTAGE in U.K., CANADA, and NEWFOUNDLAND .. 1d. Other Places Abroad 1½d.

MRS. SIMPSON OFFERS TO WITHDRAW
"Situation Rendered Both Unhappy and Untenable"

MRS. SIMPSON.

NO WISH TO HURT OR DAMAGE THE KING OR THE THRONE

Statement Issued Last Night From Cannes Villa

[OFFICIAL]

"Mrs. Simpson throughout the last few weeks has invariably wished to avoid any action or proposal which would hurt or damage his Majesty or the Throne.

"Today her attitude is unchanged, and she is willing if such action would solve the problem to withdraw forthwith from a situation that has been rendered both unhappy and untenable."

THE above statement, signed by Mrs. Simpson, was read to an international gathering of Pressmen summoned to the Hotel Majestic at Cannes last night by Lord Brownlow, a Lord-in-Waiting to the King.

Lord Brownlow said this message was the first statement she had made to the Press on the subject either in this country or in France.

DUKE OF YORK'S SIX HOURS WITH KING

The Duke of York last night visited the King at Fort Belvedere. The Duke, who is staying with the Duchess and the two Princesses at Royal Lodge, Windsor, motored through the Great Park and entered the back gates of Fort Belvedere at 6.45.

He remained with the King until one this morning.

There was a late meeting at 10, Downing Street between Mr. Baldwin, Mr. W. T. Monckton (Attorney-General for the Duchy of Cornwall) and Sir Edward Peacock (Receiver-General to the Duchy). The two visitors arrived at 9.45 p.m. and did not leave till 11 p.m. Mr. Monckton returned to Fort Belvedere.

A shooting brake, used as a conveyance for the royal luggage, and carrying articles from Buckingham Palace to Fort Belvedere, made two trips to London last night.

FIRST RAISED WEEKS AGO

Mr. Baldwin's statement in the House, printed fully on Page Thirteen, declared that the King has not yet made up his mind. When he does it will then be for the British and Dominion Governments "to decide what advice, if any, they would feel it their duty to tender to him."

The question, added Mr. Baldwin, was first raised by the King some weeks ago, when he first informed the Premier "of his intention to marry Mrs. Simpson whenever she should be free."

WHAT WILL THE KING'S DECISION BE?

By the Political Correspondent

THE news of Mrs. Simpson's statement caused a sensation when it became known at Westminster last night. M.P.s poured into the House of Commons lobbies to discuss its significance.

Late developments in the crisis suggest, however, that the statement should not be read as a portent of the King's willingness to accept the advice of his Ministers without further demur.

The crisis is now racing to its climax, and a decision by the King one way or the other is expected shortly.

Within a comparatively few hours now the Prime Minister expects to hear his Majesty's decision.

Immediate developments are likely to be a summons to Mr. Baldwin to go to Fort Belvedere today, and probably a Cabinet meeting in the afternoon or evening. But, so far as one could learn, no arrangements had been made early this morning.

GRAVE VIEW
LAST NIGHT

Should the King still defer his decision until tonight it will doubtless be conveyed to the Prime Minister in time for the Cabinet meeting already arranged for tomorrow morning.

Last night Ministers took a grave view of the situation. Following on Mrs. Simpson's statement the Prime Minister was in touch with Fort Belvedere.

The National Executive of the Labour Party last night issued the following:—

The National Executive of the Labour Party met in the House of Commons today and gave consideration to the constitutional issues and difficulties raised by the King's desire to marry Mrs. Simpson. A general expression of views took place regarding the position as disclosed by the Prime Minister's statement to the House of Commons. But in view of the incomplete character of these statements up to date no decision was taken."

The big majority view of the meeting was opposed to the marriage pro-

TURN TO PAGE 11, COL. THREE

M.P.s CHEER BALDWIN

By the Parliamentary Correspondent

The scene in the House of Commons last night when Mr. Baldwin made his statement was a remarkable demonstration of solidity.

The repeated cheers for the Prime Minister were noticeably more wholehearted and general than in the early days of the crisis. It was clear that opinion in the House, which at one time seemed to be hesitating and divided, was now overwhelmingly behind the Government.

The cheers came from all parts of the House with equal strength. Tories, Liberals, and Labour were united in expressing their approval of the stand that had been made.

ANGER AT MR. CHURCHILL

This was made all the more apparent when Mr. Churchill, in repeating his request for an assurance that no irrevocable step would be taken till a statement had been made to Parliament on the constitutional issues involved, attempted to make a speech. Cries of "Sit down!" came from all parts of the House.

When he persisted the cries became more angry. Tories were as heated as Labour. For once he seemed to have the whole House against him.

HALF MINUTE OF CHEERS

The moment he sat down, after a final rebuke from the Speaker, Mr. George Lambert rose to make the position clear. As he could only ask a question, he put it in this form : " Is the Prime Minister aware that there is in this House a deep personal sympathy with him ? "

The cheers that followed lasted for half a minute.

The tension in the air was more noticeable than before. It was obvious that the issue was in process of being narrowed down to the simple one of whether Parliament was to be supreme. There was passion in the cheers that had not been there before.

Giant Bomber Crashes

SEATTLE, Monday.

The new Boeing bomber, the world's largest land warplane, first of a fleet of 13 being built for the United States Army, crashed while landing today after a test flight.

The damage is estimated at 10,000 dollars (£2,000).—British United Press.

ATLANTIC AIR ACE MISSING

PARIS, Monday.

JEAN MERMOZ, famous Transatlantic flier, is aboard a missing air mail liner flying across the South Atlantic.

The plane left Dakar (Senegal) at 6.35 a.m. for Port Natal (Brazil), and the last wireless message received was at 11 a.m., when it was 435 miles south-east of Dakar.

It is hoped that there has been only a breakdown of the plane's wireless.—Reuter.

A Gendarme Keeps Watch

A gendarme keeps a watchful eye on one of the maids at the Villa Lou Viei, at Cannes, where Mrs. Simpson is staying, as reporters try to interview her.

It May Be Warmer Soon

AFTER a very cold night and day, temperatures over a wide area of the country last evening were several degrees below freezing point.

But, within 36 hours, the cold spell is likely to be succeeded by a rise in temperature, amounting probably to 20 degrees.

Cold is believed to have contributed to the death yesterday of Mr. Cloke (50), of Hendon, who collapsed at the wheel after his motor-van had mounted a pavement in Kilburn and injured a woman.

Crystal Palace

£120,000 INSURANCE CHEQUE

CRYSTAL PALACE trustees received a cheque for £120,000 insurance money — yesterday, within a week of the great fire.

The money, paid by Robert Gardner, Mountain and D'Ambrumenil, Ltd., the insurance brokers, represented the full amount insured, £110,000 on the building and £10,000 on the organ.

The claim had previously been taken down in the books of the underwriters at Lloyd's with whom the insurance was placed, but the collection of cheques from each individual syndicate of underwriters concerned must necessarily take a few days, so that for the time being the brokers are financing the settlement.

Other big insurance claims paid in recent years include £1,000,000 for the loss of the Titanic in 1912, and more than £1,000,000 for the gold lost in the P. and O. liner Egypt.

New Lord-in-Waiting to the King

Last night's "Court Circular" announced that Viscount Gage had succeeded the Earl of Sefton as Lord-in-Waiting to the King.

This was the first "Court Circular" issued since last Wednesday.

BRITONS DIE IN DEFENCE OF MADRID

SHELL BURSTS UNDER CHAIR

From GEOFFREY COX
"News Chronicle" War Correspondent

MADRID, Monday.

AMONG the casualties suffered by the International Column now assisting in the defence of Madrid are the following members of the British contingent:—

Killed: Steven Yeates, G. C. Maclaurin and Fred Jones.

Wounded: R. Sims.

Yeates lived in St. Pancras, N.W., and Maclaurin was a Cambridge University mathematician and founder of the Left Bookshop in the city.

David Mackenzie, student son of Rear-Admiral Mackenzie, of Caldarven, Dumbartonshire, who had previously been reported among the fallen, is alive.

EXPLOSION

Mackenzie has had a remarkable escape from death. A shell burst beneath the chair on which he was sitting.

He was unharmed, but a man near him was wounded in the face, receiving a broken nose.

Members of the International Column report that a considerable percentage of the shells fired at the Loyalist lines have been found to be duds, filled with wood or sand.

Some contain pieces of paper inscribed with the words "Red Front," in Italian and German.

"SALUD"

One Britisher in the column said to me :

" When we hear a shell go over which does not explode we now call out 'Salud,' the Republican greeting."

Meanwhile the Government is pressing on with its preparations against the expected rebel offensive.

On the fronts all has been quiet today except for the shelling of rebel

TURN TO PAGE TWO, COL. SIX

LATEST TEST SCORE

ENGLAND 211 for 8
TEA

Hardstaff st Oldfield b Ward	20
Robins c Chipperfield b Ward	0
Allen not out	41
Extras	16

—Reuter

On a wicket showing signs of wear the English batsmen had to fight hard against excellent Australian bowling. Fagg was brilliantly stumped by Oldfield; Hammond stepped back on his wicket when parrying a " shooter" from Ward, and Ames had only reached nine when he was sent back.

Ward at this stage had taken the wickets of Fagg and Hammond for 12 runs.

Leyland, having dug himself in, defended dourly, but was out at 144 to a great catch by Bradman. At 205 there was another blow to England, Hardstaff falling victim to Oldfield and Ward—the bowler's fifth wicket.

Full Description and Scoreboard on Page Three

ABDICATION OF EDWARD VIII:

Daily Mail

NORTHCLIFFE HOUSE, LONDON, E.C.4.　Telephone : Central 6000.

11th December, 1936.　346th Day.

THE KING HAS CHOSEN

WE have passed through the most anxious and astounding day in the history of our Empire. At its close no longer did King Edward the Eighth hold the most glorious heritage that ever fell to the lot of a ruler. His "final and irrevocable" abdication fills every heart with an overwhelming sense of tragedy. Indeed, the event far transcends man's capacity to realise it and all that it implies.

The King's decision was stated in an historic message, such as no English Sovereign has ever before penned. It was read by the Speaker to a hushed and deeply moved House of Commons. "The burden which constantly rests upon the shoulders of a Sovereign is so heavy that it can only be borne in circumstances different from those in which I now find myself," declared the King.

The voice of contention is stilled as the Empire sadly reflects on its great loss. The King's subjects had hoped against hope that the Throne would for many years be filled by a Sovereign so well equipped to lead a great Empire through the difficult days that lie ahead.

Yet the whole Empire is now aware that King Edward has reached his decision only after heart-searching reflection. As far back as November 16 he informed Mr. Baldwin of his intention to marry Mrs. Simpson and that he was "prepared to go."

"This Heavy Task"

When later his proposal for a morganatic marriage was rejected by the British Government after consultation with the Dominions, the King's determination became unshakable.

To no great figure in history has an issue so momentous presented itself in a form so stark and uncompromising. King Edward was faced by alternatives each awe-inspiring in its implications. He could renounce the Throne or the woman he wished to marry.

The appeals addressed to him from all parts of his loyal Empire he was led by his conscience to reject, deeply though he appreciated the spirit which prompted them. He felt that "I can no longer discharge this heavy task with efficiency or with satisfaction to myself."

Remembering his past inestimable services, both as Prince of Wales and during the few short months he has been our King, our hearts cannot but be heavy as we watch him withdraw, followed by the sympathy and regrets of his former subjects, into private life.

The thanks of the Empire are due to Mr. Baldwin for the efforts he made to persuade the King to remain, and for the unhurried consideration which the whole Cabinet gave to the King's affairs and their splendid conduct throughout the crisis. The country will share the Prime Minister's belief that where he failed no other could have succeeded; but nothing will assuage the universal disappointment that the King was unable to respond to the entreaties not only of Mr. Baldwin but of all his subjects.

Our New Ruler

By the Act of Settlement, and as the King's Message of Abdication makes clear, the Throne devolves on the Sovereign's eldest brother, Albert Frederick Arthur George, the Duke of York, who will probably elect to be known as George VI.

At the Coronation, which, it is understood, will be held as already arranged on May 12, the people will seize the opportunity of demonstrating their loyal and abiding affection for their new monarch.

Throughout the great realms to the governance of which the new King is called there will be an instant rally to his side.

It is a supreme and onerous task which he is suddenly summoned to undertake.

Like his predecessor, he has worked indefatigably for the good of his nation and has, in his own words, "travelled over the vast extent of our Empire." Like his predecessor, again, he saw front-line service in the war, fighting for his country first with the Grand Fleet at Jutland, that "battle of the mist," and then with the Royal Air Force in France.

At his side will sit a gracious and active consort, whose warm interest in social work of all kinds has earned the country's admiration.

In this hour of momentous change the heart of the nation will go out instinctively to the Queen-Mother. Once more in a period of great national stress she has stood forth as the pattern of high courage and nobility.

Long live the King!

One of the most recent portraits of King Edward in naval uniform.

This happy picture of the Duke and Duchess of York was taken during the Jubilee celebrations in May last year.

"I Have Determined To Renounce The Throne..."

AT 3.35 yesterday afternoon Mr. Baldwin, the Prime Minister, entered the House of Commons. Advancing to the Bar of the House, and bowing, he announced:

"A message from his Majesty the King, Sir, signed by his Majesty's own hand..."

The Prime Minister then bowing twice more presented the message to the Speaker, who read it out as follows:

"After long and anxious consideration I have determined to renounce the Throne to which I succeeded on the death of my father, and I am now communicating this my final and irrevocable decision.

"Realising as I do the gravity of this step, I can only hope that I shall have the understanding of my peoples in the decision I have taken and the reasons which have led me to take it.

"I will not enter now into my private feelings, but I would beg that it should be remembered that the burden which constantly rests upon the shoulders of a Sovereign is so heavy that it can only be borne in circumstances different from those in which I now find myself.

"I conceive that I am not overlooking the duty that rests on me to place in the forefront the public interest when I declare that I am conscious that I can no longer discharge this heavy task with efficiency or with satisfaction to myself.

"I have accordingly this morning executed an Instrument of Abdication in the terms following:

"'I, Edward the Eighth, of Great Britain, Ireland, and the British Dominions beyond the Seas, King, Emperor of India, do hereby declare My irrevocable determination to renounce the Throne for Myself and for My descendants, and My desire that effect should be given to this Instrument of Abdication immediately.

"'In token whereof I have hereunto set My hand this tenth day of December nineteen hundred and thirty-six, in the presence of the witnesses whose signatures are subscribed.

(Signed) EDWARD, R.I.'

"My execution of this instrument has been witnessed by my three brothers, Their Royal Highnesses the Duke of York, the Duke of Gloucester, and the Duke of Kent.

"I deeply appreciate the spirit which has actuated the appeals which have been made to me to take a different decision and I have, before reaching my final determination, most fully pondered over them.

"But my mind is made up.

"Moreover further delay cannot but be most injurious to the peoples whom I have tried to serve as Prince of Wales and as King and whose future happiness and prosperity are the constant wish of my heart.

"I take my leave of them in the confident hope that the course which I have thought it right to follow is that which is best for the stability of the Throne and Empire and the happiness of my people.

"I am deeply sensible of the consideration which they have always extended to me both before and after my accession to the Throne and which I know they will extend in full measure to my successor.

"I am most anxious that there should be no delay of any kind in giving effect to the instrument which I have executed and that all necessary steps should be taken immediately to secure that my lawful successor my brother His Royal Highness the Duke of York should ascend the Throne."

The Text Issued

Last Night of

THE BILL OF ABDICATION

THE text of the Abdication Bill was published last night. It is as follows:

A BILL to

Give effect to his Majesty's declaration of abdication ; and for purposes connected therewith.

WHEREAS His Majesty by His Royal Message of the tenth day of December in this present year has been pleased to declare that He is irrevocably determined to renounce the Throne for Himself and His descendants, and has for that purpose executed the Instrument of Abdication set out in the Schedule to this Act, and has signified His desire that effect thereto should be given immediately :

And whereas, following upon the communication to His Dominions of His Majesty's said declaration and desire, the Dominion of Canada pursuant to the provisions of Section Four of the Statute of Westminster, 1931, has requested and consented to the enactment of this Act, and the Commonwealth of Australia, the Dominion of New Zealand, and the Union of South Africa have assented thereto :

Be it therefore enacted by the King's most Excellent Majesty, by and with the advice and consent of the Lords Spiritual and Temporal and Commons, in this present Parliament assembled, and by the authority of the same, as follows :

　1 . . . (1) Immediately upon the Royal Assent being signified to this Act the Instrument of Abdication executed by his present Majesty on the tenth day of December nineteen hundred and thirty-six set out in the schedule to this Act shall have effect, and thereupon his Majesty shall cease to be King and there shall be a demise of the Crown and accordingly the member of the Royal Family then next in succession to the Throne shall succeed, thereto and to all the rights privileges and dignities thereunto belonging.

　(2) His Majesty, his issue, if any, and the descendants of that issue, shall not after his Majesty's abdication have any right, title or interest in or to the succession to the Throne, and Section One of the Act of Settlement shall be construed accordingly.

　(3) The Royal Marriages Act, 1772, shall not apply to his Majesty after his abdication nor to the issue, if any, of his Majesty or the descendants of that issue.

　2 . . . This Act may be cited as His Majesty's Declaration of Abdication Act, 1936.

There follows the Schedule of the Bill which repeats the phrasing of the Instrument of Abdication included in the King's message printed in this page.

1938

Peace for a Time

The Munich Crisis

Anyone who bought a newspaper in the 'thirties, even if he aspired no higher than to snap up the newest mackintosh offer or to qualify for the latest 'free' insurance with which the popular papers attempted to whip up their circulation in the desperate race for The Two Million, could hardly fail to be aware of a man called Hitler or identify his scrubbing-brush moustache whenever it popped up in the cartoons. But what kind of man he thought this Hitler was, and whether his motives were megalomanic or merely misunderstood, would have been coloured a variety of hues depending on which newspaper he took. Anyone who had read Lloyd George's first-hand impressions in *The Daily Express* in 1936 might well have cherished a picture of a 'born leader of men. A magnetic, dynamic personality with a resolute will and a dauntless heart', nothing less in fact than 'the George Washington of Germany' (though, to be fair, even *The Daily Express* baulked a bit at Ll.G. not mentioning his Jew-baiting or his persecution of the Calvinists). A reader of *The Daily Mirror*, on the other hand, would have been convinced the man was 'a political gangster', 'a blackmailer' and ultimately 'a maniac'.

From accounts of Lord Rothermere's fire-side chats with him in *The Daily Mail*, the Führer emerged as a man who simply wanted to make friends with Britain. Lord Kemsley, the proprietor of *The Sunday Times* and *The Daily Sketch*, also believed that all that was required for a proper understanding was a man-to-man talk (which he was continually trying to obtain). To *The Daily Herald* he was the corner-stone of 'the most powerful and most brutal machinery of oppression which has ever been created'. To H. G. Wells writing in the *News Chronicle* he was a certifiable lunatic and should be put away.

None of this, however, was immediately relevant to the editorial dilemma with which the newspapers were faced, with increasing urgency as one crisis followed hard on another: what was the answer to Herr Hitler? In 1935 the Saar was restored to Germany, and within a week he had repudiated the disarmament clauses of the Versailles Treaty. In 1936 his armies had marched into the de-militarized zone of the Rhineland unopposed, and he had denounced yet more clauses of the Versailles Treaty. In 1937 he seemed to calm down, renouncing to his Reichstag in January any further territorial claims—though the pace of German re-armament did not slacken for an instant, and a hate campaign against the London *Times* was briefly waged in the German Press (in protest against *The Times*' assertion that it was the Luftwaffe that had bombed Guernica).

But if the leader-writers approached 1938 in a happier frame of mind because Hitler appeared (to *The Manchester Guardian* at least) to be withdrawing from active politics, then they failed to sense the calm before the storm. On March 11 the German juggernaut rolled into Austria, not simply unopposed but to a tumult of welcome from the formidable Nazi party already there. The British press was more horrified at Hitler's way of doing it than by the fact of his having done it. 'The Rape of Austria' *The News Chronicle* called it, having already incurred the Führer's wrath with its 'lying and libellous allegations' in February that 40,000 German troops were massing on the Austrian frontier. 'Who's lying now?' it wanted to know. But the invasion was a fact now, and no paper was prepared to make a war out of it. *The Observer* consoled itself with the thought that from Munich to Vienna 'they drink the same beer. Naturally they want to be one people'.

Inside the British Cabinet the policy of 'appeasement' in Europe was already in its first flowering, now that the hard-liner Anthony Eden had been replaced by Lord Halifax as Foreign Secretary. It was Lord Halifax who the

CLASSIFIED RESULTS

The Premier Havana Cigar BOLIVAR CORONAS

Evening Standard

FINAL NIGHT

Brandy… MARTELL has so many uses. With a bottle in the cupboard you've a CELLAR in the house!

To-morrow's Weather—No important change. See PAGE THREE.

Lighting-up Time To-day 4.42 p.m.

No. 35,323 LONDON. SATURDAY, NOVEMBER 13, 1937 ONE PENNY

Hitler Ready for Truce

NO COLONIES DEMAND FOR TEN YEARS

If He Is Given Free Hand In Central Europe

From a Diplomatic Correspondent

THE PRIME MINISTER HAS ASKED THE FOREIGN SECRETARY, MR. ANTHONY EDEN, TO PREPARE DURING THIS WEEK-END THE GOVERNMENT'S INSTRUCTIONS FOR LORD HALIFAX, WHO IS TO MEET HERR HITLER AND GENERAL GOERING IN BERLIN NEXT WEEK.

I am able to give certain indications of the attitude of both the German and British Governments towards the coming talks.

The British Government have information from Berlin that Herr Hitler is ready, if he receives the slightest encouragement, to offer to Great Britain a ten-years "truce" on the Colonial issue. During the "truce" the question of Colonies for Germany would not be raised.

In return for this agreement Herr Hitler would expect the British Government to leave him a free hand in Central Europe.

As the Chancellor of the Exchequer informed the House of Commons yesterday, the visit of Lord Halifax to Berlin is "entirely private and unofficial."

But the news that Herr Hitler desires to avail himself of an informal conversation with a member of the British Cabinet for discussing Anglo-German relations, as well as Germany's plans in Central Europe, make it necessary to furnish Lord Halifax with relevant instructions.

A Free Vote in Austria

It has become known in London that Herr Hitler's idea of a "free hand" in Central Europe is that Great Britain shall not intervene if—

(1) Germany presses for free elections, or a plebiscite, in Austria.

(2) Germany presents a demand to Czechoslovakia for the immediate recognition of the right of the German minority in that country to administrative autonomy within the State and to cultural unity with the people of the German Reich.

Herr Hitler believes that a free vote in Austria would mean a Nazi regime in Vienna, and that political autonomy for the Germans in Czechoslovakia would paralyse Russian influences in Prague.

He attaches most importance, for the moment, to the solution of the Austrian problem in a sense favourable to Germany.

The Rome-Berlin Axis

It is taken for granted that a definite offer by Herr Hitler of terms for improved relations between Germany and Great Britain will be accompanied by a long explanation of his foreign policy, as expressed now in the Rome-Berlin axis, and in the anti-Communist pact just concluded between Germany, Italy and Japan.

That will furnish an occasion for Lord Halifax to probe the essential facts with regard to the true nature of the relations between Rome and Berlin.

Herr Hitler will find that the British Government are anxious to discover the exact extent and nature of Germany's demands for a lasting settlement of pending issues. But he will also be told that the British Government are not prepared to give away things which are not at their disposal.

At the same time, Lord Halifax will explain to Herr Hitler:

(1) The particularly close relationship in which this country finds itself to France;

(2) The desire of the British Government for a swift completion of a new Western Pact, as a guarantee for the security and *status quo* in that part of Europe; and

(3) The belief in London that international problems concerning Europe are best discussed and settled within the framework of the Covenant of the League of Nations.

German Press comment—PAGE TWELVE.

A giant figure of Atlas, which is to be erected in Capetown, being removed from the Clapham, S.W., foundry where it was cast.

SWEPT INTO SEA BY SHIP'S WASH —RESCUED

MR. A. D. REED, aged 62, of Frant-road, Tunbridge Wells, was fishing off the rocks near Newhaven breakwater to-day when he was swept into the sea by the wash of the mailboat Versailles, which was leaving the harbour for Dieppe.

Mr Reed was knocked down and dashed against the rocks. The second wash took him into deep water, 15 yards from the breakwater.

Seeing the man's plight, Mr. F. C. Brown, stationmaster at Lewes, dived into the icy water with a rope round his arm. He was forced to return. With assistance he again went to the aid of the drowning man and managed to bring him ashore.

Bulbs Instead of Onions in Soup

DAFFODIL bulbs put in soup in error instead of onions caused nine scholars to be taken violently ill yesterday at the village school at Filleigh, near South Molton, Devon.

Two senior scholars prepared the soup.

The nine who were ill had to be taken home by motorcar. The medical officer of health, Dr. W. G. Mortimer, was called in

FOOTBALL RESULTS

(Half-time scores in parentheses)

LEAGUE—Division I.

ARSENAL	(0) 1	West Brom. A.	(1) 1
Blackpool	(0) 0	Birmingham	(0) 3
Bolton Wand.	(1) 1	Stoke City	(0) 0
BRENTFORD	(3) 3	Middlesbrough	(1) 3
Derby County	(1) 2	Leeds United	(0) 2
Everton	(2) 4	**CHELSEA**	(0) 1
Huddersfield T.	(2) 2	Portsmouth	(0) 0
Leicester City	(0) 1	Preston N.E.	(0) 0
Manchester C.	(1) 1	Liverpool	(3) 3
Sunderland	(2) 2	Grimsby Town	(1) 2
Wolverhampton	(1) 1	**CHARLTON A.**	(1) 1

LEAGUE—Division II.

Aston Villa	(0) 0	Burnley	(0) 0
Blackburn R.	(0) 2	Newcastle U.	(1) 1
Bradford	(1) 1	Bury	(1) 1
Chesterfield	(1) 1	Manchester U.	(5) 7
FULHAM	(0) 0	Barnsley	(0) 0
Norwich City	(1) 2	**TOTTENHAM**	(1) 1
Plymouth A.	(0) 2	Stockport C.	(0) 1
Sheffield Wed.	(1) 4	Luton Town	(0) 0
Southampton	(1) 2	Notts Forest	(0) 0
Swansea Town	(0) 3	Sheffield U.	(1) 5
WEST HAM	(0) 0	Coventry City	(0) 0

HIGHEST SCORE

(Football League and Scottish League, Division I.)

7—Manchester United.

HIGHEST AGGREGATE

8—Chesterfield 1, Manchester United 7.
Swansea 3, Sheffield United 5.
Morton 2, Hamilton 6.
Partick 6, Ayr U. 2.

LEAGUE—Division III. (South)

Aldershot	(0) 0	Northampton	(1) 2
Bristol City	(0) 2	**Q.P. RANGERS**	(0) 0
CRYSTAL P.	(1) 4	Torquay Utd.	(0) 1
Exeter City	(0) 2	Cardiff City	(1) 1
Gillingham	(0) 0	Bournemouth	(0) 2
MILLWALL	(0) 2	Bristol Rovers	(1) 1
Newport C.	(1) 2	Southend U.	(0) 0
Notts County	(0) 1	**CLAPTON O.**	(0) 0
Reading	(0) 3	Mansfield T.	(1) 2
Swindon T.	(0) 1	Walsall	(1) 1
Watford	(0) 1	Brighton	(0) 1

LEAGUE—Division III. (North)

Barrow	(0) 1	York City	(2) 2
Crewe Alex.	(1) 1	Tranmere R.	(0) 0
Darlington	(1) 3	Carlisle Utd.	(0) 1
Gateshead	(2) 3	Chester	(0) 1
Hartlepools U.	(1) 1	Southport	(0) 2
Hull City	(3) 4	Rochdale	(0) 1
Lincoln City	(1) 2	Doncaster R.	(0) 2
New Brighton	(1) 2	Rotherham	(1) 3
Oldham Ath.	(0) 1	Accrington S.	(0) 0
Port Vale	(0) 0	Halifax Town	(0) 2
Wrexham	(2) 2	Bradford City	(1) 1

MINOR INTER-LEAGUE MATCH

Central League	(2) 2	London Com.	(0) 3

SCOTTISH LEAGUE—Division I.

Arbroath	(1) 1	Rangers	(0) 1
Clyde	(1) 2	Aberdeen	(0) 1
Dundee	(0) 1	Falkirk	(2) 4
Hearts	(0) 2	Queen's Park	(0) 0
Kilmarnock	(1) 1	Queen of South	(0) 1
Morton	(1) 2	Hamilton A.	(5) 6
Motherwell	(1) 3	St. Mirren	(1) 2
Partick Thistle	(4) 6	Ayr United	(2) 2
St. Johnstone	(1) 2	Hibernian	(0) 0
Third Lanark	(0) 1	Celtic	(1) 1

See also Back Page & Stop Press Columns

News Chronicle

No. 28,662　ONE PENNY　　SATURDAY, MARCH 12, 1938　　• • •　POSTAGE IN U.K., CANADA, AND NEWFOUNDLAND .. 1d. OTHER PLACES ABROAD 1½d.

Hitler Marches Troops Into Austria: Fuehrer's Deputy Flies To Vienna

BERLIN ORDERS SCHUSCHNIGG OUT OF OFFICE

Nation Told Not To Resist Invaders

HITLER INVADED AUSTRIA LAST NIGHT. HE THUS DROVE FROM OFFICE CHANCELLOR KURT VON SCHUSCHNIGG, WHO HAD PLANNED TO HOLD ON SUNDAY A PLEBISCITE TO DECIDE WHETHER THE NATION STOOD FOR A "FREE, GERMAN AND INDEPENDENT STATE."

At 7 p.m. Schuschnigg went to the microphone in Vienna and broadcast:

"The German Government sent President Miklas an ultimatum that unless my Government fell in with the proposals of the German Government, German troops would march into Austria.

"I declare before all the world that reports of workers' unrest in Austria, and of blood flowing in the streets, are fabrications from A to Z.

"SUPERIOR FORCE"

"The Federal President asked me to inform the Austrian people that we yield to superior force. Because we did not wish to spill German blood we ordered the Austrian Army to offer no resistance and to retire.

"General Schilhavsky has been entrusted with the command of the Army and will give all necessary further orders.

"So I take farewell in this hour of the Austrian people with a German word and a greeting—'God protect Austria.'"

HERR ENDER

Suggested As New Chancellor

DR. ENDER, who at one time last night was suggested as successor to Schuschnigg, was Chancellor of the Coalition Government in 1930-31, when an Austro-German Customs union was attempted.

As Minister with Portfolio in the Dollfuss Cabinet, he was the creator of the new Constitu-

MUNICH IN FERMENT AS NAZIS MOVE

Reservists Called Up, Cars Seized

From Our Own Correspondent

MUNICH, Friday.

MUNICH woke this morning to find itself in a state of mobilisation and to read the first news of Dr. von Schuschnigg's proposal to hold a plebiscite on Austrian independence.

Early in the day large detachments of regular troops and units of Brown Shirts and Black Guards were seen driving through the streets, curiously enough in a northerly direction.

Dispatch riders were racing along, breaking all the rules of the road.

Reservists, especially those with fast cars, were called up and their cars were commandeered.

The municipal buses were also seized and the "Motor Caravan Journalists"—a fleet of lorries with most elaborate wireless, ambulance and complete equipment—left their garages before daybreak.

Drone of Planes

Very few taxis remained in the city and private business is greatly hampered by the absence of conveyances. The noise of aeroplanes was incessant.

Inquiries in official quarters were futile, with the exception of a vague statement by the police that a large-scale transport alarm practice was taking place.

The headquarters of the Munich

MINISTERS READY IF NEEDED

The Political Correspondent writes: Cabinet Ministers had not received any instruction from Downing Street last night to "stand by" in case the Austro-German situation developed into a serious clash.

Most of them, however will be within easy reach of Downing Street, should a meeting of Ministers be necessary at any time during the week-end.

The Prime Minister has gone to Chequers. He will be constantly informed of all developments.

LATE NEWS

BRITAIN'S PROTEST

On the Government's instructions, the British Ambassador in Berlin (Sir Nevile Henderson) last night called upon the German Government and, in reference to the contents of the second German ultimatum to Austria, registered a protest in the strongest possible terms against "such a use of coercion, backed by force, against an independent State, in order to create a situation incompatible with its national independence."

"Such action," it was pointed out, "is bound to produce the gravest reactions, of which it is impossible to foretell the issue."

---

previous November had been dispatched to see Hitler (he was going there anyway, said *The Daily Telegraph*, in his capacity as a master of foxhounds to visit a hunting exhibition) to assure him that on European questions Britain was prepared to countenance 'alterations . . . through the course of peaceful evolution'. The discussions came to nothing partly because the German leader was still cross at *The Evening Standard* for scooping the news of the visit and suggesting that Hitler was prepared to trade a truce on colonial issues in return for 'a free hand in Central Europe'. But they did convince him that Britain wasn't going to interfere.

After Austria, most of the papers saw very clearly that the next target would be Czechoslovakia: three million 'Sudeten' Germans lived within its borders and already there had been riots there. The Czech Government was certainly making some effort to redress Sudeten grievances, but it was getting no support from the rest of Europe. Under Geoffrey Dawson, its editor with one short break since 1912, *The Times* was accepted rightly or wrongly as being the echo of Whitehall policy and, occasionally, its unofficial spokesman. Dawson might consider his paper truly independent in spirit, but his own closeness with the National Government and Chamberlain, in particular, gave people quite the opposite impression. Thus, when on September 7 *The Times* ran its notorious editorial 'Nuremberg and Aussig' it was analysed minutely, as giving a clue to the Government's private attitude towards Czechoslovakia. The

sentence which caused all the subsequent excitement read: '. . . it might be worthwhile for the Czechoslovak Government to consider whether they should exclude altogether the project, which has found favour in some quarters, of making a more homogeneous state by the secession of that fringe of alien populations who are contiguous to the nation with which they are united by race'. Behind all the pompous circumlocution, this was clearly advice to the Czechs to hand over the Sudetenland and not make a fuss (which was how it was read in Berlin and Prague, at any rate).

In spite of *The Times'* own protestations that it was not collaborating, the Foreign Office hastened to issue a disclaimer (which only made things worse). Nevertheless when Chamberlain underlined the crisis by making his first-ever plane journey on September 15, to see Hitler personally at Berchtesgaden, he went with just such an appeasing posture as *The Times* had suggested. On the 18th the French and British Governments formally proposed to Prague that Germany's terms be accepted. By the 22nd however Germany's terms had suddenly become considerably more stringent, demanding a settlement which no-one could doubt would lead to the ultimate disintegration of the Czechoslovak state. 'Only a miracle could avert war now' declared Mr. Chamberlain, and ordered the country to prepare itself for war. Thousands of gas masks were hastily distributed, trenches were dug in London parks and anti-aircraft guns exhumed (44 were found), evacuation plans for schoolchildren were con-

cocted and air-raid sirens tested. The Navy and part of the Auxiliary Air Force was mobilised, and many of the newspapers began to take on that slightly unreal aspect of consciously trying to 'do their bit' — no less alarming for all that.

When Chamberlain announced to a cheering, sobbing House of Commons on the 28th that he was going back to Munich for a last-ditch appeal to Hitler, the press breathed a collective sigh of relief, the more hopeful claiming 'the lamps of Europe were alight again', the less optimistic telling him to 'stand firm'. Likewise when the Premier landed at Heston airport on the 30th waving a piece of paper containing Hitler's illegible signature and recommending everyone to go home and sleep quietly in their beds, the papers were virtually unanimous in their enthusiasm (the one exception was the left-wing *Reynolds News*). On Lord Beaverbrook's order *The Daily Express* was moved to declare that 'Britain will not be involved in a European war this year, or next year either'. It has been *The Daily Express's* cruel fate to have been reminded of its untimely prediction ever since. Its real mistake, however, was to persevere with these sentiments long after the general euphoria had subsided in the rest of the press.

Some papers, like *The News Chronicle* ('. . . that price is the sacrifice of a small and noble people'), faced up to' the reckoning soon — others later, like *The Sunday Times* whose immediate reaction had been 'to go home to take all my books on Europe, place them in my garden trench and have it filled in'. In little

WEDNESDAY, SEPTEMBER 28, 1938

Daily Mirror

No. 10862   Registered at the G.P.O. as a Newspaper   ONE PENNY

EVERY MAN AND WOMAN MUST ACT

The call for 25,000 women. ★
. . . This is a member of the
Women's Auxiliary Terri-
torial Service, which is to be
formed to release men from
non-combatant duties. 2,000
officers and 23,000 members
are needed immediately.
See story on page 3.

MR. CHAMBERLAIN'S BROADCAST SPEECH
LAST NIGHT, REPORTED IN FULL ON
THE BACK PAGE, MADE IT CLEAR THAT
ONLY A MIRACLE CAN NOW AVERT A WAR.

" If I were convinced," he said, " that any nation
had made up its mind to dominate the world by fear
of its force. I should feel it should be resisted."

These were the restrained words of statesmanship.
The nation must realise what they mean.

**They mean that we are on the eve of war. Every
man and every woman must at once put himself and
herself at the disposal of the State.**

Face the facts without fear. Answer now the call
to Britain's defence.

To-day the women of England have a new chance to serve.

**The War Office needs 25,000 women—the first division
of the new women's army—for non-combatant work with the
Army and the R.A.F. Every woman from eighteen to fifty-
five is eligible.**

" I ask you to offer your services," said the Premier.

**ANSWER THAT CALL NOW. THE NEED IS URGENT.
BRITAIN NEEDS YOU.**

The British Cabinet met last night to
discuss the reply brought from Germany
by Sir Horace Wilson, the Premier's envoy.
That answer is known to be negative.

The meeting lasted ninety minutes. M.
Corbin, French Ambassador, was at the Foreign
Office at the time and in Paris Sir Eric Phipps,
Britain's Ambassador, was with the French
Foreign Minister.

IN BERLIN LAST NIGHT IT WAS KNOWN
THAT UNLESS THE CZECHS GIVE HITLER
THE ANSWER HE WANTS BY 2 P.M. TO-DAY
THE GERMAN ARMY WILL MOBILISE.

Two courses now remain to be taken by the
powers who want peace. They are:—

1. A direct appeal to Hitler from President
(Continued on back page)

Germans Mobilise

It was announced on the Berlin Radio last night (says the Exchange) that unless Czechoslovakia agreed to accept the terms of the Hitler Memorandum by 2
P.m. to-day Germany would mobilise to-morrow.

A Rome message from the British United Press quotes an " authoritative
quarter " as saying that Mussolini expects that events will develop within two
or three days at the most.

The Italian War Ministry last night formally denied rumours that Italy was
ordering a general mobilisation. It is believed, although not confirmed, that
some specialists have been recalled, says Reuter.

Hungary began to mobilise yesterday, says Reuter.

FLEET TO BE MOBILISED AS "PRECAUTION"

THE Secretary of the Admiralty announced last night that it had been
decided to mobilise the Fleet purely as a
precautionary measure.

The following are the instructions which will
be issued this morning immediately after the
King has issued the royal proclamation calling
up naval reservists.

Royal Fleet Reserve, Class B.

All men in the British Isles belonging to the
Royal Fleet Reserve. Class B. are to proceed
to their depots on Wednesday morning without
waiting for individual summonses.

Class B. men allocated to Submarine Service
are to proceed direct to Fort Blockhouse.
Gosport.

This order applies to members of the Royal
Fleet Reserve Class B only

Notices at Ports

Men of the Royal Naval Reserve should consult the notices posted at the ports.

All other Naval reservists and pensioners will
receive individual summonses in the event of
their services being required.

Officers should await individual notice of
appointment, which they will receive as soon as
their services are required.

THE QUEEN BACK TO-DAY

The Queen, who spent the night at Balmoral
after launching the Queen Elizabeth at Glasgow
yesterday, will return to London this evening to
be by the King's side

---

over a week the American press seemed to
have undergone a remarkable change of heart.
Whereas the first news of the Anglo-French
proposals for Czechoslovakia had been greeted
with a chorus of 'weakness' and 'betrayal', now
Chamberlain was being hailed as 'the peacemaker'. On the 20th, although the *Los Angeles
Times* had pointed out that the U.S. was by no
means absolved of moral responsibility 'since
Czechoslovakia was practically dictated by
President Wilson', it had been the considered
opinion of *The Boston Herald* that 'the statesmen of London and Paris . . . are in danger of
unleashing a giant who may stride through their
homes, destroy their empires and make them
one with Nineveh and Tyre'. *The San Francisco
Chronicle* had felt 'the Czechs rightly complain
that they have been betrayed' and *The Cincinnati Inquirer* that 'France and Britain have
bought peace at tremendous cost'. But a week
later the seriousness of the crisis appeared to
have sunk in, rendering Roosevelt's personal
appeal to Hitler a practical, even a popular,
move. Determination to 'stay out' was no less

strongly-voiced, but now there was a spontaneous surge of sympathy for what the Prime
Minister had tried to do. As *The Boston Herald*
said: 'the informality, understatement and quiet
seriousness of Chamberlain's radio address is
typical of the best in British statesmanship'. As
far as *The Daily Oklahoma* was concerned
'Chamberlain stands out today as the greatest
man in Europe, a man who was willing to
humble himself beyond any precedent to avoid
the destruction of another generation of fine
young men in the trenches of Europe'.

But perhaps the strongest lesson learnt
during the Munich crisis was how woefully
ill-prepared for war Britain was. Even the
isolationist papers had long been calling for
faster re-armament (Rothermere had even
commissioned a new plane to be designed at
his own expense — which later went into
production for the RAF as the Blenheim
Bomber). Now they were grateful there was a
little more time to do something about it. But
how long, no-one knew.

Daily Express

WORLD'S LARGEST DAILY SALE

No. 11,970   Friday, September 30, 1938

The Daily Express declares that Britain will not be involved in a European war this year, or next year either

| Ultimatum withdrawn at Munich | # PEACE! | Cession less than Hitler plan |

AGREEMENT SIGNED AT 12.30 a.m. TODAY

German troops may go in tomorrow: Then occupation gradually: No plebiscites

DUCE DRAWS FRONTIER

IT IS PEACE

AT 12.30 A.M. TODAY HITLER, MUSSOLINI, CHAMBERLAIN AND DALADIER SIGNED AT MUNICH A FOUR POWER AGREEMENT WHICH SOLVES THE CZECHO-SLOVAK PROBLEM.

When Mr. Chamberlain returned to his hotel at 1.35 a.m., after a series of conferences which started before noon yesterday and continued almost without interruption. he said: "Everything is fixed up now." He is returning to London today.

Tomorrow morning, October 1, the date named in Hitler's famous memorandum, German troops will cross the Czech frontier. But instead of steel helmets they will wear forage caps, and they will march in quietly to begin a progressive occupation of Sudetenland.

An international commission will define the new frontier; an international force, including British, French and Italian troops, will police the areas to be surrendered to Germany.

By October 31 the new frontier should be finally fixed and all cause for friction removed.

SUBMITTED TO PRAGUE

That is the plan; the only doubt was that the Czecho-Slovak Government might not be able to accept the plan in time. In this case London diplomats hope that Hitler might be willing to extend the time limit until Sunday.

Writing at 2 a.m., the Daily Express Political Correspondent says:—

"Proposals have been submitted to the Czecho-Slovak Government on these lines:—

"Cession of the most densely populated Sudeten German areas within ten days;

"Substitution of negotiation for plebiscite as a preliminary to cession of other areas. Parties to the negotiations to be France, Italy, Germany and Czecho-Slovakia. Time limit will be set for the conclusion of the negotiations.

"Germany will guarantee integrity of new Czecho-Slovak frontier."

AREA NOT SO LARGE

Meanwhile there is no question of Germany ordering a general mobilisation, as threatened earlier in the week.

Mussolini is described as being particularly elated as he ordered his special train to return to Rome at midnight. A German spokesman said that a revised line of demarcation between

Germans and Czechs in Hitler's map of Czecho-Slovakia was drawn by Mussolini himself.

The area to be surrendered is not quite so large as was demanded by Hitler at Godesberg.

Nazi Storm Troopers formed a cordon in the lobby of Mr. Chamberlain's Munich hotel last night. There were shouts of "Heil Chamberlain" and "Hoch Chamberlain" from the Germans when the Premier returned from the conference for dinner.

Field-Marshal Goering, in the uniform of his rank, raised a big laugh in the lobby when he strolled over to the French Premier and slapped him on the back, saying:—

"Well, Herr Daladier, you had better stay here for the October Festival."

The "Oktoberfest" is Germany's great annual beer festival, which began four days ago and is still in progress.

This is the Peace Plan

By GUY EDEN.

THIS, I understand, was the peace plan taken to Munich for discussion between Mr. Neville Chamberlain, Herr Hitler, Signor Mussolini, and M. Daladier, the French Premier:—

1. Handing over to Germany after tomorrow of "token" areas of the Sudetenland;

2. Appointment of an international commission to draw the new border-line between Germany and Czecho-Slovakia, and to see that the transfer of populations—Czechs to Czech territory and Germans to German—is carried out fairly and quietly;

3. Demobilisation of the "abnormal" rival armies on each side of the frontier, and the appointment of an international force of British, French, Italian, Belgian and Dutch troops to take over control of the areas scheduled to be ceded to Germany;

4. On stated dates, the Germans to occupy the areas under the control of the international force, the Czech troops having previously withdrawn from the areas.

One series of districts, it is suggested, should be given up on October 15, the second on October 31;

5. Formal settlement, on October 31, of the new

PAGE TWO, COL. ONE

THE PRIME MINISTER MEETS MUSSOLINI AT MUNICH. Picture wired last night: see also Back Page.

LATEST
CENTRAL 8000

Weather: cooler (see page 11)

HE MAY BE SIR NEVILLE

Daily Express Staff Reporter

MR. NEVILLE CHAMBERLAIN is likely to be offered a Knighthood of the Garter—the highest honour the King can bestow—in recognition of his services to the cause of peace.

Mr. Chamberlain's half-brother, Sir Austen, was made a K.G. for his work in bringing about the Locarno Treaty.

The honour carries with it the title "Sir." Although Mr. Chamberlain would probably prefer to remain "plain Mr." as his brother wished to do, it has been ruled that the title must go with the honour.

Sir Henry Campbell-Bannerman, the Liberal Prime Minister who relinquished office in 1908, was the last knighted Premier.

Premier's wife mobbed

CROWDS of women, rejoicing at the news from Munich, cheered Mrs. Neville Chamberlain for several minutes last night as she left St. Michael's Church, Chester-square, W., where the Archbishop of Canterbury had addressed a broadcast service.

The big crowd that waited outside the church to cheer her had grown to several thousands by the time her car had arrived.

As she stepped into her car people surged round cheering continuously.

Women with tears in their eyes clambered on the running-board, grasped her hand and congratulated her on the good news.

Mrs. Chamberlain, almost overcome by emotion, repeated: "Thank you, oh, thank you" As she drove away she smiled and waved.

Two hundred people crowded round the newspaper sellers in Piccadilly at midnight as they brought the first editions of the morning papers announcing the peace.

People wept at the Gaiety and Prince's Theatres when the shows were interrupted and peace was announced.

At a Croydon theatre three thousand people cheered for nearly five minutes when the manager announced the success of the conference.

MAP (showing areas involved) **PAGE 8**

SUNDAY PICTORIAL, Sept. 3, 1939

King-Hall . . . Page 10

No. 1,277

TWOPENCE

Sunday Pictorial

CRISIS LATEST

OUR PREMIER GIVES HITLER LAST CHANCE

"If the German Government should agree to withdraw their forces, then the British Government would be willing to regard the position as being the same as it was before German forces crossed the Polish frontier."

WEAKNESS? CHAMBERLAIN PROMISES 'NO'

'Well . . .' wrote William Connor, Cassandra of *The Daily Mirror*, after the first full day of war, in rather perkier mood than his namesake had been when the siege of Troy began, 'it's a bit of a basket, isn't it? Still we're off now, so we might as well win this race'. There really wasn't much more a paper could say. Appeasement had failed and Munich had proved to be what Churchill had said it was at the time — a 'total and unmitigated defeat'. Within six months Hitler had dismembered whatever was left of a divided and debilitated Czechoslovakia, and by the end of March 1939 it was simply a matter of conjecture where in Europe his fancy would take him next — Belgium or Switzerland, Greece or Rumania, perhaps even Russia?

After Czechoslovakia none of the British Press clung to the illusion that peace could be preserved by further surrenders. True, *The Daily Express* continued to assure its readers 'there would be no war' until as late as August 4 — but now it represented a clarion-call for armed isolation rather than a pig-headed faith in appeasement. *The Observer* had been finally and utterly converted when 'the last rag of human decency was discarded' by the occupation of Prague. *The Sunday Times*, too, articulated a firmer policy (even while, behind

the scenes, its proprietor Lord Kemsley was engaged in a futile, slightly ridiculous, one-man crusade to divert the Führer: on July 27 he tracked Hitler down at the Bayreuth Festival and button-holed him there for an hour without knowing a word of German).

The Times, of course, did not desert the National Government, but it didn't have to for by March 17 Chamberlain himself was casting about for an alternative to appeasement: in the future he would have to anticipate the next political headache rather than turn up with the aspirin afterwards. When on the 29th the Berlin correspondent of *The News Chronicle* reported in person to the Cabinet that Germany was, and had been for some time, trying to woo Poland secretly, it looked as if he was almost too late once again. But this time the Premier moved with unprecedented speed, and in two days both Britain and France had guaranteed Polish independence. The following month they extended the same courtesy to Greece and Rumania in the south.

The other obvious expedient was an alliance with Russia, which *The Daily Herald* in particular had been advocating for months. Very reluctantly Mr. Chamberlain came to the same conclusion, but with such conspicuous lack of enthusiasm

were the negotiations conducted that yet again Chamberlain was overtaken by events: on August 22 it was announced that the Russians had decided to sign a non-aggression pact with Hitler instead (complete with secret clauses, it later turned out, apportioning fair shares for both from the carve-up of Poland). War was imminent — indeed inevitable, for Hitler's invasion timetable was pre-determined. It allowed a bare 24 hours for Polish envoys to come and grovel in Berlin, and hear the German ultimatum. He knew the Poles would refuse, and they did. But just to prove to Britain that Poland had 'rejected his ultimatum' he had Ribbentrop gabble the 16 so-called points at the British ambassador in unintelligible German, then unleashed his stormtroopers on Danzig, like 'a Wagnerian Deity' as *The Observer* put it.

On the 2nd, at the unwonted hour of 7.30 on a Saturday night, MPs crowded into a House of Commons already portentously blacked-out, expecting to hear the terms of the Prime Minister's ultimatum. For a bewildering moment it looked as if Appeasement had raised its ignoble head once more: there was no ultimatum — nor, Mr. Chamberlain added hastily when the House called on the Opposition leader to 'Speak for England', any weakness either.

WANTED!

FOR MURDER . . . FOR KIDNAPPING . . .
FOR THEFT AND FOR ARSON

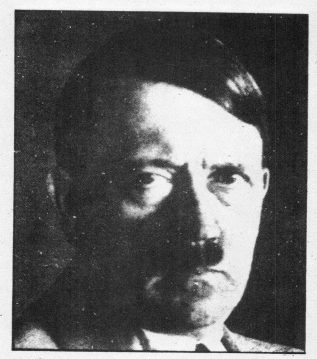

Can be recognised full face by habitual scowl. Rarely smiles Talks rapidly, and when angered screams like a child

ADOLF HITLER
ALIAS
Adolf Schicklegruber,
Adolf Hittler or Hidler

Last heard of in Berlin, September 3, 1939. Aged fifty, height 5ft. 8½in., dark hair, frequently brushes one lock over left forehead. Blue eyes. Sallow complexion, stout build, weighs about 11st. 3lb. Suffering from acute monomania, with periodic fits of melancholia. Frequently bursts into tears when crossed. Harsh, guttural voice, and has a habit of raising right hand to shoulder level. DANGEROUS !

Profile from a recent photograph. Black moustache. Jowl inclines to fatness. Wide nostrils. Deep-set, menacing eyes.

FOR MURDER Wanted for the murder of over a thousand of his fellow countrymen on the night of the Blood Bath, June 30, 1934. Wanted for the murder of countless political opponents in concentration camps.

He is indicted for the murder of Jews, Germans, Austrians, Czechs, Spaniards and Poles. He is now urgently wanted for homicide against citizens of the British Empire.

Hitler is a gunman who shoots to kill. He acts first and talks afterwards.

No appeals to sentiment can move him. This gangster, surrounded by armed hoodlums, is a natural killer. The reward for his apprehension, dead or alive, is the peace of mankind.

FOR KIDNAPPING Wanted for the kidnapping of Dr. Kurt Schuschnigg, late Chancellor of Austria. Wanted for the kidnapping of Pastor Niemoller, a heroic martyr who was not afraid to put God before Hitler. Wanted for the attempted kidnapping of Dr. Benes, late President of Czechoslovakia. The kidnapping tendencies of this established criminal are marked and violent. The symptoms before an attempt are threats, blackmail and ultimatums. He offers his victims the alternatives of complete surrender or timeless incarceration in the horrors of concentration camps.

FOR THEFT Wanted for the larceny of eighty millions of Czech gold in March, 1939. Wanted for the armed robbery of material resources of the Czech State. Wanted for the stealing of Memelland. Wanted for robbing mankind of peace, of humanity, and for the attempted assault on civilisation itself. This dangerous lunatic masks his raids by spurious appeals to honour, to patriotism and to duty. At the moment when his protestations of peace and friendship are at their most vehement, he is most likely to commit his smash and grab.

His tactics are known and easily recognised. But Europe has already been wrecked and plundered by the depredations of this armed thug who smashes in without scruple.

FOR ARSON Wanted as the incendiary who started the Reichstag fire on the night of February 27, 1933. This crime was the key point, and the starting signal for a series of outrages and brutalities that are unsurpassed in the records of criminal degenerates. As a direct and immediate result of this calculated act of arson, an innocent dupe, Van der Lubbe, was murdered in cold blood. But as an indirect outcome of this carefully-planned offence, Europe itself is ablaze. The fires that this man has kindled cannot be extinguished until he himself is apprehended dead or alive !

THIS RECKLESS CRIMINAL IS WANTED—DEAD OR ALIVE!

BLACK-OUT 9.39 p.m. to 4.17 a.m.

Sun rises 4.48 a.m.
    sets 9.9 p.m.
Moon rises 4.46 a.m.
    sets 8.23 p.m.

DAILY SKETCH. WEDNESDAY, JUNE 5, 1940.

DUNKIRK FALLS AT LAST: PAGE THREE

Daily Sketch

No. 9,697 WEDNESDAY, JUNE 5, 1940 ONE PENNY

THE enemy was hurled back by retreating British and French troops. He was so roughly handled he did not dare molest them seriously

The Royal Air Force inflicted losses of nearly four to one, and the Navy, using 1,000 ships, carried over 3,35,000 French and British men and vast supplies.

—THE PRIME MINISTER.

DUNKIRK BEACH—JUNE 4, 1940

Towards midnight, the lightning flashed and thunder rolled ominously (*Sunday Pictorial*) as the Cabinet arrived at Downing Street to draft the ultimatum, which called on Germany to withdraw. It was delivered in Berlin at 9.00 am on the 3rd, and expired unanswered two hours later. Britain and Germany were at war. Yes, it was 'a bit of a basket', and no mistake.

The evacuation of the British Expeditionary Force from Dunkirk in the last days of May 1940 not only brought a weary and dispirited army back home, it brought the war itself to the streets and skies of Britain. 'The battle for France is over' Churchill bluntly told the Commons on June 19. 'I expect that the battle of Britain is about to begin'.

Indeed that very day an isolated German raid struck down nine people in Cambridge. Inexorably over the next few weeks the blitzkrieg that was intended to bring Britain to its knees built up, until by the second week of August the Junkers and the Heinkels, the Dorniers and the Messerschmitts darkened the skies over the South Coast daily in their hundreds. As fast as they could refuel the British Hurricane and Spitfire fighters returned to the air to confront each new murderous wave. From August 11–18 Churchill's promised battle for Britain was at its height — and as the morning headlines rolled off the presses, giving 'the score at the end of each innings' as one sub-editor was inspired to call it, it became gloriously clear that the Luftwaffe had met its match. 62 Nazi planes down on the 12th, 78 the next day, 180 destroyed on the 15th and another 140 on the 18th. As August gave way to September, the Germans tried a new tactic: their bombers turned towards London in an effort to demolish British morale quicker than they were succeeding with British property.

On September 7 the signal 'invasion imminent' was flashed to the army and all home guard units. It never came. Gradually the tide of destruction receded, while winter approached and rendered the prospects of invasion more and more remote. When the final count was taken nearly 1,800 German planes littered the fields and beaches of Britain. Amazingly and in spite of heavy casualties, Fighter Command emerged from the fray with more planes than it started — largely due to the proprietor of *The Daily Express*, Lord Beaverbrook, who was now running the Ministry of Aircraft Production with the same autocratic single-mindedness he ran his newspapers (he had publicly renounced his pacifism, bravely if a little belatedly, in a signed article on May 6 — he was ushered into Churchill's new coalition less than a fortnight later).

In all this life-and-death struggle, the newspapers discovered new headline heroes: their readers. If you discounted the few Zeppelin raids of the First War (which had been regarded more as an insult than an emergency), this was the first civilian conflict in the island's history, and the man in the street (when he wasn't in his ricketty Anderson shelter, struggling with his gas mask) had come out of it battered but cheerfully unbowed. His story was the very stuff of newspapers and, what's more, there was no censorship of High Street heroism: the lady from Coventry defiantly manning her tea-urn all day as the bombs fell around her . . . the farm labourer clutching his pitchfork and capturing a Nazi pilot single-handed . . . the Portsmouth doctor ducking the shrapnel as it tore through his operating theatre but calmly returning to the operating table . . . the A.R.P. warden from Mile End plunging into a burning house to rescue a child, and not coming out again. All

BLACK-OUT ZERO HOUR TO-NIGHT UNTIL 7.53 A.M.
MOON RISES 6.32 P.M. MOON SETS 10.11 A.M.

Daily Express

No. 12,632 — Saturday, November 16, 1940 — One Penny

"It is time now for our deepest, most inspired anger
Coventry cries: Bomb back and bomb hard"

A VERY GALLANT CITY

Stricken, but keeps its courage and sanity

MORRISON: ALL THE HELP YOU NEED

The wonderful story of Mrs. Smith, who served tea through it all

By HILDE MARCHANT

COVENTRY, Friday Night.

AMID the black horror of the Nazi attack on Coventry, which was Guernicaed all through last night, two things stand out—the great courage of the people and the devotion of A.R.P. workers, who were only stopped by death.

Today I met Coventry's mayor, Alderman J. A. Moseley — deeply shocked, busy, worried. I asked if there was to be a general evacuation of the city, and he answered:

"OF COURSE NOT. WE STAY.

"I shall go on in this city even if there is no room for me to sleep in.

"Everything humanly possible is being done for our people. Everything has been planned, and it has all worked out."

Mr. Herbert Morrison, the Minister of Home Security, came to Coventry as soon as he heard of the attack and the estimated casualties of nearly 1,000. He had a conference with the mayor and other officials and told them "Go ahead. Don't hesitate."

He tramped among the ruins, getting A.R.P. officials to tell him their difficulties. And he gave orders to wipe those difficulties away.

'MAGNIFICENT'

With his wife he went among the people, helping them, talking to them, and seeing that nothing was hindering their work

He said to me: "The National Service workers have stood up to their duty magnificently.

"They have displayed great courage and determination under exceptional strain.

"I am very grateful to them for their devotion to duty and the service of their country.

"Such actions as this by the Germans can only lead to a determination by this country's people to put everything they possibly can into the war effort."

The shopping centre of Coventry is one choking mass of ruins, fire, and people who, by some miracle, have emerged alive.

They walk through this skeleton of the city centre with faces stained black, breathing the smoke of their homes, trying to find their families and friends, not sure of the way through their own streets.

The cathedral in the centre of the city is just a shell, ruined, not by time, but by one night's savage, vicious bombing. Its thick walls and heavy pillars have crashed.

Street after street of houses and

BACK PAGE, COLUMN ONE

SPERRLE — Nazi field-marshal. Sent his men to bomb Coventry. Official German communiqué says: "The attack was particularly vigorous and successful." He . . .

Gets "honourable" mention for this

"Coventry Cathedral, in the centre of the city, is just a shell, ruined, not by time, but by one night's savage, vicious bombing. . . ."

Coventry is known as the City of the Three Spires. The Cathedral of St. Michael possessing one of them, was a fine building in the Perpendicular style, dating from 1373-94.

18 to 1 *was the R.A.F.'s remarkable score against the enemy in daylight battles yesterday. And that brought the Fighter Command's score for the week up to* **69 to 5**

Blitz on Berlin for hours

AN explosion so gigantic that a whole building was lifted sky-high and Berlin's anti-aircraft batteries went dumb provided a climax for the R.A.F.'s latest and most devastating raid, in which they raked Hitler's capital for hours.

The story was told late last night by a pilot of one of the bombers which spent hour after hour pounding Berlin the night before.

He said: "The building was the centre of the biggest of several fires blazing in Berlin when we arrived. There came a terrific explosion and the whole structure went up in the air.

GUNNERS SCARED

"Burning debris falling all around started scores of smaller fires.

"The explosion lit up the inside of our machine, thousands of feet above it, and even the "flak" gunners seemed to be awed, for there was a lull in the barrage for several minutes.

"It was one of the best nights' bombing I have ever known."

Other pilots agreed that conditions, with a full moon and a clear sky, made it impossible to miss the targets they were sent to hit.

These were the great Berlin termini, which serve all the railways of central Europe and the marshalling yards where freight trains are made up.

TRAFFIC HOLD-UP

On the basis of all reports collected from the returning fliers, the Air Ministry was satisfied last night that the havoc inflicted on Berlin's vital centres would affect transport throughout Germany and in many of the countries she has overrun.

Cost to the R.A.F. of Britain's biggest blitz night, which included the bombing of a 1,500-mile-long string of German "invasion ports" was ten aircraft missing.

NURSE SAVED 86 PATIENTS

JUNIOR Nurse Violet Eleanor Reid, seriously wounded and plunged suddenly into the darkness of a bombed mental hospital, is today a heroine, entitled to wear the blue and red ribbon of the George Medal.

With ten policemen, two railwaymen and a couple of firemen, this twenty-seven-year-old Scots girl from Arbroath is in the latest list of civilian heroes who win the medal.

Nurse Reid was working with another nurse in the kitchen when the bomb fell. Part of the room was demolished. Steam and hot water spurted out from damaged pipes, and the whole place was in darkness.

Deaf and injured

She was cut on her face, hands, body and legs, the crash had made her stone deaf and she was weak from loss of blood.

Terrified patients gathered round in the darkness and added to her ordeal. There were eighty-six of them, four injured. But Nurse Reid from Arbroath remained calm and master of the situation.

First she reassured the patients, then went to the assistance of the other nurse whom she carried upstairs unaided and attended her until a doctor arrived.

Nurse Reid then returned to her patients, most of them in night clothes, pacifying them and helping them into warm coats.

Death for looters

BERLIN, Friday.—A special court at Genoa has sentenced the two ringleaders of a black-out looting gang to death by shooting, says a Milan telegram.—Reuter.

Night raider brought down

Big bombs hit houses

An enemy plane was destroyed late last night at Harlow, Essex.

Shortly after the alert in the London area—it was unusually early—a bus was lifted several feet into the air by a bomb.

The bus was crowded with late homeward-bound City workers, but none was hurt. The driver was the only casualty, and he was not seriously injured.

After a heavy bomb had fallen in a garden of a residential district, six people were extricated from the debris of houses and taken to hospital.

There was a lull during which neither guns nor planes were heard. Then guns over a big area boomed out.

One of two large bombs dropped in the same district demolished a boarding-house and a block of flats.

The other wrecked a number of houses, and it is feared that the death roll is heavy.

A public-house was also wrecked, but no one was hurt. A hospital, hit by several bombs, was only slightly damaged.

Italians abandon strategic Islands

Daily Express Staff Reporter

NEW YORK, Friday.

AS Mussolini sent his most trusted general, Marshal Badoglio, to meet Hitler's Chief of Staff, Field-Marshal Keitel, at Innsbruck today it was reported from Athens that the Italians were withdrawing from all but two of the fourteen blockaded Dodecanese Islands in anticipation of an attack.

They are said to be concentrating in the two fortified islands of Rhodes and Leros.

Official explanation of the Innsbruck meeting came from Berlin that the united command of the Axis Powers wanted to go over the entire military situation, with particular relation to Egypt and Greece.

But it was generally believed that Mussolini asked his boss, Adolf Hitler, for some help. If the Greeks, as reported, are advancing into Albania on a 120-mile front, [illegible] threat that the Italians will be cut off in Southern Albania.

The Fleet Air Arm raid on Taranto made the deepest impression in Germany. Despite extreme discretion, the German Press makes, between the lines, unmistakable allusions to Nazi disappointment at the results obtained by the Italians on sea and land and in the air.

STOP PRESS

Big R.A.F. raid on Berlin

German radio, quoted by A.P. New York message, said large numbers of R.A.F. planes attacked Berlin last night. Claimed that only twelve reached the capital and that six were brought down. Hamburg was also bombed.

GREEKS TAKE 700 PRISONERS

ATHENS, Saturday morning.—Greek communiqué last night says there was great activity by infantry, artillery and aircraft along the whole front. About 700 prisoners and ten guns were taken.

Air Force bombed enemy troops in action and three enemy planes were brought down. Two Greek planes failed to return.—Reuter.

"IT WILL RISE AGAIN"

Priest tried to save cathedral

TWELVE fire bombs fell on Coventry Cathedral. The provost, the Very Rev. R. T. Howard, and a party of watchers were putting them out with sand when more fire bombs came down, and explosives with them.

Then it was impossible to save the building—

BUT the provost said yesterday: "The cathedral will rise again. It will be rebuilt, to be a pride to future generations."

AMONG the places bombed are:—Two churches, a Methodist chapel, a library with thousands of volumes and treasured manuscripts, a hall, a ward and an operating theatre at a hospital, outbuildings of an isolation hospital, two hotels, a newspaper office, stores and office buildings.

Short of water

WITH some of the gas, electricity and water mains damaged by the bombs, shortage of water handicapped the firemen. In some cases it was necessary to use dynamite to prevent flames spreading.

A YOUNG Coventry man who had been working in Birmingham went to his home town to help the rescuers. The first victim he got out was his own wife—dead.

FIVE policemen—three specials and two regulars—were patrolling a street when a bomb was heard falling.

The three specials threw themselves down. The two regulars fell on top of them, trying to shield them. But the bomb fell almost directly on them, and all were killed.

Pavement 'shops'

SHOPKEEPERS dug their stocks out of ruined shops yesterday and carried on their trade on the pavement.

AS dusk fell last evening private cars loaded with comforts for bomb victims were pouring INTO the city.

Egypt has new premier

CAIRO, Friday.—Hussein Sirry Pasha has been appointed Prime Minister by King Farouk of Egypt in succession to Hassan Sabry Pasha, who collapsed and died while reading the Speech from the Throne yesterday.

Sirry Pasha is a former Premier and War Minister.—Reuter.

'Nazi supply ship sunk'

NEW YORK, Friday.

REPORTS, not yet confirmed, reached shipping men in New York today that British warships had sunk the German steamer Helgoland, which made a dash from Colombia, the South American republic, on October 28.

The Helgoland is said to have gone down in the Caribbean Sea.

After she had slipped out of the Colombian harbour of Barranquilla it was reported that the ship had been loaded with fuel for a Nazi raider in the South Atlantic.

It was also stated that she carried pilots of a German air line in South America.—A.P.

Moscow is silent on British proposals

It was revealed last night that the British Government have so far received no reply from Moscow to proposals submitted on October 22.

The proposals included the *de facto* recognition of the incorporation of the Baltic States in the U.S.S.R., a guarantee that Russia would take part in any peace settlement after the war, and an assurance that Britain would not be associated in any attack against Russia.

LAVAL ASKS HITLER: STOP MASS EXPULSION

Daily Express Staff Reporter C. V. R. THOMPSON

NEW YORK, Friday.

MARSHAL PETAIN called a vital Cabinet meeting in Vichy this afternoon while Laval went back to Paris to try to persuade the Germans to cancel the order for the expulsion of all French people from the province of Lorraine.

It became clear from messages reaching New York that the whole future of the delicately balanced Franco-German "co-operation" policy rests on the success of Laval's mission.

Earlier messages from Switzerland suggested that Laval had double-crossed Petain in agreeing to the expulsion policy, but it is certain now that unless Laval can get the order modified he cannot hope for even the reluctant support of his chief.

Laval is trying to get some kind of satisfaction and hurry back to Vichy by the morning.

Petain plans to go to Lyons on Monday to comfort refugees from Lorraine.

The people of France have been stirred out of their numbed lethargy by the ruthless expulsion of 100,000 French people, dumped in France with practically no notice to quit, and with no more than £6 each to face the future.

U.S. warned: "Watch for sabotage"

Daily Express Staff Reporter

NEW YORK, Friday.

Congressman Martin Dies, chairman of the committee investigating sabotage and subversive activity in the United States, today predicted that within ninety days the most crippling act of sabotage in history would hit the aircraft industry.

Mr. Dies added that his committee had given to the Department of Justice the names of employees in plants who will be responsible for sabotage as agents of totalitarian Powers.

DAILY MIRROR, Thursday, November 5, 1942.

Daily Mirror NOV 5

No. 12,136 ONE PENNY

Registered at the G.P.O. as a Newspaper.

ROMMEL ROUTED

HUNS FLEEING IN DISORDER

He dished it out

9,000 men captured
260 tanks destroyed
600 planes knocked out

The Italians have asked for an armistice to enable them to bury their dead. The message does not state whether or not the request applies to all Italian forces on the Mediterranean Qattara front.

ROMMEL'S desert army, blitzed as no German army has ever been blitzed before, is in full retreat with the Eighth Army in close pursuit of his "disordered" columns.

The dramatic story of General Montgomery's smashing victory was told in the following special joint communique from British Headquarters in Cairo last night:—

"The Axis forces in the Western Desert, after twelve days and nights of ceaseless attacks by our land and air forces, are now in full retreat.

"Their disordered columns are being relentlessly attacked by our land forces and by the Allied Air Force by day and night.

"General von Stumme, a senior General, who is said to have been in command during Rommel's absence in Germany, is known to have been killed.

"So far we have captured over 9,000 prisoners, including General Ritter von Thoma, Commander of the German Afrika Korps, and a number of other senior German and Italian officers.

"It is known that the enemy's losses in killed and wounded have been exceptionally high.

"Up to date we have destroyed more than 260 German and Italian tanks, and captured or destroyed at least 270 guns.

"The full toll of the booty cannot be assessed at this stage of the operation.

"In the course of these operations our air forces, whose losses have been light, have destroyed and damaged in air combat over 300 aircraft and destroyed or put out of action a like number on the ground.

"At sea our naval and air forces have sunk 50,000 tons and damaged as much again of shipping carrying Axis supplies to North Africa.

"The Eighth Army continues to advance."

For the first time in this war a German Army has been really blitzed. The famous Afrika Korps could not stand up to the ceaseless pounding that General Montgomery (above) and the Eighth Army have dished out. Twelve days of this terrible fighting have broken Rommel's crack troops. They are in full retreat falling back in disorder

He couldn't take it

Rommel—not so tough

Huns' road back may be shambles

NOW that the retreat has started, Rommel will have the difficult job of extricating his battered army from a narrow corridor under the full weight of Allied air power, writes a military correspondent.

To accomplish this without the command of the air is one of the most difficult of military tasks in modern warfare. It remains to be seen whether his forces can be rallied on a new line further back.

At present the retreating German and Italian forces are compelled to follow a narrow course which keeps them so tightly compressed that air attack can be made with devastating effect.

What is the reason for Rommel's lack of an effective air arm at the very moment when he needs it most? There are four answers:—

Rommel's forward aerodromes have been heavily and persistently pounded by the Allied air forces; there are few airfields between here and Sollum; Rommel's main concern must be to save as much of his air force as he can for possible operations further back; and Axis petrol supplies have been gravely compromised.

Rommel's road back is liable to become a shambles.

The description "disorderly" applied to the retreat of Rommel's army best sums up the situation.

Once demoralisation sets in, where will it be checked? In answering this, it cannot be over-emphasised that the Eighth Army, fighting fit and full of spirit, is hard on the heels of the Axis troops.

The figure of 260 tanks captured or destroyed means that more than half the Axis armoured force is definitely out of action.

We keep up 'nightmare bombing'

FIRST signs of the Axis rout were reported back to a forward aerodrome early on Tuesday afternoon, when a message flashed from the Eighth Army's land forces announced that the enemy was beginning to fall back towards the west.

It was the moment for the Allied forces to strike.

The call went out to the squadrons to "send in every available bomber and every available fighter."

This was a dramatic moment—the moment everyone had been waiting for a long time.

Though the weight of our air attacks had been very heavy for the past few days, the tempo of our operations seemed to be doubled in a few minutes.

From every desert landing ground waves of planes took off, and the desert air was shattered by a mighty roar from the engines of scores of bombers of all types.

Great dust plumes rose as one plane after another took off heading west with throttles wide open.

Down on the aerodromes tired ground crews, the sweat running down their faces, grimed with oil and dust, paused for a few seconds in their work to give the "thumbs-up" sign to the pilots.

Within a matter of fifteen minutes or so when the final waves returned the ground crews went feverishly to work to put the planes back into the air in the fastest possible time.

Throughout the afternoon heat the procession went on while the ground crews, too tired even to talk, kept the bombers turning about on their "nightmare" bombing service.

Nothing like this has ever been seen before.

Only the barest fighter cover was provided for our bombers.

The enemy, powerless to offer any effective defence, had to suffer the most violent and grim air attack seen in North Africa.

One British fighter pilot, newly returned from strafing a road, said: "There is very little future in being a German this afternoon."

The Missing Link—
OXO
LET OXO
MEAT YOUR VEGETABLES

these and a thousand stories like them flooded from Fleet Street, to show the world that Britain was not afraid to stand alone.

The newspapers themselves suffered along with their public. *The Evening Standard* and *The Daily Herald* were bombed early in the Blitz. *The Times*, too, received a direct hit as the paper went to press one morning: *The Daily Telegraph* was showered with incendiaries, and part of *The News of the World* was burnt out later in 1941. But, doubtless inspired by the bulldog spirit to which their columns bore witness, all of them kept the presses rolling without break. Far more irksome, in fact, proved to be the acute shortage of newsprint, which from the middle of 1940 restricted them to a maximum of six pages – and from 1941 to four pages (eight for the tabloids). Paper rationing even obliged some papers to cut their print-orders and urge their readers to 'share your newspaper', but this enforced lack of competition (apart from being a welcome respite from the cut-throat pre-war days) did some papers a power of good. *The Daily Mirror* in particular having vigorously and as a conscious policy identified itself with the view-point of 'the common man' who was bearing the brunt of war's hardships (especially the forces and war-workers), reaped its reward in the post-war expansion by watching its circulation soar to dizzy heights.

In this capacity *The Daily Mirror* assumed the self-appointed role of watchdog of the individual's interest in what were bound to be authoritarian times. On more than one occasion its criticism of ministers aroused Churchill's wrath, until he was finally moved to lecture Cecil King, the newspaper's chairman, on the fine distinction between criticism and fifth-columnism. Ironically, the ultimate showdown between Churchill and *The Daily Mirror* was the result of a misunderstanding: the Prime Minister interpreted a cartoon drawn by Philip Zec (below) as implying that the Government was capitalising on the sacrifices of the Merchant Navy. The cartoon in question, in fact, was intended only to make the public more conscious of the high risks seamen ran in getting petrol across U-boat infested waters. Churchill wanted to suppress *The Daily Mirror* at this point (as *The Daily Worker* had been suppressed in January 1941), but *The Daily Mirror* finally escaped with a solemn warning from the Home Secretary. Just how unpopular *The Daily Mirror* contrived to make itself in some political quarters was illustrated by the charge – which was quite seriously raised in Parliament – that the paper was the tool of William Randolph Hearst. Which was the ultimate absurdity, in view of the fact that *The Daily Mirror* was even then one of the most democratically-run papers in the country.

After the loneliness and tribulations of August and September 1940 it might have looked as if, whatever Hitler had in store, Britain 'could take it'. But there was little comfort in the headlines of 1941: Rommel pushes his way across North Africa, Tobruk falls, Greece is evacuated, Vichy France collaborates, the Germans break through to Leningrad. There were, to be sure, occasional consolations: the Bismarck finally disappearing beneath the waves and the Deputy Führer falling out of the Scottish skies. But the biggest consolation of all, the promise of imminent American participation, seemed to have been indefinitely postponed. During the battle of Britain, the papers had regularly recorded American 'shock and horror' (not least its rage, as one U.S. correspondent put it, at Hitler's 'attempt to terrorize the British Empire into submission' by bombing Buckingham Palace). Yet month followed month, missions came and went, money and munitions arrived – but no men. What was happening? Most newspapers were too preoccupied with their own problem to follow the bitter controversies that were dividing America . . .

Below: Zec's controversial cartoon in The Daily Mirror.

The price of petrol has been increased by ½d.

To a Date in Infamy
America in World War II

It was significant that, whereas Wilson at the onset of the First War had urged Americans to be neutral in thought as well as act, in his appeal to the nation in 1939 Roosevelt omitted any reference to 'thinking neutral'. Perhaps he remembered how difficult it had been even to act neutral in the face of unprovoked Japanese aggression on the Yangtze in 1937, and perhaps he understood the futility of trying to remain morally uncommitted about the ugly face of Nazism. It is even to be doubted that, as he spoke the words, he himself was eager to preserve America's neutrality at all costs. The Atlantic in 1939 was not the formidable barrier it had been in 1914, and he may already have been thinking those thoughts which he finally articulated when in 1940 Britain stood alone after the fall of France: 'If Great Britain goes down, the Axis powers will control the continents of Europe, Asia, Africa, Australasia and the high seas – and they will be in a position to bring enormous military and naval resources against this hemisphere'.

But whatever his private fears and public utterances in that first September of the war, the drift of his policies over the next eighteen months was unmistakable: the amendment of the Neutrality Act to sweep away the embargo on the sale of war materials; the sale of second-hand guns and planes to the Allies; the trading of U.S. destroyers to Britain in return for British bases in the West; the introduction of a selective draft in the fall of 1940, and above all the offering of aid to the democracies in January 1941 on a lend-lease basis, postponing payment till after the end of hostilities (staking all, in effect, on an Allied victory). Roosevelt interpreted his triumph in the 1940 presidential elections, close though it was, as an endorsement of his policy and a mandate for further actions (which soon included the seizure of German ships in US ports, the freezing of all Axis assets in America and the black-listing of a number of firms).

None of these measures, however, were accomplished without strenuous opposition from the non-interventionists who had rallied under the slogan of 'America First'. Nor could he count on the undiluted support of the newspapers. The New York Times, as always, threw its considerable weight behind his foreign policy, but the Hearst papers remained as vociferously isolationist as ever. It was widely argued that what had dragged America into the First War was precisely this kind of material support for one of the belligerents. In 1940 there were a great many newspapers which would have profoundly disagreed even with The Chicago Daily News' moderate stand: 'there is still another step to be taken. It is to help in every way, SHORT OF WAR ITSELF, those who are now fighting the bestial monster that is making a shambles of Europe, flouting every essential of international good faith, despoiling the lands and killing the men of weaker neighbours, reducing all European civilisation to the level of a cave man's morality' (May 11 1940).

But it was largely to the President's credit, and not solely to the growing awareness of America's peril, that between the summers of 1940 and 1941 so many influential papers publicly disavowed their isolationist stands. On June 2 1940 The Philadelphia Inquirer announced its conversion in a front-page statement that 'America must help Allies to beat Hitler' and reprinted it in its next issue for good measure. Exactly a year later, on June 1 1941, The Detroit Free Press joined the cause with a signed letter from its publisher: 'The Free Press has opposed every step leading toward involvement in a war which was not of our making. We have seen far too much of Europe's intrigue, the wars that have been fought to preserve its sordid commercialism disguised by noble and high-sounding slogans; yes too many comrades lying wounded and dying on the battlefield, not to be sceptical of the motives of the 'statesmen' in high places who make these wars' – then having got that off its chest it concluded – 'But now the die is cast . . . there is no turning back. To that end, the Free Press pledges its complete support to President Roosevelt as our Commander in Chief'.

Neverthless there was one newspaper that vehemently resisted intervention to the bitter end – The Chicago Daily Tribune (as it was now known). Its proprietor, Colonel Robert McCormick – the very same that had voluntarily declared war on Al Capone – was said to have possessed 'the greatest mind of the 14th Century', but it was his physical bulk (through the banner headlines of his The Chicago Daily Tribune) which the administration felt most acutely. He made no attempt to moderate his single-minded opposition to Roosevelt personally. The passage of the Lend-Lease Act through Congress drew the Colonel's fire in impassioned volleys: 'Fear of War Stirs Congress – Scheme to Lend Arms is Cast as One Man Show' snarled the front page on January 7. And on the 11th: 'Vast Power Asked by F.D.R. – Scope of Plan to Aid Britain Stuns Capital'. It was The Chicago Daily Tribune's recurring theme that the President was gradually appropriating to himself dictatorial powers.

So, when at the beginning of August 1941 Roosevelt and Churchill met secretly in mid-Atlantic to discuss their war aims, The Chicago Daily Tribune was beside itself. No doubt part of its fury was due to the fact that its great rival The Chicago Daily News scooped the whole of America with the news of this mysterious meeting. On the 5th The Chicago Daily News came out with the categorical headline 'F.D.R. Sees Churchill' after its London correspondent realised that the Prime Minister had left the country on a mission important enough for him to miss a crucial debate in Parliament. Roosevelt, it was known, had gone away on 'a fishing trip' – and it didn't take The Chicago Daily News long to work out what he was hoping to catch. Most other papers were hesitant ('Roosevelt May Meet Churchill, Conference at Sea is Rumoured': The New York Herald-Tribune on the 6th) and indeed it was not until the 14th that The Chicago Daily News was completely vindicated, when Washington announced the two leaders had met after all and were publishing an 8-point joint declaration of war aims.

To The Chicago Daily Tribune this was tantamount to declaring war: 'Pact Pushes U.S. Near War – F.D.R. Alliance with Churchill Rocks Capital' it shouted and denounced Roosevelt for being' . . . more than outside his country. He was outside his office. The spectacle was one of two autocratic rulers, one of them determining the destiny of his country in the matter of war or peace absolutely in his own will, as if his subjects were without voice.. The country rejects that idea of its government'. The Los Angeles Herald-Examiner too thought '. . . the eight points, taken as a whole, appear to be a prelude to taking this country into the European war . . . (they) have all the nobility of the late President Wilson's 14 points which were a desolate failure for Europe and America'.

But a great many other papers hailed the declaration with enthusiasm. The Atlanta Constitution likened it to the signing of Magna Carta and the adoption of the Constitution, besides which 'the mouthings of small-souled isolationists and political opportunists shrink to nothing'. The San Francisco Chronicle was under no illusions: 'The basic importance of the Roosevelt–Churchill statement is that it envisions everything that is the opposite of the foul Nazi philosophy. And that . . . is itself worth fighting for. Such a fight is the only road to peace'. For its part The New York Times was positively lyrical about 'the rendezvous with destiny' – 'The great winds of history blew the two gray ships together in the shadowy lanes of the North Atlantic. They met there . . . in the narrowing moat between two hemispheres. The passengers . . . were not merely men with a flare

U.S. Must Keep Out of Europe's War

WE can keep out of war if we want to. Europe could keep out of war if it wanted to.

There is no situation in Europe which could not have been solved by the peaceful discussion which the President urged.

But the traditional hatreds and jealousies and the long established warlike habits of Europe made war inevitable there.

But war is in no sense inevitable here.

We have not the established warlike habits. We have not the racial hatreds, the international jealousies.

We have not the greed for power and added territory.

And if we follow the injunctions of Washington, we will not have the partisanship which might lead us into war.

IF the President wants to keep us out of war— as it is evident from his broadcast that he does —if the Congress acts intelligently to keep us out of war, if the people continue their desire, so often expressed, to keep out of European conflicts, there is no reason why we should become involved in this European catastrophe.

When it is over, Europe will be prostrated, of course.

The people will be exhausted and impoverished.

A large part of what we considered civilisation, but what is apparently only an empty shell, will have been destroyed over there.

But here in America peace and prosperity will prevail, the best benefits of civilization will have been retained, and the United States in her full strength can stand for 's to lead and aid the world back to such peace and happiness as these warring peoples are then capable of securing and enjoying.

AMERICA has a great opportunity, a great mission, which it can only fulfill if it keeps out of war, and if it keeps its resources, its institutions, its democratic principles in ..t, and fully available for its own benefit, and for the reconstruction of the world.

WILLIAM RANDOLPH HEARST.

Chicago Daily Tribune
THE WORLD'S GREATEST NEWSPAPER

FINAL ★★

VOLUME C.—NO. 6 C   [REG. U. S. PAT. OFFICE, COPYRIGHT 1941 BY THE CHICAGO TRIBUNE.]   TUESDAY, JANUARY 7, 1941.—30 PAGES   THIS PAPER CONSISTS OF TWO SECTIONS—SECTION ONE   PRICE TWO CENTS   IN CHICAGO AND SUBURBS   ELSEWHERE THREE CENTS

FEAR OF WAR STIRS CONGRESS

Cubs Beat Cardinals; Braves Trim Phillies

THE CHICAGO DAILY NEWS

RED STREAK

[REG. U. S. PAT. OFF. COPYRIGHT 1941 BY THE CHICAGO DAILY NEWS, INC.]   TUESDAY, AUGUST 5, 1941—TWENTY-FOUR PAGES.   Telephone DEArborn 1111.   THREE CENTS

F.D.R. SEES CHURCHILL

Chicago Daily Tribune
THE WORLD'S GREATEST NEWSPAPER

FINAL ★★

VOLUME C.—NO. 290 C   [REG. U. S. PAT. OFFICE, COPYRIGHT 1941 BY THE CHICAGO TRIBUNE.]   THURSDAY, DECEMBER 4, 1941.—46 PAGES   THIS PAPER CONSISTS OF THREE SECTIONS—SECTION ONE   PRICE TWO CENTS   IN CHICAGO AND SUBURBS   ELSEWHERE THREE CENTS

F.D.R.'S WAR PLANS!

REDS BEGIN NEW DRIVE TO BREAK VISE ON MOSCOW

Strike at Nazi Line South of Leningrad.

BULLETIN.
BERNE, Switzerland, Dec. 4 (Thursday).—A special bulletin from Moscow early today announced soviet forces had launched a heavy attack along the entire northern line from Kalinin to Leningrad in a terrific effort to crush the German threat against Moscow. The main fighting was believed to be in the Lake Ilmen district 120 miles southeast of Leningrad where Russian forces were reported breaking thru the German lines on the Volkhov river.

(Maps on Page 17.)

LONDON, Dec. 4 [Thursday].—[P.]—Russian troops were reported early today to have captured two Italian divisions which the Germans, falling back west of Rostov, had thrown into the path of the soviet steamroller.

The Italians, identified as members of the Union and Tuscan lines, "hardly reached the battle lines before they began giving themselves up as prisoners," Moscow said. "They complained of absence of warm cloth-

LEIBER TRADED TO GIANTS; CUBS GET BOWMAN

The Chicago Cubs early this morning traded Outfielder Hank Leiber to the New York Giants for Pitcher Bob Bowman and an unannounced sum of cash. The deal was completed at the minor league baseball convention in Jacksonville, Fla. Leiber was one of three Giants sent to the Cubs after the 1938 season in exchange for Bill Jurges, Frank Demaree, and Ken O'Dea.

(Details on sports pages.)

NEWS SUMMARY
of The Tribune
[And Historical Scrap Book.]
Thursday,
December 4, 1941.

WAR SITUATION.
BERNE—Russians launch offensive to end Moscow threat. Page 1.
CAIRO—RAF presses war during lull in Libya fighting. Page 14.
HELSINGFORS—Finns begin to occupy Hango as Reds pull out. Page 17.
WASHINGTON.
Roosevelt war plan calls for armed force of 10 million. Page 1.
House passes drastic anti-strike bill. Page 1.
White House reveals Turkey put on lend-lease aid. Page 1.
President seeks to avoid shooting war over Thailand. Page 13.
LOCAL.
Country kids prove smart as quizzes.

HOUSE ADOPTS DRASTIC BILL TO BLOCK STRIKES

Goes to Senate on 252-136 Vote.

BY WILLIAM STRAND.
[Chicago Tribune Press Service.]
Washington, D. C., Dec. 3.—The house of representatives, by a vote of 252 to 136, today passed sweeping anti-strike legislation designed to prevent work stoppages because of labor disputes in arms industries.

The final vote was on a compromise measure introduced yesterday by Rep. Howard W. Smith [D., Va.]. It was regarded as the most drastic of four antistrike measures before the house.

A coalition of 123 Republicans and 129 Democrats prevailed over 108 Democrats, 24 Republicans, 2 Progressives and 1 American Labor party member in adopting the bill.

Bill's Major Provisions.
As sent to the senate, the measure—
1. Provides for a secret strike vote supervised by the federal govern-

THE STRONGHOLD OF PEACE

GOAL IS 10 MILLION ARMED MEN; HALF TO FIGHT IN AEF

Proposes Land Drive by July 1, 1943, to Smash Nazis; President Told of Equipment Shortage.

BY CHESLY MANLY.
[Copyright: 1941: By The Chicago Tribune.]
Washington, D. C., Dec. 3.—A confidential report prepared by the joint army and navy high command by direction of President Roosevelt calls for American expeditionary forces aggregating 5,000,000 men for a final land offensive against Germany and her satellites. It contemplates total armed forces of 10,045,658 men.

One of the few existing copies of this astounding document, which represents decisions and commitments affecting the destinies of peoples thruout the civilized world, became available to The Tribune today.

It is a blueprint for total war on a scale unprecedented in at least two oceans and three continents, Europe, Africa, and Asia.

The report expresses the considered opinion of the army and navy strategists that "Germany and her European satellites cannot be defeated by the European powers now fighting against her." Therefore, it concludes, "if our European enemies are to be defeated it will be necessary for the United States to enter the war, and to employ a part of its armed forces offensively in the eastern Atlantic and in Europe and Africa."

July 1, 1943, is fixed as the date for the beginning of the final supreme effort by American land forces to defeat the mighty Ger-

REVEAL TURKEY GETS LEND-LEASE

By ROYCE BRIER

NOW let us look at history, and let us look at it calmly, for we are the greatest people in history, and that imposes upon us a great responsibility.

And let us look at history in its wide and true sense in our time. The chronicle of mankind. We need not as a people worry unduly about the Japanese. We will take care of these upstarts after a while, and when we have they will be back in the murky feudalism from which they emerged 9 years ago.

But the chronicle of mankind is something else, a deep and mighty river forever flowing toward an unseen sea.

So in the beginning there lived not long ago in the great gray city of Vienna, a man, a John Wilkes Booth kind of crazy man, but not too crazy, brooding and waiting in an apparently fathomless anonymity. Yet this man was true son of our history.

In him, in his hate, his madness, his inborn treachery and peevish bent, the history of our days strained convulsively, like the white-hot core of a volcano, for he was a revolutionary and unexampled revolution was churning in many men, and after a certain number of years had passed in turmoil and confusion, then lo! the revolutionary and revolution were one.

They were one by inner predestination from the beginning, but in the reaches of the deep and mighty river they did not know each other at first. When they did, most of us did not know and far across the earth millions upon millions of the unknowing were pitched abruptly into the abyss.

"And the war came - - -"

As in Abraham Lincoln's day, it came slowly and blunderingly and in false-face. But instead of riding across a continent it rode across a world. It moved a little east and a little west, a little north and a little south, a revolutionary war which was in motion through time as well as space. It struck and recoiled, struck and recoiled, but always it engulfed a little more time and a little more space, for this is the way of revolutions.

It did not want to show its face till it had to, for this is the way of revolutions, too, especially is it true.

Continued on Page 2, Col. 1

FINAL MORNING EXTRA

San Francisco Chronicle
THE CITY'S ONLY HOME-OWNED NEWSPAPER

FOUNDED 1865—VOL. CLIII, NO. 146 CCCC°°°°• — SAN FRANCISCO, MONDAY, DECEMBER 8, 1941 — DAILY 5 CENTS, SUNDAY 10 CENTS — PER MONTH, $1.38

U.S. AT WAR!
PARATROOPS LAND IN PHILIPPINES!

America at War!
EDITORIAL

By the act of Japan, America is at war. The time for debate has passed and the time for action has come. That action must be united and unanimous. "Politics is adjourned," whether between parties, factions or economic groups. From now on America is an army with every man, woman and child a soldier in it, all joined to the one end of victory.

If war had to come, it is perhaps well that it came this way, wanton, unwarned, in fraud and bad faith, virtually under a flag of truce. For in war there can be only one side in action, and now there is only one side in thought or feeling. Its slogan is, "Americans unite, for victory and freedom."

We can not know how long this war will last, how wide it will range, nor what it will cost us, in toil, in sacrifice and in treasure. We do know that whatever the cost, we will pay it, and that our reward will be to hand down to our children the free America which our fathers bequeathed to us.

Americans, unite!

U. S. Faces War: Losses May Be Heavy, Nation Warned

WASHINGTON, Dec. 8 (Monday) (AP)—Bombs from Japan made war on the United States today and as death tolls mounted, President Roosevelt announced he would deliver in person today a special message to Congress.

In the background as the Commander-in-Chief went before the joint session of the House and Senate was a Government report of "heavy" naval and "large" losses to the Army.

Whether Mr. Roosevelt will ask for a formal declaration of war by this country, to match the action taken in Tokyo, was left uncertain after a hurriedly summoned meeting of his Cabinet and congressional leaders of both parties tonight at the White House. Also uncertain was whether that declaration might extend to Japan's Axis allies, Germany and Italy.

It was clear from a statement made by the participants, however, that Congress would be requested to adopt a resolution of some nature, and equally clear that it would quickly give its approval. A request for governmental power equivalent to that under a war declaration was expected as a minimum.

WAR CAME WHILE TALKS WERE CONTINUING

War came suddenly to the United States early yesterday afternoon. Without warning, and while Japanese diplomats were still conducting negotiations for peace, the Japanese Air Force struck at Honolulu, Pearl Harbor and Hickham Field, all in

Paul C. Smith Called to Active Service

Paul C. Smith, Editor and General Manager of The San Francisco Chronicle, has been called to active duty with the Navy.

He was ordered last night to report to the Navy Department, Washington, D. C., at once.

Smith is a Lieutenant Commander in the U. S. Naval Reserve. He leaves today.

Japs Bomb Hawaii, Invade Thailand

350 Slain----Then Tokyo Declares War on U. S., Britain; President Roosevelt Will Go Before Congress Today!

Pacific Coast Springs to Wartime Alert; Leaves Are Canceled, Guns Manned

The West Coast, from San Diego to the Canadian line, and the entire Western Continental United States were swinging to a wartime basis within a few hours of the air attack on Hawaii by Japan.

Air raid listening devices went into action. The fastest pursuit ships and bombers of the Army Air Corps were poised for any sign of raid by land, sea or air.

Leaves and furloughs of all officers and enlisted men of the 11th, 12th and 13th Naval districts were canceled and the men ordered back to their ships.

A roundup of Japanese aliens who have been under suspicion as possible subversive agents was ordered by the Attorney General of the United States. FBI agents here, as well as in other cities of the United States have taken a number of these Japanese into custody.

FACTORIES TIGHTEN WATCH FOR SABOTEURS

The outposts of the Nation's far-flung Pacific Coast defenses at Alaska and the Panama Canal were blacked out last night.

Leaves of all soldiers in the 9th Corps Area — California, Nevada, Utah, Idaho, Montana, Washington and Oregon—were summarily canceled by the War Department and all men were ordered to their posts.

The United States Coast Guard ordered all Pacific Coast craft into port, and the Customs Department canceled all departure permits. Movements of craft in harbors was restricted.

All enlisted men of Class M-2 Naval Reserve, were instructed by the navy to report today for mobilization orders.

Quickly many of the discordant elements which have been bickering over foreign policy for months,

Continued on Page 6, Col. 1

OLSON CALLS FOR GUARD VOLUNTEERS

Governor Olson issued a statement at Sacramento proclaiming the State "the most vital military objective of any attack which may be contemplated by air, sabotage or other means of destruction," and called for 10,000 volunteers to the State Guard.

Attorney General Earl Warren in a State-wide, all-points broadcast out of Los Angeles warned all law enforcement agencies and civilians to be on the alert against disorder, and urged that reason and calm judgment prevail.

He instructed citizens to call his office. In the State building, San Francisco, "in the event of need of outside civilian assistance to prevent civilian disorder of any kind."

Under these circumstances, the

FDR on Air

Network radio stations will carry President Roosevelt's address to the joint session of Congress this morning. Among them will be stations KGO, KPO and KSFO in San Francisco. Time here will be 9:30 a. m.

Raids Took a Heavy Toll, Hawaii Says

(This is the last uncensored Associated Press dispatch from Honolulu in the new war. Soon after this dispatch was telephoned a heavy censorship was imposed on dispatches from the Hawaiian islands. In Washington, some hours later, the War Department gave the White House a preliminary estimate that 104 were dead and more than 300 wounded in the army forces alone by the bombing.)

HONOLULU, Dec. 7 (AP)—War struck suddenly and without warning from the sky and sea today at the Hawaiian islands, and Japanese bombs took a heavy toll of lives.

Cannonading offshore indicated a naval engagement in progress.

Wave after wave of planes streamed over Oahu in an attack which the army said started at 8:10 a. m. Honolulu time, and which ended at around 9:25, an hour and 15 minutes later.

Witnesses said they counted at least 50 planes in the initial attack.

The attack seemed to center against Hickam Field, huge army airport three miles northwest of Honolulu, and Honolulu, where the islands' heaviest fortifications are located.

The planes streamed through the sky from the southwest, their bombs shattering the morning calm. Most of the attackers flew high, but a few came low, five down to under a hundred feet elevation to attack Pearl harbor.

An oil tank there was seen blazing and smoking. An unconfirmed report said one ship in the harbor was on its side and four others burning.

Army officials said two Japanese planes had been shot down in the Honolulu area.

Planes which did not bomb Pearl

Continued on Page C, Col. 7

INSIDE

You'll find full war coverage—news, background and pictures: See Pages A, B, C, D, E, F, G, H, 3, 4, 5 and 6. Other war news on pages 2, 7 and 11.

Hoover: Our Decision's Clear

By Associated Press

Former President Herbert Hoover last night called for an all-out fight against the Japanese, saying, "American soil has been treacherously attacked by Japan. Our decision is clear."

Wendell Willkie, Republican standard bearer in 1940, said: "I have not the slightest doubt as to what a united America should and will do."

Raiders Fly From Hidden Aircraft Carrier; Guam Is 'Surrounded'; Wake Falls

NEW YORK, Dec. 8 (AP) — Royal Arch Gunnison, broadcasting to WOR-Mutual from Manila, reported today that Japanese parachute troops had been landed in the Philippines.

He said native Japanese had seized control of some communities where they are thickly concentrated, but said that in other sections Filipino police were rounding up Japanese nationals and taking them to concentration camps.

Gunnison also reported, without detail, that "in the naval war the ABCD fleets under American command were appearing to be successful against Japanese air and sea invasions," WOR announced.

By the Associated Press

The Japanese bombed Pearl Harbor and Honolulu with murderous effect Sunday and proceeded today to assault or invade Thailand and United States and British possessions in the far reaches of the Pacific in the hasty prosecution of a war which the Japanese government declared only after it had been in deadly progress for three hours.

The Hawaiian bombing came at 7:35 a. m. (10:05 a. m., San Francisco time) Sunday.

The Japanese claimed among their successes the sinking of the U. S. battleship West Virginia and the setting afire of the battleship Oklahoma—grievous blows if true.

In general the first tidings told of heavy—"doubtless very heavy losses" — to the American

Continued on Page 11, Col. 1

Evening Standard

37,357   BLACK-OUT 10 57 pm to 5.0 am.   MOON Rises 9.50 pm; Sets 6.29 am.   ONE PENNY

FINAL NIGHT EXTRA

Churchill Announces Successful Massed Air Landings Behind Enemy in France

4000 SHIPS, THOUSANDS OF SMALLER VESSELS

"So Far All Goes to Plan"— 11,000 First Line Airplanes

An immense armada of more than 4000 ships, with several thousand smaller craft, has crossed the Channel, said Mr. Churchill to-day, announcing the invasion.

"MASSED AIRBORNE LANDINGS HAVE BEEN SUCCESSFULLY EFFECTED BEHIND THE ENEMY'S LINES," HE SAID.

MR. CHURCHILL DESCRIBED THE LANDINGS AS THE "FIRST OF A SERIES IN FORCE ON THE EUROPEAN CONTINENT."

"The landings on the beaches are proceeding at various points at the present time. The fire of the shore batteries has been largely quelled, said Mr. Churchill.

"The obstacles which were constructed in the sea have not proved so difficult as was apprehended.

"The Anglo-American Allies are sustained by about 11,000 first line aircraft, which can be drawn upon as may be needed for the purposes of the battle.

No. 1

At 9.30 a.m. to-day the following communiqué was issued from General Eisenhower's Supreme Headquarters:

"Under the command of General Eisenhower, Allied naval forces, supported by strong air forces, began landing Allied armies this morning on the Northern coast of France."

The statement was marked "Communiqué No. 1." At the same time it was revealed that General Montgomery is in command of the Army Group carrying out the assault. This Army Group includes British, Canadian and U.S. forces.

The King on the Radio To-night

It was officially announced from Buckingham Palace to-day that the King will broadcast at 9 o'clock to-night.
The King received the Prime Minister in audience at Buckingham Palace to-day, and Mr. Churchill remained for lunch.

NAZIS NAME DIVISIONS

The German official news agency said the British 1st and 2nd and the 8th Airborne Divisions are taking part in attacks in the Seine estuary area.
The US 82nd and 101st Airborne Divisions are attacking in the Cherbourg peninsula.
(Continued on Back Page, Col. Five)

'LANDINGS ON JERSEY, GUERNSEY'

German Overseas News Agency said this afternoon that landings have been made on the Channel Islands —Jersey and Guernsey—by Allied parachute troops.

Quoting the German High Command spokesman, the agency said: "Early to-day Allied airborne formations landed on Guernsey and Jersey

"They were at once engaged in extremely costly battles."

SURPRISE

"There are already hopes that actual tactical surprise has been attained," said the Premier, "and we hope to furnish the enemy with a succession of surprises during the course of the fighting.

"The battle which is now beginning will grow constantly in scale and in intensity for many weeks to come, and I shall not attempt to speculate upon its course.

"Complete unity prevails throughout the Allied Armies (Cheers.)

"There is a brotherhood in arms between us and our friends in the United States.

"There is complete confidence in the Supreme Commander, General Eisenhower, and in his lieutenants, and also in the Commander of the Expeditionary Force, General Montgomery.

"The ardour and spirit of the troops as I saw them myself embarking in these last few days was splendid.

"Nothing that equipment science and forethought can do has been neglected, and the whole process of opening this great new front will be pursued with the utmost resolution both by the commanders and by the U.S and British Governments whom they serve."

After Mr. Churchill made his war statement in the Commons, Mr. Gallacher (Com. W. Fife) said: "This is one of the (Continued on Back Page, Col. Five)

640-GUN SHELLING

The Supreme Headquarters of the Allied Expeditionary Force state that over 640 naval guns, from 16in. to 4in., are bombarding the beaches and enemy strong points in support of the armies.

About 200 Allied minesweepers, with 10,000 officers and men, are engaged in the operations.

The weight of minesweeping material used amounts to 2800 tons, and the amount of sweep wire in use would reach almost exactly from London to the Isle of Wight.

The Press Association learns that enemy destroyers and E-boats are reported coming into the operational area,

Wave After Wave of Khaki-clad Figures Surged up the Beaches

"BEACH-HEAD WAS OURS"

THE BOMBARDMENT FROM ALLIED WARSHIPS BEGAN TO-DAY AS SOON AS DAWN BROKE, REPORTS A MILITARY OBSERVER WHO LANDED WITH THE FIRST ASSAULT FORCES.

"From left, right and centre our guns opened up and from our vantage point at sea we could see that targets ashore were being pounded out of existence as the assaulting infantry sailed slowly and surely ahead to let bayonets do whatever work remained," said the observer.

'Bitter Fighting'

To-day's German communiqué stated:
"Last night the enemy began his long-prepared attack on Western Europe, which was expected by us.

"Beginning with two heavy air attacks on our coastal fortifications, the enemy dropped airborne troops at several points on the French northern coast between Havre and Cherbourg, and supported by strong naval forces also landed from the sea.

"Bitter fighting is in progress on the coastal stretches attacked

"From sea and sky the bombardment continued, until our infantry were ashore.

"It was a magnificent sight. Wave upon wave of khaki-clad figures surged up the beaches, overcoming any opposition in their way.

"Within a very short space of time the immediate bridgehead was ours; and shortly afterwards, beachmasters, beach parties and the like were ashore and putting their organisations into effect.

"When I went ashore, the organisation was complete, and as vehicles, guns, infantry and equipment of all sorts came trundling on to the beaches from the sea. It was sorted out and despatched as quickly as it had come.

"On beaches beside us, other divisions stormed the fortress and rushed in their reinforcements to coincide with ours."

Invasion Fleet "Beats All"

From HOWARD WHITHAM

AN INVASION PORT.

First ship to return to this port from the invasion armada was a landing ship for tanks commanded by a New Zealand sub-lieutenant.

He gave the first description of the invasion fleet: "I have been in the shows in Africa, Sicily and Italy, but I have never seen anything like this one.

"This one really beats all. Out where I was there were landing ship tanks stretched out as far as I could see."

Many Americans and Britons described their air cover as "superb."

Hitler in Command

Hitler is taking personal command of all the anti-invasion operations, according to news reaching London from underground sources.

(Continued on Back Page, Col. Two)

[Map showing Southern England and Northern France with distances marked, towns including SOUTHAMPTON, PORTSMOUTH, BRIGHTON, NEWHAVEN, DOVER, FOLKESTONE, CALAIS, DUNKIRK, BOULOGNE, ETAPLES, LE TOUQUET, ABBEVILLE, DIEPPE, CHERBOURG, BARFLEUR, LE HAVRE, CAEN, ROUEN, AMIENS, and others, with distances 22 MILES, 26 MILES, 67 MILES, 83 MILES, 114 MILES]

Tanks Drive South from Beach-heads

The Allies have established beach-heads in Northern France and are driving inland, according to pilots who have flown over the battle.

This afternoon the German announced that landings were continuing in the Seine Bay stretch of the Normandy coast between the two ports of Cherbourg and Le Havre and that between Caen and Isigny the Allies had penetrated several miles to the south with tanks.

They reported that the whole coast between these ports was involved, but mentioned particularly three focal points. These were:

ORNE ESTUARY the mouth of the river which runs north through CAEN into the Seine Bay. Caen itself, about 10 miles from the coast, was described as the first focal point.

Landing barges, under a strong air umbrella, were reported to be coming ashore at OUISTREHAM, at the river mouth.

Tanks have been landed at ARROMANCHES, a fishing village further west, said another German report.

"More than 200 craft approached this part of the coast nine hours after the first landings," it was added. "The enemy are trying to scale the cliffs with special ladders."

"The Germans are putting up very stiff resistance in the Caen area," said Paris radio this afternoon. "The town area itself has been sorely tried. The enemy appear to be penetrating deeper inland.

"It has now become clear that the main Allied blow is not directed against Havre, but that General Eisenhower is concentrating (Continued on Back Page, Col. Two)

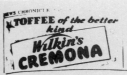

News Chronicle
No. 30,666 SATURDAY, AUGUST 26, 1944 ONE PENNY
4 a.m. EDITION

PARIS FINALLY LIBERATED AND DE GAULLE HAS ENTERED

Nazis march through jubilant capital as prisoners

PARIS IS FREE. THE GERMANS WHO LAST NIGHT MARCHED THROUGH THE CITY MARCHED AS PRISONERS. GEN. DE GAULLE HAS ENTERED THE CAPITAL AND HAS SPOKEN FROM THE TOWN HALL.

"I wish simply and from the bottom of my heart," he said, "to say simply to you, 'Vive Paris!'"

Today the capital will celebrate her victory with a great triumphal procession down the Champs Elysees.

The story of the 24 hours—from 10 o'clock on Thursday night to 10 o'clock last night—that ended in the glorious liberation is briefly this.

1. Late on Thursday night patrols of Gen. Leclerc's Second Armoured Division moved forward to make contact with the F.F.I. forces at the Hotel de Ville.

2. Early yesterday morning the main forces moved into the city. From 2 a.m. onward there was skirmishing.

3. U.S. troops moved into the city to join the battle.

4. At 7 p.m. came the word that Gen. de Gaulle had entered the city.

5. Soon after, it was announced that Gen. Leclerc had issued an ultimatum to the German commander. This was accepted.

End of the battle

6. At 10 p.m. it was announced that the Battle of Paris had ended, that no Germans save only the dead and the prisoners remained on the soil of the capital.

Thus was Paris liberated. There is so far no connected report of what happened on this great day, but from the masses of messages this picture may be drawn.

The first outside forces to move in were patriots from Gen. Leclerc's division. They went in late on Thursday night and made contact with the F.F.I. chiefs at the Hotel de Ville.

Then yesterday morning the main forces moved in.

Into the city

The tanks approached Paris from the Versailles area in two main columns.

They encountered stiff but patchy German resistance, and they also found more road blocks, demolitions and mines than they expected.

Soon after midnight, however, they had fought their way into the outskirts, and at 2.30 a.m. they were fanning out into the city.

Casualties were inflicted on the Germans both around the fringes and inside Paris itself. A number of prisoners were taken.

By the morning they had crossed the Seine in the heart of Paris by the Pont St. Michel, which crosses by way of the Ile de la Cité, on which the Palais de Justice, the Prefecture of Police and Notre Dame stand, and which was seized by the Forces of the Interior when they rose against the Germans.

Hour by hour

The story of the fighting was told in a series of bulletins by the "broadcasting service of the French nation" on the Paris wavelength. Here they are:

7 a.m.: French armoured cars circulating on the outer boulevards.

7.30 a.m.: Since 2 a.m. engage-

Continued Back Page

THE FIRST PICTURE FROM PARIS

Crowds of jubilant Parisians, free at last, throng the streets to salute the day of liberation. At Clamart (below), two miles from the city, a cheering crowd broke into the armoured column as it moved on the capital and clambered on to the vehicles

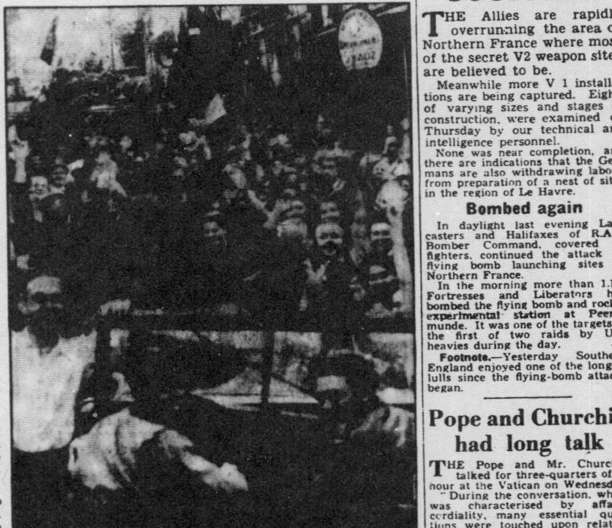

RHEIMS REACHED BY AMERICANS REPORT AT H.Q.

Advance to Troyes, within 130 miles from Reich

From STANLEY BARON
News Chronicle War Correspondent

SUPREME H.Q., Friday night.

AMERICAN patrols are reported tonight as far east as Troyes, 90 miles south-east of Paris and only 130 miles from the German frontier.

An unconfirmed report says another column has reached Rheims, 85 miles north-east of the capital and 15 miles north of the Marne.

Rheims is only 50 miles from the scene of the great German break-through in 1940 at Sedan, and is about the same distance from the Belgian border.

As this report is given, it would mean that the Americans have made the greatest advance of the war.

Gen. Patton's army east of Sens was last heard of three days ago. If the story concerns the same force, which has been stated to be meeting with very little opposition, its new advance would be over 100 miles, measured through Troyes.

Outflanking the North

An Allied army at Rheims would completely outflank the German Fifteenth Army in the north, and its presence there would negative any success the enemy may have had in getting the remains of the Seventh Army over the Seine.

The report puts in proper perspective the fighting in Paris. It has constantly been insisted here that Paris was not a major objective, militarily considered.

That the Germans have, in fact, got a fairly considerable number of men out of the Seine pocket to the north of the river now seems likely. Foul weather, grounding our air forces, enabled them, during a great part of the week, to get a steady trickle of barges over.

Any who are left on the wrong side of the river at present, including those who have fought a stubborn, well-organised rear-guard action on the west and south of the pocket, have little chance now of getting out, however.

The fight in the Seine pocket, indeed, has now reached the utmost intensity.

54 tanks destroyed

The Germans have given up any attempt at hiding their efforts to cross the river.

From daylight to dusk fighters and fighter-bombers have been screaming down on barges and the two bridges which the enemy engineers have managed to reconstruct.

In a great attack on motor transport and tanks moving east to get to these points and the crossings at Duclair and Caudebec, the Ninth American Air Force had, up to 6 p.m., smashed 158 motor vehicles, destroyed 54 tanks and damaged 50 others.

In the air the fight has gone on, too, as the Luftwaffe came up in an endeavour to put an umbrella over the river. By early evening they had already lost 41 aircraft, six probables, and 21 had been damaged.

The final tally, when the figures for the second T.A.F. have been included, will probably go well beyond these. Our own losses up to six o'clock were 18.

Beyond Honfleur

Meanwhile, the springing of the great land trap has been practically completed with a Canadian advance three miles beyond Honfleur, at the mouth of the Seine, and the capture of Elbeuf, just above Rouen, by the Americans and another Canadian force coming from south to south-east.

We are over the Risle in six places and now the bottom of the pocket is looking like a grid as forces of Americans, Canadians and British cross each other's track, pulling in prisoners and cleaning up spasmodic suicide resistance as they go.

While this great round-up has been reaching its final stages, the battle for Brest has opened.

At 3 p.m. a heavy co-ordinated attack began with the evident intention of freeing the port. While 300 Marauders and Havocs bombed strong-points, coastal batteries and the arsenal, fire was poured in from battleships standing off the coast and ground artillery opened up from behind and around the port.

Panic flight of remnants over Seine

From RONALD WALKER
News Chronicle War Correspondent

NORMANDY, Friday.

TODAY the R.A.F. found the first signs of panic attempts to cross the Seine in daylight by the elements of the German divisions hemmed in by the rapidly advancing British, Canadian and American troops.

During the past 24 hours it has been an advance at high speed, with the Germans scampering before it.

Today the different Allied armies have joined hands at several points and the large gap which existed yesterday has been reduced to a diamond-shaped area bounded on the south-west by the Risle River, on the east by a line from Louviers to Brionne and on the north-east by the Seine.

Having experienced the awful punishment inflicted upon them in the Falaise-Trun area, the German troops are obviously nervous of being exposed to our fighters and fighter-bombers.

Closer and closer

But circumstances are against them. Although comparatively little fighting has been reported today the Germans are being pushed closer and closer to the Seine. They must cross it or be rounded up.

Despite our patrols by night, it is obvious that the enemy has been able to sneak a number of his troops over the river under cover of darkness, but it now appears that circumstances will also force him to dash for it in daylight.

Today the panic seems to have begun. Our fighters found soldiers swimming the river in the vicinity of the Foret de la Londe. Their swim was not a pleasant summer exercise.

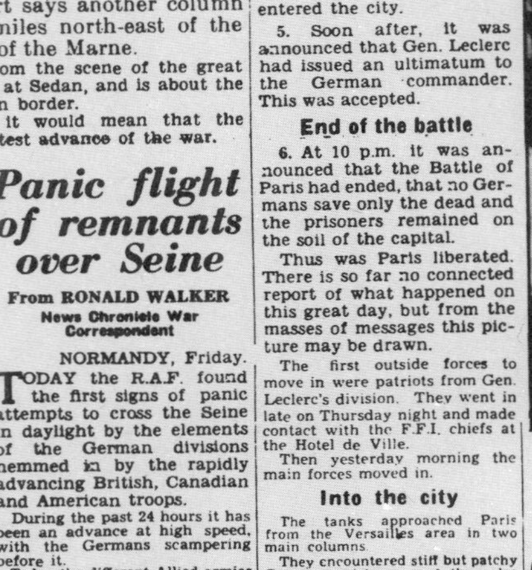

"Eternal France"

GEN. DE GAULLE, in a speech to the people of Paris late last night, broadcast from the Prefecture of Police, stated:

"France will take her place among the great nations which will organise the peace.

"We will not rest until we march, as we must, into enemy territory as conquerors.

"France has rights abroad. France is a great nation, and she has rights which she will know how to make heard. She has the right to security.

Will be heard

"She has the right to insist that she be never again invaded by the enemy who has so often invaded her. She has the right to be in the first line among the great nations who are going to organise the peace and life of the world.

"She has the right to make herself heard in all four corners of the world.

"France is a great world Power—she knows it, and she will act so that others may also know it, because this is of supreme interest—that is the interest of humanity.

"Men and women, we are here in Paris, which stood erect and rose in order to free herself—Paris, oppressed, downtrodden and martyred, but still Paris; free now, freed by the hands of Frenchmen, the capital of Fighting France, of France the great eternal.

As conquerors

"It is not enough that with the aid of our dear and splendid Allies we should drive the enemy from our soil. After what has happened to France we will not rest or be satisfied until we enter, as is only right, upon the enemy's own territory as conquerors.

"We are going to fight on to the last day, to the day of total and complete victory.

"After what happened in 1940 after France gave in and her Government was usurped, there is no other practical and acceptable way for the people to make its voice heard than by the universal and free vote of all Frenchmen and women."—Reuter.

24-hour strike in Athens

Cairo, Friday. — A 24-hour general strike was declared in Athens yesterday, the Hellenic News Service announced today, in protest against the deportation to Germany of 1,500 civilian hostages.

Later 4,000 more people were arrested.

Koenig's troops are in Lyons

FRENCH troops, commanded by Gen. Koenig, have entered Lyons, a F.F.I. general staff communique announced last night.

American forces are now in the Lyons region, according to Algiers radio, and the advance on the southern end of the Rhone Valley has brought an American column to within eight miles of Arles. The town of St. Martin has been captured.

Sertorius, the German military commentator, said yesterday that Allied troops, supported by men of the Maquis, have approached the middle Rhone between Montelimar, 45 miles north of Avignon, and Valence, 33 miles farther north.

Cannes captured

On the eastern sector of the beach-head our troops have captured Cannes, the largest of the Riviera resorts, and Grasse, about seven miles inland.

American troops who entered Cannes are already beyond Antibes, seven miles east of the town.

Prisoners taken now total 20,000.

In the south-west of France the Germans are "withdrawing according to plan," said Berlin yesterday.

Running fights in the Channel

LIGHT British and American naval forces had a series of running fights early today with enemy naval vessels trying to break out of Le Havre.

In the first, U.S. coastal craft chased a group of E-boats off Cap d'Antifer and scored many hits.

Later, British torpedo-boats torpedoed and sank an armed trawler escorting a convoy, while the Americans severely damaged one of a further group of E-boats, and the British destroyers Retalick and Talybont damaged three more E-boats, one of which sank.

The convoy then attempted to proceed under cover of heavy fire from the shore and was again attacked by torpedo-boats, one R-boat bursting into flames and another being silenced.

Shortly before dawn British torpedo-boats scored a hit on one of a group of escort vessels which was considered to have sunk. There were three slight casualties in the Allied ships.

V-weapon sites are overrun

THE Allies are rapidly overrunning the area of Northern France where most of the secret V2 weapon sites are believed to be.

Meanwhile more V 1 installations are being captured. Eight, of varying sizes and stages of construction, were examined on Thursday by our technical and intelligence personnel.

None was near completion, and there are indications that the Germans are also withdrawing labour from preparation of a nest of sites in the region of Le Havre.

Bombed again

In daylight last evening Lancasters and Halifaxes of R.A.F. Bomber Command, covered by fighters, continued the attack on flying bomb launching sites in Northern France.

In the morning more than 1,100 Fortresses and Liberators had bombed the flying bomb and rocket experimental station at Peenemunde. It was one of the targets in the first of two raids by U.S. heavies during the day.

Footnote.—Yesterday Southern England enjoyed one of the longest lulls since the flying-bomb attacks began.

Pope and Churchill had long talk

THE Pope and Mr. Churchill talked for three-quarters of an hour at the Vatican on Wednesday.

"During the conversation, which was characterised by affable cordiality, many essential questions were touched upon relating to important problems of the present hour," states an official announcement released at Advanced Allied Force H.Q.

Mr. Churchill drove into Vatican City without any police precautions. He was accompanied by the British Minister to the Vatican, Sir Francis D'Arcy Osborne.

Mr. Churchill left Rome on Wednesday evening. He is likely to meet Mr. Attlee in the Mediterranean before returning to London.

U.S. parties and world security

From Our Own Correspondent

Washington, Friday.—An informal agreement between the Democratic and Republican parties to regard the new world security organisation as above the level of partisan debate emerged today from meetings between Secretary of State Cordell Hull and Mr. John Foster Dulles, whom Governor Dewey, the Republican Presidential candidate, designated to represent him.

Mr. Dulles told correspondents at the State Department today that this development is "something unique in American politics" and implied that it is the best insurance it has been possible to devise so far against a repetition of the divisions which led the Senate to reject the League of Nations after the last war.

317,646 U.S. war casualties

Washington, Friday.—The latest announced casualties of the U.S. armed forces from the outbreak of the war total 317,646. These include 72,015 dead, 144,994 wounded, 52,549 missing and 48,288 prisoners of war.

Jap cruiser left on fire and sinking

Allied H.Q., S.W. Pacific, Saturday.—Allied planes bombed a light Japanese cruiser and left it on fire and sinking near the Celebes on Thursday, states Gen. MacArthur's communique.

Five merchantmen were sunk and two others damaged.

Japs call special session

The Jap Parliament has been summoned for a special session, to begin on September 6 and last five days, according to a Japanese announcement quoted by the German Overseas News Agency.

Gunfire heard in Straits

Explosions, believed to be heavy gunfire, were heard on this side of the Straits from the Calais region during yesterday afternoon. The rumble continued for some time at frequent intervals.

Luftwaffe makes mass attack on Bucharest, troops gun civilians, then

Rumanian Cabinet broadcasts: we are at war with Germany

A SUCCESSION of dramatic messages over Bucharest radio last night gave the news that—

1. The Luftwaffe had made a heavy attack on Bucharest. 2. Rumania had declared war on Germany. 3. The German forces in Bucharest had surrendered after heavy fighting.

The radio said that fighting broke out between Rumanian and German troops in the capital and in the country yesterday morning.

The German Legation and German High Command had been informed that the Rumanian Army would take no hostile action against Germany and would allow the German troops to withdraw. The Germans in return promised that they would take no hostile action.

Later, however, they attacked and tried to disarm the Rumanian forces. They also machine-gunned civilians.

Dive-bombed

At the same time the German Air Force in strength bombed the capital and other towns of the country, destroying non-military objectives and aiming particularly at the Royal Palace.

After a mass bombardment by Stuka dive-bombers, German troops attempted to capture the Baneasa airfield, near Bucharest, but all their attacks were repelled.

German guns and lorries were destroyed and German prisoners taken. At 11 o'clock the capital was completely freed, the German garrison having surrendered.

Outside the capital, the last German strong-points were giving in. Whole groups of soldiers were surrendering.

A Government proclamation was then read. It said: "By these acts of aggression, which occurred simultaneously in various parts of the country, Germany has placed herself in a state of war with Rumania.

"The Government therefore orders the Rumanian Army to begin the struggle against all German military forces on Rumanian territory for the liberation of the country from German usurpation."

Bulgaria collapsing

In Rumania the whole front is disintegrating—a word used by the Germans themselves—beneath the weight of the Soviet's drive.

The collapse of Bulgaria is believed to be imminent; Hungary has ordered general mobilisation; there have been frontier clashes between Hungarian and Rumanian troops; Tito's men in Yugo-Slavia are at grips with the enemy on every sector.

Bulgaria is expected to be out of the war within a few days, possibly even before the end of the week.

Armistice negotiations in Istanbul are believed to have entered the final stages. A special Bulgarian emissary has returned there after receiving fresh intructions from M. Bagrianov, Bulgarian Premier. He is understood to have taken a positive answer to certain of the Allied demands.

The general mobilisation order in Hungary followed a Cabinet shake-up. Postal, telegraph and phone communications with Rumania have been cut.

LATE NEWS

GOING BACK TO SIEGFRIED LINE

Zurich, Saturday.—Germans withdrawing from Belfort towards Mulhouse, according to special correspondent's dispatch from Belfort to "Tribune de Geneve." Paper states "on good authority" the German forces taking up positions along Siegfried Line.

LONDON BLACK-OUT

Tonight	Tomorrow
9.30–6.34 a.m.	9.28–6.35 a.m.

Moon sets, 12.16 a.m. tomorrow; rises, 4.8 p.m. Full Moon Sept. 2.

Enemy lost 204,000 men in five days

ONE of the biggest German defeats since the war began has been inflicted by the Russians in Rumania, according to a Soviet Command announcement broadcast from Moscow last night.

In battles which have gone on for five days the Germans, caught between two Russian armies, have lost 100,000 men in dead, 104,000 have been captured (including three generals).

Twelve German infantry divisions—possibly 96,000 troops, are now encircled south-west of Chisinau.

For two days they have been trying to break out of the Russian ring.

Nearing Galatz

The armies which scored these victories are commanded by Gen. Malinovsky and Gen. Tolbukhin. They have now joined up, and yesterday, in a big thrust towards the Danube basin, they took over 500 places.

German losses in material included 200 planes, 664 tanks and self-propelled guns and 3,217 guns of other kinds.

An Order of the Day announced a victory in the north. The Estonian rail town of Tartu was captured by the Third Baltic Army.

for Aeschylean drama, . . . in the play of would-be gods and self-elected giants, they are figures representing the only two great Powers left in the world that speak with human voices'. *The New Orleans Times-Picayune* put it rather more concisely: 'The war's result will be determined by deeds and not by words'.

Yet *The Chicago Daily Tribune* was not going to give up that easily. On December 4 it 'leaked' — with cries of horror — a secret Army and Navy war plan which called for an American Expeditionary Force of 5,000,000 men for an offensive against Germany, and quoted July 1 1943 as the date fixed for America's supreme war effort. The Secretary of War, understandably furious, did not however deny the report. He simply put two rhetorical questions to newsmen at a Press conference the next day: '1. What would you think of an American General Staff which in the present condition of the world did not investigate and study every conceivable type of emergency . . .? 2. What do you think of the patriotism of a man or newspaper which

would take those confidential studies and make them public to the enemies of the country?'

The Chicago Daily Tribune's report was certainly reprinted and investigated in Berlin and Tokyo. Official spokesmen in both capitals were inclined to treat the news flippantly. A Tokyo paper asserted that US military leaders were obviously 'panic-stricken'. One source in Berlin thought the notion 'a piquant, delightful idea bordering on idiocy'; another pointed out that 'the plan apparently is based on the theory that both Russia and the British Empire will be defeated by 1943, which is not exactly flattering to either. We can calmly await July 1 1943'.

And there the debate, and the recriminations, ended. For at 7.30 the next morning (Hawaiian time) more than 350 Japanese planes dived over the American Pacific fleet moored in Pearl Harbor and bombed it, unwarned and unprepared, mercilessly. Japan then proceeded to declare war on America — followed promptly by its tripartite partners, Germany and Italy. December 7 1941 was, the President declared

to Congress the next day, a date that will live in infamy'. It was also the date that finally united America; as *The San Francisco Chronicle* said 'If war had to come, it is perhaps well that it came this way, wanton, unwarned, in fraud and bad faith, virtually under a flag of truce. For . . . now there is only one side in thought or feeling. Its slogan is "Americans unite"!'

"All the News That's Fit to Print"

The New York Times.

LATE CITY EDITION
Temperatures Yesterday—Max. 72; Min. 66
Sunrise today, 5:57 A. M.; Sunset, 8:06 P. M.

Copyright, 1945, by The New York Times Company.

VOL. XCIV..No. 31,972.

Entered as Second-Class Matter,
Postoffice, New York, N. Y.

NEW YORK, TUESDAY, AUGUST 7, 1945.

THREE CENTS NEW YORK CITY

FIRST ATOMIC BOMB DROPPED ON JAPAN; MISSILE IS EQUAL TO 20,000 TONS OF TNT; TRUMAN WARNS FOE OF A 'RAIN OF RUIN'

HIRAM W. JOHNSON, REPUBLICAN DEAN IN THE SENATE, DIES

Isolationist Helped Prevent U. S. Entry Into League— Opposed World Charter

CALIFORNIA EX-GOVERNOR

Ran for Vice President With Theodore Roosevelt in '12 —In Washington Since '17

Special to The New York Times.

WASHINGTON, Aug. 6.—Senator Hiram Warren Johnson of California, lifelong isolationist who helped prevent this country's entry into the League of Nations and fought all "foreign entanglements" through a second World War, died in his sleep this morning at Bethesda Naval Hospital, nine days after, ill but consistent, he had paired his vote against ratification of the United Nations Charter. Death was caused by a thrombosis of a cerebral artery. Mrs. Johnson was with him when the end came.

When word reached the Capitol of the passing of the oldest member of the Senate in point of service, save Senator Kenneth McKellar, the President pro tempore, the mourning was deep. With great personal affection colleagues paid humble tribute to his integrity of character, his liberalism and his steadfastness to his ideals and convictions. They joined in declaring that the country had lost a great statesman.

Senator Johnson, who was serving the fourth year of his fifth term in the Senate, would have been 79 years old on Sept. 2. Although his health had been failing during the last two years and though the thundering voice which had conveyed his eloquence through innumerable stirring debates had become little more than a whisper, friends believed he planned to seek a sixth term in 1947.

He went to the hospital July 18. Five days before that he had cast the lone vote in the Foreign Relations Committee, of which he was the ranking minority member, against reporting the new World Charter to the Senate without a change. He did not participate in the floor debate on this document, which won Senate approval by a vote of 82—2. However, he clashed spiritedly with colleagues while the hearings were in progress.

Funeral arrangements awaited the arrival of the Senator's son, Lieut. Col. Hiram W. Johnson Jr., who was flying here from California.

Capper Becomes the Dean

The death of Senator Johnson made Senator Arthur Capper of Kansas, who last month marked his eightieth birthday, the Republican dean of the Senate. It also elevated him to the ranking minority membership on the Foreign Relations Committee, with which Senator Johnson had been so conspicuously identified through the many years of his unshaken position on foreign policy. Mr. Capper, too, with Senators McKellar, Carter Glass of Virginia, David I. Walsh of Massachusetts and Peter G. Gerry, was in the League fight of 1919 and 1920. He supported it, with reservations.

The career of Senator Johnson, from his entrance into the Senate from the Governorship of California in March of 1917, was one distinctly lacking in compromise or reservation. In 1912 he had bolted his party with Theodore Roosevelt and had become his running mate on the Bull Moose ticket. In 1932 he again bolted to support Franklin D. Roosevelt for the Presidency but broke bitterly with the President when he ran for his third term. In 1919 Mr. Johnson joined with Senators Lodge, Borah, Reed,

Continued on Page 23, Column 4

Jet Plane Explosion Kills Major Bong, Top U. S. Ace

Flier Who Downed 40 Japanese Craft, Sent Home to Be 'Safe,' Was Flying New 'Shooting Star' as a Test Pilot

By The United Press.

BURBANK, Calif., Aug. 6.—Maj. Richard Bong, America's greatest air ace, died today in the flaming wreckage of a jet propelled fighter plane which crashed while he was testing it.

Only 24 years old, he wore twenty-six decorations including the nation's highest award, the Congressional Medal of Honor. He had survived countless air battles and shot down forty Japanese planes without a scratch.

With a roaring sigh, the plane, like a giant blowtorch, shot over the airport just before 3 P. M. and then lurched over the trees and nosed down into the field, a mile away.

Smoke and flame surged up and crowds rushed from the airport. By the time anyone could reach the scene the ship had been almost consumed.

The crash scene was near the intersection of Cahuenga and Oxnard Boulevards and barely outside.

"The plane started to wobble up and down, then went into a left bank and hit the ground," he stated. "It exploded and burned and scattered wreckage over about a block square."

Major Bong was trying to get out of the ship when it crashed. He had released the escape hatch and was partly clear. He had pulled the ripcord to his parachute, and the silken folds lay about the body as the flames swept over it.

Witnesses did not agree on the cause of the crash. One Army flier said that Major Bong overshot the Lockheed airport. Another witness, a John McKinney of North Hollywood reported that he saw something fall out of the plane's tail.

Continued on page 15, Column 2

MORRIS IS ACCUSED OF 'TAKING A WALK'

Fusion Official 'Sad to Part Company'—McGoldrick Sees Only Tammany Aided

The No Deal ticket, headed by Council President Newbold Morris, "can only serve the interests of Tammany Hall," Controller Joseph D. McGoldrick, candidate for re-election on the Republican-Liberal-Fusion party slate, declared yesterday in a fresh attack on the third-party ticket injected over the week-end into the city Mayoralty campaign.

A short while later Gabriel A. Wechsler, general secretary of the City Fusion party, which supported Mayor La Guardia and Mr. Morris in previous city campaigns, accused Mr. Morris of "taking a walk away from the good government forces."

To both charges Mr. Morris declared he would stand on his statement of Sunday that he was not interested in "just taking votes" away from Judge Jonah J. Goldstein, Republican-Liberal-Fusion candidate for Mayor, or from William O'Dwyer, his Democratic-American Labor party opponent.

"I have no comment," he said, "since I stand on my statement of Sunday. We are waging an affirmative campaign."

Informed that Hyman Blumberg,

Continued on Page 19, Column 6

CHINESE WIN MORE OF 'INVASION COAST'

Smash Into Port 121 Miles Southwest of Canton—Big Area Open for Landing

By The Associated Press.

CHUNGKING, China, Aug. 6.—Chinese troops have broken into the South China port of Yeungkong and cleared a fifty-mile stretch of the Chinese "invasion coast" east of Hong Kong, Generalissimo Chiang Kai-shek's headquarters said today.

Swaying block-by-block street fighting is raging in the strategic coastal highway town, 121 miles southwest of Canton, a communiqué said.

By breaking into Yeungkong Chinese forces won control of a fifty-mile coastal stretch leading west to Tinpak, which lies east of Luichow Peninsula on the South China Sea. The coastal area now is open to a virtually unopposed landing should American forces choose it for a staging point for supplies to the armies of South China.

West of Luichow Peninsula another 145-mile coastal stretch extending to the Indo-China frontier is under Chinese control and observers believe the Chinese soon may launch a concerted drive from the west and east that would seal off the Japanese on the Luichow

Continued on Page 2, Column 7

Turks Talk War if Russia Presses; Prefer Vain Battle to Surrender

By SAM POPE BREWER
By Wireless to The New York Times.

ANKARA, Turkey, Aug. 6.—Russo-Turkish relations weigh heavy on Turkish minds these days. All leading editors commented today on various aspects of the Russian claims against Turkey.

The Potsdam conference leaves the situation virtually unchanged so far as the Turks can see, but they seem to agree that they would go to war, however hopeless such a war might be, rather than yield before the threat of force. Suggestions that a bilateral agreement but must be discussed at a conference of the signatories of the Montreux Convention, with America replacing Japan. The signatories were Great Britain, France, Russia, Japan, Turkey, Greece, Rumania, Yugoslavia and Bulgaria.

The grounds for the Russian claims to Kars and Ardahan are not clear, but throughout the Near and Mideast in recent months that it was a failure.

Many point out that all the really thorny questions still are unsettled. The Turks probably do not see a relative importance among world problems of Russian demands on Turkey, but point out that the important question of principle is involved. The general and apparently official argument is that the status of the Straits cannot be modified by a bilateral agreement but must be discussed at a conference of the signatories of the Montreux Convention, with America replacing Japan. The signatories were Great Britain, France, Russia, Japan, Turkey, Greece, Rumania, Yugoslavia and Bulgaria.

The grounds for the Russian claims to Kars and Ardahan are not clear, but throughout the Near and Mideast in recent months certain specific questions means that it was a failure.

Continued on Page 13, Column 1

KYUSHU CITY RAZED

Kenney's Planes Blast Tarumizu in Record Blow From Okinawa

ROCKET SITE IS SEEN

125 B-29's Hit Japan's Toyokawa Naval Arsenal in Demolition Strike

By FRANK L. KLUCKHOHN
By Wireless to The New York Times.

MANILA, Tuesday, Aug. 7.—More than 400 fighters and bombers, speeding at chimney-top level for two hours Sunday over Tarumizu in southern Kyushu in the largest single attack launched by Gen. George C. Kenney's Far East Air Forces to date, leveled that city's munitions factories and aircraft and munitions storage depots and waterfront installations.

Rockets and demolition bombs were poured by waves of B-26 Invaders, B-25 Mitchells and Mustangs and Thunderbolts of the Fifth and Seventh Air Forces from Okinawa, supported by a few B-24 Liberators carrying big bombs.

[Tarumizu, about 350 miles from Okinawa, appeared to be a site at which the Japanese might be preparing a rocket campaign against the American base, said a United Press dispatch. FEAF pilots reported seeing in the area, which has extensive cave construction, what seemed to be Japanese robot planes and also a huge catapult-like machine, extending over the water, that might be a rocket launcher.

[About 125 B-29's hit the Toyokawa naval arsenal of Japan in a demolition bombing Tuesday noon, Strategic Air Forces headquarters at Guam reported.]

The planes over Tarumizu met scant resistance, as our fliers took their time to assure the highest

Continued on Page 11, Column 2

REPORT BY BRITAIN

'By God's Mercy' We Beat Nazis to Bomb, Churchill Says

ROOSEVELT AID CITED

Raiders Wrecked Norse Laboratory in Race for Key to Victory

The text of Mr. Churchill's statement is on Page 8.

By CLIFTON DANIEL
By Wireless to The New York Times.

LONDON, Aug. 6.—The hitherto secret details of the grisly race between Germany and the Allies to develop a weapon so destructive that it would insure absolute victory—a race not only between scientists but also between under-cover agents—were recounted in London tonight after it had been disclosed that the first atomic bomb had been dropped on Japan.

"By God's mercy British and American science outpaced all German efforts," said a statement by former Prime Minister Churchill written before he left office and issued from 10 Downing Street by his successor, Clement R. Attlee.

"The possession of these powers by the Germans at any time might have altered the result of the war," Mr. Churchill said, "and profound anxiety was felt by those who were informed."

The British Isles, which endured the terrors of flying bombs and rockets, did hear repeated rumors that Adolf Hitler's V-3 weapon was to be an atomic bomb, but they never knew until tonight how close they came to being the first victims of its destructive power. Much less did they suspect what

Continued on Page 9, Column 1

Steel Tower 'Vaporized' In Trial of Mighty Bomb

Scientists Awe-Struck as Blinding Flash Lighted New Mexico Desert and Great Cloud Bore 40,000 Feet Into Sky

By LEWIS WOOD
Special to The New York Times.

WASHINGTON, Aug. 6.—A blinding flash many times as brilliant as the midday sun and a massive, multi-colored cloud boiling up 40,000 feet into the air accompanied the first test firing of an atomic bomb on July 16, three weeks ago today. Set in the remote desert lands of New Mexico, the experiment was seen against a wild background where rain poured in torrents, and lightning pierced the sky up to the zero hour of the explosion at 5:30 A. M.

A steel tower from which the atomic weapon hung was vaporized. In its place was only a huge, sloping crater. At the moment of the explosion a mountain range three miles distant stood out sharply in brilliant light.

"Then," said the War Department in a description, "came a tremendous, sustained roar and a mighty pressure wave which knocked down two men outside the control tower (10,000 yards, or more than five miles, away.)"

Before the detonation scientists waited in tense expectancy. Minutes lengthened seemingly to hours. Lying face downward, with their feet toward the steel tower, the watchers waited, nearly breathless. They were "reaching into the unknown" and did not know what would happen.

On the instant that all was over these men leaped to their feet. The terrible tension ended, they shook hands, embraced each other and shouted in glee. Behind their triumph was sober consciousness of possessing the means to "insure the speedy conclusion of the war and save thousands of American lives."

The scene of the great drama was the Alamogordo Air Base, 120 miles southeast of Albuquerque. Here the scientists strove to unlock the secret upon which $2,000,000,000 had been spent.

Graphic word pictures of the

Continued on Page 5, Column 1

ATOM BOMBS MADE IN 3 HIDDEN 'CITIES'

Secrecy on Weapon So Great That Not Even Workers Knew of Their Product

By JAY WALZ
Special to The New York Times.

WASHINGTON, Aug. 6.—The War Department revealed today how three "hidden cities" with a total population of 100,000 inhabitants sprang into being as a result of the $2,000,000,000 atomic bomb project, how they did their work without knowing what it was all about, and how they kept the biggest secret of the war.

One of these, Oak Ridge, situated where only oak and pine trees had dotted small farms before, is today the fifth largest city in Tennessee. Its population of 75,000 persons has thirteen supermarkets, nine drug stores and seven theatres.

A second town of 7,000 was built for reasons of isolation and security on a New Mexico mesa. The third, named Richland Village, houses 17,000 men, women and children on remote banks of the Columbia River in the State of Washington.

None of the people, who came to these developments from homes all the way from Maine to California, had the slightest idea of what they were making in the gigantic Gov-

Continued on Page 3, Column 2

TRAINS CANCELED IN STRICKEN AREA

Traffic Around Hiroshima Is Disrupted—Japanese Still Sift Havoc by Split Atoms

By The United Press.

WASHINGTON, Aug. 6.—The Osaka radio, without referring to the atomic bomb dropped on Hiroshima, hinted tonight at the terrific damage it must have caused by announcing that train service in the Hiroshima and other areas had been canceled.

First mention of the bomb came in a Japanese Domei agency dispatch announcing that President Truman and Prime Minister Attlee had disclosed that the new missile had been dropped on an important Japanese army center.

Japanese Solemnly Warned

What happened at Hiroshima is not yet known. The War Department said it was "as yet unable to make an accurate report" because "an impenetrable cloud of dust and smoke" masked the target area from reconnaissance planes. The Secretary of War will release the story "as soon as accurate details of the results of the bombing become available."

The Office of War Information began telling the Japanese today with them. OWI branch transmitters in San Francisco, Hawaii and Saipan beamed President Truman's statement on the atomic bomb to Japan.

Edward Barrett, director of the OWI's overseas branch, said that the President's announcement and related information on the atomic bomb will dominate the OWI's normal Japanese transmissions for the next several days.

LONDON, Tuesday, Aug. 7 (UP) —The Japanese Domei news agency, in a dispatch recorded by the British radio, said today that

Continued on Page 7, Column 3

War News Summarized

TUESDAY, AUGUST 7, 1945

One bomb hit Japan on Sunday night, but it struck with the force of 20,000 tons of TNT. Where it landed had been the city of Hiroshima; what is there now has not yet been learned.

The attack, dramatically announced by President Truman sixteen hours after the missile had struck, was with an atomic bomb, a "harnessing of the basic power of the universe," he said. "The force from which the sun draws its power has been loosed against those who brought war to the Far East. And the end is not yet."

Details of the missile are closely guarded, but the 125,000 workers who saw materials pour into their factories never saw anything go out. The bomb is the result of pooling British-American scientific knowledge begun in 1940. "We have spent two billion dollars on the greatest scientific gamble in history —and won." Mr. Truman said, and warned:

"We are now prepared to obliterate more rapidly and completely every productive enterprise the Japanese have above ground in any city. It was to spare the Japanese public from utter destruction that the ultimatum of July 26 was issued at Potsdam. If they do not now accept our terms they may expect a rain of ruin from the air."

Secretary of War Stimson detailed the story of research and production and forecast improvements to increase the effectiveness of the "atomic bomb" several times. Congress will be asked to establish a committee to control peacetime use.

Hiroshima was a major military target, a city of 318,000 persons thickly settled around a quartermaster's depot, an embarkation port, armament and airplane parts plants. [All the

All production was on the United States at two plants at Oak Ridge, near Knoxville, Tenn., and one at Richland, Wash. A scientific laboratory was installed in Sante Fe, N. M. [1:6.]

Former Prime Minister Churchill told of Britain's part, including costly attacks on German "heavy water" plants and the race to outstrip the Nazis. He praised American scientific achievement and gave full credit to President Roosevelt and his advisers. [1:5.]

Tokyo made no mention of what had happened to Hiroshima but rail service in that area was canceled. [1:7.]

Okinawa sent out 400 planes that left Tarumizu, on Kyushu's Kagoshima Bay, in flaming wreckage. About 125 "Superforts" bombed Toyokawa naval arsenal by daylight. [1:4; map p. 11.]

Chinese troops have broken into the port of Yeungkong and have cleared a large stretch of the south China coast west of Hong Kong and east of the Luichow Peninsula. [1:3; map P. 2.]

Moscow, moving to implement Potsdam decisions, has resumed diplomatic relations with Finland and Rumania. [11:4.]

The Germans received an opportunity to develop democratic talents when the United States and Great Britain authorized local trade unions and political parties in their zones of occupation. [12:2.]

France is expected to ratify the United Nations Charter and then the Bretton Woods monetary plan in the near future. [13:6.] Marshal Pétain was accused of having asked Hitler for help in settling France's colonies. [13:1.]

Argentina has lifted the state of siege in effect since Pearl Harbor. [11:6.]

Reich Exile Emerges as Heroine In Denial to Nazis of Atom's Secret

Special to The New York Times.

WASHINGTON, Aug. 6.—How Germany twice narrowly missed the secret of harnessing atomic energy by splitting uranium atoms and releasing the most powerful destructive force on earth was recalled today in War Department reports on the atomic bomb.

Development of the bomb after more than ten years of experimentation and research marks the dramatic story of the long search for a method of releasing atomic energy is Dr. Lise Meitner, a woman physicist whom the Nazis expelled from Germany as a "non-Aryan." With her associates, Dr. Otto Hahn and Dr. F. Strassmann, both chemists, she had been working in the Kaiser Wilhelm Institute in Berlin, bombarding uranium atoms with neutrons and then submitting the uranium to chemical analysis.

That the bomb may be far from its maximum devastating potential was indicated by the War Department's statement that:

"The energy we are now able to utilize in the atomic bombs, at 100 per cent efficiency, constitutes

Continued on Page 7, Column 1

NEW AGE USHERED

Day of Atomic Energy Hailed by President, Revealing Weapon

HIROSHIMA IS TARGET

'Impenetrable' Cloud of Dust Hides City After Single Bomb Strikes

Truman, Stimson statements on atomic bomb, Page 4.

By SIDNEY SHALETT
Special to The New York Times.

WASHINGTON, Aug. 6.—The White House and War Department announced today that an atomic bomb, possessing more power than 20,000 tons of TNT, a destructive force equal to the load of 2,000 B-29's and more than 2,000 times the blast power of what previously was the world's most devastating bomb, had been dropped on Japan.

The announcement, first given to the world in utmost solemnity by President Truman, made it plain that one of the scientific landmarks of the century had been passed, and that the "age of atomic energy," which can be a tremendous force for the advancement of civilization as well as for destruction, was at hand.

At 10:45 o'clock this morning, a statement by the President was issued at the White House that sixteen hours earlier—about the time that citizens on the Eastern seaboard were sitting down to their Sunday suppers—an American plane had dropped the single atomic bomb on the Japanese city of Hiroshima, an important Japanese army center.

Japanese Solemnly Warned

What happened at Hiroshima is not yet known. The War Department said it "as yet was unable to make an accurate report" because "an impenetrable cloud of dust and smoke" masked the target area from reconnaissance planes. The Secretary of War will release the story "as soon as accurate details of the results of the bombing become available."

But in a statement vividly describing the results of the first test of the atomic bomb in New Mexico, the War Department told how an immense steel tower had been "vaporized" by the tremendous explosion, how a 40,000-foot cloud rushed into the sky, and two observers were knocked down at a point 10,000 yards away. And President Truman solemnly warned:

"It was to spare the Japanese people from utter destruction that the ultimatum of July 26 was issued at Potsdam. Their leaders promptly rejected that ultimatum. If they do not now accept our terms, they may expect a rain of ruin from the air the like of which has never been seen on this earth."

Most Closely Guarded Secret

The President referred to the joint statement issued by the heads of the American, British and Chinese Governments, in which terms of surrender and warning given to the Japanese and warning that their rejection would mean complete destruction of Japan's power to make war.

[The atomic bomb weighs about 400 pounds and is capable of utterly destroying a town, a representative of the British Ministry of Aircraft Production said in London, the United Press reported.]

What is this terrible new weapon, which the War Department also calls the "Cosmic Bomb"? It is the harnessing of the energy of the atom, which is the basic power of the universe. As President Truman said, "The force from which the sun draws its power has been loosed against those who brought war to the Far East."

To their amazement, they found the element barium in the debris of the smashed uranium atoms.

Continued on Page 7, Column 1

"Atomic fission"—in other

Continued on Page 2, Column 2

If anyone (apart from the puzzled inhabitants of Albuquerque, New Mexico) had paid much attention to a small item which a number of papers carried on July 17 1945 to the effect that an ammunition magazine at the Alamagorado Air Base had exploded, it was probably only to wonder in passing at the sheer size of the explosion. It had been visible, the reports said, 235 miles away — and that made it one hell of a bang. In fact, it had been seen up to 450 miles away, but at that moment the United States Government had no desire to publicise its goings-on in the New Mexico desert. For that 'exploding magazine' was the first atomic bomb test anywhere in the world. It was the culmination of decades of theory, research, experiment and practical technology — in laboratories at Cambridge, Washington, Chicago, Los Angeles, New York and in secret complexes at Oak Ridge, Clinton, Hanford, Los Alamos; it was the climax to the work of men of many nationalities, Einstein, Rutherford, Chadwick, Lawrence, Fermi, Oppenheimer among many others. It was the end-product of $2 billion, and there was only one journalist present to see it, *The New York Times'* science correspondent William Laurence. And he was forbidden to breathe a word.

Since 1942 the 'Manhattan Project' had been working all-out, in an effort to win the race against the Germans whose researches along similar lines were known to be well-advanced. Now, of course, the war in Europe was over but the Japanese were still in arms, hopeless though their situation was and however much the President warned darkly of 'utter destruction' unless they surrendered unconditionally. No-one — not even the scientists who had observed the awesome and withering power of that mushroom cloud over Alamogordo — yet fully appreciated the cataclysmic might of their new weapon. Least of all the Japanese High Command.

At 2.45 in the morning on August 6, the B-29 Enola Gay with its two escorts lumbered into the night from the US base at Tinian. The planes were over the city of Hiroshima just as it was waking up. Many inhabitants, no doubt, were still asleep when the bomb exploded. It was probably better than being awake.

The first news of the bomb, and the attack on Hiroshima, was given to the Press at a White House news conference sixteen hours later. President Truman's statement seemed curiously flat: on Sunday an American airplane had dropped a single bomb on the city of Hiroshima; it had exploded with the power equivalent to that of all the high explosive which could be carried in a fleet of 2000 B-29s. There were no casualty figures. No estimate of the damage could be given, as the city was still lost under an impenetrable cloud of dust and smoke. Full details of the bomb, its history and technical details, were to be found in the official hand-outs (largely prepared by *The Times'* correspondent).

Yet even in those stark statistics it was, in the words of *The New York Herald Tribune* 'as if we had put our hands upon the levers of a power too strange, too terrible, too unpredictable in all its possible consequences for any rejoicing over the immediate consequences of its employment'. There were, in fact, no immediate political consequences: Japan did not surrender. On the 8th Russia declared war and invaded Manchuria, as had been agreed at the Yalta conference. On the 9th another atomic bomb was dropped on city of Nagasaki.

William Laurence accompanied this mission in his role of official historian. He described what he saw: '. . . a giant ball of fire rise as though from the bowels of the earth, belching forth enormous white smoke rings . . . a giant pillar of purple fire, ten thousand feet high, shooting skyward with enormous speed'. On the 10th, realising the futility of resisting such a monster, Japan surrendered. It was only some time later, when the war correspondents and photographers landed and went to inspect the results, that it was understood at what a price peace had been bought: children dying slowly and in agony, buildings melted, a landscape of lunar desolation. Had it been a world war to end wars? Or worlds?

HEADLINES 1945-1960

High Sierra Back

49ers Ed

San Franci

THE CITY'S ONLY HOME-

VOL. CLXXVI, NO. 125 CCCCAAA SAN FRANC

TESTS REVEAL

ane Lost

DAILY GRAPHIC

and Daily Sketch

A KEMSLEY NEWSPAPER

FOUNDED IN 1890 1d.

TUESDAY, OCTOBER 1, 1946 **

EY HEAR THEIR FATE TO-DAY

As Lord Justice Lawrence was reading the judgment at Nuremberg yesterday this picture was taken of the prisoners in the dock. Hess, without headphones, was the only one apparently not listening. From left to right in the dock are (front row): Goering, Hess, Ribbentrop, Keitel, Kaltenbrunner, Rosenberg, Frank, Frick, Streicher and Funk; (back row): Doenitz, Raeder, Schirach, Sauckel, Jodl, Papen, Seyss-Inquart and Speer. On the extreme right and hidden from view, sat Schacht, Neurath and Fritsche. More pictures on page 2 and middle page.

'Clear Proof Of Guilt' | Nazis Cowed By Verdict

From NICHOLAS CARROLL, Daily Graphic Special Correspondent
NUREMBERG, Monday night

NAZI Germany's 2† former leaders in the dock here to-day heard their collective guilt affirmed by the International Military Tribunal on the last day but one of this dramatic trial.

1,000 POLICE GUARD COURT

Their individual guilt and the sentences to be awarded, they and the world will know to-morrow.

To-day's historic judgment, read in sections by all eight judges, gave only one indication of the probable severity of the sentences.

It ruled that the German General Staff and High Command could not be considered criminal. But it added that the evidence of criminality against many of its individuals was clear and convincing.

...responsible in large measure for the miseries and suffering that ...fallen on millions of men, women and children.

...a disgrace to the honourable profession ...ent. Lord Justice Lawrence, in ...horised

YARD HUNT AGENT'S MURDERER

From Daily Graphic Special Correspondent
CALAIS, Monday night.

TWO Scotland Yard men left here for London to-night with information about a three-year-old spy murder which will begin another murder hunt in England.

After two weeks' inquiry into the death of a British agent—Christopher James Lord, found...

France in 1943 and operated with French Resistance workers.

His body was found after a village well had run dry.

Lord's wife's brother, touring in France, happened to hear about the recovery of the body of an Englishman with white hair, a gold tooth and wound marks on one leg.

He telephoned Mrs. Jane Lord, a former captain in the French A.T.S., now living at Randolph-crescent, Maida Vale, London. She identified the body.

Chief-Inspector Scardon and Detective-Sergeant Deaton checked up on a story of two Englishmen, self-styled British agents, who said they had come to execute a foreign spy.

They now have all available details about the two English-men. One is believed to have been killed during the war; the other will be a wanted man b to-morrow.

shot and dumped in a well at Tanus—Chief-Insp. Scardon and Det.-Sgt. Deaton, of the Yard, told Toulouse police that all ...dence pointed to the killer ...into

12 PAGES TO-MORROW

DAILY

FRIDAY MAY 7 1954

No. 16,805

EXPRESSMAN Peron's police hold our reporter **BANNIS**

AT LAST—TI

THIS IS IT—THE DR

BANNISTER DOES IT

English victory beats world

Express Staff Reporter

THE dream of world athletes through the years was achieved yesterday h...
Engli...
y...
Ba...
the
to r
four
His
evening
an-hour 17,560
equal in
sound bar...
Bannister...
recorded. w...
—beating

DAILY

MONDAY NOVEMBER 5 1956

The Desperate Hours: The

HUNGA

Daily Mail

FOR QUEEN AND COMMONWEALTH

NO. 18,579

TUESDAY, MARCH 22, 1960

MORNING SPECIAL

South Africa riot toll rises hourly until by midnight more than 60 lie dead

THE BATTLEFIELD

Defiant to the last
pl... ... as tanks
of ... enforce
RO...
...ship

ED

Light in the Gloom

Nothing brings out the best in British newspapers quite like a spot of pageantry. And never, was a pageant more welcome to the British public, after seemingly endless years of rationing, shortages and international indignities, than in 1953. On June 2 Queen Elizabeth II was to be crowned in Westminster Abbey, with all the pomp and circumstance that 1,000 years of accumulated ritual could muster. For weeks before the event the Press picked bare every detail of the ceremony, from the precise role of Portcullis Pursuivant to the car-parking arrangements in Central London. Coronation souvenirs, from plastic mugs to propelling-pencils, were examined and criticised: delicate points of etiquette for the visiting royals were discussed: the decor of the processional route dissected in detail (and found wanting by some). Overriding all was the universally accepted assumption that a new and glorious chapter in the country's history was about to unfold – why, even the name was of good omen, the New Elizabethan Age. One could almost believe that once again Britain would rule the waves and cast its aegis over immeasurable continents. And as if to give substance to this heady vision, on the very day of the Coronation (a grey and dismal morning, if anyone had noticed) the newspapers carried the stupendous news from Tibet that an Englishman (well, a New Zealander) had conquered the highest mountain in the world, Mount Everest. As one paper put it 'All this' (meaning Norman Hartnell's luxuriant Coronation gown) 'And Everest Too'. The cup was indeed full!

NEWS CHRONICLE

No. 33,381   TUESDAY, JUNE 2, 1953   PRICE 1½d.

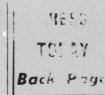

THE CROWNING GLORY
EVEREST IS CLIMBED

Tremendous news for the Queen
HILLARY DOES IT

The new Elizabethan

GLORIOUS Coronation Day news! Everest—Everest the unconquerable — has been conquered. And conquered by men of British blood and breed.

The news came late last night that Edmund Hillary and the Sherpa guide, Bhotia Tensing, of Colonel John Hunt's expedition, had climbed to the summit of Earth's highest peak, 29,002 feet high.

New Zealand's deputy premier announced it at a Coronation Day ceremony at Wellington—and within seconds it flashed round the world.

Queen Elizabeth the Second, resting on the eve of her crowning, was immediately told that this brightest jewel of courage and endurance had been added to the Crown of British endeavour. It is understood that a message of royal congratulation is being sent to the climbers.

Hillary, a 34-year-old New Zealander, and Bhotia Tensing, 38-year-old leader of the guides and bearers, are said to have made the final 1,000-foot ascent from Camp Eight on the upper slopes.

The feat was apparently accomplished on Monday. A year ago Bhotia Tensing climbed to within 800 feet of the summit with Raymond Lambert, in the unsuccessful Swiss attempt.

NEWS BY RUNNER

The latest news of the progress of the expedition hitherto—despatched by runner and received in London yesterday—was that the climbers were ready, as soon as the weather was suitable, to set out from Camp Seven, established high on the South Col at about 26,000 feet, to pitch Camp Eight high up near the summit. Events

EDMUND HILLARY, whose conquest of Everest sets the seal on the new Elizabethan age, is a 34-year-old bee farmer from New Zealand.

He learned his mountaineering in the Alps of the little Dominion of two million people, and was a pioneer in introducing winter ski-ing there.

He and George Lowe, the other New Zealander of the party, were making a free-lance climb in the Himalayas when Eric Shipton's 'look-see' expedition arrived in 1951 to choose a route up Everest.

Hillary and Lowe dropped their own project and trailed halfway across the vast range to join them.

Told of Hillary's achievement, New Zealand's Prime Minister, Mr. Sidney Holland, said :—

'What a grand achievement on the eve of the Coronation! I hope this terrific example of tenacity, endurance and fortitude in this our Coronation year may be regarded as a symbol that there are no heights or difficulties which the British

SMILING, mountain - wise

Here the forecast is rain—hail—sun—storm, BUT the crowds are singing in the rain SO—
WHO CARES NOW IF IT SNOWS?

CORONATION DAY FORECAST : Northerly winds, sunny spells, showers with hail and thunder, cold, Mid-day temperature 55 deg.

NEWS CHRONICLE REPORTERS

REPEATED heavy showers lashed the packed campers lining the Royal Way last night. Then the sky cleared and the temperature dropped 13 degrees in a few hours.

But the campers sat it out. And early this morning, cut by a chill wind under the stars, they could still raise a cheer for Britain's Everest victory.

When the news spread, people started shouting : "The new Elizabethans!" Hundreds woke from their blanket beds to dance and sing.

By 1 a.m. 50,000 people were squatting in The Mall. Another 50,000 were camped in Trafalgar Square. Along the route stretched the queue—at a temperature of 45 degrees.

And still they came—from early morning trains at main-line stations, and from 18,000 cars converging on London every hour.

FIRES LIT IN STREETS

People already on the pavements lit fires to keep warm, cooked snacks and tea on spirit stoves, played cards, sang—or tried to sleep.

Earlier, thousands of cheering people surrounded the Queen Mother and Princess Margaret as they drove from Buckingham Palace after spending two hours with the Queen in her private apartments—a last visit before the Coronation.

Reinforced police could not clear a way : the car was halted for 15 minutes beside the Victoria Memorial.

The Queen Mother, in a white feathered gown and off-the-face white hat, and Princess Margaret, in a low-cut smoke-blue gown, waved. Motor-cycle police came to the rescue. But a little later more crowds ran from their pitches and blocked the route to Clarence House.

Fifty thousand people gathered outside Buckingham Palace. Despite the bitter wind, they danced away the hours, sang hymns and popular songs and for hour after hour chanted : "We want the Queen !"

Once the curtains parted above the Palace balcony and a roar went up.

REST OF THE NEWS

ONE of the greatest footballers of the century, Alex James, died in a London hospital yesterday.

Stabbed girl dead in Thames

News Chronicle Reporter

A MURDERED girl was found in the Thames yesterday and last night the police feared her girl companion had been killed too.

The girl in the river was 16-year-old Barbara Songhurst, a chemist's assistant, of Princes Road, Teddington. She was stabbed three times in the back after being assaulted on Lovers' Towpath at Ham, Surrey.

On Sunday Barbara went cycling with her friend, 18-year-old Christina Reed, of Roy Crescent, Hampton Hill.

See Page Five

Flash kills 3 cricketers

Lightning struck three cricketers dead at a Coronation match yesterday. The flash shot through the dressing room at a soap factory's ground at Irlam, near Manchester.

The men killed were Ernest Taylor, 44, Herbert Vaudrey, 37, and George Perry, 31, all of Cadishead.

CENTRAL 5000

WEATHER. — Showers and short sunny intervals. Midday temp 50-55. Sun rises 4.45 a.m., sets 9.10 p.m. Moon 00.35 a.m.-9.56 a.m. Lights 10.07 p.m.-3.49 a.m. tomorrow. High water at London Bridge 5.48 a.m.-5.54 p.m.

Weather map, Page Two

"A SMITHS CLOCK my dear, is the Unforgettable Gift for Coronation Year"

Here is indeed a gift that will be a constant link for years and years to come with this outstanding

U.S. TRIES OUT H-BOMB

But atom men hedge on explosion

'WE ARE SATISFIED'

From HENRY LOWRIE: Washington, Sunday

SHELL-BATTERED DIEN FALLS TO 30,000 SHRIEKING REDS

MACARTHUR FIRED

Truman Ousts Him From All Jobs

Hollywood's Politics

Film Actor Sterling Hayden Tells of Being Communist In '46, Quitting in Disgust

Former Marine Combat Captain Tells Congressmen Joining the Party Was 'Stupidest Thing I Have Ever Done'

Exclusive to The Chronicle
From the New York Herald Tribune

WASHINGTON, April 10 — Sterling Hayden, motion picture actor, told the House Un-American Activities Committee today how he had joined a Hollywood Communist cell in 1946, but resigned six months later in revulsion against totalitarian ways.

Hayden, who was a marine captain during World War II and served behind the German lines in the Balkans, told the committee today he had joined the Communist party because he became enthused about the spirit of the Yugoslav partisans.

"It was the stupidest, most ignorant thing I have ever done," Hayden told the committee. "I had a very emotional, unsound approach."

Hayden said he decided to leave the party "because of the manner in which everything is predetermined." Although he had "become a victim of the idea they had the form of democracy," he said, "it only took a couple of months for me to realize that they think they have the key to everything by some occult power."

Unlike Larry Parks, another Hollywood actor who admitted former Communist membership to the committee, Hayden had no compunction about mentioning the names of others he said were Communists. The only Hollywood personality of any note whom he named, however, was Actress Karen Morley, whose connection with Communist front groups has caused comment for several years.

(Associated Press reported Hayden said he didn't know any big-name Hollywood personalities who are or had been connected with

Remmer Gives Up

Gambler Posts Bail on Charge Of Tax Evasion

Elmer F. (Bones) Remmer, San Francisco and Nevada gambler, surrendered in Reno yesterday on a Federal Grand Jury indictment charging him with evading $160,887.64 in income taxes for the years 1944-46.

The chubby gambler, released on a $15,000 property bond after being fingerprinted at first refused to discuss the charge, but his attorney attributed it to "politics."

"There is no criminal case," said John R. Golden, Remmer's San Francisco lawyer who flew to Reno to conduct the surrender. "Pressure created by the California Crime Commission and the Kefauver Committee, putting the Internal Revenue Bureau on the spot, precipitated this thing."

Remmer was angry when he later talked to reporters.

"If I am guilty of tax evasion, so is every other businessman in the country.

"I filed my returns honestly. Anything more serious than that I will tell in court."

The indictment, returned by a Federal Grand Jury at Carson City on Monday, was taken off the secret file after Remmer's surrender. It specified six counts on which Remmer "wilfully and knowingly attempted to defeat the purpose of the law and evade a large portion of his income tax payments."

The charge accused Remmer and his wife, Helen, of reporting total joint incomes of $81,997.94 for the three years when their income actually was $331,806.09. The indictment said they paid taxes of $32,751.45, when they should have paid $193,409.09.

The three years cover the time Remmer operated the Menio Club on Turk street in San Francisco.

The President's Historic Decision

Ridgway Takes Over the General's Commands; The Reaction in Tokyo: 'It's Like a Thunderclap'

'Commander Didn't Know' Says Aide

By RUSSELL BRINES
Associated Press Staff Writer

TOKYO, April 11—President Truman's removal of General MacArthur struck this headquarters like a thunderclap today (Wednesday).

Colonel S. H. Huff of MacArthur's staff said the General had no prior knowledge of the Truman announcement.

The news broke here in a broadcast over the Armed Forces radio.

MacArthur himself was at his American Embassy residence in his customary afternoon rest. He was not immediately available.

Staff officers, discussing report of the impending action a few minutes before the historic White House news conference, all said they did not believe the President would take such a step.

The report spread quickly throughout headquarters. Officers received it with evident bitterness and sadness. MacArthur's staff has been consistently loyal to him and his views.

"If the President does that," said one officer, "he will lose the next

GENERAL DOUGLAS MacARTHUR
He is relieved of all commands, "effective at once"

U.S.-British Policy Rift

'He Has Proven Himself Unable to Co-operate With United Nations Policy'

By the United Press

WASHINGTON, April 11—President Truman today (Wednesday) relieved General Douglas MacArthur of all his Far Eastern commands because of his inability to give "his wholehearted support" to the policies of the United States Government.

The President designated Lieutenant General Matthew B. Ridgway, now commander of the Eighth Army in Korea, to succeed MacArthur.

Announcement of the President's decision followed days of international controversy over the General's endorsement of policies, particularly relating to the use of Chinese Nationalist troops, in conflict with the announced policies of the President.

Mr. Truman discharged MacArthur from his commands with this statement:

"With deep regret I have concluded that General of the Army Douglas MacArthur is unable to give his wholehearted support to the policies of the United States Government and of the United Nations in matters pertaining to his official duties."

only
UNITED

flies
NORTH

The only nonstop service to both Portland and Seattle; the only DC-6s.

Fall from Eden

The Suez Crisis

Ask for RIZLA CIGARETTE PAPERS Today's smoothest smoking

DAILY HERALD

No. 12650 (c) WEATHER: Mainly dry and cold, cloudy—See Page 7. RADIO and TV—See Page 5. PRICE 2D

A1 LIGHT for HAND ROLLING!

Nasser rejects ultimatum, Israel accepts

OUR TROOPS IN TODAY

MALTA MEN PUT TO SEA

A LAND-AND-WATER armoured car rumbles through the bow doors of a tank landing craft "somewhere in Malta." Heavily-kitted Commandos wait to follow it aboard. All day long yesterday, this was the scene in Malta's ports. British troops were expected to land in the Suez Canal Zone at dawn today.

EDITORIAL

THIS IS FOLLY

THE British people's immediate interest in the Israeli - Egyptian fighting is to stop it.

Our problem is NOT which side to take. It is NOT how to turn the situation to our advantage in the dispute with Nasser over the Suez Canal.

Our problem is to end the bloodshed, in association with the Security Council, and to prevent the danger of widespread war.

That is the swiftest, surest way of protecting British interests in the Canal Zone and ensuring safe passage for British ships.

Sir Anthony Eden chooses a different course. He does not act through and with the Security Council.

ALONE

He does not act in co-operation with America and in consultation with the members of the British Commonwealth.

He "goes it alone" with France. He risks disunity among the Western Powers. He offends important members of the British Commonwealth. And he divides the British people at a grave moment in history.

The facts speak louder than any words.

The ultimatum instructing Israel and Egypt to stop fighting on pain of armed intervention by British and French forces is, in truth, aimed at Egypt alone. Egypt was bound to reject it.

PRETEXT

Eden's decision will rouse the entire Arab world against Great Britain and France and, whatever the immediate outcome, will destroy the last vestige of British influence in the Middle East. More, it will reduce the mighty moral authority our country has earned by faithful support of the United Nations.

Already, Eden's decision has reinforced the propaganda armoury of our enemies. They claim that Israel-Egypt differences are being used as a mere pretext to do now what the British Government wanted to do some weeks ago—invade Egypt.

From this final collapse of British policy, let us pray, we may yet be saved—by a nation-wide rally to Labour's lead for sanity.

Britain accused of 'trick' by Dulles

BRITISH and French troops will start invading Egypt any time after half-past four this morning.

At that hour the ultimatum sent yesterday to President Nasser expires. He was asked to let an Anglo-French force occupy key positions in Port Said, Ismailia and Suez.

And Egypt and Israel were told that unless they stop fighting and withdraw their forces ten miles from the Canal then British and French troops would move in. They were given twelve hours—until 4.30 a.m. today—to reply.

But Colonel Nasser did not wait. At 10.30 last night he summoned the British Ambassador and told him that the ultimatum was "unacceptable in any circumstances." It was an attack, he said, on Egypt's rights and dignity and a flagrant violation of the United Nations Charter.

Early this morning the Israeli Radio announced that Israel had accepted the Anglo-French ultimatum.

GRAVE DECISION

So British troops move to battle today. They go in the face of protests from the Labour Party in Britain and the opposition of almost the whole world.

In the House of Commons yesterday after Sir Anthony had announced the grave British decision, the Labour Party forced an emergency two-hour debate. Mr. Gaitskell urged the Government to stop in its tracks, to await at least for the verdict of the United Nations. He was voted down.

News of the Anglo-French decision astonished the Americans. Late last night President Eisenhower sent urgent personal messages to Sir Anthony Eden and Mr. Mollet the French Premier, begging them to withdraw their 12-hour ultimatum.

Indeed America is angry. Mr. Dulles, the Secretary of State, summoned the British Minister in Washington, Mr. J. E. Coulson, to express his Government's serious displeasure.

He is believed to have said that he has definite evidence that Britain and France have acted with Israel to trick the U.S. about their plans and so bring about the Anglo-French occupation of the Suez Canal Zone.

EVIDENCE

In New York, the Security Council of the United Nations met to discuss the Middle East crisis. Mr. Cabot Lodge, the U.S. delegate, proposed a resolution condemning Israel's action and urging all member states to refrain from force or threats of force.

But this morning Sir Anthony Eden had refused to listen to advice given at home and abroad. British troops boarded transports at Malta and at Cyprus. The Mediterranean Fleet called off its exercises and suddenly turned towards Egypt.

Egypt announced a full-scale mobilisation. Once again British soldiers, sailors and airmen are going to war.

BRITAIN VETOES U.S. MOVE

NEW YORK, Tuesday.—Britain and France tonight vetoed a U.S. resolution before the Security Council calling on all nations to refrain from force or threats in the Middle East.

Britain and France were the only opposers. Seven nations voted for the resolution, Belgium and Australia abstaining.

Alone, the U.S. tabled its resolution demanding immediate withdrawal of Israeli forces from Egypt.

It also urged member nations to refuse all aid to Israel unless her troops withdrew.

The proposal was submitted to an emergency meeting of the Council and was backed by the Soviet delegate, Mr. Arkady Sobolev.

Temporary

But Russia made a further demand — that Britain and France must be warned not to intervene in the fighting.

Sir Pierson Dixon, for Britain, called on the U.S. not to press its resolution.

"For the moment," he said, "there is no action that the Security Council can constructively take which would contribute to the objective of stopping the fighting and safeguarding free passage through the Canal."

The considerations which arose in the mind of the British Government were:

THAT fighting between Israel and Egypt must stop;

THAT unless hostilities could quickly be stopped, free passage through the Suez Canal would be jeopardised.

The action the British Government had felt duty-bound to take was of a temporary character.

"I do not believe that our motives are likely to be generally misconstrued, but they are certain to be misconstrued in some quarters," he said.

"We have done everything in our power to lower tension in the Middle East. If tension has increased, it is unhappily because neither Israel nor her Arab neighbours have seen fit to listen to our advice.

'Minimum'

"How can we have any confidence that some further injunction by the Security Council would in fact prove effective to deal in time—and time is of the essence—with a situation which is rapidly getting out of control?"

Mr. Cabot Lodge, the United States delegate, pressed for the adoption of the resolution which, if passed, he said, would cause the basis of the Anglo-French ultimatum to disappear.

"But," he added, "we do not imply that this ultimatum would be justifiable or found to be consistent with the purposes and principles of the United Nations Charter."

The resolution proposed only a "minimum of sanctions" against Israel.

"If the resolution is promptly carried out, it will meet the situation caused by the Israeli penetration of Egypt."

Russia's Mr. Sobolev said that he considered the Anglo-French action an attempt to use the situation created by the Israeli aggression for the armed seizure of the Suez Canal.

Warships mass, Commandos and tanks sail

By Gilbert Carter

A POWERFUL British fleet — including three carriers—was converging on Egypt's Mediterranean coast early this morning.

Paratroops and Commandos, with guns, tanks and amphibious vehicles, had left Cyprus and Malta for secret destinations.

At Valletta Harbour, MALTA, the embarkation hustle yesterday looked like the war-time Sicily operation all over again.

Commandos bent under heavy kit streamed into the bow doors of landing craft, as convoy after convoy rumbled towards the quays from island camps.

Civilians waved at the lorry loads of troops as they passed by in heavy rain.

At Akrotiri RAF base, near Limassol, CYPRUS, the "Red Devils" of the 16th Independent Parachute Brigade filed aboard transport planes and roared away into the blue.

All civilian workers at the base had been ordered off earlier and told not to return for 72 hours. As the paratroops flew out, Constellation airliners landed with French troops.

Nine French Navy ships which had been assembling at Famagusta moved out of the harbour and anchored off-shore.

Other French ships were loading troops last night.

Earlier the famous "Enterprise" tug Turmoil had arrived, towing a huge floating crane.

Build-up

Here is as much as has been revealed or reported of the strength and deployment of British forces in the Middle East:

THE NAVY For the last 24 hours Britain's Mediterranean Fleet has been assembled in the Eastern Mediterranean.

Three operational carriers—the Eagle, Bulwark and Albion—at least two cruisers, and a number of destroyers are there.

Marine Commandos are with the Fleet, ready to carry out landings wherever necessary. Fleet Air Arm planes are ready.

At Aden, a cruiser and two destroyers have already been detailed to cover the Red Sea area—the southern end of the Canal.

THE ARMY In Libya, there are armoured formations, and at Akaba, at the head of the Gulf of Akaba, are British military forces which may have a vital effect on the whole situation.

They are nearest to the fighting.

The 16th Parachute Brigade—which was flown out of Cyprus—consists of three battalions of the Parachute Regiment, an Independent Parachute Company of the Guards, and Sappers, Gunners and Medical Services.

It is under the command of Brigadier M. A. H. Butler, and the men recently completed a series of training drops in Britain.

The full strength of the troops embarked from Malta is not known.

THE RAF At Malta and in Cyprus, Canberra bombers and fighters have been deployed. More planes are standing by at Lybian bases.

Among the fighters are swept-wing Hunters which should be able with ease to cope with MiG fighters flown by Egyptian pilots.

AMERICAN warships of the 6th Fleet—including two big carriers, two cruisers and 20 destroyers—have sailed from Greek and Turkish ports.

Last night the force was reported between Crete and Cyprus.

'WAIT!' GAITSKELL TELLS EDEN

By Hugh Pilcher

A DRAMATIC appeal to Sir Anthony Eden to pause before plunging Britain into war was made by Mr. Hugh Gaitskell during the Commons emergency debate last night on the ultimatum to Egypt and Israel.

"I am going to ask him once again if he will defer action by Britain's armed forces and, if we can persuade the French, by the French as well until after the Security Council has completed its deliberations and until we have had a further opportunity of discussing the matter in the House of Commons," he said amid Labour cheers.

Mr. Selwyn Lloyd, Foreign Secretary, replying declared: "We cannot postpone our action until the conclusion of another Commons debate."

Bluntly, Mr. Gaitskell told the Government that the Labour Party and its supporters throughout Britain would not support it in throwing troops into Egypt.

In tremendous Commons excitement the Opposition Leader denounced the Government's threatened plunge into war without consultation either with the Commonwealth or the United States.

At the climax of his historic peace appeal—with only eight hours to go before British troops were to go into action—Mr. Gaitskell revealed that the Tory Cabinet is indeed "going it alone."

The Opposition, representing

CONTINUED ON PAGE TWO

The Red Army moves out

Russia said last night that her troops would be withdrawn from Budapest as soon as the Hungarian Government wished. Then came this dramatic cable—

From Basil Davidson

BUDAPEST, Tuesday.—Soviet troops tonight began to evacuate their main positions in the heart of the city.

Armoured cars and tanks are clattering outside my window as I write this message, the roar of their tracks echoing back and forth across the dark and fast-flowing Danube.

But the chatter of sub-machine-gun fire and occasional thump of shelling shows there is trouble still in the darkened city.

Mass lynching and other acts of terrorism disfigured the picture of happy liberation today.

Many men of the hated political police and others merely suspected of belonging to it were seized in the streets, killed and stripped and hung by their heels from trees in the public gardens.

But most of the insurgents are now actively backing the compromise attempts of Imry Nagy.

The Last Battle—Page Five.

Canal is safe, says Cairo

EGYPT claimed last night that its forces were in control in Sinai, and the Suez Canal "is not threatened at all."

But it admitted that the Israelis had penetrated up to 35 miles on a 72-mile front and fighting is going on.

And in Tel Aviv reports persisted that flying columns had infiltrated 13 miles from Suez.

Army H Q in Cairo said that invading troops were "liquidated" west of Thamad, a desert post 30 miles inside Egypt.

Egyptian and Israeli communique's indicate heavy fighting around the road junction of Kossayema, ten miles from the border.

Israel claims that the junction has been taken.

But Cairo insists that the attack was repulsed with "heavy losses."

Above the confused desert fighting, Egyptian fighter planes tangled with Israel's French-built Mystere jets.

Seven Israeli planes were shot down without loss in dog fights, said the Egyptians.

Israel counter-claimed the destruction of three Egyptian MiG-15 jets.

There were many in Britain, in the years that followed the war, who observed with mounting dismay the rapid dissolution of an Empire, who suffered in frustration the unrequited taunts of jumped-up little nations that fifty years ago would have fallen silent at the merest growl of a gun-boat. For them Gamal Abdel Nasser provided the perfect scapegoat. The newly-elected president of Egypt — a mere colonel who mouthed (via Cairo radio) torrents of Arab obloquy at all Imperialists, who conspired with the ubiquitous Russians even as he accepted Western gold to build his dams — was the embodiment of all that was un-British. Since his usurpation of power in 1954, the catalogue of his anti-colonial crimes was a slur on

Britain's prestige. Had he not forced Britain to evacuate her strategic base in the Canal Zone? Was it not at his instigation that General Glubb had been dismissed from command of the Arab Legion (more likely in fact that Hussein, himself an Old Harrovian, had read in *The Observer* how Glubb Pasha was 'the uncrowned King of Jordan')? Had he not, just in June 1956, given explicit and impertinent notice to the Suez Canal Company to quit at the end of its lease? He was, in short, the fermenter of all Britain's problems in the excitable Middle East.

So ran the argument in the most vociferous section of the British press, which was by no means disinclined to see Nasser's machinations in various other parts of the globe too. It was no

less than he deserved, therefore, when the United States (dutifully echoed by Britain) withdrew its financial support from Egypt's Aswan Dam project on July 19 1956. But if the Western Powers imagined they had effectively removed the corner-stone of Nasser's personal popularity, they discovered otherwise on the 26th when the Colonel announced that he had nationalised the Canal, and that the revenue from that would pay for his dam, to the unutterable joy of all Egyptians.

When the British Prime Minister, Anthony Eden, branded Nasser the next day in Parliament as 'the new Hitler' he was only epitomising what a large number of his followers had come to believe long ago. They were not going to make

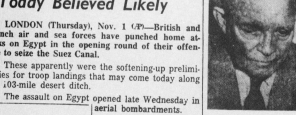

IKE VOW: 'NO WAR'

Jets Hit Egypt, Warship Sunk

San Francisco Chronicle
THE VOICE OF THE WEST

FINAL EXTRA

2nd YEAR No. 306　CCCCAAAB　THURSDAY, NOVEMBER 1, 1956　10 CENTS　GArfield 1-1112

Conflict in the Mideast

Ike: U. S. Won't Fight; Bombers Pound Egypt

Nasser Ship Is Sunk-- Troop Landings at Suez Today Believed Likely

LONDON (Thursday), Nov. 1 (AP)—British and French air and sea forces have punched home attacks on Egypt in the opening round of their offensive to seize the Suez Canal.

These apparently were the softening-up preliminaries for troop landings that may come today along the 103-mile desert ditch.

The assault on Egypt opened late Wednesday in aerial bombardments.

Cairo reported Thursday that the air raids on "all Egyptian aerodromes continued throughout the night.

Egypt has suffered the loss of two naval vessels and damage to airfields under British-French bombing.

The entry of the British and French imposed war from the West upon the four-day war of the Middle East between the invading Israelis and the Egyptians.

SEA ACTION

Jet bombers from the British-French joint command on Cyprus bombed Egyptian airfields and a British cruiser sank an Egyptian frigate in the Gulf of Suez at the Red Sea end of the canal.

Cairo radio said British jet bombers used high explosive and incendiary bombs on Cairo twice and on the great seaport of Alexandria and three cities in the Suez Canal Zone. The British denied Cairo was blasted and said only military targets were hit.

Radio Cairo said seven persons were killed in the Egyp-

The Case of The Taxpayer's Nightmare
(or this needn't happen to you)

Paul was worried. He tossed and turned all night dreaming about MONEY—the lack of it. His taxes were coming up and he didn't have the cash to pay them. But Paul had this problem every year. He just didn't have a planned saving program to accumulate money for such situations.

This year he'd have to borrow. But for *next* year—Mary had a BRILLIANT IDEA.

The President's expression was serious before speech

Israelis in Sinai Meet 2 Divisions

TEL AVIV (Thursday), Nov. 1 (AP)—Israeli troops are driving westward across the Sinai desert and have encountered two full Egyptian divisions, a government source said today.

The Israelis were reported to have partly encircled the Egyptian-held Gaza Strip on the Mediterranean.

An Israeli source said that 1000 Egyptians have been killed, injured or captured in the four days of fighting in the Sinai desert.

A military source also reported Israeli planes now have shot down nine Egyptian

Intervention An 'Error' ---President

New York Herald Tribune Service

WASHINGTON, Oct. 31 President Eisenhower told the American people tonight that "there will be no United States involvement in these present hostilities" in the Middle East.

The President declared that Great Britain, France and Israel had acted "in error" in resorting to force against Egypt.

He said that the policy of the United States will be to do all that is possible "to localize the fighting and to end the conflict."

In a 15-minute televised speech from the White House, the President announced that he had "no plan" to call Congress into special session.

The United States, the President said, would bring the Middle East crisis to the United Nations General Assembly, where the veto does not prevail. Even as the President was speaking, the Security Council voted 7 to 2 to call the Assembly into extraordinary session on the subject.

ANGLO-FRENCH STAND

As they did last night, in vetoing American and Russian proposals for an order to end fighting in Egypt, France and Britain tonight opposed

Egyptian Warship Seized

Egypt's Navy has been less than successful so far in the Mideast fighting. Two of its three frigates have been lost. The British sank one; this was heavily damaged and captured by Israeli forces off Haifa. A tug towed the prize—the frigate Ibrahim El Awal—to port. For details, see Page B.

U. P. Telephoto

Emergency Session

U. N. Assembly to Meet on Crisis

New York Herald Tribune Service

UNITED NATIONS, N. Y., Oct. 31—The United Nations Security Council tonight called for an emergency session of the General Assembly to try to halt the warfare in Egypt. The vote was 7 to 2 with two abstentions.

Dr. Joza Brilej of Yugoslavia sponsored the summons for the 76-nation session because the 11-nation Security Council "stands apparently powerless" to stop military action against Egypt by Israel, Britain and France.

Adlai Blames 'Disastrous' Ike Policies

Prop. 4 Fight Costs Near $5 Million

Oil companies supporting and fighting the controversial Proposition 4 conservation measure spent $4 million to $5 million up to October 15, reports on their campaigns indicated yesterday.

No figures have been released on amounts spent on "educational campaigns" before Proposition 4 was officially drawn up, but supporters of the measure once estimated they had spent "in the

Ahern Shifts 7 Cops for Tag Errors

Police Chief Frank Ahern and Director of Traffic Daniel W. Kiely announced yesterday that seven policemen have been transferred out of traffic duty for issuing too many defective citations.

Forty-five other members of the three-wheeled motorcycle detail have had their beats shifted.

The action followed an investigation begun a month ago when hundreds of faulty traffic tags were found to be the same mistake that was made at Munich: there would be no appeasement this time. This view was wholeheartedly endorsed by the French Government who, quite apart from their vested interests in the Canal, were incensed at Nasser's undisguised support for the Algerian nationalists. Only Foster Dulles, the American Secretary of State who had stirred it up in the first place, now seemed concerned to restore the waterway to international control by peaceful means. Over the next three months a variety of proposals emanated from all sorts of diplomatic sources, including an international control board and a Canal Users' Association. But Nasser would have nothing to do with any scheme which did not recognise Egyptian sovereignty over the Canal. What was worse, as time went on it became distressingly clear that, contrary to all expectations, the 'wogs' were proving perfectly capable of running the Canal efficiently.

In retrospect it is quite evident that the British Cabinet (or the majority of it at least) was not unwilling from the very beginning to use this opportunity to oust Nasser, by force if necessary. Eden in particular seems to have been obsessed by the thrilling prospect. It was by no means obvious at the time, though the signs were there for all to interpret as they would. Through August and September a 'precautionary' build-up of troops in the Mediterranean by both France and Britain was under way, and every 'suggestion' made to the Egyptian President contained all the deference of an ultimatum. The bellicose *Daily Express* might complain on September 22 of 57 days wasted in 'the diplomatic arts of word-spinning, phrase-finding and machinery-making' and rant at the apparent indecision and inaction, but unknown to even the most informed editor events at the highest level had been moving inexorably towards the long-desired 'showdown'.

There was, in fact, a conspiracy afoot, between the French and Israeli premiers M. Mollet and Ben Gurion, into which (according to a British Minister present) Eden was admitted on October 14. The substance of the plot was that Israel should invade Egypt (to eliminate hostile bases in Sinai and re-open sea communications in the Gulf of Akaba); Britain and France would then issue a joint ultimatum to both sides to withdraw from the Canal and when Egypt refused — as there was no doubt she would — regain control of the Suez bases themselves by force. In this way an invasion could be dressed up as 'police action' and a semblance of political morality be given to the adventure. It was a scheme fraught with difficulties and, as is now recognised, unlikely to attain its long-term objectives. It would have to be done without the knowledge or approval of America, who would be appalled at the very thought; of the United Nations, who had already obtained Egypt's agreement to six important principles on the running of the Canal; and of Parliament, whose drawn-out deliberations would inhibit the vital speed of the operation.

On the other hand, the plan would find the joyous support of the great section of hard-liners in the country, whose sentiments were being admirably expressed by *The Daily Sketch*: 'Eden Gets Tough. Tells Nasser: Ike's with Us and We're Taking Over Our Canal. It's GREAT Britain Again'. (Where the *Daily Sketch* obtained its insight into Eisenhower's intentions was never revealed). Other papers, however, viewed Britain's involvement and the outcome with some apprehension. *The Observer* warned that though 'We know our Government would not make a military attack in defiance of its solemn international obligations, people abroad might think otherwise'. *The Manchester Guardian* was even more perceptive than perhaps it knew: 'The Prime Minister's course can only lead to

disaster' it cautioned.

Nevertheless Israeli tanks rolled into the Sinai desert on schedule through the afternoon of October 29. On the 30th the Anglo-French ultimatum (drawn up several days earlier) was duly dispatched, ordering both belligerents to 'withdraw' to a distance of ten miles from the Canal. Already the transparency of the manoeuvre was beginning to show: the ill-timed ultimatum required the Israelis to advance some 100 miles nearer the Canal, and the Egyptians to retreat the same distance — from their own territory. The Opposition became further convinced of Eden's obsessive recklessness when it was learnt the next day that, for the first time in its history, Britain had used its veto in the U.N. Security Council to forestall an American resolution for a ceasefire.

At 4.30 pm on the 31st, R.A.F. bombers from Cyprus proceeded to pound the Egyptian air force into impotence. They did, in fact, a remarkably accurate and business-like job. No civilian targets were hit, though this small crumb of comfort failed to stem the Opposition's storm of rage which burst on Eden's head next day in the Commons. Amid cries of 'collusion' and some undignified fisticuffs, the House had to be suspended for half an hour. Outside

Parliament the country, too, was divided on Eden's gamble as it had rarely, if ever, been divided before. The dissension cut across all party, social, even family loyalties: bishop denounced bishop, professor cold-shouldered professor, Tory ministers resigned in protest. Never more clearly did the press reflect the divisions, the conflict of emotions of a country plunged bewilderingly into a war.

The News Chronicle called it 'folly on a grand scale' and pointed out that for the first time British policy 'had achieved the incredible feat of uniting America and Russia against her'. *The Daily Telegraph* ranged itself firmly behind the Prime Minister and believed the world would come to see things his way in due course. *The Daily Mirror*, on the other hand, declared it was 'the culminating blunder in Eden's disastrous Middle East record'. *The Daily Sketch* said that if guilt existed it lay on the heads of Eden's critics who were 'morally sabotaging' the fighting men at Suez and that the depths of real infamy were to be found in the columns of *The Daily Herald*. That particular paper was, of course, fulminating at Eden's 'power-crazy adventure' and in turn mocking *The Times* for its irresolution. Indeed *The Times* was having second thoughts: at an early stage it had

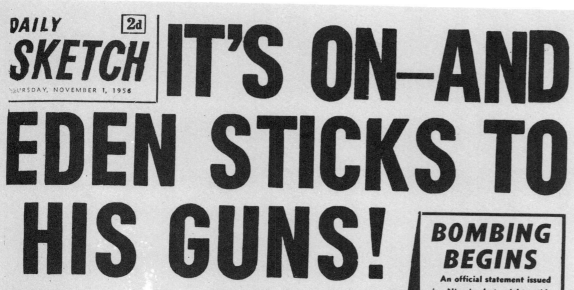

DAILY SKETCH

Thursday, November 1, 1956 — 2d

IT'S ON—AND EDEN STICKS TO HIS GUNS!

THE invasion is on—in a blackout. Sir Anthony Eden confirmed it in the Commons yesterday, but refused to give one detail of British or French military movements.

"We stand by our decision," he told the angry Opposition.

As the world waited for news, only rumours from foreign radio stations broke the silence.

One concrete fact was a Ministry of Defence statement that: "All available means, including broadcasting, are being used to inform the Egyptian people as follows:

"'All civilians in Egypt are warned for their safety to keep away from all Egyptian airfields from now onwards until the Egyptian Government accepts the request of the United Kingdom and French Governments delivered on October 30.'"

Asked to elaborate the statement, a Ministry spokesman said it was "an operational announcement".

About the reference to "airfields," the spokesman said: "We are warning civilians. Any military force would be foolish to give its plans away."

Mr. Hugh Gaitskell, the Socialist Leader, announced in the Commons a censure motion on the Government and all constitutional opposition to its policy in the Middle East.

Sir Anthony called the U.S. resolution in the Security Council "in effect, a condemnation of Israel as the aggressor".

"We felt that we could not associate ourselves with this and we said so through diplomatic channels both in London and New York," he said.

● 'Prisoners captured'

"Is there any member of this House who can consider Egypt as an innocent country who can be exonerated at the Security Council by condemning Israel as an aggressor?" Sir Anthony asked.

Israeli troops were continuing to advance towards the Canal, and the latest report was that they were approaching the Canal.

"There have been a number of prisoners captured, I understand," said Sir Anthony.

"In the light of these facts, can anybody say that we or the French Government should have waited? *

"We have no desire whatever, nor have the French Government, that the military action we shall have to take should be more than temporary in its duration.

"But it is our intention that our action to protect the Canal and separate the combatants should result in a settlement which will prevent such a situation arising periodically in the future.

"In the actions we have taken, we are not concerned to stop Egypt, but to stop war."

➡ Back Page

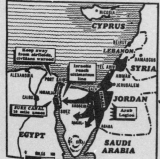

Britons told 'Quit Port Said—NOW'

A THIRD and final "Get out" notice was given to 850 Britons in Port Said yesterday. But most of them are staying on—either because they think they are in essential jobs or because there's no way out now. Said a British Consulate spokesman: "This warning carries greater urgency than previous ones."

Desert war story, Back Page.

BOMBING BEGINS

An official statement issued in Nicosia last night said:
"An air offensive by bomber aircraft under Allied command is at this moment being launched against military targets in Egypt."

The statement was issued by Allied Forces Headquarters.

THE HOUR BY HOUR DRAMA

THIS was the hour-by-hour drama of the on-off invasion as reports and rumours poured into London yesterday:

5 a.m.—Unidentified radio station announces in Arabic: "British and French forces entering Egypt now."

5.20 a.m.—Suez Canal Zone reported "absolutely quiet." No sign of any fighting.

8 a.m.—Convoy passes through Canal normally. Cairo radio reported: "We'll protect all shipping."

9.45 a.m.—Complete clamp down on news in London. Admiralty, War Office, Air Ministry have "No news."

'NO LANDINGS'

11.20 a.m.—Rumours sweep Cairo that Britain and France have climbed down, withdrawn ultimatum.

2 p.m.—French Defence Ministry confirm: No landings have been made.

3 p.m.—Cairo communique reports: Canal, Suez and Port Said all quiet.

3.30 p.m.—Sir Anthony Eden reports to the House.

6 p.m.—Norwegian Foreign Minister tells his Parliament in Oslo: "British and French forces landed at 5.30 a.m. to-day."

For Elevenses

there is nothing like **OVALTINE**

WHEN you pause for your Elevenses in the middle of the morning's work, be sure that you choose a hot drink that helps to stimulate and sustain energy.

'Ovaltine' is a delicious concentration of Nature's best foods, fortified with extra vitamins. It is an ideal dietary supplement.

Make the best of your morning break—drink delicious 'Ovaltine' every day. There is nothing like it.

1/6, 2/9 and 5/- per tin.

P8a

---

into which it seemed to have fallen'. On the other side of the fence *The Observer* took the most uncompromising stand of all (and paid a correspondingly higher penalty than other papers in lost subscribers): 'Never since 1783 has Britain made herself so universally disliked ... Nations are said to have the governments they deserve. Let us show that we deserve better'.

But it was too late. The Empire's lifeline which Eden's precipitate action was going to safeguard at all costs was now blocked in numerous places by sunken ships. And the fatal hiatus between November 1 and 4 had only served to harden world opinion against Britain rock-solid (perhaps what hurt the hardest were the decisions of several nations to withdraw from the Olympic Games due to start in Melbourne in a month's time). When the airborne assault on Port Said began at dawn on November 5, the gunfire along the Canal paled beside the explosions heard from Moscow and Washington. The Russians dropped an unsubtle and (in view of their own actions in Hungary) unprincipled hint that the invasion was bringing the world to the brink of atomic war. Eisenhower refused to extend any credit to prop up Britain's dwindling reserves, unless the advance beyond Port Said was halted. This was now a critical condition. Speculation against sterling had reached panic proportions and industry threatened to be crippled, with oil supplies from the middle east turned off like a tap.

With the United Nations having resolved on a peace-keeping force for the Middle East on the 4th, every mile advanced down the Canal by French and British troops looked more and more like unwarranted Imperialist aggression. Eden himself had broken under the pressure of the preceding week. He was a very sick man. On the 7th with the British vanguard preparing to take their lunch in Ismailia, he called a ceasefire. With a final show of bravado, however, he refused to evacuate any troops until the U.N. force arrived in strength, in spite of Russian threats to send in 'volunteers'.

So it was at the end of November, when Eden announced his departure for Jamaica to recover what was left of his health, that Britain found herself as short of friends as she was of funds, lamely occupying one end of an unusable canal, and facing the imminent prospect of severe petrol rationing. Both sides in the continuing debate were dissatisfied now: the doves felt that Britain's political integrity was indelibly stained, the hawks that the inconclusive military fiasco had opened the floodgates to Russian penetration in the Middle East.

In the weeks and months that followed the accusing eyes of the world mercifully turned away from Britain to focus on man's inhumanity in other parts of the world, towards Hungary where vicious reprisals were under way, to South Africa where the Johannesburg treason trials were opening, to Syria where conspiracy was rife. But in Britain, and in particular in the newspapers, the war continued. The issue that aroused the warmest passions was whether those papers that had denounced the war were responsible for its unhappy outcome. Had they been guilty of treason, as many protested? 'Many people question a newspaper's right or competence to examine its Government's aims and actions, once military operations have been embarked upon' *The Observer* replied. 'We conceive it to be our duty as journalists ... to follow what is done in this country's name, come to a careful and honest opinion and express that opinion as frankly, reasonably and fearlessly as possible'. That *The Observer* had done admirably, though when it came to counting the cost of fearlessness and frankness, there was little consolation in knowing that history had proved you right.

---

advocated intervention in the Suez crisis, now it was admitting '... doubts remain whether the right course has been taken'. *The Manchester Guardian* had no such hesitations — this was 'an act of folly without any justification in terms but brief expediency'. *The Daily Express* could scarcely restrain its elation that the Empire was being defended by 'a policy of courage' rather than a 'policy of cowardice'.

Alas for *The Daily Express* the Empire was not enthusiastic about being defended by this kind of 'courage'. At the U.N. only Australia and New Zealand could be persuaded to take Britain's part, and that with the greatest reluctance. By an overwhelming majority the U.N. on November 2 called on Britain and France to cease hostilities immediately, as did Britain's middle eastern allies in the Baghdad Pact. In America, whatever the 'barrack-room language' reported to be issuing from the White House, the press seemed torn between disapproval on moral grounds and admiration for a plucky try. *The Cleveland Plain Dealer* claimed '... no tears will be shed in this country if the British and French ... are successful in toppling the Egyptian dictator off his throne. He had been asking for it'. And so far as *The New York Daily News* was concerned it seemed 'to hold out the best hope of prevent-

ing large-scale war'. *The Chicago Tribune*, though, was 'witnessing the collapse of many illusions' and believed Britain and France to have brought war 'by means of a sordid conspiracy'. Nearly all leading papers endorsed Eisenhower's honourable stand of non-involvement, but many of them equally were not prepared to condemn Britain and France outright without recognising America's own shortcomings, not least the Administration's vacillating middle east policies.

For whatever reason — whether because (as was suggested later) Eden had been misinformed on the date of the Israeli invasion, or whether the wheels of gun-boat diplomacy still turned as ponderously as they had in Victoria's day — there was an uncomfortable pause after the bombing of the 31st. Though it hardly seemed like it, a fleet *was* on its way from Malta but would take four days to reach the canal. In the meantime, the Sunday papers were enabled to weigh into the debate with all guns firing. *The Sunday Times* urged that 'to draw back at this stage ... would be to invite unmitigated disaster' and predicted that success would 'restore international confidence in Britain's sagacity and power, and go far to lift the prestige of the West from the moral palsy

DAILY EXPRESS

No. 17,562   WEDNESDAY NOVEMBER 7 1956   3 a.m. forecast: Dry; rather cloudy later   Price 2d.

NAVY DIVERS BEGIN TO CLEAR CANAL AT PORT SAID

'Allies have fulfilled their mission,' says French communiqué

ISMAILIA FALLS

EDEN: 3 TERMS FOR UNO POLICE FORCE

By DEREK MARKS

NEWS that Britain and France had ordered a cease-fire at one minute to midnight was given by Sir Anthony Eden in the Commons yesterday and by UNO chief Dag Hammarskjold in New York.

MR. HAMMARSKJOLD told a Press conference that Egypt and Israel had agreed to an unconditional cease-fire.

He is speeding plans to send an international force to stand between the Israelis and Nasser's men.

For this UNO force seven nations have offered a total of about 7,700 men. But Britain, America, France, Russia, and Nationalist China are barred from the force by a resolution passed in UNO's General Assembly two days ago.

The demand

SIR ANTHONY EDEN told the Commons that if acceptance of the unconditional cease-fire by Egypt and Israel is confirmed, and if the international force is competent to secure and supervise objects already set out by UNO's General Assembly —then Britain will agree to stop further military operations.

But Britain is also making another demand — clearance from the Suez Canal of obstructions planted there by Nasser's men, mostly ships.

Said Sir Anthony: "Clearing of the obstructions in the Suez Canal and its approaches, which is in no sense a military operation, is of great urgency in the interests of world shipping and world trade.

"The Franco-British force is equipped to tackle this task and the British Government therefore propose that technicians accompanying the force shall undertake this work at once.

"Pending confirmation of the above, the Government are ordering their forces to cease fire at midnight unless they are attacked."

Resolution

The objectives which Britain demands that UNO's international force must be able to "secure and supervise" were set out in a resolution passed last Friday. This resolution, introduced by the U.S., urged —

As an immediate cease-fire; a halt to the movement of military forces and supplies into the area; immediate withdrawal by the Egyptian and Israeli forces behind their former lines; and effective steps to open the Canal and secure freedom of navigation.

In his statement yesterday the Prime Minister claimed that British action had limited the area of conflict and had forced the United Nations to set up a police force.

Other Arab nations had been prevented from intervening by "the knowledge and presence of our forces."

Immediately after he had spoken in the Commons, Sir Anthony received a personal telephone call from President Eisenhower in Washington congratulating him on the cease-fire. "It's wonderful," said the President.

Here is the story behind the day's news—no less dramatic than the news itself.

Sir Anthony Eden called a full meeting of the Cabinet at 9.45 a.m.

Before the Ministers were the messages from Marshal Bulganin threatening Russian intervention in the Middle East, and the equally firm warning of President Eisenhower that the U.S. would oppose any Russian intervention.

Three threats

Reports were widespread in Westminster last night that the Cabinet had been split on the question whether Britain's interests demanded that the fighting in Egypt should continue or not.

It is said that Sir Anthony, Mr. Macmillan, and Lord Home, Minister for Commonwealth Relations, were strongly in favour of carrying on at least until the Anglo-French forces had obtained complete command of the Canal.

The opposing argument was that Britain could not continue a military operation which was being opposed in Parliament by the Opposition, and at UNO by our principal allies and Commonwealth states.

I am informed that at no time did any Cabinet Minister oppose continued intervention in the Suez area if only for the time being or not.

All-along-Canal race—and then it's cease fire at midnight

Express Military Reporters

BRITAIN AND FRANCE yesterday ordered their forces in Egypt to cease fire at midnight—40 hours after the fighting began.

And almost on the deadline the French Defence Ministry revealed that Allied troops had raced 50 miles south from Port Said and captured Ismailia.

This town, a former British base, is the halfway mark on the Canal.

The French Defence Ministry said the cease-fire was agreed because the Allies "have fulfilled their mission and attained their objectives."

It added: "The Egyptian ground forces along the Canal have been destroyed or scattered."

Nasser's navy has been "seriously damaged."

And by midnight "his air force will be destroyed 95 per cent."

Royal Marine commandos went ashore with tanks at Port Said yesterday morning, helped the paratroops mop up the town, then moved across the causeway to El Kantara for the final drive south.

Divers began to clear the blocked Canal.

CAIRO RADIO was saying up to the last minute that Egyptian troops would "keep fighting."

IN SINAI yesterday Israeli troops held a victory parade.

'Russian bombers moving'

ANKARA, Tuesday.

A FORMATION of jet bombers — officially unidentified but thought to be Russian—was reported flying over Eastern Turkey today.

Turkish Air Force planes were alerted but, it is believed, they had to identify the bombers.

No official information is available.

LONDON: Last night there were no reports of any Russian aircraft landing in Egypt.

MOSCOW yesterday broadcast an Egyptian Government appeal for "volunteers."

DAMASCUS: Syrian Air Force fighters claimed last night that they shot down a Canberra bomber—British built, but not identified as R.A.F. — which "violated Syrian air space."

A Free radio station called Roka (it means Fox) reported continued fighting in two other towns where the people are still holding out valiantly.

Helicopter Commando

MEN of No. 45 Royal Marine Commando landed at Port Said yesterday by helicopter.

As their comrades splashed ashore from landing craft, the men were shuttled high and dry from an aircraft-carrier.

This is the first time such a Commando lift has been made.

And the Admiralty disclosed yesterday that, also for the first time, it has a carrier in the Suez task force—the Theseus—working solely with helicopters.

Rear - Admiral G. B. Sayer leads the helicopter group.

The Navy has more than 100 ships involved in the operations.

Nasser calls in tanks

AS the cease-fire neared, Nasser was reported to be gathering his tank units under one command between Cairo and the Canal.

He started with around 500 tanks, including 40 British Centurions of the latest design, 200 old American Shermans, 100 light T34s of Czech origin.

and a gaggle of older tanks of British, French, German and Italian make.

The troops have been trained by former German officers.

So far the toughest opposition to Allied troops has come from S.U.100 "tank destroyers."

These consist of a 100mm. gun mounted on a T34 tank chassis with 3in. armour plate.

And these are the British wounded

From KEITH MORFETT

NICOSIA, Tuesday.

FIRST British casualties evacuated from the battle zone told their stories in hospital today —

Private Sydney Williams, aged 20, from Newport, Mon.: "I was with my commanding officer trying to knock out a tank when a mortar landed behind me, and I was hit in the back.

"My colonel took me in his truck to the first-aid post, and

I was evacuated by the French."

Private George Stanger, aged 22, of Watford, married 36 hours before he left England: "I was pulling down my lifebelt when I felt a knock in the arm from a bullet. I landed in a heap."

Private Dennis Russell, aged 20, a Regular soldier from Wolverhampton who landed in the middle of a minefield: "My legs and feet were injured. I crawled across the road and into the dropping zone itself. Two corporals picked me up."

aged 27, from Worcester, a paratroop medical officer: "I was a bit blinded in one eye by shrapnel as I floated down. Otherwise it was a good landing.

"It was not half as bad as we had expected. I noticed the lads were walking about rather than digging in."

At Bedford last night the doctor's wife, 29-year-old Barbara Cavenagh, who is expecting a baby, said that living with her mother, said "Sandy was Oxford stroke in the Boat-race of 1950 and he rowed No. 2 in this. He is a very athletic type."

Lieutenant Sandy Cavenagh.

---

3 A.M: IKE LEADING

HOW THE VOTING WENT

HERE are the voting figures this morning: Needed to win: 266 of the 531 votes contributed by the 48 States to the Electoral College. Whoever wins a State wins all its electoral votes.

These are the latest voting figures, but counting is not ended in any State:—

EISENHOWER		STEVENSON	
States	27	States	12
Popular votes	1,700,844	Popular votes	1,344,746

House of Representatives			Senate		
	New	Old		New	Old
Democrats	73	232	Democrats	36	49
Republicans	7	203	Republicans	30	47

1952 Election—Eisenhower (Republican): Electoral votes, 442: States, 39; popular votes, 33,936,252. Stevenson (Democrat): Electoral votes, 89; States, 9; popular votes, 27,314,992.

He forges ahead of Adlai—even in big industrial centres

Express Staff Reporter: Washington, Tuesday

THE U.S. presidential election looks like being a victory for Eisenhower with an increased majority.

Tonight, with many returns still to come in, he is leading in 27 States.

His Democrat opponent Adlai Stevenson is leading in 12. So far 1,700,844 votes have been cast in favour of Eisenhower. 1,344,746 for Stevenson.

In voting for the House of Representatives there has been one Democrat gain from Republican.

Most of the States in which Stevenson is leading are in the traditionally Democratic "solid South."

One exception is Illinois. Stevenson's home State, where there have been scandals in the Republican State administration.

There Democrats are in front in contests for a Senate seat and the governorship, but most of the results so far come from Chicago. The rural areas, mostly Republican, may change the picture.

Eisenhower is winning some of the big industrial cities, where forecasters said Stevenson must carry if he were to have a chance.

Record poll?

The Republicans have won New Haven, Connecticut, and are sweeping the "precincts"—districts—in such big industrial centres as Bridgeport, Connecticut, and the steel town of Pittsburgh, Pennsylvania.

In the days of Roosevelt and Truman those cities—with large Negro populations—always voted Democrat.

In Kentucky, also traditionally Democratic, the trend to the Republicans continues.

Also grim for the Democrats is the position in Tennessee. There Eisenhower's lead is increasing with each return, though the margin between h.m and Stevenson continued to be smaller than the vote for Coleman Andrews, vote-splitting State Rights candidate.

Warm, sunny weather—and the international situation — brought the voters out in force. Early returns showed that it may be a record poll.

He votes—and dies

HOLLYWOOD, Tuesday.— Paul Kelly, veteran U.S. film actor, died in Hollywood from a heart attack today shortly after casting his vote.

Russian spare-nobody hangmen wipe out Freedom Fighters

THE MONGOLS MOP UP IN HUNGARY

From RICHARD KILIAN: Vienna, Tuesday

OUT of murdered Hungary today came reports that the fight to a finish with the might of Russia goes on. The overwhelming Soviet forces—mainly Mongolian—are sparing no one as they wipe out the groups of Freedom Fighters battling on to the end.

Reports from refugees, rebel radio stations, and diplomatic sources, picked up in Vienna tonight, say that the Budapest Freedom Fighters have recaptured Parliament Buildings.

They say that two roads leading from the city, besieged since Saturday, have been opened into the countryside. Yet in Hungary are 200,000 Russians with 4,600 tanks. More Russian troops are poised on the frontier.

But food is running out—as well as bullets. These are the desperate hours.

LITTLE ARMY

And Dunapentele, south of Budapest, was still free tonight. The people were shooting it out. Plucky little Hegyeshalom, the frontier post which has never surrendered to the massed Russian tanks a few hundred yards away has increased its little army to a hundred men.

The Russians sent them an ultimatum: "Give in or we'll wipe you out with heavy guns and destroy the whole place." The hundred resolved to stay to the death.

It seems impossible that this defiance of overwhelming might should continue. It goes on because the corpses of 20,000 citizens of Budapest now lying in the broken streets. Yet the survivors snipe away at the Russians.

A conservative estimate puts the wounded in Budapest at 40,000.

Another diplomatic source confirmed that Russian casualties up until last Saturday—were 3,000 dead and 6,000 wounded. The high proportion of dead to wounded comes only when no mercy is given in the battle.

Meanwhile the Hungarian secret police, fighting side-by-side with the Russians, are indulging in a wild fury of revenge, sad refugees who came over the border tonight.

HANGINGS

"They are hanging people from the nearest lamp-post, said a Budapest man who crossed the frontier at Furstenfeld in southeast Austria.

"Russian troops are hanging captured civilian rebels from the Danube bridges. But Hungarian soldiers are being given the concession of being shot instead of hanged."

Centres of resistance named tonight were around the uranium mines in the south-west. Over in the west, and Budapest itself.

U.S. warns: 'Hands off Austria'

From DONALD LUDLOW

WASHINGTON, Tuesday.

CLOSE watch is being kept by the U.S. State Department tonight for any development that may indicate that Russia, using the Hungarian rebellion as an excuse, is about to interfere with neutral Austria.

Chief spokesman Lincoln White said in a prepared statement that any attempt by Russia on the territorial integrity and internal sovereignty of Austria would be regarded by the United States as a grave threat to peace.

The statement was an answer to Russian charges that people backed by the United States and operating from Austria had encouraged the Hungarian rebellion. These charges were condemned as "grossly false."

U.S. sends ships

WASHINGTON, Tuesday.— Twelve American destroyers leave Newport, Rhode Island, for the Mediterranean today in what the U.S. Navy described as "routine deployment."

Whisky galore

All restrictions on imports of whisky from anywhere in the world are to end next Monday.

Lloyd's radio talk

Foreign Secretary Mr. Selwyn Lloyd is to broadcast today after 9 p.m. news on the Middle East.

Fog visibility 10ft.

Fog in Kent Surrey and Essex last night cut visibility to 10ft. in the west, and Budapest itself.

4.30 a.m. LATEST: IKE WINS TWO STATES

WASHINGTON, Tuesday.— Ike has so far won two States—Maine (five electoral votes) and Maryland (nine votes).—Reuter.

HELI-TROOPS KILL 35 TERRORISTS

ALGIERS, Tuesday.—French troops flying back to base today after killing 20 terrorists in the Turenne region, spotted another band and killed 15 more.—Reuter.

FLEet-street 8000

Parcel bomb kills Briton

NICOSIA, Tuesday.—Mr. Douglas Williamson, 45-year-old assistant district commissioner in the Troodos area of Cyprus, was killed today by a parcel bomb which exploded at his office at Platres.

Woman dies after knife attack

Sixty-year-old Mrs. Amy Salter, found knifed last night in her home at Hillmarton, near Calne, Wilts, died in hospital at Bath. Police were early today seeking a young woman seen in the village earlier yesterday.

The 'poacher'

A British frigate was sent out last night to protect a Polish fishing boat off Margate. Whitstable fishermen had complained that it was poaching and that several smaller Polish boats were in the area.

"I'm just back from the Pole, Mummy!"

Woman stabbed in Soho street

A woman was found lying stabbed in the road at Berwickstreet, Soho, shortly before midnight. She was taken to hospital. Police arrived with two tracker dogs. People in the area were being questioned early today.

IT'S HARD WORK playing at Polar exploration. And even in this so-called temperate climate the wind can soon chill little fingers—especially when he just won't keep his gloves on all the time. But now he's back at Base Camp—with a good hot cup of Bovril to warm him up and see that the weather's done him no harm.

What a blessing children are so fond of Bovril! It's the grandest winter drink of them all. Tempting. Warming. Fortifying. Because Bovril is made from beef.

It will do you good, too, to have a piping hot Bovril when you're cold or tired. Bovril cheers and revives you as nothing else can. And because it's prime lean beef that Bovril's made from, you needn't have any worries about your figure. Get the Bovril habit now. It will help you and yours to ward off colds and chills this winter.

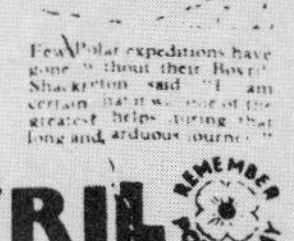

BOVRIL puts beef into you

THE SUEZ CANAL

PORT SAID
KANTARA
EL BALLAH
EL FIRDAN
MOASCAR
ISMAILIA
ABU SULTAN
Lake Timsah
Great Bitter Lake
FAYID
Little Bitter Lake
FANARA
SHALLUFA
SUEZ
PORT TEWFIK

50 MILES

50 MILES

EDEN to BULGANIN: DO NOT TALK OF BARBARISM

SIR ANTHONY EDEN, during his cease-fire speech, read to the Commons his reply to Marshal Bulganin's message of Monday night —

"I have received with deep regret your message and I cannot leave unanswered the baseless accusations in your message.

"This a.m. has now been virtually achieved.

"As regards the future you know that the Canal area has in the past been able to discuss issues vital for the whole world.

"The British Government has repeatedly said that the essential aim of the action by the British and French Governments was to stop the fighting between Israel and Egypt and separate them.

"This aim has now been virtually achieved.

"As regards the future you accuse us of waging war against the national independence of the peoples of the Near and Middle East. We have already proved the absurdity of this charge by declaring our willingness that UNO should

"taken the first steps to organise such a force. The British Government fully approves the principle of this force. Indeed, we suggested it ourselves.

"Our aim is to find a peaceful solution, not to engage in arguments with you.

"But I cannot leave unanswered the baseless accusations in your message.

"You accuse us of waging war against the national independence of countries in the Near and Middle East. We have already proved the absurdity of this charge by declaring our willingness that UNO should

take over the physical task of maintaining peace in the area.

"You accuse us of the barbaric bombardment of Egyptian towns and villages.

"Our attacks on airfields and other military targets have been made with the most scrupulous care in order to cause the least possible loss of life.

"The world knows that in the past in Hungary have been ruthlessly crushing the heroic resistance of a truly national movement for independence, a movement which by declaring

take over the physical task of maintaining peace in the area — its neutrality, proved that it offered no threat to the security of the Soviet Union.

"At such a time it ill becomes the Soviet Government to speak of the actions of the British Government as barbaric.

"UNO has called on your Government to desist from all armed attack on the peoples of Hungary, to withdraw its forces from Hungarian territory and accept UN observers in order that the peoples of Hungary shall have freedom to decide their own destiny.

"Her Majesty's Government would..."

■ PAGE TWO, COL. SEVEN.

EDEN'S WAR

WAR

THREE DECLARATIONS BY THE MIRROR

① ## WHEN SHOULD EDEN GO?

SIR ANTHONY EDEN'S Government is crumbling.   Eden is on the way out.

The Economist said yesterday: "There may rest upon Eden a painful but inescapable decision."

That decision is to resign the Premiership. The dominating question in politics today is: "When should Eden go?"

The MIRROR verdict will be published on Monday.

② ## HAS BUTLER GOT THE GUTS?

WHO can take over from Eden?

Two names stand out: MACMILLAN, Chancellor of the Exchequer.   BUTLER, Lord Privy Seal and Leader of the House of Commons.

One quality is needed from the Tory who will take over the Premiership. That quality is the courage to come out into the open against Eden. Now. Has Butler got the guts to do this?

Watch for the MIRROR declaration on Tuesday.

③ ## WHO SHOULD BE LABOUR'S FOREIGN SECRETARY?

A GENERAL Election may be near.

Hugh Gaitskell is Labour Party Leader.   When Labour wins the election, he will be Prime Minister.

Labour's biggest question is this: Who should be Gaitskell's Foreign Secretary?

Should Gaitskell appoint Aneurin Bevan—the man who challenged him for leadership?

The MIRROR declaration will appear on Wednesday

Willingly to School

Little Rock and the Colour Question

PRESIDENT SENDS TROOPS TO LITTLE ROCK, FEDERALIZES ARKANSAS NATIONAL GUARD; TELLS NATION HE ACTED TO AVOID ANARCHY

New York Times

'In this stormy world' declared *The Arkansas Democrat* on September 8 1957, 'with its lightnings of Red power threats, flickering in the international skies', there was 'only one centre of strength for peace. We are that centre'. And indeed, with the fate of Berlin in the balance and Hungary still a vivid memory, many in America would have agreed that internal unity was vital for a bulwark against the ever-present threat of communism. But even as *The Arkansas Democrat* was voicing its fine sentiments, it was being an unwilling eye-witness of a schism on its very doorstep which was to tear the country apart over the next decade.

The 1955 Supreme Court ruling that all schools in the USA should be de-segregated should have been a major landmark in the struggle for negro civil rights. The fact that it wasn't was due to the reluctance of many states in the South to comply. But in the fall of 1957 in the town of Little Rock, Arkansas, at any rate, integration looked like becoming a reality. The Little Rock board of education had designated September as the beginning of a six-year programme which was to open all the schools in the area to blacks. That month, nine carefully-selected black children were to be admitted to the Central High School for the first time.

But the authorities had reckoned without the militantly white Mothers' League and its champion, Governor Orval Faubus. Having sought and obtained an injunction on the proposed integration from a state court, Faubus calculatedly ignored its immediate reversal by Federal District Judge Davies and surrounded the High School with National Guardsmen on September 2. It was, he said, 'to maintain law and order' in the certain event of rioting. But the next day it became transparently clear that his real intention was to prevent the nine children from entering the building. It was a direct challenge to Eisenhower's civil rights programme and suddenly, as *The Arkansas Gazette* (which subsequently won a Pulitzer Prize for its coverage of the crisis) said, 'the eyes of the nation were on Little Rock'.

Judge Davies, and the Administration, stood firm and ordered Faubus to remove his troops, which he eventually agreed to do. On September 23, however, when the nine children had at last succeeded in being smuggled in to school, a white mob caught wind of the manœuvre and attempted to invade the school. In the riot a negro newspaperman was badly beaten up, and some of the black children were attacked, demonstrating, as Faubus would have it, that he had been right to put a guard on the school in the first place. Eisenhower, on the other hand, took the view that it had been the Governor's actions which had inflamed the situation, and immediately ordered Federal troops into the town. In the weeks that followed the negro children were escorted to school under armed guard, as the members of the session of Westover Hills Presbyterian Church (Little Rock) called on God to see that our law-enforcement agencies provide protection for all of our citizens, regardless of race, and that they promptly disperse any mobs'.

It took two months for their prayers to be answered completely, but on December 2 the negro students were enabled to enter the school unmolested and unguarded for the first time. It looked like a triumph of reason over prejudice, but the spark which had been ignited at Little Rock had elsewhere begun a conflagration which proved unstoppable. The following year was marked by a series of bomb

WEATHER FORECAST
Bay Area: Fair except for morning cloudiness near the coast. High temperature today in the 70s; low, 52 to 55 with winds.

Full Report on Page 23

San Francisco Chronicle

THE VOICE OF THE WEST

FINAL

93d YEAR No. 267   CCCCAAA   TUESDAY, SEPTEMBER 24, 1957   10 CENTS   GArfield 1-1112

NEW VIOLENCE IN LITTLE ROCK

Basilio Wins; N.Y., Braves Take Flags

Carmen Basilio became the new middleweight champion of the world last night by defeating Sugar Ray Robinson in New York.

In baseball, the Milwaukee Braves and the New York Yankees became opponents for the 1957 World Series. The Braves won the National League pennant with an 11-inning 4-2 victory over the St. Louis Cardinals while the idle Yankees coasted home by the American League by virtue of the second-place Chicago White Sox losing to Kansas City, 6-5.

Details in Sporting Green.

Burial at Estate For Sibelius

HELSINKI, Finland, Sept. 3 (AP)—Composer Jean Sibelius, who died last Friday, will be buried next Monday in the garden of his estate, Ainola.

not only
MUSIC LESSON PLANS

but everything fine in music for the whole family

You can test their interest before you buy an instrument . . . with lessons at the School of Music . . . and bring music to the whole family with radios, phonographs, sheet music, pianos and organs.

5 Lost Ship Survivors Spur Search

H..., Germany, Sept. . . — Five survivors of the German bark Pamir were rescued by a U. S. freighter today and an intensive search was pressed in the hope at least 25 more men got off the sinking vessel.

The five survivors found in a lifeboat told rescuers two lifeboats were launched, indicating a maximum of 30 men of the 86 aboard might possibly be alive. They said five comrades were swept into the sea from the lifeboat and drowned shortly before the rescue.

Lights and flares spotted in mid-Atlantic also raised hopes that others of the 86-man crew lived through the hurricane that struck the four-masted sailing ship 550 miles west-southwest of the Azores.

The Isbrandtsen Lines freighter Saxon made the first rescue in the hunt under way since the Pamir radioed this SOS Saturday:

"Heavy hurricane. All sails lost, 45-degree list, danger of sinking."

The Saxon told Isbrandtsen's New York office of picking

See Page 16, Col. 7

You Don't Have To Be Drafted

Volunteers Will Find Many Service Choices

(This is the third of four exclusive articles.)

By Jack Foisie

Should you wait to be drafted—and hope you'll not be tapped before working your way into a deferred category?

Or should you volunteer for the service of your choice at a time of your choosing, and with the added benefits in uniform of being a "regular?"

For Men on the Fence

Young men on the fence about the question may like to know how 12,301 local draft-age men now in service decided. Five out of six decided to volunteer.

There is a third choice: Sign up for the Reserves and serve only six months active duty. Then put in at least 2½ years at one-night-a-week drill sessions or an all-day drill once a month, plus two weeks of summer camp each year.

Four Groups of Reserves

Right now it is tough to get into the Army, Air Force, Marine Corps or Coast Guard Reserves under this program because of a cutback in military spending. (The Navy does not have the six months program. Only the California National Guard has the gates wide open for the "six months" applicant.

Before making a decision on what to do about military service, take time to shop around and dis-

See Page 16, Col. 3

The mob chased Alex Wilson, a Negro reporter . . .

. . . and one man kicked him as he tried to get away

New Gas War Flares in the Bay Area

The Bay Area was in the throes of still another gasoline price-cutting war yesterday, with regular gas selling for as low as 24.9 cents a gallon at a few "cut-rate" stations.

The previous price war petered out about six weeks ago.

But today "it's worse than ever," said William Gray, executive field director for the Bay Area Council of Petroleum Retailers.

Gray said the price cutting was "general throughout the Bay Area" with prices for regular ranging from 26.9 cents a gallon in Santa Rosa to 29.9 in San Francisco. In the East Bay and on the Pen-

insula the price was about 27.9 at most stations, he said. Stations with less well known brands of gasoline were selling their product for 2 and 3 cents a gallon cheaper in most areas.

The normal price for gas has been 32.9 cents a gallon for regular and 36.6 for premium.

Ike Orders Halt, Hints Troop Use

NEWPORT, R. I., Sept. 23 (AP)—President Eisenhower tonight signed a history-making proclamation clearing the way for possible use of Federal troops to quash any further school integration violence at Little Rock.

Mr. Eisenhower put his name to the document at the vacation White House shortly after he denounced "disgraceful occurrences" in the Little Rock racial disorders.

In an earlier statement, he asserted:

"I will use the full power of the United States—including whatever force may be necessary—to prevent any obstruction of the law and to

See Page 6, Col. 1

The Crisis At a Glance

• Integration at Little Rock was halted by mobs. President Eisenhower ordered the people to stop defying Federal law and Federal court orders.

• Press Secretary James Hagerty said the proclamation did not necessarily mean Mr. Eisenhower would use troops. Hagerty said the first test would come today, if crowds again tried to keep Negroes out of Central High School.

• Violent flareups continued into the night. "Hundreds" were arrested—Negroes and whites.

• Negro leaders said they didn't know whether Negroes would again try to enter the school today.

Cities League Warned of Big Problems

By James Benet

The dizzying growth of the U. S. in general and California in particular will confront the cities of this State with giant problems, the cities' representatives were told here yesterday.

Keynote speakers at the conference of the League of California Cities sounded the warning at the opening general session of the four-day meeting.

In the next 20 years the Nation will probably gain one-third more people, double its industry and increase its working force by only one-fourth to one-third—working perhaps one-eighth less time — said Dr. Weldon Gibson, associate director of the Stanford Research Institute.

But California's population will increase by 75 per cent, and its economic activity may triple, he said.

This will mean new crises

See Page 2, Col. 8

Turncoat's Spirits Fail

RAVENNA, Italy, Sept. 23 (Reuters) — Fourteen Yugoslavs, who left Fiume in a motorboat last Friday, arrived in Ravenna today and 13 of them asked for political asylum.

But the fourteenth, the captain of the launch, asked to be sent back, saying he had left Yugoslavia under the influence of liquor.

School Riots ---City Still Jittery

From Associated Press and United Press

LITTLE ROCK, Ark., Sept. 23 (AP)—The bloody assaults of an inflamed crowd of white men and women thwarted an integration attempt at Little Rock Central High School today.

Nine Negro students slipped into the school during a wild melee this morning but were removed about noon when officials feared the frenzied crowd would become an uncontrollable mob.

It was a wild day of hate and violence in which at least 11 newsmen were assaulted.

The violence flared anew into the night. Riot calls were being answered past the midnight hour. Officials reported hundreds arrested. In one incident shots were fired at a car of Negroes which refused an order to halt for inspection, grazing an officer as it sped away. (For details, see page 4.)

Mrs. L. C. Bates, president of the Arkansas chapter of the National Association for the Advancement of Colored People, said Negro leaders had not decided whether to let the nine students make another attempt to attend school tomorrow.

The Negro teen-agers said they were not hurt inside the school and that "Nothing much happened."

Terrence Roberts, 15, said: "I was pushed, but I don't know that anybody was hit. It was quiet after we got into classes. Some of the white students walked out. Just a few of them."

There are 1900 white students at Central.

The day's violence started at 8:45 a. m. and continued

See Page 4, Col. 1

INDEX

THE WEATHER
Today: Fair, with seasonable temperatures.
Tomorrow: Partly cloudy; little change in temperature.

Temperature: Max. 71, Min. 85.
Probable Range: Max. 77, Min. 58.
Humidity at 4 P.M. Yesterday 47%
Expected Humidity this afternoon: 40-50%

Reports, Maps—Sec. 3, Page 6

NEW YORK
Herald Tribune

A European Edition Is Published Daily in Paris

117th Year   VOL. CXVII   NO. 40,492

830 West 41st Street, New York 36, N. Y.
Telephone PEnnsylvania 6-4000

THURSDAY, SEPTEMBER 26, 1957

© 1957, New York
Herald Tribune Inc.

10c in areas 100 miles
from New York City

Late City Edition

FIVE CENTS

School Integrated, Guardsmen on Duty; President to See Governors, Not Faubus

Hoffa Is Indicted Here in Perjury

Teamsters Get Month to Clean Up; Probe Told He Paid Jailed Aids

James R. Hoffa, campaigning in Miami Beach for the presidency of the Teamsters, had a bad day in three other cities yesterday:

1. In New York a Federal rackets grand jury handed up an indictment in United States District Court charging him with five counts of perjury. This involved testimony he gave in April on an alleged wire-tapping conspiracy in his Detroit headquarters.

2. The A.F.L.-C.I.O. Executive Council, also in New York, gave the Teamsters thirty days to cashier all officers responsible for corruption in the union. It was understood that Mr. Hoffa's name led all the rest. The 1,400,000 member union faces possible expulsion if it fails to comply.

3. In Washington, Senate investigators heard testimony that Mr. Hoffa had approved spending $170,000 in Teamsters' dues to defend union officials accused of extortion and dynamiting—and also to support their wives while the men were in jail. They also heard that Detroit restaurant owners were paying off the Teamster boss, apparently to buy labor peace.

4. In Detroit, some teamsters from Local 337 said a slate of Hoffa-pledged delegates to the Miami Beach convention had been "railroaded" through at a local union meeting. Forty members voted for them, the

U.S. ICBM Fails Again In 2d Test

Rises 5,000 Feet, Tips, Explodes

By Tom Lambert

WASHINGTON, Sept. 25.— The United States failed again today in its second attempt to test fire an Intercontinental Ballistic Missile, which the Soviet Union claims to have perfected.

The missile, the giant Air Force Atlas, was fired this afternoon at Patrick Air Force Base, Florida. Reports from Florida observers said the flame - trailing Atlas climbed 5,000 feet, tipped, wobbled and exploded.

Reliable sources here said ground controllers had destroyed the weapon by actuat-

Herald Tribune—United Press   Associated Press wirephoto

THE INTEGRATION OF ELIZABETH ECKFORD—Three weeks ago yesterday the fifteen-year-old Negro was barred from Central High School in Little Rock by the National Guard called out by Gov. Faubus (picture at left). Yesterday she was in school under protection of the Army, called out by President Eisenhower—picture at right shows her with white classmates.

Bayonets Obeyed in Little Rock

1,200 Army Men Take Negroes In

By Walter Lister Jr.

LITTLE ROCK, Ark., Sept. 25.—Central High School was integrated today at bayonet point of the Army, and tonight federalized Arkansas National Guardsmen relieved the paratroopers around the high school perimeter.

It was not known whether the National Guard, used by Gov. Orval Faubus from Sept. 2 to Sept. 20 to keep Negro pupils out of Central High, would still be around the high school tomorrow morning.

An Army officer said it was not planned to keep the paratroopers off duty permanently. Several platoons of the Regular Army men remained in bivouac directly behind the high school.

The Arkansas Military District noted that the 153d Infantry Regiment, the National Guardsmen placed on duty tonight, was composed of officers from Texarkana, Hope, Malvern, Prescott, and Arkadelphia.

The Integration

This morning, nine Negro teen-agers, protected by 1,200 men of the 101st Airborne "Screaming Eagle" Division, were escorted into the school at 9:23 o'clock.

Paratroopers surrounding the school had bayonets fixed to their M-1 rifles. They wore steel helmets and carried gas masks.

THE AFRO AMERICAN

66th Year, No. 9   Contents of Newspaper Copyrighted 1957 by The AFRO-AMERICAN Company   BALTIMORE, MD., SEPTEMBER 28, 1957   ★★★★★★★   NATIONAL EDITION   28 Pages Price: 15 Cents

Faubus Backs Down

FED UP AT DEALE

Will enroll son in D.C. doctor says

DEALE, Md. — Dr. Harry N. Jones, physician, has withdrawn his 6-year-old son, Harry Jr., from the formerly white public school here and says he will enroll him in Washington.

Dr. Jones withdrew the child from the first grade after receiving threats by telephone, mail, having a cross burned in front of his home and seeing 12 carloads of white men drive past his home with rifles.

Threats had been made to bomb the school. Declaring "There'll be no Little Rock in

Alleged Bishop Held; Bail Set At $25,000

WASHINGTON

"He can heal, too. Police and newspapers just don't know what they're talking about."

This is what a 50-year-old woman of the 1000 block Third St., NW, told the AFRO Wednesday after learning of the arrest in New York of her pastor, Louis Tousana, 56, an alleged Brooklyn and Washington "bishop" and faith healer who operates the Temple of Truth in a converted store at 311 K St., NW.

Tousana, a stout, balding man who wears flashy sports clothes, was arraigned in Brooklyn Felony Court and charged with grand larceny. He was held in bond of $25,000

INSIDE THIS WEEK

HOW TO WIN $50

Second big cash prize puzzle contest now going on.— See Magazine section.

THE ENRAGED READERS

Little Rock, Ark., incident sets off angry volume of letters-to-editor.—See page 7.

'DEEP FREEZE' GIRL

Ten years ago the name of Dorothy Mae Stevens was

Arkansas now opens its schools

By MOSES J. NEWSON
AFRO Staff Correspondent

LITTLE ROCK, Ark.—Rather than come into court and face FBI testimony that no violence threatened when he called out the National Guard, Gov. Orval E. Faubus backed down, last Friday.

Faubus had said colored youngsters were buying knives and guns, and he feared trouble if Central High School opened its doors to nine colored pupils as the local school board had directed.

The FBI checked over 100 stores whose owners reporting sale of weapons was below normal.

The Washington Post

Times Herald

FINAL

The Weather

Today—Increasing humidity, scattered thundershowers late in day, high 85. Tonight—Low 68. Friday—Clearing, less humid Wednesday: High 83 at 4.20 p.m.; low, 63 at 5.50 p.m. Weather Map and Details on Page 23

86th Year · · · · No. 267   Phone RE. 7-1234   Copyright © 1963 The Washington Post Co.   THURSDAY AUGUST 29, 1963   WTOP-TV (9) Radio (1500)   TEN CENTS

Mammoth Rally of 200,000 Jams Mall In Solemn, Orderly Plea for Equality

outrages (mostly against schools) all over the South. In 1960, 'sit-in' demonstrations were staged by black protesters in one city after another, and the next year the first 'freedom riders' (in protest against 'white only' signs on public transport and elsewhere) were on the move. Victories came, but painfully slowly: in 1962 James Meredith won admission to the University of Mississippi and engaged the attentions of 3000 Federal troops in maintaining his rights.

But other, more tragic, confrontations were beginning irrevocably to fan the flames of race war. The murder of Medgar Evers in Jackson, Mississippi, and the bombing of a negro church in Birmingham, Alabama, in 1963, hardened the spirit of black militancy which had already been nourished in the ghettoes of the Northern cities of Harlem, Chicago, Detroit. Moderate black leaders, like Nobel prize-winner Martin Luther King, and peaceful demonstrations like the unprecedented march on Washington of August 1963, attempted to find peaceful solutions to the issue which by then was consuming the nation. Sadly, the intransigence of Southern administrators and Black Power leaders alike— and ultimately the assassin's bullet — belied all hopes for a non-violent conclusion to the continuing struggle.

Hurt in Harlem Riot. Bleeding from head wounds, showgirl Carolyn Fawcett is aided by police after she and her escort, Jack Lambert (left), were attacked by mob of Negroes when he stopped his auto at 127th and Lenox Ave. red light. Harlem experienced one of the worst riots in its history.
(NEWS foto by Alan Aaronson)
—Story p. 3; other pics, centerfold

The Official Lie

The U-2 Affair and the Paris Summit

When Krushchev bade farewell on the television to the American people after his personal and popular visit to the United States in September 1959, it really looked as if the cold war was thawing out at long last. He had dined in Hollywood with Marilyn Monroe and Frank Sinatra, he had played with President Eisenhower's grandchildren, he liked 'your beautiful cities and wonderful roads'. Most of all, he loved 'your amiable and kind-hearted people'. All that was needed to clinch matters was Eisenhower's return engagement in Moscow the following Spring 'when the blossoms would be out'. As Harold Macmillan observed, watching this sudden detente from Whitehall with mild astonishment, all the talk the previous November had been in threats and ultimata. Now it was of personal visits and discussions.

It all seemed like a dream. And, in reality, it was. Nik (as he was now affectionately known to American newsmen) might exude all the goodwill in the world, but back in Moscow he was no match for the hard-liners or for anxious allies in Peking, and the more realistic Sovietologists in the West knew this in their bones. There was no knowing how he would react at the Paris Summit meeting which, once all the preliminaries were completed, was arranged for May 16 1960. In particular the fate of Berlin, the flash-point of East-West relations, still hung in the balance.

Then, at the beginning of May, an incident occurred which upset everyone's calculations. For some years it had been standard American practice to keep tabs on current Soviet defence arrangements by means of a fleet of U-2 'spy planes'. These aircraft, equipped with sophisticated photographic apparatus, made regular sorties over Russian territory at a height (it was said) of 12 miles — high enough to elude any retaliatory measures, though not entirely out of range of high-powered radar equipment. On May 1, however, one such U-2 on a routine flight from Pakistan to Norway over forbidden Russian airspace was shot down — or 'crashed' (depending on whether you accepted the Russians' ability to shoot that high or not) inside the U.S.S.R. Canny Mr. K did not in fact inform the United States officially of this coup until May 5, and then with remarkable restraint as if the matter was but of passing interest. He omitted to mention that the pilot, Gary Powers, was alive and well and so were his secret photographs.

Washington fell straight into the snare laid for them. It was an accident, they said, just a weather reconnaissance plane that had strayed off-course, probably because the pilot had blacked out. That was Secretary of State Herter's story, and the newspapers grasped uncritically at it. Some even reported it straight without any editorial comment whatever. At that point Krushchev sprung his trap, producing the pilot and his poison phial in one hand and brandishing a sheath of photographs in the other. The majority of American newspapers, when the State Department admitted on the 7th that it was indeed a spy plane that had been grounded, were understandably annoyed. Either way, they had been made to look ridiculous — whether it was by appearing to connive in what *The Cleveland Plain Dealer* called 'a colossal blunder', or whether they had seemed so out of touch with the realities of nuclear diplomacy as to take Washington's statement at face value. *The Baltimore Sun* declared: 'To take exceptional chances of getting caught at the wrong time and then to be found out in flimsy fiction . . . is not good intelligence operation'. *The Toledo Blade* believed that 'all in all, it looks as though this is the most colossal diplomatic blunder ever committed in this nation's history'. *The San Francisco Chronicle* demanded that 'this Government tell the truth when it tells anything'.

Other papers weren't so concerned with the

The San Francisco Chronicle.

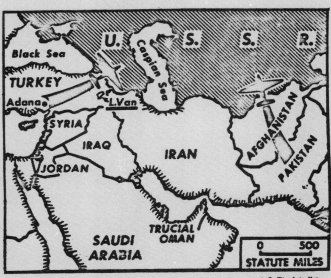

FRIDAY, MAY 6, 1960   10 CENTS   GArfield 1-1111

Russ Down Secret U.S. Jet; Nikita Charges 'Aggression'

State Dept. Launches Inquiry

WASHINGTON, May 5 (UPI)—The United States lodged an immediate "inquiry" with Russia today to determine whether a U. S. plane shot down by Soviet forces Sunday was an unarmed weather craft with an unconscious civilian pilot at the controls.

Acting on President Eisenhower's orders, the State Department instructed the U. S. Ambassador to Moscow, Llewellyn E. Thompson, to ask the Soviet government about the incident, "with particular reference to the fate of the pilot."

WEATHER PLANE

The plane was a one-man weather reconnaissance Lockheed U-2 jet operated by the National Aeronautics and Space Administration. It disappeared in the Turkish frontier area after the pilot reported he was having trouble with his oxygen equipment.

In Burbank, Calif., Lockheed officials identified the civilian pilot as Francis G. Powers, 30, Albany, Ga.

The State Department said the plane might have violated the Russian border accidentally after the pilot

See Page 8, Col. 5

Crackdown On Student Chiefs at UC

Student leaders at the University of California were sternly warned yesterday to rescind their support of an Illinois professor fired for his outspoken views on premarital sex.

Premier Khrushchev said U.S. planes violated Soviet territory near Lake Van (left) on May 1 and near the Afghanistan border (right) on April 9

Plane Was Lost From Turkey

MOSCOW, May 5 (UPI) Premier Nikita S. Khrushchev said today a United States plane had been shot down over the Soviet Union, and in one of his bitterest attacks said Russia wanted peace but the U. S. should realize it "could also suffer retaliatory blows" with rockets.

Khrushchev said there now it "little hope" for success at the Summit conference and charged that the downed plane was sent in by aggressive U. S. circles to "impress and frighten" Russia before the Paris meeting May 16.

Khrushchev did not actually threaten to send rockets or planes over American territory "because that might signify war." but he repeated an old Russian saying that "he who comes to us with the sword shall perish by it."

The Soviet Premier did not say what type of plane was involved. He said it flew in from Turkey and although the markings had been painted over it was established the plane was American.

Khrushchev reacted angrily to President Eisenhower's recent statement that he might be able to spend only a week at the summit conference in Paris and would have Vice President Richard M. Nixon serve as his deputy if necessary.

Khrushchev said this

See Page 8, Col. 1

Reston Reports

But What Did U. S. Expect to Happen?

By James B. Reston
Copyright, 1960 by the New York Times

WASHINGTON, May 5 — Every time an American plane is shot down over or near the Communist empire, it is useful to recall certain basic facts about the Cold War.

It is a war, much as we'd like to forget it. The forces of two hostile coalitions face each other across half the world, and they are constantly watching each other from the skies and probing each other's lines.

Moreover, the disposition of these forces is spread along the whole vast periphery of the Eurasian continent from the north cape of Norway through the heart of Europe to the Middle East and thence into South Asia and the Far East.

The preponderance of ground power and rocket fire may lie with the Russians and the Chinese, but it is the United States that has military and air bases close to the Soviet and Chinese borders and not the other way round.

These are the unpopular facts which are seldom mentioned in this part of the world, but they help explain Soviet Premier Nikita S. Khrushchev's melodramatic and bad-mannered outburst over the American plane today.

There is a tendency here to dismiss Khrushchev's tantrum as part of the usual Soviet tactics just before a summit meeting with President Charles

See Page 8, Col. 1

Russ Boost Ruble Value, Alter Taxes

From Associated Press and New York Times

MOSCOW, May 5—Premier Nikita S. Khrushchev announced today that the Soviet Union will abolish almost all income taxes by the end of 1965.

He said this will boost Soviet workers' take-home pay by 74 million rubles.

Khrushchev also announced a revaluation of the ruble, effective January 1, 1961, to make it worth as much as the U. S. dollar.

CONSUMER GOODS

The greater take-home pay, the Premier said, will be matched by increased stocks of consumer goods in stores.

He promised a great new drive for production of consumer goods once his current ambitious seven-year economic plan is fulfilled.

Khrushchev told a joint session of the Supreme So-

INDEX

NewYork World-Telegram
The Sun

Local Forecast: Mostly cloudy, with some rain tonight and tomorrow. Weather Fotocast on Page 9.

VOL. 127—NO. 209—Second class postage paid at New York, N. Y. and at additional mailing offices.

NEW YORK, SATURDAY, MAY 7, 1960 — Copyright, 1960, By New York World-Telegram Corp. — TEN CENTS

SPORTS
FINAL
Feature Section
Aqueduct Monday Entries

Khrushchev's 'Amazing' Story!

Downed U.S. Flier Is Alive, Admits Spying, Reds Say

Underground Atom Tests To Be Resumed, Ike Says

Plan Aimed At Peaceful Nuclear Use

United Press International

GETTYSBURG, Pa., May 7.— President Eisenhower today announced plans for the United States to resume underground nuclear tests by the end of this year as part of the "non-weapon development" of detection systems and peacetime uses of atomic energy.

Announcement of the plan to resume underground test was made here while the Chief Executive is spending the weekend.

Press Secretary James C. Hagerty said the resumption of tests, which have been suspended under a voluntary moratorium since October, 1958, would require additional funds for the Atomic Energy Commission which will be requested shortly by the President.

Research Needed.

Mr. Hagerty would not es-

The Derby Field

Special to the World-Telegram and Sun

LOUISVILLE, Ky., May 7.—Field in post position order for today's 86th running of the Kentucky Derby, mile and a quarter for 3-year-olds.

HORSE	OWNER	JOCKEY	ODDS
f-Spring Broker	M. H. Van Berg	Rotz	30-1
Yomolka	Valley Farm	Grimm	30-1
Bally Ache	L. Fruchtman	Ussery	2-1
Cuvier Relic	S. I. Crew	Sellers	20-1
Lurullah	T. A. Grissom	No boy	30-1
Tony Graff	A. Graffagnini	Chambers	30-1
Hillsborough	Calumet Farm	Brooks	12-1
f-Henrijan	Mrs. S. Elmore	A. Valenzuela	30-1
Venetian Way	Sunny Blue Farm	Hartack	6-1
Bourbon Prince	Adele Rand	Rogers	20-1
Victoria Park	Windfields Farm	M. Ycaza	10-1
Divine Comedy	Llangollen Farm	I. Valenzuela	20-1
Tompion	C. V. Whitney	Shoemaker	6-5

All carry 126 pounds. f—Field.

Cost to file entry, $250; additional $1250 to be posted Saturday to start.

Air coverage—CBS television and radio, 5:30 p.m. New York time.

Gross value if 14 start—$160,202; net winner, $116,100; second, $25,000; third, $12,500; fourth, $5000.

Latest News

Associated Press

TALLAHASSEE, Fla., May 7.—A judge convicted

Tompion Tops Field of 13 For Derby

Associated Press

LOUISVILLE, May 7.— Thirteen 3-year-old horses, tuned as fine as humanly possible at a total cost of more than $240,000, waited quietly in their stalls today for the signal sending them after gold and glory in the 86th Kentucky Derby. The field was reduced early today by the withdrawal of Hillsborough.

Post time for the start of this tradition-steeped 1¼ mile run around ancient flower-bordered Churchill Downs is 5:30 p.m. (New York time). It will be televised and broadcast nationally over the Columbia Broadcasting System TV network from 5:15 to 5:45 and on radio from 4:30—4:45.

In a little more than two minutes (the record is 2:01 2/5 by Whirlaway in 1941) it all will be over except for the

Francis G. Powers, 30-year-old civilian pilot shot down by Russians. He was an Air Force captain before joining the National Aeronautics and Space Administration.

United Press International Telephoto

Eisenhower Studies Khrushchev Charges

'Incidents' Risk H-Bomb Reprisal, Premier Hints

By HENRY SHAPIRO,
United Press International

MOSCOW, May 7.— Premier Nikita Khrushchev said today the pilot of a United States plane shot down 1300 miles inside Russia May 1 was alive and would be tried on spy charges. He warned that such incidents could result, under the worst circumstances, in immediate retaliation with a hydrogen bomb.

Khrushchev referred to a U.S. State Department statement that the pilot may have suffered giddiness and drifted across the border because of an oxygen failure and said:

H-Bomb Warning.

"In this case one could recall the statement of the Soviet government to the effect that a similar adventurous person who is subject to giddiness could drop a hydrogen bomb on other people's territory. And that means that the country in which such an adventurer has been born will receive immediately and unavoidably a no less destructive hydrogen bomb in return."

Khrushchev said the American plane was spying specifically on Russian missile bases and radar installations, and that it violated the air sovereignty of Afghanistan.

Khrushchev claimed the American civilian pilot, Francis G. Powers, 30, of Albany, Ga., confessed he had left the U.S. Air Force Base at Inprlik, Turkey, and was flying all the way across the Soviet Union to Norway to spy on Russian defenses.

The premier exhibited what he said were aerial

---

ethics of the whole thing. Some, like *Newsday*, were appalled at the timing of the flight: 'The people of the United States have the right to demand a complete explanation from the President and the State Department as to how such a frightening lack of coordination could exist, virtually on the eve of the summit meeting. What has happened is inexcusable'. Others like *The New York Journal-American*, in worldly fashion, wanted all and sundry to stop beating about the bush: 'The State Department . . . should put together a documented bill of particulars of Soviet spying and be ready to slug Kruschev with it if he continues to use this single incident as a diplomatic hydrogen bomb'. Mr. Krushchev, as it happened, had his own answer to the Hearst newspapers. 'I warn you Messr. foreign journalists' he announced at a press conference at the height of the tension, 'don't sell your souls to the devil . . . When I read the bourgeois journalists' stories slandering Soviet realities and Communism, I get angry sometimes but on second thoughts I say to myself "Not all the journalists are John Revs. Indeed they are ordinary men hired by such publishers as Hearst who, like spiders, seize a man and enmesh him in their web". And if such a journalist fails to supply slanders against Communism what then will Hearst or any other publishing concern need him for?

Hearst will not keep such a correspondent for a single day . . . Indeed he is a capitalist, but most of you are not capitalists, nor will you ever be. So why have you got to serve capitalism?'

But what now were the prospects for the Summit, only a week away? The British *Daily Worker* quoted the Russian premier as saying: 'Let those who sent the plane worry about its effects upon the summit. It is not for me to worry about that. They should have thought about that earlier'. It did not sound very promising. Nevertheless it was still on, and Eisenhower alighted at Paris with a smile on his face and prepared to 'go every foot that safety and honour permit' to reach a settlement. That, too, was not a statement to be taken entirely at face value, for when given an opportunity by Krushchev to disown the U-2 flight, he had refused — like the born army commander he was, Ike accepted total responsibility. Open confrontation at the highest level was now inevitable. What was unexpected was the speed and virulence with which it came.

No sooner had the Big Four, Eisenhower, Khrushchev, Macmillan and de Gaulle, seated themselves comfortably around the table in the Elysee Palace on the 16th than the Soviet leader launched out into his denunciation of the American action and called on the President to

punish those responsible. He suggested another Summit meeting in 'six to eight months' time. That, at least, was the gist of his message. In the next two days he held two press conferences, one informal one in a Paris street and one official 'farewell' one, where he expressed himself somewhat more forcibly. He ranted and jeered, and banged his fist on the table. When he found himself heckled by some of the West Germans present, he inveighed against the 'riff-raff (*The New York Herald Tribune* — 'bastards' *The Daily Mirror*) who were not entirely beaten at Stalingrad. He thanked the British Prime Minister for his fruitless efforts to keep the conference together, he absolved President de Gaulle as a 'man of lofty moral principles', but as for President Eisenhower, well, he'd 'thought there was something fishy about this friend of mine' when he'd been at Camp David and he warned that if any more planes were sent over the Soviet Union, not only would they be shot down but the bases and 'those who have set up these bases and actually dispose of them' would be shattered. He also withdrew his invitation to the President to visit Moscow.

And with that, he flew off. The Summit was over before it had even begun, and the sword of Damocles hung more dangerously over Berlin than it had ever done. Why, the question was now asked, had Khrushchev deliberately wrecked the conference. Surely not because of the U-2, for, as de Gaulle had drily pointed out at the time, a Soviet space satellite was passing over France eighteen times a day. *The New York Times* conjectured that the leaders of the Red Army had ganged up with new and old Stalinists to harden up Soviet policy. *The St Louis Post-Dispatch* believed the President ought to share the blame: 'There has been too much reliance on good-will tours and not enough continuous leadership at the top. Waging peace is not a part-time job to be intermittently carried on at the personality level, but a consuming responsibility'. *The Chicago Daily News* thought the same: 'The U-2 incident and the contradictory statements that U.S. officials made after it constitute one of the most discreditable pages in the history of American foreign relations. They raise grave questions concerning the competence of the hands now directing United States foreign policy. . . .'

On the problem of what to do about it, *The San Francisco Chronicle* was for the Americans 'giving what reassurance they can to the people of Russia'. Its fellow citizen *The San Francisco Examiner* would have nothing to do with the 'blustering Communist dictator who has sought to treat the United States as though it were a Banana Republic'. *The Boston Herald* advised the West to do its best to pick up the pieces: 'Despite Mr. Khrushchev's latest display of brinkmanship it is unlikely he will risk open war'. In the event it was right. Unstatesmanlike mutterings against Eisenhower continued to emerge from the Kremlin (at one point K. sarcastically offered Ike the job of managing a kindergarten) and even in September, when he arrived in New York to address the U.N., Khrushchev was still insisting he would have no truck with the United States while Eisenhower was still President (and later emphasised this by pummelling the lectern with his shoe).

The New York Herald Tribune.

DAILY HERALD

No. 13747 (C) — Tuesday, May 17, 1960 — Price 2½d.

PAPER THAT CARES

Peacemaker Macmillan—last night

ON or OFF? Ike gives spy-flights pledge—now the West waits . . .

MAC TO THE RESCUE

Night call on Mr. K in bid to save Summit

From W. N. EWER: PARIS, Monday

MR. MACMILLAN called on Mr. Kruschev late tonight in a desperate bid to save the Summit conference from being wrecked almost before it has been launched.

He talked with the Russian leader for one-and-a-half hours. When he left, Mr. K. saw him off from the steps of the Soviet embassy.

Afterwards it was reported that Mr. Macmillan would continue his talks with Mr. K. tomorrow.

Earlier, in his dramatic Save-the-Summit round of the French capital, Mr. Macmillan held separate meetings with President Eisenhower and President de Gaulle. It is understood he made his call on Mr. K. with their full approval.

Mr. Macmillan will report back to President Eisenhower and General de Gaulle at 10 a.m. tomorrow.

Journalists swarmed round first aid men at their quarters in the Palais de Chaillot clamouring for aspirins. Hundreds were issued.

After the battle of words: Mr. K leaves the conference hall

when the Western big-three have scheduled their own Summit session.

Frankly, Mr. Macmillan's chances look slim. But the Prime Minister is not entirely without hope that Mr. Kruschev, after a pause for thought, may after all agree to sit at the Summit conference table this week, NOT in "six or eight months' time" as he threatened at today's meeting.

Mr. K. said at the frigid, three-hour meeting that U.S. policy in endorsing spy flights over Russia could only condemn the Summit talks to failure in advance. He also withdrew his invitation to Ike to visit Russia next month—because "provocative actions" had created "unfavourable conditions."

Mr. Eisenhower replied by accusing Mr. K. of issuing an ultimatum and trying to sabotage the Summit.

He said that American "overflights" had been suspended after the shooting down of the U.S. U2 plane on May 1.

LATE TONIGHT it was announced that Ike ordered a halt to high-altitude reconnaissance flights over Russia last Thursday.

And U.S. sources said later that the U.S. does not intend to resume its high-level flights over Russia even if the Summit conference ends in failure.

The feeling in the British delegation is that President Eisenhower went very far to meet any reasonable objection which Mr. K. may genuinely have.

Kruschev's "statement" had—evidently deliberately—been personally galling to the President. The reference to the Moscow visit now being undesirable was, at this stage, unnecessary.

The suggestion that the Summit had better wait for another six or eight months seemed like a personal affront. For the U.S. Election is in six months' time. The new President will take over from Ike in eight months.

CALM

But President Eisenhower remained calm, and refused to be provoked. He ignored the personalities, and picked on the one point of substance.

He at once gave a firm pledge that the American over-flights will not be resumed so long as he is President.

He also repeated his offer to

CONTINUED ON PAGE NINE

WE SAY

NOW or NEVER

IF the chance of peace the Four Men of Paris have now is thrown aside, then with it will die, cruelly and maybe forever, the hopes of millions upon millions of ordinary folk.

For it is now or never at the Summit. The world cannot wait six or eight months.

APPEAL

Britain's Prime Minister knows that already he has appealed to Kruschev and Eisenhower to end their row over the spy plane.

And it is to Macmillan the fearful nations look this morning.

CURSE the folly of the American intelligence services for giving Kruschev this gold-plated opportunity.

CURSE the stupidity with which the U.S. Government handled the matter afterwards.

PROMISE

But at last Eisenhower has done what he should have done before he left for Paris.

He has said that spy flights have been stopped and WILL NOT BE RESUMED.

He offers to have direct talks with the Russians on the spy planes.

It is impossible for Kruschev to say now that he is being threatened by aggressive Americans.

And it will be monstrous if this leader of a great country can still think of throwing the world's hopes in the ashcan.

I'm as mixed up with this — as that girl with her boy friend !
says Julie

See Margaret Shaw Page 4.

My soul is pure —Kruschev

Belsky's Cartoon

"We were all set for the Summit weren't we? Espionage service on overtime—combat alert for all world bases. Was it our fault the Russians wouldn't co-operate?"

---

from **ANTHONY CARTHEW and GERARD KEMP**

Paris, Monday

IN a boiling cauldron called Room C at Chaillot Palace, today Jim Hagerty, Ike's Press secretary, gave the American answer to Kruschev.

High on the platform above 1,000 sweltering journalists, sat three hunched figures: Hagerty; the Under-Secretary of State Andrew Berding; and Charles "Chip" Bohlen, the President's adviser on Russian affairs.

There were constant shouts of "For God's sake speak up!" and "Jim, we can't hear you over here!"

Sweat poured off everyone, but the three behind the high mahogany desk kept their coats on.

Glasses were broken in the crush.

Hagerty's face was, as usual, expressionless.

From time to time he tapped the ash off the end of his cigarette on the mike.

All three chain-smoked. Berding sat glum throughout and hardly spoke.

At one point when Hagerty suddenly swivelled round on Bohlen for an explanation, Bohlen's glasses nearly slipped off his nose.

Hagerty read Ike's statement. A careful statement.

Logical, reasonable, sincere phrases . . . "to see if any possibility existed through the exercise of reason and restraint to dispose of this matter of overflights . . ."

The questions followed:

How long will the President stay in Paris, Jim? — That depends on what happens tomorrow.

Did Mr. K. reply to Ike's statement? — Partially. He repeated the three points of his ultimatum.

Then came the 64,000 dollar question.

Someone shouted: "Well, is the conference over, Jim?" — Hagerty stumbled. "I think . . . I could, I mean, I should say . . . just wait a minute, fellers."

He whispered with Bohlen.

"Well, Kruschev said he didn't consider this a meeting of the Paris conference but a prelim-

CONTINUED ON PAGE NINE

U.S. AIR CREWS GET WAR ALERT

A WAR scare hit the U.S. Pacific coast yesterday when the North American air defence squadron at San Diego was ordered to stand by.

Bomber and fighter pilots who were off duty were instructed by messages on radio and TV to report to base.

At the time newspapers were carrying huge headlines on the Summit crisis and many people rang up radio stations to ask if war was imminent.

Captain Russel Trudeau of the U.S. Navy said: "It's not a drill. I believe the alert was ordered on high authority. Things are in bad shape round the world and the situation could quickly become serious."

Practice alerts were also ordered for all U.S. forces at home and abroad. A few hours later all the alerts were cancelled.

IKE AND K's SPEECHES—PAGE 8

DIANA DORS DIDN'T MEET THE QUEEN

By DAN SLATER

DIANA DORS was not presented to the Queen at last night's Royal Variety Performance. She stood wearing a low-cut black velvet, diamante-decorated dress in the fourth row of onlookers while the Queen met other stars.

The selection of Diana Dors for the show has been hotly discussed and criticised by the *Church of England Newspaper.*

After the presentations Miss Dors and her husband, Dickie Dawson, walked quickly to their dressing-rooms and refused to comment.

CRAMPED

The show, with its teeming talent, went over with a bustle of warmth and exuberance. The brief time allowed to many stars cramped their style.

Singing, dancing Negro Sammy Davis, jun., excelled himself inside his few minutes. His own numbers as well as his imitations of Dean Martin, Jerry Lewis, Frankie Laine and Nat King Cole—who was also on the

bill — went down well everywhere including the Royal box.

After the show he stood at the end of the row of 15 stars presented to the Queen and Prince Philip.

The Royal Variety Show nearly didn't come off—because of an unexploded-bomb scare.

And while the Queen watched the show bomb-buster Major Bill Hartley was probing a 32ft. shaft at the back of the theatre.

A few hours earlier a giant cylinder churning out earth like an apple-core on a site 150 yards from the theatre, had struck something hard.

And it was not until 90 minutes before the Queen arrived at the theatre that 46-year-old Major Hartley said: "I have advised the police that the show can go on."

Daily Mirror

Tuesday, May 17, 1960   No. 17,547

MR. K!

(*If you will pardon an olde English phrase*)

DON'T BE SO BLOODY RUDE!

PS

Who do you think you are? STALIN?

10 cents beyond 50-mile zone from New York City
except on Long Island. Higher in air delivery cities.

FIVE CENTS

SOVIET TROOPS ENCIRCLE BERLIN TO BACK UP SEALING OF BORDER; U.S. DRAFTING VIGOROUS PROTEST

ALLIES IN ACCORD

Britain and France Due to Join in Challenge on German Action

Text of Rusk's statement on Berlin appears on Page 7

By TAD SZULC
Special to The New York Times

WASHINGTON Aug. 13—Secretary of State Dean Rusk charged today that the East German closing of the West Berlin border was a double violation of agreements between the Soviet Union and the Western powers.

In a statement issued with President Kennedy's approval, Mr. Rusk declared "these violations of existing agreements will be the subject of vigorous protest through appropriate channels."

Mr. Rusk said that the travel ban was in contravention of accords on free circulation within the city and of a decision by a four-power meeting of foreign ministers in 1949 assuring access to Berlin from what are now the former occupation zones.

Allied Access Unaffected

He noted, however that the Communist measures did not "thus far" interfere with the access by the Western Allies to Berlin.

The threat that this may occur later has been raised by the Soviet Union's announcement that it will sign a peace treaty with East Germany and turn over to East Germany the control of routes to the disputed city.

[In London and Paris officials viewed the East German action with extreme concern. Britain denounced the new restrictions as a violation of Berlin's four-power status.]

According to a State Department spokesman, a protest is expected to be made tomorrow in similar notes to be handed by the United States, British and French military commanders in Berlin to their Soviet counterpart.

There was also the possibility diplomatic sources indicated, that the protest delivered by the military commanders might promptly be followed with a direct protest to the Soviet Union by the Western Allies.

With the closing of the bor-

Continued on Page 7, Column 1

NO EXIT: An East German couple walks away from barbed-wire barrier on border between East and West Berlin. East German troops blocked their entry to West Berlin.
Associated Press Radiophoto

ADENAUER IS SURE ALLIES WILL REACT

Tells Germans Reds' Berlin Decree Will Be Countered —Economic Step Hinted

By GERD WILCKE
Special to The New York Times

BONN, Germany, Aug. 13—Chancellor Adenauer assured Germans on both sides of the Iron Curtain tonight that Bonn "with its Allies will take the necessary measures" to counter the Communists' closing of the border between East and West Berlin.

In a statement issued after consultation with some of his top advisers. Dr. Adenauer said:

"It is the law of the hour to meet the challenge from the East firmly but calmly and to do nothing that can worsen the situation."

Although Dr. Adenauer did not say what counter-measures the West was contemplating, it was generally felt here that economic sanctions might be high on the list.

Dr. Adenauer suggested at election rallies last week that the Communist bloc could be hurt economically if Western trade was cut off. Premier Khrushchev, he said, would use different language if the partners of the North Atlantic

Continued on Page 6, Column 8

Closing of Border Is Seen As First of Soviet Moves

By SEYMOUR TOPPING
Special to The New York Times.

MOSCOW Aug. 13—The closing of the border between East and West Berlin was regarded by informed Western observers here today as the first in a series of acts the Soviet Union will take in respect to Berlin.

These observers also viewed the Berlin action as signifying that Premier Khrushchev had decided irrevocably to conclude a separate peace treaty with East Germany.

Mr Khrushchev has been under pressure from East Germany for years to curb the westward flow of refugees by sealing the Berlin border For reasons of broader policy, the Soviet Premier withheld his consent.

Mr. Khrushchev apparently felt that any one-sided abrogation of the four-power accord on free movement within Berlin would prejudice the chances of the West's joining in a peace treaty that would recognize the status quo in Eastern Europe.

Action Was Expected

It has been regarded as inevitable, however, that the border would be closed if a heavy flow of refugees continued from East to West Germany through Berlin.

The draining away of East German manpower through the West Berlin refugee centers was dislocating the economy of the Communist state.

According to well-informed

MOOD OF BERLIN: CONTROLLED FURY

Sunday Motorists Flocking to Checkpoints Jarred by Sight of Guns

By HARRY GILROY
Special to The New York Times.

BERLIN, Aug. 13—At times today East Berlin looked like a new tourist attraction. Then it was a war camp. Next it was the picture of an ominous mob with a flicker of revolt in the air.

West Berlin was alternately a family strolling in its Sunday best, a woman crying.

It depended on where you moved and what you stumbled upon. The 3,300,000 people of this metropolis were put under sudden violent strain when the East German regime sealed the East-West Berlin border.

Churchgoers answered the call of church bells in the morning in what was described as

TEAR GAS IS USED

Reds' Police Disperse Crowds—Workers Kept From Jobs

Soviet bloc communiqué, East German decree, Page 6.

By SYDNEY GRUSON
Special to The New York Times.

BERLIN, Monday, Aug. 14—Two battle-ready Soviet Army divisions were reported to have ringed Berlin yesterday in support of East Germany's sudden and dramatic closing of the border between East and West Berlin.

The Soviet divisions were said to have armor and artillery with them. Other Soviet Army divisions among the estimated total of twenty in East Germany were reported on the move throughout the restive country

The new Communist measures shut off West Berlin to East Berliners and East Germans. They did not affect the movement from West Berlin into the Communist-controlled Eastern sector of the city or the vital communications linking West Berlin to West Germany.

Barrier Effective

According to preliminary reports to West Berlin authorities, none of the 53,000 East Berliners with jobs in West Berlin had crossed the border by 9 A. M. today. Also, it was reported, no refugees had reached West Berlin under the cover of darkness.

The East German action brought angry exchanges yesterday between East Berliners and the Communist People's Police near some of the thirteen border crossing points left open.

Smoke and tear-gas bombs and water hoses were used to disperse one crowd of several hundred youths who had taunted the police and armed Communist factory brigades trying to explain the necessity for the new measures.

Rope Barrier at Gate

At one border point, the East German police also hurled tear gas to break up a crowd of West Berliners facing them across the road. The crowd melted into side streets until the gas had cleared, but then most of them came back. The police then left them alone.

As the night wore on, the Berliners drifted to their homes. Along toward dawn, fewer than 100 young people stood behind

The New York Times.

Period of Quarantine

The Cuban Missile Crisis

On October 15 1962 President Kennedy was informed that the CIA had every reason to believe that the Russians were building nuclear missile sites on America's back doorstep. A U-2 photographic reconnaissance plane had returned the day before from a mission over Cuba with pictures that indicated highly offensive activity in a field near San Cristobal. It was no secret that Moscow had been supplying arms in indecent quantities for some time to Cuba's accommodating president Castro. Inasmuch as these were publicly declared to be of a purely defensive nature, and in view of Khrushchev's repeated promises not to send anything really dangerous to the island, there was no alternative but for the United States to suffer these thorns in its Achilles heel with as good a grace as it could muster — and especially since Washington's role in the abortive 'invasion' of the Bay of Pigs in April 1961 had been ignominiously revealed.

But these were something entirely different. These missiles, with their maximum ranges up to 2,000 miles, threatened almost every major city in America with obliteration inside twelve minutes. Kennedy revealed the gravity of the situation to a hastily-convened but none the less high-powered committee (which included his brother Robert, Dean Rusk, Robert McNamara, McGeorge Bundy, Lyndon Johnson, Theodore Sorenson among others) at the White House on the 16th. CIA agents trundled in the photographs to be scrutinized — it looked more like a football field than a missile base to the President, but the experts were convinced nevertheless — and opinions were canvassed as to what form American retaliation should take.

Some of the committee, noticeably the military, were all for blasting the rockets off the face of the earth before the engineers had finished assembling them. Others, reasonably enough, argued that this was also the quickest known way of triggering off a universal holocaust. Another school of thought favoured the notion of an air-sea blockade of the island to prevent the import of any more war-heads. Critics of this proposal contended this was tantamount to shutting the stable door after the horse had bolted. The committee was instructed to remain in permanent session until it emerged with a plan of campaign that the President could consider. Meanwhile he would return more or less to his normal engagements, so that the papers would not get the impression there was 'something up'.

But it was not long before the press did get wind that something rather critical was up, as the circle of officials admitted to the deliberations widened. It so happened that *The Miami News* had earlier in the month published a story about rocket bases in Cuba, but that had been based on the paper's own information. The air of crisis in Washington seemed to have no necessary connection with that. On the 21st *The Washington Post* reported that the capital was humming with unusually tense activity: but that was the nearest any paper got to the real story. Certain papers (which included *The New York Times*)

who had their suspicions were prevailed upon by the President himself not to print anything.

Kennedy broke the news to the nation by radio and TV on the evening of October 22. Gravely, he told the people of the danger, accused the Russians of downright deceit, and announced his decision to force a confrontation at once by imposing a blockade (a 'quarantine' was the word he used) on Cuba. He added that if the Soviet Union cherished any thoughts of reprisals on Berlin, the United States was

prepared to risk a major war. It was a tough speech, blunt and effective. The papers the next morning showed just how effective America thought it was: it was approved unanimously from coast to coast. *The Baltimore Sun* applauded the fact that 'he was not deterred by thought of the Russian reaction from taking the firm measures he thought necessary to protect American security, and his firmness deserves the wide and non-partisan support it appears to be getting'. *The Atlanta Constitution* believed the

FINAL ★★ 5¢ **New York Mirror**

WEATHER: Cloudy, partly clearing in afternoon. High 55 to 60.   Vol. 37, No. 417.   TUESDAY, OCTOBER 23, 1962   C

WE BLOCKADE CUBA WITH 40 WARSHIPS

JFK's Orders: 'Search, And If Necessary, Sink Any Arms Ship'

The Presidents 7 Points; His Ultimatum to K:

1 The U. S., "to halt this offensive buildup" in Cuba, is imposing "a strict quarantine on all offensive military equipment under shipment to Cuba." All ships of any kind bound for Cuba are to be turned back if they are found to contain cargoes of offensive weapons. This embargo also will be extended to "other carriers" if need be—meaning planes.

2 Surveillance of Cuba and its military buildup will be stepped up, and the U. S. armed forces have been ordered "to prepare for any eventuality."

3 U. S. policy will be to regard any nuclear missile launched from Cuba against any nation in the Western Hemisphere as an attack by Russia on the U. S. requiring full retaliation against the Soviet Union.

4 The U. S. Naval Base at Guantanamo, on the eastern tip of Cuba, has been reinforced, U. S. dependents there have been evacuated, and additional military units have been ordered to stand by on alert.

5 An immediate meeting of the OAS has been called to "consider this threat to hemispheric security" and to invoke the Inter-American Defense Pact provisions "in support of all necessary action."

6 The U. S. is asking for an emergency meeting of the United Nations Security Council without delay. The U. S. will call for "the prompt dismantling and withdrawal of all offensive weapons in Cuba" before it lifts the blockade.

7 Kennedy called on Soviet Premier Khrushchev "to halt and eliminate this clandestine, reckless, and provocative threat to world peace."

"All the News That's Fit to Print"

The New York Times.

LATE CITY EDITION

U. S. Weather Bureau Report (Page 91) forecasts: Partly cloudy, breezy, cool today. Fair and cool tonight and tomorrow. Temp. range: 54—45; yesterday: 66—44.

VOL. CXII..No. 38,258. © 1962 by The New York Times Company. Times Square, New York 36, N. Y. NEW YORK, TUESDAY, OCTOBER 23, 1962. 10 cents beyond 50-mile zone from New York City except on Long Island. Higher in air delivery cities. FIVE CENTS.

U.S. IMPOSES ARMS BLOCKADE ON CUBA ON FINDING OFFENSIVE-MISSILE SITES; KENNEDY READY FOR SOVIET SHOWDOWN

U. S. JUDGES GIVEN POWER TO REQUIRE VOTE FOR NEGROES

High Court Upholds Order Forcing the Registration of 54 in Alabama County

Special to The New York Times

WASHINGTON, Oct. 22 — The Supreme Court held today that Federal judges have the power to make state registrars put specific Negroes on the voting rolls.

Alabama had challenged an order by Federal District Judge Frank M. Johnson Jr. requiring the registration of 54 specific Negroes in Macon County, Ala. The order was upheld by the United States Court of Appeals for the Fifth Circuit.

Today the Supreme Court unanimously affirmed the disputed order. And it did so in a way that indicated once again its mood of impatience with Southern efforts to maintain denials of Negro rights.

One-Sentence Ruling

All that was before the court was an application for review of the Fifth Circuit decision. The usual alternatives would have been to deny the petition or to grant it and hear oral argument later.

Instead, the court granted review and then, summarily, affirmed the lower courts. It did so in a single sentence, with just one citation in the way of explanation.

The citation was to a decision in 1960 upholding a Federal Court order in a Louisiana voting case. There, a district judge had told Louisiana registrars to put back on their books 1,377 Negroes whose names had been removed in a purge by the segregationist Citizens Council.

Action by Congress

The Macon County case was one of the first brought by the Department of Justice under the Civil Rights Act of 1957. It is especially significant because the county is in the so-called Black Belt, with a predominantly Negro population.

In 1958, when the suit was started, virtually all of the 3,000 white persons of voting age in the county were registered. But only about 1,000 of the 12,000 potential Negro voters were actually eligible.

In a further move, the registrars resigned, and this was held to leave no defendants to be sued. Congress in 1960 handled this problem by providing

Continued on Page 24, Column 4

102 SAVED AT SEA AS PLANE DITCHES

Rescue Is Made off Alaska Minutes After Accident

By The Associated Press.

SITKA, Alaska, Oct. 22—A military-charter airliner ditched in the ocean near here today, but all 102 persons aboard were saved in a quick rescue operation.

The plane, a DC-7C of Northwest Airlines, was going from McChord Air Force Base in Washington to Anchorage, Alaska. It carried 95 passengers and a crew of seven.

The rescue was reported by Northwest and the Alaska Coastal-Ellis Airline at Sitka, which also reported that there apparently were no serious injuries.

The plane went down shortly after the Federal Aviation Agency at Anchorage got word that it was being ditched because of propeller trouble.

A Coast Guard plane alighted on the water nearby; the Air Force sent two rescue planes, and small boats from Sitka, about seven miles north of the

Continued on Page 8, Column 3

WHAT'S That Over-The-Counter Stock Worth Today. Consult G. E. C. DIAL PL 2-5174 For Quotes, Free. Adv.

Chinese Open New Front; Use Tanks Against Indians

Nehru Warns of Peril to Independence —Reds Attack Near Burmese Border and Press Two Other Drives

Special to The New York Times

NEW DELHI, Oct. 22—Prime Minister Jawaharlal Nehru told the people of India tonight that the Chinese Communist attack was a threat to their liberty.

His grave warning followed word that the advancing Chinese had opened a third front in the Himalayas, near the Burmese border, and had used tanks for the first time. Five more Indian posts fell to the Chinese on the third day of savage fighting.

Excerpts from Nehru's speech will be found on Page 2.

[A bid for negotiations for a peace accord was broadcast by the Chinese Communist radio early Tuesday, The Associated Press reported from Tokyo.]

In a broadcast, Mr. Nehru denounced the Peking regime as "a powerful and unscrupulous opponent, not caring for peace or peaceful methods."

"The time has come," he said, "for us to realize fully this menace that threatens the freedom of our people and the independence of our country."

Prime Minister Nehru said India would not abandon her economic development program and policy of nonalignment with international blocs, but called on the nation to switch "from the slow-moving methods of peacetime to those which produce results quickly."

"We must build up our military strength by all means at our disposal," he said.

The third front in the Himalayan fighting was opened early today when the Chinese attacked an Indian post at Kibitoo, on the border between

Continued on Page 3, Column 1

U.S. Bids U.N. Bar China; Denounces Attack on India

By SAM POPE BREWER

Special to The New York Times

UNITED NATIONS, N. Y., Oct. 22—Adlai E. Stevenson told the General Assembly today that Communist China's "naked aggression" against India was new proof that it was unfit for membership in the United Nations.

The chief United States representative at the United Nations spoke as the Assembly took up the perennial question of admitting Peking.

Mr. Stevenson told the members that by their actions on the Indian frontier the Chinese Communists "again show their scorn for the Charter of this organization."

The Vice President of the Philippines, Emmanuel Pelaez, told the Assembly that there were more than 40,000,000 Chinese living outside China who would become "a Trojan horse" if the United Nations accepted the Communist Government.

Mr. Pelaez said that the Chinese abroad, 1,000,000 of them in the Philippines, would be used for subversion by the Peking Government. He said they could now be controlled because the Communist Government did not have the means to get at them.

On the fighting in India, Mr. Stevenson declared: "Should there be some among us who think that perhaps the whole thing is a mistake that will right itself before long, let me point out that when a nation moves its troops with tanks and armor, it is no mistake. It is a premeditated act. It is naked aggression. And it has been going on with gathering momentum for some three years."

He quoted Prime Minister

Continued on Page 5, Column 3

U. S. SAID TO EASE KATANGA POLICY

Reported Willing to Put Off Any Economic Sanctions —Congolese Disturbed

By LLOYD GARRISON

Special to The New York Times

LEOPOLDVILLE, the Congo, Oct. 22 — Authoritative sources said today that the United States was no longer insisting that Katanga Province strictly meet the deadlines of the United Nations plan to end its secession from the Congo.

This has alarmed Congolese officials. They say that the United States shift is reflected in United Nations policy.

The United Nations plan, introduced Aug. 2 by U Thant, Acting Secretary General, was said to have been conceived largely by the United States.

As outlined by Mr. Thant, the plan's first stage called for the following timetable:

Within thirty days a program was to be decided on for the reintegration of Katanga's army into the Congolese National Army. Sixty days were to be allowed for the program to be carried out.

Recall of Missions

All Katangese foreign missions were to be recalled immediately, and all Katanga's foreign currency reserves were to be put under the control of the central Government, with 50 per cent of these reserves rebated to Katanga.

Unification of the Congo's currency was to have begun within 10 days.

Katanga was to have started immediately to share 50 per cent of her tax revenues with the central Government.

Not one of these conditions has been met.

Last week Cyrille Adoula, Premier of the central Government, declared that "the deadline for the first stage has passed." He said that it was now time for the United Nations to consider the second stage — economic sanctions.

A shift in United States policy became apparent over the weekend after the departure of George C. McGhee, Under Secretary of State for Political Af-

Continued on Page 3, Column 6

Stocks Plunge Early On Crisis, but Rally

By RICHARD RUTTER

An already badly battered stock market was hit by massive selling yesterday as talk of a new international crisis spread in Wall Street.

The selling was of dimensions reminiscent of late May when the market experienced its worst break in a generation. Yesterday, the tape ran as much as 19 minutes late before a half-hearted recovery set in that cut losses by about one-third.

Both tape lateness and volume were the greatest since July 10. Two million shares were traded in the first two hours.

Stock markets in London, Frankfurt and Brussels, following Wall Street's lead, also took large losses.

The selling was directly ascribed to news in the morning about an air of crisis in Wash-

Continued on Page 48, Column 6

SHIPS MUST STOP

Other Action Planned If Big Rockets Are Not Dismantled

By JAMES RESTON

Special to The New York Times

WASHINGTON, Oct. 22—President Kennedy drew the line tonight, not with Cuba, but with the Soviet Union. After almost a generation of trying to keep the "cold war" from reaching a direct confrontation between United States and Soviet power, a decision has been made to force Soviet missile bases from this hemisphere at the risk of war.

This is the official interpretation of President Kennedy's speech tonight, and the orders to American forces bear it out. On the highest authority, it can be said that these orders include the following:

¶Ships carrying to Cuba weapons capable of striking the continental United States must either turn back or submit to search and seizure, or fight. If they try to run the blockade, a warning shot will be fired across their bows; if they still do not submit, they will be attacked.

¶This applies not only to ships but to any planes suspected of carrying additional offensive weapons to Cuba. There is no evidence that there are nuclear warheads in Cuba, but long-range aircraft suspected of carrying these or any other offensive weapons, will be intercepted, and instructions have been issued to do everything possible to check all Communist-bloc planes en route to Cuba via Newfoundland or Africa.

Prepared to Risk War

Even this will not satisfy the new policy announced by President Kennedy. Not only must new offensive weapons be stopped, under the President's orders, but those already in Cuba must be dismantled, or the United States will take whatever additional action is necessary, beginning with a much more rigorous blockade of such things as Cuba's essential oil supplies, to force compliance.

If this leads to Soviet retaliation, such as a counter-blockade of Berlin, the United States is prepared to risk a major war to defend its present position in the former German capital. Accordingly, American forces, not only in Berlin and West Germany but all over the world, have been placed on emergency alert. The new policy has been defined in a private communi-

Continued on Page 19, Column 1

Canada Asks Inspection of Cuba; Britain Supporting Quarantine

Diefenbaker Comments

By RAYMOND DANIELL

Special to The New York Times

OTTAWA, Oct. 22 — Prime Minister John Diefenbaker of Canada declared tonight the time had come for an impartial inspection of what is happening in Cuba by eight of the "nonaligned nations."

Interrupting debate of the Canadian economic crisis in the House of Commons, Mr. Diefenbaker described President Kennedy's speech on Cuba as "somber and challenging."

"Naturally," he said, "there has been little time to give consideration to positive action that might be taken. But I suggest that if there is a desire—and I am sure there is on the part of the U.S.S.R.—to have the facts, if a group of nations, perhaps the eight comprising the unaligned members of the 18-nation disarmament committee, were given the opportunity of making an on-site inspection of Cuba to ascertain what the facts are, a major step forward would be taken."

Meanwhile it was disclosed that Canada has barred the use of her airfields, including that

Continued on Page 21, Column 2

British Note Peril

By DREW MIDDLETON

Special to The New York Times

LONDON, Oct. 22—Qualified sources said today that approval for President Kennedy's military quarantine of Cuba could be expected from the British government.

A Foreign Office spokesman declared, "Revelation of the Soviet build-up in Cuba will come as a shock to the whole civilized world."

Official comment cannot be given until after Prime Minister Macmillan and his Cabinet have discussed the President's statement.

Initial reaction among diplomats was that the President had taken the most reasonable course to frustrate what military circles regard as evident danger to the United States: a buildup of Soviet nuclear capacity in Cuba.

The danger that war might result from a Soviet attempt to break what amounts to a military blockade of Cuba is accepted. But one experienced airman expressed the general feeling this way: "War can come from any one of a number of causes,

Continued on Page 21, Column 1

Associated Press Wirephoto

ANNOUNCES HIS ACTION: President Kennedy speaking to the nation last night on radio and television. He told of moves to keep offensive equipment away from Cuba.

TRAFFIC DELAYED AT BERLIN BORDER

Reds Start Intensive Check of Civilian Trucks an Hour Before Kennedy Speech

By SYDNEY GRUSON

Special to The New York Times

BONN, Oct. 22—The East German police began to slow down civilian traffic between West Berlin and West Germany late tonight.

About an hour before President Kennedy announced the United States countermeasures against the Soviet build-up in Cuba, the police started intensive examination of the papers of trucks moving into East German territory.

The connection, if any, between the two actions was not immediately clear. Similar harassment of civilian traffic has occurred periodically over the years. The immediate reaction in West Berlin was to consider tonight's harassment as part of the regular order of things, rather than as an advance countermeasure to the American moves against Cuba.

Nevertheless, there was deep anxiety that the Soviet Union would retaliate by causing trouble on the West's access lines to the city.

The outcome of tomorrow's meetings between Andrei A. Gromyko, the Soviet Foreign Minister, and East German Communist leaders was awaited with concern. Mr. Gromyko

Continued on Page 17, Column 8

Moscow Says U.S. Holds 'Armed Fist' Over Cuba

By SEYMOUR TOPPING

Special to The New York Times

MOSCOW, Tuesday, Oct. 23—In a broadcast before President Kennedy's speech on the missile build-up in Cuba, the Moscow radio said that the unusual activity in Washington indicated that the United States "once again was raising its armed fist over Cuba." The broadcast said there was "real hysteria" in Washington.

A Soviet reply to the United States note on Cuba that was given last night to Anatoly F. Dobrynin, the Soviet Ambassador to Washington, was expected to be delivered in 24 hours. It was expected that the reply would take the form either of a diplomatic communication or a message to President Kennedy from Premier Khrushchev.

Western observers said it appeared inevitable in view of recent Soviet statements that the reply would be a denial of any offensive Soviet intent and a charge of United States aggression against Cuba.

Veracity Questioned

The veracity of the Soviet Government was directly questioned in President Kennedy's speech, which was given after delivery of the note. The President said evidence had been obtained that Moscow was constructing offensive missile bases on Cuban territory.

The Soviet Government statement of Sept. 11, which warned the United States that an attack on Cuba would mean war, contended that the Soviet weapons supplied to Cuba were of a defensive nature.

Western observers said the crisis over Cuba would enter a critical phase when and if United States war vessels sought to halt and search a Soviet ship bound for Cuba.

A number of Soviet vessels carrying civilian goods and pos-

Continued on Page 18, Column 3

All Military Forces Mobilized by Castro

By The Associated Press

KEY WEST, Tuesday, Oct. 23—All of Cuba's military forces have been mobilized as a result "of the news from the United States," the Havana radio said today.

The broadcast said the order was issued by Premier Fidel Castro, who will address the nation later today.

"Our combat units rapidly placed themselves on a fighting basis," said the Havana broadcast.

"Hundreds of thousands of men were mobilized in the course of a few hours," added the broadcast, which followed by some hours President Kennedy's announcement of a naval blockade against Cuba.

During the evening, Havana appeared slow to react to President Kennedy's broadcast and

Continued on Page 20 Column 5

BIG FORCE MASSES TO BLOCKADE CUBA

Armada Is Under Orders to Open Fire if Necessary— All Troops Are Alerted

By JACK RAYMOND

Special to The New York Times

WASHINGTON, Oct. 22—American ships and planes began preparing tonight to impose a blockade of Cuba. United States forces are under orders to thwart any attempt to deliver offensive weapons to Havana.

A Defense Department spokesman said that a large force of ships and planes concentrating in the Caribbean area had instructions to use force if necessary, including sinking of ships, to carry out President Kennedy's orders for a "quarantine" of Cuba.

The Pentagon said also that United States military units throughout the world, including the garrison in Berlin and the nuclear-armed Strategic Air Command, had been placed "on alert."

Dependents of servicemen at the Guantanamo Bay Naval Base in Cuba have been evacuated, the department said.

Forces at Base Doubled

It added that the military forces there, which were previously put at 3,300 naval officers and men and several hundred Marines, have been doubled.

Air defense units in the United States, particularly radar warning stations, interceptor aircraft and ground-to-air missiles, "have been redeployed," the department spokesman said.

The orders for additional defense precautions were taken the spokesman continued, on the basis of aerial photographic evidence of long-range ballistic missile bases and the arrival of Soviet Ilyushin-28 bombers in Cuba.

The spokesman displayed some of the aerial photographs and pointed to some missiles sites that, he said, had been established only in the last 10 or 15 days.

He said some of the missile

Continued on Page 20 Column 1

NEWS INDEX

PRESIDENT GRAVE

Asserts Russians Lied and Put Hemisphere in Great Danger

Text of the President's address is printed on Page 18.

By ANTHONY LEWIS

Special to The New York Times

WASHINGTON, Oct. 22 — President Kennedy imposed a naval and air "quarantine" tonight on the shipment of offensive military equipment to Cuba.

In a speech of extraordinary gravity, he told the American people that the Soviet Union, contrary to promises, was building offensive missile and bomber bases in Cuba. He said the bases could handle missiles carrying nuclear warheads up to 2,000 miles.

Thus a critical moment in the cold war was at hand tonight. The President had decided on a direct confrontation with — and challenge to — the power of the Soviet Union.

Direct Thrust at Soviet

Two aspects of the speech were notable. One was its direct thrust at the Soviet Union as the party responsible for the crisis. Mr. Kennedy treated Cuba and the Government of Premier Fidel Castro as a mere pawn in Moscow's hands and drew the issue as one with the Soviet Government.

The President, in language of unusual bluntness, accused the Soviet leaders of deliberately "false statements about their intentions in Cuba."

The other aspect of the speech particularly noted by observers here was its flat commitment by the United States to act alone against the missile threat in Cuba.

Nation Ready to Act

The President made it clear that this country would not stop short of military action to end what he called a "clandestine, reckless and provocative threat to world peace."

Mr. Kennedy said the United States was asking for an emergency meeting of the United Nations Security Council to consider a resolution for "dismantling and withdrawal of all offensive weapons in Cuba."

He said the launching of a nuclear missile from Cuba against any nation in the Western Hemisphere would be regarded as an attack by the Soviet Union against the United States. It would be met, he said, by retaliation against the Soviet Union.

He called on Premier Khrushchev to withdraw the missiles from Cuba and so "move the

Continued on Page 18, Column 1

KENNEDY CANCELS CAMPAIGN TALKS

He and Johnson Take Step to Concentrate on Crisis

By CABELL PHILLIPS

Special to The New York Times

WASHINGTON, Oct. 22—The White House announced tonight that President Kennedy and Vice President Johnson would make no further political appearances in the Congressional campaign because of the Cuban crisis.

The move by the Administration was considered evidence not only of the seriousness of the situation but also of the desire of the President to unify the country behind his blockade order and keep the issue out of partisan politics.

In this connection, the White House said the President personally informed former Republican Presidents Dwight D. Eisenhower and Herbert Hoover, as well as former Democratic President Harry S. Truman, of his decision.

And the White House announced that John J. McCloy, former disarmament adviser to the Kennedy Administration and a Republican, had been as-

Continued on Page 18, Column 7

NEW YORK
Herald Tribune

THE LATE CITY

Established 122 Years Ago. A European Edition Is Published Daily in Paris

VOL. CXXII No. 42,329

230 West 41st Street, New York 36, N. Y. Telephone PEnnsylvania 6-4000

WEDNESDAY, OCTOBER 24, 1962

© 1962, New York Herald Tribune Inc.

10c in areas 50 miles from New York City except on Long Island

FIVE CENTS

WEATHER
Today: Partly cloudy, breezy and cold.

Tomorrow: Fair and seasonably cold.

TEMPERATURE RANGE
Yesterday: 53-60; Today: 45-50.

HUMIDITY
Yesterday 3 p.m. 75%; Today: 45-55.

Reports and Maps—Page 31

IN THE NEWS THIS MORNING

[FROM THE HERALD TRIBUNE'S OWN WORLD-WIDE SOURCES. FULL COVERAGE OF ALL IMPORTANT EVENTS IN THIS EDITION]

TOPIC A: THE CUBAN CRISIS—

❮Momentous alert. As a tense world grimly considered the war or peace prospects of the gravest crisis to confront the nuclear age, President Kennedy signed the proclamation establishing (at 10 a. m. today) the blockade of Soviet Cuba. How near the brink? U. S. warships were ready to intercept, search, and sink if necessary, 25 Soviet ships presumed to be carrying rockets and atomic warheads to Cuba. *The delay in the blockade's timing was a forewarning to Moscow—an 11th hour chance to avert a showdown.* Defense Secretary McNamara ordered all Navy and Marine Corps personnel kept on active duty.

❮The Communists. The Soviets canceled all troop leaves, ordered Communist-bloc Warsaw pact countries to beef up their military preparedness. The Russians also sent our Ambassador, Foy Kohler, a note warning the U. S. is "playing with fire," moving on the road to a thermonuclear war. *Fidel Castro called President Kennedy a pirate, said the blockade violates international law.*

❮At the UN. After some dilly-dallying, the UN Security Council met in emergency session to take up a U. S. resolution calling for the dismantling and withdrawal of Soviet-supplied offensive missile bases from Cuba. UN Ambassador Stevenson lashed into both Soviet Cuba and Russia in an hour-long speech. *The best guess is the Soviets will block any action by invoking its 101st veto. Next step: The General Assembly.* Afro-Asians urged U Thant to intervene, promote a cooling off.

❮OAS. Latin American republics gave overwhelming approval to a U. S. resolution to use armed force, if necessary, to stop Soviet Cuba from becoming a dangerous offensive force. *The Organization of American States voted 19 to 0 to back our blockade.*

❮Reaction. Nearly 2,000 demonstrators beseiged our embassy in London, shouted "Viva Fidel! Kennedy to hell!" New York police tailed known pro-Castro Cubans. The British, French and West German governments backed President Kennedy. *West Berliners (outwardly confident) braced for possible Soviet retaliation, began stocking up on food staples.*

❮Big Board. Wall Street was rocked by one of the heaviest selling days. The Dow Jones industrial average plummeted 10.54 points (closed at 558.06) on a heavy turnover of 6,110,000 shares. *It was the heaviest selling day since July 10, the jitteriest since May and June.*

❮Gold. Heavy demand from the European continent pushed up the price of gold in London, but orders fell off during the day, prices dropped slightly. Chief cause: The Cuban crisis. *How it affects us: If the demand (and the price) continue to increase, it would threaten a new drain on U. S. gold reserves.*

IN THE WORLD—

❮China-India war. Red China suddenly proposed a cease-fire and summit talks between Chinese and Indian leaders to peacefully settle their border dispute. The peace feeler came after Chinese troops, under orders to ignore boundaries, scored new gains. *Note: A previous call for troop pullbacks was rejected by India, which did not want to talk under duress.*

❮Soviet anti-Semitism. Following a two week trial in a Ukrainian city, six Jews have been condemned to death. Their crimes: Alleged dealings in gold and foreign currencies. *Among the condemned: An 81-year-old, accused of remaining a bachelor to avoid sharing his wealth.*

❮Ecumenical Council. Bishop Willem Van Bekkum (a Catholic missionary in Indonesia since 1936) called for sweeping liturgical reforms. He said liturgy (public forms

Zero Hour—10 A. M.; A World in Suspense

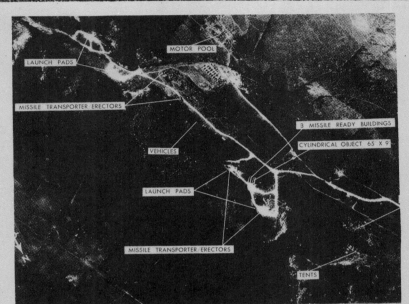

"UNMISTAKABLE EVIDENCE," said the President of the United States, "has established the fact that a series of offensive missile sites is now in preparation" in Cuba. This picture shows a medium range (1,100 miles) ballistic missile base in Cuba in operational status. The photograph was among a group of air reconnaissance shots released by the American Embassy in London but not by Washington. Why? State Department officials said the Embassy released them "by mistake." Not until early today did the Pentagon make them available in the United States.

Associated Press radiophoto

Proclamation By President— Castro Tirade

By Seymour Freidin
Executive Editor, Foreign News

An alert—meaning stand-by emergency—beeped, clacked and jangled around the world spelling out the stark crisis gripping East and West over Cuba last night.

And zero hour comes today at 10 a. m. President Kennedy declared it so by issuing a proclamation of embargo empowering the United States armed forces to blockade Cuba, beginning at that time this morning.

There will be no let-up in suspense. Breathlessly, it carries the world over until 9 o'clock this morning to a second special session of the Security Council of the United Nations here. War or peace is certain to tumble from the lips of men of state as they hear the U. S. charges against the Soviet Union and Communist Cuba and vice-versa. Over the microphone-stacked tables, though, they will concentrate on the clocks that creep toward 10 o'clock, the no-nonsense U. S. Embargo time.

SOLID SUPPORT

A line-up of sides, excluding the nervous neutrals, was evident from continent to continent. In pulsating, minute-by-minute consultation, the Organization of American States stood by this country unanimously in a historic decision of calculated risk and mutual self-defense.

It approved, 19 to 0, a U. S. resolution calling for armed force to prevent any further buildup of offensive weapons in Cuba. This same Soviet buildup of nuclear-tipped rockets caused President Kennedy to tell the world that we intended to eliminate this threat by massive blockade as a first step. The OAS action paves the way for the next step.

The Russians, trying to show off their cool side, said that American action added up to a big step toward A-war. They gave no hint of how they'd act, but 25 of their ships bearing nuclear and other weapons were strung out on the high seas of the North Atlantic.

'REPERCUSSIONS'

Far from the USSR, where Mr. Khrushchev has got himself committed so far in a 5,000-mile pipeline and prestige, the Cuba ruled by Fidel Castro ordered all-out mobilization. To try to rally the Cuban people around him, Castro launched into a fiery attack on the U. S. last night, beginning by calling President Kennedy a "pirate."

In a brief speech—short for the marathon talks to which he is accustomed — Castro warned the U. S. that the blockade "will very soon have repercussions." He spoke on TV for 83 minutes.

But the mystery and tension in the world's gravest whodunit so far were not even partly clarified by:

A massive blockade at sea by U. S. naval flotillas. It was a blockade in everything but name which became official with a proclamation by President Kennedy last night.

MYSTERY AT SEA

These vessels, on a round-the-clock quest, plow through the ocean troughs from the Caribbean to the North Atlantic.

Our UN Stand on 'Piecemeal Aggression'—Soviet Outlook

U. S. STANCE
By Darius S. Jhabvala
Of The Herald Tribune Staff

UNITED NATIONS, N. Y. The United States yesterday called on the UN Security Council, meeting in emergency session, to save the peace of the world by ending Soviet penetration of Cuba and forestalling "piecemeal aggression."

Adlai E. Stevenson, U. S.

The reaction was swift and sweeping. Announcement of the military blockade of Cuba reached into every area of the globe. Nations had to stand up and be counted; the world was choosing sides. For many of the people in the world life was changing—a wife separated from her husband in Guantanamo, a Communist soldier denied leave. The story, full words and pictures, on this page and pages 6 through 17 and on page 25.

RED STANCE
By Marguerite Higgins
Of The Herald Tribune Staff

WASHINGTON.
The Soviet Union appears to have been taken by surprise by America's decision to quarantine Cuba and seems uncertain about what stance to take. This was the official assessment here yesterday in wake of significant clues from Moscow, including a

President had 'acted bravely, responsibly and well' and *The Los Angeles Times* insisted that 'these will be months in which the President must have the support of every American'. Not one major paper that morning had the slightest doubt that his action was the right one – some regretted only that it had not come much earlier. After years of fearing the brink, it almost seemed a relief to be there. 'If the Russians want war they can have it' barked *The Chicago Tribune*. 'Blockade is war, if anyone chooses to challenge our blockade' *The Hartford Courant* warned. 'It is up to Mr. Khrushchev. Let him not misread the mood of America or misjudge her'.

Nor would it be long before the world would discover if Khrushchev misjudged the mood of America or not, since 25 Russian ships were at that very moment sailing towards Cuba. The quarantine went into effect on the 24th and a letter was delivered to the Soviet Chairman telling him so – it was one of the more breath-taking aspects of the episode that throughout the entire crisis the two leaders communicated only by letters, which often took several hours to reach their destination (a nuclear rocket took several minutes). At 10.00 am on the 24th two Russian ships were within a few miles of the American blockade barrier. A Russian submarine was also reported to be in the area.

At 10.30 a message reached the White House that six of the ships had stopped dead and seemed to be turning back (presumably the ones whose holds were stuffed with rocket components). By that night twelve of the ships had turned back to Russia – round one to Kennedy. But it was no more than a breathing-space: the work on the launching-sites in Cuba had been speeded up, as the latest U-2 pictures revealed, and efforts by the U.N. Secretary General to ease the tension were met by Kennedy with the insistence that only removal of the rockets would end the crisis. Meanwhile letters passed daily between Moscow and Washington. At first Khrushchev merely accused Kennedy of 'pushing mankind to the abyss of a world missile-nuclear war' and it began to look to those with a nose for the niceties of diplomatic prose that the strategy had not, after all, paid off.

Then, on the 26th at 6.00 in the evening, an extremely long and somewhat emotional letter arrived: it talked on a very personal level explaining how he (Khrushchev) had 'participated in two wars through cities and villages, everywhere sowing death and destruction'. He wanted, he said, not to destroy America but to compete peacefully, not by military means – and hinted the missiles might be removed, if the blockade was lifted and a guarantee was given by America not to attack Cuba. 'Let us not only relax the forces pulling on the ends of the rope' it concluded, 'let us take measures to untie that knot'. This encouraging letter was not made public, because the next day (27th) another more formal, hard-bargaining communication emerged from the Kremlin. The deal this time was: Russia will remove the missiles from Cuba if America will move hers from Turkey. This had partly been expected, but although the missiles in Turkey were obsolete and of little importance to American defence any longer, Kennedy was loath to dismantle them now at the point of a gun. Instead he chose to ignore this second letter and concentrated on following up the spirit of the first.

In the meantime, the rest of the world had been charting the course of events with trepidation, impotent to affect the outcome of what at times seemed, from the outside, the arrogant and reckless brinkmanship of two mighty Powers. Although NATO officially supported the American stand, the British press was beginning to criticise Kennedy's intransigence. Bertrand Russell had written to the President calling for a more conciliatory

attitude on his part, and had received the reply: 'I think your attention might well be directed to the burglar rather than to those who caught the burglar'. Many British papers began to share Russell's view, and suggested it would be only fair to trade in the Turkish bases. *The Observer* believed 'The wiser way is to negotiate. But Mr. Kennedy must have something to offer in return. Is it really insulting to suggest that the United States should offer to give up her missile bases in Turkey, as Mr. Khrushchev has proposed?' *The Sunday Times* said this 'alarming dance on the brink' must be stopped, and that world opinion was overwhelmingly in favour of submission to the Russian plan. *The Chicago Tribune* took some time off to reply to the 'scores of British politicians and editors' who 'paused in their rush for the bomb shelters just long enough to issue statements and dash off editorials with such headings as "A Chance To Save The World"!'

On that Sunday, however, there had looked

precious little chance to save the world. A U-2 pilot had been shot down over Cuba by a surface-to-air missile and it was widely believed that Washington was all ready to take military action on Monday, or Tuesday at the latest.

But on the 28th the tempest abated as suddenly as it had arisen. Khrushchev announced he would dismantle the bases, as requested, under U.N. supervision (Castro nearly precipitated another crisis by refusing to permit these on-site inspections but for once the U-2s proved they could avert crises as well as bring them on and produced enough evidence to convince Washington that the Russian was as good as his word). There was an outcry by the press when the Defence Department which had begun monitoring interviews by reporters on the 27th looked like continuing to do so, but the matter was dropped when the practice was discontinued the following month. Everyone had had enough crises for one year.

Johnson Takes
Nation's Helm,
Pages 4 and 5

The Dallas Morning News

John F. Kennedy
Life History,
Pages 16 and 17

VOL. 115—NO. 54   TELEPHONE: Riverside 7-4611   DALLAS, TEXAS, SATURDAY, NOVEMBER 23, 1963—50 PAGES IN 4 SECTIONS   ★★★★   PRICE 5 CENTS

KENNEDY SLAIN ON DALLAS STREET

★ ★ ★ ★   ★ ★ ★ ★   ★ ★ ★ ★   ★ ★ ★ ★   ★ ★ ★ ★

JOHNSON BECOMES PRESIDENT

Receives Oath on Aircraft

By ROBERT E. BASKIN
Washington Bureau of The News

In a solemn and sorrowful hour, with a nation mourning its dead President, Lyndon B. Johnson Friday took the oath of office as the 36th chief executive of the United States.

Following custom, the oath-taking took place quickly—only an hour and a half after the assassination of President Kennedy.

Federal Judge Sarah T. Hughes of Dallas administered the oath in a hurriedly arranged ceremony at 2:39 p.m. aboard Air Force 1, the presidential plane that brought Kennedy on his ill-fated Texas trip and on which his body was taken back to Washington.

Mrs. Johnson and Mrs. Kennedy, her stocking still flecked with blood from the assassination, flanked the vice-president as he raised his right hand in the forward compartment of the presidential jetliner at Love Field. About 25 White House staff members and friends were present as Johnson intoned the familiar oath:

"I do solemnly swear that I will perform the duties of President of the United States to the best of my ability, and defend, protect and preserve the Constitution of the United States."

The 55-year-old Johnson, the first Texan ever to become President, turned and kissed his wife on the cheek, giving her shoulders a squeeze. Then he put his arm around Mrs. Kennedy, kissing her gently

Lyndon B. Johnson

Gov. Connally Resting Well

By MIKE QUINN

Gov. John Connally — felled Friday by a sniper's bullet in the back—rested in "quite satisfactory" condition late Friday night at Parkland Hospital following nearly four hours of surgery in the afternoon.

An aide for the governor reported at 10:30 p.m. that the governor was comfortably asleep and resting comfortably following the incident which claimed President Kennedy's life.

Meanwhile, Dr. Tom Shires, chief of surgeons at University of Texas Southwestern Medical School, said Connally barely missed a fatal wound:

"After consulting with Mrs. Connally and others on the scene, the consensus is that the governor was quite fortunate that he turned to see what happened to the President. If he had not turned to his right, there is a good chance he probably would have been shot through the heart—as it was, the bullet caused a tangential wound."

Dr. Shires rushed to Dallas by Air Force jet after word of the shooting was flashed.

Connally was operated on by Dr. Robert R. Shaw, thoracic

CONTINUED ON PAGE 2.

Impact Shattering To World Capitals

Pro-Communist Charged With Act

A sniper shot and killed President John F. Kennedy on the streets of Dallas Friday. A 24-year-old pro-Communist who once tried to defect to Russia was charged with the murder shortly before midnight.

Kennedy was shot about 12:20 p.m. Friday at the foot of Elm Street as the Presidential car entered the approach to the Triple Underpass. The President died in a sixth-floor surgery room at Parkland Hospital about 1 p.m., though doctors said there was no chance for him to live when he reached the hospital.

Within two hours, Vice-President Lyndon Johnson was sworn in as the nation's 36th President inside the presidential plane before departing for Washington.

The gunman also seriously wounded Texas Gov. John Connally, who was riding with the President.

Four Hours in Surgery

Connally spent four hours on an operating table, but his condition was reported as "quite satisfactory" at midnight.

The assassin, firing from the sixth floor of the Texas School Book Depository Building near the Triple Underpass sent a Mauser 6.5 rifle bullet smashing into the President's head.

An hour after the President died, police hauled the 24-year-old suspect, Lee Harvey Oswald, out of an Oak Cliff movie house.

He had worked for a short time at the depository, and police had encountered him while searching the building shortly after the assassination. They turned him loose when he was identified as an employe but put out a pickup order on him when he failed to report for a work roll call.

He also was accused of killing a Dallas policeman, J. D. Tippit, whose body was found during the vast manhunt for the President's assassin.

Oswald, who has an extensive pro-Communist background, four years ago renounced his American citizenship in Russia and tried to become a Russian citizen. Later, he returned to this country.

Friendly Crowd Cheered Kennedy

Shockingly, the President was shot after driving the length of Main Street through a crowd termed the largest and friendliest of his 2-day Texas visit. It was a good-natured crowd that surged out from the curbs almost against the swiftly moving presidential car. The protective bubble had been removed from the official convertible.

Mrs. Connally, who occupied one of the two jump seats in the car, turned to the President a few moments before and remarked, "You can't say Dallas wasn't friendly to you."

At Fort Worth, Kennedy had just delivered one of the most well-received speeches of his ca-

CONTINUED ON PAGE 2.

John F. Kennedy

GRAY CLOUDS WENT AWAY

Day Began as Auspiciously As Any in Kennedy's Career

(Robert E. Baskin, chief of the Washington Bureau of   suit with a pert matching hat, made an instant hit at Love   agreed it was one of the most cordial receptions the President

It was 12.30 pm precisely on November 22 1963 when President Kennedy's motorcade, travelling at 12 mph through the cheering streets of Dallas, reached the junction of Houston and Elm Streets. Ahead lay an underpass, beyond that the destination at the Trade Mart. As the Presidential car turned into the sharp bend, it passed a tawdry-looking building which advertised its function as the Texas School Book Depository. At that place and at that moment, President Kennedy was fatally injured by two shots, through the neck and head. He died at 12.57 in the trauma room of the city's Parkland hospital. A few minutes after 1.00 three empty cartridge cases were discovered near a sixth-floor window of the Depository — at almost exactly the same time as an employee of the building, Lee Harvey Oswald, shot and killed a police officer who had stopped him for questioning. At 1.50 Oswald was arrested in a movie theatre and subsequently charged with the murder of the President. It was discovered that he had once been a Marine, had absconded to Russia where he had been refused citizenship; that he played a desultory role as a Castroite agitator, that he was mentally unstable. His motive for murder was never ascertained, however, for two days later as he was being transferred to a new jail he was himself shot (in full view of the television cameras and 40 million witnesses) by a local night-club owner, Jack Ruby. Also on television Ruby was sentenced to death on March 14 1964, but died of cancer before sentence was carried out.

New York

Journal American

Period Of Sorrow
Jimmy Cannon on Page 30.

Did the 'Pros' Upset Wall St.
See Leslie Gould—Page 34

★★★★★   MONDAY, NOVEMBER 25, 1963   ·27

MYSTERIES OF DALLAS
Ruby Plea: 'Out of His Mind'

Did Police Get FBI's Warning?

By DOUGLAS ANDERSON

A mysterious call warning that accused assassin Lee Harvey Oswald would be murdered on route from the City to the County Jail was received by the FBI at 2:15 a.m. Sunday, it was disclosed today.

The call was immediately relayed to the Dallas County Sheriff's office and full security precautions for the transfer of Oswald to the County Jail were put into effect, a spokesman said.

Authoritative sources said the FBI then notified Dallas City police. But Capt. Glenn King insisted it had not been.

TELL OF MEETING

This development came as the puzzle surrounding the sniper's shadowy past deepened with reports that he met secretly with both Soviet and Cuban envoys a month before President John F. Kennedy was assassinated on Friday.

The revelation was made shortly after Oswald was slain by Jack Ruby, a nightclub operator with enigmatic dealings on the fringes of the underworld.

The newspaper Excelsior in Mexico City reported that Oswald visited the Soviet and Cuban consuls late last September and requested visas so he could travel to the Soviet Union via Cuba.

NOT MENTIONED

Curiously the double-dealing Oswald made no mention of either Russia or Cuba when he applied to the U. S. State Department for a new passport which he received.

At the same time, fresh evidence pointed to possible earlier links between Oswald and Ruby. It became known that Oswald reportedly visited Ruby's Dallas nightclub a week before President Kennedy was assassinated and — by coincidence or design—rented a room in the same neighborhood where Ruby maintained an apartment.

QUESTIONS POSED

The new developments posed these questions:

● What if any was the exact relationship between Oswald and Ruby, both known as "loners"?

● Was the motive for Oswald's killing really the obvious one of retribution, or was he actually slain to seal his fate?

● Was the reported reason for Oswald's Mexico City trip a cover-up to shield the real reason for his visit?

● Was the assassination of President Kennedy and murder of Oswald part of some political conspiracy?

● Who provided funds for Oswald's mysterious trip to Mexico City?

● Who was to finance his projected journey to Cuba and Russia.

SEEK ANSWER

Investigators from city, state and Federal law enforcement agencies are seeking the answers to these questions today.

However, they are handicapped by the slaying of Oswald—just as he began to cooperate with his questioners.

The fact that the once-arrogant Oswald was beginning to soften was the final irony

Continued on Next Page

The Death Penalty to Be Sought

DALLAS, Nov. 25—Jack Ruby will plead temporary insanity in the fatal shooting of Lee Harvey Oswald in Police headquarters basement, his attorney said today.

"I think he was probably temporarily out of his mind," attorney Tom Howard said. District Attorney Henry Wade last night said he would demand the maximum penalty for the 52-year-old nightclub owner. Ruby was booked on charges of murder with malice.

"I will seek the death penalty for Ruby even if he pleads guilty because shooting a handcuffed man deserves the death penalty," Mr. Wade said.

WILL SEEK BOND

Mr. Howard, one of four defense lawyers, said he would seek to win freedom for Ruby on bond at a hearing later this week before Criminal Court Judge Joe Brown.

"If he was in the same state at the time of the shooting as when I saw him, I think he is emotionally disturbed," Mr. Howard said.

Mr. Howard said the Dallas police are capable and "absolutely" will take special precautions to protect Ruby's life.

Two detectives rushed Ruby from City Jail to the County Court House today. He pressed down on the car seat so passersby would not see him.

This was a trip similar to that which ended in death for Oswald as it barely got under way.

KEPT UNDER GUARD

Mr. Wade said he would present his case against Ruby to the grand jury "within the next week."

Meantime officers are guarding Ruby around the clock, taking extraordinary precautions. Police Sgt. M. O. Rogers said they have taken away his belt and shoes.

Rogers said Ruby told him this morning he had slept well in his city jail cell through the night.

Sgt. Rogers said Ruby ate a light breakfast this morning and has made no special requests through the sergeant.

REVEAL EVIDENCE

Earlier, the District Attorney revealed the evidence which convinced Dallas officers they had an airtight case against Oswald.

"There is no doubt in my mind that Oswald was the killer," Mr. Wade said.

"This is it—I've sent men to the electric chair on less evidence than we have against Lee Harvey Oswald.

MAJOR FACTS

Mr. Wade said two facts stood high in the mass of evidence linking the slim, brown-haired Oswald to the slaying.

First, a palm print on the underside of the rifle which fired the bullets that killed Mr. Kennedy was identified as Oswald's.

Secondly, Oswald had definitely been placed inside the building at the time the shots were fired from there at Mr. Kennedy.

The gun was here, his prints were on the gun, the gun was the gun that killed Kennedy, his palm prints were on the box on which the killer sat, and

Continued on Next Page

Torn by a bullet fired point-blank, Lee Harvey Oswald, President Kennedy's accused assassin, cries out in agony before falling mortally wounded in basement of Dallas, Tex., police headquarters during transfer to county jail. In this spectacular photo Oswald's killer, Dallas nightclub owner Jack Ruby, is still pointing the revolver at the handcuffed prisoner. A split second later Ruby was swarmed over by police before he could squeeze off another shot.

Copyright, 1963, The Dallas Times-Herald and Photographer Bob Jackson, via AP Wirephoto

A Surfeit of Spies
From Portland to Profumo

The tantalizing thing, for any newspaper, about spy dramas, is that the best bits are invariably secret. At the critical moment the official blanket of equivocation or flat denial will descend, to stifle the newsmen's sacred quest for the truth. And then — the undignified confrontation between government and press on what constitutes 'the national interest'. The one will insist it is not served by portraying Security as a leaky sieve: the other will declare it undoubtedly is. Both are apt to invoke their own high-minded concepts of duty, honour and patriotism: both will accuse the other of falling abysmally short on all counts.

Defence secrets, always the illicit coinage of cold war diplomacy, were particularly precious in the icy years that followed the 1960 Summit fiasco. The trade of espionage was flourishing, and nowhere more so than in a faceless semi-detached in a discreet Drive at Ruislip, England. Number 45 was the home of bookseller Peter Kroger and his wife Helen — an amiable couple who, apart from the friend who came regular as clockwork on the first weekend of each month, had few visitors. The neighbours were astounded to read in their papers on January 9 1961 that police had swooped on Cranley Drive and hauled off the kindly Krogers as master-spies. But they were. It took several days to uncover the high-powered radio transmitter under piles of rubble at No. 45; someone was still frantically trying to raise the Krogers — nameless M15 engineers pinpointed it to a radio station just outside Moscow.

Three others were arrested the same day, outside Waterloo station: two Admiralty clerks Harry Frederick Houghton and his fiancé Ethel Gee, whose shopping basket was stuffed full of secret atomic submarine plans from the Naval base at Portland, and a 'company director' called Gordon Lonsdale. What his Russian name was, or where the real Gordon Lonsdale from Cobalt, Ontario was, no-one ever did discover. But this bubble-gum machine manufacturer was a highly-trained Russian agent, with a network that extended to the Continent. The papers recorded in horror that he had been working undisturbed in Britain for six years, and demanded a full inquiry into national security arrangements. Their worst fears were realised when the Romer committee reported a few months later that Houghton had been known to the Admiralty as a security risk since 1956.

In the meantime the Russians had not been idle. In March they had successfully launched another dog into space (even if their much-vaunted horses in the Grand National had come a satisfying cropper the same day) and were stirring up trouble again at the U.N. *The Sunday Telegraph* reported enigmatically that Scotland Yard's files on Lonsdale's spy ring were not yet closed: there was 'thought to be a minor civil servant operating in a similar way to that mentioned at the trial'. Unfortunately there was no clue to his identity.

The Romer report had not even been published when the next hammer-blow fell. On April 18 another spy, George Blake, was charged with having passed secret documents to the Russians for no less than nine years. Blake made no bones about his fervent conversion to the Communist cause — indeed he seemed so garrulous that the Government took good care this time to have him tried in camera. In vain did *The Daily Mirror* batter the Prime Minister with its 'five grave questions'. To no purpose did *The Observer* fly its paper kite 'Was Blake a

double agent?', and *The Daily Express* complain that the American press seemed better informed than the British. The news black-out was absolute, to the approval anyway of *The Times* who saw no useful purpose in starting a witch hunt.

At least the next spy was someone else's problem — or so it seemed. Dr. Robert Soblen had already been convicted as a Russian spy in America, escaped to Israel and was being returned to prison on an El Al airliner when he was thrust into the arms of astonished British immigration officials, with blood pouring from his wrists and stomach. The Home Secretary however was deaf to all Soblen's appeals for asylum and ordered the El Al airline to take their troublesome passenger back on board. That was in July; on September 6 Soblen was still in Britain, several El Al aeroplanes having developed mysterious 'technical faults'. And in Britain he was determined to stay. As a car was driving him to Pan Am's flight 101 to New York on the 6th, he collapsed and was returned to Brixton jail. Five days later, still unconscious from an overdose of drugs, he died. This time, even *The Times* called on the government to 'clear the air by explaining, from beginning to end, what exactly did happen'.

In the same month as Soblen's fateful car ride to London airport, a car catalogue was delivered to a flat in Dolphin Square, Westminster. It was the signal for another spy to resume operations, now that the Portland fuss was forgotten. Not until the following spring did British agents in Moscow begin to suspect that the trickles of secrets to the Kremlin had started once more. In London the leak was painstakingly narrowed down once again to — the Admiralty.

William John Vassall was arrested on September 12 1962, and came up for trial at Bow Street court on October 9. Even before they were fashioned by the hands of seasoned crime reporters into epic narratives, the bare details of the life of this humble Admiralty clerk were bizarre: the lonely son of a London curate, homosexual, posted to Moscow as an Embassy clerk, compromised by a diligently-planned seduction at a Moscow restaurant . . . brow-beaten, blackmailed, frightened. Then back in London, the secret code-signs, pink circles on a tree-trunk, meetings in phone-booths, parcels of money, miniature cameras, secret cupboards, men called Gregory and Nikolai. None of the trappings of high espionage, it seemed, were omitted — even the high-living, the expensive flat, the luxury fittings, exclusive club, fine suits: all of which were to be his undoing when the inquisitive eyes of Special Branch were finally directed on his department.

The trial raised some disturbing questions. How did a clerk earning £800 a year have access to highly secret documents? Why was his lavish life-style not suspected and reported sooner? How had such an obvious security risk contrived to evade routine vetting procedures? All these questions were echoed and re-echoed by the newspapers, who looked for answers — and double-quick — from the heads of the Admiralty, Lord Carrington the First Lord and John Galbraith the Civil Lord (who had also for a time been Vassall's immediate boss). Galbraith, especially, was exposed to a sustained barrage of innuendo, for it seemed he had even been visited by his clerk at his Scottish home.

The Sunday Express alleged Galbraith had

seen Vassall's opulent Dolphin Square flat for himself and said nothing. *The Daily Mail* contended that Vassall had been known as a homosexual in his department, in fact was nicknamed 'Auntie' by his colleagues. *The Daily Express* claimed that the Admiralty had known for 18 months that there was a spy at large. *The Sunday Pictorial* (which was currently running Vassall's exclusive life-story) scooped everyone by turning up a batch of letters in Vassall's apartment which appeared to give a clear picture of 'friendly relations' between Vassall and 'some high officials for whom he worked', and handing them over to the official enquiry team. It was not many days before papers were putting names where *The Sunday Pictorial* had gallantly omitted them. *The Guardian* complained that Galbraith was being made the subject of a personal press campaign, and pointed out to its fellows that none of the charges against Vassall related to Galbraith's incumbency at the Admiralty.

It made no difference. The Prime Minister was obliged to kill the rumours by publishing the letters. They were indeed from Galbraith, and though they revealed him as a kindly and informal (perhaps too informal?) employer, they contained not one hint of complicity. Nevertheless the former Civil Lord resigned from the Government — and still the rumours persisted, the most tenacious one being that it had been Vassall's intention to join Galbraith in Italy and 'do a Pontecorvo' (after the atomic scientist who had defected while on holiday in 1950). When this reached the Premier's ears he was determined to sweep away the 'dark cloud of suspicion and innuendo' by appointing an independent tribunal. Perhaps a little prematurely the Press hailed his decision, for almost in the same breath he had referred to newspaper reports and spoken of 'the growth of what I can only call the spirit of Titus Oates or Senator McCarthy'. 'Truth' he declared 'is on trial'. He might also have added, so is the Press.

In mid-January 1963 an endless procession of journalists from nearly every national paper in Fleet Street trooped before the Tribunal. The members had read literally hundreds of newspaper articles and were quite prepared, if necessary, to get to the bottom of all of them. For some newspapers this posed two distinct problems. In the first place, it had the effect of subjecting certain time-honoured practices to a scrutiny which they could not survive: 'informed speculation' very often turned out to be based on tendentious information or unsubstantiated gossip, 'revelations' were revealed to be merely the result of diligent research among cuttings from other newspapers (thus perpetuating 'facts' which may or may not have had a sound basis in the first place). On this score, in the words of *The Times*, 'The press comes badly out of the report . . . the judgement (of the public) is likely to be harsh'. *The Times* concluded: 'The newspapers will be well advised not to put up a smokescreen of indignation or justification'.

The second problem was that the Tribunal had the power to insist that reporters reveal the source of their information or be referred to the High Court for contempt. At the same time it was fundamental (always had been, and still is) to the journalist's code that he *never* revealed his sources. After all, this was the basis of trust on which Cabinet Ministers found it convenient to leak information and disclaim it afterwards if necessary. In a number of cases

Daily Mail
News Chronicle

NO. 20,190   FOR QUEEN AND COMMONWEALTH   THURSDAY, MARCH 23, 1961   PRICE 3d.

FIRST LORD ORDERS OVERHAUL
Macmillan tells Kennedy: Agents didn't get any U.S. secrets

The extraordinary story behind the espionage ring begins in **PAGE SEVEN** →

SPY STORM BURSTS

Comment

A SECURITY SCANDAL

FIRST there was NUNN MAY. Then FUCHS, PONTECORVO, and BURGESS and MACLEAN. In all these notorious cases British security broke down.

Now comes another. Behind the unprecedented sentences awarded to the spies LONSDALE, the KROGERS, HOUGHTON, and MISS GEE lies a story of almost unbelievable slackness in our Intelligence services.

A spy ring had been operating for years before these five were caught—and then only by chance. After that, security officers and police worked fast, and deserved the tributes paid them by the LORD CHIEF JUSTICE.

B was what went before that is so terrifying. HOUGHTON, known to be unreliable, is taken on at a top-secret naval base. Why? The KROGERS, associates of convicted spies in the U.S., can work in Britain. Why?

A blow

THE answer lies in the way these matters are handled by untrained staff. The vision of an alert, unsleeping corps of first-class brains keeping watch and ward has taken another blow.

The Fuchs case led directly to a breakdown of Anglo-U.S. talks, which deprived us of nuclear know-how for years. Goodness knows what our allies will think of these latest revelations.

And will they be the last? Were HOUGHTON and MISS GEE alone in their treachery? We should be naive, indeed, to think so.

An inquiry is to be held, and high time too. If there is no improvement the next in the dock should be our security system — on a charge of gross negligence.

VAGUE JUSTICE

EVEN the suspected drunk at the wheel is entitled to the protection of British ideas of justice, but under the new Road Safety Bill he may not get it.

The old definition of the drunken motorist was one "incapable of having proper control." The new one, that "ability to drive properly is for the time being impaired," is less precise.

This will cover the man who is not drunk but has had a drink or two—and that is right enough. But the test for alcohol in the blood is far too vague.

Onus

MOREOVER, if a driver refuses the test it will be taken as an admission of guilt. The onus of proof will thus be removed from the police and it will be for the accused to prove his innocence. This is something new—and wrong.

Punishments for many driving offences are rightly made heavier. Except, strangely enough, for drunken driving. We should have thought that harsher penalties would have been more effective than playing around with breathing tests.

In the end the real recipe for safety is better roads. This is proved by the M1, where deaths are one-third the average. And where there are no licensed premises.

Worst blunder since Fuchs?

A DAILY MAIL SPECIAL INVESTIGATION

A MAJOR political storm is expected over the grave weaknesses revealed in Britain's security services by the Old Bailey spy case.

It ended yesterday with sentences of 25 to 15 years for the five members of the Russian spy ring.

Lord Carrington, First Lord of the Admiralty, will announce the establishment of an immediate Naval board of inquiry to investigate the gaps disclosed in naval security.

Commons question

He has ordered a world-wide overhaul of the Navy's security system. At least one senior security officer is likely to be prematurely retired.

But this is unlikely to satisfy the Opposition. Mr. George Brown, the deputy leader, is to question the Prime Minister on the failure of security services shown up by the case. Opposition leaders are expected to press for a full-scale inquiry into what is regarded as the worst penetration of our security system since Klaus Fuchs gave the atom-bomb secrets to Russia. An attempt will be made to raise the issue in the Commons today.

There will undoubtedly be serious repercussions on Anglo-American relations. It is only recently that the Americans have got over their mistrust of British security caused by the Fuchs case, the Pontecorvo case, and Burgess and Maclean.

It is understood that the Prime Minister has sent a personal letter assuring President Kennedy that no U.S. naval or atomic secrets were compromised by the spy ring.

A similar letter has gone from Lord Carrington to Admiral Arleigh Burke, head of U.S. naval operations.

A ten-week investigation by a Daily Mail team, ranging from Portland to Hongkong, Brussels to New Zealand and the Canadian frozen North, has revealed an astonishing situation. These facts emerged :

1. Neither Ethel Gee nor Henry Houghton, who each got 15 years yesterday, was security cleared to work at the Admiralty Underwater Weapons Establishment at Portland (where they stole the Navy's secrets). The reason : "They were only minor servants."

2. Houghton, while working as the personal assistant to the British Naval Attache in Warsaw in 1951, was declared a security risk—for drunkenness and other reasons—and sent home.

3. When Houghton was found to be unsatisfactory at the A.U.W.E it took the Admiralty six months, through the antiquated and complicated Civil Service system, to persuade the Civil Service Commissioners to transfer the spy from the top-secret establishment to less secret work in Portland dockyard.

Like a novel

4. Houghton's ex-wife Peggy, who divorced him in 1958, reported that he was engaged in spying activities and had secret documents in his home. But this was consistently ignored by the naval authorities.

5. Commander Stuart Erskine Crewe-Read, 60-year-old retired destroyer commander and security officer at Portland, admitted to the *Daily Mail* that he had not passed on information about Houghton to the Chief of Naval Intelligence in London. Why? Because "it all sounded like a novel, and I was afraid that the laws of slander would be invoked if I recommended an investigation into his activities."

6. The spy ring operated for a minimum of five years without Britain's security agencies being aware of it.

7. In all three Services security officers are often untrained and underpaid. Some tend to regard their jobs

Turn to Page 13, Col. 1

Lonsdale and a friend in convivial mood at a London party

THEY FACE GIANT NAVY PROBE

COMMANDER CREWE-READ

HE is Security Officer at Portland. He says he was never told Houghton was a security risk in Warsaw.

CAPTAIN AUSTEN

HE was naval attache in Warsaw and ordered Houghton's return "because I considered him a security risk."

CAPTAIN SYMONDS

HE is director of the anti - submarine warfare department. He will estimate what secrets the spy ring obtained.

---

95 years
THE OLD BAILEY'S TOUGHEST PEACE-TIME TOTAL

By Daily Mail Reporter

IT was two minutes to four by the clock in the No. 1 Court at the Old Bailey when the spy case jury returned with their verdict of "All guilty."

Within the next hour the Lord Chief Justice, Lord Parker had sentenced the three men and two women in the dock to a total of 95 years jail—the biggest collective sentence in the Old Bailey's peace-time history.

The sentences—which far exceeded the ten passed on atom spy Allan Nunn May and the 14 years on atom spy Dr. Klaus Fuchs—were :

Russian. It is the heaviest spy sentence on record, and the longest by any British court for nearly a century.

20 years each — white-haired Peter Kroger, 50, and his 47-year-old wife, Helen.

15 years each — ex-Navy man Henry Houghton, 56, and his fiancee 46-year-old Ethel Gee.

Lord Parker said the charges of spying had been proved "on the clearest possible evidence," and added : "This must be one of the most disgraceful cases that has ever come before the court."

Addressing Lonsdale, Lord Parker said : "You are clearly a professional spy. It is a

Turn to Page 13, Col. 1

Envoys held in Cuba

NEW YORK, Wednesday.—The second and third secretaries at the British Embassy in Havana, Mr. Frederick Jeffers and Mr. John Macdonald, were arrested by Cuban police when they went to inquire about the arrest of a third Briton. All three were freed later.—D.M. Reporter.

Butler in charge

Mr. R. A. Butler, Home Secretary, will be in charge of the Government and preside at Cabinet meetings when Mr. Macmillan leaves tomorrow on his visit to the West Indies, United States and Canada.

Spurs lose

Tottenham Hotspur, chasing the F.A. Cup and League double, were beaten 2—1 at home last night by Newcastle United—but still lead the First Division by four points.

Full report—BACK Page.

WALL STREET

NEW YORK, Wednesday. — Markets closed mixed after very heavy trading. Dow Jones Index rose 0.65 to 679.380.—Agencies.

Grave British warning on Laos

By JOHN DICKIE

BRITAIN and the United States decided last night on a showdown with Russia over Laos.

The British Ambassador in Moscow, Sir Frank Roberts, was instructed to warn the Russians: Accept new peace proposals or face the consequences of hostilities spreading, with disastrous results for the Far East.

This is the toughest stand taken against the Communists since the famous Dulles threat of "massive retaliation" to China seven years ago.

It follows a rapid deterioration of the military situation in Laos —where the Pathet Lao troops, backed by a Russian airlift of 45 tons of military supplies a day, are within a few days of reaching the outskirts of Vientiane, the capital.

Two proposals

The text of the British Note to Russia was not published, but it is believed to contain two major proposals :

(1) Reconvene the three-Power international control commission to supervise a cease-fire.

(2) Assemble an international conference, including Communist China, to draft a political settlement.

Last night, Britain's Defence Minister, Mr. Harold Watkinson, was flying back to London from Washington with a full briefing from the U.S. Defence Secretary, Mr. Macnamara, on American military preparations for Laos.

These preparations involve the use of American forces sufficient to hold the military balance in Laos. President Kennedy is determined Vientiane shall not fall.

DAILY MAIL: FLEET ST. 6000

WEATHER: Bright periods. Details : Page ELEVEN.

CROSSWORDS: Page EIGHTEEN.

COURSE CORRESPONDENT'S LATE WIRE—Best at Liverpool : CARDINAL WOLSEY (2.0, nap), and BETTER HONEY (3.40). 5

Daily Mirror

3d. Thursday, May 4, 1961 • No. 17,846

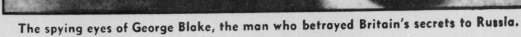

The spying eyes of George Blake, the man who betrayed Britain's secrets to Russia.

TREACHERY

42 years for the traitor, but the Mirror puts—

FIVE GRAVE QUESTIONS TO MACMILLAN

THE Lord Chief Justice yesterday passed the most severe sentence in British history on a spy convicted in peacetime.

He sent George Blake to prison for 42 years. Blake had confessed to spying for a foreign Power—Russia—over a period of 9½ years.

The appalling facts disclosed by this case of treachery arouse alarm.

The Daily Mirror, in the public interest, puts these five urgent questions to the man directly responsible for national security—Mr. Harold Macmillan, the Prime Minister.

1 HOW was it possible for a man in key British Government posts to be a top Soviet spy for nine and a half years without being discovered?

2 WHY was Blake, who had been a prisoner of the Communists in North Korea for three years—and thus exposed to brainwashing—afterwards appointed to posts where

CONTINUED ON BACK PAGE

THE TRAITOR—GEORGE BLAKE

This is the self-confessed traitor . . . the man whose treachery has, in the words of the Lord Chief Justice at the Old Bailey yesterday, "rendered much of this country's efforts completely useless."

Mr MACMILLAN

As Prime Minister he is directly responsible for the security of Great Britain.

SUNDAY PICTORIAL

November 4, 1962   No. 2,481   © Sunday Pictorial Newspapers, Ltd., 1962   5d.

THE LETTERS IN VASSALL'S FLAT

This was Vassall's flat, mentioned by Mr. Peter Thorneycroft, Minister of Defence, when he told the Commons on Friday: "When a clergyman's son is seen doing a job, perhaps a little below his educational value, in the Admiralty, maybe as a clerk, and if he has a flat in Dolphin Square—which at that time was not the most expensive type of flat in London—that would not necessarily be a highly suspicious thing by itself."

The Pictorial sends them to the spy inquiry

A **NUMBER of** letters received by John Vassall, the £15-a-week Admiralty clerk who spied for Russia, were sent last night to the Government's three-man inquiry team by the Sunday Pictorial.

They are letters written to Vassall—now serving eighteen years' imprisonment for selling secrets — on officially-embossed Government notepaper.

One is on House of Commons notepaper and another on official Admiralty paper.

These letters and a post-card, appear to give a clear picture of the friendly relations between the Admiralty junior clerk and some high officials for whom he worked.

In the light of the Commons' debate last Friday, the letters may well be of importance to the investigation into security.

Other vital letters sent to Vassall, who is 38, and

By NORMAN LUCAS and BILL HAMILTON

seized from his flat by detectives, may also be handed over. They are in a safe at Scotland Yard.

Before Vassall was sentenced for spying he talked of the urgent need for an inquiry into sex blackmail of people who work in Government departments.

But he warned that such an inquiry—to weed out homosexuals and bi-sexuals

in high office—would be unlikely to succeed.

"Many of the types who would be vetted in such an investigation are respectable married men holding senior posts. No one would suspect them of abnormal sex practices," he said.

His comments were made shortly before the Premier ordered the inquiry.

The traitor Vassall added: "I also feel that if the Government tried to start any McCarthy-style purge, the Civil Service will deteriorate.

"They will only get second-rate diplomats, since first-class ones do not like working in an atmosphere of constant suspicion."

Vassall also said that security could be tightened if junior clerks were not allowed to handle keys to top-secret files.

HOW RED SPY CHIEFS BROKE ME.—PAGE 8.

journalists appearing before the Tribunal refused point blank to name their informants. Two of them, one from *The Daily Mail*, the other from *The Daily Sketch*, were sent before the High Court and sentenced to prison.

To the Press these two journalists took on the aspect of martyrs. But beyond Fleet Street the reaction was disconcertingly different: relations between newspapers and government continued to deteriorate, and the public seemed to be hostile or, at best, indifferent. It got to a pitch in March when *The Times* was moved to publish a passionate defence of the Press's rights and duties. *The Daily Mirror* was so impressed it spread the editorial over a full page and reprinted it for the millions the next day.

Indeed there were events occurring during and immediately after the Tribunal which seemed to call for more, not less, curiosity on the part of the press, whatever its faults. In December another civil servant, Barbara Fell, was sentenced to two years imprisonment for revealing 'confidential' (as opposed to 'secret') documents to a Yugoslav official. On January 31 a Labour MP revealed in Parliament that some confidential Naval documents had turned up in an ex-Ministry filing cabinet in a Wolverhampton garage. In March a former Foreign Office official Kim Philby disappeared (and later re-appeared in Moscow, revealed as 'the third man' concerned in the defection of diplomats Burgess and Maclean in 1951).

On the 10th of the same month another Labour MP alleged that the Admiralty had 'hushed up' accusations of homosexuality against a senior Naval officer during the Vassall Tribunal 'to avoid embarrassment'. On April 13 more secrets (this time, detailing the whereabouts of regional seats of the government in the event of a nuclear attack) were found to have been distributed in leaflets to the public on a ban-the-bomb march. On April 18 the Russians announced the public trial of a British spy (what a relief!) Greville Wynne, but on the 28th a scientist from the Atomic Research Establishment, Giuseppe Martelli, was arrested and found to be in possession of a complete spy-kit. The director of the Atomic Establishment pointed out that 'we have no secrets here that are not known to Soviet scientists'. Perhaps he missed the unconscious irony of his remark — but it would have come as a surprise to the British public to learn that at that point there were any worthwhile secrets left in Britain anyway.

It began to look as if the entire fabric of national security had crumbled irretrievably. But there was *worse* to come. Almost as a diversion from the rigours of the Tribunal and bitterness of its aftermath, the popular papers turned to a promising story of an attempted murder of a model girl, by an ex-boyfriend, in the flat of a fashionable London osteopath and society artist. The model was Christine Keeler, the osteopath Stephen Ward.

Privately, none of the papers were surprised when Miss Keeler fled the country on March 14, on the eve of the Old Bailey trial. For weeks, amid all the recriminations attending the Vassall case, lobby correspondents at Westminster had been tuning in to veiled references of Christine Keeler's affair with a Soviet naval attaché, Eugene Ivanov, and even more startling with the Minister for War, John Profumo. These rumours gained momentum in February when it was learnt that security men had been having quiet words in the Government's ear. When Christine disappeared the papers were in a quandary: they had a story, but they couldn't very well print it. *The Daily Express* solved it on the 15th by leading with the story of Profumo's alleged resignation (which was denied instantly) and carrying the story of Christine's vanishing act with only a column in between for decency's sake. On the 17th *The Sunday Pictorial* ran an exclusive interview with Stephen Ward, which was a potpourri of titillating insinuations — gay young Christine, 'romances', country-house parties, MI5, 'MPs and leading industrialists', Ivanov — the one missing name was, of course, Profumo. (It was subsequently claimed this article was in exchange for some letters between Christine and Profumo). On the 20th *The Daily Mail* ran a front-page story on a Commons question concerning Keeler's disappearance, and another entitled 'MPs, Rumour and Mr. Profumo'.

On the 21st the Commons was debating the case of the two imprisoned journalists, when suddenly a Labour MP got to his feet and called on the Home Secretary to answer the 'rumour involving a member of the Government front bench'. At last it had been said. The next day Mr. Profumo answered it publicly himself. No, there had been no impropriety in his relationship with Miss Keeler. No, he was not involved in her disappearance — but most emphatically he would not 'hesitate to issue writs for libel and slander if scandalous allegations are made or repeated outside this House'.

The British press fell silent — unlike the foreign press which became more voluble than ever — even when on May 21 Stephen Ward issued a statement to them saying he had 'placed before the Home Secretary certain facts of the relationship between Miss Keeler and Mr. Profumo, since it is obvious now that my efforts to conceal these facts . . . have made it appear that I myself have something to hide'. Labour MPs, though, were not to be gagged: they compiled a dossier for their leader, Harold Wilson, to take direct to the Prime Minister and gave notice of private questions which demanded an answer. The House broke up for Whitsun — on its return it learned that Profumo had resigned, admitting and regretting his lie to the House of Commons. The Prime Minister's reply, understandably in the circumstances, was a curt acknowledgement.

The Press couldn't wait to underline the moral for its readers. *The Times* affirmed 'It is perfectly easy to understand the reluctance of people in any kind of authority to reveal information which would disclose error or weakness. What is serious is the public apathy in the face of all this. We need a new attitude on the part of the public, because it is they who ought to be dissatisfied if they are not getting the news'. Or as *The Daily Sketch* explained to a different section of the public: 'Authority tries to sway the people with cries of "Irresponsible" when stories it dislikes are printed. But the truth is that the fight of the newspapers for liberty is your fight, too. For Democracy and a free press cannot be divided'. Or as *The Washington News* put it bluntly: 'We can think of no better time for an American President to stay as far as possible away from England'.

THE TIMES said it yesterday. THE MIRROR agrees with every word..

IT IS HAPPENING HERE

"THE predominant note in the letters The Times has received about the two imprisoned journalists has been that of hostility to the Press.

The bitterness has gone far beyond what could be justified by a reasonable reading of the published proceedings of the Vassall tribunal.

It has overflowed and at times sought to sweep away the principle at stake in these cases. They have broken the dam to a long pent-up, ever rising, flood of resentment against the practices of some newspapers.

Intrusion, triviality, distortion, muck-raking, the inversion of values—the list of offences is long. They are real offences.

The newspapers were warned years ago that if they went on the way they were going they would end by alienating those very sections of society upon whose good will the freedom and the working conventions of the Press depend. This has now happened.

GRAVE

What makes the business so grave is the degree of ignorance, complacency and apathy towards the particular dangers perpetually threatening every free society that now stands revealed.

There really are people who believe that the encroachments of authority, the corruption of society, and maladministration can safely be left to the powers-that-be to put right.

There seem to be even more who are convinced, though on what evidence is not clear, that after centuries of questioning, evolution, and amendment, the Law has at last reached so perfect a state that it must no longer, even on a matter of the deepest conscience, be defied.

★ ★ ★

There is the assertion that such defiance can never be right. There are denials that our liberties can ever be preserved or enlarged by such means.

And all this is taking place in

● Reprinted from
THE TIMES
yesterday

a society that is supposed to be the most widely educated Britain has yet had, which has the means to be the best informed about the story of its past, and to which the crumbling of freedom among so many peoples during the past half-century should have taught inescapable lessons

Part of the rot is shown by the accusations of exaggeration and hysteria against anyone who sees the issue in such terms. How ridiculous to imagine that in Britain anything could ever go seriously wrong. The truth is that in a quiet way very much is going seriously wrong.

POWER

The Executive has taken over power from Parliament. It rules, or fails to rule, by a tacit agreement with outside forces in the community that their authority also shall not be challenged. The administrators at all levels decide more and more without the citizen having effective redress.

Many ways of thought in the Law are restrictive, secretive, and hamper efforts to preserve the true public interest.

And all these hazards are faced by a middle-class that, either through comparative affluence, weariness, or disgust, has thrown in its hand or lost sight of its responsibilities

Grant all this—so runs a strong line of thought—that still does not give the Press any position or competence to put things right. Who are journalists to regard themselves as the censors of power?

Whatever may have been the role of newspapers in the past, they have long since forfeited any right to confidence or respect. Newspapers are now run to

---

make money New means of expression and communication have arrived that are more effective.

Even if there used to be a convention whereby sources of information were preserved from disclosure, it is now unnecessary and out of date

The answers to these arguments are what they have always been. Journalists have no authority beyond that of other citizens

They do have in their hands an instrument which, when courageously and responsibly used, has so far proved in free societies to be the most effective in informing, in promoting discussion, in exposing error and malpractice, and in preserving liberties.

CHALLENGE

Acting responsibly, moreover, is not a matter of obeying authority or accepting unchallenged what the lawyers say. It is to put first things first and to have a declarable reason for any challenge.

Admittedly newspapers have to make money; Parliament was concerned not so long ago lest some of them could not make enough to survive.

Some proprietors may put that object uppermost (Let it be said there is as great a proportion of these in the provinces as in London.)

That should not obscure the fact that the greater part of journalism does have an active conception of public service, and that is sometimes true even among those who have the oddest way of showing it.

The new media have their attractions: their nature precludes them from fulfilling the role of the Press.

★ ★ ★

Satire is not enough Authority will, for the time being at any rate, accept a few snooks as a cheap price to pay for the prohibitions it has been able to enforce in all countries without exception upon sound broadcasting and television.

The lesson of the events of the past month is that, in the final analysis, the only people who can preserve the freedom of the Press are the journalists themselves. It will not be done by the Law or by Government; it cannot be done by Parliament.

It is mistaken escapism to believe the responsibility can be concentrated in a Press Council. Neither taste nor ethics can be authoritarianly laid down.

The way journalists behave, the

---

spirit in which they go about their business, and the kind of business they go about are what will be decisive.

This does not mean they can never be brash but must always be genteel, never rebellious but always docile. It does mean their seeming excesses should be for some discernible conception of the public good, and their manners be at least tolerable.

This is in essence one side of the contract a free society makes with its journalists There is also the other.

★ ★ ★

This is the recognition that the effective discharge of their duties, however self-chosen, depends upon certain freedoms or conventions. And among the most important of these is that journalists shall receive information from sources which they will withhold from all questioning because if there were ever the slightest doubt about this many other sources also would dry up.

Far more serious than anything that has been uncovered about the behaviour of any journalist in the Vassall case is the inability of so many people to see this need, or to accept it as valid even when it is recognised

From the incredibly naive, who say that any source that will not bear disclosure is untrustworthy, to the ultra-sophisticated, who assert that it would be quite easy to pick and choose among the occasions when sources should or should not be revealed, there is all too wide a strand of opinion that cannot, or will not, acknowledge what is at stake.

RIGHTS

This is the preservation of the rights of every individual citizen against the usurpations of every form of authority, the ensuring of efficient and beneficent administration and of good government, and the defence of society against those forces that would corrupt it.

It is not an arrogant claim on the part of the Press to have a role to play on this stage. Traditionally, and by the means at its disposal and the nature of its responsibilities, it has. Large sections of opinion would now apparently deny this, or would wish so to hobble the Press as to make it ineffective

If some things that have happened have shown that a part of the Press is sick this desire, and so much acquiescence in it, shows much of public opinion is bemused

Never is a nation so vulnerable as when those sections of it which should be well informed and are inherently progressive lose their way because of the weeds."

Death of Churchill

THE TIMES

No. 56,228 LATE LONDON EDITION LONDON MONDAY JANUARY 25 1965 PRICE SIXPENCE

SIR WINSTON CHURCHILL DIES

Highlights of his Career

Born : November 30, 1874
Entered Harrow : 1888
Commissioned in the 4th Hussars : 1895
Escaped from the Boers : 1899
Entered Parliament : 1900
Under-Secretary of State for the Colonies : 1905
President of the Board of Trade : 1908
Home Secretary : 1910
First Lord of the Admiralty : 1911
Chancellor of the Duchy of Lancaster : 1915
Rejoined the Army in France : 1915
Minister of Munitions : 1917
Secretary of State for War and Air : 1919
Secretary for the Colonies : 1921-22
Chancellor of the Exchequer : 1924-29
First Lord of the Admiralty : 1939
Prime Minister and Minister of Defence : 1940
Leader of the Opposition : 1945
Prime Minister : 1951
Retirement from Office : 1955
Retired from Parliament : 1964

THE GREATEST ENGLISHMAN OF HIS TIME

WORLD LEADER IN WAR AND PEACE

Sir Winston Churchill, whose death in London yesterday is reported on the centre page, led Great Britain from the peril of subjugation by the Nazi tyranny to victory; and during the last four years of his active political life he directed his country's efforts to maintain peace with honour, to resist another tyranny, and to avert a war more terrible than the last. In character, intellect, and talent he had the attributes of greatness.

An indifferent schoolboy, he was indifferent at nothing else which he attempted. Inheriting Lord Randolph Churchill's energy and political fearlessness, and being granted twice as many years, he carried to fulfilment a genius that in his father showed only brilliant promise. Leader of men and multitudes, strategist, statesman of high authority in the councils of nations, orator with a command of language that matched the grandeur of his themes, able parliamentary tactician, master of historical narrative, his renown is assured so long as the story of these lands is told.

The great war leader of his age, he lived through the fastest transformation of warfare the world has ever known, charging with the 21st Lancers at Omdurman in his youth, and in his old age arming his country with the hydrogen bomb.

He first entered Parliament in the sixty-fourth year of the reign of Queen Victoria. Sixty-four years later, in the thirteenth year of the reign of her great-great-granddaughter, he retired from it. Through more than half a century of British history there was not a year—barely a month—in which he was not actively and prominently engaged in public affairs.

Churchill's outstanding political virtue, which never deserted him, was his courage. There was the sheer physical courage which led him to seek more risks on active service before he was 25 than many professional soldiers know in a lifetime; and which gave him the will, when he was past 75, to overcome an affliction which would have laid other men low from the start. But there was moral and intellectual courage in equal degree. He served in Kitchener's Army in the Sudan—but attacked Kitchener publicly for his desecration of the Mahdi's tomb. He was returned as a Conservative in the "Khaki Election" of 1900—only to devote a passage in his maiden speech to a generous tribute to the Boers. No sooner was his maiden speech over than he shocked the Conservative front bench again by turning on one of his own party leaders, the Secretary of State for War, with a scorn which would have been startling even in a member of the Opposition.

Change of Party

He was still under 30 when, finding himself at odds with the tariff reform policy of Joseph Chamberlain, he crossed the floor of the House. So it continued all through his life—the habit of following his own judgment, his own intuition, and his own impulses. When he resigned from the Conservative "Shadow Cabinet" in 1931, as a protest against its attitude to India, he was acting with the same courage and independence which—they were inherited from his father—he had displayed from the very beginning. His independence frequently baffled his contemporaries, who tended to conclude, as did Margot Asquith in 1908, that he was a man of "transitory convictions". But the point is not that they were transitory but that they were his own. His mind was always restlessly surveying the political scene. He was for ever testing, courting, encouraging new ideas. No politician of this century has been less conservative and less hidebound.

This adventurousness, of course, had its disadvantages, of which his colleagues were often painfully aware. His mind never stopped roaming, and Asquith's Cabinet was described by one of its members as "very forbearing to his chatter". During the 1939-45 War—as the famous memoranda published as appendices to his history of *The Second World War* show—any question however trivial or however far removed from the central direction of the war might gain his attention. He seized on new ideas so indiscriminately that it became necessary for some of those closest to him to act as a sieve, and so prevent valuable time from being wasted on the wilder schemes. Yet, when the dross had fallen through, there remained in the sieve one or two nuggets. There is in Printing House Square a letter written early in the 1914-18 War by a high personage accusing Churchill of madness because of some impracticable scheme which he was pressing through in the face of much expert opposition. The "scheme" was the tank.

The independence of his ideas always made it difficult to define Churchill's political position. He was more of a Tory than a Conservative. The symbols of Toryism—Crown, Country, Empire—which might seem abstractions to some were to him realities. There was, indeed, always a personal element in the service he gave to his Sovereigns, which found quite different expressions in his attitude to the abdication of Edward VIII and in the tributes he paid when George VI died and Queen Elizabeth II was crowned. But it was a Toryism infused by another abstraction which to him was equally a reality: the People. He believed deeply that the People existed - not different and warring classes of people. In an earlier age he would have stood committed to the idea of the King and the People against the great Whig magnates—the cardinal principle of Disraelian Toryism. He was, in brief, a Tory Democrat, and in a speech to the Conservative conference in 1953 he proclaimed again the creed of his father, the first prophet of Tory Democracy.

Sense of History

Least of all was he a "Little Englander". No statesman has ever been more aware of his country's position in the world and its responsibility to the world. It was not merely his awareness of the facts of Germany's rearmament which made him speak so clearly from the beginning of the thirties: it was, even more (as befitted a descendant of Marlborough), his fundamental assumption that Britain was a part of Europe. He could no more have talked of Czechoslovakia as a far-away country than of Blenheim and Ramillies as far-away towns.

His politics were infused with a sense of history. It was a common gibe of his opponents that he lived in the past—that he was, in the words of Harold Laski, a "gallant and romantic relic of eighteenth-century imperialism". Nothing could be farther from the truth. He was as aware of the present, its opportunities and its challenges, as any of his contemporaries. But he drew from the past a profound conviction in the greatness of Britain, her people and her heritage. Romantic? It may be. But it was from this reserve that he drew the inspiration which he communicated to his fellow-countrymen in their and his finest hour. He was the symbol of British resistance, but of how much more as well. In his voice spoke the centuries which had made Britain as they had made him, and those who heard him in those days will never forget the echoes of Burghley, of Chatham, of Pitt, and countless more. "The last of the great orators to reach the heights."

The Right Honourable Sir Winston Leonard Spencer-Churchill, K.G., O.M., C.H., F.R.S., was born on St. Andrew's Day, 1874, at Blenheim Palace. He was the elder son of Lord Randolph Churchill and a grandson of the seventh Duke of Marlborough. His mother was the beautiful and talented daughter of Leonard Jerome, a New York businessman. Surviving her husband until 1921, she lived to see her son's fame firmly established.

Soldier and Journalist

The year had been an eventful one for Lord Randolph. Apart from his marriage and the birth of a son and heir, it had begun with his election as Conservative M.P. for Woodstock and included a maiden speech which drew from Disraeli, who had a good eye for a duke's son, a warm commendation. Lord Randolph's rise to power and influence was to be rapid, but his decline was even more rapid, and when he died in 1895 he left his son with memories of defeat and failure which carried a moral he was often to remember. Winston Churchill's education was conventional in its pattern: from a preparatory school at Ascot, to a small school at Brighton, to Harrow in 1888, and then, after twice failing to gain admission, to the Royal Military College at Sandhurst. But his verdict on Harrow was individual, for he left there, as he later confessed, convinced that he was "all for the public schools, but I do not want to go there again".

In 1895, soon after his father's death, he entered the 4th Hussars at Aldershot, and immediately obtained leave to go to Cuba for the *Daily Graphic* to watch the Spanish Army at work. While he was there he participated in the repulse of the insurgents who tried to cross the Spanish line at Trocham. After enjoying the London Season in 1896 he embarked for India, where he relieved the monotony of morning parades and evening polo by indulging his delight in reading. He was back in London for the Season in 1897, and then left in September to join the Malakand Field Force on the North-West Frontier of India. After being mentioned in dispatches for "making himself useful at a critical moment", he had to return to the 4th Hussars at Bangalore early in 1898, and there he occupied himself with the writing of his first history, *The Story of the Malakand Field Force*, which had considerable success at the time and is still consulted.

While he was at Bangalore he also wrote his only novel, *Savrola, a Tale of the Revolution in Laurania*, which he later urged his friends not to read. It contained, however, the sentence which seems to be as autobiographical as any he wrote: "Under any circumstances, in any situation, Savrola knew himself a factor to be reckoned with; whatever the game, he would play it to his amusement, if not to his advantage." During these early years Lieutenant Churchill, enjoying a liberty not likely to be granted nowadays to a serving officer, was able to combine the roles of a soldier and a newspaper correspondent, and it was as the representative of the *Morning Post* that at last, after three rebuffs from Kitchener, he joined the Sirdar's Army in Sudan. He reached Cairo in time to take part in the advance south into the Mahdi's country, and was present at the final victory at Omdurman.

Prisoner of the Boers

The strategy, tactics, and what a later generation has learnt to call the logistics of the campaign were set out by Churchill in *The River War, an Account of the Reconquest of the Sudan*, which was immediately successful when it was published in 1899. His early military writings showed a grasp, remarkable in a man of his years, of the operations of war, which was best revealed in the clear separation of the essential from the accidental. They were also distinguished by a dogmatic self-confidence which never hesitated in its criticism of senior officers. His outspokenness did not improve his prospects and he was doubtless wise to resign his commission after wearing the Queen's uniform for only four years. Moreover, his success as a journalist had enabled him to think of giving up the Army as a career, and he had even turned his attention to politics, addressing a Conservative garden party at Bath (his first political speech) and fighting a by-election (unsuccessfully) at Oldham.

It was as a correspondent, again for the *Morning Post*, that he left for South Africa within a fortnight of the outbreak of war in the autumn of 1899. There he met with sensational adventures very much to his taste. Taken prisoner on an armoured train expedition by a Boer by the name of Louis Botha he succeeded in escaping from the prison camp at Pretoria within three weeks, "jumped" a train, and after an extraordinary journey reached Delagoa Bay. He saw the campaign out until he could reenter Pretoria with the victorious Army, and when he returned to England he was received tumultuously at Oldham, where, in the "Khaki Election" of 1900, he won the seat from Walter Runciman. He was not yet 26, and contemporary accounts record that Joseph Chamberlain sat up and nudged his neighbour on the front bench when, in his maiden speech, Churchill declared: "If I were a Boer fighting in the field—and if I were a Boer, I hope I should be fighting in the field. . . ."

Tariff Reform

Chamberlain was right to take notice: there was an ominous smack about the words, and in his first session in the House not only did Churchill speak vehemently against the Conservative Government's plans for Army reform—and their unfortunate advocate, Mr. Brodrick—but he voted against them as well. His unorthodoxy had deep roots. He was at work on his life of his father, who had remained in a party with whose orthodox leaders he was at war and had suffered in the end only isolation and defeat. At the very beginning of his political career Churchill was in much the same position. He was as much a Tory Democrat as his father, in a party led by Balfour, who had always seemed to Lord Randolph to be the main opponent of Tory Democracy. Moreover, there was little intellectual adventure to be found in the Conservative Party of 1902, and Churchill, who always retained a great respect for the academic and cultured intellect, felt drawn to the company of Morley, Asquith, Haldane, and Grey.

Then, in the summer of 1903, Joseph Chamberlain made his great effort to revive protection—"playing Old Harry with all party relations", as Campbell-Bannerman excitedly remarked. With the Duke of Devonshire and Lord Hugh Cecil, Churchill declared himself a Unionist Free Trader, and by September, when it became clear that the Protectionists in the Cabinet had won, he was publicly exclaiming to a meeting at Halifax, "Thank God for the Liberal Party". Not unreasonably, the Oldham Conservative Association took exception to this and disowned him, and in the following year he crossed the floor of the House. How many who were there on that May 31, 1904, could foresee the irony in the incident as Churchill took his seat by the side of none other than David Lloyd George?

Before the end of 1905 Churchill had completed the life of his father. It stands, over half a century later, as one of the most brilliant political biographies of all time. The prose was perhaps never excelled by Churchill—later in his life the influence of the platform and the House of Commons made his prose too rhetorical—and the bringing to life of the political scene is so vividly and precisely done that the reader never loses his interest.

No sooner was this work of filial vindication done than Balfour—after months of trying to pacify his party and the House by "expressing no settled conviction where no settled conviction exists"—threw in his hand, and Campbell-Bannerman took office. Churchill accepted the office of Under-Secretary of State for the Colonies and was the spokesman of his department in the House of Commons. A month later, at the general election, Churchill was returned as a Liberal for North West Manchester while Balfour was defeated in the adjacent seat. In the House it fell to him to maintain the Government's decision to grant full self-government to the annexed Boer Republics—a controversial issue—and he began to develop his parliamentary style in the thick of a major parliamentary battle. At the same time his mind was moving to a new outlook on home affairs. Before leaving the Conservative Party he had looked back to the time "when it was not the sham it is now, and was not afraid to deal with the problem of the working classes". Now he confidently declared that the Liberal Party's cause was "the cause of the left-out millions".

He was a Radical, describing the obstructive attitude of the House of

At Hyde Park Gate on his ninetieth birthday.

Lords as "something very like an incitement to violence". In 1908, when Asquith succeeded Campbell-Bannerman, Churchill was promoted to the Cabinet as Lloyd George's successor at the Board of Trade, having turned down the Local Government Board on the ground that he refused "to be shut up in a soup-kitchen with Mrs. Sidney Webb". Under the law then still in force his promotion forced him to submit himself for reelection and a tempestuous by-election ended in his defeat by Mr. Joynson-Hicks. But he was found a seat at Dundee, and he returned to London, his official career uninterrupted, to marry Miss Clementine Hozier.

In the political field he became a less conspicuous figure in the House of Commons, but in the country was second only to Lloyd George in his advocacy of the new Liberalism. A natural association developed between these two dissimilar men. Side by side they tried to check the rising naval expenditure, for, war-leaders though they were both to be, in 1908-09 their whole interest was focused on the first experiments in the "welfare state".

Bitter Attack

Churchill hesitated for a moment when Lloyd George introduced his People's Budget in 1909, but then threw himself into the fight in the country. Bitterly he denounced the House of Lords—especially the backwoods peers "all revolving the problems of Empire and Epsom"—and as president of the Budget League he enthusiastically praised the social policies which had made the Budget necessary. There were Conservatives who, though they could have overlooked his treason to his party in 1904, never could forgive his treason to his class, as they saw it, in 1909. They were later to have their revenge. He was now becoming—though still only 35—one of the leading members of the Government. In Cabinet, where one of his colleagues thought him "as long-winded as he was persistent", he distributed long memoranda to the rest of the members on all subjects—however far removed from the affairs of his own department. (In the Board of Trade he was teaching his subordinates the duties which now belong to the Ministry of Labour.) "Winston", recorded Grey, "will very soon become incapable from sheer activity of mind of being anything in a Cabinet but a Prime Minister."

After the bitter general election of 1910 Churchill was promoted to the Home Office, where his interest in the future welfare of prisoners helped to launch the movement for penal reform. But the most famous episode of his term at the Home Office was the Sidney Street "siege", which he characteristically insisted on witnessing personally. Germany's intervention in Morocco had made it imperative to put a term to the controversy over the British naval programme which was dividing the Liberal Party, and Asquith took what proved to be the decisive step of inviting the First Lord of the Admiralty (Reginald McKenna) and the Home Secretary to exchange offices. Churchill went to the Admiralty, with a mandate to maintain the Fleet in constant readiness for war with Germany.

Preparing for War

Germany's threat had completely changed Churchill's attitude to naval and military armaments, and he became (as 25 years later) a powerful advocate of preparedness, so much losing his interest in party differences and social policies that Lloyd George said he was apt to approach him with "Look here, David", and then "declaim for the rest of the afternoon about his blasted ships". In fact, the post exactly suited Churchill's temperament and gifts. His speeches in introduction of the Navy Estimates rank with Gladstone's Budgets as classical expositions of the relationship of policy to departmental practice. In the face of considerable service opposition he created a Naval War Staff. At weekends and when the House was in recess he familiarized himself with the work of the Navy, going everywhere, seeing everything, and exercising a magnificent judgment in his selection of officers.

When war came Churchill mobilized the Fleet on his own responsibility, forcing from Morley a sad reflection on "the splendid *condottiere* at the Admiralty". But two years later, when he was dismissed to satisfy the Conservative Party leaders, Kitchener took to him the personal message: "Well,

The Moon Landing

Not everyone in the world was happy when astronauts Armstrong and Aldrin of the Apollo 11 mission touched down on the moon in their module Eagle. One angry gentleman telephoned the Houston control centre complaining that man's first landing on the moon had caused it to set earlier than usual over his home. All the same, as Neil Armstrong eloquently declared as his boot hit the first lunar dust – 'that's one small step for man; one giant leap for mankind'. This was news the press had been preparing for since Commander Alan Shepard had made the first American flight into space in May 1961. And here, almost predictably, was the first man on the moon saluting the Stars and Stripes, chatting to the President and picking up lumps of purple rock from the dead planet. Here, by any standards was the greatest news story of the decade; and even if Red China was studiously ignoring the tremendous feat, it had the Pope's blessing, they were dancing in the streets of Chile and millions upon millions, from Japan to Yugoslavia were sitting glued to their television trying to make sense of the fuzzy blurs which purported to be historic pictures from the moon. But, if it was not an unequivocable triumph for the miracle of television (yet), neither could it have been any great consolation to the press. Wherever else newsmen had succeeded in penetrating, they could not get to the moon. Even the front-page pictures had been seen in millions of homes the night before. Yet nor was it a defeat. Was it one's imagination, or did the fantastic achievement seem truer the next morning, after one had read it in the papers – there in black and white?

COUNT DOWN
First men land on moon

Good Evening

Weather
NORTHWEST OHIO: Partly sunny today with the highs in the upper 70s and lower 80s. Fair tonight and Tuesday with little change in temperature. Lows tonight in the 60s. Highs Tuesday from middle 70s to 80s.

Wapakoneta Daily News

UPI—EXCLUSIVE WIRE SERVICE DAILY—NEW YORK TIMES SERVICE

PHONES
Business 8-3318
News 8-2128

VOLUME 65 NUMBER 14 | News Department Phone 738-2128 | WAPAKONETA, OHIO (Over 17,000 Readers Daily) | MONDAY, JULY 21, 1969 | News Department Phone 738-2128 | Single Copy—55c a Week

NEIL STEPS ON THE MOON

"All people one," Nixon tells pair

WASHINGTON (UPI)—President Nixon, in a telephone call to the moon, told astronauts Neil A. Armstrong and Edwin E. Aldrin Sunday night they have brought all mankind closer together.

"For one priceless moment in the whole history of man all the people on this earth are truly one. One in their pride in what you have done and one in our prayers that you will return safely to earth," Nixon said.

"Thank you, Mr. President, it's a great honor and privilege for us to be here representing not only the United States but men of peace of all nations, men with interest and curiosity, and men with the vision for the future," Armstrong replied, his voice tinged with emotion.

Capsule communicator Bruce McCandless, the astranaut's contact with mission control, asked Armstrong and Aldrin to both move into camera range shortly before Nixon spoke to the astronauts.

"The President of the United States is in his office now and he would like to say a few words to you," McCandless said.

"That would be an honor," Armstrong said.

"Go ahead, Mr. President, this is Houston, out," McCandless said.

"Hello Neil and Buzz. I'm talking to you by telephone from the Oval Room at the White House. And, this certainly has to be the most historic telephone call ever made," Nixon said.

"I just can't tell you how proud we all are. . .for every American this has to be the proudest day of our lives. And, for people all over the world I am sure they too join with Americans in recognizing what an immense feat this is.

"Because of what you have done the heavens have become a part of man's world. And, as you talk to us from the Sea of Tranquillity it inspires us to redouble our efforts to bring peace and tranquility to earth."

Moments before Nixon made his call to the astronauts, they unfurled the American flag, planting it on the moon surface on an aluminum staff.

Nixon made the call on a green telephone while sitting at his large ornate desk in the Oval Room. Flags were on his left and bowl of flowers was on the table behind him.

Navy beefs up armada in Pacific

ABOARD USS HORNET (UPI)—The Navy today ordered extra ships and aircraft deployed in the Apollo 11 splashdown zone as a safeguard for the visit of President Nixon.

The Chief Executive was scheduled to greet the astronauts following their recovery in the mid-Pacific Thursday by this aging aircraft carrief.

Meanwhile, space agency officials aboard the ship ordered a final practice exercise today.

NASA officials released a detailed schedule for recovery day, starting at 4:2o a.m. ship time when helicopters and radar planes will leave the flight deck for their assigned positions.

The extra precautions for Nixon were ordered by Pacific Fleet headquarters in Honolulu, some 1,040 miles nor heast of the recovery area. The President is scheduled to fly from Johnston Island by helicopter Wednesday evening and stay overnight aboard the communications ship USS Arlington.

Early Thursday, the Chief Executive will take another helicopter trip to the Hornet in time to witness the reentry and 12:51 p.m. splashdown.

The Navy ordered the guided missile destroyer USS Goldsborough to a position between the Arlington and Hornet. The destroyer USS Carpenter will be deployed between the Arlington and Johnston Island, 450 miles northeast of the recovery zone.

Additional protection will include a Navy Super Constellation from Guam, an Air Force HC130 from Hawaii, a helicopter carrying Navy swimmers and a radar plane from the Hornet.

The President's three-hour schedule aboard the Hornet includes breakfast, then a chat by intercom with the astronauts, who will be sealed inside a shiny aluminum quarantine trailer on the hangar deck.

Breathless wives watch

HAPPY COUPLE GREETS PRESS — Mr. and Mrs. Stephen Armstrong, parents of Commander Neil Armstrong of the Apollo 11 mission, were joyous Sunday night when they met the press and were interviewed on television. The couple emerged from their home after their son, Neil, had emerged from the lunar lander to become the first man in history to set foot on the moon.

"Moon trip answers challenge"

350 gather for services

WAPAKONETA, Ohio (UPI)—Worshipers at Neil Armstrong's hometown church paid tribute to the first man on the moon Sunday by singing new lyrics for two favorite humns.

To the tune of "Arise, The Kingdom is at Hand," the congregation at the St. Paul United Church of Christ sang:

"They blaze a pathway to the moon,
The heroes of the hour
They make the outer darkness feel
Man's growing mighty power
They move through God's enormous home
Of stars and worlds and space
Away beyond this earth we know
And still within his grace."

To the tune of "Hymn to Joy," they sang:

"Come, oh Lord of all creation,
God of worlds in outer space,
By Whose help through automation
We explore in every place..."

Pastor Herman Weber said Sunday in his sermon that the moon mission proved God wanted man to have a "significant place" in the universe.

He told his congregation mankind always was under "tremendous challenges" from God.

"The moon trip is one way of answering the challenge," he stated.

The little white church near the downtown section was filled to capacity with about 350 friends of the astronaut's parents, Mr. and Mrs. Stephen Armstrong, who also attended services.

"As insignificant as we seem in the light of God's power, we have a very significant place in nature," Weber said. "If we cease to be challenged by new frontiers we will become stagnant."

Timetable

1:51 p.m.—Liftoff of ascent stage of lunar modulel, boost to intermediate rendezvous.

2:49 p.m.—LM raises orbit for rendezvous with command module.

5:11 p.m.—LM and CM rendezvous and dock.

9:2. p.m.—LM is jettisoned and abandoned.

Tuesday

12:53 a.m. EDT—Command module fires its main engine to break out of moon gravity and start trip homeward.

Armstrong, Aldrin set for hazardous return

BULLETIN PRECEDE

SPACE CENTER, Houston (UPI)—Nail A. Armstrong and Edwin E. Aldrin launched off the moon at 1:54 p.m. EDT today in the Eagle, ending a lunar surface stay of 21 hours 36 minutes.

By EDWARD K. DELONG
UPI Space Writer

SPACE CENTER, Houston (UPI)—America's two moon pioneers, winding up the first exploration of the moon, gave earthlings a fascinating description today of its ghastly, shattered surface.

Near the Sea of Tranquillity, where they established the first space base on another world, Western scientists said Russia's Luna 15 might have landed.

Aldrin and Armstrong were given a long rest after taking the first human steps on the moon, planting the American flag in the dust-covered surface where their Eagle spaceship touched down late Sunday and gathering priceless moon nuggets.

At midday they started running over instrument and procedure checks with ground controllers for a liftoff at 1:54 p.m. EDT and the hazardous maneuvers to rejoin Michael Collins, circling above in the main Apollo 11 command ship.

Braking Blast

At Jodrell Bank, England, a spokesman said the indications were that Luna 15, which has been mysteriously circling the moon since Thursday, had fired a braking rocket blast apparently intended to put it down near the Sea of Tranquillity.

Ground controllers awakened Collins at 10:30 a.m. to start the complicated Eagle liftoff and rendezvous operations which will last until all three astronauts are reunited in the Columbia command ship late tonight.

Astronaut James Lovell, commander of the Apollo 11 backup crew, radioed his congratulations today to Armstrong and Aldrin for their moonwalk, seen by millions on television.

"Thank you," Armstrong told him. "We were getting a lot of help down there, Jim."

Then Aldrin radioed a description of the dead and airless lunar landscape where Armstrong spent more than two hours and Aldrin nearly that long—hopping and jumping like slow-motion ballet dancers in a dreamlike, shadowed world.

Many Craters

"We are landed in a relatively smooth crater field," he said. "There are elongated secondary crater fields. Most of them have rims but there are a few which do not have discernible rims. They are covered with very find sand or silt.

"The thing that would be most like it on earth is powdered graphite," Aldrin said.

Mom, dad worries lighter after walk

WAPAKONETA, Ohio (UPI)—The mother of Apollo 11 astronaut Neil Armstrong said today she was concerned her son would "sink in too deeply" when he set foot on the moon.

"I was worried that the moon might be too soft and that he would sink in too deeply," Mrs. Viola Armstrong said. "But I'm so thankful they got there safely."

Mrs. Armstrong said she slept for about only "two hours" early today but felt refreshed.

"I think they are going to be all right now," said Mrs. Armstrong. "I slept for about two hours, but that's all. I hope they're still sleeping. I'm worried they may be cramped and uncomfortable in there."

Mrs. Armstrong said she could tell by her son's voice that he was "pleased, tickled and thrilled" when he uttered man's first words on the lunar surface Sunday night.

She said Neil's words as he stapped on the moon, "One small step for man, one giant leap for mankind," came as a surprise to her.

"Same Old Neil"

Neil's father, Stephen, said, however, "It was the same old Neil."

Mrs. Armstrong said when her son stepped onto the moon a roomful of friends and relatives, watching the historic space venture on television at the Armstrong home in this small western Ohio community, "became absolutely quiet."

When the moon cameras snapped on, Mrs. Armstrong leaned forward in her chair and said, "Oh, there he is."

When Armstrong and fellow astronaut Edwin "Buzz" Aldrin bounced on the lunar surface Mrs. Armstrong said, "He looks like he's having fun."

"I hope this increases man's concept of God," Mr. Armstrong said. "I hope this brings us closer together and does much for man and the world."

"Nice of Nixon"

The elder Armstrong said it was "real nice" of President Nixon to talk with the astronauts on the moon.

He said the Russian Luna 15 spacecraft circling the moon was "uncalled for and unfair." He did not elaborate. Mrs. Armstrong wished the Russians well in their space venture.

Report Luna is on moon

JODRELL BANK, England (UPI) — Jodrell Bank tracking station said today indications were Russia's Luna 15 satellite has landed on the moon.

A spokesman at the station said Jodrell Bank's giant dish antenna detected a rocket blast that evidently was intended to drop the craft out of orbit down toward the lunar surface.

Luna 15 apparently landed on the moon near the Sea of Tranquillity—the vast, desolate plain where America's Apollo 11 astronauts came down Sunday—at 11:50 a.m. EDT today, the spokesman said.

There was no indication immediately how far Luna 15 was from the U.S. Eagle lunar lander carrying astronauts Neil A. Armstrong and Edwin E. Aldrin.

BULLETIN

Governor James Rhodes will arrive in Wapakoneta early this evening to visit with the Stephen Armstrongs, according to wire reports received this afternoon.

The governor will fly in, arriving at the Neil Armstrong airport.

Matter of Responsibility

The Pentagon Papers and the Watergate Affair

When *The New York Times*, on June 13 1971, published the first in a series of extracts from a secret official study of the origins of the Vietnamese War (the 'Pentagon Papers'), America had been intimately involved in the affairs of South Vietnam for 17 years, and virtually inextricably for ten of those years. This involvement was based on a deceptively simple and plausible premise, that communist expansion in South-East Asia had reached alarming proportions, that its containment was beyond the means of local governments without the moral — and if necessary the physical — presence of the United States, that the place to make this stand was in what was still democratically 'free' of Indo-China after the collapse of French imperial power there in 1954. Out of this theory sprang another hypothesis, which came to be known as the 'domino theory' and which strongly influenced American policy in the early 1960s: that if South Vietnam fell, Laos and Cambodia would also fall, that Burma, Malaysia and the Philippines would be threatened, and so on like, of course, a pack of dominoes. To forestall this disagreeable prospect, a policy of 'graduated overt military pressure' (to use the euphemistic Pentagonese) was embarked upon.

By the middle of the '60s this graduated overt military pressure stood revealed as nothing less than total war, which was devouring American men, money and machines at a gargantuan rate. By the summer of 1967 an articulate minority within America was demonstrating its profound disquiet at the manner and depth of U.S. involvement (and the apparently underhand way in which it had come about) in song, on stage, in the streets, on badges proclaiming the superiority of love over war. The "silent" majority continued mutely to support the decisions of the Administration and to suffer increased taxes in what it was assured was a good cause: if any misgivings existed, they were over the patent lack of success that attended this vast outlay. It was in the same year (1967), though very few knew it at the time, that a secret history of the war within the Pentagon was commissioned by Defence Secretary Robert McNamara, who had himself become increasingly uneasy about America's motives in the war and, in particular, about the whole process of decision-making. This study, over $1\frac{1}{2}$ million words or 40 volumes of narrative, reports and memoranda, took a year to prepare and was compiled by 30 or 40 officials of the government (none of whom, however, had access to the White House files).

One of this select band which wrote the history was Daniel Ellsberg, then a member of the Rand Corporation's 'think-tank' in California. Like McNamara, he too had undergone a disillusioned transformation from being a fiercely committed hawk to being a conscientious dove (he later declared that reading parts of the Pentagon Papers to which he had contributed was what finally converted him). Having unlimited access to a report denied even to Congress, he began laboriously to photocopy page after page of it until he possessed the only unauthorized copy in America. The more convinced he became that Nixon's policy in Vietnam would lead to an irrevocable escalation of the war, the more he came to believe that the

public had a right to see how these decisions were being made in its name. Late in 1969 he showed some of the secret documents to the Chairman of the Senate Foreign Relations Committee, Senator Fulbright. But as the months passed the elected representatives remained impotent, or still uninformed. By the beginning of 1971 the Vietnam War had become *the* major issue which threatened to tear the country apart, and irreparably to damage America's prestige abroad (the shock-waves following the revelation of a massacre in the village of My Lai were even then being felt all round the world).

In March 1971 Ellsberg took the plunge: he leaked the report to *The New York Times*, not all the report — he wisely witheld parts relating to sensitive exchanges between Hanoi, Washinton and Moscow — but enough of it to cause a sensation if published. *The New York Times* did publish, two months later, huge incriminating chunks, verbatim. Among other things, the first three instalments showed that for months before the so-called Tonkin Incident (where North Vietnamese gun-boats had allegedly fired, unprovoked, on two U.S. destroyers) which President Johnson had used as justification for escalating the war, America *had* been secretly conducting military operations against North Vietnam: that during the 1964 Presidential campaign, while Johnson was projecting an 'acceptable' image of caution and responsibility against Goldwater's insistence on bombing the North, plans for an air war were actually in the process of being formulated: that the CIA had challenged the validity of the 'domino theory', and that America had deliberately sabotaged the Paris Conference on Laos.

On June 13, 14 and 15 these and other revelations spilled out of the pages of *The New York Times*. On the evening of the 14th John Mitchell, the U.S. Attorney General 'requested' the publishers to refrain from putting out any more extracts — which *The New York Times* respectfully declined to do, 'believing that it is in the interest of the people of this country to be informed of the material contained in this series of articles'. On the 15th, however, the honeymoon ended abruptly, by order of the Federal Court. And at this point began a cat-and-mouse game between American editors, united by this threat to their privileges under the First Amendment, and the Administration's lawyers.

On the 18th *The Washington Post*, having obtained a copy of the report apparently from the same source as *The New York Times*, began publishing its own summary, in essence what *The New York Times* would have printed as its next instalments but for the court injunction. Furthermore *The Washington Post* took the precaution of distributing the copy to more than 300 clients of its syndication service. The news agencies immediately picked up extracts and it wasn't long before every paper in the United States was running part of the Pentagon Papers — including, ludicrously, *The New York Times* which printed the A.P. summary as a news story. The New York paper could now — and did — complain that it was being discriminated against. In reply the Justice Department attempted to show that publication of the documents would be a disaster to national security, and

that they had been obtained by criminal means. The latter point could not be sustained, but on the 23rd the New York court ruled that *The New York Times* could resume publication but could *not* use any material which the government thought posed 'such grave and immediate danger to the security of the United States as to warrant their publication being enjoined'. The next day *The New York Times* appealed to the Supreme Court.

In the District of Columbia, however, the Justice Department was getting a rougher ride. On the 18th the judge ruled that it had no constitutional right to seek prior restraint, its only course would be to bring a criminal prosecution after publication. On the 23rd an appeal by the Justice Department was over-ruled on the grounds that 'The Washington Post had a constitutional right to publish the articles'. Now it was the Justice Department's turn to appeal to the Supreme Court, which delivered its judgement exactly a week later. To the delight of the American press, it announced that government restraints were incompatible with the First Amendment — and both *The New York Times* and *The Washington Post* resumed their interrupted articles on July 1.

Meanwhile, almost eclipsing all this judicial excitement, the newspapers and TV were abuzz with speculation about who had leaked the report in the first instance. According to *Newsweek* 'those privy to the feelings' of ex-President Johnson were saying he 'saw the ghostly hand of Robert Kennedy' in all this (*The New York Times* then revealed that LBJ was putting this story about personally). As early as the 16th a former *New York Times* reporter named Ellsberg as the informant on the radio. The following day Ellsberg went to ground — though later made himself available to CBS for a lengthy interview. The FBI were less successful in bearding Daniel in his den, and on the 25th a warrant was issued for his arrest: on the 28th he gave himself up voluntarily to the Federal authorities in Boston, uncontrite and regretting only that he hadn't released the report long ago. In May 1973 all charges against Ellsberg were dropped, ironically because the Administration itself was alleged to have used the same dubious methods in pursuit of evidence as those with which Ellsberg was accused.

Before Daniel Ellsberg was finally acquitted of all charges (for lack of evidence) in spring 1973, a potentially far more dangerous storm burst over the White House. In summer 1972, while the election bandwaggons were rolling, five men were caught red-handed breaking into the Democratic Party's Watergate headquarters in the process of 'bugging' the whole building. Seven men were charged, including Howard Hunt, a former aide to Mr. Nixon, and Gordon Liddy and James McCord, senior officials of the President's election campaign.

In spite of what Senator McGovern called 'the collapse of morality in the White House', Mr. Nixon was swept back into office — but his problems had hardly begun. Even before he was inaugurated, the *Washington Post* began a painstaking enquiry into the scandal and cover-up (two of its reporters were later awarded the Pulitzer Prize for their work), and found itself increasingly ostracised by the government.

JUDGE, AT REQUEST OF U.S., HALTS TIMES VIETNAM SERIES FOUR DAYS PENDING HEARING ON INJUNCTION

PUBLIC WORKS BILL CLEARS CONGRESS; VETO THREATENED

House Votes 275 to 104 for a $2-Billion Program to Help the Unemployed

By MARJORIE HUNTER
Special to The New York Times

WASHINGTON, June 15—Ignoring threats of a Presidential veto, the House gave final Congressional approval today to a $5.5-billion economic development bill embracing a $2-billion program to create jobs for the unemployed.

Joining an almost solid Democratic majority in approving the bill were 65 Republicans, most of them from areas of high unemployment. The final vote was 275 to 104.

The measure cleared the Senate last week by a nearly party-line vote, 44 to 33.

Republican leaders warned that inclusion of a $2-billion public works program in what they termed an otherwise acceptable measure would almost certainly bring a veto by President Nixon.

Aid Programs Extended

In addition to the public works program, the bill would do the following:

¶Extend for four years, at a cost of $1.5-billion, the 14-state Appalachian regional development programs for highway construction, housing, education, health and airport safety.

¶Extend for two years, at a cost of $1.9-billion, the Public Works and Economic Development Act, under which other regional commissions receive Federal grants and loans to upgrade their economies.

Only the emergency public

U.S. Plans Ways to Bolster Saigon for '72 Enemy Push

By WILLIAM BEECHER
Special to The New York Times

WASHINGTON, June 15—The Nixon Administration is engaged in a broad policy review aimed at determining courses of action that might improve South Vietnam's ability to withstand military assaults next year, after most American forces have been withdrawn.

"In my view," one senior Government planner said, "this is the most important review we've made since the decision to pull out the first troops two years ago."

The review is being conducted against a backdrop of increased Congressional demands to speed up the disengagement process and of budgetary pressures to cut costs in the war zone.

Other key developments include an estimate by the National Security Council that North Vietnam is building toward a new offensive in the South next year. The Administration is also concerned about the effects a major South Vietnamese military defeat in the spring of 1972 might have on Republican fortunes in the

U.S. May Block Contract To Import Algerian Gas

By TAD SZULC
Special to The New York Times

WASHINGTON, June 15 — The White House is delaying, and may possibly block, approval for import to the United States of liquefied natural gas from Algeria under a 25-year contract signed last year by a Texas corporation.

If approved, the contract, which involves investments of

Presidential election in November.

Well-placed Administration sources disclose that, against the expected North Vietnamese threat, officials are focusing on the following major questions:

¶How rapidly can most of the remaining United States forces be withdrawn after the 184,000-man level is reached on Dec. 1? Many planners expect President Nixon to scale down to a residual force of 30,000 to 70,000 men by July 1, 1972, but to leave enough flexibility in the pace of reductions so that many of them can be timed for May and June.

¶Should this residual force include many helicopter and artillery units to "stiffen" South Vietnamese defenses, or should it be made up primarily of advisers to Saigon's forces plus large numbers of supply teams to pack up the billions of dollars, worth of weapons and equipment that are to be returned home?

¶Should all or most of the

Continued on Page 15, Column 1

mission expressing concurrence with the contract, which is between El Paso Natural Gas Company and Sonatrach, the Algerian oil and gas state monopoly.

Mr. Flanigan intervened just as the letters were ready to be sent out.

SENATE STUDY SET

Roots of Involvement Sought—Disclosure Worries Rogers

By JOHN W. FINNEY
Special to The New York Times

WASHINGTON, June 15—Amid continuing Administration criticism of the publication by The New York Times of data from a secret Pentagon study on Vietnam, Senator Mike Mansfield said a Senate committee would hold public hearings on how the United States had become involved in the war.

The Senate Majority Leader told newsmen that he had been "surprised, shocked and astounded" by the revelations in the documents printed by The Times largely because it was now apparent that the Lyndon B. Johnson Administration had made the crucial decision to enlarge the war in Vietnam without informing Congress.

At a State Department news conference, Secretary of State William P. Rogers said the publication of the material was "a very serious matter" that was going to cause "a great deal of difficulty" in relations with foreign governments. These, he said, will question whether they can deal with the United States on a confidential basis.

No Comment From Johnson

In Texas, a spokesman for former President Johnson said that Mr. Johnson would have no comment on the Pentagon study under his policy of not granting interviews.

In Atlanta, the secretary of former Secretary of State Dean Rusk said that he also would have no comment.

Senator Mansfield, who heads

ARGUMENT FRIDAY

Court Here Refuses to Order Return of Documents Now

By FRED P. GRAHAM

United States District Judge Murray I. Gurfein yesterday ordered The New York Times to halt publication of material from a secret Pentagon study of the Vietnam war for four days. Argument on publication thereafter will be heard Friday.

The judge granted a request by the Justice Department for temporary relief, but he gave no hint as to how he would

Text of complaint and court restraining order, Page 18.

eventually rule. He also refused to order The Times to return the massive report immediately to the Government.

Declaring that the case could be an important one in the history of relations between the Government and the press, Judge Gurfein said that any temporary harm done to The Times by his order "is far outweighed by the irreparable harm that could be done to the interests of the United States" if more articles and documents in the series were published while the case was in progress.

Times Says It Will Comply

The Times, in a statement issued after the hearing, said:

"The Times will comply with the restraining order issued by Judge Murray I. Gurfein. The Times will present its arguments against a permanent injunction at the hearing scheduled for Friday."

Lawyers for The Times and the Justice Department told

SUPREME COURT AGREES TO RULE ON PRINTING OF VIETNAM SERIES; ARGUMENTS TO BE HEARD TODAY

THE SUPREME COURT: Chief Justice Warren E. Burger with Associate Justices. From left, front: John M. Harlan, Hugo L. Black, Mr. Burger, William O. Douglas and William J. Brennan Jr. Behind them, from the left, are Thurgood Marshall, Potter Stewart, Byron R. White and Harry A. Blackmun. They posed early this year.

United Press International

RESTRAINT HOLDS

In Dissent, 4 Justices Support Publication Without a Hearing

By FRED P. GRAHAM
Special to The New York Times

WASHINGTON, June 25 — The Supreme Court agreed today to hear arguments tomorrow on the Government's effort to enjoin The New York Times and The Washington Post from publishing material from the Pentagon papers on Vietnam.

In two brief orders signed by Chief Justice Warren E. Burger, the Court also placed both The Times and The Post under equal publication restraints, based upon the restrictions imposed upon The

---

Yet it persisted, and in April its efforts bore fruit. A series of resignations and admissions stunned the nation. They included Attorney-General Richard Kleindienst, Patrick Gray, the acting head of the FBI, then two aides, Robert Haldeman and John Ehrlichman. A special prosecutor was appointed and a public enquiry set up under Senator Sam Ervin. The underlying question was always, did the President know what had been going on and had he tried to hush it up? At first all incriminating evidence rested on the testimony of John Dean, another aide who had quit, but as spring turned into summer another bombshell burst. There had, it seemed, been a recording system in the White House which switched itself on whenever anyone opened his mouth. Taking refuge in the 'separation of powers' concept of the Presidency, Mr. Nixon flatly refused to release any tape recordings there might be. The indefatigable *Washington Post* was now on the tail of Vice-President Spiro Agnew for tax evasion and possible corruption. To avoid going to prison on the more serious charge, Agnew accepted the tax rap and promptly resigned.

The whole fabric of the Presidency seemed to be crumbling. To stave off demands for impeachment, Nixon finally agreed to release some of the tapes. But then it was discovered that some crucial ones were 'missing' and, worse still, nineteen minutes of conversation on one of them had been mysteriously erased.

At the time of writing (March 1974) the issue remains a major preoccupation in the columns of the American and British papers. But, whatever the outcome, it is fitting that this book should begin and end with examples of total confrontation between Press and Government. For whatever the temporary ills a nation may be suffering, they cannot be pronounced incurable as long as such confrontations *can* exist.

Los Angeles Times

LARGEST CIRCULATION IN THE WEST, 1,026,499 DAILY, 1,210,556 SUNDAY

VOL. XCII † FIVE PARTS—PART ONE CC S TUESDAY MORNING, MAY 1, 1973 96 PAGES Copyright © 1973 Los Angeles Times DAILY 10c

WATERGATE FORCES OUT NIXON AIDES

President Accepts Responsibility, Vows Thorough Probe

FBI Urges Nixon to Pick Director From the Ranks

But Telegram Supposedly Signed by 'All Officials' Prompts One Dissension

H. R. Haldeman

Kleindienst, Ehrlichman and Haldeman Quit; Dean Is Fired

BY RONALD J. OSTROW and ROBERT L. JACKSON
Times Staff Writers

WASHINGTON—President Nixon's two top aides, H. R. Haldeman and John D. Ehrlichman, resigned under pressure of the Watergate scandal Monday along with Atty. Gen. Richard G. Kleindienst.

And climaxing Mr. Nixon's most embattled period in office, White House counsel John W. Dean III was fired.

The President named Secretary of Defense Elliot L. Richardson as his

Richardson Granted

The Weather

Today—Partly cloudy, high in the 70s, low around 50. Chance of rain is 20 per cent today, 10 per cent tonight. Friday—Partly cloudy, high in the 60s. Temp. range: Today, 75-51; Yesterday, 61-46. Details, C12.

The Washington Post

Index 142 Pages 7 Sections

Amusements	B15	Metro	C 1
Classified	C17	Obituaries	C16
Comics	F 6	Outdoors	D12
Editorials	A30	Panorama	F 1
Fed. Diary	F 7	Sports	D 1
Financial	D13	Style	B 1
Food	E 1	TV-Radio	B18

97th Year · No. 92 © 1974, The Washington Post Co. THURSDAY, MARCH 7, 1974 Phone (202) 223-6000 Classified 223-6200 Circulation 223-6100 15c

Nixon Says He Called Hush-Money 'Wrong'

From News Dispatches

President Nixon said last night that he rejected as wrong any payment of hush money or offer of clemency to the original defendants in the Watergate breakin.

Mr. Nixon thus restated the position described by H. R. (Bob) Haldeman, his former chief of staff, in Senate testimony. Haldeman has been indicted on perjury charges in connection with that testimony.

The President said other persons might reach a different conclusion in reading a transcript or listening to a tape of the White House conversation last March 21.

But Mr. Nixon said he knows what was said and what he meant about payoffs for the silence of the Watergate defendants.

It was on March 21, the President said, that Dean first told him money raised for the defendants was to buy their silence.

He said he questioned Dean at length on the matter and "then we came to what I considered to be the bottom line. I pointed out that raising the money was something that could be done. I pointed out that that was linked to clemency . . . that unless a promise of clemency was made, the objective of hush money would not be achieved . . .

"I then said the payment of clemency would be wrong. In fact, I think I can quote it directly, I said the promise of clemency would be wrong."

Then he added, "I know what I meant . . . I meant that the whole transaction was wrong."

"I never at any time authorized clemency for any of the defendants. I never at any time authorized the payment of money to any of the defendants," Mr. Nixon added.

The President said that after Dean failed to bring back a report on March 30—he misspoke and said Aug. 30—he directed John D. Ehrlichman to make the investigation and received a report in mid-April.

He was asked if he would consider clemency to any former associate.

The President said such offers are based on individual cases. No defendant, he added, had been offered clemency or will be offered clemency.

Later, the President said he was not flatly ruling out clemency "to any individual depending on a personal tragedy or something of that sort.

"What I'm saying is that I will not be granting clemency because of Watergate," he said. "That I'm ruling out."

Before starting to respond to questions about the Watergate scandal, Mr. Nixon opened the session by saying that the Senate, by sustaining his veto of an emergency energy bill, had "vetoed longer gas lines and vetoed nationwide rationing."

Mr. Nixon said—as his chief Watergate lawyer James D. St. Clair had said earlier in U.S. District Court yesterday—that he would provide the House Judiciary Committee all the evidence he also has given Watergate Special Prosecutor Leon Jaworski.

He said he also would answer—under oath—written questions from the committee on matters not covered by tapes and documents. But he declined to say whether he would give the committee, which is considering his impeachment, any more material than Jaworski got.

"Those matters continue to be under discussion," he said, adding he would submit to an interview with a few committee members at the White House if his written answers do not satisfy them.

Mr. Nixon said he already has given Jaworski 19 tape recordings and "more than 700 documents," and that Jaworski had indicated that was all he needed to conclude has grand jury investigation of the bugging scandal.

But Jaworski has said he has not

See PRESIDENT, A18, Col. 5

Energy Bill Vetoed; Hill Fights Back

By Spencer Rich and Mary Russell
Washington Post Staff Writers

President Nixon vetoed the emergency energy bill yesterday, contending that a provision rolling back crude oil prices would discourage oil production and worsen the oil shortage.

The Senate promptly sustained the veto by an 8-vote margin, killing the bill after months of dispute. The vote was 58 to 40, 8 short of the required two-thirds needed to override.

However, the House, acting on an entirely separate bill dealing with the powers of the Federal Energy Office, just as promptly wrote into the measure, on a 218-to-175 vote, a price rollback provision similar to the one in the vetoed bill.

The House Ways and Means Committee, meanwhile, indicated it may vote today to phase out the oil depletion allowance, the most controversial of all tax loopholes and one worth more than $2 billion a year to the oil industry.

The indication came from Rep. Herman T. Schneebeli (R-Pa.), the committee's senior Republican, who surprised his colleagues by breaking ranks and saying that he would support a phase-out. The phase-out — a way of increasing oil company taxes—has been looked upon in Congress as an alternative to the vetoed price rollback.

The House action, plus a statement from Sen. Henry M. Jackson (D-Wash.), sponsor of the vetoed bill, signaled that the long battle between Congress and the White House over the control price of crude oil is far from over.

"The rollback provision is going to be an ongoing fight," declared Jackson. "We can always put a rollback in a bill they must have." Jackson said the maximum price for oil in the vetoed bill—$7.09 a barrel—is more than enough to provide incentives to production, in view of the fact that oil was selling a year ago for under $4 a barrel and producers had told him a few months ago that a price of anywhere from $4.50 to $6.50 a barrel would be high enough.

The emergency bill contained broad authority for the President to ration gasoline, to set aside some environmental con-

See VETO, A7, Col. 1

Senate Kills Hill, Judges' Pay Raise

By Spencer Rich
Washington Post Staff Writer

The Senate, dreading to vote itself a pay raise in an election year, killed all proposals for a congressional pay boost by a 72-to-26 vote yesterday.

Also rejected on the same vote, which is final and doesn't require any confirming actiin by the House, were raises requested by President Nixon for federal judges, Cabinet members and top-level administrators in executive pay levels I to V.

Before the final vote, the Senate invoked cloture and shut off a filibuster that was seeking to keep the pay raise measure alive. The cloture vote was 67 to 31—one more than the needed two-thirds.

President Nixon in his budget message last month had recommended a three-step 24 per cent boost for Congress—from $42,500 a year to $52,800 by January, 1976—and corresponding raises for federal judges and top-level executives, under a procedure set up in a 1967 law.

The boosts would have gone into effect automatically at midnight Saturday unless either the House or the Senate altered or rejected them.

The Senate Post Office and Civil Service Committee chairman, Gale W. McGee (D-Wyo.), and members Hiram L. Fong (R-Hawaii) and Ted Stevens (R-Alaska)—with strong backing from GOP Leader Hugh

See PAY, A4, Col. 5

United Press International

Nixon: "I meant that the whole transaction was wrong."

2 Parties Hopeful After Election Split

By Jules Witcover
Washington Post Staff Writer

Today's split result in two special congressional elections—in Ohio a third straight 1974 victory for a Democrat and then in California the year's first Republican victory—generated optimistic talk yesterday from leaders of both parties.

Predictably, each side sought to accentuate the positive in the wake of an election day that first plunged the Republicans into deeper gloom with the loss of the GOP-stronghold seat in Cincinnati, then brought them solace with success in the California district.

But even in that first GOP victory of 1974, post-election analyses indicated, there was considerable slippage in the normal Republican vote, especially in light of the special circumstances in California's 13th Congressional District race.

In the district that encompasses most of Ventura and Santa Barbara counties northwest of Los Angeles, Republican state Sen. Robert J. Lagomarsino drew 53 per cent of the vote, enough to win a House seat for the remainder of the term of the late Rep. Charles M. Teague, also a Republican.

The special race, in which seven Democrats sought unsuccessfully to force Lagomarsino into a runoff, was subjected to intense scrutiny as mostly outside state and national media sought to gauge the impact of the so-called Watergate factor on local elections.

The Democrats played the Watergate scene with heavy flourish, emphasizing Lagomarsino's support for Gov.

See ELECTION, A5, Co. 1

Nixon to Give Hill Watergate Material

President To Reply to Questions

By George Lardner Jr.
Washington Post Staff Writer

President Nixon has decided to give the House Judiciary Committee all the tapes and documents he submitted to federal grand juries investigating Watergate-related scandals, his lawyers disclosed yesterday.

White House special counsel James D. St. Clair made the announcement at a dramatic and tangled hearing in U.S. District Court here involving all three branches of the government. He said Mr. Nixon would also be willing to respond in writing to questions from the House panel and then to sit down with several members of the committee for an "oral interview."

St. Clair refused to say, however, whether the President would give the House impeachment inquiry any more documentary evidence than the grand juries got.

Both Watergate Special Prosecutor Leon Jaworski and the House Judiciary Committee have already asked for more. Committee Chairman Peter W. Rodino (D-N.J.) said yesterday afternoon that he would not be satisfied with just the grand jury evidence. "We've made a request that goes beyond that," Rodino said, warning that a subpoena may still be necessary. "We'll stick by our request."

Speaking to newsmen during a recess at the court hearing on the other points in Mr. Nixon's proposal, St. Clair said at first that the President would be willing to submit to the oral interview under oath, but later in the day, the White House lawyer took that back and said this was not part of the President's offer.

At this point, St. Clair said, Mr. Nixon contemplates taking an oath only for his written responses—which presumably would be drafted by his attorneys.

At his press conference last night, however, Mr. Nixon returned to the original formula and said he would be willing to give the personal interview "under oath," too.

Despite its rough edges, the offer still blunted the impact of the court hearing itself

See HEARING, A18, Col. 1

By James K. W. Atherton—The Washington Post

Presidential attorney St. Clair during a break in hearing before Judge Sirica.

British Strike Ends, Miners Get Raises

By Bernard D. Nossiter
Washington Post Foreign Service

LONDON, March 6 — The nationwide coal strike and the three-day work week it caused were coming to a swift end here tonight as leaders of the miners' union agreed to accept a wage increase more than double that proposed by the defeated government of Edward Heath.

The 250,000 striking miners are now expected to be back at work on Monday after a four-week shutdown which plunged the nation into its gravest industrial crisis since before World War II.

The rapid settlement fulfills the first pledge of the new administration of Harold Wilson to "get Britain back to work." It comes just two days after Wilson returned to 10 Downing St.

Ironically, however, the settlement terms are almost identical with new ones that Heath had pledged he would offer, had he been returned to office.

The new deal will raise the base pay of the best-paid miners, those who extract the coal, from $86 to $105 a week. The base wage of other underground workers will rise from $62 to $84 a week. Clerical and other men on the surface will go from $57.50 to $74 a week.

The wage bill for Britain's nationalized coal industry will jump about $240 million a year. Until the election, Heath had insisted that anything more than $100 million would break his anti-inflation pay curbs.

On the very day he called for an election based on his firm stance against the miners, however, Heath also said

See BRITAIN, A10, Col. 1

Meir Revives Coalition in New Cabinet

By Yuval Elizur
Special to The Washington Post

JERUSALEM, March 6 — Prime Minister Golda Meir presented her new Cabinet to President Ephraim Katzir tonight and announced that the National Religious Party would rejoin in a coalition, giving her a majority in Parliament.

The Cabinet retains Defense Minister Gen. Moshe Dayan and other key ministers. Both Mrs. Meir and Dayan had earlier reversed their decisions to quit their posts, amid reports of a Syrian military buildup on the Golan Heights.

Mrs. Meir's announcement that she had formed a Cabinet came just an hour before the midnight deadline, after a week of internal feuding in her Labor Party Alignment and intermittent negotiations with other parties.

"I plan to ask the speaker of the Knesset [Parliament] that he be ready to convene it on Sunday so that the new government can be presented before the Knesset, according to the guidelines of its policies, its composition, the apportioning of duties among its ministers and seek a vote of confidence," she said.

A crucial factor in ending the political squabbling appeared to be Israeli reports

Transit Aid Bill Blocked In House Unit

By Jack Eisen
Washington Post Staff Writer

The House Rules Committee dealt a probably fatal blow yesterday to the first legislation passed by both houses of Congress that would grant federal subsidies to help pay transit deficits in Washington and other big cities.

With final House action on the measure postponed indefinitely by a voice vote of the Committee, the transit industry now will pin its hopes on an administration-backed bill that would authorize more money each year but may

Tax Ruling Revoked In Big ITT Merger

By Morton Mintz
Washington Post Staff Writer

The Internal Revenue Service yesterday revoked a controversial tax ruling that cleared the way in 1969 for International Telephone and Telegraph Corp. to acquire Hartford Fire Insurance Co.—the largest merger in American history—by allowing for a tax-free exchange of shares.

The rare IRS action was announced in New York by ITT, which immediately requested domestic stock exchanges to suspend trading in its stock until further notice.

The IRS action—taken less

Commodities Unit Gains In Congress

By Selig S. Harrison
Washington Post Staff Writer

The House Agriculture Committee yesterday approved landmark legislation to tighten regulation of the swelling $400-billion-a-year commodity futures market.

The bill would set up an agency to control speculative pressures on consumer prices and protect small investors.

It comes in the wake of 1973's record volume of futures trading, which surpassed the dollar volume of trading on the stock market.

New Khrushchev Tapes

By Dan Morgan and John Sharkey
Washington Post Staff Writers

In a sequel to his recollections published in the West in 1970, the late Soviet Premier Nikita S. Khrushchev dictated

on Khrushchev's observations and recollections, to be entitled "Khrushchev Remembers—The Last Testament." Time magazine will publish excerpts from the book.

FINAL ★★★ **DAILY NEWS** 15¢

NEW YORK'S PICTURE NEWSPAPER ®

Vol. 55. No. 93 New York, N.Y. 10017, Thursday, October 11, 1973 WEATHER: Sunny, breezy and cool

AGNEW QUITS

Fined $10,000 on Tax Charge

Spiro T. Agnew leaves Baltimore Federal Court yesterday.

By WILLIAM SHERMAN
Staff Correspondent of The News

Baltimore, Oct. 10—In one of the great dramas of American history, Spiro T. Agnew resigned as vice president today, pleaded no contest to income tax evasion charges and walked into private life with a $10,000 fine and three years' probation.

With head bowed and his politi-

(Continued on page 3, col. 4)

METS IN SERIES!

CHICAGO

Sun-Times

Tuesday, May 1, 1973

WET
Rain probable Tuesday. High in the 60s. Details on Page 52.
© 1973 by Field Enterprises Inc.

★★★★
FINAL

96 Pages — 10 Cents

NIXON TAKES BUG BLAME

Kleindienst, Haldeman and Ehrlichman quit

'Downers'
No. 1 drug
problem

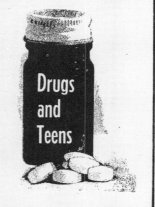

Drugs
and
Teens

3d installment
is on Page 4

Dean is fired by President

189

Index

Entries in bold refer to individual newspapers. Page numbers in brackets refer to illustrations of newspapers.